The Organization and Performance of the U.S. Food System

The Organization and Performance of the U.S. Food System

Bruce W. Marion
U.S. Department of Agriculture
University of Wisconsin-Madison

NC 117 Committee

Lexington Books
D.C. Heath and Company/Lexington, Massachusetts/Toronto

Library of Congress Cataloging-in-Publication Data

Marion, Bruce W.
    The organization and performance of the U.S. food system.

    Bibliography: p.
    Includes index.
    1. Food supply—United States. 2. Food industry and trade—United States. 3. Produce
trade—United States. 4. Agriculture—Economic aspects—United States. I. NC 117
Committee. II. Title.
HD9005.M327   1985   338.1′ 9′ 73   85-45106
ISBN 0-669-11220-8 (alk. paper)

Published simultaneously in Canada
Printed in the United States of America
Casebound International Standard Book Number: 0-669-11220-8
Library of Congress Catalog Card Number: 85-45106

The paper used in this publication meets the minimum requirements of American National
Standard for Information Sciences—Permanence of Paper for Printed Library Materials,
ANSI Z39.48-1984.
∞ TM
The last numbers on the right below indicate the number and date of printing.

10   9   8   7   6   5   4   3   2   1

95   94   93   92   91   90   89   88   87   86

Contents

Part III   Food Manufacturing and Distribution   197

Part IV   The Legal Environment of the U.S. Food System   367

Part V   Conclusions   413

List of Figures

List of Tables

Authorship

This book is a product of North Central Regional Research Project 117 (NC 117). Bruce Marion, as executive director of NC 117, coordinated much of the research reported in this volume and the writing of this book, and coauthored several parts. However, this was far from a one-person effort. The authors of the various parts of the book are as follows.

Foreword   *A.C. Hoffman*
Introduction and Overview   *James D. Shaffer* and *Bruce W. Marion*
Part I   *David Harrington* (coordinating author)
    Chapter 1   *David Harrington* and *Alden Manchester*
Part II   *Bruce Marion, Lee Schrader,* and *Ronald Ward* (coordinating authors)
    Chapter 2   *Lee Schrader, Marvin Hayenga, Dennis Henderson, Raymond Leuthold,* and *Mark Newman*
    Chapter 3   *Bruce Marion* and *Ronald Ward* (coordinating authors)
        Dairy Subsector   *Bruce Marion*
        Beef Subsector   *Bruce Marion*
        Pork Subsector   *Bruce Marion*
        Broiler and Egg Subsectors   *Lee Schrader*
        Wheat, Corn, and Soybean Subsectors   *Mack Leath, Lowell Hill,* and *Bruce Marion*
        Potato Subsector   *Eugene Jones, Ronald Ward,* and *Bruce Marion*
        Citrus Subsector   *Ronald Ward*
        Tart Cherry Subsector   *Donald Ricks* and *Larry Hamm*
        Looking across Subsectors   *Bruce Marion* and *Ronald Ward*
Part III   *Bruce Marion* and *John Connor* (coordinating authors)
    Chapter 4   *John Connor, Richard Rogers, Bruce Marion, Willard Mueller,* and *Robert Wills*
    Chapter 5   *Bruce Marion, Russell Parker,* and *Charles Handy*
Part IV   *Dale Dahl* and *Willard Mueller* (coordinating authors)
    Chapter 6   *Willard Mueller* and *Thomas Paterson*
Part V   *Bruce Marion* (coordinating author)
    Chapter 7   *Bruce Marion* and *V. James Rhodes*
Appendix A   *Paul Farris*

Foreword

The food marketing system has historically been of great interest, and sometimes of considerable concern, to the people of the United States. Concerns about the marketing spread, the middle man, what goes on in the dark between farmer and consumer, go all the way back to the Granger movement and populism. In economic terms, these concerns relate to competition, efficiency, and the best possible use of economic resources in getting agricultural products from farmer to consumer. Economists refer to all this as market performance, and that is what the research work of NC 117 is all about.

Economic performance is directly related to, and to a considerable extent determined by, industrial structure. Structure is a broad concept, but as used here it relates to the number, size, and kinds of business firms that make up an industry. We will begin with an overview of the changes that have occurred in the structure of the U.S. food marketing system in this century.

When the century began, the food marketing system was comprised mainly of large numbers of small and medium-sized firms, with a few notable exceptions, such as meat packing and sugar refining, where large-scale corporate enterprise had made its appearance. Agricultural products moved from farmer to consumer through a series of ownership transfers at each stage of the marketing system: from local assembler or processor to final manufacturer, to grocery wholesaler, to independent retailer. The whole process was aided at each stage by dealers, brokers, and jobbers whose function it was to help bring buyers and sellers together.

By the classical definition of competition (no seller in a position to exercise any significant degree of control over the supply or price of the product), the food marketing system prior to World War I was the most competitive major sector of the economy. The main criticism of it was that it was not very efficient, mainly because most of the firms comprising it were too small and unintegrated to achieve the economies of scale associated with the new techniques of mass production and mass distribution.

But this was about to change, and drastically, during the 1920s. In food manufacturing there was a wave of mergers, and almost overnight the big food corporations were put together. In food distribution, the corporate chains had grown to importance and were driving independent wholesalers and retail grocers out of business.

There were numerous reasons for this development, most of them related to economies of scale and vertical integration. In addition to applying new technology to the physical processes of food manufacturing, the big food manufacturers sought national distribution for their products in order to take full advantage of newly available national advertising media. In the case of the corporate chains, they not only modernized the function of retailing itself but integrated the wholesale and retail functions and even began the manufacture of some of their private label merchandise.

In terms of efficiency, the food industries made great progress during the 1920s. The spectre of monopoly power had not yet appeared except to a few discerning observers. With the onset of the Great Depression and World War II, the merger movement largely came to a halt, although the major food companies continued to grow and the position of the smaller companies continued to erode. The structural situation in the food industries seemed fairly stable, but great changes lay ahead.

These fundamental changes in the food marketing system did not receive much attention from the agricultural economists of the day. For the most part, the economists were concerned in their marketing work with cooperative marketing and the first-stage handling of farm products, and they had neither the training, the conceptual framework, nor the research facilities to go much beyond this. So it is understandable, if not entirely forgivable, that they largely missed the significance of what was happening to the U.S. economy.

Among the first to perceive the revolutionary changes being wrought by the rise of big business were A.A. Berle and Gardiner Means, whose monumental work, *The Modern Corporation and Private Property*, was published in the early 1930s. They clearly saw that price making in a large corporation was administratively determined and inherently restrictive in the sense that supply tended to be controlled to achieve the desired price. Shortly after, Gardiner Means developed the concept fully and gave it a name: administered prices.

At about the same time, another seminal work appeared, Edward Chamberlin's *Theory of Monopolistic Competition*. Like Berle and Means, Chamberlin clearly saw that the competitive model was no longer valid for many parts of the economy, but his work was largely cast within the paradigms of neoclassical economics and lacked some of the depth and perception of Berle and Means.

Soon thereafter, two young agricultural economists, working independently, began research for their doctoral theses on structural changes and imperfect competition in the food industries. They were A.C. Hoffman, whose work was published in 1940 by the Temporary National Economic Committee of the U.S. Senate (TNEC Monograph No. 35, *Large-Scale Organization in the Food Industries*, and William H. Nicholls, *Imperfect Competition in the Agricultural Industries*, published in 1941 by Iowa State University.

Although the work of both Hoffman and Nicholls stemmed from that of Chamberlin and Berle and Means and both covered much the same ground, there was a fundamental difference between them. Hoffman's was grounded in economic determinism and the economies of enterprise scale (the Galbraithian thesis), whereas Nicholls held more closely to the tenets of neoclassical economics. Both were concerned about the imperfections in the marketplace, but Hoffman favored a public policy that went in the direction of government control of economic power where needed; Nicholls favored the antitrust approach. This basic difference still remains the central policy issue of research in the field of industrial organization.

Politicians are frequently quicker than economists to sense important economic developments. This has been true with the rise of big business in the United States. The Sherman Act at the beginning of the century was not inspired by the textbooks and teachings of economists of that time. And again in the 1930s it was the Congress, without much help from mainstream economists, that sensed the growing problem of concentration of control in the U.S. economy and set up the Temporary National Economic Committee (TNEC) to investigate it.

The TNEC made the most thorough study ever done of the structure, conduct, and performance of the U.S. economic system. It published the results of these studies in its well-known monograph series. On the basis of these studies and a series of public hearings, the U.S. Senate began an in-depth consideration of public policy for the all-important problem of concentration of control. This effort was summarily ended by World War II.

Following the war, Congress never reactivated the TNEC, although it had some residual effect in the passage of the Cellar Kefauver Act of 1950 and other legislation intended to strengthen the antitrust approach to public policy. But the basic problem of economic power and concentration of control remained and was destined to grow. Thus ended the first half of the twentieth century.

After World War II, the trend toward large-scale organization in the food industries was resumed but not at the feverish pace of the 1920s. The leading food manufacturers, with increased emphasis on advertising and product differentiation, continued to grow and increase their share of market, while the products of their small competitors had all but disappeared from the supermarket shelves by 1960. Some of the small food manufacturers were acquired by the big corporates as they sought to round out their operations and increase their product lines, but many of them simply went out of business and disappeared.

Among the regional and national corporate food chains, there was lively merger activity in the post–World War II period, but since none of them had more than a small percentage of the total national market, there was no great public concern. However, in most urban markets the grocery business was shifting rapidly into the hands of a few chain competitors. A welcome development in food distribution during this period was the rapid expansion of cooperative and voluntary wholesaler systems that enabled independent retailers to achieve most of the operating advantages of the corporates. This general situation in the food industries—steady growth of the larger firms and continued erosion in the position of the smaller ones—continued until about the mid-1960s, when a new era of merger activity was to come.

Meanwhile, agricultural economists for the first time showed a broad and growing interest in agricultural marketing problems beyond the farm gate. It was sparked by the passage of the Research and Marketing Act of 1946, which provided generous funding for research in agricultural marketing. The purpose of this legislation was primarily to improve the efficiency of the marketing system in order to raise farm income rather than to investigate changes in structure and concentration of control, as had been the purpose of the TNEC. So long as the funds lasted, there was a great deal of agricultural marketing research during the late 1940s and the 1950s, but with a few notable exceptions, the studies were largely descriptive, uncoordinated, and not of much lasting significance in terms of major marketing problems. Not the least of the benefits was the introduction of the agricultural economics profession to the food industries.

In 1959 an important and much-needed book was published: *Industrial Organization*, by Joe Bain. Essentially this book developed and rounded out the conceptual framework laid down by Chamberlin twenty-five years earlier so as to show in much greater detail how the structure of an industry tends to affect the conduct and performance of the firms comprising it. Almost immediately Bain's work became the bible for those working in the field of oligopoly and industrial organization, and it remains so to this day. But as so often happens, events tend to outdate the work of even the best economists, and this was destined to happen to Bain. His concepts were basically those of neoclassical economics, and his work neither anticipated, nor was it adequate to treat, the great changes in the structure of U.S. industry that lay just ahead.

In the mid-1960s, the Congress again became concerned with changes taking place in the food industries and established the National Commission on Food Marketing (NCFM) to study these industries. This time agricultural economists were ready for the task, and under the able direction of George Brandow of Penn State, the profession did a splendid job—in my judgment, one of the best it has ever done in any field. The NCFM was greatly aided in its task by the Federal Trade Commission, which at the time was doing some of the most significant work on the structure and performance of the food industries. The NCFM had subpoena power which contributed greatly to its ability to obtain data and information relative to its purposes. Most researchers working in the field of industrial organization do not have subpoena power but perhaps should in some circumstances.

The conclusions reached by the NCFM were essentially in accord with the conventional wisdom of the day among industrial organization economists. There was some concern over the emphasis being put on advertising, product differentiation, and selling, and the report clearly recognized these factors as contributing greatly to the advantages of the big food manufacturers. The commission found some degree of monopoly power in certain sectors of food manufacturing and by the retail chains in some urban markets, but on the whole the system was judged to be workably competitive. No remedial action was proposed beyond a more vigorous enforcement of the antitrust laws. For efficiency, technological innovation, and general progressiveness, the NCFM gave the food industries fairly good marks. As for the future, no great changes were foreseen. (Economists have never been very good at predicting this kind of thing.)

The ink was hardly dry on the final report of the NCFM when an avalanche of mergers broke loose in the U.S. economy. It has aptly been called "merger mania." For nearly two decades it has continued unabated and unchecked. No one knows where it will end, and no end is in sight. It caught nearly the entire economics profession by surprise and flat-footed, including myself.

Although all the major food manufacturing companies had been thought to be relatively mature in terms of growth, there were none among them which were not caught up in merger mania. The leading firms in several different sectors have merged with each other (Standard Brands with Nabisco, General Foods with Oscar Mayer, Pillsbury with Green Giant, Esmark with Hunt Foods, Beatrice with Esmark, Nestles with Carnation), and several have been acquired by the makers of cigarettes and soft drinks, which have large capital flow. One was bought and then sold by a bus company (Armour by Greyhound). Another was acquired by an energy and chemical conglomerate (Iowa Beef by Occidental). Others have gone outside the food industries to merge with nonfood companies (Dart/Kraft and Beatrice are outstanding examples).

It is important to note that the present merger movement is fundamentally different, both as to its causes and its consequences, from those that have gone before. Most of the earlier mergers in the food industries were engineered for operating reasons: horizontal mergers to achieve greater geographical distribution, acquisitions to broaden product lines, and vertical ones to reduce costs and achieve greater functional depth for operating purposes.

But operating efficiencies directly associated with economies of scale can hardly be claimed for most of the recently formed conglomerates. The chief management function they perform is the control and allocation of capital among their operating units. It is sometimes argued that conglomerates provide a sort of synergistic benefit in terms of renewed vigor and improved operating performance, but it is difficult to identify this in most cases. Frequently it is claimed that conglomerates turn around companies that they acquire by improving their profitability, and sometimes they do. But it usually turns out that they do this mainly by firing employees and selling off the least profitable lines of the acquired company. Good management should involve a little more than this.

The current merger movement is being fueled by numerous factors, most of which have received relatively little attention from economists. One of these is that the corporate management team—what Galbraith calls the technostructure—is inherently growth oriented. That is, it measures its performance and progress from year to year in terms of increasing every phase of its operations: sales, profits, share of market, capital investment, and product proliferation. Any corporation that does not grow, merge, acquire, or do something else beyond trying to improve the operations in which it is engaged is regarded as stodgy and old-fashioned. This is a powerful factor in the economy today.

There are, of course, numerous other reasons for the current merger movement. Financial considerations and tax benefits are a factor in many of them. Many family-owned companies are eager to sell to larger ones for a variety of reasons, and their assets frequently represent a good buy for the acquiring company. Further encouragement is given by a whole congeries of enterprisers whose purpose (and profit) is to engineer mergers—bankers, brokers, finders, fee takers of many kinds.

Some companies have fallen into financial difficulties, and in order to avoid bankruptcy they merge or sell their assets to stronger companies. But such motives explain few mergers in the food field thus far. Typically the medium and large companies being acquired are sought out because they have a strong cash position or are being profitably and successfully managed, sometimes more so than the acquiring corporation.

Contrary to what most economists thought a generation or so ago, we are learning that an oligopolistic industrial structure is highly unstable. The weaker of the big firms tend to fall behind, even in good times. Chrysler, International Harvester, and the A&P Tea Co. are examples, but the same thing is happening in greater or lesser degree in most other sectors of U.S. industry.

This raises some questions of great and ominous portent for the future. Can we permit a great firm employing tens of thousands of people to go down the tube? Should two firms in a concentrated industry be allowed to merge in order to provide more effective competition for the stronger firms? And if so, where is the stopping point in this process? Are we indeed faced with the prospect of simple one- or two-firm monopolies in major sectors of U.S. industry, including some parts of the food industry?

The economic consequences are even more disconcerting. Industrial organization economists have traditionally thought of the problem of monopoly in terms of a single product in its relevant market, and they have analyzed it in terms of profits, prices, and output in the industries directly involved. Joe Bain essentially cast the problem in these terms, and most economists working in the field of industrial organization still use this approach.

There is nothing wrong in doing this, but obviously the social and economic consequences of what is happening go far beyond this. Never before in the history of capitalism have such great aggregations of economic power been created—and by organized labor as well as the corporations. Cost-push inflation, unemployment, an almost intolerable welfare burden, an adverse balance of trade (what has been called the deindustrialization of the United States): all are directly related in greater or lesser degree to the exercise of economic power. As the twentieth century draws to a close, this is one of the greatest problems it leaves to the twenty-first.

Since the inception of NC 117, its main purpose has been to study the changes in the organization of the food production and marketing system and to assess their effects on system performance. In doing this, it has tackled some of the most significant problems in agricultural marketing, which by their very nature are highly controversial. It is to the great credit of the committee that it has consistently sought to put the public interest above that of any particular group: the food industries, the cooperatives, or even farming itself.

Several generalizations of great public interest have emerged from the committee's work. Among the most important of these is that increasing concentration of control, both in food manufacturing and food distribution, has been clearly associated with higher food prices and profits. However controversial, research in this important field must go on.

Another major undertaking of NC 117 has been to study the role that advertising, particularly on television, has had on the organization and performance of the food industries. Clearly advertising has been a major factor in the growth of the big food manufacturing companies and the demise of the smaller ones that cannot use this medium effectively. It also has had a deleterious effect on several aspects of food system performance and represents a major entry barrier in many industries.

Although not widely understood, structural changes of this kind have affected the way the firms involved do business with each other. Earlier most firms in the food industries dealt with each other at arms length through the impersonal forces of competitive markets, and prices were the key determinant of economic behavior. But large-scale organization has largely transformed this system of market dealings into one of highly personal, firm-to-firm transactional arrangements. Private treaties between buyer and seller, standing market agreements, production contracts, vertical integration, collective bargaining, and formula pricing are the new bromides of agricultural marketing. NC 117 has tried to discern the implications of these changes for price discovery, vertical coordination, equity, and the efficiency and progressiveness of the food system. The research by the committee on pricing and information systems, the organization of subsectors, and the role of cooperatives have often plowed new theoretical and empirical ground. On the whole, this work has made an important contribution to our understanding of how commodity systems are organized and coordinated.

It is to the credit of NC 117 that it has addressed the broad problem of merger mania and the rise of economic power in the economy despite the declining interest in these topics among economists and politicians. In 1969, NCR 20 (precursor of NC 117) held a symposium on the emerging conglomerate movement, attended by participants from the land grant universities, the government, and business. The proceedings were published by Oregon State University (*Economics of Conglomerate Growth*, edited by Leon Garoyan). By the standards of the day, it was a good contribution. The research efforts of NC 117 have added significantly to our understanding of the market positions and competitive consequences of conglomerates in the food system. The committee has also provided valuable insights into merger trends and effects in the food manufacturing and distribution industries.

In the long sweep of history, the economics profession has given much attention to perfecting its economic constructs, but its work has often been bypassed by the onrush of events. Probably this has never been truer than it is today. As we look back over the twentieth century, one of its most important developments has been replacement of the unseen hand of competition by economic power as the regulator of economic activity. As will be evident in the report of its work that follows, NC 117 has taken the lead in trying to analyze and appraise this development as it has affected the food marketing system. It may take several more swings of the political pendulum, but sooner or later the Congress, spurred by public pressure, will once again address itself to this problem. It is hoped that the profession will be ready.

A.C. Hoffman
Retired Vice President
Kraft Foods Co.

Acknowledgments

This book is the product of North Central Regional Research Project 117 (NC 117). The regional project is a mechanism for coordinating research among participants from the land grant experiment stations and U.S. Department of Agriculture (USDA). Participation in such projects is not limited to researchers in the region but may include researchers from states outside the region and federal agencies. The NC 117 project is national in scope of subject matter and in participation. Background information on the evolution of events leading to the formation of NC 117 is presented in appendix A.

The book brings together the results of research from the NC 117 project and also draws on research done outside the project. The project personnel have not attempted to do original research on all aspects of the U.S. food system. Unnecessary duplication of research was avoided.

The book is more than a summary of research. It uses research results to address significant questions about the organization and performance of the food system. The book is also less than a summary of NC 117 research in that no attempt has been made to include findings from all the research that has been conducted. The project has produced more than 110 individual reports; titles are listed in appendix B. It is not possible to do justice to these many publications in this book. Nor is this a final report of the NC 117 project. The original research of the project continues. The U.S. food system is very dynamic; understanding that system requires continued research attention. One of the functions of this book is to summarize what we know so that areas needing further research can be identified.

This book reflects the dedication and contributions of scores of people who have been involved in the NC 117 project during its more than ten years. Of particular importance has been the core of committed scholars who played a major role in designing the project, obtaining fundings, and providing guidance and support. Willard F. Mueller, James D. Shaffer, Paul L. Farris, and Dale Dahl have been the core members of the executive committee from the beginning and have stuck with the project through thick and thin.

Other members of the executive committee for shorter periods have been Kenneth Farrell, John Lee, Randall Torgerson, Daniel Padberg, and Dennis Henderson. Willard Mueller has been chairman of the NC 117 committee throughout and more than any other person has been responsible for the success of the project. As executive director of NC 117, I have deeply appreciated the consistent support of these men, both for the project and for me personally. I could always count on them.

The project has been fortunate to have had three dedicated administrative advisers who have helped obtain funding, provided valuable counsel and served as our liaison with experiment station directors: Elmer Kiehl, dean at the University of Missouri, Walter Fishel, associate dean of the Ohio Agricultural Experiment Station, and Kenneth Schneeberger, associate dean of the University of Missouri. Their contributions have been behind the scenes but have been essential.

Projects with innovative organizational designs often encounter difficulty in obtaining funding. This was true of NC 117. We are particularly indebted to Kenneth Farrell, former administrator of the Economic Research Service (ERS), who took the first leap in faith in funding the project. John Lee, current administrator of ERS, was instrumental in maintaining strong support for the project. The Agricultural Cooperative Service and its administrator, Randall Torgerson, have also been consistent supporters of the project from the beginning. William Manley and the Agricultural Marketing Service have provided important support since 1977. Because of the commitment of these three USDA agencies, the project has been a true collaborative effort between the land grant universities and the USDA. However, the views expressed are not necessarily those of the USDA. The North Central Experiment Station directors have also been a vital source of ongoing financial support for the project through off-the-top funds. Last but certainly not least, the U.S. Congress has helped support the project through annual special grants since 1976. We are deeply indebted to the many senators, congressmen, and their staffs who helped maintain this source of funding.

The manuscript for this book went through several versions. I am particularly indebted to the coordinating authors who hung in through this process: A.C. "Oscar" Hoffman (foreword), James Shaffer (introduction), David Harrington (part I), Lee Schrader and Ronald Ward (part II), John Connor (chapter 4), Willard Mueller (part IV), V. James Rhodes (chapter 7) and Paul Farris (appendix A). Paul Farris reviewed the entire manuscript and provided many helpful suggestions.

Nearly all members of the committee, as well as people not involved in the project, reviewed various versions of the manuscript and offered helpful comments. Inevitably some contributed more than others. In addition to those identified as authors of various chapters and sections, we are particularly grateful for the contributions of Edward Jesse, Thomas Sporleder, and R.A.E. Mueller to chapter 2, Lee Schrader, Edward Jesse, Marvin Hayenga, and Dennis Henderson to chapter 3, and Frederick Geithman, Elizabeth Schiferl, John Schmelzer, Michael Van Dress, Ronald Cotterill, and William Lesser to chapter 5.

I have been blessed throughout the preparation of this book with a patient, conscientious, and highly competent secretary, Dorothy Snyder. I will forever be indebted to her for making this undertaking both manageable and bearable. She is a gem.

Finally, I owe much to my wife, children, and friends for their support, patience and loyalty. I am especially grateful to my beloved wife, Ruth, who has been my happy companion of thirty years and has always been my number one cheerleader. I have also appreciated the encouragement, love, and understanding of our three children, Brad, Betsy, and Carol. Finally, the unwavering support, encouragement, and assistance of my friend and colleague Willard "Fritz" Mueller is gratefully acknowledged. Without him, this book would probably not have been written, and I certainly would not have done the writing.

Introduction and Overview

The industrialization of the U.S. food system has been one of the most important economic phenomena of the past century. As national markets have grown, a decentralized, market-coordinated system of food production and distribution has been transformed to a capital-intensive system coordinated through ownership, contracts, and other vertical ties. Associated with this transformation has been a great increase in production and productivity, a movement of activity from farm to nonfarm firms, increased integration and interdependence of the food system with the general economy, and a changing role of government in the food system.

In addition to the increased industrialization of the food system in the United States, the system has also become increasingly involved in international markets. International trade of agricultural commodities has mushroomed; domestic U.S. farm prices are increasingly exposed to world supply and demand forces and political actions. Macroeconomic policies that affect U.S. interest rates and exchange rates for the U.S. dollar have a profound influence on the U.S. food production and distribution system.

The internationalization of the U.S. food system has also occurred in the food manufacturing and food retailing industries. Most of the large food marketing companies operating in the U.S. are multinational companies. While most of these are U.S. companies that have operations in other countries, the 1970s witnessed a sharp increase in the acquisition of U.S. food companies by foreign companies. To an increasing extent, the U.S. food system in intertwined with the world food system.

Some of the causes of these changes originated in farming; however, to an increasing extent, the forces shaping the organization and performance of the food system have originated from the input-supply or food marketing sectors or from national or international economic or political policies.

The industrialization and internationalization of the U.S. food system have wrought important changes in the organization of the system. Farming in the United States is becoming increasingly concentrated; the largest 30 percent of farms produced nearly 90 percent of U.S. farm output in 1983. Nearly changes and causes of change in the organization of these subsectors, and determine the effects of alternative vertical organizations, price discovery systems, and systems of coordination.

3. To describe the legal environment of the food system, determine the effects of the law on the organization and performance of various parts of the food system, and evaluate the effects of alternative legal environments.

4. To identify and evaluate the consequences of alternative public and private actions that could be taken to alter the future organization, control, and performance of the food system.

The research followed three general lines of inquiry, which are reflected in the organization of this book. The first was industry studies. Attention was focused on farming (chapter 1), food manufacturing (chapter 4), and food distribution (chapter 5). Food distribution includes food wholesaling and retailing and the away-from-home food market. The major general areas addressed in the industry studies were the structural characteristics of the industries, the factors that have influenced the structure, and the relationship of structure to conduct and performance. These studies relate to objective 1.

The second line of inquiry focused on commodity subsectors and vertical coordination. The industry studies emphasize horizontal relationships; that is, they look at structure and competitive relationships among firms producing similar products and services, such as food retailing. The subsector studies emphasize vertical relationships. Coordination within subsectors takes place within firms and across markets. Coordination across markets is directed mainly by prices, contractual agreements, and market information. The general areas addressed in the subsector studies include how the subsector is organized, what the systems and mechanisms of coordination are, how the subsector is changing, and how subsector organization affects subsector performance. An important aspect of vertical organization is the extent of vertical integration—that is, the extent to which coordination is controlled within firms in contrast to interfirm mechanisms such as contracts or spot markets. A number of subsectors were investigated in order to identify the variety of coordinating mechanisms (part II). Considerable attention was paid to the differences in pricing mechanisms. The potential for improving pricing effectiveness and reducing costs of price determination through the introduction of electronic technology was thoroughly examined. These studies relate to objective 2.

The third line of inquiry focused on the legal environment of the food system (part IV). This included extensive documentation of laws and regulations that directly influence the organization and performance of the food system and intensive examination of several specific areas of law, especially as related to antitrust, competitive practices, cooperatives, collective bargaining, and food safety. These efforts relate to objective 3.

The final chapter of the book deals with alternative public and private actions to affect the organization and performance of the food system, addressing objective 4. An attempt is made to relate changes in policy to expected resulting changes in performance. This chapter draws on the research reported previously in the book but, more than the other sections, draws on research and information beyond the specific studies of the project. Not all areas of food policy are considered. Emphasis is on policy most relevant to the basic organization of the system. Some areas of policy, such as farm commodity price and income policy, are not included because they have been dealt with extensively in other research projects. Other policies, such as those affecting interest rates and foreign trade, are not considered because our research has not generated information that would enlighten policy in these areas.

Methodological Orientation

The Weltanschauung of the researcher—how one views the world—has a strong effect on the type of research he or she conducts, the questions that are considered relevant, and the hypotheses that are tested. Thus, the academic discipline and training of a researcher tells a good bit about the type of research he or she is likely to undertake. Even within the same academic discipline, such as economics, there are major differences in the orientation of researchers.

One of the strengths of regional research is that a large group of scholars can work cooperatively without necessarily agreeing on either methodological approaches or policy, since each scholar is free to pursue independent inquiry. Rather than being a handicap, the diversity produces a creative tension. Policy-oriented research, such as the NC 117 project, has three functions: description, diagnosis, and prescription. Each of these is influenced by the theoretical and world views of the researchers, which in turn influence the relative importance placed on different variables, interpretations of data, and policy inferences.

All participants were trained in neoclassical economics and were influenced to varying degrees by the theoretical notion of efficiency of the purely competitive market as the performance norm. Beyond traditional neoclassical economics, the dominant paradigms that guided the research were industrial organization theory, a pragmatic institutionalism, and systems theory.

The analytical framework of industrial organization focuses attention on the relationship among the structure of the market, the conduct of firms associated with that structure, and the resulting performance. The central hypothesis is that only a few characteristics of the market structure have a strong influence on conduct and thus on performance. Traditional industrial organization theory deals with a limited set of performance norms and conduct variables. Pragmatic institutionalism argues to include attention to institutional variables of the market, especially a broad notion of property rights, with more attention to behavior and to a broader set of performance criteria. Systems theory raises still other dimensions. Vertical relationships, feedback and control procedures, and the dynamics of vertical coordination and system evolution are identified as important factors to examine. In contrast to schools of economics that concentrate on defending theoretical models as accurate portrayals of the real world, most of the research in this project has sought to identify market imperfections and failures and the alternative ways of eliminating them.

Description in this project focused on identifying how various parts of the food system are organized—including the institutional infrastructure—how the system behaves, and the cause-effect relationships. It included testing the validity of alternative theories. For example, to what extent is the theory of contestable markets or the theory of strategic groups useful in explaining the organization and performance of markets in the food system?

Descriptive research also helps to develop or expand theories through an inductive approach. The studies of agricultural subsectors and vertical coordination have largely been inductive in nature. For example, what generalizations can be drawn about subsector organization and performance from several case studies of selected subsectors?

The project placed a high priority on empirical testing of theoretical concepts. Much of the current debate in the policy arena concerns the validity of alternative theories of how the world operates. In many cases these theories have not been subjected to empirical validation. Validation may be impossible in some instances; however, in many cases, some form of validation is possible. This has been one of the emphases of NC 117, particularly in examining alternative theories of market behavior through cross-sectional econometric analysis.

Unlike the physical and biological sciences, economics seldom has the opportunity to test or develop theories by experimentation. In this project, some experimentation was possible to test different market institutions (electronic marketing system) and to determine the effects of altering the level and distribution of information. Rather than describing the existing food system, these efforts focused more on changing the system and studying the effects.

One of the most important differences in the descriptive research done by different committee members was the emphasis placed on the structure of markets and industries. Those conducting industry studies generally viewed the structure of markets as key variables, while those doing subsector and pricing studies placed heavier emphasis on business behavior and institutional factors. Another major difference was the extent to which dynamic factors were emphasized. Those with a systems orientation tended to place more attention on the evolving and dynamic dimensions of the food system.

Regional Research

NC 117 stands for North Central Regional Research Project 117. This means the project was sanctioned by the experiment station directors of the land grant universities of the North Central Region. However, the project is not only national in scope but also national in participation, for many researchers from universities outside the region and from several government agencies have contributed to the research. Similarly the funding of the research has come from many sources.

The origin of the project is documented in appendix A. One of the major goals in designing the project was to overcome the difficult and important problem of fragmented research. A major criticism of agricultural marketing research has been that it has not been additive or comprehensive. The scope of much of the needed research requires a critical mass beyond that which can usually be provided by a single researcher or university. Since the food marketing system is ever changing, monitoring the system's performance requires systematic research over a period of years, a task beyond the capacity of uncoordinated research. The regional research concept was intended to provide a mechanism to plan research so as to coordinate the efforts of a group of researchers with a common mission.

Regional research frequently has been criticized for the lack of close coordination. Traditionally coordination has been provided by a committee of researchers without strong incentives to contribute to the coordination function. An important innovation of the NC 117 project was to employ a full-time executive director and a small core staff under his direction. While the planning of the project research involved a committee of all contributing researchers, the executive director was essential for leadership and follow-up. The core group was also able to engage in major research beyond the capacity of individual researchers and to contribute to the integration of research results.

The NC 117 project was an experiment in regional research organization. Although the organization did not solve all of the problems of coordination, critical mass, comprehensiveness, additivity, and timeliness of research, it did prove to be a workable model significantly more effective in organizing research than has been the experience with previous regional research. Agricultural research administrators should consider adopting the NC 117 model in establishing other regional projects. It is a workable and cost-effective model.

Authorship Responsibility

Each chapter of this book is identified as to authorship. Although all chapters were reviewed by other members of the project, the responsibility for the content of each chapter rests with the authors. They could accept or reject suggestions. The project does not have or impose a collective point of view. This book and other reports of the project do not necessarily represent a consensus position, and thus the positions taken by authors should not necessarily be attributed to other participants of the project. We believe this is an important principle for cooperative research, especially in respect to research that deals with policy.

Part I
Agricultural Production

T he desired organization of farming and the effects of public policies on
it have been issues in U.S. public life since independence. For the first
eighty years, culminating in the Homestead Act, the principal issue was
the basis on which public land was made available to settlers. Other public
policies in the period from 1862 to 1929 included establishment of the Department of Agriculture (USDA) in 1862, at first primarily as an information and
research agency; the Hatch Act of 1887 to encourage research; the establishment
of the Federal-State Extension Service in 1914; and the addition of a number of
marketing services by USDA between about 1914 and the early 1920s.

The agricultural depression of the 1920s brought concern with the generally low level of farm income and attempts to deal with it through the first
commodity programs. These came to a head during the even more depressed
conditions of the 1930s, the Great Depression, and the advent of New Deal
agricultural programs. Concerns began to be expressed about the separation
between farms run actively as businesses and those that were the homes of
powerless, low-income families (Brewster 1979b).

The primary concern during the 1930s was with the great bulk of family-
operated farms that had severe income problems. The Agricultural Adjustment
Act of 1933 (AAA) and later programs attempted to deal with that problem.
Other programs were initiated to help the farmers at the bottom end of the
scale. A submarginal land purchase program was begun to buy out farmers on
units too small for successful operation as business enterprises. These programs
were consolidated with others, attempting to deal more directly with the problems of tenants and black sharecroppers in the South that were the historical
aftermath of slave-operated plantations. These activities of the Resettlement
Administration were consolidated into the Farm Security Administration in
1937 and later into the present-day Farmer's Home Administration, which
concentrates on farm operating and ownership loans (Brewster 1979b, p. 67).

This part was coordinated by David Harrington of the Economic Research Service, U.S. Department of Agriculture. The views expressed are not necessarily those of USDA.

The debate on agricultural policy following World War II focused on an agriculture composed primarily of family farms, which were defined at the time as viable operations, providing full employment for the operator and adequate support for the farm family (Brewster 1979a, 1974b, p. 68). In general, the consolidation of part-time, marginal, or subsistence operations into larger farms was part and parcel of a family farm policy. The major policy issue relating to small farms during the 1940s, 1950s, and into the 1960s was seen as the problem of getting the excess human resources out of agriculture and off the small farms. Rural development programs were seen as a major solution to the problems of small farmers. Thus, the small farm issue came to be seen as a welfare matter that had little to do with commercial agriculture (Brewster 1979b, p. 70). The major structural problem of the 1940s—the overabundance of resources, especially labor—was largely solved by events of the 1950s and 1960s. By the millions, these farms were absorbed by remaining family farms, as older generations retired or died and younger generations moved to the cities or to nonfarm occupations.

Today's commodity policies are the lineal descendants of the AAA programs of the 1930s, differing in many ways but more alike than different. There are many objectives of public policy relating to farming, ranging from conservation to nutrition (Lee 1981). The objectives of federal commodity policy appear to be concentrated on improving income levels, both averages and for subgroups; improving income stability and risk management; and fostering countervailing market power (which also contributes to both of the other objectives).

During the past half-century, the organization of farming and its economic and financial situation have changed markedly. The basis for public intervention in agriculture may have changed so much that the policies appropriate for the 1980s need to be examined anew. The principal policy issues relating to commodity programs in the mid-1980s are these:

To what extent should policies contribute to significant income enhancement for producers of specific commodities? What is the desired balance between income enhancement and income stabilization?

In the light of the significant growth in the shares of very large farms, to what extent should policies be size neutral?

Is there an intent to provide income enhancement for small farms that are not commercial producers of agricultural products?

Reexamination of the basis for these commodity program decisions requires a current description and assessment of the farm sector—its production, financial, institutional and policy structures. Four perennial policy issues are briefly discussed:

1. Income parity: Are farmers' incomes chronically depressed compared to those of other groups in society?

2. Small farms: Are small farms a chronically disadvantaged group in society?

3. Large farms: Are larger-than-family farms and corporate farms likely to force out family-sized units? Could they exercise market power to force up food prices?

4. Stability: To what extent should stability be pursued as a policy goal?

1
Agricultural Production: Organization, Financial Characteristics, and Public Policy

Organization of Farming

The organization of the farm sector has undergone major changes since World War II. Especially prominent among these changes are a decline in farm numbers from a prewar peak of 6.5 million farms to 2.3 million today, increased concentration of production (the largest 5 percent of farms produced 50 percent of output in the 1980s compared to 42 percent in 1960, and changes in the technology and specialization of farm production that have encouraged the formation of very large, highly capitalized farms, and very small, part-time farms, leaving farms in the middle of the size distribution relatively disadvantaged. Correcting for inflationary changes in the price level, however, the change in the distribution of farm sizes is much smaller than it first appears. Thus, although structural change in the farm sector has been occurring, there is little evidence that the farm sector will rapidly evolve to a monolithic structure of large farms. At the beginning of the 1980s, some of these trends, such as the rapid decline in farm numbers, appear to have ended, and new directions may be emerging in the structural and organizational development of the farm sector.

Farm Numbers and Sizes

The decline in farm numbers that began in the late 1930s has slowed dramatically since the 1950s and 1960s (figure 1–1 and table 1–1). The rate of decline in the number of farms, which was running at over 200,000 per year in the early 1950s, had slowed to about 2,000 farms per year by 1979. Then it increased to about 30,000 per year from 1981 to 1984.

The authors of chapter 1 are David Harrington and Alden C. Manchester of the Economic Research Service, USDA. The views expressed are not necessarily those of USDA.

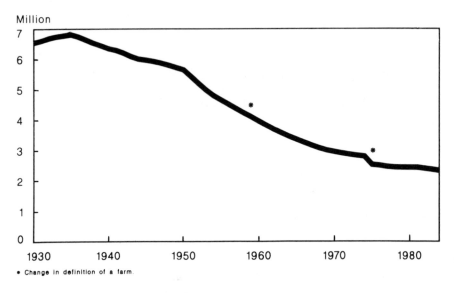

Source: Statistical Reporting Service, USDA.

Figure 1–1. Number of Farms in the United States

When approximately corrected for price change, the numbers of smaller farms in all sales classes declined sharply between 1949 and 1983 (table 1–2). Numbers in the three largest sales classes rose sharply. Most of the declines in number of farms with sales in 1980 dollars of $1,000 or more occurred in the 1950s and 1960s and virtually all of it by 1980.

Rural residences declined sharply in the 1950s and 1960s and then approached stability in the late 1970s or 1980s. The movement out of small family farms slowed during the 1970s. Among family farms, those with sales of $40,000 to $99,999 in 1980 dollars increased to 1970 and then declined. All larger farms increased throughout.

The larger-than-single-family farms—those with sales of $200,000 or more—include more cotton, fruit, vegetable, horticultural specialty, dairy, poultry, and egg farms than average (table 1–3). Among the family farms and small family farms, cash grain, cotton, and dairy farms are more heavily represented than the average. Among rural residence farms, cattle, hog, or sheep farms, general crop farms, and fruit and tree nut farms are more heavily represented than average.

Only 55 percent of all farm operators were primarily engaged in farming in 1982 (table 1–4). About 90 percent of those with sales of $40,000 or more were principally farmers but only 22 percent of those with sales of less than $2,500. And many of these farmers were sixty-five years old or older.

Table 1–1
Farm Numbers and Sizes

Year	Number of Farms (thousands)	Land in Farms (million acres)	Average Size of Farm (acres)
1950	5,648	1,202	213
1960	3,963	1,176	297
1970	2,949	1,102	374
1980	2,433	1,039	427
1981	2,434	1,034	425
1982	2,401	1,028	428
1983	2,370	1,024	432
1984	2,333	1,020	437

Source: Statistical Reporting Service, USDA.
Note: Definition of farm changed in 1959 and 1974. Whereas a farm had been defined as 3 or more acres and $150 or more in sales, in 1959 it was changed to 10 acres or more *and* $50 in sales, or over $250 in sales. In 1974, the acreage requirement was eliminated; a farm had to have $1,000 or more in sales of agricultural products.

Concentration

The share of sales accounted for by the largest 5 percent of farms has gradually increased from 39 percent in 1949 to 42 percent in 1960, 47 percent in 1970, and 50 percent in 1982. The share of value-added or of harvested acreage would be lower than the share of sales, due to the concentration of cattle feedlots, and poultry and egg operations among the largest farms (Raup 1980).

Concentration of production, as measured by the Gini concentration ratio, has remained stable since 1974 (table 1–5). The most highly concentrated commodities are eggs, vegetables, fed cattle, and fruit production. The least concentrated are sorghum, rice, wheat, beef, and dairy products. The coefficient for broilers appears relatively low because the concentration in broiler production is among the 150 or so contractors rather than among the contract producers measured here. All of the most concentrated commodities are those without price supports. The price-supported commodities are found among the least concentrated commodities. Cash grain farming and dairying are the least concentrated of all enterprises and have the highest proportion of family-sized farms. The stability provided by the commodity price-support programs probably contributed to this situation (see Manchester 1983 for dairy).

Specialization

One of the more prominent features of U.S. farming since the end of World War II has been increased specialization at both the regional and farm levels. Improved and expanded communication and transportation networks, which facilitated rapid, low-cost movement of agricultural commodities over long

Table 1–2

Approximate Distribution of Farms and Farm Product Sales at 1980 Prices, by Sales Class, 1949–1983

| Year and Item | Larger-Than-Single-Family Farms | | Family Farms | |
	$500,000 and Over	$200,000 to $499,999	$100,000 to $199,999	$40,000 to $99,999
Number of farms (in thousands)				
1949			50	239
1960	16	32	76	455
1970	16	68	122	566
1980	24	84	179	388
1982	25	87	186	393
1983	24	83	177	381
Percentage of farms				
1949			1.0	4.8
1960	0.4	0.8	2.0	12.0
1970	.5	2.4	4.2	19.7
1980	1.0	3.4	7.4	16.0
1982	1.0	3.6	7.7	16.4
1983	1.0	3.5	7.5	16.1
Percentage of sales				
1949			21.0	18.7
1960	14.6	8.6	10.9	29.2
1970	22.5	16.5	15.3	29.6
1980	30.0	18.8	19.0	19.3
1982	30.1	19.0	19.3	19.2
1983	30.2	19.1	19.3	19.2

Source: Calculated data from Statistical Reporting Service, USDA.

Note: Includes only farms with sales of $1,000 or more at 1980 prices. Empty cells are included in $100,000–$199,999 sales class.

distances, were major factors leading to increased regional specialization. The interstate highway system spurred a major expansion in long-haul trucking and enabled production of various commodities to concentrate in the areas of greatest comparative advantage.

Specialization in the production of agricultural commodities is much more apparent for individual farms than for regions (table 1–6). The proportion of farms that have more than half of their sales in a single commodity group increased from 86 percent to 96 percent between 1969 and 1982. The share of production accounted for by such farms increased by 81 percent to 84 percent over the same period. Increased specialization at the farm level is largely the result of the development of specialized, capital-intensive production technologies that increased the advantages of size, aided by govern-

Small Family Farms		Rural Residences		
$20,000 to $39,999	$10,000 to $19,999	$5,000 to 9,999	$1,000 to $5,000	All Farms
601	878	1,002	2,205	4,975
594	636	675	1,300	3,784
314	376	338	1,075	2,875
279	286	332	856	2,428
273	281	331	824	2,400
272	279	325	829	2,370
12.1	17.7	20.1	44.3	100.0
15.7	16.8	17.9	34.4	100.0
10.9	13.1	11.8	37.4	100.0
11.5	11.8	13.7	35.2	100.0
11.4	11.7	13.8	34.4	100.0
11.5	11.8	13.6	35.0	100.0
24.4	18.3	9.5	8.1	100.0
17.9	10.2	5.1	3.5	100.0
6.8	4.5	1.9	2.9	100.0
6.3	3.2	1.9	1.5	100.0
6.1	3.1	1.8	1.4	100.0
6.0	3.0	1.8	1.4	100.0

ment farm programs that reduced the need for farm diversification as a method of lessening risk. But specialization has increased for all commodities, not just for those with government programs.

Just as farms are becoming more specialized in producing specific commodities, they are also becoming more specialized in performing the various functions required for the production and marketing of agricultural commodities. Much of the work and many of the functions formerly performed on farms have shifted to nonfarm firms (Dorner 1980). The most dramatic shift probably has been in power inputs. Until 1910, almost all of the power on farms was supplied by people or animals. Over the next fifty years, the introduction of petroleum-powered machines and, later, electrically powered machines brought about nearly a total replacement of horses and mules. Now practically the only workhorses left are on farms operated by the Amish, who refuse to use mechanical power for religious reasons. Horses are now used almost entirely for recreation. The virtual disappearance of horses and mules

Table 1–3
Percentage of Farms, by Sales Class and Type of Farm, 1982

	Larger-Than-Single-Family Farms		Family Farms	
Type of Farm	*$500,000 and Over*	*$250,000 to $499,999*	*$100,000 to $249,999*[a]	*$40,000 to $99,999*
Crop farms				
Cash grain	14.6	28.9	35.5	39.6
Cotton	4.1	3.1	1.8	1.5
Tobacco	.5	1.4	2.1	3.3
Other field crops	5.0	3.8	2.6	2.4
Vegetable and melon	5.1	1.9	1.0	.9
Fruit and tree nut	6.7	3.8	2.8	2.8
Horticultural specialty	5.4	2.5	1.4	1.2
General crop farms	3.4	2.8	2.1	2.0
All crop farms	44.8	48.2	49.3	53.8
Livestock farms				
Cattle, calves, hogs, and sheep	28.9	25.6	22.0	21.9
Dairy	11.1	13.6	20.8	20.2
Poultry and eggs	13.2	10.9	6.0	2.1
Other livestock	2.0	1.8	2.0	2.0
All livestock farms	55.2	51.8	50.7	46.2
All farms	100.0	100.0	100.0	100.0

Source: Census of Agriculture, 1982.

[a]Census of Agriculture breaks their sales class data at $250,000 in 1982, whereas Statistical Reporting Service and ERS break their series at $200,000.

from U.S. farms freed up 90 million acres—about a quarter of all cropland—which had been used to produce feed for them. It also freed up 8 percent of total farm labor man-hours, which had been used in caring for horses and mules. These resources could then be used for other tasks, including producing food for humans.

Feed, seed, and livestock—other major farm inputs—still come from farms and are used on farms. But higher proportions are now produced on one farm and used on another, with ownership passing through nonfarm firms along the way. More feed and feed ingredients are purchased rather than grown on the farm where they are used. Most seed is produced by or for seed companies under careful quality control. The entire cattle feedlot business was built on the separation of cattle feeding from cattle raising.

Small Family Farms		Rural Residences		
$20,000 to $39,999	$10,000 to $19,999	$5,000 to $9,999	Less than $5,000	All Farms
39.5	32.6	23.8	12.0	25.7
1.3	1.0	.6	.2	1.0
5.9	8.6	10.1	6.1	5.9
2.9	4.2	5.8	6.0	4.5
1.3	1.5	1.7	1.4	1.4
3.5	3.4	3.1	4.7	3.8
1.4	1.5	1.4	1.0	1.3
2.4	2.4	1.7	3.4	2.6
58.2	55.2	48.2	34.7	46.2
28.6	37.3	47.4	56.4	40.4
10.2	3.9	1.2	.3	7.3
.9	.4	.3	.9	1.9
2.2	2.4	3.0	7.7	4.2
41.8	44.8	51.8	65.3	53.8
100.0	100.0	100.0	100.0	100.0

All of these changes mean that many of the inputs farmers use are now purchased rather than produced on the farm itself. Intensive use of purchased inputs has increased farmers' vulnerability to rising prices and interruptions of input supplies.

Contracting and Integration

The specialized functions of input supply, production, and marketing are becoming more integrated with farm production through the use of contractual arrangements and vertical integration. The percentage of total farm output produced either under contractual arrangements or by vertically integrated firms increased from 25 percent in 1960 to 31 percent in 1980. As a consequence, the traditional farm is playing a more restricted and specialized role than formerly. Some functions formerly performed by farmers have been contracted, and certain decisions are being made by input-supplying or output-marketing firms.

Table 1–4
Age and Principal Occupation of Farm Operators by Sales Class, 1982
(percentage)

Sales Class	Farming[a]			Other Occupations			Total Farming and Non-Farming
	Under 65	65 Years and Older	Total Farming	Under 65	65 Years and Older	Total Non-Farming	
$500,000 or more	81.9	9.1	91.0	7.7	1.3	9.0	100.0
$250,000 to $499,999	86.2	6.8	93.0	6.2	.8	7.0	100.0
$100,000 to $249,999	86.5	6.2	92.8	6.5	.7	7.2	100.0
$40,000 to $99,999	79.0	9.2	88.2	10.7	1.1	11.8	100.0
$20,000 to $39,999	57.5	14.4	71.9	25.4	2.7	28.1	100.0
$10,000 to $19,999	39.7	17.8	57.5	38.1	4.4	42.5	100.0
$5,000 to $9,999	24.8	16.8	41.6	50.8	7.6	58.4	100.0
$2,500 to $4,999	18.7	14.8	33.6	57.6	8.8	66.4	100.0
Less than $2,500	12.9	9.8	22.7	66.9	10.4	77.3	100.0
Total	42.9	12.2	55.1	39.3	5.6	44.9	100.0

Source: Census of Agriculture, 1982, Vol. 1, Part 51, pp. 48–49.

[a]Farm operator spent 50 percent or more of his time in farming.

The extent of formal coordination through contracts or integration ranges from virtually 100 percent for sugar beets and sugarcane to almost none for hay (table 1–7). The growth in contracting and vertical integration in the 1960s and 1970s was due largely to increased contracting and vertical integration of egg and turkey production and to an increase in contract marketing of grains, cotton, and oil seeds. Changes in support programs for these crops greatly increased market price risk to producers. Many turned to using forward delivery contracts as a risk management strategy.

For some agricultural commodities, particularly those produced on a lot or batch basis for processing, little or no production is undertaken without a contract between the producer and the processor. Most of the broiler industry in the South was built on this basis. However, contracting did not replace open-market selling of broilers in the South since almost no broilers were produced there prior to contracting.

Vegetables for processing are mostly produced under contract. The exceptions are those that are perennials or where the same varieties are used for both processing and fresh market. Most asparagus, a perennial, is purchased on the open market for processing. The same varieties are used both for processing and fresh market. A number of varieties of potatoes are used for both processing and fresh market. Contracting accounts for a significant share of such production. Frequently the processor sorts the potatoes received from the grower, sending the top grades in selected size ranges to the fresh market and the remainder to processing.

Most other vegetables for processing are produced only under contract. Without an assured market provided by a contract, a grower will not plant

Table 1–5
Gini Concentration Indexes of Commodity Production, 1974, 1978, 1982

Commodity	1974	1978	1982
Corn	0.5697	0.5406	0.5422
Cotton	.6559	.6073	.6222
Fruit and tree nuts	.7072	.8006	.8088
Peanuts	.5794	.5494	.5437
Rice	n.a.	.4276	.4463
Sorghum	.4928	.4078	.4359
Soybeans	.4700	.4728	.4688
Tobacco	.5306	.5785	.5803
Vegetables	.7850	.8485	.8431
Wheat	.4916	.4151	.4706
Beef cows	.3834	.4724	.4793
Broilers	.5331	.5622	.5555
Eggs	.9119	.9291	.9343
Fed cattle	.8210	.8374	.8374
Hogs	.5051	.5789	.5995
Dairy products	.5167	.5370	.5203
Sheep	.5456	.6015	.5645

Note: A Gini coefficient of 0.0 would result from all firms producing equal quantities of output. The higher the index, the greater the concentration of production. A Gini coefficient of 1.0 would result from all production coming from one firm.

such vegetables. Production contracts date back to the early days of processing vegetable production. In most cases, contracts and production of such vegetables started together. In the early days, processors specified very tightly the product to be delivered and the terms and conditions. They often supplied seed and other inputs. As growers became accustomed to the specifications of the buyer, contract terms had a tendency to become less inclusive.

Production of vegetables for processing in some areas is a minor activity for many growers. Producing sweet corn for processing in the Midwest provides farm work and cash income on a different schedule from most other crops. The grower does not generally depend on the income from sweet corn— it is a sideline—so the processor must offer sufficient inducement to get the acreage he needs, even though he may be the only processor in the area. In such cases, competition is provided not by other processors but by other enterprises that the farms may undertake. Such sideline production is becoming less common as canning and freezing have moved to more specialized areas such as California.

Marketing contracts involve much less shift of decision making from producer to contractor than do production contracts. They accounted for about 60 percent of the value of agricultural products sold under contracts in 1980. Marketing contracts, written or oral, have been the usual way of selling continuously produced products such as milk and eggs for many years. Such contracts provide a method for setting prices and other terms of trade. This is essential for commodities that move from farm to market every few days.

Table 1–6

Farm Specialization by Type of Farm, 1969 and 1982

(percentage)

	1969		1982	
Type of Farm	Percentage of Farms	Share of Sales from Primary Commodity[a]	Percentage of Farms	Share of Sales from Primary Commodity[a]
Cash grain	21.3	81	25.7	86
Tobacco	5.2	80	5.9	76
Cotton	2.3	69	.9	80
Other field crops	1.8	82	4.5	79
Vegetables	1.1	86	1.4	86
Fruits and nuts	3.1	95	3.8	95
Horticultural specialty	n.a.	n.a.	1.3	98
Dairy[b]	15.1	78	7.3	84
Poultry	3.3	94	1.9	95
Animal specialty	n.a.	n.a.	2.9	95
Other livestock	32.8	84	40.5	86
Total	86.0	81	96.1	84
Other farms	14.0	Less than 50	3.9	Less than 50

Source: Census of Agriculture, 1969, 1982.

[a]Share of sales of this type of farm which are of the primary commodity.

[b]Sales are dairy products only, not including dairy animals.

n.a. = not available or not applicable.

Production contracts have increasingly come into use for eggs in the last twenty years. These are more like broiler contracts than the older marketing contracts for eggs.

Marketing contracts (forward selling) for staple commodities—grains, oilseeds, and cotton—came into use during the 1970s, permitting the grower to shift some price risk and the buyer to remove some uncertainties as to supply. Their use varies markedly from year to year (see chapters 2 and 3).

Both contracting and vertical integration are associated to some extent with larger sizes of farms. Contracts tend to be made with larger producers, since there are economies for the contractor in dealing with fewer and larger producers. Also, nonfarm firms that engage in farming are much more likely to do so on a large scale.

Technology of Production

U.S. agriculture achieved tremendous gains in productivity between 1930 and 1980. Total output rose by almost 150 percent, while total inputs increased only slightly, by 7 percent (figure 1–2). Land inputs have remained

Table 1–7
Percentage of Farm Output Produced under Contracts and by Vertically Integrated Firms
(percentage)

Products	Production and Marketing Contracts[a]			Vertical Integration[b]		
	1960	1970	1980	1960	1970	1980
Crops	11.6	12.4	16.7	6.3	7.0	7.2
Feed grains	.1	.1	7.0	.4	.5	.5
Hay	.3	.3	.5	0	0	0
Food grains	1.0	2.0	8.0	.3	.5	.5
Vegetables for fresh market	20.0	21.0	18.0	25.0	30.0	35.0
Vegetables for processing	67.0	85.0	83.1	8.0	10.0	15.0
Dry beans and peas	35.0	1.0	2.0	1.0	1.0	1.0
Potatoes	40.0	45.0	60.0	30.0	25.0	35.0
Citrus fruits	60.0	55.0	65.0	20.0	30.0	35.0
Other fruits and tree nuts	20.0	20.0	35.0	15.0	20.0	25.0
Sugar beets	98.0	98.0	98.0	2.0	2.0	2.0
Sugarcane	24.4	31.5	40.0	75.6	68.5	60.0
Cotton	5.0	11.0	17.0	3.0	1.0	1.0
Tobacco	2.0	2.0	2.0	2.0	2.0	2.0
Oil-bearing crops	1.0	1.0	10.0	.4	.5	.5
Seed crops	80.0	80.0	80.0	.3	.5	10.0
Other crops	5.0	5.0	5.0	1.0	1.0	1.0
Livestock	27.5	29.2	33.0	3.6	4.5	4.8
Fed cattle	10.0	18.0	10.0	6.7	6.7	4.5
Sheep and lambs	2.0	7.0	7.0	5.1	11.7	9.0
Hogs	.7	1.0	1.5	.1	.1	.1
Fluid grade milk	95.0	95.0	95.0	2.9	2.1	1.4
Manufacturing grade milk	25.0	25.0	25.0	2.0	1.0	1.0
Eggs	5.0	20.0	45.0	10.0	20.0	44.0
Broilers	93.0	90.0	89.0	5.4	7.0	10.0
Turkeys	30.0	42.0	62.0	4.0	12.0	28.0
Other livestock	3.0	3.0	3.0	1.0	1.0	1.0
Total farm output[c]	20.6	22.3	24.8	4.8	5.5	6.0

Source: Estimates by ERS specialists.

[a]Vertical coordination of farm production and marketing under agreements between farmers and processors, dealers, cooperatives, or others.

[b]Production and marketing by the same firm.

[c]Omits forest, greenhouse, and nursery products.

essentially constant. The catalyst for the productivity gains was technological change. Mechanization, hybrids and improved varieties, commercial fertilizers, pesticides, and irrigation all increased the productivity of land and labor, encouraged the substitution of capital for labor, and led to a large outmigration of labor from agriculture (Lu 1979). In the last two decades alone,

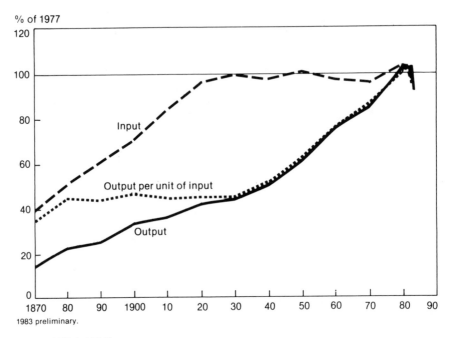

% of 1977

Source: USDA 1984f.

Figure 1–2. Farm Productivity Trend, 1870–1983.

labor use dropped by nearly half (figure 1–3), and now a larger share is hired than is provided by the farm family. Current agricultural production technologies were developed in an era of abundant, low-cost energy and were designed primarily to replace human labor with mechanical power and chemicals. This input substitution has been a key factor behind the decreasing number and increasing size of farms.

Technological changes, especially those that allowed substitution of capital for labor, combined with specialization of production, had the effect of making traditional-sized family farms too small to employ fully a farm operator family. The resulting low net income of these farms provided a strong incentive for the farmer to adjust. In the 1950s and 1960s, the incentive seemed to be to get bigger or get out. In the 1970s and 1980s, it seems to be to get bigger or get smaller (become a part-time farmer) in order to achieve a desired standard of living.

Economies of size were another source of productivity gains, but the potential contribution of further farm expansion to enhance productivity is unclear (Miller 1979; Miller et al. 1981). Economies of size arise from:

Technical economies (efficiency in use of inputs).

Buying economies (quantity discounts and better terms for larger purchases).

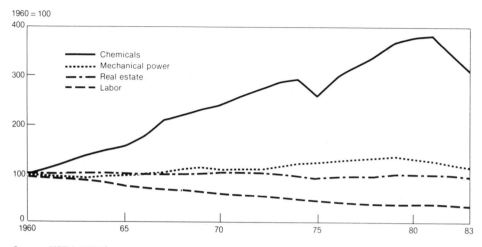

1960 = 100

Source: USDA 1984f.

Figure 1–3. Changes Since 1960 in Real Value of Inputs Used in Farm Production

Marketing economies (higher prices for larger quantities and lower unit marketing costs).

Tax advantages (nonmarket gains for delaying or avoiding taxes on income from any source).

Managerial economies (more effective mangement through specialization, including purchased services). Risk management is one significant aspect. The management of hired labor—techniques of recruiting, supervising, compensating, training, negotiating labor contracts, and handling mandated fringe benefits—is another advantage for larger farms (Holt 1979).

For the bulk of production, technical economies of size do not hold the promise of reduced food costs. Empirical estimates of long-run average cost curves for various farm types and sizes based solely on technical economies of size suggest that costs per dollar of gross income consistently decline as small farms expand, then taper off for medium-size farms, and fall very little for large farms (figure 1–4). Thus, today it appears most likely that farmers enlarge their operations to achieve higher net income rather than to reduce unit costs (Swanson and Sonka 1980, p. 66). Virtually all technical economies of size inherent in the current technology have already been exploited by family-sized crop farms. Consequently net farm income after technical economies is almost directly proportional to gross farm income over the range of commercial production, which encompasses 70 percent of all production. In addition, Hottel and Harrington (1979) and Jensen, Hatch, and Harrington (1981) have demonstrated that financial, tenure, and equity considerations are capable of overshadowing likely gains due to technical economies of size for typical family farms.

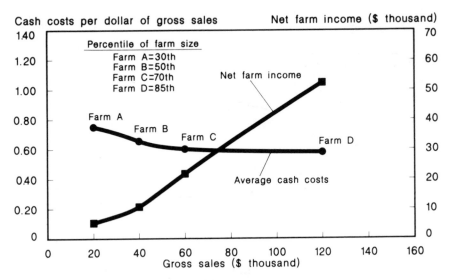

Source: Miller, Rodewald and McElroy 1981.

Figure 1–4. Average Cash Costs per Dollar of Gross Sales, 1980

These estimates of production economies of size, however, do not take into account any procurement and marketing advantages and tax regulations that can further increase the net returns of larger farms (Davenport, Boehlje, and Martin 1982; Krause and Burbee 1982; Krause and Kyle 1970, 1971). There are significant economies of scale in buying inputs. The larger farms can obtain quantity discounts and more favorable terms.

Form of Business Organization

Farm businesses are organized in three principal ways: sole proprietorships, partnerships, and corporations. Sole proprietorships are the simplest and most common form of organization (86.8 percent of farms in 1982), followed by partnerships (10.0 percent) and corporations (2.7 percent) (figure 1–5). Although sole proprietorships are what are ordinarily thought of as family farms, all three types are chiefly family organizations: in partnerships, the partners are usually related by blood or marriage, and most corporate farms are family owned and operated (Harrington et al. 1983; Reimund 1979a).

The growth in corporate farming during the 1970s is almost entirely attributable to an increase in the number of family and other closely held farming corporations. The number of corporate farms with ten or fewer shareholders, which are mostly family farm corporations, nearly doubled between 1974 and 1982 (table 1–8).

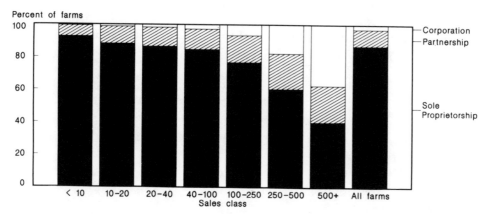

Source: 1982 Census of Agriculture

Figure 1–5. Form of Business Organization, 1982

Over the same period, widely held (nonfamily) corporations declined in number, in farmland operated, and in value of products sold. In 1982, farming corporations with more than ten shareholders accounted for only 0.1 percent of all farms, less than 2 percent of land in farms, and just over 4 percent of the value of agricultural products sold.

Federal tax policies probably have had more influence on the conversion of farms to the corporate form of organization than any other single policy or program of the federal government (Boehlje and Krause 1981; Davenport, Boehlje, and Martin 1982; Krause 1982; Krause and Burbee 1982). Federal income tax policies, in particular, encourage farm business incorporation because corporate tax rates are much lower than individual rates for taxable incomes above $25,000 to $35,000 (Boehlje and Krause 1981). Corporate income tax provisions enable farming corporations to increase equity capital through retained earnings at a faster rate than sole proprietorships or partnerships. Further, federal tax policies encourage certain nontaxable fringe benefits for corporate farm owners. On the other hand, social security taxes are higher on the salaries that incorporated farmers pay themselves than on the earnings of unincorporated farmers. Corporate farmers who reinvest a significant portion of farm earnings in the business can still make substantial total tax savings (Jeremias and Durst 1984).

Industrial corporations are not taking over the ownership and operation of U.S. farms. The 1974 Census of Agriculture (the only data on this topic) found 3,460 business-associated corporate farms. These were farms owned by corporations more than half of whose business income came from nonfarm sources. This was less than 0.1 percent of all farms, and accounted for 0.6 percent of all land in farms and 3.4 percent of the value of agricultural products sold. These business-associated corporate farms were most important

Table 1–8
Number, Landownership, and Value of Sales of Corporate Farms
(Share of all farms)

Item and Year	Ten or Fewer Shareholders	More Than Ten Shareholders
Number of farms		
1974	1.0	< 0.1
1978	2.0	.1
1982	2.5	.1
Percentage change in share, 1974–1982	160.0	220.0
Land in farms		
1974	7.3	2.1
1978	10.1	1.6
1982	11.7	1.9
Percentage change in share, 1974–1982	60.0	– 10.0
Sales		
1974	12.3	5.7
1978	17.4	4.2
1982	19.8	4.1
Percentage change in share, 1974–1982	81.0	– 28.1

Source: *1974 Census of Agriculture*, vol. IV, pt. 5, *1978 Census of Agriculture*, vol. I, pt. 51, and *1982 Census of Agriculture*, vol. 1, pt. 51.

in the category Other Field Crops, where they accounted for 13.5 percent of sales. These were mostly sugarcane farms in Hawaii, Florida, and Louisiana. Other commodity groups where such business-associated corporate farms accounted for more than 5 percent of sales included:

Commodity group	Percent of sales
Seeds, hay, and forage	12.2
Poultry	8.3
Fruit and nuts	8.0
Other livestock	7.8
Nursery and greenhouse	7.7
Vegetables	7.1
Beef	5.2

There have been a few celebrated cases of nonfarm corporations going into agricultural production in recent years. United Brands decided to transfer what it had learned about banana and vegetable production in Central America to

California. It purchased a large producer-shipper of lettuce in the Salinas Valley in the 1970s. In 1983 Sun Harvest (half owned by United Brands) announced that it was leaving the lettuce business. Superior Oil Company also decided to sell its produce-growing subsidies. Similar ventures in vegetable production by Purex and Tenneco lasted for only a few years. Only Castle and Cooke has remained in vegetable farming over an extended period.

Ventures by Ralston Purina and other feed manufacturers into poultry production did not change the cyclical nature of that business, and they mostly moved on to other enterprises. Kentucky Fried Chicken purchased an integrated broiler operation; however, this production operation supplies only a portion of the broilers that the company sells in its restaurants, and not all of the broilers produced by the company are sold through Kentucky Fried Chicken outlets.

Tenure

Some farmers own all their land, some rent all their land, and others own some land and rent the rest. The importance of full tenancy operations has declined noticeably, and the acreage rented by farmers from nonoperator landlords has increased. As a percentage of total land in farms, rented farmland dropped from 45 percent in 1935 to 37 percent in 1969 with the decline in tenant farming. It has remained roughly constant since then, being 35 percent in 1982.

Farms in the lower sales classes are overwhelmingly full owners. Over 75 percent of those in the rural residence category are full owners, while only 8 percent are full tenants and 15 percent part owners. Among family-sized farms, 30 percent are full owners, 14 percent are full tenants, and 56 percent are part owners. The larger-than-single-family farms have a slightly higher proportion of full ownership, 36 percent, and slightly lower proportions of full tenancy, 12 percent, with part ownership at 52 percent (figure 1–6).

The decision to lease or own land depends on the operator's need for current realized returns versus deferred, unrealized returns from capital appreciation of land (Hottel and Harrington 1979). Throughout the 1970s, leasing generally returned a higher net farm income to the operator, whereas landownership produced strong capital gains. Large and rapidly growing farms tended to make greater use of rented land in their operations in order to have less real estate debt to service out of cash receipts. The situation in the 1980s is uncertain. Land values have been dropping, but land rental rates still appear to be holding steady in the face of declining farm profitability.

Farmland Ownership

While there were 2.4 million farms in 1978, there were about 6 million farmland owners, nearly the same number as in the previous documentation of

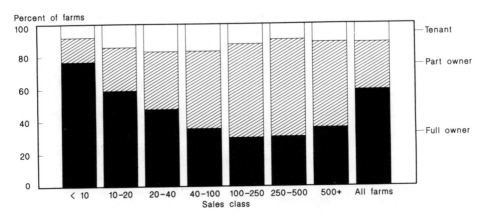

Source: 1982 Census of Agriculture

Figure 1–6. Tenure of Operator, 1982

U.S. landownership in 1946; however, there was a significant change in the composition of farmland owners. In 1978, only a third of the farmland owners were farm operators, compared with 70 percent in 1946. Most farmland (90.3 percent) is owned by individuals or close family units, including family corporations.

Foreign entities and individuals own a very small amount of farmland in the United States (DeBraal and Majchrowicz 1983). As of October of 1984, foreign ownership of agricultural land was reported to be 14 million acres, only 1 percent of all privately held agricultural land. However, 57 percent of this was classified as forest land, and nearly two-thirds was owned by U.S. corporations with 5 percent or more foreign ownership.

Summary: Profiles of Farm Size Classes

Inflation, changing technology, increasing off-farm income, and increasing specialization of farms have changed the distribution of farms by sales classes. After correcting for these changes, however, there is a surprising similarity of the profiles of farm-size categories defined earlier: rural residences, small family farms, family farms and larger-than-single-family farms (table 1–9).

The sales of the farm-size categories in 1982 are four to five times the corresponding sales class values of 1960, yet the percentage distributions of numbers of farms and total production are nearly unchanged. Roughly half the farms are noncommercial, rural residences; roughly 5 percent are larger-than-single-family operations. The noncommercial half of the farms produce only 3 to 5 percent of total output, but the larger-than-single-family operations have increased their share of total output from one-third to one-half in the last two decades.

Table 1–9
Profiles of Farm Size Categories, 1960 and 1982

Measure	Rural Residences	Small Family Farms	Family Farms	Larger-Than-Single-Family Farms
Sales class				
1982	Less than $10,000	$10,000–39,999	$40,000–199,999	$200,000 and up
1960	Less than $ 2,500	$ 2,500– 9.999	$10,000– 39,999	$ 40,000 and up
Percentage of farms				
1982	49	23	23	4
1960	46	32	19	3
Percentage of production				
1982	3	9	39	49
1960	5	22	40	33
Approximate cropland used[a]				
1982	Up to 40 acres	40–160 acres	160–640 acres	640 acres and up
1960	Up to 45 acres	45–175 acres	175–700 acres	700 acres and up
Approximate labor input at most common technology[b]				
1982	Up to 5 person weeks	5–20 person weeks	20–100 person weeks	Over 100 person weeks
1960	Up to 9 person weeks	9–36 person weeks	36–144 person weeks	Over 144 person weeks
Ratio of production expenses to cash receipts				
1982	2.35	1.20	0.96	0.76
1960	.84	.71	.74	.75
Net farm income per farm				
1982	$ −737	$ −121	$ 10,100	$ 169,402
1960	$ 806	$ 2,594	$ 6,030	$ 17,274
Off-farm income per farm				
1982	$ 19,894	$ 15,092	$ 10,746	$ 16,696
1960	$ 2,732	$ 1,706	$ 1,390	$ 2,177
Assets per farm				
1982	$134,493	$313,372	$791,174	$2,337,491
1960	$ 18,600	$ 40,000	$105,000	$ 260,000

Source: Calculated by authors.

[a]Approximate acres of corn, at yields and prices of the day, that would be required to provide gross sales equal to sales cutoff points of size category: 1982 = 109 bu./acre @$2.10, 1960 = 54 bu./acre @$1.05.

[b]Approximate labor input required to reproduce the acreage of corn required in footnote a, assuming common field crop technology of the day.

Because of rapid technological change, labor inputs in each of these farm-size categories have declined since 1960. Also, it takes slightly fewer acres of crops to equal the dollar sales of the various size classes in 1982 than in 1960. Forty acres of corn at 1982 yields and prices would put a farm at the $10,000 break between rural residences and small family farms. In 1960, it would have taken 45 acres to produce $2,500 worth of corn, the break between the two size categories at that time. In 1982, a family-sized farm would require between 160 and 640 acres of land—if it were all used for crops as intensive as corn. Larger-than-single-family farms, beginning at about 640 acres, are usually multiple-operator or multiple-generation family farms rather than large, nonfamily corporations.

Most striking has been the decline in labor input required by a crop farm in each of the size categories. Because of more mechanization, the introduction of pesticides and herbicides, increasing yields from new varieties, and higher rates of fertilization, the amount of labor that would be required to be in the rural residence category dropped from 9 weeks to 5 weeks. Similarly, the labor required by a corn farm at the cutoff point between family farms and larger-than-single-family farms was 144 weeks in 1960 but only about 100 weeks in 1982. This fact helps explain the squeeze on the incomes of family-sized farm operators; comparable-sized farms are, in fact, using less labor now than they did in 1960.

The next several measures relate to income and well-being. The ratio of production expenses to cash receipts illustrates that all size categories returned some net income to their operators in 1960. By 1982, the smaller two size categories appeared to return tax or paper losses to their operators. Family-size farms were feeling the pinch in 1982, with production expenses almost equaling cash income. Larger-than-single-family-farms displayed similar ratios in 1982 and 1960, indicating similar profit orientation and similar economic performance in both periods.

Off-farm income increased sharply for all farm sizes between 1960 and 1982. By 1982 neither the rural residence nor the small-family-farm category primarily depended on farming for their livelihood. Family-size farms show about equal dependence on net farm income and off-farm income. Larger-than-single-family farms realized large net farm incomes, but these were often split between several owners and/or operators. In 1960, only the rural residence category had higher levels of off-farm income than of net farm income.

The value of assets in each of these farm size categories increased eightfold while inflation as measured by the gross national product (GNP) deflator tripled over the same period. The result was a significant increase in the real wealth of owners of agricultural assets. Thus, while much of the farm sector suffered a decline in net income compared to the economy in general over the two decades, farm asset owners accumulated real wealth, and still retain much of it in spite of recent declines in farm asset values.

Financial Structure of the Farm Sector

The financial structure of agriculture encompasses the income and wealth positions of farm operators and the farm sector. As with individuals and businesses, the financial position of the farm sector is indicated by income and balance sheet statistics. This section concentrates on the incomes of farmers in a typical year (1982), the growth of farm assets and debts over the 1970s, and the current financial situation of farmers.

Current Income

The average income of farm operator families, which includes net farm and off-farm income, was well below the national average family income in 1982, a year that typifies the income situation of the early 1980s (figure 1–7). (The Payment-in-Kind (PIK) program of 1983 temporarily distorted the level and distribution of direct government payments for 1983 and 1984.) Income of farm operator families in the $200,000 and over sales classes significantly exceeded the national median family income. The distribution of income among farm families has become U shaped due chiefly to the growth of off-farm income in the lower sales classes and the continued profitability of large farms (Carlin and Ghelfi 1979). Farm operator families on small family farms ($10,000–39,999) have incomes below the U.S. median family income in

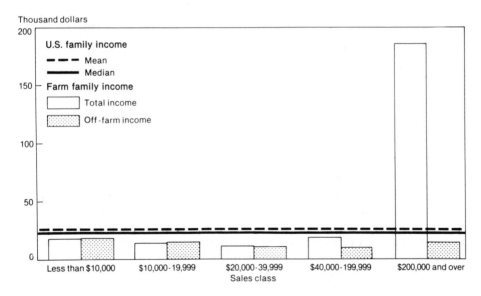

Source: USDA 1984f.

Figure 1–7. Average Farm Family Income by Farm Size, 1982

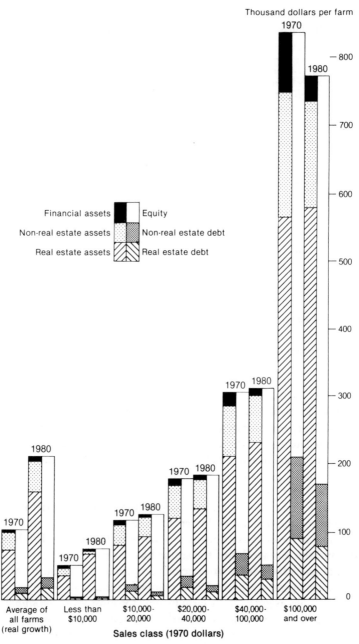

Figure 1–8. Balance Sheet of Farms by Sales Class, 1970 and 1980

Source: USDA 1984f.

losses, unless a farm experiences such severe cashflow problems and declining equity levels that liquidation or bankruptcy occurs. The most highly leveraged farms—those that expanded in the late 1970s or that used a lot of their equity to cover past cashflow losses—were the first to feel the stress of declining rates of capital appreciation and, more severely, declining values of farm assets.

Credit Usage and Requirements in Agriculture

The farm sector has some unique credit requirements due to its ownership and operating characteristics. The traditional owner-operator farm, the dominant type of farm, requires recapitalization with inherited or internally generated equity once each generation. With larger farm sizes, rising values of farmland, and increased capital requirements of farms, recapitalization became increasingly difficult over the 1970s. Financial credit for farm ownership is necessary, but lenders and borrowers must recognize the uncertainty of annual net returns and, more recently, the uncertainty of farm asset values. Hence both farmers and lenders should attempt to maintain modest debt-to-asset ratios. When farms need to be refinanced to weather periods of unfavorable yields or prices, the owner's equity is the cushion that allows such refinancing. Highly leveraged farms have difficulty surviving such periods.

Farm real estate debt has more than tripled between 1970 and 1985 (table 1–11). One reason for the rapid rise in real estate debt was that current returns to farm assets constituted a relatively small portion of total returns (current returns plus capital gains) throughout the postwar period. Another is that during the 1970s, inflation raised both interest rates and input prices, increasing farmers' needs for current cash returns to service debt and meet cash production expenses. Thus, many farmers found it necessary to monetize their capital gains by borrowing against the increased value of their assets, but this increased their vulnerability to income swings. These borrowing trends contributed to a significant increase in the debt burden of many farmers and to the declining financial stability of the farm sector.

Operating credit needs of farms also increased—more than quadrupling since 1970—primarily due to increases in outlays for production inputs and capital items. Farm operations, being biologically based, tend to have annual production cycles requiring credit to purchase inputs early in the year in the expectation of salable products later in the year. If credit is unavailable or prohibitively expensive when planting decisions are made, the size of a crop may be greatly reduced. Similarly, if credit is unavailable when livestock carryover decisions are made, both immediate and long-term meat and livestock supplies can be affected by reduction of breeding herds.

Summary: Financial Strength of the Farm Sector

The most commonly accepted measure of financial strength is the debt-to-asset ratio of the firm. It is a measure primarily oriented toward ensuring

Table 1–11
Real Estate and Other Farm Debt Outstanding, January 1, 1970, 1985

Type of Creditor	Real Estate Debt				Other Debt			
	1970		1985		1970		1985	
	Million Dollars	Percentage of Total	Million Dollars	Percentage of Total	Million Dollars	Percentage of Total	Million Dollars	Percentage of Total
Federal land banks	6,671	22.9	48,444	43.1	n.a.	n.a.	n.a.	n.a.
Farmers Home Administration	2,280	7.8	9,956	8.3	785	3.3	15,206	15.0
Life insurance companies	5,734	19.6	12,375	11.7	n.a.	n.a.	n.a.	n.a.
Commercial banks	3,545	12.1	10,179	7.7	10,330	43.3	40,551	40.0
Individuals and others	10,953	37.5	29,900	29.2	5,340	22.4	18,200	18.0
Production credit associations	n.a.	n.a.	n.a.	n.a.	4,495	18.9	18,129	17.9
Federal intermediate credit banks	n.a.	n.a.	n.a.	n.a.	218	.9	877	.9
Commodity Credit Corporation	n.a.	n.a.	n.a.	n.a.	2,676	11.2	8,312	8.2
Total	29,183	100.0	110,854	100.0	23,844	100.0	101,275	100.0

n.a. = not applicable.
Source: Harrington et al. 1983; USDA 1984g.

adequate security for a lender. It is the ratio of two total value indicators: total assets and total debts. It provides little information about the flows of income and contractual payments or other important cash flow variables. Debt-to-asset ratios have increased in unfavorable years and decreased in favorable years. As of January 1, 1984, farms in the highest sales category had the highest debt-to-asset ratios, and farms in the lowest sales classes had the lowest debt-to-asset ratios (table 1–10). These ratios imply, on average, adequate security for lenders and strong financial positions. Nevertheless farmers with debt-to-asset ratios above approximately 40 percent generally must delay debt payments or refinance their debts when faced with a year of unfavorable income. A few years of poor returns, closely spaced, as have occurred since 1981, can bring a reasonably well-established farm with 60 percent equity and 40 percent debt to the point of forced liquidation. The financial problems wrought by several low-income years are exacerbated if asset values are declining at the same time. The current financial crisis in agriculture is the result of just this combination of events.

Data available as of January 1985 on the severity of farm financial problems (table 1–12) suggest the following:

At current interest rates and levels of net returns in farming, farms with debt-to-asset ratios of over 40 percent are likely experiencing cash shortfalls. Farms with ratios of over 70 percent are almost certain to have serious cash shortfalls.

Some 194,000 farms have debt-to-asset ratios from 40 to 70 percent. Termed highly leveraged, these farms tend to have serious cash shortfalls and owe one-third of all farm debt.

As many as 72,000 farms have debt-to-asset ratios between 70 and 100 percent. These very highly leveraged farms make up only 7.3 percent of all farms, but they owe over 15 percent of all farm debt.

A further 50,000 farms have debt-to-asset ratios of over 100 percent. These farms are technically insolvent in that their assets, if sold, would not bring enough money to discharge the debts of the farm. These farms owe almost 15 percent of all farm debt.

Not all of the farms in the highly and very highly leveraged categories are under serious financial stress. Farms with less than $40,000 in sales obtain much of their income from off-farm sources and often qualify for and repay their loans on the basis of off-farm income. On the other hand, very large farms with over $500,000 in sales tend to be highly industrialized specialty operations (feedlots, sod farms, nurseries, orchards, and poultry operations) and typically operate with high debt-to-asset ratios. Higher proportions of these very large farms have positive cash flows.

Table 1–12
Distribution of Farms and Farm Debt by Debt-Asset Ratio and Sales Class, January 1985

Sales Class	Highly Leveraged (debt-asset ratios of 40 to 70 percent)			Very Highly Leveraged (debt-asset ratios 70 to 100 percent)			Technically Insolvent (debt-asset ratios over 100 percent)		
	Percentage of Size Class	Number of Farms	Percentage of Debt	Percentage of Size Class	Number of Farms	Percentage of Debt	Percentage of Size Class	Number of Farms	Percentage of Debt
$500,000 and over	21.1	6,417	5.3	8.6	2,611	2.6	6.0	1,827	3.7
$250,000–499,999	23.6	16,184	5.9	8.9	6,118	2.8	5.7	3,993	1.9
$100,000–249,999	20.7	47,411	10.8	7.7	17,583	5.1	4.5	10,391	3.1
$40,000–99,999	16.8	51,285	6.5	6.1	18,540	3.1	4.6	13,982	2.3
$20,000–39,999	10.4	20,708	1.9	4.2	8,328	0.8	4.0	8,011	0.9
$10,000–19,999	8.1	15,623	1.1	3.4	6,581	0.7	3.0	5,820	0.5
Less than $10,000	5.8	36,577	1.5	1.9	12,069	0.7	1.0	6,185	0.7
All farms	11.6	194,205	32.9	4.3	71,830	15.8	3.0	50,209	13.1

Source: USDA 1985h.

Table 1–13
Farms with Cash Flow Shortfalls: Numbers, Proportions, and Proportions of Debt Owed

Sales Class	Highly Leveraged			Very Highly Leveraged			Technically Insolvent		
	Percentage of Group	Number of Farms	Percentage of Debt	Percentage of Group	Number of Farms	Percentage of Debt	Percentage of Group	Number of Farms	Percentage of Debt
$500,000 and over	50	3,221	3.1	47	1,250	1.5	53	973	3.0
$250,000–499,999	47	7,550	3.3	69	4,248	2.3	60	2,378	1.3
$100,000–249,999	57	27,173	7.5	71	12,515	3.9	69	7,528	2.7
$40,000–99,999	70	35,678	5.2	85	15,669	2.8	76	10,657	1.9
$20,000–39,999	92	19,020	1.8	73	6,095	0.6	91	7,264	0.9
$10,000–19,999	60	9,439	0.7	87	5,921	0.6	76	4,416	0.5
Less than $10,000	48	19,030	0.8	73	8,930	0.5	78	4,820	0.4
All farms with cash shortfalls	62	121,111	22.3	76	54,628	12.4	76	38,036	10.7

Source: USDA 1985h.
Tables 1–12 and 1–13 were calculated from slightly different samples.

Farms that have both high debt-to-asset ratios and cash flow shortfalls have the most serious financial stress problems. Table 1–13 summarizes the numbers of farms and proportions of debt that experienced cash shortfalls in 1984. These farms with cash shortfalls in 1984 (table 1–13) should be considered as the minimum numbers and proportions of farms that are experiencing financially related income problems. Table 1–12 should be considered as the maximum estimate. Thus, between 225,000 and 315,000 farms had financial problems ranging from difficulties in meeting principal repayment commitments to technical insolvency. These farms owe between 45 and 60 percent of all farm debt; thus poor loan performance is a significant problem for farm lenders. Half or more of farm debt needs special attention in the form of loan stretch-outs, reamortizations, renegotiation, or perhaps foreclosures.

The farm sector is subject to extreme variability of net income, with attendant cash flow problems. Low and variable realized returns and high fixed interest payments contribute to the financial instability of the sector. In short, the farm sector is becoming increasingly prone to boom or bust cash flow situations. Without some form of cash flow stabilization or diversification of income sources, many farms may be able to support relatively modest debt-to-asset ratios. The resulting restrictions on debt acquisition would inhibit the ability of farms to make capital investments in improved technology or to adopt specialized, capital-intensive, cost-reducing production methods. This financial instability influences the patterns of farm consolidation in the sector. Acquiring additional farmland would place many small and medium-sized farms in highly vulnerable, leveraged positions. Thus, only large, well-established farms have the financial means to absorb other farms or large tracts of land.

Institutional Structure

The farm sector operates in a unique economic and institutional environment, which has led to a number of public policies aimed at altering its performance.

Technological Adoption

Since individual farmers are price takers, they have quickly adopted new cost-reducing or output-increasing technologies of production, storage, and marketing to increase profit margins (Cochrane 1979; Lu 1979; Swanson and Sonka 1980). Early adopters of a technology derive only temporary benefits from it. The cost-reducing technology results in an increased total supply of the products affected, driving down the prices and profits of early adoptors and forcing late adopters to use the new technology merely to stay in business. This is known as the technological treadmill (Cochrane 1979). Because of the technological treadmill, the farm sector has been progressive and efficient, and the benefits of technological advances and productivity increases have been passed on to consumers of farm products.

Instability of Prices and Incomes

After remaining relatively stable through the 1950s and 1960s, net farm income gyrated widely in the 1970s and early 1980s (figure 1–9). Instability of income in agriculture stems from many sources, all important. Farming is subject to yield and production variability caused by weather, disease, and natural hazards. For example, national average yields and total production of corn dropped by almost 20 percent between 1979 and 1980.

Because of the inelastic demands for agricultural products in domestic markets, total income to producers of a commodity can be severely depressed by bumper crops—or, conversely, greatly increased by crop shortfalls. Increases in supplies result in proportionally larger decreases in prices, causing total incomes to fall. Conversely, crop shortfalls cause greater increases in

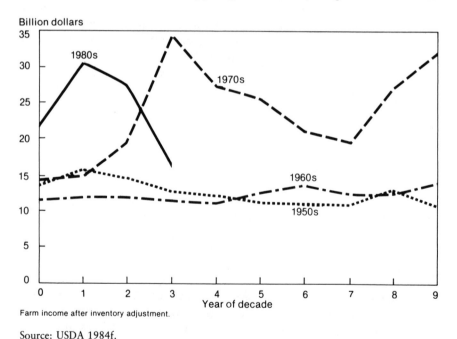

Farm income after inventory adjustment.

Source: USDA 1984f.

Figure 1–9. Instability of Net Farm Income over Three Decades

prices, and total incomes rise. As a result, current income to the farm sector can be very volatile from year to year. Over a period of several years, however, the responsiveness of the farm sector—in increasing the supplies of products that show short-run profits—causes reductions in all commodity prices and increases in factor prices (primarily land) to levels that just cover the cost structure of farms, including the opportunity costs of selling resources to other farmers (Hoffman et al. 1981).

World demand for U.S. agricultural products is likely elastic, but it is highly variable, especially as large international customers alter their trade practices and policies. Variability of cash receipts and income of farm operators have increased in recent years (table 1–14). Net farm income changed from one of the most stable portions of farmers' income to one of the most unstable portions.

Inflation

Variability of net returns stemming from production, demand, and cost variation is only part of the problem. Concurrent changes in the economic environment and the inflation expectations of investors in farmland have amplified the problem of instability. In the 1970s and early 1980s, several changes in the economic setting of agriculture occurred, largely linked to inflation in the general economy and to the value of the dollar in international exchange.

Changes in Cash Flows and Rates of Return. Persistent inflation throughout the 1970s caused cash incomes and expenditures to diverge from economic

Table 1–14
Variation in Farm Income, 1950–1983

	Coefficient of Variation[a]	
Item	*1950–1971*	*1972–1983*
Gross income from farming	20.4	25.2
All cash receipts	19.3	25.2
Crop receipts	17.4	27.4
Livestock receipts	21.4	25.5
Income of farm operator families		
Net farm income less government payments	16.0	17.3
Net farm income	11.9	23.4
Nonfarm	25.8	22.6
Income from all sources	17.7	15.9

Source: Calculated from USDA 1984f.

[a]The coefficient of variation is the standard deviation of the data series divided by the mean and expressed as a percent.

costs and returns. In a stable economic environment without inflation, there is an exact correspondence between cash flows and economic costs and returns in the long run, when all returns are realized and all costs are covered. However, when inflation and the institutional rules governing income taxation and the use of credit are introduced into the economic environment, there is no longer any fixed correspondence between cash flows and economic costs and returns in the short run (Harrington 1983).

In the 1970s, the combination of several institutional factors—inflation, capital gains treatment of certain returns, cash accounting, and credit terms—caused the realized cash income portion of farm returns to shrink and the unrealized capital gains portion of returns to expand (Melichar 1979). Thus, farmers and investors in farmland felt that they could benefit from inflation by aggressive investment and expansion of their farms.

Farmland Values. Most farm assets—75 percent on January 1, 1985—are in the form of real estate, chiefly farmland. This farmland is valued mostly by its expected return in farming (Boxley and Walker 1979). It is physically and economically impossible for most farmland to be converted to nonfarm use within any short period, except on urban fringes and in a few other localized areas, such as where urban or industrial development is taking place. Thus, the value of farmland largely reflects the expected returns (both cash returns and capital gains) from continued agricultural use of the land (Melichar 1979). These expectations are frequently conditioned by long-term return factors that may be unrelated to the current year's cash return to farm assets. As a consequence, owner-operators of farms are frequently caught between cash outflow that reflects the long-run expected value of farmland and cash inflow that reflects temporarily different current incomes.

The value of farm assets, especially land, also adjusted to the conditions of the 1970s as farmers and investors in farmland came to recognize two new and important aspects of land ownership. In addition to being a necessary production input (for which it could be rented), farmland became a superior hedge against inflation and, by the mid-1970s, it had become analogous to a growth stock (Melichar 1979). The inflation-hedge motive attracted more nonfarm investors to the land market and induced more farmland owners to hold on to their investments. The former led to a higher demand for land and the latter to a lower supply of land offered for sale; the combination of the two raised the price of land much faster than the inflation rate throughout the 1970s. And farmers and investors were led by a long history of favorable capital gains on land investments to acquire more land and use more financial leverage.

The growth-stock characteristic of land was that its value increased because of expected future increases in returns to land ownership through operation or later resale. Investors in farmland, like investors in any other growth stock, had to be prepared to experience negative cash flows for several years.

Thus, farmland investors, farm or nonfarm, had to subsidize their land purchases from either previously owned farmland for which the net cash flow was positive or off-farm income sources.

With any growth stock, when growth expectations decline or even taper off, its price must fall. Hence, one would expect a decline in farmland values if any of the following were to occur: a sustained decline in the level of current returns, a change from an expectation of future growth in returns to an expectation of no growth, or a reduction in potential returns from tax treatment or from control of inflation in the general economy. Each of these has occurred to some extent since 1981, and the trend of increasing land values has been broken, at least temporarily. Current prices for farmland are down from their 1980–1981 peaks. Declines of as much as 48 percent have been recorded in some states in the corn belt and upper Midwest.

The land market is a thin market; only about 3 percent of farmland changes ownership in any year. Also, all farmland is valued on the basis of the few arm's-length sales that do occur each year. In years of favorable incomes or expectations, land prices are likely to be high; in the face of poor incomes or expectations (such as forced sales), the land market is likely to be severely depressed.

International Markets

Another factor contributing to increased instability in the agricultural sector is the increased reliance of the rest of the world on U.S. supplies of crops. In the three decades from 1950 to 1980, exports increased from 5.5 percent to 18.4 percent of gross farm output—highest for crop commodities. For many important agricultural exports, up to 60 percent of the world's exportable supplies have been produced in the United States in recent years. The competitiveness of U.S. agricultural exports in the 1970s was due to the devaluation of the dollar in the early years of the decade and to exceptionally strong foreign demand. Exports have been as high as 77 percent of production for wheat and 50 percent for soybeans. International markets are typically thin, volatile, and subject to the vagaries of international politics and currency exchange relationships. World grain production did not deviate more than 5 percent from trend in 1972–1973, but this shortfall, exacerbated by policies of trading partners, resulted in large commodity price increases and massive income transfers to farmers.

While the expanded markets for U.S. farm products have contributed to growth in the farm sector, they have also contributed to the instability of agricultural markets. U.S. producers and consumers have absorbed most of the costs of the resulting variability. The variability of net farm income was more than twice as great in the 1970s and early 1980s than in the 1950s (table 1–14). The sensitivity of international markets to changes in currency exchange relationships is underscored by the fact that since 1982, the realized dollar value of U.S. agricultural exports has declined, though foreign buyers paid more in their own currencies than they did in 1981. The strengthening of the dollar in international exchange is closely related to the high real interest rates that accompany large federal budget deficits and efforts to fight inflation through monetary policy.

Policy Responses

Different commodity subsectors have reacted differently to the economic and institutional structure of the agricultural sector. Producers of grains and fibers have obtained governmental stabilization and support of their prices through commodity programs since the 1930s (Johnson et al. 1979; Miller and Sharpels 1979). Producers of fresh fruits and vegetables have reacted to intraseasonal, as well as interseasonal, instability of prices and to disparities in bargaining power between producers and handlers by seeking governmental authority partially to regulate markets under marketing orders (Thor and Jesse 1981; Jesse and Johnson 1981; USDA 1981b). Producers of processing vegetables have utilized negotiated production contracts to manage their risks, and processors have used these contracts to ensure timing, quality, and quantities of raw product supplies (Reimund, Martin, and Moore 1981). Dairy farmers have obtained marketing orders, governmental support of prices, and strict control of importation to reduce the risks of cyclically unstable prices as dairy herds expand or contract in response to price signals. Since the national dairy herd can be expanded only by raising heifers to twenty-four to twenty-seven months of age, milk prices can be depressed or elevated for long periods before the industry can adjust to bring supply and demand into balance (Manchester 1983). Cattle producers, too, have been subject to cyclical expansion and liquidation of beef herds for the last fifty years. The beef subsector has not resorted to any governmental regulations except import quotas to control the risks of production. Instead beef producers have used various market means to spread their risks: hedging on futures markets, spreading ownership of cattle on feed among many off-farm investors through custom feeding, and more recently increased contracting (Reimund et al. 1981). Poultry producers do not have governmental programs to stabilize prices. The broiler subsector is the classic case of private sector adjustment to risk (Dorner 1980; Reimund, Martin, and Moore 1981). It is almost entirely vertically integrated, with broilers owned by an individual firm (the integrator) all the way from hatchery flocks to the supermarket loading platform. The traditional farm production portion of this integrated process is the grow-out phase, where farm operators contract their labor and facilities to integrators and raise broilers for a contractual margin.

Eggs and turkeys are not as integrated, but their organization is still highly industrialized and coordinated through contracts and ownership integration.

Farm Commodity Programs

Farm commodity programs have been used to raise and stabilize returns to farming since the Great Depression (Ericksen et al. 1981; Johnson et al. 1979; Lee 1981; Lin, Johnson, and Calvin 1981; Miller and Sharpels 1979). Direct payment programs or loan and storage programs are currently in effect for wheat, feed grains, cotton, soybeans, and rice; production or marketing quota programs exist for peanuts and tobacco; and milk prices are supported through a direct purchase program.

The effects of these programs on the organization of agriculture have been mixed. Four effects have been evident in various subsectors of agriculture:

1. Public assumption of some of the price and production risks of farming may have stimulated farm growth and consolidation by allowing farmers to assume more debt with less risk. Farmers could thus adopt new, specialized technologies faster and acquire more land as it became available, thus leading to a high and stable demand for land (Cochrane 1979).

2. Insuring or protecting farmers against low prices or natural hazards has prevented highly leveraged farms from being forced out of business in periods of low prices or poor production. This may have slowed the consolidation of farms by reducing the amount of land forced to change ownership because of financial difficulties, leading to a low and stable supply of land offered for sale (Lins 1979; Lins and Barry 1980).

3. The combination of high demand and low supply of land for sale has led to high and increasing prices of land (Boxley and Walker 1979).

4. Supporting the prices of farm products above what they would otherwise be, while simultaneously increasing productivity through technological advances, led to returns to farm assets higher than they would be if product prices were not supported (Cochrane 1979). This reinforced the expectation of increasing returns to farm assets and, consequently, the expectation of capital gains for owners of farm assets (Melichar 1979).

Other Market Policies

Marketing orders have very different effects from private sector means of stabilizing and sharing risks of production. Federal marketing orders for fruits, vegetables, and specialty crops (forty-eight orders) have the potential for increasing economic efficiency by stabilizing returns to producers, providing buyers with assured supplies of products of known quality, and facilitating such activities as product research and container standardization. But because some orders can limit quantities marketed, either in total or for certain uses, marketing orders can raise farm income at the expense of consumers (Jesse and Johnson 1981; USDA 1981b).

Not all marketing orders contain provisions that allow allocating supplies between different uses or markets, controlling the seasonal flow of products to market, or creating a reserve pool. Only two orders (hops and mint oil) restrict entry of new producers, and these provisions are being phased out. Losses from misallocations and inefficiencies are offset to varying degrees by gains from price and quantity stabilization. Detailed analysis of each order would be required to assess the balance of gains and losses for each market.

Marketing orders for fluid grade milk utilize classified (use) pricing and pooling to provide somewhat more stability than would otherwise exist in three principal dimensions:

1. Seasonal price relationships have been stabilized through the classified pricing system so that class prices and, to some extent, blend prices in the flush production season are above short-run market-clearing levels and those in the short season are below short-run market-clearing levels.

2. Spacial price relationships have been stabilized so that intermarket differences in prices reflect the cost of transportation and varying supply and demand conditions in individual markets.

3. Competitive relationships—the behavior of processors as milk buyers— have been stabilized through pooling so that processors equally situated pay more nearly the same class prices for milk and producers equally situated receive similar prices. Put differently, the effect is to minimize free-riding.

Income enhancement for producers of fluid grade milk through price discrimination was of some significance in the 1950s and 1960s but is now minor (Manchester 1982).

Public policy has been modestly supportive of agricultural cooperatives during most of this century, largely on the grounds that farmer cooperatives provide countervailing power in the marketplace that individual farmers lack when dealing with the relative few and generally larger buyers of their products and sellers of farm inputs. Marketing cooperatives are provided a partial exemption from the general antitrust laws, which allows them to exist and to engage in some activities (primarily in concert with other cooperatives) not allowed to other firms (Manchester 1982).

Tax Policy

Tax policies have made farming a tax-favored industry (USDA 1979b). The tax-sheltering possibilities of farm assets have exacerbated the capital barriers to entry facing new owner-operators through the following:

Making current cash income and expenditures a downward-biased indicator of economic returns in agriculture (Harrington 1983).

Inflating asset values by their expected return as possible tax shelters, further depressing the apparent rates of return based on cash income and expenditures (Harrington 1983).

Stimulating more investment in farm assets than would otherwise be warranted, thus depressing commercial returns by stimulating greater production of farm products, which in turn lowers their prices (Davenport, Boehlje, and Martin 1982).

Fostering ownership of farm assets with tax-sheltering possibilities by those who can best reap the benefits of the tax treatment of these assets (Davenport, Boehlje, and Martin 1982).

Biasing farmers' investment decisions toward assets with lower effective tax rates. Since there are wide differences in effective tax rates between various classes of farm equipment and structures, investments tend to be concentrated where the tax treatment is best rather than on the economically most efficient types (Jeremias, Hrubovcak, and Durst 1983).

Some of the effects of income tax rules can be seen by comparing individuals who reported farm profits with those who reported farm losses to the Internal Revenue Service (IRS) in 1976 (table 1–15) (Simunek and Poirier 1983). It seems highly likely that most of the 12,000 persons who reported farm losses of $50,000 or more, averaging $104,000, were primarily interested in farming to offset those current losses against their large off-farm incomes and later reap capital gains on sales of the assets.

Additional tax policy factors that influence the structure of agriculture include estate and inheritance tax policies and institutional rules governing incorporation. The estate tax and the gift tax—federal taxes on wealth transferred during life or at death—have several provisions that can influence the ownership of farms and the maintenance and accumulation of wealth across generations. Among the most important are special use valuation of farm assets and deferred payment of estate taxes. Special use valuation, within certain limits, allows farm assets to be valued on the basis of the prevailing rental rates for these assets capitalized at the prevailing Federal Land Bank interest rate. This method of valuing agricultural assets ignores several components that contribute to the market value of farmland: its inflation-hedging, growth-stock, and tax-sheltering potentials. These components have been estimated to contribute up to 50 percent of the market value of farmland in some areas and at some times (Davenport, Boehlje, and Martin 1982). The deferred payment of estate taxes, with preferential interest rates on the first $1 million of taxable estate values, provides heirs with very valuable financing breaks. Access to these provisions is focused toward farmers by requiring material participation and qualified use tests for eligibility (Davenport, Boehlje, and Martin

1982; Krause and Burbee 1982). Other institutional rules surrounding incorporation of farms, provision of fringe benefits, and liabilities for certain employment taxes such as workers' compensation have been shown to provide significant means for farms to obtain favored tax positions (Krause 1982).

Issues in the Organization of Agriculture

The causes and effects of structural change are highly interdependent, with many feedback effects. There has been insufficient research to establish a complete understanding of structural change. This much has been established: structural change and structural policies affect farmers and the farm sector by influencing individual farms and households at one or more stages of their life cycle: entry, survival and growth, and succession. Aggregate structural change is determined by who (or what types of organizations) can outcompete whom at each stage. Structural change issues can be viewed from three vantage points: The farmers' problems, the industry's problems, and the policymakers' problems.

Farmers' Problems

Farmers' problems are concrete and revolve around how to enter, how to survive and grow, and how to pass the farm on to the next generation. Entry was made difficult in the 1970s by high and rising capital requirements. Rapid inflation raised barriers to entry by stimulating even more rapid increases in farmland values. With lower inflation rates and declining farmland values in the 1980s, entry may again become favorable for operators who can maintain low debt burdens.

Farm survival and growth is as much a matter of financial management as production or marketing management. The rapid increase in farm asset values in the 1970s followed by the shocks of the early 1980s resulted in financial strategies being the key to growth and survival of farms. Financial strategies that led to success in the economic environment of the 1970s frequently resulted in financial disaster in the 1980s. Farmers' financial growth and survival problems center around adjusting to the economic instability of the agricultural sector (balancing growth and security), adjusting to the disparity between cash flows and economic returns (balancing returns from current net income and capital gains), and adjusting to farm and nonfarm opportunities for investment and employment (balancing farm and nonfarm income sources). These financial decisions are superimposed on day-to-day production and marketing decisions and are currently of equal, if not greater, importance.

The third problem from the farmer's point of view is passing the farm on to the next generation—whether to his or her own family or to a new entrant.

Table 1–15
IRS Farm and Off-Farm Income, by Individuals Reporting Farm Profits and
Losses, per Farm, 1976

Item	Number of Returns (thousands)	Adjusted Gross Income	Farm Income or Loss	Off-Farm Income
Farm profits				
$50,000 or more	17	$81,673	$ 74,911	$ 8,706
$25,000–49,999	81	37,671	32,979	5,684
$10,000–24,999	231	21,196	15,624	6,110
$ 5,000–9,999	210	13,291	7,178	6,507
$ 2,000–4,999	252	11,027	3,233	8,226
$ 1,000–1,999	179	9,872	1,441	9,148
$1–999	358	10,512	397	10,851
All farms with profits	1,328	15,366	7,716	8,245
Farm losses				
$50,000 or more	12	16,362	− 104,448	122,080
$25,000–49,999	24	17,366	− 33,942	51,602
$10,000–24,999	93	15,423	− 15,154	32,348
$ 5,000–9,999	191	13,571	− 6,836	20,641
$ 3,000–4,999	228	13,638	− 3,842	18,151
$1–2,999	917	13,329	− 1,184	14,864
All farms with losses	1,465	13,631	− 4,568	18,669
All individuals	2,793	14,533	1,268	13,877

Source: Simunek and Poirier 1983.

Most concern is centered on estate taxes, but most farms except the multiple-
operator, larger-than-single-family farms can be passed to a qualified heir
without being subject to a heavy estate tax burden under current federal law.
A potentially more important problem is that of equitably sharing the estate
(or the proceeds from operating it) among many nonfarm heirs. Farming and
farmland ownership have traditionally returned low rates of current return
and high rates of capital gains and are likely to do so in the future, so it is difficult for the farm-operating heirs to buy out the nonfarm heirs, but it is
equally difficult for the nonfarm heirs to receive a fair share of returns without selling the land to realize the capital gains.

The actions of individual farmers at these three stages—entry, growth and
survival, and transfer to the next generation—determine over time the number
and size of farms, and hence the structure of farming. They are influenced by
government policies, the management decisions of farmers, and a number of
other factors over which neither the farmer nor the government has much control, such as world supply and demand, new technology, and the weather.

Industry's Problems

The farm sector as an industry faces two problems as a result of structural change. Agriculture is losing its uniqueness and, with it, may be losing control over the policies that affect it most.

The one-farm, one-owner, one-operator model of agriculture is no longer strictly applicable to farming. This model still characterizes small farms and rural residences, but among family farms and larger farms it is becoming less common. With the decline of the owner-operator model of farming, the sector has lost some of its resilience and flexibility because every factor—land, labor, capital, management, and risk bearing—must be rewarded every year. This is a far different and far less flexible system than that of low-debt owner-operators allocating an undivided margin above short-run variable costs to their most pressing needs in any year. As a result of this decreased financial flexibility, the industry is in a poorer position to withstand economic or natural shocks. Its ability to cope with instability is weakened at just the time that the probability and magnitudes of external shocks have increased.

U.S. crop production capacity has far outstripped the domestic market for food and fiber, making it mandatory to export the surplus. This has made agriculture dependent on foreign markets to absorb the production of two acres out of every five. The policies that most vitally affect the well-being of farmers are no longer under the control of the agricultural policy process—not the USDA or the farm lobby. Trade policies and international political stances are forged largely by nonagricultural interests. General economic policies as reflected in inflation, interest rates, and international exchange rates are of overwhelming importance to the economic well-being of farms. Yet agriculture has a very small voice in the formulation of these policies—no more than the share that agriculture makes up of GNP.

Policymakers' Problems

Policy analysts and policymakers face several problems in dealing with structural change in agriculture. The first is that structural change has been mostly an unintended side effect of policies designed to accomplish other ends. The United States has not had overt farm structure policies since the Homestead Act. Certain programs such as land reclamation, commodity support payments, or lender-of-last-resort programs have had size limitations, but most were set at levels such that the policies would not affect structure any differently than would an unassisted free market. While the intention seemed clear, the realization was not. Unintended structural side effects of policy have abounded and have been described since the 1930s (Johnson and Short 1983; Lin, Johnson and Calvin 1981; Schertz et al. 1979; USDA 1981a).

Policymakers and analysts are faced with a difficult task in assessing the likely structural impacts of policies. The combined effects of policies and programs are seldom the sum of their individual effects. Given real-world behavior of advantage seeking, institutions that are complex and interrelated, and policies that are full of exceptions, the combined effects of a group of policies can be to negate, attenuate, or potentiate the direct effects of the individual policies.

One general relationship appears clear. This can be termed the policymaker's dilemma: public assistance policies can help the current group of family farms to survive, but they tend to hinder the long-term survival of family farming as a system. The converse appears equally true: eliminating existing farm programs will hinder the survival of the current group of family farms but may allow others to enter farming and help preserve the system of family farming. These relationships have resulted largely from establishing policies that are applicable to all types of ownership and operating units in farming. Policies that create an economic environment favorable to family farms may create a more favorable climate for other types of farm organization. The existence of the policies and programs has likely induced nontraditional investors and farm organizations to enter the industry.

Historically agricultural policies and programs have been viewed as economic policies required to deal with a chronically depressed and chronically unstable sector of the economy. Programs traditionally have been justified on the basis of controlling the undesirable effects of unstable prices or depressed incomes in agriculture. Programs aimed at mitigating instability should be justified by the improved welfare or efficiency of a more stable industry as opposed to a less stable one. Programs aimed at increasing the income or wealth of farmers should address the question of whether farmers are in fact a disadvantaged group in society or would be without the programs.

Some programs do contribute primarily to controlling either price or income instability or both: the Farmer Owned Reserve for grains, Commodity Credit Corporation (CCC) nonrecourse loans at or near world price levels, crop insurance, lender-of-last-resort and economic emergency lending policies, and marketing orders for fruits, vegetables, and milk. Other aspects of federal commodity programs, however, contribute primarily to increasing the income or wealth of farmers at taxpayers' expense (such as target price programs, direct costs of dairy support purchases, and credit at subsidized rates) or at the expense of consumers (indirect costs of dairy support purchases, consumer price effects of tobacco and peanut quotas, or supply management provisions of marketing orders). At present, the total budgetary costs for income transfer programs greatly exceed the costs of programs aimed at controlling or coping with instability in agricultural markets. In addition, the benefits of these programs are strongly skewed toward larger farms because direct payments and indirect benefits conferred through raising prices in the marketplace are proportional to volume of production.

Linking payments to volume of production is easily justified for the programs that deal with instability but is much more difficult to justify for programs that transfer money from taxpayers to the farm sector. The benefits of federal programs go heavily to the larger-than-single-family farms, which account for nearly 50 percent of production and have current incomes and net worths that are usually above the average of the population.

It will become increasingly hard to justify the income-transfer aspects of agricultural programs, whether or not provisions for controlling instability can be justified. If the instability-oriented programs are turned down because they contain unacceptable elements of subsidy or income transfer, then the industry and the farmers and investors who make it up will need to find private ways of dealing with the instability and uncertainty that are inherent in agriculture. Possible adjustments might be farm enterprise diversification, financial (farm and off-farm) diversification, capital rationing, and bidding down the prices of agricultural assets. Again these adjustments point up the policymaker's dilemma: terminating or even reducing existing levels of public support causes hardships for the individuals and families currently making up the farm sector.

Policy Issues

Four specific policy issues perennially appear:

1. Income parity: Are farmers' incomes chronically depressed compared to those in other sectors of the economy?
2. Small farms: Are small farms a chronically disadvantaged group in society?
3. Large farms: Are very large farms a privileged group? Are there dangers that they could exercise market power at a cost to consumers?
4. Stability: To what extent should stability be pursued as a policy goal?

Income Parity

At least since the 1920s one major goal of federal policy relating to agriculture has been income parity for farm operators. In other words, public policy has sought to move the incomes of farm operators to a level comparable with that of nonfarm people.

One time series compares the income per person after taxes of the farm-resident population and of the rest of the population over about a 50-year period. This includes only farm operators living on the farm and farm laborers living on the farm where they work. It is available only on a per capita basis. By this measure, the income per person of the farm population was only a third of that of the nonfarm population in 1934 (figure 1–10). It has generally risen since that time but with much variation. In 1973, the income of farm residents was slightly above that of nonfarm residents, and since then it has varied from 68 to 98 percent of the level of the nonfarm population. This comparison is strongly affected by the decline in the number of farm laborers, the decline in the proportion living on the farm where they work, and by the marked closing of the gap in family size between farm and nonfarm families.

Comparing the current incomes from all sources of farm operator families with those of all other families, the average income of farm operator families was 66 percent of the income of other families in 1960 and was above 100 percent from 1973 to 1975. In 1981, average income of farm operators' families was 90 percent of that of other families, and in 1983 it was 69 percent. This calculation assumes that there is one family per farm, a simplifying assumption that is not entirely correct. Partnership and corporate farms typically provide a living for more than one family, and farms owned by trusts, estates, and institutions are typically not associated with families in any direct fashion.

If capital gains on assets are included with current income, the average income of all farm operator families averaged 49 percent above that of nonfarm families in the 1970s; however, this does not include any capital gains

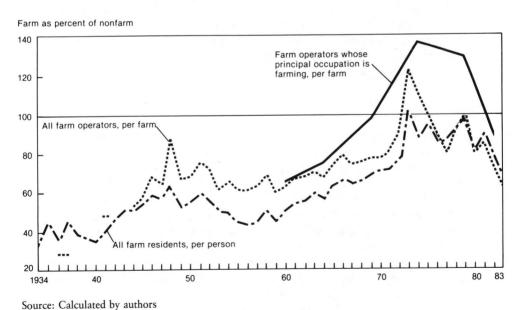

Source: Calculated by authors

Figure 1–10. Comparison of Farm and Nonfarm Incomes

by nonfarm families. Obviously there were significant capital gains on owner-occupied housing throughout much of that period.

The final comparison is for farm operators whose principal occupation was farming. Current incomes of this group were above those of nonfarm families during most of the 1970s and still remain the highest of all measures of farmer income.

Small Farms

The policy issues relating to small farms are numerous, varied, and charged with emotion. What constitutes a small farm is often defined differently by different observers. No effort will be made in this chapter to confront the highly charged issues that figure in the small farm debate.

In the 1980s, in each of the size classes with sales of less than $40,000 per year, substantial off-farm income of the operator and his or her family offset losses from farm operations. For farms with sales of $40,000 to $99,000, farm and off-farm income were about equal in the 1980s. It is difficult to see how either commodity policy or credit policy could raise the income from farm operations in the smaller sales classes sufficiently so that one could make a living from farming. If that is the objective, the small farms must become at least middle-sized farms. Credit could help some, but probably not all, small farmers become larger.

The incidence of poverty is higher among farm residents than among others. It seems unlikely that either commodity policy or credit policy can make a significant impact on poverty among those living on farms. The social insurance and welfare programs would appear to be the main vehicles to deal with poverty.

Large Farms

The questions about larger-than-family farms are more directly related to commodity, credit, and tax policy issues. The benefits of price support and related programs are roughly proportional to the sales of supported commodities, so they are concentrated among the largest farms, which make most of the sales. To what extent should the government assist such farmers? To the extent that public policy is intended to assist family farmers, limitations on the assistance to larger-than-family farms are one option. Past attempts to limit direct government payments have not been very effective in limiting assistance to large farms. Limiting price-support levels and related activities to stop-loss levels in line with the stability objective would be one way of approaching the possible problem.

The issue of who will control agriculture means many different things to different people. If the question is looked at simply in terms of the potential ability of small numbers of farmers to control output and thus raise prices, it appears highly unlikely that farm numbers could become sufficiently small under anything remotely resembling present circumstances to become an issue. Even if all of the production of a commodity were to be concentrated in the hands of farmers in the largest sales category, the numbers would still be so large that the possibility of oligopolistic influence would be negligible. Numbers of firms would have to decline to a handful—not to thousands or even hundreds—for such control to become an issue.

Stability

One objective of public policy has been to introduce a greater element of stability into the markets for farm products, at least on the down side. The introduction of target prices and direct payments for many crops in the mid-1960s to some extent allowed the stability-of-income objective to be pursued without interfering with the operations of the market. Incomes were maintained through direct government payments of the difference between the target price and the loan rate.

The rationale for commodity programs has shifted in the past thirty years from an emphasis on raising farmers' incomes to providing stability on the down side. Farm incomes are much more variable than they were up until a decade ago, and the sources of increased instability are not likely to disappear. The issues involved here are the following:

Are there industry performance benefits from stabilization of prices or incomes? How do producers, consumers, product marketers, input suppliers, and factor owners share in these benefits?

Are there industry structure benefits from stabilization? What types of structures are favored?

Do the social or public benefits exceed the social or public costs of stabilization?

Part II
Food System Coordination

The organization and coordination of many agricultural commodity subsectors have undergone significant changes in recent years. For a variety of reasons, some subsectors have moved from arrays of small firms linked only by markets toward systems with much of production and processing linked by contracts, vertical ownership, or joint ventures. Large farm supply, processing, and nontraditional farm firms play an increasingly important role in many subsectors.

Changes in organization and coordination of subsectors raise a number of questions:

1. Who has control over strategic decisions in a subsector? Regardless of the observable effects on performance, it is important to understand the distribution of rights and authority over strategic aspects of a subsector and the degree that decision control is shifting.

2. What are the effects of alternative vertical organization and coordination patterns on subsector performance? At least five performance dimensions are of particular interest:

    a. The extent to which supply matches demand at prices consistent with the opportunity cost of resources.

    b. The level of technical and operational efficiency of the entire subsector.

    c. The extent to which returns, rights, risks, information, and responsibilities are distributed equitably.

    d. Accessibility to the subsector, including the widening or narrowing of markets, market foreclosure, vertical squeezing opportunities, and the conditions of entry.

    e. The reliability and stability of subsector performance.

This part was coordinated by Bruce Marion, Lee Schrader, and Ronald Ward. Bruce Marion was the coordinating author of the introduction to the part.

These are some of the concerns that led NC 117 to include the analysis of subsector organization and coordination as one of its principal areas of inquiry. The early work of this committee revealed two important obstacles to answering the above questions. There is inadequate information on the organization of various commodity subsectors and the extent to which these have changed in recent years. Second, subsector analysis is a relatively recent undertaking for economists. Although there are a variety of theories about firm and market behavior, there are no well-developed theories of subsector organization and performance.

An agricultural subsector is viewed as an interdependent array of organizations, resources, laws, and institutions involved in producing, processing, and distributing an agricultural commodity. A subsector normally includes several industries (firms that are similar in functions performed and products produced), such as the egg packing or the food retailing industries. Subsector analysis is more than an analysis of the various industries that are part of a subsector, however. Although such industry analyses may be useful, the essential characteristic of subsector analysis is focusing in on the total vertical complex as *a system*. In a real sense, subsectors are small economic systems.

Viewed as a system, a subsector is analogous to a pipeline with inlets, outlets, and valves or an assembly line in which functions are performed and value added at several succeeding stages. This view focuses attention on the total vertical value-adding process leading to the final products of the subsector, on control of critical parts of the subsector, and on the coordination needed to synchronize and integrate efficiently the contributions of each stage and to ensure that what comes off the end of the assembly line is in fact what is demanded.

In subsector analysis, NC 117 researchers have attempted to meld the horizontal (industry) and vertical dimensions of a subsector. Efforts to develop a conceptual framework for subsector analysis have met with modest success. Henderson (1975) and Marion (1976) adapted the structure-conduct-performance paradigm of industrial organization theory to subsector analysis. Figure II–1 is the result of their efforts. This is the general framework and classification scheme that has been used by NC 117 subsector task forces.

The subsector studies conducted by NC 117 researchers have been base studies in nature; the emphasis has been on providing a detailed description of particular commodity subsectors and to the extent possible, identifying problems. Although the analytical framework in figure II–1 has served as a useful guide to conducting these case studies, it has not been possible to test the causal relationships suggested.

The conceptual framework used in the subsector studies posits that basic conditions plus subsector structure strongly influence conduct in the subsector, which in turn has an important effect on subsector performance (figure II–1).

Particular attention has been focused on vertical coordination. Understanding vertical coordination is probably the most difficult and critical part of subsector analysis. Mighell and Jones (1963, p. 1) defined vertical coordination as "all the ways of harmonizing the vertical stages of production and marketing." Vertical coordination includes the system of prices and other mechanisms that direct the allocation of resources in a subsector.

Vertical coordination is unnecessary in very simple economic systems where the product is immediately available (such as spring water) and requires neither prior commitment nor the combination of several inputs. The more complex the subsector in the number of stages and types of resources involved, the length of the production period, the geographic dispersion of the organizations performing various functions, and the perishability or storeability of the product, the more complex and important vertical coordination is for good performance.

Economists have focused little attention on vertical coordination. Prices are assumed to provide the signals necessary to regulate and synchronize economic activity in a market economy. Economic theory tends to focus on a single interface between a group of sellers and a group of buyers. Given this setting and the frequent assumptions of perfect information, perfect mobility of resources, and stable demand, price signals can be assumed largely to direct the allocation of resources.

The realities of commodity subsectors, however, suggest that vertical coordination is one of the central dimensions of the organization and conduct of economic activity. Prices perform part of the coordinating task but only part. A variety of other institutions and arrangements such as government programs, marketing orders, contracts, and vertical integration often replace or supplement prices in the coordination task.

The process of coordination depends heavily on the extent to which supply and demand are controllable, the random shocks that affect either the quantity supplied or demanded (thereby affecting their predictability), and the decisions made by subsector participants concerning supply or demand. The dispersion of decision control within a subsector (which is determined by subsector structure) affects the process of vertical coordination. Consider the following illustration. In a subsector in which 1,000 similar-sized firms operate at each of five stages (5,000 firms in total), control would be highly dispersed. Each of the 5,000 firms managers would assess future supply and demand conditions based on available information, and commit resources that reflect his or her assessment of future prices. The total quantity and quality of products supplied at different times and locations would thus depend on the aggregate resources initially committed to production, the shocks that shift either supply or demand, and the short-run adjustments (within the production period) made in supply. Given the number of decision makers involved, some variations in the resulting market price are to be expected over time.

BASIC CONDITIONS

- Production trends; geog. distribution
- Consumption characteristics
  - growth or decline
  - price, income & cross E of D
- Time char. of production & mkt. cycles
- Type & degree of uncertainties
  - Commodity price patterns
- Trade; world markets
- Laws & gov't. policies.

FIRM DECISION ENVIRONMENT

- Alternatives
- Incentives
- Control & influence

CONDUCT

Industry
- Product strategy
- Pricing behavior
- Advertising
- Research & innovation
- Mergers & divestitures
- Risk mgt. practices

Subsector
- Efforts to shift control
  - Type of exchange used
- Coordination activities
  - Prediction of future S, D, and price
  - Information communicated
  - Quality specification
  - Scheduling and timing synchronization
  - Efforts to influence inter-stage cooperation/ conflict
- Process of determining terms of exchange (private treaty, administered, bid-offer-acceptance, etc.)
- Response to change forces

STRUCTURE

Industry Structure	*Subsector Organization*
- Nr. & size of buyers & sellers	- Functional structure
- Entry & exit conditions	- Location, timing and clustering of
- Product characteristics	functions
- perishability	- Nr. of stages
- quality requirements	- Nr. of parallel channels
- differentiation	- Information system
- Technol. char./cost functions	- type of information (grades, mkt.
- Capital intensity; minimum	conditions, etc.)
efficient firm size	- distribution
- Rate of change	- cost
- Capacity	- Structure of authority, rights & control
- Specialization/diversification	- Decision anatomy
- Vertical integration	- Exchange institutions (auctions, buying
- Financing & credit characterist.	stations, etc.)
- Collective organizations	- Types of exchange (spot, contracts,
- Cooperatives	tying agreements, etc.)
- Trade assoc.	- Risk sharing institutions & arrangements
- Business objectives, attitudes	- Inter-stage differences (location, size
and capabilities	of enterprise, seasonality, prod. char.)
- Frequency of purchases and sales	- Nature of assembly, sorting and
	synchronizing tasks

PERFORMANCE

Industry	*Subsector*
- Technical & operational efficiency	- Allocative accuracy
- Pricing efficiency (profit &	- Extent to which S offerings
output levels)	match D preferences re:
- Product characteristics	quantity, quality, timing,
- quality/wholesomeness	& location
- variety	- Stability of output, prices &
- Progressiveness (process & product)	profits
- Selling activities	- Technical & operational efficiency
- Expense	- at each stage and in linking
- Influence on consumption	stages (transaction costs)
pattern & social values	- Equity re: distribution
- Market access and/or foreclosure	- Returns vs: investments and
	risks
	- Rights and control vs.
	investments and risk
	- Accuracy, adequacy & equity of
	information distributed
	- Subsector adaptability
	- Level & type of employment
	- Waste & spoliation
	- Product waste
	- Resource conservation
	- Capacity utilization

Figure II–1. Subsector Structure, Conduct, and Performance Paradigm

Even assuming adequate information on supply and demand conditions, some managers may respond by adjusting supply in the direction suggested by market conditions, while others may try to outguess their competitors and adjust supply in the opposite direction.

The opposite extreme in dispersion of control would be for a single firm to replace all 5,000 firms. Then control would be concentrated both vertically and horizontally in the hands of one decision maker. If demand was highly predictable and random shocks were unimportant, a relatively stable price could result.

These two extreme organizational arrangements suggest that concentrated control leads to improved coordination. Baligh and Richartz (1969) suggest that this may be true when horizontal control is highly concentrated at one or more stages. For example in subsector A shown in figure II–2, the manufacturing monopolist has complete control over the quantity, quality, form, and timing of products sold to retailers. Although the manufacturing monopolist would likely restrict the quantity produced—and hence performance would be suboptimal in this respect—the quality mix, timing, and location of products might be consistent with demand preferences if the monopolist exerts sufficient control over producers (through contracts for example) and over retailers.

By contrast, subsector B has centralized vertical control without concentrated horizontal control at any one stage. In this subsector, every firm is vertically integrated from production through retailing. Under this organizational arrangement, we would expect each firm's vertical network to be carefully synchronized. Except for uncontrollable shocks, management should be able to control the quantity, quality, timing, and location of output within the firm's system. The aggregate output of the subsector would not necessarily be consistent with consumer demands, however, particularly if numerous firms are involved. Total subsector output would depend on the aggregate of individual firms decisions.

The U.S. broiler subsector is illustrative of subsector B. Although the individual broiler integrator's vertical network is tightly controlled so that it can be assured of a certain quality and quantity of broilers four months or six months hence, total subsector supply depends upon the aggregate decisions made by 100 or more integrators. Oscillations in price continue to plague this subsector, indicating that although centralized vertical control may have resulted in more streamlined and efficient vertical networks, it has not led to aggregate supply control. Whether this has been due primarily to the lack of horizontal control over decisions, to the magnitude of random shocks affecting supply or demand, or both, is not clear.

Changes in subsector organization occur for a variety of reasons: to reduce costs, shift risks, improve coordination, circumvent institutional barriers such as price controls or union contracts, and increase monopoly power,

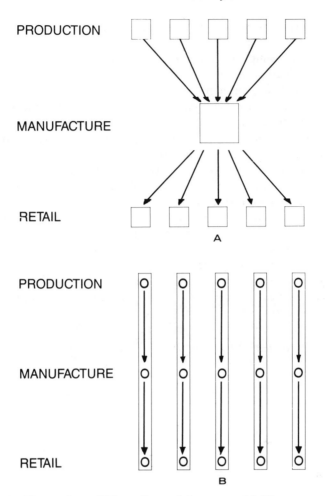

PRODUCTION

MANUFACTURE

RETAIL

A

PRODUCTION

MANUFACTURE

RETAIL

B

**Figure II–2. Illustration of Three-Stage Subsector with Two
Alternative Organizations**

to name a few. The consequences of different organizational arrangements
are important to understand. It appears that aggregate supply control
depends more heavily on horizontal control at one or more stages in a
subsector than on vertical control. The centralization of vertical control,
however, may increase the efficiency and synchronization of the subsector.
Vertical control may also overcome deficiencies in the pricing, grading, and
information systems and in the process increase the likelihood that the mix
and timing of products produced are consistent with demand. To the extent
that firms closer to consumers are also in a better position to interpret and
influence demand, centralization of vertical control in the hands of pro-

cessors or distributors may reduce price volatility or problems of surpluses or shortages.

Chapter 2 attempts to summarize the state of knowledge on pricing and vertical coordination in the food system. The focus of the chapter is on pricing and coordination mechanisms and the impact of alternative mechanisms on system performance. The emphasis on the producer and first handler levels reflects the research focus of agricultural economists interested in pricing and coordination issues. Much less is known about pricing and coordination at the food manufacturer–food distributor stages. The space devoted to various topics is more a reflection of what we know than of relative importance. Although we have learned a good bit about pricing and vertical coordination, they remain rather elusive topics.

In chapter 3, summaries of several subsector case studies are provided. The commonalities among the subsectors are then discussed. There is no well-defined methodology for doing subsector studies. The focus of such studies depend to some extent on the questions considered important by those conducting such studies. In some studies, the physical flow of products may be emphasized; in others the mechanisms of coordination or the competitive organization of industries receive major emphasis. In the case studies reviewed here, a common conceptual framework was used to achieve some uniformity in the discussions (see figure II–1).

2
Pricing and Vertical Coordination in the Food System

I n any economy characterized by specialization or division of labor, exchange of products and resources among individual economic agents is
necessary. Appropriate incentives and constraints on economic behavior
are needed to coordinate production and consumption activities of these
agents. Coordination and exchange ensure specialized agents that commodities are available, with a certain degree of reliability, in amounts and
qualities when and where they are needed.

In the ideal world of a perfect and competitive economy with perfect
foresight and no transaction costs, exchange and coordination are integrated.
Prices are sufficient to coordinate individual behavior such that a social optimum will be attained. Market prices reflect all the information needed by
economic agents to plan and adjust their activities.

In actual markets the future is shrouded by the fog of uncertainty, price
signals are bent by transaction costs, and a small number of participants may
encourage rivalry and exploitation of the powerless or uninformed. The
perfect market is, at best, useful only as a norm, and some might question
that (Pasour and Bullock 1975). When the perfect and competitive market
model is used as a standard to appraise the operation of an existing market,
the result is predictable; the actual market will be regarded as inefficient and
prices as insufficient for coordination. Given this state of affairs, the task of
the economist cannot be to declare all existing markets to be inefficient and ill
coordinated. Rather it is to identify alternative or supplementary systems of
coordination and to point out their virtues and shortcomings under various
economic conditions.

Coordination of agricultural production and marketing has been the object of research attention for many years. Mighell and Jones's 1963 study of
vertical coordination in agriculture provided a framework that has served
well in this endeavor. Goldberg (1968) brought coordination to the center of

Lee Schrader was the coordinating author for chapter 2. Other authors were Marvin Hayenga,
Dennis Henderson, Ray Leuthold, and Mark Newman.

his systems approach to the study of commodity production and marketing. More recently interest has focused on pricing mechanisms and systems and their impact on prices, price reporting, and coordination (Hayenga 1979a; Hayenga and Schrader 1980). Interest in pricing has been stimulated by allegations of acute pricing problems, particularly in the beef and egg subsectors (USDA 1979a). The application of computers and modern telecommunications to commodity trading and pricing has also stimulated interest in the pricing process.

A number of NC 117 studies have focused directly on issues in pricing and price reporting, electronic marketing, and coordination mechanisms in the study of commodity subsectors. The problems that have motivated these studies are by no means unique to the U.S. food system but appear in most or perhaps all market economies. For example, Pickard (1982, p. 264) of the United Kingdom, while discussing the proper role of government in agricultural marketing, said, "For one thing it implies considerably more interest in the efficiency of the critically important price-finding mechanism, in the accuracy of the messages which result, and in the ability of the participants in the system both to receive the messages and to respond to them." Similar problems were also identified by Boeckenhoff et al. (1976) for the West German food system.

In this chapter, we review the concept of vertical coordination and draw on the work of NC 117 researchers and others to place pricing and coordination mechanisms into appropriate perspective. We attempt to provide a basis to evaluate these mechanisms in different commodity settings as they affect coordination and the performance of the subsector involved.

Vertical Coordination of Commodity Systems

The concept of vertical coordination is well characterized by Mighell and Jones (1963, p. 1): " 'Vertical coordination' is the general term that includes all the ways of harmonizing the vertical stages of production and marketing. The market-price system, vertical integration, contracting and cooperation singly or in combination are some of the alternative means of coordination." They define a stage as follows: "As a working definition, we shall consider that an *economic stage* in production is any operating process capable of producing a salable product or service under appropriate circumstances" (p. 7). We take the definition of a stage to include any value-adding process, whether a change in location, time, or form of the commodity. It is any step that takes the commodity closer to final consumption.

These definitions imply that a transaction may exist at each stage boundary. When adjacent stages are completely integrated, the transaction point at this boundary disappears. Mighell and Jones (1963) define coordination as activities or processes employed to harmonize stages. Lang (1978, p. 1) has observed that coordination is also used to describe the objective of a perfectly harmonized state. Thus, coordination has been used to refer to both a *process* and a *state*.

The process of coordination is amenable to positive analyses as an economic activity that employs limited resources to achieve desired ends. Coordination as an ideal state is identical to the notion of economic efficiency, including temporal and spatial dimensions. By definition, a less than optimally coordinated state represents a market failure. The study of coordination as a process, the concern of this chapter, deals with this market failure.

Different concepts of coordination can and have been employed in past analyses. In normative studies, historical states of coordination (perhaps best described as arbitrarily chosen segments of historical coordination) are compared to the ideal state. Divergences are identified and policy conclusions to rectify the situation are drawn. An obvious limitation of this approach is equating the objectives of those agents who perform the coordination activities with those assumed by the researcher. In addition, divergences may arise from external constraints on coordination activities (such as transaction cost) and events not controlled by system participants that are omitted from the researcher's model of the ideal.

In positive studies of vertical systems, the objective is to identify and quantify the relationships between coordination activities (processes) and the resulting performance of the system. The purpose of such studies is to gain insight into how a vertical system actually operates given multiple dimensions of performance and multiple goals of market participants.

Pricing and Pricing Systems

Price usually refers to the monetary terms of trade arrived at as part of the process of voluntary exchange (market price). It also includes terms determined exogenous to the particular exchange where the price is related by formula to factors not known when the exchange contract is made (transfer price). Excluding concerns about price level, commodity pricing and pricing systems have attracted little public attention when market price performs all or even a major part of both long- and short-term coordination or resource allocation functions. The grain and oilseed subsectors provide examples. Pricing attracts attention when other methods of coordination become dominant and the transfer price is based on a market price generated in much diminished open markets. When market price is the major allocator of goods between stages, income allocation is incidental to the process of pricing. When the product allocation decision is made by prior arrangement but priced based on a market quote, price is performing only the income allocation function in the short run. It is little wonder that the price discovery or price reporting system can become a center of controversy in that situation.

Market price may be the major means to coordinate exchange between stages, or it may be used as an adjunct to other means of coordination, such as contracts that specify all terms of trade except price. Price may play no role at all if adjacent stages are integrated with the coordination function internalized by the firm. Nevertheless, the final transfer to consumers is usually price coordinated.

The focus of NC 117 concern with pricing has been on price discovery and its reporting. Price discovery is the process of interaction between and among buyers and sellers by which they identify alternatives and arrive at a transaction price; that is, price discovery is the process of finding a set of prices that clears the market at a given time. Price is *determined* by the fundamental factors that affect the amounts actually supplied and demanded—the stuff of economic theory. But the prices implied by these behavioral relationships are not self-evident. They must be discovered by market participants, none of whom possesses complete information and each of whom may possess some unique information.

Interest in price discovery and price reporting represents recognition that price discovery is neither automatic nor costless, that it may be accomplished by any of several means, and that most coordination systems short of integration continue to rely on market price to some extent. Intelligent choices among alternative pricing and coordination systems can be made only when the characteristics of and interactions among these systems are known.

Impact of Pricing and Coordination on Performance

Project (NC 117) research has shown theoretically and empirically that methods of coordination and pricing affect the performance of the commodity subsector involved. Interactions among coordination methods, pricing, and performance were treated as part of subsector studies and in other studies of pricing. The inferences that one may draw from studies of pricing systems are limited. Experiments such as the testing and evaluation of electronic markets are rare. Even with an opportunity to experiment, it is difficult to draw definitive conclusions. Experimentation, however, does reveal relations between controlled variables that often cannot be discovered in markets without controls. A change of trading practices in one area cannot be isolated completely from the remainder of the market. Comparisons of performance before and after a change suffer from the inability to control for other factors that may have been changing at the same time.

Prices, price reports, and other market news are, to some extent, public goods (Henderson, Schrader, and Rhodes 1983). That is, the additional use of the information, once developed, adds little or nothing to cost, nor does added use interfere with its use by others. The value of information to an individual may, however, be affected by its possession by others. Public goods bring free riders, and market price is no exception. As long as a sufficient proportion of traders participate in the price discovery process, it is advantageous for some to use the prices generated in the open market institution to establish prices for exchanges arranged outside that institution. Acceptance of price from one institution as a valid indicator of equilibrium value makes possible the use of some nonprice coordination mechanisms, such as contracts for which price is not established until the date of shipment or delivery.

Relation to Vertical Market Structure

Free riders in open market price discovery illustrate the potential for pricing and coordination methods to affect and to be affected by vertical market structure. The existence of a published market price may facilitate the use of formula-priced contracts that bypass the open market to gain from more direct exchange. Some may believe this is undesirable. But if the advantages of coordination by means other than spot markets are large, the only viable alternatives may be integration or contract coordination.

Coordination methods and system structure evolve simultaneously. There may be little incentive for individual actions to move the system in a direction that would benefit all participants in the system. Given the free rider aspect already identified, there may be little incentive for the individual to participate in voluntary group action to change the system.

Performance Dimensions

What do we expect from a system of vertical coordination? Ideally it would be a system that delivers the quantity and quality of products at the time and place that maximizes the benefit to society from the resources available. This goal is beyond the range of methods yet invented or evolved. It requires a degree of foresight that cannot be achieved.

Thus, at best, one may search for a system that can maximize social satisfaction given that which is known or subject to being known when key resource allocation decisions must be made. Neither information about exchange or production possibilities nor estimates of the relevant probabilities of uncertain events can be obtained without cost. Rarely is a future state so uncertain that nothing can be learned about the probability of various outcomes. Clearly the coordination mechanism is a variable in a commodity system. It is unlikely that any one system of coordination or pricing will be best with respect to all relevant dimensions of performance. The object of this section is to identify and discuss the criteria or performance dimensions by which one may evaluate coordination and pricing.

Resource Allocation

Resource allocation is optimal when, given property rights as defined and available knowledge when allocative decisions must be made, the allocation is such that no reallocation could be made that would increase the satisfaction of anyone without reducing the satisfaction of another (Pareto optimality). The allocation of resources to information gathering, analysis, and distribution must be included. One must recognize time, information, and risk. Efficient allocation implies maximization of the value of resources to their owners.

In agriculture, commitments of resources must be made using only the information that is known when the decision is made. Revisions in allocation decisions as uncontrolled events occur cannot be considered as suboptimal performance. Performance must be judged moment by moment in the light of what was known or could be known, not by looking backward to what might have been given a state of knowledge attainable only after the fact. For example, idle capacity for processing or wasted raw product may not be evidence of inefficiency when planning was based on appropriate yield distributions and the deviation due to unusual weather. In contrast, it is difficult to argue that year-to-year variation of pork production of 10 to 15 percent is consistent with efficient use of resources.

Persons or firms acting in their own self-interest when subjected to the competitive forces of others acting in their own interest can be presumed to make choices that lead to a Pareto-optimal solution. The efficacy of the process is limited by the information available to these persons or firms. Thus, likely causes of deviations from Pareto optimality are constraints on competition and inadequate or unequal information. Cycles of price and production indicate inappropriate expectations. Limited knowledge of exchange alternatives may also result in nonoptimal allocation.

The extent to which coordinating mechanisms provide for risk sharing may also affect the efficiency of allocation. Fixed quantity forward contracts accent production risks, whereas spot market sales bring large price risks. In both cases, uncertainty may restrict resource use. If coordination mechanisms include some risk sharing, individuals may be able to benefit from reduced uncertainty. A coordination system that pools individual risks may result in resource allocation that is more nearly a market-wide optimum than that represented by decisions based on individual risk positions. Arrangements such as market pools that average returns to producers where there is substantial random variation may reduce individual uncertainty to the level of aggregate variation. Market pools ordinarily are managed such that the variation in returns to individuals is lower than would be the case for individual spot market selling. Futures markets are separate institutions that provide opportunities for risk shifting.

Group action to correct some problems may create others. Lang (1978) identified several instances of nonoptimal allocations between growers and processors due to flaws in collectively bargained contracts. In these cases the bargaining process was also used to modify the contracts in such a way that both parties to the contracts benefited.

Equity

Property rights, taken as given in the resource allocation discussion, are at the center of the discussion of equity. Equity is viewed in the sense of equal treatment of all system participants to the extent that they can deliver equal performance. Efficiency requires recognition of differences in value to users resulting from differences in quality, location, and timing. Equity means that these rewards accrue to the persons or firms who control the product attributes involved. Contracts that place production practices or harvesting under control of the buyer and penalize the grower for problems caused by the buyer are considered inequitable.

Grade standards established when end uses and processing technology were different than at present may be a source of inequity. Tradition plays a major role in determination of standards used and in the detail of their application. Premiums and discounts for quality have been shown to reflect end use value poorly even in the relatively competitive grain trade (Schrader and Lang 1980; Nichols, Hill, and Nelson 1983).

One would expect the largest inequities to be found where market power and information are most unbalanced. In this situation the party on one side of the transaction may be able to dictate the coordination mechanism, if not exact terms of trade. Collective bargaining where representatives of growers negotiate terms for the group may reduce inequities caused by power imbalance.

Cooperatives at times have confused equal treatment with equity. In some cases they may have erred in the direction of equal prices to all patrons when some differentiation reflecting cost of service would have been more equitable. One is less likely to find this today with quantity discounts as common for cooperatives as for other firms (Johnson and Schrader 1981). However, price averaging across quality is not necessarily inequity. When the attributes are not controllable by the producer, there may be efficiency reasons for pooling the risk. That is, a pooled price may send an appropriate signal at the time production decisions are made even though it may give equal reward for unequal products ex post.

Transaction Costs

Transaction costs vary greatly among alternative vertical coordination methods. In fact, transaction costs may be as much a determinant of vertical coordination methods as an outcome. Coase (1937, p. 390) saw transaction costs as the primary reason for the existence of firms: "The main reason why it is profitable to establish a firm would seem to be that there is a cost of using the price mechanism. The most obvious cost of 'organizing' production through the price mechanism is that of discovering what the relevant prices are." His observation implies that market price coordination is sometimes more costly than vertical integration.

Transaction costs include the costs of searching for alternatives, the costs associated with physical exchange, and the costs added because of uncertainty associated with exchange. These costs are influenced by the availability of information. If every participant were aware of all other bids and offers in a commodity system and statements regarding quality were accurate, transaction costs might be quite small, representing little more than physical transfer cost. Thus, the cost associated with knowing the alternatives may be the major transaction cost. Search is not simply finding a buyer or seller of the commodity but finding the time, quality, location, and minimum cost (highest price) for the buyer (seller). Economies of size in performance of the search function bring the broker, a specialist, into the system. Quality uncertainty may be a major factor. If, for example, product quality is inherent in the production process but not verifiable at moderate cost prior to its use, this quality uncertainty may be sufficiently high to move the system away from market price coordination toward integration. Grades may reduce quality uncertainty and transaction costs, but their benefit may be limited if not based on the product characteristics that determine the product's value to the customer.

Large segments of the food system have made specific quality promises to consumers. The retail hamburger restaurant chains will not tolerate much quality variation. Avoiding the risk of an out-of-specification delivery (considered very damaging to the firm) increases the costs of open market procurement for that type of firm. If these tight quality specifications are beyond the consumer's ability to detect and if they are not related to safety, the degree of coordination demanded may be beyond the optimum and the transaction cost higher than necessary. The imposition of industrial-style specification buying on a production activity dependent on biological processes has been a major factor encouraging movement away from market price coordination systems in several subsectors.

Accessibility of Markets and Information

Access is a key performance criterion. Access to buyers and sellers is necessary to enter (or to remain in) a stage of a subsector. The question is whether a firm is precluded from entry to a particular stage of a subsector even though it is able to perform the activity at lower cost than other firms currently performing the activity. The satisfaction of market participants is probably related to the perception of having alternatives, as well as the profitability of their current arrangements. That is, the lack of alternatives increases uncertainty as to whether the market participant has the best deal, or whether any alternative will be available in the future. Access to a subsector level (to buy from or to sell to a particular stage) varies greatly. When adjacent stages are coordinated by transacting in a spot market, the system is open to anyone with product or money. At the other extreme, if adjacent stages are completely integrated and there are high exit costs or high transaction costs, access may be foreclosed to the unintegrated firm.

Access also varies with time. While spot market access (produce, then sell) may be restricted, access may be relatively free over a period longer than a production cycle. Even the integrated firm must review its make-or-buy decisions from time to time. Some large industrial firms ask wholly owned subsidiaries to bid competitively for the business of the parent or sister firms. Integration in the food sector has received much attention, although disintegration of the functions once performed on the farm has been much more dramatic. Production of power, fertilizer, feed, pest control, and other inputs has been separated from the farm enterprise to a large extent. Thus, access to these activities by nonfarm firms is less proscribed now than in the past.

Much of the concern about market access has been in terms of the produce, then sell, operator. Possibly such an approach to coordination is an anachronism. Its cost in terms of instability may be quite high. Access at the time resources are committed to production may be much less restricted. Size economies (in transactions as well as production) may well preclude the small operator from some or all stages of a subsector.

Access to information is an important aspect of market access. While not all known markets are accessible, those that are not known to the potential participant are certainly not accessible. The definition of property rights may determine to some degree what can be known to an individual firm. Although our earlier definition of efficiency was given in terms of all alternatives known, not everyone need know all. Some knowledge of alternatives is key, but the amount needed by individuals is limited.

We must be careful to distinguish between equal possession of information and equal access. Almost by definition, a larger firm will possess a larger amount of information than a small one, but equal information may be available to the small firm at a cost. The cost of a given information level per unit of trade is expected to be higher for the smaller firm. The amount of information required for a particular level of performance may be greater for the larger firms trading in a larger geographic area. The public good aspects of price and other market information have led to a government role in price and other market intelligence reporting for agricultural products.

Given the impossibility of knowing all, what should be known? Ewart (1972) constructed a computer simulation of the U.S. soybean market. The actions of farmers, processors, and speculators in futures and cash markets were simulated, with the accuracy level and distribution of crop estimates subject to experimenter control. As one would expect, more accurate crop size forecasts result in less price variation. The simulation experiments also suggested that information received by any group of market participants before it is made available generally is transmitted rather rapidly throughout the market by means of price signals. The advantage to the early receivers was much smaller than expected. Apparently having the information in the market was sufficient. Clearly access to information is necessary for coordination and appropriate functioning of markets. The extent of information needed and who needs how much is not at all clear. If information comes only at some cost, the rule that more is preferred to less is hardly sufficient. The fact that some market participants do search the market and create market information is a benefit to others even if such information is not made public directly. Beales, Craswell, and Salop (1981, p. 503) state the idea clearly: "The first and most ubiquitous market failure arises from the fact that information has public good properties. The purchase, production and use of information by consumers generate a market perfecting external benefit to uninformed consumers."

Dynamic Stability

Cycles in production and prices are common in the food system. Decision makers at the production stage tend to react to current market conditions as if all other market participants will make no adjustment. The result is periodic overcommitment of resources. Ideally the coordination system would be able to avoid such periodic resource waste. These cyclic tendencies persist even though production decisions have been concentrated in fewer hands and information has become more accessible than ever before.

Information and its interpretation may be at the heart of the problem. If information is sufficient to generate accurate expectations, one should see little cyclical behavior. Reports on farmers' intentions to raise livestock or to plant crops are steps in that direction, but the once-per-season surveys used today provide no information on how farmers will react to the reported intentions. Percentage swings in production are larger for hogs than for broilers, and both of these are more variable than milk or eggs. Are these differences the result of coordination methods in use and availability of information, or are they inherent in the biological process, extent of specialization, and asset fixity that are responsible for the behavioral lags that characterize the commodity system itself?

Methods of Pricing

Pricing is the key economic activity in a market economy. Without a pricing system, an economic system could not survive. Pricing is the way in which, with no one in charge, the continuous process of allocating limited resources to meet unlimited wants occurs. Even when someone is in charge (such as an administered or command economy), some type of pricing system emerges—the black, grey, or underground market—to create order out of the chaos of the resulting imbalance of amounts supplied and demanded.

There does not yet exist an adequate explanation of how pricing systems evolve. Microeconomic theory assumes the existence of a pricing system but does not address how it came about, nor does it inquire into the possibility that market solutions may be influenced by the type of pricing system that exists. Yet different pricing systems do evolve in similar situations, and an appreciable body of experimental economics literature has emerged that demonstrates that different pricing systems have differential impacts on market behavior and performance in the same structural circumstances.

The purpose of this section is to classify pricing systems into a limited number of categories, each of which has common application in markets for agricultural products and reasonably consistent performance implications. Many such classifications have been attempted. Breimyer (1976), after surveying many of those classification schemes, suggested seven general categories and twelve variations that are distinguishable in terms of behavior and application. His seven general classes are auction, private treaty, administered, group bargained, marketwide supply-demand estimation, formula, and government regulation.

For sake of brevity and simplicity, we have condensed these into four classifications: auction (similar to Breimyer's but with more variations), private treaty (including all types of private negotiations over price, whether done individually or collectively on either or both sides), administered (or any situation in which one party announces a price and others accept it or do not complete a transaction, including price listing and government regulation), and formula (similar to Breimyer's but including any value indicator, thus including his marketwide supply-demand estimation scheme).

Auction

Probably the most extensive investigations of pricing systems have focused on auction pricing procedures. Certainly as Smith (1982) points out, most of the laboratory experiments in microeconomics have dealt with various types of auction pricing behavior. Thus, probably a more complete understanding exists of the performance implications of these pricing systems than of others.

Variations of auction systems are found in many markets for agricultural products; terminal produce auctions, country livestock auctions, and tobacco auctions have achieved a certain status in American folklore.

The essence of an auction is competitive bidding by persons on one or both sides of the market for what persons on the other side are offering to sell or buy. The common image is probably best captured by the country livestock auction where farmers consign their livestock for sale, an auctioneer chants and calls for successively higher bids from among an assembly of buyers, and sales are awarded to the highest bidder amid much hoopla and fanfare.

There are many variations. Schrader and Henderson (1980) identified five types of auctions, each with somewhat unique pricing behavior, performance implications, and applications in the food system: (1) English or ascending bid, (2) Dutch clock or descending bid, (3) double or converging bid, (4) simultaneous, and (5) sealed bid, including bid acceptance and offer acceptance variations.

The English auction, used in casual sales that many attend such as those for used household furnishings, antiques, and liquidation sales, is probably the most familiar type. The Latin root of auction, *auctus,* literally means "to increase." Thus, the increasing bid behavior of the English auction best exemplifies an auction pricing system.

Nonetheless, variants of the auction procedure are important in many agricultural markets and deserve analysis. The Dutch clock auction, more extensively used in Canada and Europe than in the United States, operates on a declining price offer basis, with the sale awarded to the first and only bidder on each sales lot. The auctioneer starts the bidding at a price above the expected sales price and then lowers it in decrements until a buyer signals acceptance. Compared to the English auction, the Dutch procedure is generally faster but often results in a less efficient and lower price (Coppinger, Smith, and Titus 1980).

The double auction is characteristic of most commodity futures exchanges where each trader acts as his or her own auctioneer. Bids are raised and offers lowered by different traders simultaneously until they converge at a price at which a transaction is recorded. The double auction procedure requires each trader, both buyers and sellers, to be a competent auctioneer and thus does not accommodate passive sellers, as do the English and Dutch procedures. Considerable research has shown that prices are most efficient in the double auction; they converge rapidly toward the competitive equilibrium as trading progresses (Smith 1976).

The simultaneous bid auction, sometimes referred to as the Japanese auction because of its predominant use in Japanese fish markets, requires all bidders to submit single bids for the lot being sold to the auctioneer at the same time, on the auctioneer's signal. Sales are awarded almost instantly on going up for bid. No research regarding the performance implications of simultaneous bid auction can be found, but because typically only the winning bid is announced and there is little opportunity to observe bidder behavior, it is likely that the performance is similar to that of Dutch auctions.

Sealed bid auctions take many forms but in general require the buyer (seller) to submit secret bids (offers) to an auctioneer during a specified time period, at the end of which the auctioneer views all bids (offers) and awards the sale. The sale is normally awarded to the highest (lowest) bidder (offerer) but may be at either the price bid (offered) by the successful trader (the first price sealed bid auction) or the next to highest (lowest) price bid (offered) (the second price sealed bid auction). Sealed bid auctions are often used for large transactions where considerable effort goes into determining the bid or offer. Available evidence suggests that, in terms of price levels and pricing efficiency, second price sealed bid auctions are comparable to English auctions, while first price auctions result in less efficient and lower prices but are more efficient than Dutch auctions (Coppinger, Smith, and Titus 1980).

Private Treaty

Private treaty pricing systems are those in which prices are privately negotiated between buyer and seller. The negotiation process is not governed by formal, structured rules as are auctions. Rather, negotiators utilize whatever strategies they find to their advantage. Negotiations may occur between individuals (such as a cattle feeder negotiating price with a feedlot cattle buyer), between an individual and a group (such as a canner negotiating with a group of tomato growers who are organized for collective bargaining), or between two groups. Seldom are more than two parties (potential buyer or buying group and potential seller or selling group) directly involved in private price negotiation at one time; however, both buyers and sellers can search for others with whom to negotiate, and knowledge of alternatives may be important to the results.

Available evidence shows that some traders are better price negotiators than are others, although it has not been shown whether advantages are due to increased shopping, making more credible promises or threats, or other factors (Houg and Plott 1982). Limited evidence suggests that as price negotiations between two parties are repeated, prices tend to approach but not converge with the competitive equilibrium (Plott 1982). Prices would be expected to move toward the competitive equilibrium from below (above) when the buyer (seller) dominates the private negotiation process. Overall, however, private treaty prices appear to be less efficient (in terms of converging with the competitive equilibrium level) than are auction prices, particularly those in double auctions.

Rhodes (1978) lists convenience and physical efficiency as advantages of private treaty pricing. These stem in part from the fact that a third party, the auctioneer, is not necessary to the pricing process and because prices can be negotiated whenever and however buyer and seller get together, even by telephone, without waiting for a preannounced sales date and/or time. As disadvantages, he mentions that knowledge of alternative marketing opportunities is less complete and more difficult to obtain and that many farmers lack sufficient negotiation skills.

Administered

Administered pricing refers to all situations in which the seller, or in some cases the buyer or a third party regulator, announces in advance of the sale a nonnegotiable selling (or buying) price (sometimes called price listing or price posting). Typically the firm that announces the price has an obligation to accept whatever volume of sales occurs at the listed price as long as it remains unchanged.

There are numerous examples of administered or posted prices in the food system. Governmentally regulated prices are one example, including minimum buy-up or support prices for various commodities and price ceilings for various food products that are sometimes established during war or other national emergencies or as a means of controlling inflation. Price listing is the predominant pricing method used in the retail trade for food products, and it is often used by food manufacturers, particularly on branded products. It is also frequently used in pricing farm production inputs and some farm products. In particular, most grain elevators post a nonnegotiable price at which they will purchase grain from farmers. Some livestock slaughterers follow the same practice.

Administered pricing is at least implicitly assumed in much of microeconomic theory of imperfect competition. As a result, this pricing system has received considerable scholarly attention. Evidence from experimental markets clearly shows that prices administered by a monopoly seller converge fairly rapidly to the monopoly equilibrium, and those administered by a single buyer converge to the monopsony equilibrium (Smith 1981). Also, consistent with theory, administered prices tend to move toward the competitive equilibrium as the number of sellers or buyers on the posting side of the market increases, but the movement toward competitive equilibrium is slower than in double auctions, and there is no assurance that prices will converge with the competitive equilibrium price (Plott and Smith 1978). Thus, both theory and available evidence indicate that administered pricing systems result in less than efficient prices.

Formula Pricing

A formula pricing system is one in which the price in any given transaction is established on the basis of a mathematical formula that relates transaction price to one or more indicators of value. In some sense, formula pricing is a hybrid between private treaty pricing and administered pricing; that is, the terms of the mathematical formula may be privately negotiated between buyer and seller, and the indicator(s) of value used in such formulas are usually estimated or quoted by a third party. In cases for which the agreement allows one party to take any amount at the formula price, the effect is similar to an administered price.

In the truest sense of the words, formula pricing is trading on someone else's price. The actual formula used by any pair of buyers and sellers is almost always determined privately and is often different for the same seller and different buyers (or vice-versa). Generally the formula is negotiated prior to a transaction and in many cases stands without modification over an extended period of time and numerous transactions. The actual transaction price varies only in proportion to changes in the value indexes or reference price over the duration of time that a given formula is in use.

Formula pricing is used extensively in the markets for some farm commodities and processed products. For example, egg prices are generally formulated relative to the Urner Barry quote, which is published daily and recognized as a reference price in most of the United States. Prices for grade A milk sold under federal market orders are based on a formula (determined through a public hearing process) that often uses the USDA's public report on market prices for manufacturing-grade milk that is purchased by creameries and other milk handlers throughout Minnesota and Wisconsin (the so-called M-W price series) as a reference price. Some slaughter cattle are sold to meat packers on the basis of a price that is formulated from a publicly reported average price at a specified central livestock market (such as the Omaha stock yards). A major portion of trading in fresh meat products is also formula priced. Hayenga and Schrader (1980) found that 70 percent of carcass beef and 10 to 20 percent of boxed beef were formula priced relative to price quotations published daily by National Provisioner, a commercial publishing firm. About 40 percent of fresh pork was priced by formula. Futures prices are commonly used as reference prices for grain, soybean, and soybean product pricing formulas.

Relatively little empirical research has been reported on the performance implications of formula pricing. Assessment appears to turn largely on two issues: how well are terms of formulas arbitraged, and how relevant are the indexes used in formulas to the specific exchange situation? Little insight regarding the first issue can be found in the literature. However, it seems reasonable to argue that the less frequently terms of formulas are negotiated, the less opportunity there is to arbitrage these terms to reflect changes in conditions that alter the relationship between the index values and the value of product in a specific transaction. Thus, prices are probably less than efficient, and the amount of distortion from efficient prices is probably positively correlated with the age of the formula.

Considerably more research attention has been devoted to the relevance of prices used in pricing formulas. As formula pricing increases, the number of transactions for which prices are negotiated necessarily decreases. This thin market problem has received considerable attention by NC 117. The market, thinned by formula-priced transactions that are not immediately responsive to spot market prices, may be less likely to arrive at a price that approximates a competitive equilibrium. Furthermore, firms with formula-priced contracts based on a thin market price may have an incentive to attempt manipulation of the reference price quotation. These propositions have not been proved but nevertheless remain appealing to many. With no assurance that either formula terms or value indexes are efficient and with considerable argument in the literature that the latter are not, it seems reasonable to view formula pricing systems as price inefficient. Formula pricing does result in low transaction costs and reduces individual firm risks under certain circumstances.

Formula pricing using futures market prices escapes much of the above criticism. Use of futures prices as the value index for formula pricing does not necessarily diminish trading in the futures contract. The typical pattern of grain trading focuses contract negotiation on the formula or basis and allows the discovery of base value to be accomplished in a highly competitive auction market.

Coordination Mechanisms

The concept of a coordination mechanism includes the set of institutions and arrangements that are used to accomplish the harmonization of adjacent stages of commodity systems. Coordination mechanisms include a method of pricing if the adjacent stages are not integrated. A given commodity subsector may, and usually does, employ a number of coordination mechanisms. The predominant mechanism may vary from stage to stage, and more than one may be used at the same stage interface.

Alternative coordination mechanisms span a continuum from those that rely on separate decisions by firms with exchange in a spot market to integration where coordination is internalized. Contracts, bargaining, and cooperative integration are intermediate forms.

The objectives of this section are to describe the major methods of coordination and certain auxiliary mechanisms that are used in coordinating the U.S. food system and to characterize their performance. The classifications used are neither exhaustive nor mutually exclusive but serve to illustrate significant differences and provide a basis for discussion of the relationship of coordination methods to the organization and performance of commodity subsectors.

Terminal Markets

As used here, terminal markets refer to all public assembly markets for agricultural goods. This includes local and country auction markets, as well as central markets located in major railroad or truck terminal cities such as Chicago, St. Paul, and Omaha. Distinguishing characteristics of these markets are public trading and product assembly. That is, trading on these markets is in general open to anyone (although they may have to hire a representative, such as a commission agent, to sell or buy), and the products traded are physically assembled in the market facility at the time of sale.

Because of the public nature of trading, rules governing trader behavior may be subject to government scrutiny or regulation, and in many cases the tariffs charged for buying and/or selling at these markets are also government regulated. The purpose is to maintain the public trust—that is, to ensure that people have confidence that they are treated fairly. Also because of their public nature, information on trading in terminal markets is generally considered to be public property. Anyone who wants information on trading, including quantities bought and sold and at what prices, is presumed to have a right to it. In many cases it has also been presumed that the government has an obligation to provide such information to the public at large.

Because of the physical assembly of goods, buyers, and sellers, costs associated with terminal market trading are relatively high. Physical facilities for loading and unloading products, for weighing, storing, sorting, and displaying them, and for accommodating traders must be constructed and maintained. Goods must be shipped in, unloaded, inspected, handled, reloaded, and reshipped. Buyers, sellers, and agents must come, interact, and go. The guardians of the public interest must be provided with accommodations.

Pricing in terminal markets occurs by private negotiation or auction. Historically private negotiation between the seller's commission agent and the buyer was the dominant trading means used on terminal markets. Farmers would ship their products to the market consigned to a commission agent, who would seek out a buyer, negotiate a price, collect payment, deduct commission and other marketing fees, and reimburse the seller. Government price reporters conferred with agents and buyers to learn prices and other trading details. As assembly markets sprang up in the country, auction pricing procedures were used more frequently. Today an increasing proportion of transactions at the large terminal livestock markets use auction pricing. Private treaty pricing predominates at terminal produce markets.

Terminal markets were once the nexus of trade in agricultural products. Farmers by and large were small and located at considerable distance from the major cities where the major food processing plants were situated. In some cases farmers shipped directly to commission agents or merchant traders who handled sales on their behalf at these markets. More often, products arrived from local assembly points via country merchants. In time some farmers joined to form shipping associations, which carried out many of the functions of the country merchant and in some cases the functions of commission agents. Regardless of how these functions were performed, however, considerable effort and cost were involved in getting products to the terminal markets due to the small size and dispersed location of most farms. Terminal markets provide a large assemblage of product from which wholesale buyers can choose and a reasonable assurance to the seller that a buyer can be found.

In 1932, Clark and Weld (p. 392) praised these wholesale terminal exchanges as "the highest type of organization and the highest development of efficiency in marketing farm products that can be found." By that time, however, the seeds of change had already been sown. Railroads, which were the supply lifeblood of the central terminal markets, were giving way to trucks. Processors were beginning to specialize, making it more feasible for farmers to deal directly with buyers and increasing the amount of direct trading with farmers and ranchers.

Many country markets emerged to give structure and order to agricultural marketing as it moved away from the central cities. Because these are scattered across the countryside, they typically handle smaller volumes than central markets while retaining the basic operating pattern of physically assembling both products and buyers at the time of sale. Because of smaller volume, these generally attract fewer buyers; thus auction selling is frequently used to ensure the greatest possible buyer competition. Also because of relatively small volume, most country markets do not operate daily; many hold sales only one day each week.

The importance of both country and central terminal livestock markets has declined since World War II as use of direct trading, contracting, integration, and other means of coordination increased. In many cases a marginal volume of trade remains for many products at the terminals. Often this volume represents distressed product (product that is of low quality or that represents a temporary market surplus). As such, this trade may not reflect accurately the broader supply and demand forces. Yet prices in these markets are frequently used as reference points in settling terms in private trades and contracts.

Terminal markets remain an important coordination mechanism for the produce trade. The share of produce handled in these city markets has decreased, but volume remains significant. The city produce market serves independent distributors and local stores whose volume does not justify shipping point trading.

Terminal markets, when used for a major share of exchange, are generally regarded as pricing efficient. The assembly of buyers encourages buyer competition, the assembly of large product volume provides a reasonably accurate supply picture, and the organized nature of trading, along with frequent public scrutiny, helps to ensure reasonably fair exchange. Although stories of exclusion, manipulation, and price rigging are part of the lore of these markets, belief in their pricing efficiency is common. This explains much of the willingness of buyers and sellers to use terminal market prices as base prices in private trades, but they are a rather expensive means of establishing efficient prices.

High transaction or trading costs, with increased concentration of agricultural production and processing, have encouraged many to bypass terminal markets in favor of direct trading. As large volumes of trade have bypassed these markets, their volumes have frequently declined enough to bring even higher costs per unit handled. Also, while prices established in these markets may be efficient in terms of what was actually traded, in many cases they may not well represent the broader market factors that affect product value. Thus, use of prices from low-volume terminal markets in settling other transactions may increase price distortions and cause resource misallocations in the longer term.

Direct Marketing

Direct marketing, in the context of this book, refers to decentralized, individual transactions between seller and buyer. It is private (as opposed to public) trading in that both the sales negotiations and the outcome of those negotiations (price and other terms of trade) are known with certainty only to the parties to the trade. It is guided by informal rules of trader behavior rather than the formal procedures typical of terminal markets. In general, direct marketing is considered to be a means for completing spot transactions, although in many cases repeated trades with implied agreements have some of the characteristics of a longer-term market contract.

Direct marketing transactions normally occur at the place of business of either the buyer or seller rather than at a neutral site that exists primarily for exchange purposes. In some cases, direct trading occurs by telephone conversations between buyer and seller, with actual delivery being made shortly after the transaction is negotiated. This is more likely to occur when a given buyer and seller have a long-standing trading relationship that has established the confidence of the buyer in the quality of the seller's products and the seller's confidence in the buyer's payment intentions. In many cases at the producer–first handler level, the farmer delivers the product to the buyer's facility, and the transaction is made at that point; in other instances, the buyer visits the seller's farm, inspects the product, negotiates a deal, and takes delivery.

Direct selling dominates exchange at nearly all levels of commodity subsectors beyond the producer–first handler exchange. Some brokers of nondifferentiated products function much like a public market because the bids and offers of many firms are matched almost simultaneously. Other so-called brokers, who act as exclusive agents for a firm, function essentially as the firm's own sales representative in a typical direct trade.

Because of the private nature of direct marketing, it is difficult to characterize this method of vertical coordination. Indeed the nature of direct trades varies considerably. In some, personal inspection of seller's products by buyers is considered essential; in others, product description by the seller suffices. In some, delivery is made when the transaction occurs; in others, delivery is made before or after the actual deal is struck. In some, payment is made on delivery; in others, payment is made well after delivery or, on occasion, before. In some, price is negotiated separately for each transaction; in others, price is negotiated in advance, on a delayed basis, or calculated as a formula price. In some, the buyer is sought out by the seller for each transaction (or vice-versa); in others, a long-standing trade arrangement is worked out between a seller and buyer, and new trading partners are sought only rarely. In some cases, market reporters seek out information on prices and other terms of trade for more general disclosure; in others, only the buyer and seller know such trading details.

Pricing in direct sales typically occurs by private treaty or private negotiations between seller and buyer, although prices in public markets or price reports on other private trading in similar products are often used as a base for such negotiation. Private treaty pricing is the dominant practice in the direct market for livestock, processed meat, fresh fruits and vegetables, manufactured dairy products, and ice-packed broilers.

In some instances, private treaties have evolved into long-standing price formulas; individual transaction prices are settled accordingly. For some commodities, most notably eggs and beef carcasses, this has become the industry norm. In situations where trade has been routinized and long-standing price formulas used, the situation probably more closely resembles contract coordination than direct marketing. A stable exchange relationship between a processor and a producer, viewed by some as potentially exploitive, may be evidence of an efficiently operating system. Where quality is difficult to determine, a buyer may pay a premium to the producer based on prior experience with the product. The producer, recognizing that the price from a familiar buyer is likely to exceed that from a new outlet, has diminished incentive to search for new markets. The practice indicates a lack of information, but the missing information is not the type amenable to third party reporting.

In still other situations, administered pricing or price listing is practiced. Generally this is where a buyer posts the purchase price and farmers agree to sell at that price or go elsewhere. Direct trade in grain and oilseeds between farmers and local elevators is often done on a posted price basis.

Direct marketing has displaced terminal markets as the most prominent means of market coordination for agricultural products since World War II. It dominates the trade for farm commodities such as eggs, livestock, food and feed grains, oilseeds, and fresh produce and in processed products such as meat, broilers, and manufactured dairy products.

Rhodes (1978) lists convenience and physical efficiency as major advantages of direct marketing. The physical efficiencies relative to assembly markets, are obvious: less movement, handling, loading and reloading of products; reduced stress on livestock and other perishable products during the process of being physically transferred from seller to buyer; the elimination of costs associated with physical facilities for assembling products and buyers; and often the elimination of fees for commission agents, auctioneers, and other market intermediaries. Convenience is related to the ability of buyer and seller to strike a deal whenever it is consistent with their other business operations rather than having to time sales to coincide with the operating schedule of an organized market. Also, the farmer may have more control in the selling process when selling directly from the farm. At the farm, the farmer can refuse a bid that he or she considers to be unsatisfactory with relatively little cost, whereas costs may be considerable if he or she rejects a bid after having already shipped the product to a terminal market or a buying station.

The major disadvantages of direct marketing are market access and pricing problems. Market access is generally not a limitation for farmers who have a large enough market volume to facilitate efficient shipment to a buyer (such as a truckload) and are located in physical proximity to at least one buyer station or buyer representative. For the smaller and more geographically isolated farmer, however, finding a buyer with whom to deal directly can be difficult, and, in many cases, finding an alternate buyer to ensure competition and equitable treatment is virtually impossible.

Pricing efficiency and equity are probably the most serious limitations to the direct marketing means of vertical coordination. Market information is relatively unavailable and uncertain in quality due to the private nature of this trade. Parties to direct trades are frequently not equally informed of market conditions and alternative trading opportunities. This information imbalance frequently works to the disadvantage of farmers, who typically are less active in the market than are buyers. Even where information is widely disseminated, the potential for such information to present an incomplete and thus misleading perspective of market conditions is considerable, as it is a virtual impossibility to compile a complete census on private trades. And even if such a census was compiled, it would serve only as a historic record rather than an accurate picture of market conditions at the time of actual transaction.

Further, direct marketing utilizes pricing procedures that do not ensure efficient prices. Indeed when pricing practices such as price listing are used in direct trade situations characterized by a dominant trader on one side of the market, prices are most likely to converge toward a monopoly or monopsony rather than to a competitive equilibrium. Overall, therefore, direct marketing brings a trade-off of reduced pricing efficiency for greater operational or technical efficiency in comparison with terminal markets.

Electronic Markets

Electronic markets are the newest of the market-oriented mechanisms for vertical coordination in agriculture. Although efforts to establish electronic trading mechanisms for fresh produce in the United States were made as early as 1948, the first commercially successful application in North America was not until 1962 when the Ontario Pork Producers Marketing Board launched a teletype auction for butcher hogs. Concurrently telephone auctions (teleauctions) were being tried for livestock in Virginia, and over the succeeding ten years, several small but successful teleauctions were established for feeder pigs in various areas of the United States.

The potential benefits of electronic markets began to receive more general attention with the analysis by Schrader et al. (1968) of a proposed electronic exchange for eggs in 1968. Some progress was made shortly after in developing a workable electronic egg market. In 1975 the Plains Cotton Cooperative Association in Lubbock, Texas, devised a computerized auction for pricing cotton that had previously been tied to government support prices. Substantial impetus was given to the development of electronic markets in 1978 when the USDA's Agricultural Marketing Service embarked on a program of matching fund grants for the development of such markets.

To date, there has been a variety of experiences with these markets. The teletype auction for Ontario butcher hogs has flourished, while similar systems were tried and eventually abandoned in several other Canadian provinces. Teleauctions have grown in importance in local feeder pig markets in the United States and have been adopted for feeder cattle in several southeastern U.S. markets. After starting as a manual trading system in 1972, the egg exchange emerged into a full-fledged computerized auction by the mid-1970s; however, it has never attracted more than a tenth of its potential volume. The cotton exchange, TELCOT, has become a commercial success, spreading well beyond the initial cooperative, and is now an accepted institution in the U.S. cotton market.

Experimental computerized auctions, partially funded by USDA, were conducted with limited success for slaughter hogs in Ohio and feeder cattle in Texas, with no success for wholesale meat nationally and slaughter cows in Virginia and with more success for market lambs in Virginia and surrounding states. The experimental computerized lamb auction has since become a commercial venture, the National Electronic Marketing Association (NEMA). It has expanded to lamb sales in many parts of the United States, has become a base system for use in other livestock markets, and eventually may expand to other commodities. In early 1985 the system was being used by three selling organizations and three packer buyers for market hogs in the Midwest. This was, however, fewer on both sides of the market than were involved at the inception of hog trading two years earlier.

Observations on the performance of electronic markets as a coordination mechanism in agriculture are limited by the still-infant nature of these markets. Nonetheless, enough study of the experimental and operational systems has been completed to allow some generalizations.

Performance is a function of concept and design. Henderson (1982) has identified five characteristics common to all such markets: (1) organized trading, that is, trading occurs in accordance with a known and formal set of rules of behavior; (2) centralized sales negotiaton, meaning that numerous buyers and sellers interact more or less simultaneously; (3) remote market access, that is, buyers and sellers are not necessarily physically present in the central sales arena but enter into sales negotiations by long-distance communication devices such as telephones, teletype, and computer terminals; (4) description selling, which means that products are sold based on verbal and/or pictorial description rather than personal inspection by the buyer; and (5) postsale shipment, that is, products are not shipped by the seller until after successful sales negotiations have been completed. While none of the above characteristics is unique to electronic markets, electronic exchanges are unique in combining all five features in a single marketing system.

The premise on which electronic marketing rests is that both the pricing efficiency benefits associated with large-volume central terminal markets and the technical efficiency benefits associated with direct marketing can be achieved. The idea is to separate price establishment from physical delivery, centralizing the former through the use of organized trading rules and remote communications between traders and decentralizing the latter through description selling and direct shipment after a transaction has occurred.

Pricing in these markets generally occurs through some type of auction. Dutch and English auction procedures have been used most frequently to date, with a unique combination of the two being used in the NEMA system. The egg exchange uses a variation of the price-efficient double auction. TELCOT uses first price, sealed bid auction pricing plus a price listing option. Private treaty pricing was attempted in the wholesale meat experiment, but there was not sufficient trading in that venture to generate much insight into the adaptability of this pricing technique to electronic exchange.

Trading results on both experimental and commercial electronic markets reveal remarkably consistent results. In comparison with direct markets and some terminal markets, competition among rival buyers has been enhanced, the accuracy and availability of market information is greater, and market access for smaller and geographically remote traders is improved. All of these factors have helped electronic markets to achieve more efficient prices and less monopsonistic price distortion.

The unit costs of electronic trading have generally been high. Trading costs have often been comparable with or perhaps modestly lower than those in assembly markets. The expected cost efficiencies of direct markets, for the most part, have not been realized because of insufficient volume to realize the substantial scale economies associated with most existing electronic market designs. The potential exists to lower trading costs to levels more competitive with direct trading given adequate trading volume. Innovative systems are evolving that appear to hold promise of lower trading costs than have been achieved so far.

Two factors that observers expected to present problems for electronic markets have not proved limiting in the experimental markets. Description of products has been generally successful, with the methods developed for the electronic markets generally adopted for trading by other means. And, the use of prices generated on the electronic market to facilitate trading off the market has not been a major factor limiting participation.

Integration

The mechanisms treated in the preceding sections represent alternative means to coordinate by market price. Spot markets are at the heart of the processes. Integration represents the opposite extreme, where two or more adjacent stages, under single ownership, are coordinated by intrafirm administrative direction. Although internalized coordination is usually associated with common ownership of two adjacent stages, it is not in all cases. Firms that own operations at more than one stage may rely on market mechanisms partially or entirely for coordination.

Coase (1937) and Williamson (1975) argue that, in a competitive market, transaction costs provide a rationale for combining stages within a firm. Most of the gains from the organization of economic activity are from specialization and exchange, quite the opposite of integration. Economies of size provide the major incentive for specialization. Thus, until a firm in a competitive market has exhausted the size economies at one stage, there would be no reason to extend into another in the absence of transaction costs.

Uncertainty is a major component of transaction costs. In a market transaction, there is always some question as to whether the seller can deliver the quality and quantity that is promised and some cost of policing quality. There is also some question as to whether suppliers (or buyers) will be available exactly when needed. The flow of product (quantity and quality) may be rather uneven when individual decision makers respond to price signals in a less than perfect market. Search cost may be quite high when specifications are exacting, as they often are in the industrialized food sector.

Integration may also reduce profit variation. Firm theory implies that competitive marketing firm margins will be low when quantity is low and producer prices (and profits) are high. Conversely, marketing margins are likely to be high when quantity is large and producer prices are low. Combining the production and marketing stages may well reduce income variation, as well as transaction costs.

When quality is important at later stages in the system and is not easily measurable short of actual use in processing, control of the production process may be the least-cost means to ensure quality. In some situations there may be technological interdependence to the extent that separation of the nominally separate stages is costly. For example, there appears to be substantial cost reduction associated with the combination of egg production and the grading and packing operation at the same site.

An imbalance of market power and excess profits at one stage may also provide incentive to integrate by firms at adjacent stages. Joint profit maximization will result in greater total profit to the two stages if firms on either side of the stage interface have market power. A noncompetitive firm is not expected to integrate into a competitive stage except for transaction cost reasons.

Integration is found in nearly all commodity subsectors. The poultry and egg subsectors provide a number of examples. Food retailing and wholesale distribution are substantially integrated. Processing and distribution are integrated to some degree in both red meat and poultry. Some restaurant chains have integrated the distribution of food and supplies to the stores. Several grocery chains have integrated into fluid milk processing. Changing technology has resulted in both integration and disintegration of the production level. Production of power, fertilizer, pest control, breeding, and so forth have been separated from the traditional farm enterprise to a large extent, while some commodity subsectors have become noted for integration of stages formerly operated by separate firms.

Joint ventures, associations of two or more business entities (persons, partnerships, corporations, or cooperatives) to carry on a specific economic operation, enterprise, or venture but with the identities of participants remaining apart from their co-ownership or co-participation in the venture (Hulse 1976), represent another approach to coordination. The participants share on agreed basis the expenses, profits, losses, risks, and some measure of control. Joint ventures of cooperatives with corporations and other cooperatives at adjacent stages have received some research attention. To be effective coordinating mechanisms, substantial control over adjacent stages must be given to the joint venture management. Its effect may vary from equivalent to integration to that of contract coordination.

Integration, when undertaken because of high transaction costs, contributes to the efficiency of the subsector. This is true by definition. The gains are from precise scheduling and quality control. An integrated unit is expected to be able to operate more nearly at capacity than its nonintegrated counterparts.

When the combination includes what would otherwise be a non-competitive stage, the final output is expected to be more nearly at the economically efficient point than would be the case for separate decisions at the two levels. If integration is motivated by a market power imbalance, coordination may not be accomplished most efficiently by administrative decision. The option to coordinate by the means having the lowest transaction cost remains; thus, common ownership of two stages need not be a cause of inefficient resource allocation.

Equity in the sense of appropriate payment for quality, time, and location is not diminished by integration. Within the integrated firm, equity is not a consideration. Integration of two or more stages may affect participants at other stages positively by more accurately reflecting values in final use. The process of combining stages into a single firm may certainly affect the welfare of the original firm owners differentially. If accomplished by merger, the outcome would reflect the relative bargaining positions of the original firms. If integration is into a noncompetitive stage, the former occupants of that stage are the losers.

Integration and coordinaton by administrative direction of only a portion of the total flow of a product inevitably leave a thinner market at the transaction points involved. For example, with a smaller amount of produce being allocated by the market, the chance for inequitable treatment (if only by accident) increases. Further, the greater the transaction cost relative to value, the greater the potential for inequitable pricing. In particular, high search cost in a thin market may result in greater divergence from a Pareto-optimal solution.

Transaction costs are expected to be low or absent for the integrated stages. Search cannot cease entirely because the firm must have information on alternatives, and some market participation may be necessary to adjust for inevitable planning errors or uncontrollable variation. In fact, per unit transaction costs may be quite high for these incidental transactions, but the average over all units is expected to be quite low. Transaction costs in the remaining unintegrated portion of the market may increase as volume decreases.

Similarly, access to markets or sources is reduced for those not integrated. If integration is economically justified, exit of the nonintegrated firm is inevitable. If it is not justified, the integrated firms will find it in their own best interest to participate in the market and to give access to those who can provide the intermediate product at lower cost or buy it at a higher price than possible for the integrated firm. If two stages are completely integrated, access to the intermediate product is foreclosed short of a technical innovation, which encourages disintegration. Shifts in integration patterns do occur. Much of the cutting and packing for retail sale once done in the store is now done by the meat and poultry packers. Here the cutting stage remains integrated but with a different stage.

Integration of stages is expected to increase the dynamic stability of a subsector if it has any effect at all. Simultaneous planning of more than one stage should reduce the tendency to overreact to short-term stimuli. It can reduce the errors within the integrated stages but may have little impact outside them. The persistence of price and production cycles in the highly integrated (and contract coordinated) broiler subsector provides evidence for the latter view.

Cooperatives

Cooperatives play major roles in the U.S. food system. As such, they are treated in greater detail than might be expected if discussion were limited to their role as a coordination mechanism. Although cooperatives exist at other levels of the system (grocery wholesale and retailing), their largest role is at the farm supply and first handler levels. Farmers' cooperatives function as an extension of the farm business into other stages of the system (integration) and as bargaining agents for farmers.

Cooperative Integration. Farmers have extended their business cooperatively backward into petroleum products, fertilizer, feed, and other inputs to the production stage. They have extended forward into assembly, processing, and wholesaling to some extent in all subsectors of agriculture. The horizontal (market share) extent of integration of at least one stage varies from quite high for milk and some specialty crops to very low for poultry and eggs. The shares of farm products and inputs handled by cooperatives for 1973 and 1983 are shown in table 2–1.

The vertical extent (number of stages combined) also varies substantially. Cooperatives have typically integrated backward to refining and even production of petroleum, mining, and basic manufacture of fertilizer and feed manufacture on the input side. Forward integration from the farm has been more limited, with most grain, oilseed, and livestock cooperative activity at only the assembly or first handler stage. Even in those commodities, some cooperatives (for example, American Rice, Riceland Foods, and Land O'Lakes) are engaged in processing and, to some extent, the manufacture of branded products for the consumer.

The motivation for cooperative integration has probably more often been related to farmers' perception of a market power imbalance between themselves and the small number of buyers of their products and sellers of their production supplies than to transaction costs and improvement of coordination as such. Reduction of transaction costs is difficult to accomplish through cooperation. Coordination is usually internalized to a lesser extent than would be the case for an integrated noncooperative firm. Cooperatives must depend on contracts or marketing agreements with members to provide for any surrender of member decisions to the cooperative entity. The length of contracts is limited by state statute to ten years or less in most states, and

Table 2–1

Number of Cooperatives and Cooperatives' Share of Farm Supplies
Purchased and Products Marketed, 1973 and 1983

	Number of Co-ops		Share of Market	
	1973	1983	1973	1983
Marketing				
All farm products	5257	4175	23	30
Milk and dairy products	657	418	76	77
Grain and soybeans	2567	2271	29	38
Cotton and products	507	488	21	31
Fruits, vegetables, and products	447	394	23	19
Dry beans and peas	47	23	23	18
Livestock and wool	748	402	9	11
Poultry and eggs	174	63	7	8
Supplies purchased				
All major farm supplies	5574	4243	23	27
Fertilizer and lime	3990	3226	36	38
Petroleum and products	2647	2562	38	38
Farm chemicals	3353	3202	19	35
Feed	3790	3097	18	19
Seed	3591	3121	17	14

Source: Wissman 1985, pp. 18–19.

several require an annual withdrawal option. The major broiler chicken co-operative is an exception, with the entire process, from breeder placement through processing, centrally coordinated. Pooling of farm products is probably also motivated by the reduction of the transaction costs of search and the gathering and processing of information. Usually one finds only a buy-sell relationship between farmers and their purchasing cooperatives.

Where economies to size are substantial, farmers may feel that a cooperative is needed to prevent exploitation by a firm of minimum efficient size if it were not a cooperative. Farmers have formed cooperatives to maintain market access when a noncooperative firm leaves or threatens to leave an area without an outlet for certain products.

Extension of the cooperative firm into stages that are not adjacent to the production stage (for example, from fertilizer blending and retailing into manufacture and mining) may be motivated by transaction costs and/or market power reasons. Preserving access to a supply or market is seen as market power motivated.

In response to changing conditions beyond the first handler level, some cooperatives have become involved in nontraditional forms of integration. These generally involve horizontal and vertical growth through interregional cooperation and joint ventures among cooperatives or with proprietary firms.

The merger of hundreds of smaller dairy cooperatives into Associated Milk Producers, Mid-America Dairymen, and Dairymen, Inc. during the late

1960s and early 1970s is the most vivid example of horizontal cooperative growth. This consolidation allowed more efficient milk assembly by eliminating duplicate pickup routes and receiving and manufacturing facilities. It also increased cooperatives' bargaining power in dealing with fluid handlers, thus increasing their antitrust visibility, as evidenced by Department of Justice prosecution of all three for alleged anticompetitive practices.

More recent examples of interregional cooperation include the development of a number of entities involved in grain transportation, storage, and marketing, such as Mid-States terminals, St. Louis Grain Company and Farmers Export Company; the development of origination capacity in fertilizer as with CF Industries; and efforts to become more self-sufficient in energy production. These and similar arrangements are often characterized by vertical extension, leading to sharing of significant risks and seeking of economies of size and scale through pooling of the resources of a number of cooperatives.

A number of other cooperatives have either merged recently or are in the process of merger. These include cooperatives at the local level, as well as federated regional cooperatives, as represented by the recent mergers of Land O'Lakes, Inc. and Midland, Inc.; Tri/Valley Growers and California Canners and Growers; Landmark and Ohio Farmers; and FCS and Central Carolina Farmers Exchange. Other mergers are part of a strategic effort to harmonize interests of producer-owned organizations. While some mergers are necessary for mere survival of cooperatives, merger of regional cooperatives is often accomplished at the same time that local cooperative members of the federated regional cooperatives are finding that other local cooperatives are their primary source of competition. In the case of a number of centralized cooperatives in California (Diamond Walnuts, Sunsweet Prunes, Sun Maid Raisins, and Valley Fig Growers), a joint marketing agency (Sun-Diamond) apparently offered the opportunity to achieve economies in management, marketing, and data processing that could be passed on to their membership as higher returns.

A recent example of joint ventures among cooperative partners involves collaboration between Ocean Spray Cranberries, Inc. and Sunsweet Growers, Inc. Sunsweet processes, packs, and ships cranberries from the Pacific Northwest, and Ocean Spray handles prune juice in eastern markets for Sunsweet (Harris, et al. 1983).

A recent cooperative–proprietary firm joint venture of interest involves U.S. and European cooperatives' purchase of a 50 percent interest in the commodity trading portion of Alfred C. Toepfer, a grain trading organization with offices and an information network worldwide. The cooperatives participating in this venture hope to be able to use the Toepfer organization to improve market information and market access. The arrangement is expected to permit returns to producers to increase as a result of improved marketing decisions and market access flowing from better market information and first refusal options for Toepfer sales of U.S. grain (Newman and Riley 1982). Interestingly, Archer-Daniels-Midland has also purchased a portion of the Toepfer organization.

Another approach to joint ventures and mergers involves combinations that make use of the tax advantage of purchase-leaseback arrangements for facilities. Agway, Inc., was the catalyst in developing a fruit and vegetable grower cooperative, Pro-Fac, which purchased vegetable canning facilities and leased them to Curtice Burns, a vegetable canning corporation in which Agway is part owner. A long-term supply contract between the two entities was part of the arrangement. More recently Agway entered the dairy business through a joint milk marketing venture whereby Agway, Yankee Milk, and others formed a joint venture, Agri-Mark, which purchased the fixed assets of H.P. Hood, the major New England dairy processor, and then leased the fixed assets back to Hood, as well as making a supply agreement that provides for Hood to receive all of its milk requirements from Agri-Mark (Harris, et al., 1983).

Cooperative Bargaining. Cooperative bargaining is a means to establish terms of trade at a stage interface characterized by unequal numbers of buyers and sellers. Only producers have the legal protection to organize and market cooperatively. One might argue that bargaining should be considered a method of pricing or as a special case of contracting. Because of its importance in the food system, we treat it separately here. Discussion is limited to bargaining associated with contracts; the operation of cooperative marketing agents in spot markets will not be treated.

Cooperative bargaining is more limited than labor union bargaining for wages. With the exception of the 1973 Michigan Agricultural Marketing and Bargaining Act, which applies to perishable fruits and vegetables, and a recently enacted New York law, which applies to apples in a limited area, there is no legal sanction for exclusive agency bargaining. Only in these limited cases is it possible for the bargaining association to obtain the authority to represent all farmers in a bargaining unit, members and nonmembers alike. The U.S. Supreme Court decided in 1984 that nonmembers could not be held to contract terms negotiated under the Michigan law. Furthermore, "undue price enhancement" by producer cooperatives is proscribed by section 2 of the Capper-Volstead Act. No such limits apply to organized labor.

Lang (1978) found that the most frequent trade terms that are bargained for by associations include price, time of payment, quality provisions, rights and responsibilities during production, provision of seeds, and premiums and discounts. Lang also questioned bargaining association managers regarding their goals. Those ranking highest included higher grower income, stable prices, assured markets, expanded membership and markets, higher prices, and better market information.

Lang (1978) found some interesting differences in the approaches of bargaining cooperatives handling annual crops and those handling perennial crops. Since annual crops are generally planted after contracts have been signed, bargainers can use expected production costs, opportunity costs of alternative crops, and overall market supply and demand information in their bargaining process. In contrast, the associations handling perennials were found to place substantially greater emphasis on supply and demand conditions in the marketplace than on production costs.

Bargaining cooperatives differ from operating cooperatives in the types of services rendered to members. Where the only service provided is to set price, there are economic incentives for the individual producer to become a "free rider" in that the producer does not pay to support the bargaining association but benefits from any price advantage achieved by the association. Lang (1978) found that associations attempt to reduce the incentive to free ride by providing additional services to members of the association, including market information, newsletters, public relations, fieldmen, legislative representation, research, commodity programs, industry representation, and other factors.

The key question with respect to bargaining associations deals with their actual and potential impact on prices. Measuring the price effect of bargaining is, however, complicated because it entails evaluating what would have happened in the absence of bargaining. Empirically the analysis is handled by measuring (adjusted) prices before and after the start of bargaining or relationships between prices in bargained and nonbargained areas. In both cases, it is assumed that the only difference is the existence of bargaining.

Helmberger and Hoos (1965) examined twenty-nine bargaining agreements for various periods from 1910 to 1962. In only one case, processing tomatoes in Ohio, were the results positive and statistically significant, and in several instances a negative effect was measured. The researchers even questioned the one significant result, noting that prices in the region were rising generally around the time bargaining was instituted. Comparing Ohio prices to other regional but nonbargained prices led to a rejection of even the conclusion of a significant effect in Ohio.

Using data from a more recent period (1960–1975) Garoyan and Thor (1978) contrasted the annual rates of price changes between bargained and nonbargained fruit and nut crops produced in California. Overall they found a statistically significant average annual difference of about 4 percent. This falls in the range expected by Hoos (1970).

The Garoyan and Thor 1978 sample is unique in the sense that all but one of the commodities (cherries) were covered by marketing orders (see Armbruster and Jesse (1983) for a discussion of these orders). In addition, several of the crops, including the stone fruits, processing tomatoes, and raisins, are limited to California, giving the bargaining association the potential for representing a large share of the national production of these products. Moreover, the crops in the nonbargained group were largely handled by producer processing and marketing cooperatives. Thus, the comparison is really between prices paid by processing cooperatives and bargaining associations, not between bargaining groups and proprietary firms. Since processing cooperatives without supply controls are well known for overproducing compared to proprietary firms, the base prices used in the comparison may be at the lower limit. Hence, the results shown by Garoyan and Thor may not be reproducible elsewhere.

Skinner (1981) evaluated the experience in Michigan following the passage of the mandatory good-faith bargaining legislation in 1973. Since this legislation is the most comprehensive of the sort, the impact on Michigan prices might be expected to exceed that in other areas. For the two crops Skinner analyzed, processing apples and asparagus, he found only a modest increase in prices. Using average annual price changes as the more appropriate comparison, price changes were not significantly different, either between the before and after period or between producing areas. One explanation for this result is the small share Michigan has of these products. Specifically, the law does not prevent Michigan processors from importing products from outside the state, which, according to industry observers in the area, they have been doing in increasing amounts.

Bargaining facilitates coordination in two ways. First, many bargaining cooperatives provide information on supplies and prices. For products not reported by the Crop Reporting Service, this may be the only source of public supply and price information. The dissemination of information is further enhanced by its use as a means of attracting and holding association members. Without such member-only services, bargaining groups are weakened by "free riders," who benefit from any group-negotiated benefits without incurring the costs and other responsibilities of membership.

Second, when quality is difficult or expensive to measure ex post, a bargaining arrangement can assist in quality assurance or screening. Often reputation will serve as an unwritten term of the agreement (Campbell 1981, p. 128). This is but one example of how cooperation between growers and handlers can help coordination and assist adaptation. The California Tomato Growers Association, for example, formed an advisory committee with canner representatives to work out problems associated with mechanization and bulk handling (Kautz 1978).

The pattern of performance is mixed. Its impact may depend on industry structure (particularly the share of production represented by the cooperative), commodity characteristics, and the skill with which bargaining is undertaken. The somewhat cumbersome machinery of bargaining is not expected to result in a maximum of allocative or technical efficiency. The process may result in terms that encourage efficient allocation and resource use when the change in terms benefits all individuals in the bargaining group. Adjustment of terms that affect members of the group differently are much more difficult to resolve. Any mistake in terms probably generates a subgroup who would be worse off if the error is corrected. It may then be necessary to compromise on efficiency in order to obtain agreement. Bargaining may well move a market characterized by unequal market power in the direction of efficiency. Also, given that bargaining is most likely found in a situation of great disparity of numbers and market power, it is expected to move the system toward a more nearly equitable state. However, the rigidities inherent in bargaining and compromise, which are needed to maintain the group, may create some inequities within the bargaining group that would not exist in a competitive market.

Transactions costs under bargaining are likely to be fairly low. The expense of maintaining the bargaining organization and necessary policing of contracts keep costs higher than the integration case. The larger the group, the larger the structure needed, and the larger the expenditure needed to maintain group solidarity.

Access to markets is usually ensured to members of a bargaining cooperative. The inability to deny access to nonmembers limits the price gains of many bargaining efforts. Foreclosing access with long-term full supply contracts may be possible. It may also be possible to control volume through linkage to marketing orders. It will suffice to say that cooperative bargaining provides greater market access than integration but, to exploit market power, it must restrict access to some extent.

Dynamic stability should be enhanced if the bargaining agent represents a large proportion of the product and if there is bargaining for both quantity and price. The information flow should reduce the tendency of separate decision makers to overreact to a price signal. Much depends on the extent to which the impact of marginal tonnage on price can be conveyed to producers.

Although these benefits are difficult to measure directly, they are observable indirectly in one dimension: price variability. With agricultural crops, weather fluctuation and other environmental factors can have a widespread effect on supplies from year to year. Wide supply variability in turn contributes to price uncertainty, which increases the uncertainty for the producers. Under these circumstances, the bargaining association, in the words of Garoyan and Thor (1978), "would seek to achieve greater price stability by tempering widely swinging prices by foregoing highest short-run returns to achieve long-run demand stability through lower than maximum prices" (p. 138). This effect of stabilizing prices may be seen as an improvement in coordination, at least for growers.

The results of the Garoyan and Thor (1978) analysis on California fruits were not strong but did show some tendency toward price moderation following bargaining. The effect was apparent only for crops with moderate price variability. In Michigan, Skinner (1981) found that the variability (measured as a percentage of the mean) of both prices and income for apples was reduced following bargaining; however, for asparagus an increase was found.

Contract Coordination

Contract coordination between independent firms represents an intermediate position between spot market coordination and integration. The class covers a variety of arrangements that might also include bargaining (treated separately). Contracts involve commitments to deliver and receive goods at some later time. Usually contracts involving farm production extend over at least one production period. Producer–first handler contracts have received the most attention from agricultural economists, but forward contracts are found at all levels of the food system short of the retailer-consumer interface. Futures markets will be treated separately because futures contracts are not usually settled by delivery.

Mighell and Jones (1963) classified production (producer–first handler) contracts as market-specification contracts, production-management contracts, and resource-providing contracts. A great deal of variation in contract terms exists within each category.

Market specification contracts establish the amount, time, quality, and place for a future delivery. Price for the product to be delivered may be established at the time the contract is made, in which case it would be what is usually called a forward contract. Forward contracts are common in grain, oilseed, and oilseed products trades and for many transactions beyond the first handler level in a number of subsectors; however, the commodity price may not be established at the time of trade but left to be determined by formula at the time of shipment or delivery. Substantially all the risk of production remains with the producer. The major difference from some form of spot market coordination is that the seller is sure to have an outlet and the buyer a supply. If quality is rigidly specified, the producers' risk may be increased. Price risk may or may not be shifted depending on pricing terms.

Production management contracts call for more direct participation by the contractor in production management. This participation is usually in the form of specification of inputs or cultural practices. It will often include the presence of the contractor's personnel to ensure compliance. In these cases, the contractor often accepts part of the production risk. For example, the contract often specifies input quantities, not output quantity. Price of the commodity may be established at the time the contract is negotiated or may be determined by formula included in the contract.

Coordination by resource-providing contracts may approach that of integration in the extent to which production and price risks and coordination responsibility are assumed by the contractor. Broiler contracts are near the integration end of the continuum. Chicks, feed, and often other inputs are provided by the contractor, and the grower is paid on a piece basis, often with no direct relationship to a market price at any level of the subsector. In contrast, Florida citrus growers often contract for processing and marketing services from the processors on a toll basis. That is, the grower is paid the amount received for processed products, less processing cost and processor's profit margin. This is almost the direct opposite of the chicken case. The citrus grower accepts much of the risk of marketing, as well as that of growing.

Contracts are used in the coordination of the food system under appropriate conditions for a variety of reasons. They allow participants to capture some of the benefits of internalizing coordination while retaining the benefits of remaining as separate business entities. Appropriately applied contracts can reduce transactions costs, reduce risks associated with availability of markets or supplies, and reduce the risks associated with quality variation. Contracts may also contribute toward the stability of the businesses involved. The equity of contract arrangements is as variable as is the bargaining position or benevolence of the parties. Contracts may restrict short-run access to markets but probably do not in the longer term. They do limit the access of the produce-and-then-sell operator. In most areas it would be quite risky to produce turkeys without a marketing agreement with a processor, but such an agreement would probably be available prior to starting production. The method of contract negotiation and information made available is more relevant to access than the existence of contracting.

A major complaint related to the use of forward contracts, particularly where formula pricing is used, is that price discovery in the spot market is degraded. This effect is external to the decisions of the contract participants. If contracting at or near the time resources are committed to production results in sufficiently lower transaction costs or more appropriate resource allocation than spot markets, it serves no purpose to lament the demise of an inferior system. The problem arises when participants desire to contract but leave the pricing to the spot market that they are replacing.

Choice of contracting as the means of coordination may be compatible with open markets. If fixed price forward contracts were traded on an open exchange, pricing accuracy would be enhanced, and these contract options would be more accessible to potential market participants. Forward deliverable contract markets (FDCM) have been proposed by Holder and Sporleder (1976).

An FDCM is a publicly organized exchange for trading standardized forward contracts which mandate delivery of the commodity. Its distinction from existing futures markets is the emphasis on delivery. Buyers and sellers enter the FDCM only when they wish to procure or sell a commodity for later delivery. When an FDCM contract is made, the buyer and seller are known to each other, as are the time and place of delivery. Producers and processors may enter the market directly, without the services of a broker. This market would centralize the price discovery process for forward contracts.

A FDCM can be justified on the basis of information theory, bargaining theory, and vertical coordination theory. It should achieve the benefits of open market trading, along with the benefits of contracting. Such a market could result in more accurate and timely prices, more efficient allocation of resources, greater access to markets, less opportunity for processors to exercise market power, and reduced transaction costs for processors. FDCM would be applicable to any subsector now using forward contracts. Kauffman (1983, p. 38) emphasizes the potential for a FCDM for hogs to dampen the hog cycle. He sees it as "the only way to force enough long-run price information into the system so that chronic mistakes in long-run production plans might be reduced."

Skepticism about FDCMs abounds, however. Despite all the stated advantages, their introduction and implementation have been slow. Problems exist in obtaining adequate information, the existence of inequitable bargaining power, planning production for a specific date, and assuring quality. Also, firms that have market power, such as some processors or bargaining agents, do not want to lose their power base. It may be that FDCMs can be successful only if participation is made mandatory.

The standardization necessary to establish a contract market diminishes the value of a forward contract as a coordinating device. One reason stated for the use of contracts is to obtain exactly the quality desired; this may entail the specification of production practices or use of other special means to achieve the quality desired by the buyer.

It may also be the case that neither buyer nor seller wishes to shift the price risk that currently exists. For example, the meat packer buys raw material in a daily cash market, and the customer, a restaurant chain, wants to be sure of a price no higher than its competitors but does desire quantity and quality assurance. The formula-priced contract that results is preferred by both parties to either spot market transactions or fixed-price forward contracts.

Futures Markets

Futures markets do not serve directly as coordination mechanisms. Typically few contracts are settled by delivery. Rather futures markets serve as an adjunct to or facilitate the use of other coordination mechanisms. The essential difference between futures contracts and what have been referred to as forward contracts is that a futures contract obligation can be completely discharged by an opposite transaction in the same commodity and option. In effect it is as if every trade is with the exchange clearinghouse. Thus a futures transaction can be used "as a temporary substitute for an intended later contract to buy or sell on other terms" (Working 1953, p. 137). Futures serve a major role in price discovery and as a pricing base for formula-priced contracts for a number of commodities in the food system.

Leuthold's (1973, 1976) studies have illuminated the role of futures in coordinating vertical systems. As stocks of storage commodities decreased and price variability increased in the 1970s, use of futures markets became more prevalent. First handlers offset their purchases, whether spot or forward contract, by selling futures contracts. Shippers and merchandisers reduced their exposure to subsequent price risks through the use of futures contracts. Producers signed more forward contracts or delayed pricing contracts with first handlers, who simply offset risks in the futures markets. The prices for nearly all of these contracts were strongly influenced by prevailing futures market prices.

A significant role of a futures market is the providing of information. Whether pricing a spot transaction or forward cash contract, the futures market is often used as a base for pricing. Surveys show that no more than 10 percent of producers use futures markets directly, but up to half watch the market and rely on it in their cash market decision making (Helmuth 1977). Futures prices aid in efficiently allocating resources and in reducing information costs. Futures markets are more liquid than cash markets, meaning that large positions can be accumulated more quickly in futures. They reflect the current and anticipated demand and supply conditions for a commodity, give highly standardized price information to both producers and processors, and thereby help coordinate activities of economic agents. Futures markets may limit the power of very large firms to dictate terms of trade by providing a readily available value indicator.

Futures trading is concentrated into standardized contracts with a limited number of delivery points and times. This concentration of trading limits usefulness to some market participants but provides the liquidity necessary for successful use as a hedging tool. It also facilitates use of the market by speculators and economizes on information that must be distributed to and processed by users. Concentration of trading results in very low transactions costs for the trading of futures. One may infer that the transactions cost of a combination of the cash and futures transactions used in hedging is lower than a cash market transaction alone. Reduced uncertainty and search costs in the hedged transaction set more than offset the added costs due to increasing the number of transactions and participants involved.

The efficiency of resource allocation is increased where a futures market allows the pricing function to be separated from the search for and completion of the cash side of the transaction. That is, finding a willing trader at a price level may be easier than finding one with the exact quantity, quality, and delivery terms *and* price desired at any given time. Use of futures expands the time available to complete a transaction.

Futures markets are open and accessible with nearly full parity of information for all participants. Despite beliefs to the contrary, futures markets are probably more competitive and less subject to the influence of individuals or firms than are most spot cash markets. Regulation by both government and the exchanges has been reasonably successful.

Market Information

Market information, although not a coordination mechanism, is a central issue in vertical coordination. Cost and availability of information are key determinants of performance. In the discussion of resource allocation as a performance dimension, it was implied that information can be treated as a commodity; that is, resources are used in its production, and it can be sold. But the seller can have it and sell it too, which implies that information has attributes of a public good.

Riemenschneider (1979) examined the implications of the fact that information possesses many public good attributes. Uncertainty, indivisibility, and nonappropriability are all characteristics of information. Enforcement costs limit the effectiveness of copyright protection. The externality that use of information by others reduces the individual's need for the same information is a further complication, which reinforces Riemenschneider's argument: "it does seem clear that the social returns to information often exceed the sum of individuals' private returns, particularly in a decentralized economic system where information is needed to coordinate activity among firms" (p. 18). He sees the alternatives as information provided by specialized firms, voluntary collectives, or government and builds a strong case for public information.

The efforts of specialized information firms are limited because of the nonappropriability of information. Voluntary efforts tend to fall short of the optimum, and the shortfall is likely to be greater the larger the number of participants involved. The case for public provision of information is also strengthened by its potential impact on market structure. Public information may reduce the advantage of large firms and may reduce the incentive to integrate to achieve closer coordination.

Coordination can be facilitated by information services such as price reporting, production estimates, inventory data, and intentions of market participants. Interpretation of data (creation of information) may be at least as important as the provision of raw data. The latter point has important implications for equity, given the likely greater analytical capability of large firms. Private information networks (including grain firms, brokerage firms and specialized firms) do play an important role, particularly in the market price and current news area. Specialized firms serve the meat, poultry, fats and oils, and other markets. Large trading firms maintain their own information networks, and the information clearing function of brokers should not be overlooked. Their product is primarily information, though it is not sold as such. Trade associations also provide information services. Livestock producers and feedlot operators have initiated services to gather and disseminate information on a subscription basis. Few private firms or trade associations gather primary data on production, use, and stocks except to supplement or anticipate government reports.

Public market information and price reporting services can reduce information-gathering costs and duplication of similar functions that private firms may perform for themselves. The incidence of the cost is transferred from the firm to the taxpayer, yet in many cases the public may be the ultimate indirect beneficiary. The roles of information in maintaining competitive markets, increasing equity, increasing access, and assisting in planning of production and use assure its place as a key food system policy variable.

Widespread use of contract coordination suggests a need for public reporting on contract terms, as well as spot market prices. The task is complicated by the complexity of most production contracts. Campbell (1981) evaluated an experimental contract reporting program in Wisconsin with mixed results and concluded that contract reporting is feasible. But although a majority of users indicated the report was a valuable addition to market information, they did not indicate a willingness to pay for the information. Little impact of contract reporting could be shown in this limited experiment. The very limited number of contract alternatives open to individuals may mean that the information provided by contract reporting is interesting but not of much value in decision making. Most of the contracts reported may not be available to the individual, who is in a take-it-or-leave-it position.

Government Programs

Government programs have direct impacts on coordination of the food system through price supports, direct production controls, and federal and state marketing orders and agreements. Price supports probably add to physical efficiency through a reduction of uncertainty but, unless accompanied by controls, can hardly be said to increase coordination. Large surpluses of dairy products in the 1980s illustrate the opposite effect. Direct controls such as those exercised over tobacco and peanuts effect some degree of coordination at a substantial cost in terms of resource allocation.

The Secretary of Agriculture's task group on marketing orders (USDA 1981b) gave federal marketing orders a mixed review:

> These regulations [qualities and/or quantities marketed] are designed to compensate for, or overcome certain characteristics of agricultural markets—imbalances in marketing power, instability, incomplete information, and the external effects of individual firms' actions—that prevent free trading from being fully efficient. But some of the regulations themselves have potentials

for reducing economic efficiency mainly by causing too little or too much of certain products to be produced or, once produced, to be used where the value to society is less than it could be. [p. 81]

Price stabilization is viewed as aiding efficiency, whereas distortion of prices may increase costs in the short run. With provision for entry, orders may increase efficiency sufficiently to offset the short-run costs. Marketing orders may favor small producers to the exent that some of the benefits of an order might be achieved without an order by large, integrated farms but not by small farms acting without an order. Federal orders, while mandatory after being voted into existence by producers, can also be terminated by producer vote. To at least that extent, orders preserve more freedom for producers than do government controls associated with price-support programs.

Pricing, Coordination, and Performance of the Food System

Pricing and coordination are interrelated, and usually several coordination mechanisms are found in a given subsector. Different mechanisms are used at different levels in a system, or parallel channels often exist at each level of exchange in a commodity system. The vertical structure and coordination of commodity systems has shifted to accommodate technological change and institutional change, but it is not one-way causation from technology and institutions to vertical coordination and structure. Existing vertical structure has also affected the adoption of technology and adaptation of institutions.

The performance attributes of coordination systems and their associated pricing methods are summarized briefly in table 2–2. The focus of this section is on the performance of the mixture of systems that one finds in existing commodity systems and on the trade-offs in the selection of coordination and pricing systems.

Regardless of the predominant coordination methods in use, spot exchange is likely to exist at least to some degree at every stage interface in a subsector. These exchanges may be too rare to be considered a market, but they do occur even when the stages are, as a practical matter, fully integrated. Unplanned variation of output or demand results in unplanned exchange of intermediate products even by integrated firms. Generally transfer to the final consumption stage is coordinated by market price. One is unlikely to find the consumer willing to contract for food a full production period ahead. Risk to the consumer is reduced by the use of spot market coordination for most items since the risk of unforeseen changes in wants or needs is likely to be greater than the risk associated with spot market transactions.

The fact that some spot exchange will occur to sort out the errors made using other coordination methods does not mean that these systems have failed

Table 2–2
Relationship of Coordination Achieved to Coordination Mechanism and Associated Pricing Method

Coordination Mechanism	Pricing Method				Performance				
	Auction	Private Treaty	Administered	Formula	Efficiency	Equity	Transaction Cost	Access	Stability
Terminal market	X	X			A high – T med	High	High	High	Low
Direct trade		X	X	X	A med T med +	Variable—vulnerable to information imbalance	Medium	High[a]	Low
Electronic market	X				A high T high	High	Low with volume	High	Low
Contract coordination		X	X	X	A low T high	Variable	Low per unit	Low in the short run, medium in the long run	Medium
Bargaining		X		X	A low T med	Depends on balance of power	Low + per unit	Variable	Medium +
Cooperative integration					A med T high	High	Low –	Variable	Medium
Integration					A high T high	NA	None	Low –	Medium
Forward contract	X	X		X	A high T ?	High	Medium	High	Medium +
Futures	X				A low T high	Variable	Low	High	Low
Government control			X		A low T low	Variable	High	Variable	High

Note: A = allocative; T = technical.
[a]May be limited for the small producer.

or that a spot price is a sufficient coordination signal. Dynamic instability and limited ability to convey the quality message are major problems for some systems. In fact, a spot price reflects both the quality differentials and price level, which at any moment represent partly the realization of plans and partly random variation. The most important information for coordination is not the spot price or price differentials as such but what they indicate about changes in demand or supply relationships. The function of a spot price is to clear the market at an instant of time.

There has been some tendency to assume that if spot markets were made sufficiently efficient in terms of costs of exchange and accuracy of price discovery, spot market prices would be the preferred method of coordination. But uncertainty regarding quality and product availability may be the major component in transactions cost. Contracts and integration are used to reduce some types of uncertainty and may result in lower search and physical transfer costs than market price coordination.

Given the reality of integration, forward contracts, and nonprice coordination arrangements, the impact of these methods on the remaining market-price-coordinated segment needs to be considered. The fundamental concern most often identified is the thin markets problem.

Thin Markets

Thin markets is the term economists and traders in the food industry use to describe markets with low trading volume and low liquidity in which individual firms (purposefully or inadvertently) can sometimes exert undue influence on price or other terms of trade, usually to the detriment of others but sometimes of themselves. An additional concern is that prices in thin markets may mislead if they do not reflect appropriately conditions in the whole market.

Some writers emphasize the number of market transactions per unit of time as the distinguishing characteristic of a thin market; others emphasize the number and size distribution of buyers and sellers in the market where price is established; and still others focus on the absolute or relative volume of product for which prices are negotiated. The last is most common with a thin market viewed as one in which only a small portion of total quantity of the product to be marketed is priced through open bids and offers by traders. The larger portion of the total is either unpriced (that is, no change in ownership takes place between stages), or ownership is transferred by contractual arrangements that use formula pricing or some other predetermined system for payment. Each of these market characteristics is important in appraising market performance.

It is important to distinguish between *thinly traded* markets and *thinly reported* markets. In the latter there is little public information on price and other terms of trade, regardless of the volume of product traded openly.

Thinly traded markets are not necessarily thinly reported, and vice-versa. Each of these market characteristics has important but different implications for market performance. Although the primary concern here is with thinly traded markets, market reporting inadequacies are discussed as they relate to market thinness (Jesse 1980).

Although the increased use of vertical integration or formula-priced contracts may lead to thinner markets and certainly may be prompting some current concerns, one should not overlook the fact that thin markets are quite natural as new products or commodities are developed and when new market institutions are developed that are unfamiliar to market participants. In a similar vein, the use of products or market institutions that are circumvented by improvements, become incompatible with current consumer or trade needs, or become unprofitable to producers normally declines. This results in thin markets, at least during the period of transition.

Problems of Thin Markets

As vertical integration or longer-term contractual arrangements remove product from other market institutions, those residual market institutions become thinner with less trading volume and fewer buyers and sellers negotiating cash or spot prices. Although the overall market concentration among buyers and sellers may not change greatly, the stresses of accommodating unexpected changes in the rate of production or consumption in the entire market may fall on the residual market. The price impact of the necessary adjustments may be greater than if all buyers and sellers were in the market. If so, price volatility would be increased. The impact on price variation depends largely on the adjustment process. When pricing formulas are based on past market prices, the price signal and adjustment of quantity are delayed and variation accentuated. But if the market participants regularly use the spot market to make the final quantity adjustments, a rather small open market volume need not imply greater price variation than if all transactions were in that market. The combination of a thin market and very few participants on one side of the market may accent price volatility and inequity. Anxious traders opposite the few may be vulnerable to exploitation in an illiquid market. Where a large firm has a large volume involved in formula-priced contracts, a thin spot market may provide a setting where relatively small shifts in that firm's spot market buying or selling activity can influence prices in their favor. On the other hand, a firm might take a relatively large position in a thin cash or futures market and subsequently find that lack of market liquidity makes it difficult to adjust to changed circumstances or liquidate a position in futures without acquiring unwanted supply or disastrously affecting the market price.

Problems are associated with the dynamics of market evolution; as markets become thinner, firm behavior and market institutions must change to accommodate the changing environment. However, many firms and market institutions either do not realize the nature of the environmental change, do not know how they should change their organization or behavior, or because of vested interests resist accommodation to the changing market environment. A spot corn market was quoted in Chicago long after even token trading had ceased.

Concerns about thin markets appear to be related to the short-term dynamics of market behavior and consequent performance, an area of increasing public concern and attention in futures and cash markets. Firms or individuals may temporarily be in a position to exert undue influence on market price and the corresponding welfare of themselves and other market participants. While individual occurrences may be short term in nature, they may be sufficiently severe or chronic that they lead to demands for long-term remedial action to eliminate recurrence.

Thin market concerns are frequently voiced where several kinds of market arrangements (for example, vertical integration, long-term contracts, spot or cash markets) are used to serve the same marketing function, leaving individual market institutions with less volume and fewer buyers and sellers. Since firms may deem it undesirable or too costly to shift from one market institution, product form, or delivery date to another, the relevant submarkets may be temporarily separate and distinct. Yet the transfer arrangements may be closely entwined in other ways (for example, contract prices based on the spot market price, futures contracts with different delivery dates, processed versus raw commodity markets). Here inquiry into the interplay over time among closely related markets where one or more is thin may provide a clearer understanding of the market dynamics, and the potential success of (and need for) possible remedies.

Other concerns are related to externalities that changes in transfer arrangements between some participants inflict on other firms in the same industry and on consumers. Firms faced with the risk of a competitive disadvantage may be forced to follow the leader and adopt similar transfer mechanisms, making the residual market even thinner, or to develop other more costly ways to compensate for the benefits associated with viable markets (for example, adequate price or supply information at low cost) that may be lost in the process. This raises the specter of significant changes in market structure, behavior, and performance, which may warrant careful analysis and evaluation.

Available Evidence on Thin Markets

Several NC 117 conference or task forces have focused on the organization of food and agricultural commodity markets (NC 117 monographs 2, 5, 6, 7, 8, and 9, listed in appendix C). In many cases, evolving market structures have led to thinly traded spot markets. Some examples include beef carcasses, bulk cheese, butter, live broilers, cartoned eggs, live turkeys, and several fruit and vegetable markets. Most of the analyses of market behavior have been descriptive in nature, relying on statements of market participants to determine whether significant problems were present in the market. For example, Hayenga and Schrader (1980) found that formula pricing was not considered a major source of problems by market participants even when the resulting spot market volume was thin in several commodity markets.

Some of the greatest criticism has been voiced about the carcass beef market price determination and reporting systems. The analyses of these markets have been both qualitative and quantitative. An investigation by the U.S. House of Representatives' Small Business Committee staff into the National Provisioner's Yellow Sheet reporting of beef carcass prices led members to conclude that many price reports were based on very few, if any, market transactions. Nelson's (1980) analysis of actual transaction prices and the price reports by the Yellow Sheet found no indication that price quotes by the Yellow Sheet were inaccurate representations of market prices. In response to concerns raised by Representative Neal Smith of the House Small Business Committee, a special meat pricing task force assembled by the secretary of agriculture appraised the meat pricing and price reporting system (USDA 1979a). The task force concluded (p. 20) that "No proof was submitted to support the contention of improper pricing or price reporting, but the beef carcass market is thin and is likely to become thinner in the future." They also indicated that "A thin beef carcasses market is of major concern because of the increased potential for manipulation."

In another study of a thin market, Tomek (1980) analyzed the pricing accuracy on the Denver terminal market for fed cattle. Tomek demonstrated that Denver price movements were increasingly disassociated with price movements in other terminal markets as volume on the Denver market declined in the late 1960s. Further, he proposed a statistical procedure that one could use, admittedly based on some arbitrary judgments, to determine the minimum volume of trading that might be adequate for fairly accurate pricing in a market.

Futures Market Issues

Futures markets play a significant role in vertical coordination and have considerable impact on the organization and performance of several agricultural commodity cash markets. For those commodities that have corresponding futures contracts, theory and practice suggest close interrelationships between the cash and futures market prices. The existence or nonexistence of active corresponding futures contracts affects the way agents in the cash markets organize themselves for decision making, gathering information, discovering prices, and managing risks. These in turn affect market performance.

Futures markets have a role to play in the vertical coordination of market activity. They enable marketing agents to make partial future commitments, discover prices, and transfer risks. Historically futures contracts developed as an extension of existing cash (including forward contract) marketing practices. These contracts arose out of the specific needs of the cash commodity trade and the existence of agents willing to participate as speculators. Where these contracts developed, the cash markets had to be viable and liquid. Since fulfillment by delivery is not the norm for futures markets, these contracts usually are complementary to cash market trading and pricing.

Futures contracts have been most successful for storable agricultural commodities such as grains, cotton, coffee, cocoa, and frozen concentrated orange juice and for some nonstorable livestock commodities. In most of these cases, active forward cash contracting complements the futures contracts. Termination of futures trading in these cases would probably hinder market performance. Finally, there are few active futures contracts at levels in commodity systems where vertical integration or federal market orders are dominant, such as fruits and vegetables, seed crops, and milk. Egg futures trading declined as fresh eggs became available the year around. Contracts for broilers and turkeys failed although frozen turkeys are storable.

The primary role of futures markets is to assist market participants in forward pricing their inputs and/or output and in hedging their price risks. Early literature has documented that futures markets could not exist without hedgers. Hedging patterns follow seasonal storage patterns, and speculators seem to respond to these marketing pressures. Trading activity peaks when storage peaks, not when seasonal price uncertainty is greatest. The fact that hedgers of storable commodities can reduce their risks through futures markets is so broadly accepted that it is not often tested empirically. Hedgers give up price level risks to accept basis risks, and as long as the latter is less than the former, their risks can be reduced by hedging. A study of basis charts indicates it is highly unusual for basis risks not to be less than price level risks.

Whether risks could be reduced by hedging in livestock markets was less obvious because cash and futures prices are not as functionally related as in the case of storable commodities. Leuthold and Tomek (1982) reviewed several empirical studies and concluded that hedging can reduce risks while maintaining income levels for producers provided that selective strategies are followed. The successful strategies usually involve economic common sense, such as forward pricing only when profitable feeding margins can be established (futures prices exceed break-even prices). Hence, futures markets aid cash market participants in their management of risks.

A second major role of futures markets is that of forward pricing. Tomek and Gray (1970) found that futures prices for storable commodities such as corn and soybeans are much more accurate as indicators of future cash prices than for potatoes, which are semistorable. However, springtime futures prices for harvest delivery are more stable year to year for potatoes than for the storables. Thus routine hedgers of potatoes can stabilize annual income to a greater extent than can corn and soybean producers.

The forward pricing role has been most closely examined for livestock. Leuthold and Hartmann (1979, 1981) examine whether futures prices reflect all publicly available information. Econometric forecasting models are used as a norm against which to test forward pricing abilities. Examinations of the live hog, live cattle, and frozen pork belly markets have shown that the futures markets do not at all times reflect all available information. Martin and Garcia (1981) used a different procedure to confirm that cattle futures add little forecasting information beyond that available in lagged cash prices. Hog futures perform well as an indicator of forward price except during times of economic instability. In a broad test across several commodities, Just and Rausser (1981) show that futures markets seem to forecast as well as and sometimes better than commercial forecasters using econometric models.

Theoretically futures markets should reduce seasonal cash price variability of storable commodities. Speculators are willing to assume ownership of grain at harvest, resulting in higher prices and more grain storage than otherwise might be the case. Their acceptance of price risk during storage will tend to prevent prices from rising as high as they might have otherwise later in the season. Furthermore, the ability of commercial processors and storers to shift unwanted risks to speculators allows the commercial agents to operate with a smaller margin. Futures markets can generate more information that is of a higher quality and disseminated faster and to more people than would be possible without futures markets. In sum, futures trading should decrease the variability of the corresponding cash prices and reduce seasonal price variation.

Empirical results have supported these propositions. The short-lived onion futures contract provided an interesting case study. Research by Working (1960) and by Gray (1963) found that futures trading in onions reduced spot price variation and the seasonal price range. After a congressional ban on onion futures trading, the seasonal price range increased to the level it had been before futures trading had begun. Johnson (1973), in a comprehensive analysis, disagreed somewhat with these two studies by concluding that there was no significant shift in cash onion price performance during the period of futures trading.

Tomek (1971) has shown that seasonal price variations of wheat prices are lower because of futures trading. Powers (1970) found that pork belly and cattle cash price variability was reduced after the introduction of futures trading, a result confirmed over a longer time span for cattle by Taylor and Leuthold (1974).

Oellermann (1985) concluded that futures prices for live cattle and feeder cattle were used extensively to price cash market transactions. He interpreted this to imply that the futures market is the center of price discovery for these commodities. He also found that the speed of cash price adjustment increased as trading in live cattle futures increased.

The additional information provided by the existence of futures markets should improve price behavior. Cox (1976) built a model relating information, expectations, and price behavior. Testing numerous agricultural commodities, he found that futures trading improves market information and that cash markets become more efficient with futures trading. That is, spot prices reflect the available information resulting from the futures market.

A recent interest among researchers has been the cash-futures interrelationships. Miller and Kenyon (1980) found evidence of a linear causal daily price relationship running from near-term live hog futures to cash prices for hogs. Purcell, Flood, and Plaxico (1980) found that information flows both ways for live cattle—from futures to cash and cash to futures. Also, live cattle futures exerted influence on cash feeder cattle prices. Further work in this area is needed as the statistical methodology is developed, but it is apparent that cash and futures prices are closely interrelated and the performance of one market may easily influence the performance of the other.

Various proposals have been made concerning how the government might stabilize farm prices through the futures market (Houthakker 1967); however, simulation of Houthakker's plan has yet to demonstrate empirically that increased price stability would result (Richardson and Farris 1973).

To date, researchers have not examined the larger question of the net private and public value of futures markets. Is society better off with these markets? If they did not exist, what would replace them? Presumably they perform important economic functions because hedgers continue to use them, and they have lasted over one hundred years. Entry and exit in these markets is relatively easy, and no one is required to use them. Many studies, especially those examining forward pricing efficiency, have examined only a small aspect of market behavior and have not investigated the overall contribution to market performance.

What Have We Learned?

The questions that remain unanswered are remarkably similar to those that were asked twenty years ago. With few exceptions technology has continued to favor larger operations and has made processing less tolerant of quality and quantity variation. But the concept of a perfect and competitive market survives as the norm as if the spot market price were *the* appropriate allocating and coordination device for all occasions. Increased interdependence has accompanied the industrialization and associated specialization of agricultural production and marketing. The cost to the firm of not having a specific quantity and quality at the appropriate time and place has increased;

that is, the risks have increased, and risk considerations are central to coordination and pricing.

The desire to reduce these quality and availability risks for the food processor or vendor has encouraged the use of formula pricing, contract coordination, and integration. The road has not been one way toward integration, however. Integration patterns do change. Feed manufacturers were once the major poultry contractors. Today the processor or producer processor has taken the leading role. Several of the large feed firms have left the poultry and egg subsectors. Technological change has also resulted in the disintegration of some functions, such as pest control, from the farm firm. Powerful tax and credit incentives were factors in the integration of grain storage and conditioning by the farm firm.

Current coordination and pricing mechanisms perform well in the sense that the food stores and food service firms are seldom unable to supply the products consumers desire at posted prices. There is little waste due to failure to find a market. Thin or otherwise, the markets clear effectively in the short term.

Cycling of quantities and prices for the nonregulated commodities indicates a less than ideal state of coordination over time. Even the largely integrated and/or contract-coordinated broiler subsector with relatively few firms making production decisions is unstable.

Spot markets will continue to play an important coordinating role in the food system. Even when other coordination mechanisms dominate, firms are seldom able to match exactly the output from biological production processes to the changing demands of consumers at competitive prices. One finds frequent exchange of raw, semifinished, or final products among food processors, including exchange at levels not commonly recognized as markets. Prices are established by private treaty and are often arrived at with little difficulty. Price may be secondary to obtaining or disposing of the quantity or quality needed or not needed, which may be only a small proportion of the firm's total production. Depending on the reason for the short-term imbalance, the prices arrived at in this type of incidental spot exchange may carry little information of use for the allocation of resources to future production.

Preserving Markets

Given the high values placed on access and equity, one finds considerable emphasis on maintaining open and competitive markets. Despite the shortcomings, the focus is often on spot markets. Few will advocate the existence of markets at every stage interface (defined as a potential market), but if a market ever existed, an advocate to preserve or revive it can be found easily. The state of Arkansas reports a live broiler price, and USDA's Statistical Reporting Service also provides live broiler and turkey prices, though neither exists in the usual sense of a reportable market.

Markets serve a function, and they appear and disappear for reasons not fully understood. Although the egg market seems in danger of expiring despite professions of desire to keep it alive, the market for cocaine thrives despite the considerable efforts of the U.S. government to stifle it. The price of cocaine also appears to be readily available after each raid. Apparently, then, there is an information system available, whether the market is legal.

Given a desire to preserve market exchange at some level of the system, what means are available? If one accepts the idea that transactions costs are a major determinant of the integration of stages, the reduction of transaction costs should be a means to delay or reverse integration. Institutional changes can modify search, transfer, and uncertainty costs of exchange. Throughout the chapter it has been argued that the institutional arrangements are, to at least some extent, endogenous to the commodity system. It has not been established, however, whether there are forces that will drive a system toward global optima with respect to exchange institutions and vertical structure patterns. On the contrary, there is some evidence that failure of a market institution to respond appropriately results in an accelerated move away from the open competitive market, a process that further weakens the market institution. We have also argued that less than an optimal amount of information may be generated because of its public good properties.

Electronic markets, measures to improve information, and measures to increase the accuracy of product description would be expected to augment market exchange as a means of vertical coordination. Accurate description is a prerequisite for and increased information is a product of electronic markets. Despite the advantages perceived by their advocates, electronic markets have had a mixed reception. The reluctance of already existing systems to fade away without resistance, high volumes needed to achieve low costs, hesitance to abandon a working system for an unknown, and the temptation to take a free ride are all impediments electronic markets must overcome.

Any action (short of mandating trade) that increases the amount of information on exchange prices also makes contract coordination a more attractive alternative since value establishment is made easier. Mandatory reporting of transactions prices involves a change in property rights with respect to information and depends on the existence of reportable transactions. To some firms it may be a weak incentive for integration to eliminate reportable transactions. Reporting of contract terms may be useful, but that has not yet been proved.

Restrictions on integration or contract coordination restrict decision freedom and may reduce efficiency by preventing avoidance of transactions costs. A mandate for all firms over a certain size to procure (sell) some part of their input (output) in an open market may achieve the pricing benefit at lower cost in terms of efficiency. No research is available to indicate what proportion should be traded to achieve a particular level of pricing accuracy or market information.

Contracts Revisited

Contract coordination is often seen as the antithesis of market price coordination when it may more properly be viewed as an intermediate state on the open market to integration continuum. A contract with a firm price entered into at the time of production commitment may serve very well as a coordination device. It is the unpriced contract that provides an incentive to manipulate the market that will determine the final contract price. The formula-priced contract does allow the participants to reduce some uncertainties when no shift of price risk is desired. The futures-based contract can accomplish the same end but allows each party the option to establish a price at any time. The problem of contracts is the way in which they are negotiated (private treaty with little information available on completed contracts) and the use of formula pricing against a spot market thinned as a result of contracting. An open market in forward contracts could overcome this problem. But even in a world of forward contracts, there probably will remain a spot market in some form to compensate for errors in the estimation of demand or amounts actually supplied.

No single type of forward contract fits all exchange situations. Broiler processors benefit sufficiently from close coordination of time and quality that nearly all details of production are specified. Only a nonassignable contract can accomplish this degree of specificity. In contrast, a grain processor may be prepared to forward contract for grain at a fixed price but probably has no interest in the identity of the producer. Uncertainty regarding quality may, in fact, be reduced if grain from any origin can be used to fulfill a contract. The processor's quality discount schedule will result in some sorting by elevators for the product that will generate the smallest discount and thereby provide more nearly what the buyer wants, as well as the highest net price to the seller. When the processor desires specific qualities that require special production practices or special handling, the contract style more nearly approaches that of the broiler or vegetable production contract.

Cooperatives

Cooperative integration by producers would seem to offer the benefits of integration without the possible inequity or pricing problems posed by private treaty contracts. But individual producer commitment necessary for effective marketing programs has been uneven among commodity lines. Difficulties associated with obtaining initial capitalization for cooperative marketing ventures and problems of gaining access to and maintaining markets may have constrained development in some instances.

Cooperative integration backward into fertilizer and petroleum basics seems to be accomplished more easily than forward integration into processing and food manufacturing. Member commitment necessary to accomplish backward integration may have been less than that required for successful marketing programs.

Tradition

Tradition or historical accident must be recognized as a major factor in the explanation of currently employed coordination and pricing means. A tradition of independence inhibits farmers' exploitation of cooperatives to improve coordination. Corn belt soybean growers shun pooling, while Arkansas growers use pooling extensively. The explanation must be in terms of people, not commodity or market characteristics.

There is an element of simultaneity in the shaping of people's behavior and institutions. Hog farmers' attitudes toward markets are different from dairy farmers' attitudes, in part because those who like the way hog markets function became hog producers, not dairymen. However, the commodity characteristics are probably the major factor in the difference between pork and dairy coordination systems.

When technological change is as sweeping as has been the case in the poultry subsectors, the coordination system changed despite tradition. To some extent the activity moved to areas where tradition did not impede the adoption of a new system.

3
A Comparison of Agricultural Subsectors

A gricultural economists have long been interested in vertical commodity systems: the array of firms, markets, rules, and arrangements involved in producing a commodity and moving it through to the point of consumption. Some refer to these vertical commodity systems as industries. We prefer the term *subsector* since *industry* is frequently used to refer to a group of firms involved in the same business at one stage in a commodity system (for example, the beef packing or food retailing industry).

Research on agricultural subsectors has largely been case study in nature. There have been few attempts to do comparative analysis across subsectors (for one such attempt, see Reimund, Martin, and Moore 1981). The NC 117 project conducted comprehensive case studies and published monographs on five subsectors: dairy (Cook et al. 1978); eggs (Schrader et al. 1978); citrus (Ward and Kilmer 1980); tart cherries (Ricks, Hamm, and Chase-Lansdale 1982); and pork (Hayenga et al. 1985). In addition, less comprehensive studies were done of the beef, broiler, wheat, corn, soybean, and potato subsectors.

The major guideline for selecting these subsectors was that they represent a cross-section of U.S. agricultural commodities where most types of coordinating mechanisms can be found. Substantial differences exist in the organization and coordination of these subsectors and the types of problems involved. The selection of subsectors does not imply that it is a representative sample of U.S. agriculture. Although the primary guide for selecting the subsectors was theoretical, implementation of the studies was limited by the persons willing to take on the responsibility for a subsector.

Bruce Marion and Ronald Ward were the coordinating authors of chapter 3. The authors of the various parts of chapter 3 were as follows: Dairy, B. Marion (drawing heavily on Cook et al. 1978); Beef, B. Marion; Pork, B. Marion (drawing heavily from Hayenga et al. 1985); Broilers and Eggs, L. Schrader; Wheat, Corn, and Soybeans, M. Leath, L. Hill, and B. Marion; Potatoes, E. Jones, R. Ward, and B. Marion; Citrus, R. Ward; Tart Cherries, D. Ricks and L. Hamm; and Looking Across Subsectors, B. Marion and R. Ward.

The boundaries of a subsector are arbitrarily defined. In some instances such as the broiler and egg subsectors, important inputs such as feed and breeding flocks are included. In other instances, this is not the case. Although there are some differences in how subsectors are defined, the major emphasis in all case studies is on the vertical system from farm production to retailing.

In this chapter, eight vignettes of the various subsectors are presented. Because of the similarities of the broiler and egg subsectors, they are discussed together. The wheat, corn, and soybean subsectors are also discussed as a group. The case study summaries will focus on four characteristics:

1. Basic conditions such as consumption trends, characteristics of production, and types of uncertainty.
2. Subsector organization, including the vertical stages and functions, the structure of markets, and changes that are occurring.
3. Major modes of coordination and changes that are occurring.
4. Major attributes of performance.

The subsector case studies are attempts to examine vertical commodity complexes as isolated economic systems. Particular emphasis is placed on understanding the nature and organization of the vertical value-adding process for each commodity and the mechanisms used to coordinate each vertical system. For example, to what extent are markets relied on to guide resource allocation decisions, and to what extent are government programs or industry-wide mechanisms (such as marketing orders) used either to supplement or replace markets in their coordinating function? To what extent are contracts or vertical integration changing control over resource allocation decisions?

Although the case studies provide some assessment of subsector performance, they are rather subjective and modest efforts for the most part. Given the unique characteristics of each commodity and each subsector, subsector performance evaluation is difficult. For similar reasons, comparisons across subsectors and hypothesis testing are difficult. We believe some valuable insights are gained from the comparisons of subsectors in the final section of this chapter. At the same time, we had hoped to be able to say more—to have a stronger bottom line. Given the present status of subsector theory and the research approach used, we were unable to test scientifically subsector organization-coordination-performance relationships.

We expect that many readers will elect to read a sample of the case studies. Each case study stands independent of the others, so readers can select those in which they have the most interest. A few comparative comments may help in the selection process.

The livestock and poultry case studies are presented first and are ordered from those commodities with long biological production periods and relatively complex subsector organizations (dairy and beef) to those with short production periods and simpler subsector organizations (broilers and eggs). The pork subsector falls in between.

The crop case studies follow, with wheat, corn, and soybeans discussed first because of their importance as feed for livestock and poultry. Potatoes, also an annual crop, are discussed next, followed by citrus and tart cherries, both perennial tree fruits.

In general, commodities that are transformed into several end products are more complex in organization than those with primarily one end product. For example, eggs, broilers, beef, pork, and tart cherries have few alternative uses. In contrast, milk, potatoes, wheat, corn, and soybeans have many alternative uses. Parallel channels have developed in the latter subsectors for the alternative end uses (for example, fluid milk versus cheese).

The nature of production has an important effect on the speed of producer supply response and the existence of production cycles. With annual crops such as potatoes, wheat, corn, and soybeans, production assets are relatively fluid. Substantial shifts in acres planted can occur from one year to the next. Tree fruits are at the opposite extreme, with land committed to a particular crop for many years and with few ways of expanding supply from one year to the next. Whereas production cycles exist to some extent with the fruits, they do not with annual crops.

Supply response in the livestock and poultry subsectors tends to be quickest in broilers, next in eggs, and slowest in dairy and beef. This is not only due to the length of the production period (eight weeks from chick hatching to a grown broiler compared to two years from birth of a heifer calf to a milk-producing cow) but also because of differences in the time required to adjust the number of offspring from breeding stock. In poultry, if the number of eggs produced by breeding flocks exceeds the number needed for hatching into broiler or laying chicks, they can be diverted to the table egg market. Thus, some surplus capacity in breeding flocks can be maintained without substantial losses. With beef and pork, this is not the case. Beef calves and pigs—once born—are largely raised either for breeding stock or the slaughter market. Excess breeding herd size is not maintained as it is to some extent in poultry. Thus, to expand beef or pork supplies, the first step is to expand breeding herds. Supply response is therefore considerably slower than in the poultry subsectors. In most subsectors, expansion of output requires more time than contraction.

Although there are seasonal highs and lows, the livestock and poultry subsectors studied are essentially "flow" commodities since production is consummated throughout the year. By contrast, the crops examined are harvested primarily once per year and are a "stock" that must be stored if supply is to be available at other times during the year. Storage of unprocessed or processed commodities is important to coordinate supply with consumer demand in all of the crops and in dairy and pork to some extent.

Temporal coordination is important both within a market period and across market periods. In chapter 2, the degree of stability in production and prices across market periods was referred to as dynamic stability. Whereas most of the subsectors have developed mechanisms to achieve reasonable temporal coordination *within* a market period, most are plagued by dynamic instability and volatile long-run prices. Dairy has had by far the most stable prices and has largely avoided the boom or bust cycles of many of the other subsectors examined. This is due in large part to the government price-support and marketing order programs in dairy.

Government price-support programs remain important in dairy. Since the early 1970s, government programs for corn and wheat have generally involved direct supplemental payments to farmers while allowing U.S. market prices to respond to world supply and demand forces. In addition to price-support or income supplement programs, federal and state marketing orders have an important effect on prices and/or the quantity flowing to market in dairy and citrus. There are government programs that affect supply or prices in the remaining subsectors (such as import policies on boneless beef), but these tend to be of smaller importance.

While dairy is clearly the subsector in which government programs play the biggest role in price determination and the allocation of milk to different uses, the broiler subsector is clearly the most vertically integrated subsector. Thus whereas prices are largely administered in the dairy subsector, coordination is largely administered within individual firms in the broiler subsector. For this reason, the two subsectors make for an interesting comparison.

Resource-providing or production management contracts—both of which transfer some control and risk to the contractor—are primarily important in broilers, eggs, and potatoes. Forward sale contracts are quite widely used in several of the subsectors but involve little transfer of risk or control.

These are some of the important differences and similarities of the subsectors studied. The most fundamental difference, however, is the nature of each individual commodity. The production, perishability, end uses, and coordinating needs of each is unique. That makes them both fascinating to study and difficult to compare.

Dairy Subsector

Although milk is produced in all regions of the country, over 60 percent is produced in the Northeast, the Lake States, and California (figure 3–1). The Pacific and Mountain regions have grown fastest in milk production since 1976. Total pounds of milk produced in the United States increased from 1924 to 1964, then went on a downward trend through 1975. From 1975 to 1983, milk production increased 21 percent (USDA 1984b). Milk production

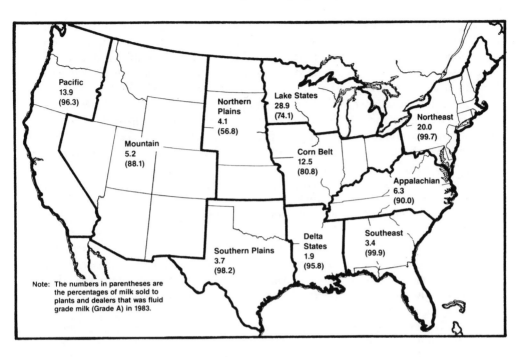

Source: USDA 1984a.

Figure 3–1. Percentage of 1983 U.S. Production by Region and Percentage of Milk Sold to Plants and Dealers That Was Fluid Grade Milk (Grade A) in Each Region

varies seasonally as a result of calving seasonality, the availability of feed, and the effect of seasonal temperature variations.

Milk of drinking quality (grade A) accounted for 86 percent of all milk produced in 1983. The remaining 14 percent was manufacturing grade milk (grade B) (USDA 1984a). In 1983, 41 percent of grade A milk was processed into fluid milk products (fluid milk, cream, and some soft dairy products); this represented 36 percent of all milk marketed. Thus, 2 out of 3 pounds of milk produced in 1983 went into manufactured dairy products (cheese, butter, nonfat dry milk, and frozen products).

Total per capita consumption of all dairy products declined from 1945 to 1976 and has increased slightly since. From 1970 to 1983, per capita consumption trends were generally down for fluid whole milk, evaporated and condensed milk, nonfat dry milk, and cottage cheese and generally up for lowfat fluid milk, American- and Italian-type cheese, and yogurt. Butter consumption, after declining for years, appears to have reached a plateau since 1974 (USDA 1984b).

Import quotas provide the dairy subsector considerable protection from foreign competition except on cheese and casein. In 1983, the United States imported nearly 286 million pounds of cheese and 160 million pounds of casein (approximately one-third of world casein production, equivalent to 480 million pounds of nonfat dry milk) (USDA 1984b). The U.S. exports of dairy products are almost entirely noncommercial (such as for CARE, religious relief efforts, and the Food for Peace program). Government dairy price-support minimums result in U.S. products' being noncompetitive in world markets. Both dairy import and price-support policies have been the subject of considerable controversy in recent years, with some consumer groups contending that the dairy subsector should be more fully exposed to competition in international markets; however, the international markets for dairy products are heavily influenced by the government policies of European Economic Community (EEC) countries. These countries subsidize exports in order to dispose of surpluses. Opening up U.S. markets to foreign competitors would reduce the cost of dairy products to consumers but would also reduce the cost of export subsidies to European countries, increase the cost of dairy subsidies in the United States, and expose the U.S. dairy industry to competition that many consider unfair.

Sanitation and health regulations are extensive throughout the dairy subsector, particularly for grade A milk producers and processors. Federal product grades are also used extensively on most dairy products and facilitate commercial exchange.

Subsector Organization

The dairy subsector produces and markets several major products—fluid milk, cheese, butter, nonfat dry milk, ice cream—plus many minor products. In addition, cull cows and bulls from the subsector provide about 20 percent of all beef consumed. Tracking the vertical system for all of these products is too much for this summary; therefore, the discussion concentrates on fluid milk, cheese, butter, and, to a limited extent, nonfat dry milk. Figure 3–2 is a simplified flowchart of the main stages and channels for fluid milk. In the fluid milk system, nearly 90 percent of grade A milk is controlled by cooperative bargaining associations, many of which physically assemble the milk from farms. The milk is then processed into bottled milk and soft products by proprietary dairy processors, food chains, or cooperatives and distributed to a variety of retail and food service customers.

The vertical systems for manufactured products are similar except for an intermediate handling stage between manufacturing and retailing. Many smaller manufacturers of butter and cheese sell their output to intermediate handlers, who cut and package the products, brand and advertise in some cases, and supply retail outlets. Larger companies like Kraft and Land O'Lakes perform both the manufacturing and intermediate handling functions.

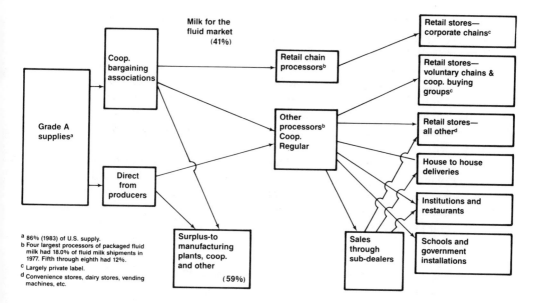

Source: Cook et al. 1978.

Figure 3–2. Marketing Channels for Grade A Milk

Vertical integration in fluid milk is most significant between farmers and their cooperatives that bargain, perform services for processors, and manufacture surplus grade A milk and between corporate food chains and their milk bottling facilities. In cheese and butter, cooperatives and investor-owned companies frequently vertically integrate manufacturing and the various intermediate functions such as packaging, branding, and physical distribution.

Market Concentration and Entry Barriers
in the Dairy Subsector

The structure of dairy farms can be characterized as a large number of small, atomistically competitive producers. Most dairy farms have thirty to one hundred cows and have become larger and more specialized.

The minimum efficient plant size for fluid milk processing, butter manufacturing, or cheese manufacturing has increased sharply due to new technology and the large volume requirements of many retail accounts. The number of fluid milk processing plants declined from 8,392 in 1948 to 1,439 in 1976, while average processing capacity increased substantially (Cook et al. 1978). The share of national packaged fluid milk sales by the four largest dairy processors in 1977 was only 18 percent; however, concentration was much higher in smaller geographic markets. For example, Manchester (1974) estimated that in the smaller geographic markets in which fluid milk plants effectively compete (areas within a radius of 250 miles from each major metropolitan area in 1970), the average market share of the four largest firms was 46.9 percent.

Large producer cooperatives and large-volume retail chains tend to have the most bargaining power in fluid milk marketing; however, product differentiation and capital requirements for fluid milk plants represent modest entry barriers. In addition, the distance that bottled milk is shipped has expanded, thereby expanding the size of processor-retailer markets. These factors have tended to limit monopolistic behavior.

Continuous advances in cost-reducing technology and other factors caused butter plants to decline from 4,022 to 231 between 1944 and 1982, a decline of 94.3 percent. In the last fifteen years, the continuous churn and soft butter printing technology, especially as used by the regional co-ops, has been an important factor in the decline of the butter factory numbers. In nonfat milk powder, the numbers of plants for making spray process powder for human food declined from 496 in 1944 to 108 in 1982 (USDA 1983b). Spray equipment is usually in the same plants (or at least the same companies) that make sweet cream butter.

In the American cheese industry, plant numbers declined by 79 percent from 2,144 in 1944 to 457 in 1982. Half of this decline was before 1960 when the small one- and two-vat family cheese operations were eliminated by the rindless block technology and competition for milk. Since the mid-1960s, demand for cheese has strengthened, and advanced technology has sharply increased average plant size and reduced labor costs.

National concentration in butter and cheese manufacturing is modest, with the largest four companies manufacturing 30 and 38 percent of these products, respectively, in 1977 (Bureau of Census 1977d). However, concentration is much higher at the intermediate handling stage for both of these products. At this stage, companies such as Kraft (which manufactures some cheese) buy cheese from other manufacturers, transform natural cheese into processed cheese products, and cut, package, and distribute both natural and processed cheese. Kraft was estimated to market about 50 percent of the cheese in the United States in the late 1970s (Hayenga 1979b).

A similar situation exists for butter, where Land O'Lakes buys butter from other manufacturers, as well as making some themselves, and cuts, packages, and distributes butter at the intermediate handling stage. Land O'Lakes is estimated to control over two-thirds of the butter that moves through U.S. retail channels.

Product differentiation is moderate in cheese and butter. Kraft and Land O'Lakes have dominant brands in cheese and butter, respectively, and likely enjoy some market power; however, retailer brands hold important shares of both products. Entry barriers into the private-label segment of cheese and butter are much lower than into the advertised brand segment.

Vertical Coordination

The coordination task in dairy is made easier by the multiple products made from milk, some of which are storable. Temporal coordination of supply and demand is easier to accomplish without large price changes than in beef or broilers, which lack manufactured product options for surpluses. Manufactured dairy products act as a cushion to balance fluid milk supply and demand. With the current price-support program, surplus butter, cheese, and nonfat dry milk are removed from the commercial market so that the prices of these products are often not allowed to drop to the market clearing level. Government purchases neutralize mistakes in both short-run and long-run supply-demand coordination.

Enduring vertical linkages between various levels of the marketing system have been established. For example:

Most dairy bargaining cooperatives have a written contract with producers, usually requiring producers to deliver their entire milk production to fluid milk processors designated by the cooperative.

Contracts between cooperatives and processors establish the proportion of processor milk needs that will be supplied by the cooperative. These contracts normally extend over a year.

Contracts or agreements frequently exist between manufacturers, including cooperatives, and major intermediate handlers of manufactured dairy products. Such contracts generally call for independent manufacturing plants to deliver all of their production to the marketing firm.

Supply contracts have become prevalent between fluid milk processors and retailers of fluid milk, who require an assured supply of their private label milk.

Producer cooperatives have vertically integrated into milk bottling, butter-powder manufacturing, and cheese manufacturing. Food chains have also integrated backwards into fluid milk processing.

Most of these contracts are indefinite quantity contracts and usually include some type of formula price. Compared to spot market transactions, these arrangements reduce the risk of having a market outlet (or supply) but do not alter the price risk.

Prices for cheese and butter are typically formula prices based on the National Cheese Exchange prices or the Chicago Mercantile Exchange butter price. Both of these exchanges are auction-type spot markets that trade a very small percentage (about 1 percent) of total cheese and butter volume. Federal price-support levels for American cheese and butter provide an approximate lower bound for the prices on these exchanges. Although there have been periodic concerns about the thinness and possible manipulation of these markets, studies have provided no evidence that prices are unrepresentative of broad supply-demand forces (H. Cook and T. Graf in Hayenga 1979a).

Prices within the subsector are heavily influenced by government price supports and federal market order programs. The Commodity Credit Corporation (CCC) buys cheese, butter, and nonfat dry milk when supplies exceed demand at the support prices for these products. When market prices move above support prices, CCC stocks are sold into commercial channels. In this way, CCC activities tend to reduce variations in the prices of manufactured dairy products.

Federal milk marketing orders classify milk according to end uses, set minimum prices by class, and pool proceeds to allow uniform (blend) prices to be paid to producers. The price for fluid milk use is based on the price for manufactured grade milk plus a differential established through market order hearings that varies by distance from the upper Midwest. The dairy industry faces a relatively inelastic demand for fluid milk and a more elastic demand for manufactured products; thus, a classified pricing system can increase total revenues for producers (Babb and Bohall 1979). Eighty-one percent of the fluid grade A milk produced in the United States was priced administratively under one of forty-nine federal milk marketing orders in 1982, and an additional 17 percent was regulated under state orders.

Producer Cooperatives

Dairy producers have relied heavily on cooperatives to perform marketing functions and to represent their interests in establishing prices and other terms of trade. Of the 119,000 dairy farmers marketing milk under federal orders in December 1980, 84 percent were members of a cooperative association, down from 87 percent in 1970 (Manchester 1983). Co-ops are more prominent in the handling of grade A milk than in manufacturing milk.

In two-thirds of the federal order markets, the largest cooperative had more than one-half of the producers as of December 1980, which is enough to disapprove the order in a referendum. However, for the purposes of bargaining for over-order premiums with handlers, even a fairly small percentage of producers who are determined to be free riders often can undermine effective bargaining by the principal cooperative. The percentage of producers in each federal order that are members of the largest cooperatives has declined; the four largest cooperatives in each order had 78 percent of the producers in 1965 and 66 percent in 1980 (Manchester 1983).

The larger milk co-ops have been criticized by the antitrust agencies, some elements of Congress, the press, and others for abusing the power given to farmers under the Capper-Volstead Act. Three co-ops were charged in the early 1970s with monopolization and predatory behavior. Two of these,

AMPI and Mid-America Dairymen, signed consent decrees. Dairymen, Inc. was exonerated.

Dairy cooperatives have a number of vertical coordination roles.

1. They perform the balancing function for milk supplies; this may require short period storage, milk movement, and/or surplus manufacturing. Premiums above the federal or state order prices are negotiated, at least in part, to compensate cooperatives for this service.
2. They represent the interest of producers at hearings on federal orders or state milk regulations; administration of orders would be difficult without strong, responsible co-ops.
3. Cooperatives are vertically integrated into primary manufacturing and are especially prominent in butter-powder manufacturing.
4. Some co-ops are vertically integrated into intermediate handling of butter, powder, and cheese.
5. Only a few co-ops have had much success in processing and distributing bottled milk and fluid milk products as their primary activity. In total, co-ops bottle approximately 15 percent of all fluid milk (Manchester 1983).

Subsector Performance

Many would view the dairy subsector from 1965 to 1980 as a very stable, well-coordinated subsector providing an adequate supply of high-quality perishable products to consumers. The combination of the government price-support program, the federal marketing order program, and producer cooperatives provided long-term and short-term stability in milk production and prices. Figure 3–3 compares producer all-milk prices with the producer price index (PPI) for all commodities, farm and nonfarm, from 1950 through 1980 (both indexes are expressed as a percentage of 1967). Variations in milk prices were low, whether month to month, over six-month periods, or over twelve-month periods. Similar analyses showed much greater price variability in the prices of all of the other commodities reviewed in this chapter.

The pricing system for dairy, however, has encouraged an unnecessary expansion of grade A milk and a decline in manufacturing-grade milk. In addition, dairy price-support levels have periodically encouraged considerable more milk production than can be sold in commercial channels. The greatest period of surpluses was during the mid-1950s and early 1960s, when 8 to 14 percent of all dairy products (on a solid-not-fat basis) were removed from the commercial market by programs of the USDA. Between 1980 and 1983, surpluses again ran high; dairy products representing about 10 percent of milk marketings were purchased by the USDA at a cost of about $2 billion annually.

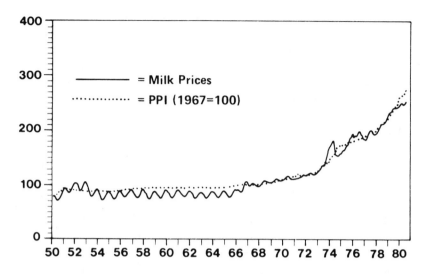

Source: Cook and Marion 1981.

Figure 3–3. Index of Prices Received by Farmers for All Milk, 1950–1980

Thus, from time to time, the coordinating system of the dairy subsector gets out of kilter, resulting in surplus production, high government costs, and some product wastage. By September 1983, government stocks of dairy products had grown to 458 million pounds of butter, 929 million pounds of cheese, and 1.35 billion pounds of nonfat dry milk, totaling approximately $3.33 billion in value (USDA 1984a). The dairy program became a major national issue. In January 1984, the Dairy and Tobacco Adjustment Act went into effect. This program paid farmers to reduce milk production, the first time such an approach has been tried in dairy. In addition, the act mandated a national dairy product promotion, research, and nutrition program for which assessments in 1984 provided approximately $200 million.

Milk marketing orders also have been challenged, with allegations that these orders unduly raise the price of milk to producers and for consumers. A study by Kwoka (1975) alleged that orders raised the price of milk more than 20 percent above competitive levels in 1970, resulting in a social cost to consumers of $800 million per year; however, an extensive quantitative analysis by Dobson and Buxton (1977) indicated that the net social cost of marketing orders was approximately $13.2 million per year in 1974, roughly 2 percent of the Kwoka estimate.

The subsector has been relatively progressive at both the farm and processor-manufacturer levels. The adoption of new technology by milk bottling plants, butter-powder plants, and cheese plants has significantly increased minimum efficient plant size. The subsector has also introduced a significant number of new products and/or packages. The slowness of milk bottlers and unions to adjust the wage rates and services of delivery personnel, however, was one factor contributing to the rapid integration of chains into milk processing. Retail chains bottled about one-fifth of the fluid milk in 1977 (Cook et al. 1978).

Although reliable profit figures are not available for firms operating at different stages in the subsector, the evidence indicates that average profit rates are reasonable among dairy farms and milk bottling plants. Proprietary bottling firms have found themselves squeezed between the bargaining pressures of large cooperatives that typically supply them with milk and grocery chains and large wholesalers that are often their primary customers. As a result, several large dairy companies have closed or sold some of their bottling plants. Dairy cooperatives have purchased some of these plants to ensure a market for their members' milk.

Profits appear to be somewhat higher in cheese and butter manufacturing and among intermediate handlers that sell advertised brands of these products; however, private label products are an important check on the pricing discretion of advertised brands.

Farmer access to markets is not a serious problem in dairy, in part because cooperatives dominate the first handler stage and are committed to serving all their members.

From the farmer's viewpoint, the performance of the dairy subsector would probably be given high grades on average. Prices have been highly stable and predictable. Dairy farmers have not been subject to the seriously depressed prices that periodically afflict many other subsectors. Producers, through their cooperatives, have exercised greater control over pricing and coordination in the subsector than in most other subsectors.

Dairy cooperatives have also been active politically in representing their member interests. The consolidation of cooperatives into a few large regional cooperatives in the 1960s and 1970s has resulted in greater political power by cooperatives. At least in part, the surpluses that have plagued the subsector since 1980 can be attributed to the political influence of dairy cooperatives on the 1977 farm bill, which raised the minimum dairy price-support level to 80 percent of parity. Together with the decline in grain prices in the late 1970s, this bill encouraged an expansion in milk production that has not yet been reversed.

From the standpoint of the public, the classified pricing system of federal marketing orders and the tendency for the price-support program periodically to encourage large surpluses represent important weaknesses in subsector performance.

Beef Subsector

The 1970s were particularly difficult for the beef subsector. The sharp rise in feed grain prices in 1974–1976 coincided with a large cattle herd on U.S. farms.

The steer-corn price ratio during these three years hit its lowest point in over twenty years and resulted in an unprecedented liquidation of breeding herds. Per capita consumption of beef peaked at 127 pounds in 1976, double the level in 1950. By 1979–1981, cattle prices had reached a new plateau, nearly double the level of the early 1970s, and the steer-corn price ratio had returned to slightly above its historic level. Per capita consumption dropped to 104 pounds during 1979–1981 (USDA 1983c). Chavas (1983) estimated that a fundamental shift in the demand for beef occurred from 1975 to 1979; both the own-price elasticity and income elasticity for beef dropped sharply.

A cattle cycle, about ten years in length, characterized the subsector from 1940 to 1980. The subsector has typically experienced six or seven years of growth followed by three or four years of decline when measured by total cattle numbers. Cattle prices are also cyclical, varying the most for calves, followed by feeder cattle, and least for slaughter cattle.

Subsector Organization

The fed beef subsector has five major stages: cow-calf operations, growing or stocker operations, feedlots, slaughtering and processing, and distribution (wholesaling, retailing, food service) (figure 3–4). Beef calf production is highly dispersed throughout the United States. Thirty states each produced at least 1 percent of the U.S. beef calf crop in 1980. The top five states accounted for 37 percent of the calf crop. Most producers are relatively small; about 70 percent of the beef calves in 1978 came from beef cow herds of fewer than 200 head (USDA 1978). Feeder calves are weaned at about 400 pounds; 80 to 90 percent are then placed in growing operations, where they add 300 to 400 pounds while on pasture and roughage. At about 700 to 750 pounds, they are sent to a feedlot for finishing to slaughter weights of 900 to 1,200 pounds. The on-feed weight changes considerably over time, depending on the steer-corn price ratio.

The production of beef calves, the weaning of these calves, and the placement of feeder cattle on feed are highly seasonal. Henderson and Schwart (1977) found that in 1975, 89 percent of beef calves were produced in the first two quarters, and 77 percent were weaned in the last two quarters (calves are weaned at seven to eight months). By varying the weaning age and growing time, seasonal calving patterns are substantially reduced for cattle placed on feed. Additional smoothing occurs within feedlots. For example, between 1970 and 1982, the number of cattle placed on feed in the peak month (October) averaged 190 percent of the low month; however, the number of fed cattle marketed in the peak month (October) averaged only 114 percent of the low month (USDA 1983a).

The growing stage is the least distinct of the five stages. Henderson and Schwart (1977) estimated that growing operations that were integrated with

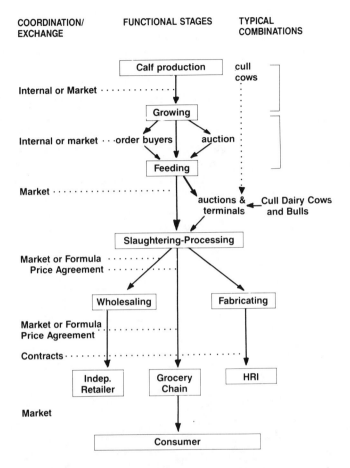

Figure 3–4. Organization of Beef Subsector

cow-calf operations handled 40 to 50 percent of feeder cattle; growing operations owned by feedlots handled an additional 20 to 30 percent. Total integration of calf production, growing, and feeding is uncommon, accounting for 5 to 9 percent of fed cattle. Although feedlots have become large, specialized operations, this is not as true of cow-calf and growing operations.

Larger feedlots (one-time capacity of 1,000 head or more) accounted for 68 percent of U.S. fed cattle marketings in 1982, nearly double the share in 1962. The 381 feedlots with capacity of 8,000 head or more fed 50 percent of the fed cattle in 1982 (USDA 1983c). The vast majority of these are commercial feedlots (as opposed to farm feedlots) in which almost all the feed is purchased and nearly all the labor is hired. Several of the larger feedlots are owned by large grain-feed companies such as Cargill and Continental. Cargill also owns Excel, the second largest beef packing company in the United States. Packer feeding, however, has gradually declined from over 7 percent of fed cattle marketings in the mid-1960s to 4.2 percent during 1980–1982 (USDA 1984c).

The geographic distribution of cattle feeding in 1981 is shown in figure 3–5. Cattle feeding has shifted sharply to the western corn belt and high plains since 1960. Five states—Texas, Nebraska, Kansas, Iowa, and Colorado—accounted for 66 percent of the fed cattle marketed during 1978–1982 (USDA 1983c). In large part, the shift of feeding to the high plains occurred because of new milo varieties and expanded irrigation that greatly increased grain supplies in that region. The development of large feedlots was encouraged by scale economies and tax shelters. Depletion of irrigation water and higher pumping costs in the southern plains states is expected to reduce future grain production in these states sharply. Cattle feeding may shift north toward the western corn belt. The geographic distribution of steer and heifer slaughter closely parallels the distribution of cattle feeding. Most cattle are slaughtered within 100 miles of where they are fed.

Cull cows and bulls accounted for about one-fifth of the cattle slaughtered during the 1970–1982 period. Cow and bull slaughter is much more dispersed

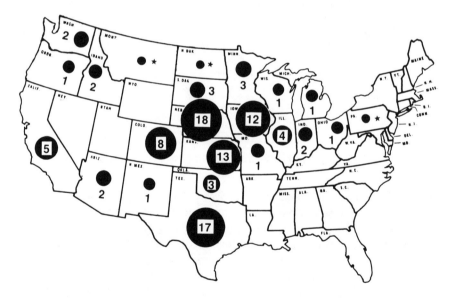

Source: USDA 1983a.

*% < 0.5

Total = 23,014,000

Figure 3–5. Fed Cattle Marketings in 23 States, 1981 (Percentage by States)

than steer and heifer slaughter, reflecting the distribution of cow-calf operations and dairy herds. Since cows and bulls are sold a few at a time, auctions continue to be the most important market outlet, accounting for 51 percent of cow and bull sales in 1982 (USDA 1984c).

Packer concentration of steer and heifer slaughter in relevant procurement markets is high and increasing. The four leading beef packers in each of the twenty-three major fed cattle states, on average, accounted for 56 percent of the steers and heifers slaughtered in each state in 1969, 62 percent in 1972, 66 percent in 1978, and 81 percent in 1982 (Helmuth 1984). When procurement markets are defined somewhat broader as thirteen regional markets, the share of steers and heifers slaughtered by the top four firms (four-firm concentration ratio) ranged from 33 to 97 percent in 1980 (Quail et al. 1985). Only four regional markets had four-firm concentration ratios below 50; seven exceeded 70.

The beef slaughtering and processing industry has undergone dramatic changes in the last twenty-five years. As cattle feeding shifted out of the eastern corn belt, several new packing companies emerged, led by Iowa Beef Packing Co. (IBP). This new generation of packers located large, efficient, specialized beef slaughtering plants in cattle feeding areas and hired workers at substantially lower wages (and fringes) than the old-line packers. The employees of most of the old-line packers were covered by the master labor union contract, which had a cost of living adjustment clause (COLA). The automatic wage increases that were triggered by double-digit inflation during the 1970s exacerbated the cost disadvantage of old-line packers. Several companies closed plants, reopened them under separate ownership, and negotiated new labor contracts.

The growth of Swift Independent and the decline of the Spencer division of Land O'Lakes has resulted in three dominant beef slaughtering companies in the United States. By the end of 1983, the three (IBP, Excel, and Swift Independent) were slaughtering approximately half of the nation's fed beef.

The most dramatic development in beef packing in the last twenty years is boxed beef. Whereas in the 1960s nearly all beef left the packer as forequarters or hindquarters, much of it is now cut into primal or subprimal cuts by the packer, sealed in vacuum-pack bags, and shipped in cardboard boxes. Boxed beef has grown rapidly in acceptance and accounted for about 43 percent of beef sold in 1979 and 58 percent by 1982 (Helmuth 1984). Boxed beef has provided an important means for packers to differentiate a commodity—USDA choice carcasses—but also provides many benefits to the packer-retailing stages in transportation and labor cost savings, product quality and shelf life, and merchandising flexibility.

Most small and medium-sized packers do not have boxed beef operations and sell their output in carcass form. The largest three beef packers have boxed beef processing operations. Carcass sales by these companies primarily involve those carcasses that do not meet the standards for boxed beef. Firms engaged in processing carcasses and selling boxed beef often purchase carcasses from other meat packers; thus, the concentration of boxed beef sales is significantly higher than the concentration of steer and heifer slaughter. Four-firm concentration ratios for boxed beef sales were 60 percent in 1979 and 66 percent by 1982 (Helmuth 1984).

Economies of scale exist in beef slaughtering and processing but are difficult to assess. In the major cattle feeding areas, a specialized slaughtering plant that kills 250,000 head per year using two shifts will apparently realize most of the scale economies available. This represents about 1 percent of the U.S. fed cattle slaughter in recent years. Economies of scale appear to be greater in boxed beef processing (Cothern, Peard, and Weeks 1978). Most of the new combination beef slaughtering-processing plants have a slaughtering capacity of 500,000 to 1 million head per year.

The beef packing industry seems to be evolving toward two subsets of companies. One includes the slaughterers with large efficient plants (often exceeding 500,000 head annual slaughter) that specialize in a narrow range of cattle (U.S. Choice, yield grade 2s and 3s) and sell much of their output as boxed beef. These companies cater particularly to medium and large supermarket chains. The second subset of packers generally operates smaller plants, slaughters cattle of varying quality, and caters to the smaller, specialized market niches such as restaurants selling U.S. Prime beef, stores handling lower-quality lean beef, and similar markets. The two subsets of the beef packing industry may compete only indirectly both in buying live cattle and in the wholesale meat market.

Most fresh beef is sold through retail supermarkets. Close to half of the beef sold through retail stores is sold directly by packers to supermarket chains, which usually perform the warehousing and distribution functions. The remaining half is largely sold to grocery wholesalers, which service independent supermarkets and small chains, or to specialized meat wholesalers.

Food service outlets also sell substantial volumes of beef. Fast food hamburger chains are an important part of the market for ground beef products and hence the demand for cull cows and beef trimmings. Beef sold to food service firms usually goes through one or two intermediate stages. Independent beef processing-fabricating firms buy beef on a negotiated price basis from packers and fabricate specified cuts for food service companies. Fabricated beef products are either delivered directly to retail outlets by beef fabricators or channeled through food service distributors. Large, limited menu food service companies seldom perform either the beef fabricating or distribution functions. The food service firm's purchasing department controls the procurement process through a system of contracts and distribution agreements with both feed fabricators and food service distributors.

Subsector Coordination

The coordination task in the beef subsector is relatively difficult. The seasonal output of atomistic and geographically dispersed cow-calf producers must be synchronized with the demands of meat packers and retailers for a stable supply of consistent quality beef. This synchronizing task is performed by growers (also called stockers or backgrounders) and feedlots but largely without contracts or vertical integration to provide greater vertical control.

Auctions and order buyers are the primary means by which small lots of feeder cattle are sorted and consolidated into truckloads of relatively homogeneous cattle for shipment to feedlots. In the exchange between feedlots and packers, there has been a sharp decline in the importance of terminals and an offsetting increase in direct marketing. Whereas 39 percent of steer and heifers were sold direct in 1960, this had increased to 88 percent by 1982 (USDA 1984c). Although contracts or formula-pricing arrangements are rarely used in feedlot-packer exchange, the price packers are willing to pay for fed cattle depends on the price they expect to receive in the wholesale meat market. Since the National Provisioner Yellow Sheet is the most heavily used source of price information for the wholesale market, the prices of fed cattle tend to follow the Yellow Sheet quotes.

Packer sales of carcass beef are predominantly formula priced using the Yellow Sheet. One-third or less of carcass sales are priced by private negotiation or offer-acceptance arrangements. In contrast to carcass pricing, most boxed beef sales involve negotiated prices. A major exception is IBPs Cattle-Pak, which is formula priced based on the Yellow Sheet. Formula pricing is also heavily used in cost-plus procurement arrangements between food service firms and beef fabricators.

Formula pricing is controversial because of concerns about the price base most commonly used, the Yellow Sheet. Concerns include: 1) the small volume of negotiated prices on which price reports are based (several large chains that negotiate prices refuse to report them to the National Provisioner); 2) price quotes are sometimes based on no trades; and 3) the small number of reported trades may allow price manipulation, particularly via packer-to-packer trades. Although research on the Yellow Sheet provides some support for the first two concerns, the existence of price manipulation has been neither confirmed nor refuted.

Suggested solutions to concerns about the Yellow Sheet include abolishing formula pricing, instituting mandatory price reporting or instituting electronic marketing. A pilot electronic marketing system for wholesale beef was not widely enough accepted to be commercially viable (Faminow and Sarhan 1983). Most observers are reluctant to advocate elimination of formula pricing because of low transaction costs, the benefits to small buyers and sellers, and the strong preference of many traders.

Although contracting and vertical integration is not widespread in the beef subsector, two relatively new vertical arrangements deserve note. One is the joint venture between IBP and North West Feeders Cooperatives (NWFC). Six feedlots in Idaho and Washington formed a cooperative and entered into a five-year agreement with IBP to supply about three-fourths of the slaughter needs of two IBP plants. IBP and NWFC share profits or losses from feeding, slaughtering, processing, and distributing the cattle supplied by NWFC under the agreement. Such an arrangement is more likely in fringe production areas where both feeders and packers face greater market uncertainties than in major production areas.

A more complex vertical network was organized by Keystone Beef, a major fabricator of ground beef for McDonald's restaurants. A subsidiary of Cargill, Inc. (Caprock feedlots) purchases and feeds feeder cattle for Keystone. These cattle are then custom slaughtered by Excel, another Cargill subsidiary, processed into boxed beef and shipped to Keystone, where they are further processed into hamburgers that meet McDonald's specifications. This contractually tied network is an attempt to ensure dependable supplies that meet rigid specifications regardless of the stage of the cattle cycle.

Agricultural cooperatives play a minor role in the beef subsector. Cooperatives operate some feeder cattle auctions and may help connect buyers and sellers of fed cattle. Land O'Lakes is the only cooperative that has had a significant involvement in beef packing. In 1978, Land O'Lakes acquired Spencer Packing Co., one of the largest five beef slaughterers at the time. In 1983, Land O'Lakes attempted to sell the spencer plants to Excel but was blocked by private antitrust action (*Monfort of Colorado, Inc.* v. *Cargill, Inc.,* 1983). Government programs have long played a role in beef grading and health and sanitation inspections. Federal grades for beef facilitate coordination in the subsector. Import limitations on processed beef (mostly frozen) are the primary means by which the federal government influences beef supplies or prices. Imports would undoubtedly be much higher than the present 1 billion pounds without import restrictions.

Subsector Performance

Given the series of major changes that have affected the beef subsector since 1960, the subsector has demonstrated both adaptability and organizational progressiveness. New firms that entered the cattle feeding and beef packing stages have had a particularly strong effect on subsector progressiveness.

There has been a cost to this progressiveness, particularly for employees of meat packing companies and the owners and managers of "old-line" packing plants and many smaller slaughtering plants. Hourly employees have seen many jobs eliminated and their wages and fringes reduced substantially. Some packers have been criticized for encouraging rapid turnover of employees and recruiting immigrants and foreign nationals willing to work for lower wages.

The counterargument is that new-generation firms have substantially reduced costs in the beef subsector and provided an infusion of keen competition. Technological changes in meat packing such as on-rail slaughtering and on-line processing have increased labor productivity and reduced the level of skills required. Red meat output (in pounds) per man-hour increased by 49 percent from 1960 to 1970 and by 20 percent from 1970 to 1980 in meat packing plants (SIC 2011). The introduction of boxed beef by newer firms has brought significant labor, transportation, and marketing efficiencies to the subsector. Boxed beef has also led to a greater market orientation of the subsector since retailers can buy the specific subprimals demanded in their markets.

Prices and profits in the beef subsector have been highly variable. Prices are the most volatile for calves, followed by feeder cattle and then fed steers and heifers. The beef cycle persists, although its length is more difficult to predict. Since current fed beef supplies reflect breeding and marketing decisions made over two years ago by cow-calf producers, it is difficult to correct shortages or surpluses quickly.

Considering the complexity of coordination in the beef subsector, market period coordination is quite good. Seasonal calf production is largely smoothed out by stockers and feeders. The quality of fed beef has gradually changed in response to consumer desires for leaner beef and packer-retailer desires for higher-yielding cattle.

Price information and formula pricing remain major issues in the subsector. Although there appears to be a sufficient volume of negotiated trades on carcass beef to discover equilibrium prices, only a tiny fraction are included in price reports. The volume of carcass trades is also steadily declining. The current price reporting system for carcass beef is vulnerable to manipulation and selective reporting. Because of formula pricing, distortions in reported carcass prices affect prices throughout the wholesale meat and fed cattle markets.

The changes affecting the subsector have resulted in relatively high and increasing levels of concentration in the procurement of live cattle and the sale of boxed beef. These appear to be the markets in the subsector where some deterioration of competitive forces may be occurring. Research at the University of Wisconsin indicates that fed cattle prices tend to be significantly lower in the more concentrated markets (Quail, et al. 1985). Thus, feeders in some areas may be receiving lower prices for their cattle than they would in more competitive markets.

The development and acceptance of boxed beef has been the most important change affecting the beef subsector since the mid-1960s. Within ten years, most industry observers expect the U.S. beef subsector will have completed its conversion to this form of meat handling. Boxed beef subprimals have gradually become smaller and freer of bone and fat, and require less store-level fabrication. It appears only a matter of time before boxed beef processors will provide packaged case-ready retail cuts. At that point, the development of packer brands of fresh beef cuts would be feasible. Fresh beef marketing could become similar to the marketing of wieners and bacon.

Pork Subsector

Unlike beef, cured products play an important role in the pork subsector. Approximately one-half of the hog carcass is sold as cured products (such as bacon and ham) and one-third as fresh cuts; lean trim and fat make up the remaining one-sixth and are used in sausage products (wieners, sausage, luncheon meat). Fresh cuts are highly perishable. Processed products vary in perishability from fresh sausage to canned hams.

Per capita consumption of pork has fluctuated considerably over time but exhibits no definite trend. The relatively flat consumption pattern for pork contrasts with the sharp increase in per capita broiler consumption and the more gradual long-run increase in per capita beef consumption until 1976. Consumer expenditures on pork are roughly twice their expenditures on chicken and about one-half their expenditures on beef.

There are important seasonal variations in hog production and pork consumption, which make coordination more difficult. Farrowings peak in the spring and fall; slaughter levels peak during the same periods (six months after farrowing). Per capita consumption of perishable pork products generally follows the seasonal pattern of hog production. Bacon consumption is highest during summer months; ham consumption peaks in November-December and at Easter. Frozen pork bellies and ham storage are required to satisfy peak consumption periods.

Geographically hog production and slaughter (and to a lesser extent feeder pig production) are concentrated in the corn belt. Twelve states accounted for 84.6 percent of all market hogs produced in 1982. The same states produced 83.9 percent of all feeder pigs in 1982 (USDA 1983c).

Subsector Organization

Figure 3–6 indicates the stages and primary channels of the pork subsector. The breeding stock supply stage has gradually become a more important and distinct stage. Although hog producers typically produce their own female breeding stock, most boars are supplied by commercial breeders. In recent years, a few large corporate suppliers have gained a small but growing share of the breeding stock market. These firms emphasize crossbred breeding

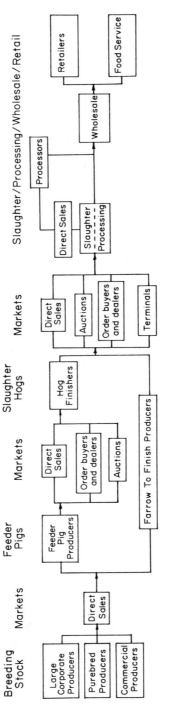

Source: Hayenga et al. 1985. Reproduced by permission of Iowa State Press.

Figure 3–6. Organization of Pork Subsector

stock and a more scientific approach to breeding and are challenging small purebred breeders.

Feeder pig production and market hog production, the next two stages, are organized in several ways. Some firms specialize in either feeder pig or market hog production, in which case a transaction occurs between the two stages; however, about 80 percent of the nation's pigs are farrowed and finished in the same operation in which the two stages are integrated (Hayenga et al. 1985). A new type of firm is the farrowing corporation, which is owned by a small group of hog finishers. It supplies its owners with feeder pigs of known breeding and health. The number of feeder pigs supplied to each owner may be less flexible than desired, however.

Only about 20 percent of all pigs farrowed are sold as feeder pigs. About half of these are sold through organized markets (mainly teleauctions and auctions). Concern about feeder pig quality and health has encouraged direct sales and integrated farrow to finish operations.

Pig and hog production is in the second phase of a major structural reorganization. The elimination of hogs as a small-scale enterprise on 4 million farms occurred from 1920 to 1970. Since 1970, the second phase, industrialization of production, has been taking place. Consistently successful production of hogs (and pigs) in large-scale confinement, first accomplished in the 1970s, may be the most significant factor affecting farm structure in the pork subsector in the 1970s and 1980s. Pig and hog production has rapidly moved into total confinement, with an attendant substitution of capital for labor, and in units large enough to utilize specialized management. The greater capital investment in confinement operations encourages high utilization and results in greater reluctance to cut back the number of hogs fed.

The number of farms selling over 1,000 pigs and hogs per year increased from 6,600 in 1969 to 21,700 in 1982. Research indicates that some economies of size are realized up to 5,000 head marketed per year and possibly beyond (Hayenga et al. 1985). Some of the largest hog units (defined as 15,000 head or more marketed) are owned by feed companies or food processing companies. Completely integrated vertical complexes, such as in broilers, do not appear to be developing in hogs. In 1982, 34 percent of the hog farms produced 88 percent of the nation's hogs. A majority of hog producers also raise feed grains, but some specialize entirely in hog production.

The sale of finished hogs to meat packers occurs in relatively local markets. Most hogs are sold to plants within 100 miles of the farm. Over three-fourths are direct sales in which the producer delivers the hogs to a packing plant or packer buying station (USDA 1984c). Sales are predominantly negotiated spot sales, with pricing on a live weight basis. Although there are some short-term marketing contracts between packers and producers based on futures market quotations, the volume involved is relatively small.

Accurate estimates of buyer market shares in producer–first handler markets are not available. Data on concentration of hog slaughtering by state probably overstate the level of buyer concentration in relevant geographic markets but are the best data available. The largest four slaughterers of hogs in each state in 1982, based on unpublished Packers and Stockyards Administration data, slaughtered 84.5 percent of the hogs in each state on average (concentration weighted by head slaughtered). Concentration of hog slaughter on a regional basis is significantly lower. For the eight regions used by Packers and Stockyards Administration, the four largest slaughterers of hogs slaughtered 55.5 percent of the hogs in each region in 1982. The regional concentration figures probably understate the level of concentration in relevant geographic markets, while the state figures likely error in the opposite direction. The halfway point between the two is a concentration ratio (CR4) of 70, a very high level of concentration. Except for very dense production areas, hog producers often have few buyers from whom to choose.

Increasing concentration of packer procurement is in part the result of substantial changes in the meat packing industry. Changes in pork slaughtering and processing have come more slowly and have been less dramatic than in beef. Some of the causal forces have been similar, however. Slaughtering and processing plants have become larger and more specialized in both pork and beef. Labor contracts have also had strong effects in both pork and beef. Employees of old-line pork processors, such as Wilson, Armour, Hormel, Swift, and Oscar Mayer, were on the master union contract, which had much higher wages and more restrictive work rules than the labor contracts of their smaller competitors.

Many of the companies on master contracts closed plants and either reorganized them as a new corporation or sold them to other companies. The plants were then reopened with lower wage agreements (for example, Dubuque Packing became FDL Foods; Esmark plants were spun-off to Swift Independent; Armour plants were sold to Swift Indep. and ConAgra). Wilson, the largest slaughterer of hogs, went into Chapter 11 bankruptcy proceedings and renegotiated its union contracts. The older plants in older locations continue in operation but are often under new ownership and new wage agreements.

Unlike beef, where new firms entered the industry with new-generation plants and low wages, competitive pressures in pork processing have come primarily from older regional companies such as Frederick and Herrud, which took advantage of their lower labor costs and gradually built market share. However, the announcement by IBP in 1981 of plans to open a hog slaughtering plant in 1983 substantially increased the efforts of incumbent firms to reduce costs and improve efficiency.

In 1982, the largest four hog slaughtering firms nationally accounted for 36 percent of hogs slaughtered in the U.S. (Helmuth 1984). Since then, three Armour hog slaughtering plants have been sold to Swift Independent. IBP, the largest beef slaughtering company, has taken steps to enter hog slaughtering in a serious way. Another new entrant, ConAgra, recently acquired two hog slaughtering and eleven pork processing plants from Armour, as well as the Armour brand. ConAgra is the nation's largest broiler processing company. Both IBP and ConAgra have adequate financing and reputations as aggressive, low-cost competitors. It appears likely that some additional restructuring of this industry may still lie ahead.

There appear to be economies of size in operating very large, modern plants with double shifts that slaughter 2 million to 4 million hogs per year. Such plants need to be in areas of heavy production in order to minimize the cost of obtaining sufficient hogs.

Pork slaughtering and processing companies sell their products in regional and national markets to grocery retailing chains, wholesalers serving independent supermarkets and food service firms, and other pork processors. Although formula price contracts are used some on fresh pork transactions between meat packers or processors and their customers, there is very little vertical integration. Fresh products are largely undifferentiated, whereas processed products are often branded and advertised by processors. A recent innovation is boxed fresh and boneless pork, an attempt to differentiate fresh pork products to retail and food service buyers.

Two companies, Oscar Mayer and Hormel, have developed strong national brand franchises: Oscar Mayer on hot dogs, luncheon meat, and bacon and Hormel on hams and canned meat (Spam). Most other processors have brands that are strong in certain markets or regions but not nationally. The structure of processed pork product markets therefore varies greatly in different areas.

Subsector Coordination

The pork subsector is essentially market coordinated. Market prices are free of direct government controls. There are no marketing orders or price-support programs. Recently import duties were imposed on subsidized Canadian hog imports. Organized markets still play significant roles in price discovery of feeder pigs and slaughter hogs. Approximately half of all feeder pigs are sold at auctions and teleauctions. Packers purchased about 21 percent of their slaughter hogs through terminals and auctions in 1982 (USDA 1984c). Direct marketing of slaughter hogs has steadily increased; these are generally spot sales in which price is negotiated.

Formula pricing in the hog subsector is mainly used in the sale of fresh pork by packers to retail and food service customers. An estimated 40 percent of fresh pork was formula priced in 1978, while approximately 50 percent was sold with negotiated prices (Hayenga et al. 1985). Since then the use of formula pricing has increased substantially. The Yellow Sheet is usually the base for formula pricing arrangements. Processed pork products, which are generally branded, are largely sold with administered prices (price lists) by processors.

Vertical integration and contract arrangements are relatively unimportant in the pork subsector except at the sow farrowing–hog finishing stages, where 80 percent of the pigs are fed out by the same farm firm. Recently contract feeder pig finishing has begun to develop in the financially stressed corn belt as a way for hog producers with inadequate capital to utilize their facilities.

A more uniform pattern of sow farrowings has reduced the seasonal pattern of hog production; however, seasonal price fluctuations for slaughter hogs have changed little since 1960 and are relatively large.

The large, cyclical but erratic price fluctuations for live hogs reflect the difficulties of long-run coordination in the subsector. Current pork supplies are largely determined by the sow breeding decisions of thousands of farmers nine months earlier. Such decisions are made amid considerable uncertainty about future hog and feed prices. The trend toward highly capitalized confinement finishing operations may stabilize hog production but also may result in more serious price depressions if such firms are slower to reduce output.

Viable futures contracts for live hogs and feed grains provide a vehicle for hog producers to manage price risks. Interest in hedging and marketing contracts appears to be cyclical, with greater interest after periods of losses.

Retail prices on pork products tend to be sticky; there is an estimated lag of two to six weeks between changes in farm level and retail prices. This tends to accentuate the magnitude of price fluctuations at the farm level.

Agricultural cooperatives are more important in the pork subsector than in beef or broilers but far less important than in dairy. A few cooperatives (Genetics Unlimited, Farmland, Land O'Lakes) have developed marketing programs for their purebred breeder members. Cooperatives have also played an important role in developing and operating feeder pig auctions and teleauctions. Cooperative-operated markets handled about 20 percent of the feeder pigs sold in 1980. At the slaughtering-processing stage, Farmland Industries, the largest U.S. farmer cooperative, operates three plants and is one of the ten largest slaughterers of hogs in the United States (Hayenga et al. 1985).

Government activities affect subsector coordination, but the government does not directly determine prices or output. USDA grades facilitate communication and commercial exchange. Market news reports aid in marketing decisions and pricing. Health and sanitation laws contribute to wholesome products. Government action on the legality of nitrites could have a strong effect on the subsector. Total elimination of nitrites from cured pork products would eliminate the present system of producing and marketing these products. Most firms are marketing cured pork products with reduced levels of nitrite.

Subsector Performance

Although hog production and prices have historically been highly cyclical, hog production has generally been profitable. This is in contrast to other cyclical commodities such as beef and eggs in which producers have periodically suffered large losses. Apparently hog production is not a preferred enterprise for many farmers. Barriers to entry and exit have been low. Thus, farmers have been able to enter hog production, stay in it as long as profits were significantly better than alternative enterprises, and exit without sacrificing large sunk costs. This is not true for the large confinement hog operations that have grown rapidly in importance. These producers have large sunk costs and specialized facilities. They are committed to the hog business.

The profitability of pork slaughtering-processing firms has been highly variable, particularly for firms with substantial fresh pork sales. The profitability of cured products has been higher and more stable due to the differentiation of these products and the ability to even out variations in supply through storage.

Producer-packer markets are highly concentrated. Particularly in fringe production areas, producers have few market alternatives. One study found a significant negative relationship between slaughter hog prices and state concentration of hog slaughtering (Miller and Harris 1982). Thus, monopsonistic power may depress hog prices in certain markets. Markets at other stages in the subsector appear to be relatively competitive.

Price discovery and pricing signals in the subsector are enhanced by the existence of effectively functioning markets at several stages in the subsector. Formula pricing is used for more than half of the fresh pork sold in wholesale markets. The price base for formula pricing of pork has recently been questioned but historically has been more acceptable than in beef.

The subsector has been relatively progressive in adopting new technology and streamlining the flow of products. New organizational forms have been developed in breeding stock and feeder pig production and are filling a need.

The subsector was relatively slow in shifting to leaner-type hogs. In part this was due to the inability of consumer preferences to be expressed in market signals throughout the subsector. However, over a thirty-year period, a substantial shift in hog type has taken place. Recent efforts by producers and packers to develop more accurate carcass merit buying systems should result in more accurate transmission of quality preferences in the future.

The subsector continues to be plagued by cyclical production and prices. Hog cycles have become more severe since 1980. Considerable excess capacity exists in the subsector at low points in the cycle. The inefficiencies and misallocation of resources resulting from these cycles is the major deficiency of the subsector. A forward deliverable contract market for hogs, if effectively developed, could provide much better information on production plans and hog prices ten to fifteen months in the future (Kauffman 1983). Producers could also lock in a price using these contracts in advance of sow breeding and farrowing. Thus, such a contract market appears to hold the potential for reducing the extreme volatility of hog production and prices; however, such a market remains to be operationally tested.

Broiler and Egg Subsections

The identity of both broilers and eggs is preserved from farm to retail store. Relatively little change occurs in product form. The vast majority of production is marketed fresh. Approximately 7 percent of broiler meat is processed for input into other food products; about 15 percent of eggs are broken commercially for use by food manufacturers. Unlike dairy, processed broiler and egg products are unable to absorb surplus egg or broiler production.

Per capita consumption of eggs has declined almost continuously from over 390 eggs per year in 1951 to 261 in 1984 (USDA 1985a). The quantity of eggs consumed is relatively unresponsive to changes in the price of eggs, the prices of other products, or consumer income. Egg prices exhibit a pronounced seasonal pattern, with the low occurring usually in May or June and the high in the September to December period. Within-year price variations are usually much larger than between-year variation (figure 3–7). The seasonality of egg production has been reduced substantially over time and has resulted in some decline in the seasonal variations in prices in recent years. In the long run, prices tend to follow a cyclical pattern, about two to four years in length. These price variations remain a major problem to the subsector.

Per capita consumption of broilers has increased sharply from less than 20 pounds in 1950 to 53 pounds in 1984 (USDA 1985a). Unlike eggs, which have no close substitutes, broilers compete with beef, pork, fish, and other meats. Broiler consumption is relatively responsive to the price of broilers, the price of other products, and consumer income.

Total broiler production exhibits more variation from year to year than eggs; however, because the demand for broilers is more price elastic than the demand for eggs, the price of broilers varies less than the price of eggs. Still, both broiler and egg prices vary considerably from year to year (figure 3–8). When combined with volatile feed prices, periods of boom and bust create considerable risk in both broilers and eggs.

Eggs are produced in all regions of the country. The north Central region, which at one time produced about 50 percent of all eggs, declined sharply until 1970 and since has stabilized at about 25 percent of U.S. production. The south Atlantic and south Central regions grew from 24 percent of U.S. production in 1950 to 42 percent in 1970 and have held that share (USDA 1985a).

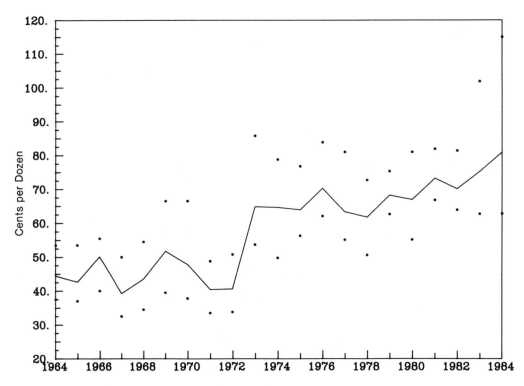

Source: Developed by Lee Schrader from USDA data.

Figure 3–7. Grade A Large Eggs, Prices to New York Retailers, 1964–1984 (Annual Average and Monthly Extremes)

Broiler production is more geographically concentrated than eggs, with the south Atlantic and south Central regions producing 85 percent of the total in 1982. The top ten broiler-producing states accounted for 84 percent of U.S. production in 1982; the comparable figure for eggs was 60 percent (USDA 1985a). The geographic distribution of production for both broilers and eggs has been relatively stable since 1970.

Subsector Organization

Both subsectors have several stages prior to farm production (figure 3–9). Basic breeding companies sell foundation breeding stock to hatching egg producers. From the hatching egg stage on, both subsectors are tied together with vertical integration and contract arrangements. In broilers, integrators typically own the hatching facility, feed mill, and processing plant

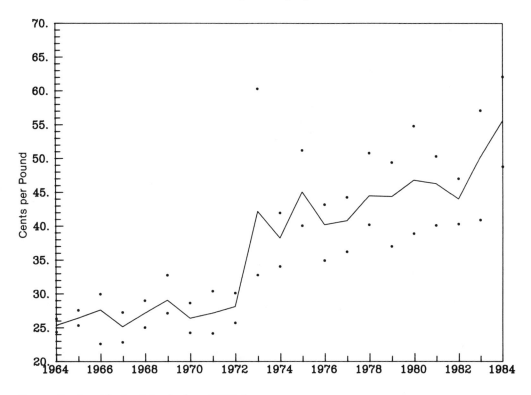

Source: Developed by Lee Schrader from USDA data.
Note: Prices for 1983 and 1984 are twelve-city weighted average.

Figure 3–8. Prices of Broiler-Fryers, Ice Packed Ready-to-Cook, Nine-City Weighted Average 1964–1984 (Annual Average and Monthly Extremes)

and contract for hatching egg production and for broiler growing. Initially feed companies were the primary integrators of the broiler subsector. Over time processors have become the focal point of control.

Eighty-two percent of total broiler production in 1978 came from 12,300 farms, each of which sold at least 100,000 broilers in 1978 (Lasley 1983). Typically contracts between integrators and broiler growers call for the integrator to retain ownership of the birds, provide feed, medication, and certain other inputs, pickup fed broilers at the farm, and deliver them to the processing plant. Growers maintain ownership of their facilities but largely operate as employees of the integrator. They are generally paid so much per pound produced, regardless of market price. The integrator retains all the risk of broiler price or feed price fluctuations; however, they also have almost

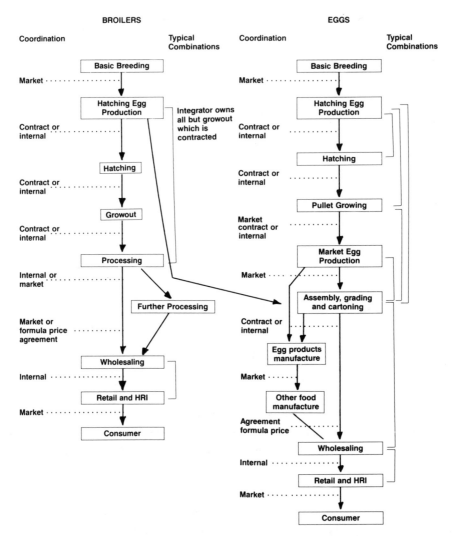

Figure 3–9. Organization and Coordination of Broiler and Egg Subsectors

total control over the production process. Approximately 90 percent of broilers are produced under contracts, with the remaining 10 percent produced by integrators in their own grow-out facilities.

There is greater variation in the organization of the egg subsector. Pullet growing tends to be combined with either the hatching or egg production stage. Approximately 37 percent of egg production comes from large-scale production-processing complexes in which eggs move directly from the production house to grading and cartoning machinery at the same site. Contract production, in which feed and pullets are provided by the integrator, accounts for an additional 43 percent. Feed suppliers have retained an important share of contract production. Most egg production contracts provide for producer payment based on the number of eggs produced or the number of hens producing, and many provide for adjustments for feed conversion, death loss, egg grade, or in some cases egg price. One finds a wide variety of contract terms in use, ranging from profit participation to fixed fee per unit produced. The remaining 20 percent of egg production is largely independent. Even the independent producer usually has a marketing agreement (formal or informal) with an egg packer. In these cases, transfer prices are determined by a formula based on a market quote.

National concentration of sales is high in the breeding industries in both subsectors. For example, the largest five breeders of layers account for 80 to 90 percent of total breeder pullets placed in the United States. Entry barriers are high because of the long periods to develop new poultry strains and then get them accepted.

National concentration of sales of ready-to-cook broilers is considerably higher than for shell eggs. The largest twenty broiler firms accounted for about two-thirds of the broilers slaughtered and 73 percent of the ready-to-eat broilers sold in 1981 (Broiler Industry 1982). Due in part to mergers, the largest four broiler processors increased their share from 23 percent in 1980 to 34 percent in 1984. The top four broiler processors in 1984 were Con Agra, Tyson Foods, Gold Kist, and Holly Farms (Broiler Industry 1984). Central Soya and Cargill ranked among the top twenty broiler companies.

In 1984, an estimated sixty-three companies had 1 million or more laying hens. The largest twenty accounted for about 30 percent of the U.S. egg production (*Poultry Tribune,* December 1984). Cargill, Cal-Maine, Seaboard Foods, and Rose Acre Farms were the top four egg firms. Con Agra ranked as the twenty-sixth largest egg firm.

The cost of supplying production inputs, supervising cultural practices, and collecting products for market encourages relatively small producer-contractor markets. In areas of dense broiler or egg production, producers generally have several integrators with which they can contract. In fringe production areas, however, growers may have only one or two contractors from which to choose.

Product differentiation is relatively unimportant in either subsector. Eggs are almost all marketed using USDA grades; differences in quality are not sufficient to be easily detected by consumers. Advertised brands of eggs have an insignificant share of the market. Branding of broilers has gradually increased as ice-packed broilers have declined in market share and broilers prepackaged at the processing plant have gained market share. Perdue Farms has been relatively successful in differentiating its broilers in the New York market. Although the majority of broilers are still sold as undifferentiated ice-packed broilers, a National Broiler Council survey indicated that about 38 percent of broilers reached consumers with a processor's brand in 1981.

Subsector Coordination

The egg and broiler subsectors operate without government price supports or direct controls over output. Although contracts and vertical integration result in both subsectors being largely administratively coordinated, ultimately both must respond to market prices at the processor-retailer interface. The coordination task in the short run is made easier because the spatial and temporal dimensions of both marketing channels are short and product changes are not large. The task is made more complex because the products are perishable, the demand for eggs is relatively unresponsive to price changes, and production and demand for both products vary seasonally.

In most market-coordinated subsectors, coordination depends on the decisions of subsector participants. Ownership integration and production contracts are vehicles for transferring decision authority from one or more stages to a single stage. In effect, several vertical stages are controlled by a single decision maker. Output decisions, coordination of product flow, and harmonization of stages can then consider the total interests of the vertical subsystem.

Contracts and integration do not eliminate the fundamental causes of long-run coordination problems in most agricultural subsectors. Production commitments must be made several months before the product will be ready for market. The factors that may affect future supply and demand conditions —such as the output of other producers, the supply of competing products, demand fluctuations, weather, and disease—are extremely difficult to foresee. The managers of large, integrated egg firms may be no more omnipotent than a small egg producer. In eggs, there is a lag of seven to eighteen months from a decision to change output to its full realization. In broilers, the lag is three to nine months.

The processor-retailer exchange of broilers is the only point of price discovery in the subsector. Weekly negotiated prices predominate in the exchange of ice-packed, ready-to-cook broilers at the processor-retailer interface. Prepackaged and special cut broilers, which are growing in market share, tend to be formula priced against the ice-packed quotation. Negotiated trades account for about half the volume. While there is some concern about the amount of formula pricing, the ice-packed price as quoted by the USDA Market News is considered to be an accurate reflection of broiler values.

Open negotiated trades of eggs are few and often not reported. Formula pricing is used to establish transfer prices throughout the United States at almost every level of trade for table eggs. Urner Barry spot market quotations, a private market report, is the most common base for formula pricing, although USDA Market News price quotations are also used. Urner Barry provides market quotations that attempt to reflect the current market situation. They have been criticized because they are not a compilation of actual market prices; however, these quotes generally are viewed by subsector participants as objective indicators of egg value.

Participants in the egg subsector may want to use a market price but evidence very little desire to participate in the process of discovering that price. As a result, prices and pricing are much more a point of conflict than is the case in the broiler subsector. Apparently the benefits of formula-priced transfers outweigh the desire for open market pricing. The assembly of eggs from the farm and distribution of cartoned eggs to retailers is more efficiently accomplished when the exchange partners are established by long-standing arrangements. A relatively new institution, Egg Clearinghouse, Inc., provides a forum for exchange of members' eggs; however, trading there represents only about one-half of 1 percent of all U.S. egg production.

Collective bargaining cooperatives are of little importance in either the egg or broiler subsectors. Except for Goldkist, marketing cooperatives are also relatively unimportant in both subsectors. Goldkist was estimated to be the third largest slaughterer of broilers in 1984 (Broiler Industry 1984). Goldkist has similar arrangements with its contract growers as noncooperative integrators.

In the egg subsector, cooperatives have typically performed the assembly-packing-distribution function for members or the sales and distribution function for eggs packed by integrated producer-packers. Relatively few cooperatives have provided feed and chicks. Several egg cooperatives have gone out of business in recent years so that the role of cooperatives in the subsector has diminished. Goldkist was estimated to be the twenty-eighth largest egg producer in 1984 (*Poultry Tribune* 1984).

Subsector Performance

The broiler and egg subsectors are models of production and marketing efficiency. Gains in efficiency have more than offset cost increases, resulting in decreasing real prices to consumers. Net returns from production and marketing activities, while somewhat variable from year to year, have not been high.

Feed use per unit of product has been cut more than 25 percent for eggs and nearly 30 percent for broilers since 1955. Production per man-hour has increased by a factor of 6 in the poultry group (including turkey). Similarly, gains in productivity in marketing have been substantial, totaling almost 40 percent since the mid-1960s alone. Most of these gains have accrued to the consumer.

Although the primary product of the egg subsector is still eggs in shell form, the quality of eggs reaching the consumer has greatly improved. Product changes in broilers have been more significant. Sales of prepackaged branded broilers have increased. Processors have also developed value-added products made with poultry meat and new types of products for the fast food industry. Efforts to expand domestic markets have generally emphasized products that are less vulnerable to commodity price cycles.

There appear to be more problems of equity in broilers than in eggs. The alternatives for broiler growers are much fewer than for egg producers. In the egg subsector, no single system of vertical arrangements dominates as it does in broilers. The in-line egg production and processing complex, where eggs are conveyed directly from the layer cage to grading and packing, appears to yield consistently lower costs than production on separate farms. Most new construction has been of the in-line complex type, which may be the dominant system in another ten years. This trend may reduce the alternatives available over time. At present, however, the existence of more alternatives for egg producers may provide at least an illusion of fairer treatment for egg producers.

The grower contracts of different broiler integrators are difficult to compare and tend to be more complicated than in eggs. Potential returns from alternative broiler contracts have been shown to vary substantially. Formal producer bargaining for contract terms has been strongly resisted by integrators, with alleged backlisting of growers involved in organizing efforts.

Price and income stability continue to be the major problems facing participants in these subsectors. The technological and organizational changes that have transformed these subsectors over the last three decades have wrought important benefits to consumers but have had little effect on the cyclical pattern of fortune in these subsectors.

Wheat, Corn, and Soybean Subsectors

These three subsectors are similar in organization and coordination. Storage, transportation, temporal price risk, and exports are extremely important in all three. Government programs have played an important role in attempting to adjust annual supply to expected demand, particularly in corn and wheat. Periodic large government inventories of corn and wheat are testimony to the difficulty of this balancing task.

Whereas most of the other commodities reviewed maintain their identity to the retail store, corn, wheat, and soybeans lose their identity at the processing level. All three are ingredients in a large number of products (such as feed, flour, breakfast cereal, bakery products, margarine, and shortening). At some point, the notion of a subsector no longer has meaning with these commodities. For example, flour milling is a logical part of the wheat subsector; cookie and bread baking are not. Wet corn milling is a logical part of the corn subsector. The use of high-fructose corn syrup in soft drinks is not. In this review, we will largely confine our analysis to the farm through initial processing stages.

In 1982 (a fairly normal year) the harvested acreage of these three crops totaled 223 million acres, nearly two-thirds of the land devoted to crop production in the United States. As a result of the Payment-in-Kind (PIK) program in 1983, acreage dropped sharply, especially for corn (figure 3–10). Whereas the acreage in corn for grain has been relatively stable over time, soybean acreage tripled from 1960 to 1984. In 1984, the acreage devoted to each of these crops was about equal. The yield per acre of corn has been much higher and has increased faster than either wheat or soybeans. As a result, total production of corn (in bushels) has continued to increase and was three to four times the total production of either wheat or soybeans in 1984 (figure 3–10). Acreage and yield variations of these crops from year to year are due to production decisions, weather, government programs, and production technology.

In contrast to other commodity subsectors reviewed in this chapter, which are primarily domestic in focus, the grain subsectors are heavily influenced by international markets. U.S. exports of these crops represented 30 to 60 percent of U.S. production in recent years. The United States is the dominant world exporter of all three crops (table 3–1).

Organization of Subsectors

Figure 3–11 provides a comparison of the institutions and channels that characterize the three subsectors. Many intermediate marketing and processing firms are involved in assembly, handling and storing, grading and inspecting, merchandising, and processing as grain and oilseeds move from farms to final users. The volume of wheat, corn, and soybeans marketed from U.S. farms has expanded rapidly in recent years, and this has led to considerable changes in the marketing system.

Corn and soybeans are produced in the same geographic areas. The five corn belt states have accounted for 55 to 60 percent of the production of both corn and soybeans since 1970. In 1982, nine states accounted for 81 percent of the volume of corn produced (Iowa, Illinois, Indiana, Nebraska, Minnesota, Ohio, Wisconsin, Michigan, Missouri); the nine leading soybean-producing states (including seven of above) produced 73 percent of U.S. soybeans (USDA 1985b).

Wheat production is more dispersed geographically than either corn or soybeans. The top nine wheat-producing states in 1982 accounted for 65 percent of U.S. wheat production. The northern plains is still the most important wheat-producing region but declined from 46 percent of national acreage in 1970 to 38 percent in 1981 (USDA 1985b).

Country elevators traditionally have been the primary outlet for grain and soybeans sold from U.S. farms. A 1977 survey by the Statistical Reporting

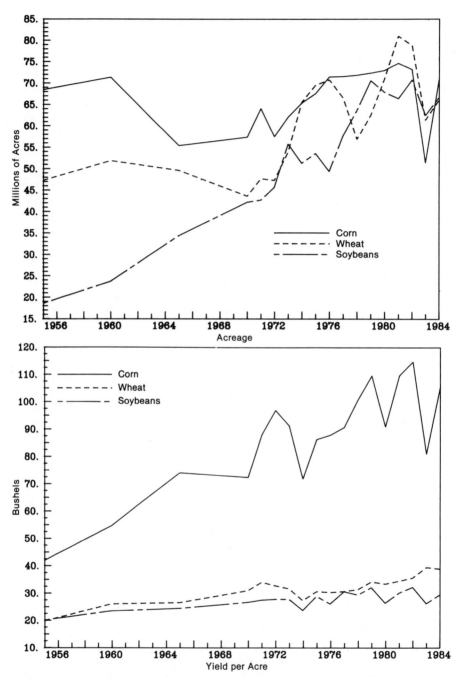

Source: USDA 1985b.

Figure 3–10. Production Trends for Corn, Wheat, and Soybeans, 1955–1984

Figure 3–10 continued

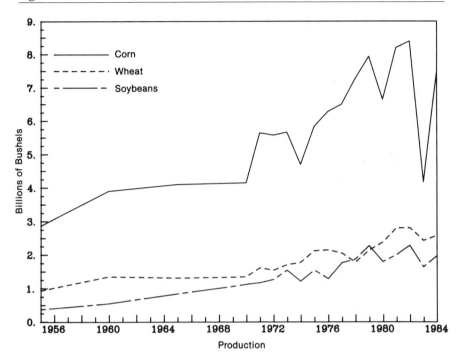

Production

Service found that 78, 80, and 87 percent, respectively, of the corn, soybeans, and wheat were sold by farmers to local elevators. Some large farmers can deliver sufficient volumes to bypass country elevators and sell directly to subterminal and terminal elevators. In 1977, 13 percent of the corn, 14 percent of the soybeans, and 5 percent of the wheat were delivered directly to subterminals and terminals (Hill and Leath 1985).

Producer–first handler markets are characterized by many grain producers selling to a relatively small number of elevators, usually within 50 to 100 miles of the farm. In major grain-producing areas, there are probably enough alternative buyers and sufficient market information to provide effective competition. In fringe producing areas producers may have only one or two elevators to which they can sell.

Storage by farmers, country elevators, and inland terminal elevators is necessary to distribute available supplies throughout the marketing year. Grain producers have invested heavily in on-farm storage and grain conditioning facilities in recent years, in part to store farmer-owned reserve (FOR) grain and earn storage payments under the program. In 1982, grain storage capacity on U.S. farms represented about 60 percent of the total grain storage capacity (Hill and Leath 1985). As on-farm drying and storage has increased,

Table 3–1

Importance of United States in World Production and Exports of Corn, Wheat, and Soybeans, 1978–1979 to 1981–1982 Marketing Years

	Corn	Wheat	Soybeans
U.S. production as percentage of world production	46	14	64
U.S. exports as percentage of U.S. production	30	65	43 (beans only)
U.S. exports as percentage of world exports	79	45	82 (beans) 35 (meal) 30 (oil)

Source: USDA 1985f, 1985g.

producers have become less dependent on country elevators for these services and are better able to sell directly to inland terminals, river elevators, or processors. Country elevators may be increasingly bypassed in the future.

Just as grain storage is essential for temporal coordination within these subsectors, transportation is essential for spatial movements and coordination. Rail and barge are the dominant modes of interstate grain movement (most of which are for export). Deregulation of the railroads has eliminated fixed rail rates, greatly increased the variability of rates between points, and resulted in less information about the rate structure. The introduction of user charges for river locks has changed the costs of barge transportation of grain. At present, there is sufficient uncertainty about future rail and barge rates that companies face considerable risk in locating facilities based on current rate structures.

Grain that is exported moves through stages that are increasingly concentrated as it goes from country terminals to port terminals. A few large multinational grain trading companies do nearly all the exporting of U.S. grain. Many of these companies are privately held so that market share, profit, and other financial information is difficult to obtain. Because they operate in world markets, proprietary international information networks may provide significant economic benefits and may be an important barrier to entry. It is not clear whether economies of size in information networks dictate the present large size of these companies.

Wheat. Of the 2.4 billion bushels of wheat utilized in the 1982–1983 marketing year, about 1.4 billion was channeled through port elevators for export (Hill and Leath 1985). Port elevators obtain their supplies from country and terminal elevators. A large proportion of port elevators are owned (or leased) by multinational grain trading companies, which also own some country, subterminal, and terminal elevators.

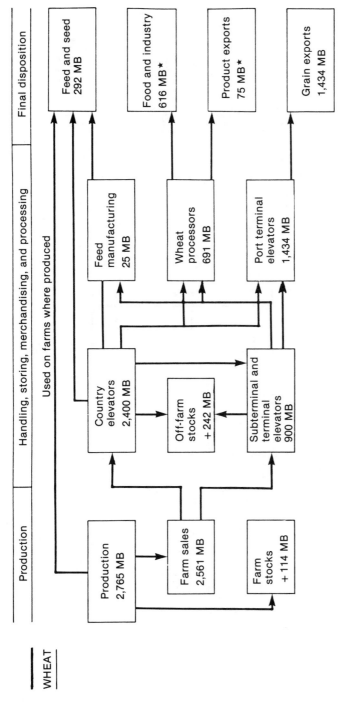

★ Product quantity expressed in grain equivalents. MB = million bushels.

Source: Hill and Leath 1985.

Figure 3–11. Marketing Channels for Corn, Wheat, and Soybeans, 1982–1983 Marketing Year

Figure 3–11 continued

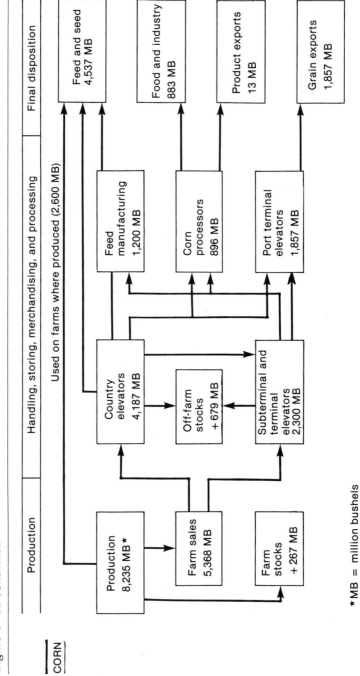

CORN

★ MB = million bushels

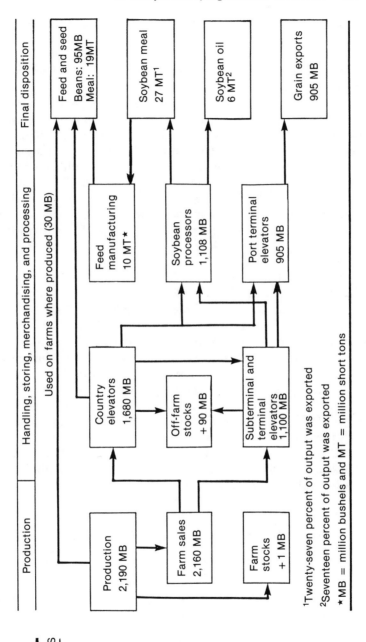

SOYBEANS

| Production | Handling, storing, merchandising, and processing | Final disposition |

Production 2,190 MB

Farm sales 2,160 MB

Farm stocks +1 MB

Used on farms where produced (30 MB)

Country elevators 1,680 MB

Off-farm stocks +90 MB

Subterminal and terminal elevators 1,100 MB

Feed manufacturing 10 MT★

Soybean processors 1,108 MB

Port terminal elevators 905 MB

Feed and seed Beans: 95MB Meal: 19MT

Soybean meal 27 MT[1]

Soybean oil 6 MT[2]

Grain exports 905 MB

[1]Twenty-seven percent of output was exported
[2]Seventeen percent of output was exported

★MB = million bushels and MT = million short tons

Domestic flour millers utilized about one-fourth of the wheat marketed in 1982–1983. Several of the large flour milling companies own country elevators; wheat is then shipped directly to the mills. Millers that are not vertically integrated rely on terminal elevators; the latter can blend wheat to the quality specifications of millers.

Of the five major types of wheat produced in the United States, hard red winter is the most important, accounting for 45 percent of total U.S. wheat production in the 1980–1982 crop years. Soft red winter has become the second most important type, accounting for 22 percent of production during 1980–1982, while hard red spring wheat ranks third with 16 percent of production. White wheat follows with 12 percent, and durum wheat makes up the remainder (USDA 1985e). The principal domestic use of hard wheats is in the production of bread flour. Soft wheats are lower in protein and are milled into flour for cakes, cookies, pastries, and crackers. The durum wheats are hard varieties used mainly in the production of semolina, a granular type of flour used to make pasta products.

In 1982, U.S. flour mills utilized 640 million bushels of wheat to produce 285 million hundredweight (cwt) of flour (USDA 1985e). Approximately 9 percent of the wheat flour tonnage produced in 1977 was marketed by flour millers in consumer packages of flour or flour mixes (Bureau of Census 1977e). The remainder (except for 7 percent that was exported) was used by various other food manufacturers, repackagers, and food service establishments.

The number of flour mills has dropped sharply from 423 in 1965 to 247 in 1982 (*Milling and Baking News* 1982). Mills larger than 5,000 cwt in capacity increased from 65 to 89 and accounted for 82 percent of industry capacity in 1982. This was primarily due to the construction of large, modern mills near major flour consumption centers. Total industry capacity has increased slowly from 942,000 cwt in 1965 to 1,071,000 cwt in 1982.

Concentration in flour milling—though historically relatively low—has increased sharply during the last eighteen years. Based on industry estimates, four-firm concentration increased from 28 percent in 1965 to 37 percent in 1981 and then, propelled by two large mergers between the third and fourth largest firms and the fifth and eighth largest firms, jumped to 49 percent in 1983. The market share held by the largest eight millers increased from 45 in 1965 to 69 percent in 1983 (*Milling and Baking News* 1982).

Corn. The marketing channels for corn are similar to those for wheat. An important difference is the large proportion of corn used for feed (59 percent of production in 1982–1983). Exports have gradually increased over time (figure 3–12) and accounted for nearly one-third of total production in 1979–1980. In 1982–1983, this dropped to less than one-fourth of total production. Domestic use of corn for food and industrial products has more than doubled since 1971–1972 but still utilizes only about 11 percent of total corn produced. About

Bil. bu.

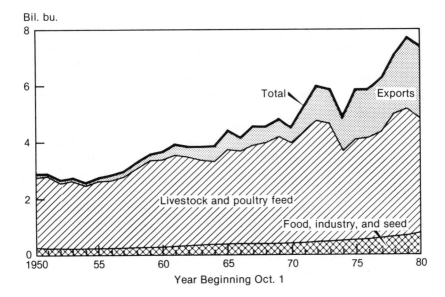

Source: USDA 1985c.

Figure 3–12. Major Uses of Corn, 1950–1980

880 million bushels of corn were domestically processed for food and industry uses in 1982–1983, roughly 30 percent greater than wheat (USDA 1985c).

Most of the corn moving into food and industrial uses is processed by either the wet corn processing industry or the dry corn milling industry. A large proportion of the primary products of these industries (meal, grits, flour, and starch) is further processed into breakfast foods, snack foods, corn sweetener products, ethyl alcohol, pet foods, and other products. The growth that has occurred since 1971–1972 reflects to a large extent the expanding markets for corn sweetener products, especially high-fructose corn syrup (HFCS). Large commercial users such as soft drink manufacturers have increasingly substituted HFCS for sugar in satisfying their sweetener needs. Dry corn milling used about 30 percent as much corn as wet corn milling in 1982 and had about one-fifth the value of shipments.

The wet corn milling industry (corn sweetener industry) is highly concentrated, with only eleven firms listed in a 1982 industry directory (*Milling and Baking News* 1982). These companies operated nineteen plants, most of them located in the corn belt. Census data indicate that the top four and top eight companies accounted for 61 and 86 percent, respectively, of the industry shipments in 1977. Four- and eight-firm concentration figures for dry corn milling were 62 and 85 percent, respectively, in 1977 (Bureau of Census 1977d).

Soybeans. Soybeans fall between corn and wheat regarding the importance of exports and the proportion of production used for feed. Soybeans account for about 85 percent of total U.S. oilseed production. During the five crop years 1978–1979 to 1982–1983, 52 percent of soybean production was crushed; 41 percent was exported as whole beans (USDA 1985d). Approximately one-fourth of the soybeans crushed domestically were exported as meal or oil, resulting in over 50 percent of soybean production being exported in one form or another. During those five crop years, about 45 percent of the world exports of soybeans were as meal and oil. The United States accounted for only about one-third and one-fourth of world meal and oil exports, respectively, whereas it provided over 80 percent of the whole beans exported (table 3–1).

In 1982–1983, approximately, 1,100 million bushels of soybeans were crushed domestically, yielding 53 billion pounds of soybean meal, flour, grits, and by-products and 12.0 billion pounds of crude soybean oil. The majority of soybean oil (65 to 80 percent) was used to manufacture shortening, cooking oil, salad oil, and margarine (USDA 1985d).

As the soybean processing industry has expanded, large, efficient plants have been constructed; smaller, obsolete plants have been closed. The four largest soybean crushers in 1977 accounted for 50 percent of the shipments of U.S. soybean mills (Bureau of Census 1977d). Two of the four largest soybean processing companies also rank among the top four firms in flour milling and corn milling.

Agricultural cooperatives are particularly important in these subsectors at the first handler level. In 1983, about 2,300 cooperatives marketed 38 percent of the U.S. grain and soybeans (excluding rice), up from 29 percent ten years earlier (Wissman 1985). Cooperatives have also increased their involvement beyond the first handler level through ownership of rail cars and barges, as well as subterminal, terminal, and port elevators. Several cooperatives have integrated into processing, particularly of oilseeds. In 1977, eight of the largest 100 marketing cooperatives operated soybean oil mills and accounted for about 16 percent of industry shipments (Combs and Marion 1984).

With the rapid growth in grain exports, cooperatives have attempted to penetrate export markets by setting up export departments (such as Far-Mar-Co, Union Equity, Agri-Industries, Indiana Farm Bureau) and interregional cooperatives such as Farmers Export and by joint ventures such as Intrade/Toepfer. These efforts have met with mixed success.

Coordination of Grain Subsectors

The corn, wheat, and soybean subsectors are essentially market coordinated but with considerable influence from government programs. During the 1950s, the prices of wheat and corn were supported at 75 to 90 percent of parity. Price-support levels generally exceeded market clearing prices, resulting in a buildup of government-purchased grain in CCC storage in spite of programs that paid farmers to take land out of production (figure 3–13). During the 1960s, the wheat and feed grain programs required producers to divert a specified percentage of their acreage to conservation uses in order to be eligible for price supports. In spite of these various land diversion programs, government stocks of surplus corn and wheat continued to be a problem until the early 1970s, when worldwide grain shortages dissipated the U.S. surplus.

The Agricultural Act of 1973 substituted costs of production for parity as a basis for price supports. This program used CCC "loan prices" to provide a floor for market prices and somewhat higher "target prices" to establish the prices participating producers would receive. Direct payments were made to producers when market prices fell below target prices. This program was designed to allow crops to move freely in international trade while providing

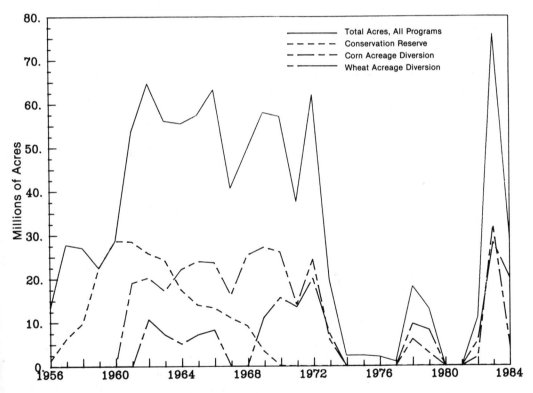

Source: USDA 1984e.

Figure 3–13. Cropland Acreage Withheld from Production under Various Government Programs, 1956–1984

participating producers some price and income protection. The production response of U.S. producers once again resulted in a buildup of surplus grain. Corn and wheat in storage reached 2,286 million and 1,164 million bushels, respectively, in 1982. Much of this surplus was stored in on-farm storage as a result of the Farmer-Owned Reserve (FOR) program initiated in 1977. In 1983, the USDA introduced the PIK program. Heavy participation in this program resulted in corn acreage dropping from 73 million in 1982 to 52 million in 1983; wheat acreage dropped from 79 to 61 million (figure 3–10).

Government programs have had a substantial effect on acreage planted, price levels, stocks in storage, and international trade. It has proved extremely difficult for government programs to regulate supplies so that market clearing prices are at desired levels. Although these programs have increased the stability of grain prices from year to year, they also have been plagued by almost continual problems of grain surpluses.

Coordination within a marketing year in these subsectors is largely achieved by market prices and an extensive network of public and private information. Administrative coordination via vertical integration occurs to some extent as some U.S. and foreign grain processors and grain exporting companies also own country and/or terminal elevators. Even in these cases, however, market prices ultimately determine how much grain is purchased at various times and locations, how much is stored, how much is exported or domestically processed, and so forth.

The interaction of the forces of supply and demand establishes the overall price level at central markets. All points in the market channel are tied together by prices and the cost of transformation across the dimensions of time, form, and space. The storability of grain and oilseeds and the ready availability of market information make these markets quite broad in scope. Large aberrations in spatial price alignment cannot endure for long periods of time because of easy arbitrage. Few problems of market access are encountered by producers except, perhaps, at the far reaches of the major producing areas.

Coordination of these subsectors is facilitated by actively traded contracts on the futures exchanges. These contracts indicate expected future prices and are important means for transferring risks. Risk management is one of the key ingredients to survival in the grain subsectors. In addition to their role in risk transfer and temporal coordination, futures contracts also facilitate contracting in the cash market and allow arbitrage without possessing the physical commodities. Thus, futures trading has a strong and pervasive influence on pricing and coordination of these subsectors.

The present system of grades and standards has serious limitations; the most important is the lack of correspondence between official grades and quality factors of economic importance. In part because official grades and standards do not allow some buyers to obtain the quality of grain desired, various types of contracts and vertical integration have developed. Dry corn millers are especially sensitive to quality differences and use market specification contracts to supplement open markets. Some foreign buyers use production contracts to gain additional quality control. In addition, several Japanese firms have acquired country elevators both as a means of controlling the quality of grain exported and to reduce the risk of market interruptions through government action.

Although contracts and vertical integration exist, most transactions within these subsectors are either spot transactions or forward sale contracts in which the price is pegged to a futures market contract. Thus, most contracts involve relatively little transfer of decision control.

In the exchange between farmers and first handlers, pricing and physical delivery are often separated. As a result, there is an increased demand by farmers for a variety of pricing arrangements. Four basic methods of pricing are used in these subsectors:

1. Cash sales: Price is established at time grain is delivered.

2. Forward price contract: A fixed price is agreed upon for grain to be delivered in future.

3. Delayed price contract: Price is established at a time selected by the seller after the grain is physically delivered.

4. Basis contract: Similar to forward price contract except price is established relative to the basis at a future date.

These pricing and exchange methods, used throughout the grain and oilseed subsectors, provide considerable flexibility in the type and magnitude of risk to which buyers and sellers are exposed. Nearly all of these methods are used in combination with futures markets transactions executed by either the seller or buyer.

Subsector Performance

The corn, wheat, and soybean subsectors have been progressive in adopting cost-reducing, output-increasing, and labor-saving technology. Comparative studies of grain subsectors in different countries have concluded that the U.S. subsectors rank high for progressiveness and operational efficiency, particularly at the farm level.

In general, the pricing systems in the corn, wheat, and soybeans subsectors are efficient in accurately reflecting time, form, and space utility for these commodities once they have been produced. Futures markets have proved to be a relatively low-cost, easily accessible, and highly responsive system for pricing time utility. Studies of pricing patterns over space indicate that price differences generally reflect transportation costs but also reveal some cases where price differentials between elevators cannot be explained by cost differences. Three factors appear to distort spatial pricing patterns:

1. Producers often lack adequate information on which to base delivery decisions. Differences across elevators in measuring quality and determining prices and discounts make it difficult for farmers to compare prices and choose the best alternative.

2. Local gluts at harvesttime generally depress prices and provide elevators with an opportunity to increase margins temporarily. The increase in on-farm storage during the last decade should help to even the flow of grain to market and ease this problem.

3. High transportation rates and limited availability of transportation sometimes result in imperfect pricing patterns. The variability in rail and barge rates over time also results in long-run investments in elevator and processing facilities that may be uneconomic. There is a need for improved long-term coordination of production of grain, transportation capacity, and demand at processing plants and export terminals.

The ability of the pricing system to reflect form utility is hampered by outdated federal grades and standards. Proposed revisions to make grain standards more consistent with commercial priorities have met with limited success.

Corn, wheat, and soybean prices were relatively stable fom 1950 to 1972. Since 1972, prices of the major grains have been much more volatile, both within and across years. The subsector has generally been responsive in creating arrangements to redistribute or reduce risk. In addition to contracts on the futures market, cash grain contracts with forward or delayed pricing allow some shifting of risk.

Compared to countries like Canada, which operate with grain marketing boards, the market-coordinated system of the U.S. experiences much greater variation in price within a marketing year (from day to day, week to week, and month to month). In Canada all wheat producers are paid the same average base price for sales during any specific year. On a year-to-year basis, however, Canada's producers experience as much variation in average prices as do U.S. producers (Hill and Leath 1985).

Greater stability in both domestic and international markets is desired by many participants in these subsectors; however, most proposed solutions involve greater government involvement, isolation of the domestic from the international market, or other departures from a market system that currently are not widely accepted in the United States.

Although the pricing systems in these subsectors generally do an effective job of allocating supplies already produced, the mechanisms for coordinating supply and demand across market periods are often ineffective, resulting periodically in either surplus production or volatile prices. Government farm programs increased grain price stability during the 1950s and 1960s but were plagued with surplus production and large quantities purchased and stored by the CCC. Since 1973, government programs have resulted in less intervention in grain markets and more interaction between the U.S. and world markets. Prices have been much more volatile. Surplus corn and wheat supplies appear to be a persistent problem under most government programs but might be even worse with no government programs. Volatile corn and soybean prices are particularly troublesome for livestock and poultry producers, for whom feed costs are a major cost of production.

The corn, wheat, and soybean subsectors have generally been quick to respond to incentives to expand production but slow to reduce production. When worldwide grain shortages in 1972–1973 resulted in a sharp increase in U.S. exports, the grain subsectors responded quickly to increase production and transportation capabilities and reorient the U.S. marketing systems toward world markets. The more frequent problem has been the tendency of firms in these subsectors to overreact to annual price changes.

Although occasionally there are markets within these subsectors in which the forces of competition have been eliminated, most markets in these subsectors appear to be effectively competitive. Based on structural characteristics, the firms in these subsectors that have the greatest likelihood of enjoying some market power are the railroads, international grain trading companies, and some domestic processors. Unfortunately, too little is known about some of these markets to evaluate accurately the extent to which market power exists.

Potato Subsector

This subsector has changed dramatically over the last thirty-five years. In 1950, the subsector was almost entirely devoted to fresh potatoes, with the Northeast the dominant producing area. Contracts with growers were unusual. By 1983, the Pacific Northwest states produced nearly half of total production. Processed potatoes, which tend to be coordinated by contractual arrangements, exceeded fresh potatoes in tonnage.

Changes in utilization of potatoes have been dramatic. Processed potatoes (chips, dehydrated, frozen) comprised less than 6 percent of total supplies in 1950; by 1983 they accounted for 50 percent of total production and 60 percent of the potatoes used for food. Processed potatoes increased from 43.1 million cwt in 1956 to 166.7 million cwt in 1983 (USDA 1984d). Frozen potato products accounted for 55 percent of the potatoes processed in 1983 and have accounted for two-thirds of the growth in processed potatoes. Potatoes for fresh consumption declined from 155.4 million cwt in 1956 to

109.0 million cwt in 1983. On average, about 18 percent of total production each year is utilized for nonfood purposes (seed, shrinkage and loss, and livestock feed) (USDA 1984d).

Excluding potato starch and flour that go primarily for manufacturing, per capita consumption of processed potatoes increased from 6.3 pounds in 1950 to 66.9 pounds fresh-weight equivalent in 1983. Fresh potato consumption declined from 100 pounds per capita to 54.1 pounds during this same time period (figure 3–14). Per capita consumption of all potatoes has remained nearly constant since 1968. The share represented by processed potatoes has been relatively stable since 1973.

Subsector Organization

Irish potatoes are commercially produced in most states and over four seasons. Most potatoes, however, are harvested in the fall and marketed during the winter and spring. During 1982–1984, for example, 87 percent of

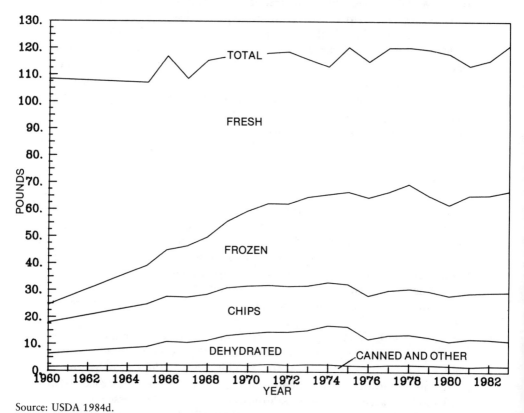

Source: USDA 1984d.

Figure 3–14. U.S. per Capita Potato Consumption, 1960–1983

total production was from the fall crop. The winter crop represents approximately 1 percent of production, and the remaining 12 percent is distributed nearly equally between the spring and summer crops (USDA 1984d).

The fall crop is produced mainly in a band of states from the Northeast through the North Central to the Northwest. Idaho, followed by Washington, are by far the largest producers of all potatoes. Maine, Oregon, Wisconsin, and North Dakota are next in importance and were nearly equal in production during 1982–1984. The total fall crop has increased dramatically, with most of the expansion occurring in the Northwest.

The potato subsector can be visualized as four parallel channels depending on the utilization of the product (figure 3–15). The channels for frozen potatoes and potato chips are the most distinct. Potato freezers use largely russet potatoes and generally are not involved in the other three potato channels. Freezers contract with growers for a significant portion of their supply and obtain the balance in the open market. The percentage contracted is somewhat lower in the Pacific Northwest but is still around 50 percent of freezer needs. At harvest time, freezers take title to potatoes grown under contract and store them until processed.

The channel for chipping potatoes uses round white varieties of potatoes. Because chippers make potato chips daily to maintain freshness, they require a continual flow of potatoes. The large chipping companies contract directly with growers to supply their needs. The smaller chippers often use potato chip stock brokers to obtain supplies. Chippers generally bypass wholesalers and deliver their products directly to retail stores and foodservice outlets.

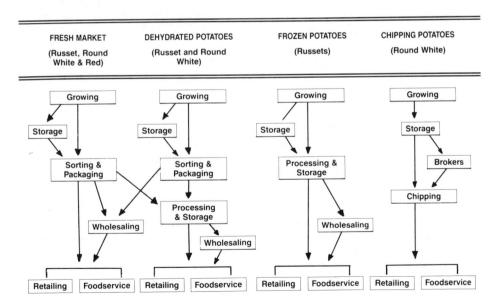

Figure 3–15. Channels Making Up the Potato Subsector

The dehydrated and fresh market channels tend to be interconnected. Several of the largest dehydrators, such as American Potato and French's, are also large packers of fresh potatoes. These firms generally contract for some of their supply. Contracted potatoes are sorted, with the best quality packed for fresh market and the residual being dehydrated. Dehydrators obtain a major portion of their remaining needed supply from the culls sorted out by fresh market packer-shippers. Since dehydrators can use a wide range of qualities, they provide a market for potatoes that at one time went into starch, flour, and cattle feed.

In the fresh market channel, many growers and packer-shippers special-ize in the fresh market. Some growers in the Midwest and Northeast have in-tegrated growing-storage-packing operations for the fresh market. Except for the potatoes purchased by dehydrators, there is little contract production in the fresh market channel.

Although a large percentage of potato chips and canned potatoes are sold through retail grocery stores, about 80 percent of frozen potatoes are sold to foodservice outlets (Judge 1983). Fast food establishments are estimated to account for 60 percent of the frozen potatoes sold through foodservice outlets. The foodservice market is also the major outlet for dehydrated po-tatoes. This is particularly true for mashed potato products. Dried sliced potato products (such as hash browns and au gratin) are marketed more through retail stores. Foodservice outlets account for only 25 percent of potato chip sales.

Potato production has become more concentrated geographically. Whereas the Pacific Northwest (Idaho, Washington, and Oregon) accounted for 18 percent of U.S. production in 1950, by 1982–1984 this had increased to 47 percent (USDA 1984d). The Northeast dropped from 29 percent to 12 percent of U.S. production during the same period. During 1982–1984, the top six potato-producing states accounted for 65 percent of U.S. production.

Average yields in the Pacific Northwest have increased sharply, in part because of increased irrigation and improved varieties. Yields increased from 197 cwt per acre in 1950 to 350 cwt during 1982–1984. This compares to the modest increase from 212 to 243 cwt per acre in the Northeast during the same period. U.S. total production increased from 259 million cwt in 1950 to 349 million cwt, on average, during 1982–1984 (USDA 1984d). Total acres planted to potatoes have gradually declined.

As indicated by figure 3–15, different types of potatoes have different uses. Russet and round whites, the two major types, are used both for fresh market and dehydrated products. Frozen products use russets almost ex-clusively, and potato chip companies use only round whites. Since the varieties grown in different regions vary, this influences the marketing chan-nels that are important for different regions. The regional differences are as follows:

Region	Major Varieties	Major Food Uses
Pacific Northwest	Russet Burbank > 90 percent	Frozen: about 50 percent Remainder: fresh markets, dehydrated
Northeast	Round whites ≅ 80 percent Russets ≅ 20 percent	Fresh market: over two-thirds Remainder: dehydrated, chipping, frozen
Red River Valley (North Dakota and Minnesota)	Round whites ≅ 70 percent Reds ≅ 18 percent Russets ≅ 12 percent	Chipping: about 45 percent Fresh market: about 30 percent Remainder: frozen, dehydrated
Wisconsin	Russet Burbanks ≅ 65 percent Round whites ≅ 35 percent	Fresh markets: about 60 percent Remainder: frozen, dehydrated, chipping

The Pacific Northwest accounted for approximately 80 percent of all frozen potatoes packed during 1980–1982 (Judge 1983). Nearly half of the potatoes marketed for food from this region are sold as frozen potatoes. This compares to 15 percent for the remainder of the country.

Structure of Industries at Various Stages in Subsector

Potato-producing farms have dropped sharply in numbers and increased in size and specialization. Only 30,000 farms produced potatoes in 1978. As the tonnage of processed potatoes has increased, storage has tended to shift off the farm. Processors now provide much of the storage for potatoes used for processing. Most of the storage of fresh market potatoes is still done by growers. Grower packing of fresh market potatoes has declined, particularly in the Pacific Northwest where specialized packers are important.

The structure of the processing stage varies for the three main processing channels. In general, different firms operate in the three channels. The two major processors of frozen potatoes are Ore-Ida (H.J. Heinz Co.) and J.R. Simplot, a private company. Heinz acquired Ore-Ida in 1965. According to Heinz's 1984 annual report, Ore-Ida holds about 50 percent of the retail frozen potato market. Since control brands (private labels) have about 30 percent of this market, other national brands have small market shares. Whereas Ore-Ida concentrates on the retail market, Simplot sells most of its potatoes to foodservice outlets. Although Simplot is reputedly the largest supplier of frozen potatoes for the foodservice market, several other large freezers serve this market. The number of plants processing frozen potatoes increased from about thirty in 1960 to ninety-one in 1964 but then declined to thirty-three in 1980 (USDA 1984d).

Advertising is primarily used to differentiate brands of frozen potatoes sold through retail stores. During 1981–1983, Ore-Ida spent $25.3 million in the six media covered by Leading National Advertisers (1983). This was roughly 98 percent of the advertising of frozen potatoes.

The American Potato Co., a subsidiary of Basic American Foods, is the leading dehydrator. Although American sells most of its output to the foodservice market, it is also the primary supplier to General Mills. French's (Reckitt and Coleman Co.), Carnation, Pillsbury, and Idahoan are other important dehydrators. Dehydrating potato plants increased from twenty-one in 1960 to twenty-eight in 1964 and then declined to nineteen by 1980 (USDA 1984d).

Although General Mills operates no potato dehydrating plants, its 1983 annual report states that the company "continued as the leader in the $195 million (retail) dehydrated potato market." General Mills accounted for 95 percent of the advertising of dehydrated potato products during the three years 1981–1983 (Leading National Advertisers 1983). Although French's, Carnation, and Pillsbury have national brands of dried potatoes, Betty Crocker is clearly the dominant national brand. Private label and generic products hold about 20 percent of the market (Nielsen Co. 1980). Instant mashed potato products accounted for about 30 percent of the retail dried potato market in 1982 (*Chain Store Age* 1983). Scalloped, au gratin, hash brown, and other dried potato products made up the balance.

The manufacture of potato chips is more fragmented than either the frozen or dehydrated potato markets. Potato chip plants are generally located near consumption areas, whereas frozen and dehydrated potato plants are located in producing areas. In 1982, there were 168 potato chip plants, which processed 40 million cwt of potatoes. A decade earlier, 261 plants processed 34 million cwt of potatoes (USDA 1984d). Although potato chips use only 45 percent as many cwt of potatoes as frozen potatoes, the total sales value of chips is estimated to exceed slightly that of frozen potatoes.

Frito-Lay (PepsiCo) is the leading manufacturer of snack foods in the U.S. (PepsiCo Annual Report 1983) and estimated to be the clear leader in potato chips; however, a large number of regional companies also have strong market positions in certain areas. For example, Wise Potato Chips (owned by Borden) is probably the market leader in the Northeast; Buckeye Potato Chips (also owned by Borden) is thought to be the leader in Ohio. The market share held by the four largest chip processors increased sharply from 36 percent of the U.S. market in 1959 to 60 percent in 1982 (Jones and Zepp 1985).

Retail sales of potato chips through supermarkets in 1982 was estimated at $1.2 billion (*Chain Store Age* 1983). This compares to $331 million for frozen potatoes (only 20 percent of frozen potatoes are sold through retail stores). In part because advertising has more influence on retail sales than on foodservice sales, potato chips receive about three times the advertising of frozen potatoes. Two companies accounted for 89 percent of the media advertising during 1981–1983: Frito-Lay (55 percent) and P&G-Pringles (34 percent) (Leading National Advertisers 1983). However, there were twenty-five companies in each year that spent $10,000 or more advertising potato chips. Some of the regional potato chip companies are important competitive factors in certain areas and are also potential entrants into markets adjacent to the areas they serve. The market share held by private label potato chips is estimated to be small.

To what extent are fresh potatoes, frozen potatoes, dehydrated potatoes, and potato chips direct competitors? Are they in the same relevant economic market? For certain foodservice establishments, these products may be close substitutes. Baked potatoes, french fries, mashed potatoes, or potato chips can be served in school cafeterias, hospitals, and similar outlets. For other foodservice firms, such as fast food outlets, this is not the case.

For potatoes sold through retail stores, the question is the extent to which consumers perceive the four forms of potatoes as close substitutes. Jones (1984), using time-series data, found that fresh potato consumption was relatively sensitive to the price of processed potatoes. When the latter increased 1 percent in price, fresh potato consumption increased 0.34 percent. Cox (1984) examined the demand characteristics for fresh, frozen, and dehydrated potatoes and came up with somewhat different results in a cross-sectional analysis of household food consumption data for western households. Fresh and frozen potato consumption was not significantly affected by the prices of other potato products; however, the consumption of dehydrated potatoes was significantly affected by the price of fresh potatoes but not by the price of frozen potatoes. At this point, the results are somewhat inconclusive on the extent to which consumers consider these products as close substitutes.

Subsector Coordination

Coordination of the potato subsector has important spatial, temporal, and product-type dimensions. Coordination in the fresh market channel is largely provided by spot prices. Marketing orders to regulate the grades and standards of potatoes marketed to the fresh market exist for the major producing regions. In most cases, however, the grades and standards demanded by distributors and hence reflected in commercial transactions exceed those called for in the marketing orders. Thus, orders appear to have little effect on coordination.

Contracts are actively used in the processed potato channels, although this varies some by region and by type of processing. Whereas in Wisconsin, a major portion of the processed potatoes are grown under contract with a processor, in the Pacific Northwest, as much as half of the processed potatoes are purchased in the open market. Grower contracts are generally for all the production from a specified number of acres. A base price is usually specified with premiums and discounts for variations in quality. Processors usually specify variety and certain agronomic practices (such as irrigation or crop rotation) but provide few inputs to growers. To obtain potatoes with desirable processing characteristics, processors often provide technical assistance to producers as part of the contractual arrangement. The preference of processors to contract with large growers has probably accelerated the trend toward fewer but larger potato growers.

The decreasing number of potato processors has resulted in fewer alternative buyers for some growers. It some areas, the inequality in bargaining positions led growers to form bargaining associations to negotiate contracts with processors. Producers' cooperatives are primarily involved in bargaining; cooperative processing plants account for a minor share of the market.

Although grocery retailers rarely contract for their supplies of either fresh or processed potatoes, contracting by large fast food chains for frozen french fries is common. These contracts, negotiated annually in November, specify the quantity to be supplied and have well-defined quality specifications (variety, color, dry matter content, and so forth). Since these contracts are negotiated after fall harvest, they do not provide a means for freezers to hedge the price risk exposure from grower contracts. The futures contract for Maine round white potatoes on the New York Mercantile Exchange is apparently of limited value for risk management by producers or processors of russet potatoes.

Generic advertising, which has emphasized the nutritional characteristics of potatoes, has had some influence on subsector coordination. Fresh potato sales have increased substantially in selected retail markets featuring generic potato promotion (Jones 1984); however, the overall effect of generic advertising is difficult to assess because expenditures are small relative to brand name advertising of potato products.

Subsector Performance

The subsector has been responsive in adjusting to shifts in consumer demand from fresh to processed products. This rapid shift was facilitated by industry efforts to improve the taste and nutrition of processed potatoes. For example, innovative steam peeling methods were adopted to reduce greatly the loss of nutrients. Potato processors have also been relatively innovative in developing new processed potato products. A greater variety of processed products is available to consumers and foodservice firms, which has likely increased consumption. In addition, Talburt and Smith (1975) contend that processed potatoes compare favorably with fresh potatoes in terms of nutrients and costs.

Increases in the consumption of frozen potatoes have served to expand greatly the growth rate of processed potatoes relative to that of the seven major processed vegetables (asparagus, cabbage, cucumbers, snap beans, spinach, sweet corn, and tomatoes). Leading the growth of frozen potatoes are frozen french fries, which in 1980 constituted 30 percent of all frozen retail vegetables and 65 percent of all institutional vegetables (Jones 1984).

The increased use of contracts has redistributed risk and control in the subsector. Contract growers of processed potatoes usually are assured of a market and a certain price when they plant potatoes, although they retain the risks associated with production. Some potato growers argue that large processors have an unfair advantage in the procurement of raw potatoes because of their bargaining strength relative to growers. Growers feel that processors have adversely influenced prices at the farm level. There are also complaints of processors' rejecting shipments of potatoes, ostensibly because of poor quality but in fact because of overcommitments by processors (Halloran 1983).

The use of contracts throughout the subsector has probably improved coordination and operational efficiency, on balance, although some coordination problems persist. Production and processing costs have been reduced, quality has shifted in response to demands, and the overall synchronization of the various stages has probably improved. Grower contracts may have resulted in greater price volatility for those potatoes sold on the open market. Since potatoes grown under contracts are committed to particular processors at a predetermined price, shifts in total supply and demand must be absorbed by open market transactions. As the proportion of total production traded on open markets declines, the same variation in total production may lead to greater price swings. Fresh market potato prices tend to be extremely volatile, both within and across crop years.

Ward (1982) found the wholesale market to be the focal point for establishing the value of fresh potatoes. Wholesale price decreases were consistently reflected in terms of lower shipping point prices, whereas wholesale price increases were not proportionally reflected in higher shipping point prices. Between the retail and wholesale levels, wholesale price decreases were passed through to retail to a greater extent than were wholesale price increases.

Each of the three processed potato channels tends to be dominated by a few large firms. Some degree of market power is most likely for companies whose advertised brands have large market shares in the retail market (Ore-Ida for frozen potatoes, General Mills for dehydrated potatoes, and Frito-Lay for potato chips). Frozen and dehydrated products sold to the foodservice market tend to be unbranded. Rigid quality specifications are common for frozen potatoes sold to large fast food firms. These characteristics suggest less pricing discretion may be possible in potatoes sold in the foodservice market. There is also excess capacity in potato freezing and dehydrating. Economic theory indicates that this is likely to result in more aggressive competitive behavior and make oligopolistic coordination more difficult than when capacity is fully utilized.

The potato-processing industries have actively sought means of expanding the total demand for potatoes. Although new products have been the primary avenue used, some companies are also seeking to expand exports to Europe and the Far East.

The Citrus Subsector

Although a variety of specialty fruits fall within the citrus classification, the current discussion is limited to oranges and grapefruit, which accounted for 87 percent of all U.S. citrus production in 1983–1984. Most of the institutions and related coordinating mechanisms found within these two commodity systems also facilitate the flow to market of specialty fruits.

U.S. citrus production is concentrated in Florida, California, Arizona, and Texas. Florida accounts for about 75 percent of the U.S. orange and grapefruit production (figure 3–16). California is the second largest domestic producer of oranges (21 percent of U.S. total), and Texas is the second largest domestic supplier of grapefruit (16 percent of U.S. total). In each region, supplies vary over time with changes in bearing acreage and weather conditions.

Total U.S. citrus production more than doubled from the early 1960s to the late 1970s and then tailed off in the early 1980s (figure 3–16). Total U.S. orange-bearing acreage increased to around 887,000 acres in 1970–1971 and then gradually declined to 744,700 acres by 1983–1984. Grapefruit acreage consistently increased from 137,000 acres in the early 1960s to 192,000 by 1983–1984. The sharp declines in orange and grapefruit production since 1980 have been primarily due to an unusual series of Florida freezes.

In 1970 the United States accounted for 26 percent of world production; by 1980–1981 this share had increased to 32 percent. Because of subsequent freezes, this share decreased to 25 percent by 1983–1984. Much of the citrus from the rest of the world does not compete in the same markets with the United States. Brazil, the major competitor of the United States in processed citrus, increased its production from 38.2 million boxes (90 pound boxes) in 1966 (7.5 percent of world production) to over 249 million boxes in 1983–1984 (30 percent of world production). This phenomenal growth plus the strong U.S. dollar in the 1980s led to sharp increases in imports of frozen concentrated orange juice from Brazil.

U.S. citrus is harvested from late November through July depending on crop conditions and production region. Once harvested, the fruit flows through either fresh packinghouses and related fresh outlets or to processing plants. During the six crop years 1978–1984, around 77 percent of all U.S. oranges were processed. In contrast, about 44 percent of the grapefruit supplies were marketed as fresh fruit during this period (figure 3–17).

There are major regional differences in citrus utilization: 94 percent of the Florida orange crop is processed into juice and related products, whereas California markets 66 percent of its oranges as fresh fruit. In total California supplies around 75 percent of the domestically produced fresh oranges, while Florida accounts for approximately 88 percent of the domestically produced processed oranges (Florida Crop and Livestock Reporting Service 1985). As these figures suggest, international trade in processed citrus products has a particularly strong effect on the Florida citrus industry.

Processed oranges are utilized in the production of three major citrus juices: frozen concentrated orange juice (FCOJ), canned single-strength juice (CSSOJ), and chilled orange juice (COJ). During the 1983–1984 season, 83 percent of Florida's oranges were used to produce FCOJ, 15 percent for COJ, and 2 percent for canned juice products (Florida Citrus Mutual 1985). Roughly half of the grapefruit processed in Florida is utilized for juice; the remainder is used for canned fruit.

Chilled and canned orange juices are sold in retail or institutional packs that are ready to serve, whereas frozen concentrate must be reconstituted before consuming. Concentrate in retail packs (42 degree brix) is readily reconstituted with water. Concentrate initially processed into bulk (58–65 degree brix) is a high-solids juice that must be commercially reconstituted before being consumed. Processors usually store their juice stocks in bulk form and then reprocess the bulk stocks into retail or institutional pack concentrate (42 degree brix) or single-strength juices (11 degree brix).

U.S. consumption of citrus products has changed along with general adjustments in life-styles. Per capita consumption of fresh oranges and grapefruit has remained reasonably stable, with a slight decrease in the late 1970s. Consumption of frozen citrus juices increased from under 20 pounds (single strength juice) per capita in the late 1960s to over 37 pounds per capita in 1983. Chilled juice per capita consumption increased to 5.8 pounds by 1980 but declined somewhat in the 1980s because of the substantial price increases following Florida freezes (Florida Citrus Mutual 1985). Recent demand estimates for FCOJ, COJ, and CSSOJ indicate that COJ has a lower price elasticity of demand and a much higher income elasticity than for either FCOJ or CSSOJ. These estimates also indicate that FCOJ and COJ are only weak substitutes. As incomes increase, consumers are willing to pay for the convenience of having a ready-to-serve product such as COJ. The increasing demand for chilled juices supports the trend toward reconstitution of bulk concentrate at locations nearer consuming centers.

The major uncertainty in the citrus subsector stems from the effects of a freeze or related weather conditions on total production. Prior to the growth

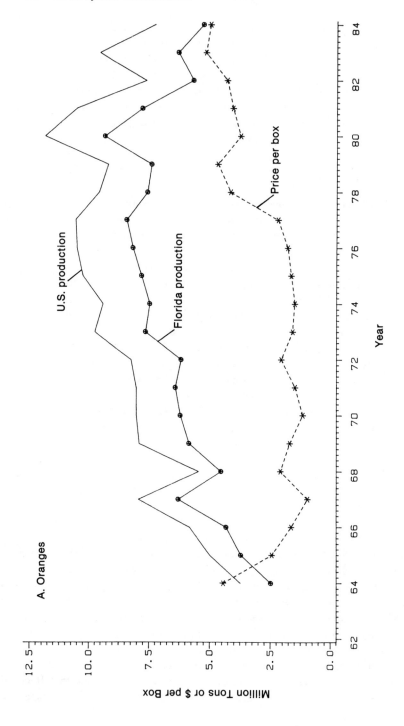

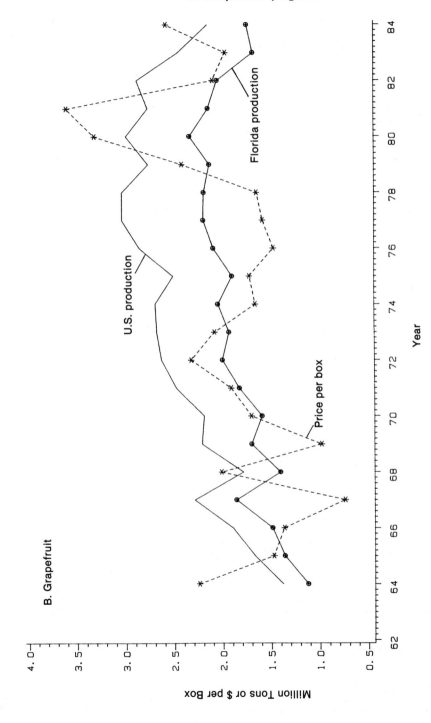

Source: Florida Crop and Livestock Reporting Service 1985.

Figure 3–16. Orange and Grapefruit Production for the United States and Florida and On-Tree Prices

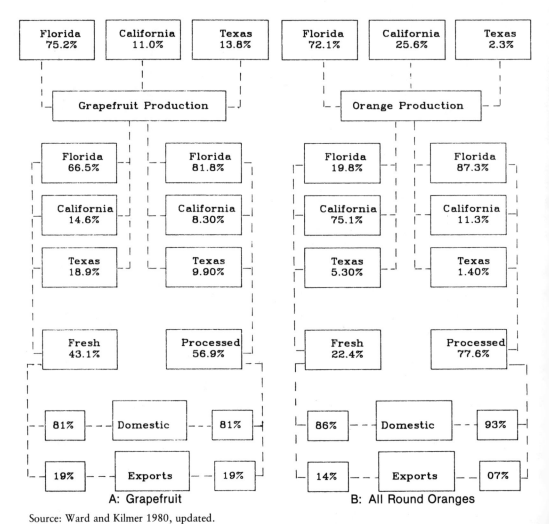

Source: Ward and Kilmer 1980, updated.

Figure 3–17. Product Flow, Utilization, and Regional Shares for All Grapefruit and All Round Oranges, 1978–1979 through 1983–1984

in imports, prices would rise in direct response to the severity of the freeze, and total industry revenues would usually increase. However, the growth in imports has dampened the price response to changes in domestic supplies. Furthermore, prices have become more volatile throughout the seasons as more economic forces enter the price-making process.

Subsector Organization

Fresh Citrus. The system for packaging and distributing fresh citrus differs considerably among the regions. Within California one dominant producer cooperative, Sunkist Growers, accounts for nearly 70 percent of all supplies. Most of the marketing leadership and industry policies for both fresh and processed citrus in California emanate from this one cooperative. In contrast, Florida's fresh packing industry is made up of private and cooperative packinghouses. No packinghouse has a dominant position. Competition among Texas packinghouses is even more fragmented.

In all three regions fruit is shipped directly from the packinghouses to wholesale and retail markets with minimal delays. This linkage is accomplished through brokers, packinghouse selling staff, and some consolidated cooperative selling agencies. Selling prices are determined at the time of sale, and there are few if any forward prices between citrus handlers and wholesale buyers. However, the industry often provides a "buy-in" policy where the buyer is assured that for a given period of time (say three weeks) he or she can buy in at the lower price if prices drop.

The subsector has a number of state and federal marketing orders that are used to influence quality standards and product allocations. Florida's citrus federal marketing orders apply only to the 7 percent of Florida's oranges that are sold fresh and around 46 percent of Florida's grapefruit sold fresh. Their use is generally limited to setting standards and providing some limited controls on product flow. In contrast, the majority of California's citrus is sold fresh and is affected by the marketing orders for that region. California's citrus market orders have been the source of considerable controversey in recent years, primarily as a result of concerns over the potential for achieving unreasonable profits to producers and unreasonable enhancement of prices to consumers. The Federal Trade Commission and the Justice Department have charged that citrus marketing orders potentially elevate prices relative to prices for similar nonorder commodities. Because the California citrus order exists where one cooperative has a substantial share of the market, it has been particularly subject to scrutiny.

Processed Citrus. In California the relatively small amount of processed product is largely controlled by Sunkist. The Florida processing industry can be characterized as a loose oligopoly. The combined market shares of the top five Florida processors remain around 50 percent, with the largest having 10 to 12 percent, depending on the season. Price leadership and storage policies are exercised by one or more of the top processors. In most situations, the remaining processors follow the adjustments made by one or more of the top five firms.

The larger processors include proprietary and cooperative organizations. Many of the proprietary processors are subsidiaries of large food manufacturing corporations. The recent increase in mergers has increased the market shares of these processors. Most large processors have integrated backward into citrus production to supply some of their needs (tapered integration). Many also have their own container manufacturing facilities. Approximately 45 percent of the processed citrus is sold under processor brand, and the remainder is sold as private labels or institutional packs.

Historically most institutional and retail packaging of citrus juices was completed in Florida. With the growth in capabilities to transport large volumes of bulk concentrate from Florida or Brazil, a larger share of the ready-to-consume juices is being reprocessed and packaged nearer consumption areas. This has changed the oligopolistic power of the larger Florida processors. Although the volume reprocessed in consumption areas is still relatively small, this trend will be of increasing importance to the subsector.

Superimposed on the Florida fresh and processing industry is a state marketing order that allows the industry to exercise some self-regulation and to support a strong generic advertising program for Florida's products. The maintenance of high-quality products and substantial investments in generic promotions have been important contributors to the long-range growth in demand for citrus products.

This subsector is somewhat unique in having a major generic advertising program plus substantial advertising by brand manufacturers, among them Minute Maid and Tropicana. The leading advertised brands have differentiated their product sufficiently to enjoy a significant price premium over private label products.

Subsector Coordination

The linkages between growers and processors or packers are of three general forms. In California, most product is committed to Sunkist Growers, the dominant cooperative. In Florida, approximately 20 percent of the fruit is sold in the spot market directly to packers or processors. Price is determined at the time of delivery. The remaining supplies are committed either to cooperatives or proprietary firms with participation plans. In both Florida and California, the final price to be paid to a large share of producers is not determined until after the product is sold by the packers or processors. Fruit enters a pooled supply accumulated over a designated period of time. Once these pooled supplies are processed or sold fresh, the returns from the sales are used to determine payments to producers. All producers in the pool (cooperative or participation plan) receive the same average price. Under this arrangement the producer bears nearly all price risks but is assured of an outlet for the fruit. In principle, there is little difference in the payment arrangements of cooperative and participation plans.

Processors or packers sell to foodservice or retail firms on a direct purchase basis established for short time periods. When formal contracts are made, they are generally only for a few weeks. Discount buying policies and price promotions are often part of the total marketing program of processors.

Prices are set by the leading processors in accordance with market conditions, seasonal movements, and inventory levels. Prices can be adjusted quickly when supplies are drastically changed, such as following a freeze.

While the price for most processed products is an administered price, the price of bulk concentrate is adjusted continuously with the market. The price for retail pack frozen concentrate is used as the index from which all other prices are generally derived.

Production and consumption information is well documented and widely disseminated. Processors and producer organizations, as well as government agencies, provide detailed statistics on the subsector. Data on the performance of the Florida processing industry are reliable and available in greater quantity than for other producing regions.

Federal government involvement in the citrus subsector has been minimal relative to many other subsectors. There are no direct price-support programs for citrus. Federal grades and standards affect the overall coordination effort and, hence, indirectly affect prices. Federal marketing orders provide the subsector with a mechanism for internally regulating quality and, to a limited extent, quantity. Probably the most direct influence of the federal government is the establishment of import tariffs and special import adjustment taxes. Imported frozen concentrate is taxed at a minimum of 34 cents per pound of solids, with an additional 3 cents equalization tax. Without this tariff, imports would be substantially larger, and probably more reprocessing would occur. Processors that import concentrate may regain the tariffs paid if within a three-year period they export an equivalent volume of juice.

The federal government is also involved in joint advertising efforts with the citrus industry and foreign importers to develop international markets for U.S. citrus products. A three-party program provides a formula for sharing in the cost of promoting citrus products in Europe and, to some extent, in Japan.

Subsector Performance

Over time the citrus industry at the producer and processor levels has been very profitable; however, the subsector faces continued cost increases and often must deal with excess plant capacity, partly because of the seasonal nature of production. Prices have increased over time, and there appears to be reasonable equity of return among producers. Data on relative returns to producers and processors are incomplete.

The subsector has been progressive and innovative in new product development and in the promotion of its products. The subsector has been particularly innovative in expanding its foreign markets for fresh grapefruit, especially to Japan. In general, the subsector at the producer and first handler levels is self-regulating, with minimal external controls.

In addition to marketing innovations, inventory management has been well coordinated and reasonably stable. Supplies of processed products accumulate through July when the harvest season ends. These inventory accumulations supply the various markets until the new crop year beginning in

December. There have been minimal changes in the seasonal patterns except during seasons of crop losses.

The most dramatic change affecting the subsector has been the growth of world citrus production. Imports of Brazilian juice into the United States increased over tenfold in the last two decades; in 1984 approximately 33 percent of U.S. supplies of frozen concentrate were from imports. This growth has changed the market power of processors, affected prices, and caused significant structural shifts in reprocessing. Year-to-year coordination of supply and demand continues to be a problem, particularly because of weather variability and the factors affecting exports and imports.

Tart Cherry Subsector

Tart cherries are highly perishable and as a result are almost entirely frozen or canned. Most cherries are purchased by consumers as an ingredient in cherry pies and other manufactured desserts. Tart cherries are a minor crop commodity, and their production is relatively geographically concentrated. All of these characteristics influence the organization and coordination of the subsector.

Variable weather conditions, particularly early spring freeze damage, result in large fluctuations in annual production and market prices for tart cherries (figure 3–18). National tart cherry production in a short-crop year is frequently only about 50 percent of aggregate production is a large-crop year.

Cherry trees begin to bear small amounts about five years after planting and continue to produce for twenty to twenty-five years. The aggregate long-term production cycle for tart cherries has been about twenty to twenty-five years. Peak production occurred during 1961–1965, with substantial surplus productive capacity and very unprofitable price levels to growers (figure 3–18). This was followed by a long-term decline in bearing acreage and production during the late 1960s and 1970s.

Between 1976 and 1981 a number of short-crop, high-price years occurred. This was during a low point in the bearing acreage cycle and was also influenced by several weather-reduced crop years. During this period cherry prices were unusually high except in 1980. As a result, growers expanded orchard acreage considerably with new plantings of young trees; these are now coming into the early bearing stages. Therefore the subsector in the mid-1980s is beginning a decade of substantial production expansion. U.S. tart cherry production averaged 155 million pounds during the late 1970s. By the late 1980s, it is predicted, national productive capacity may reach 400 million pounds.

Unlike some other agricultural subsectors, tart cherries do not have government price supports or major tax-supported government programs. Producer group-action institutions have been used to reduce the instability of supplies, expand demand, and provide growers with a more active role in the

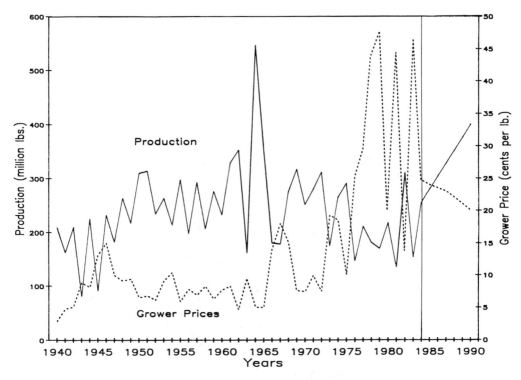

Source: USDA 1985i.

Figure 3–18. U.S. Tart Cherry Production and Grower Prices, 1940–1984

subsector. These institutions include cooperatives, a federal marketing order, cooperative-corporation joint ventures, and a farmer bargaining association.

Subsector Organization

The tart cherry subsector involves several stages in its organization. The vertical stages are growing, initial processing, food manufacturing, wholesaling and retailing (including foodservice) (figure 3–19).

Approximately 90 percent of U.S. tart cherry production comes from the Great Lakes states of Michigan, New York, and Wisconsin. In recent years Michigan alone accounted for 72 percent of the nation's production. Tart cherries are produced by 2,900 growers, nearly all of them owner-operators. Although cherry farms are getting fewer and larger, they are still moderate in size. For example, farms with 30 to 200 acres of cherries accounted for 59 percent of the tart cherry acreage in Michigan in 1982.

Initial processors freeze about 60 percent of the cherries produced. Approximately 30 percent is canned as pie fillings, and about 10 percent is processed

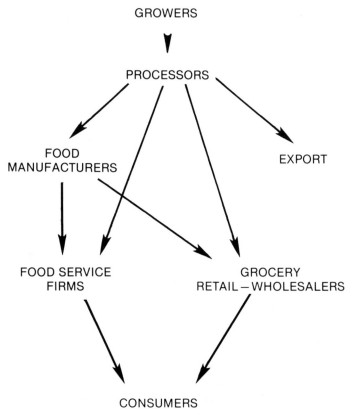

Figure 3–19. Tart Cherry Marketing Channels

as canned cherries. Most processors produce only one of these three products. Some processors are highly diversified into a substantial number of fruit and vegetable items, while some process only two or three other commodities in addition to cherries. About 30 percent only pack tart cherries.

The number of processors has gradually increased since 1970. In recent years, approximately seventy-five processors operated in the Great Lakes states. Most new processing firms are small, grower-owned, cherry freezing operations.

Economies of size in cherry processing are relatively small. A few of the largest cherry growers can obtain most of the potential processing economies of size with their own farm's production. Three or four moderately large growers can also jointly build a processing plant and have sufficient volume to obtain most of the economies of size for processing. Grower integration into processing allows better coordination of mechanical harvesting with processing and ensures growers of a processing outlet for their farm's production.

Because of relatively low profits and high risk, many investor-owned processors have left cherry processing. Some of these firms have become grower cooperatives or have sold their facilities to existing grower cooperatives. As a result, the ownership pattern of cherry processing has changed drastically. In 1970 approximately 83 percent of the processor capacity was in investor-owned firms. In 1984, 80 to 85 percent of the processing capacity was owned by cooperatives and by grower-processors.

Market channels for frozen cherries differ somewhat from the market channels for canned cherries or cherry pie filling. Initial processors sell frozen cherries as an ingredient commodity to manufacturers of pies and cherry desserts. Very few cherries are sold to retail consumers as frozen cherries. The market for frozen cherries is a highly competitive commodity market with almost no product differentiation. Some of the new grower-owned processors have formed a federated marketing cooperative for cherries and other processed fruits.

Large dessert manufacturers, the major buyers of frozen cherries, have become fewer and more concentrated. Several of these companies market advertised brands of pies, desserts and other products (such as Mrs. Smith, Sara Lee, and Pillsbury) through retail stores and foodservice outlets. Apples, cherries, and blueberries are typically the major fruit ingredients in their branded product lines. These companies promote their entire product lines, only a few items of which are made of cherries.

The cherry pie filling channel is more streamlined than the frozen cherry channel. Using raw or frozen cherries, cherry pie filling is packed by cherry processors and sold to either grocery retailer-wholesalers or to foodservice firms. Retail-size cherry pie filling is packed mainly by three cooperatives, each with a regional brand. One of these cooperatives, Pro Fac, has a long-term joint venture arrangement with Curtice Burns, an investor-owned food marketing firm. The cooperative provides raw product supplies, facilities, investment, and some financing, while the marketing firm provides the brands, marketing activities, and management. Two or three smaller processing firms emphasize private label pie filling, which has increased its share of the market. Pie filling manufacturers market a complete line of pie filling items, although tart cherry is the most important item in the pie filling line.

The channel for canned cherries is similar in organization to the pie filling channel. Canned cherries are a low and declining volume product in both the retail and foodservice markets. Export markets have taken primarily canned cherries but recently have been of minor importance.

Vertical Coordination

Aggregate demand for tart cherries and tart cherry products tends to be relatively stable from year to year, while supplies, by contrast, vary greatly.

The magnitude and consistency of annual fluctuations in tart cherry supplies (often double or half of the previous year) are one of the most pronounced for any agricultural commodity in the United States. This creates substantial coordination problems. Although consumer demand for cherries can change significantly over the years, it is nearly impossible to alter demand in a magnitude even approaching the size of the fluctuations in annual supplies.

As a result, prices fluctuate widely, reflecting the large swings in annual supplies. For example, frozen cherry prices fluctuated from a low of 45 cents per pound in the large-crop year of 1980 to 75 cents per pound for the short crop of 1981; prices then dropped for the large crop of 1982 to 37 cents per pound, rising again to 83 cents per pound in the short-crop year of 1983. Farm prices in the same four years were 20 cents, 46 cents, 13 cents, and 49 cents per pound.

Manufacturers of cherry pie and desserts tend to maintain more stable prices for their products over a period of several years. Consumer prices in grocery stores and particularly in foodservice markets largely do not reflect fluctuations in cherry supplies. Thus prices in the subsector transmit signals of changing supply rather ineffectively to consumers. This exacerbates the price variations at the producer level.

In an effort to stabilize market supplies and prices, the tart cherry subsector uses an industry-wide storage program as a supplemental coordinating mechanism. The primary purpose of the storage program, operated under a federal marketing order, is to store supplies in the large-crop years to supplement supplies in the short-crop years. Secondary objectives for the program include stabilizing prices within the marketing season and encouraging new markets, new product development, and market expansion.

The storage approach is feasible because the price increases from large crop to short crop are typically several times greater than the costs for storage, interest, and handling of the stored cherries. There are, however, substantial risks and uncertainties in storing cherries. The major risk is that of having two or more large crop years in succession. Although this happened only once per decade in the 1960s and 1970s, the risks are sufficiently high to pose a major deterrent to storage by individual processors or growers. Even in the recent large-crop year of 1982 when the federal marketing storage program was not allowed to operate by the federal government, there was very little year-to-year storage by individual firms. Risks are substantially reduced with an industry-wide storage program. Aggregate storage levels can be coordinated with overall cherry supplies and prices.

Demand expansion programs are another mechanism to help coordinate supply and demand. Each major cherry-producing state has a generic demand expansion program for tart cherries. These are supported by grower check-offs, which are mostly mandated through state marketing orders. Expenditures for promotion, advertising, and demand expansion are somewhat greater in large-supply years than in short-crop years. Demand expansion efforts by processors and branded food manufacturers are also increased somewhat in large-crop years. The annual supply fluctuations are, however, much greater than the ability of these efforts to shift demand.

The changes in processor ownership have altered the pricing mechanisms between growers and processors. Most cooperatives and grower-processors base their net return to growers on the revenues received from the sale of processed cherries (such as frozen cherries) less the costs for processing. The remaining investor-owned processors tend to use similar procedures for determining returns to growers except in short-crop years when a firm price may be offered at harvesttime. The move to participation plans for determining grower prices has resulted in a very thin cash market for cherries.

Some cooperatives and all grower-processors pack all of the production their growers produce. Under these arrangements, the grower has a processing home for the entire farm's production even in a large-crop year. Since this practice requires plant capacity sufficient to handle members' production in large-crop years, underutilization of facilities occurs in short-crop years.

There have been a few initial attempts to use multi-year contracts between processors and food manufacturers as a means to improve vertical coordination. The volume involved, however, has been very limited. These contracts may specify a price or a price basis with inflation adjustments over a period of two to five years. The quantity may or may not be specified.

A cooperative bargaining association representing the majority of the tart cherry production has made some attempts to reduce annual price fluctuations. By using market information and price-influencing activities, the bargaining association has attempted to raise the very low prices in large-crop years; however, the bargaining association has bargained with investor-owned processors only. As the percentage of tart cherries purchased by investor-owned processors has declined, the role of bargaining has also declined.

A major challenge in the tart cherry subsector is the coordination of long-term productive capacity with consumer demands over a period of ten to twenty years. Orchard planting decisions are made by several thousand independent cherry growers. Because they have little information about market demand ten to twenty years in the future, growers tend to make planting decisions based heavily on prices received during the most recent two or three years. Periodic excesses or shortages in production capacity are the result. The composite effect of the lack of long-term coordination is dynamic subsector inefficiency and resulting welfare losses to society.

Subsector Performance

The tart cherry subsector has shown improved cost efficiency through the progressive adoption of new technology, particularly at the farm level. A major improvement in labor efficiency occurred with the adoption of mechanical harvesting between the mid-1960s and mid-1970s. With modern mechanical harvesting equipment, a grower's family-sized crew of four to five people can harvest as many tart cherries as formerly required a hand harvesting crew of 250 people. Total per pound costs of mechanical harvesting are often 50 percent or less of hand harvesting costs. Increased economies of size resulting from harvesting equipment investment (often exceeding $100,000 per unit) are partially responsible for structural change at the farm level. On-farm adoption of high-yielding planting systems, more efficient plant-protection technology, and trickle irrigation have also improved on-farm productivity and efficiency. These and other changes have enabled cherry growers to have smaller increases in costs than have occurred in many other sectors of the economy. Average grower prices of cherries in 1980–1982 were 173 percent of prices in 1967–1969. By comparison, in 1980–1982, the consumer price index was 262 and the index of prices paid by farmers was 300 (1967–1969 = 100).

Cherry processors have also adopted new technology, including electronic sorters, to improve in-plant efficiency and produce better-quality processed cherries. Pitting equipment has been improved. In recent years, the lowest-cost processors have tended to be the relatively small, vertically integrated grower-processors. Plants of these grower-processors involve relatively low building investments and obtain cost efficiencies by using some key management and labor in the plant during the short processing season and on the farm during other seasons of the year. Thus, the vertical integration of growing and processing has improved processing efficiency and has also improved the coordination of mechanical harvesting and processing, which must be done within hours after harvest in order to maintain product quality.

Despite the high risks in growing tart cherries, growers continue to produce and even expand production with rates of return on investment lower than much of the rest of the economy. Because of long-term orchard investments, cherry growers frequently produce for a number of years at prices that average considerably below average costs. From the point of view of the growers, low net returns on investments reflect poor subsector performance. Many processors also have earned less than market interest rates on their investments for a number of years.

Development of new cherry products and uses has been hampered by the wide annual fluctuations in supply and prices and the several years of relatively short production during the 1970s. Recently the cherry industry has given more emphasis to cherry juice, unsweetened snack products, and low calorie cherry pie filling. All of these products are consistent with the rising demand and consumer preference trends for more natural, nutritious, and low calorie products.

The tart cherry subsector has attempted to reduce supply fluctuations through new institutional marketing arrangements and improved technology.

Research has been conducted on improved strains and varieties, more productive orchard planting systems, orchard hedging, improved nutrition, trickle irrigation, and frost reduction techniques. To date, however, these technologies have not appreciably reduced the wide annual fluctuations in production.

The industry-wide storage program, instituted by a federal marketing order, has reduced some of the fluctuations in supplies and prices from large-crop to short-crop seasons. In the 1984 large-crop year, 15 percent of supply was placed in the storage pool; however, substantial fluctuations in market supplies and prices have continued even with the storage program.

Pricing practices of pie and dessert manufacturers and retailers result in relatively stable retail prices for cherry products despite wide fluctuations in grower and freezer prices. It appears that retail prices are more comparable to the grower prices in the short-crop, high-price years than to the large-crop, low-price years. Rather than changing prices, manufacturers and retailers are more likely to alter the quantity sold from year to year by varying advertising, promotion, and merchandising activities and in some cases the availability of cherry products.

Retail price stability may be regarded by consumers as desirable performance. On the other hand, because changing supply and demand conditions at the farm and processor levels are not reflected in the prices to consumers, subsector performance suffers.

Looking across the Subsectors

The case studies presented in this chapter have attempted to highlight some of the key characteristics of a cross-section of subsectors within the U.S. food system. Although each subsector is unique, several subsectors have similar problems, organizational features, or coordinating mechanisms. In this section, we will draw from the case studies to make comparisons and provide generalizations. First, however, a few comments are warranted concerning the problem of comparing subsectors.

The case studies are useful in understanding how these subsectors work as small economic systems. The case studies have adapted the structure-conduct-performance paradigm of industrial organization theory to examine the organization-coordination-performance of subsectors. Implicit in this approach is the premise that the three elements are linked. Does a simple three-stage subsector perform better than a complex five-stage subsector? In what ways does a contractually coordinated subsector outperform a subsector coordinated through organized markets? What are the gains and losses from vertical integration?

It was initially hoped that these and other questions could be answered by examining the organization-coordination-performance of a number of different subsectors; however, we find that comparative analysis of different subsectors provides rather tentative conclusions on subsector organization-performance relationships. With our present knowledge level, normative judgments about different subsectors are hazardous. It is difficult to evaluate subsector performance in anything but a crude way and even more difficult to establish the cause of various levels of performance. For example, we might conclude that the potato subsector outperforms the cherry subsector in certain respects. But we may be unable to determine whether the difference in performance is due to certain organizational features or to the fact that cherries are a tree fruit subject to frequent frost damage, whereas potatoes are an annual crop with few weather hazards. Would the organization of the potato subsector work for cherries? Perhaps the potato subsector has been lucky that fast food chains have helped to rejuvenate potato consumption and stimulated some changes in subsector organization. The simple truth is that potatoes are not cherries, eggs are not oranges, and fluid milk is not beef. What works or makes sense in one subsector may not work or make sense in another.

The problem is analogous to the challenge of defining workable competition, a task to which economists devoted considerable attention in the 1940s and 1950s. Rather than trying to define workable competition, Jesse Markham (1950, p. 361) suggested:

> An industry may be judged to be workably competitive when, after the structural characteristics of its market and the dynamic forces that shaped them have been thoroughly examined, there is no clearly indicated change that can be effected through public policy measures that would result in greater social gains than social losses.

Since that article, substantial progress has been made, theoretically and empirically, in determining what affects the performance of markets, although defining workable competition remains rather controversial. Perhaps in another thirty years we will understand better what affects subsector performance. With our present state of knowledge, however, Markham's approach has appeal in trying to evaluate subsector organization and performance.

Markham's approach would require an assessment of the social gains and losses from alternative public policies. In many cases, some trade-off would be involved. This approach would be largely subsector specific. Although some insights might be gained by examining different subsectors, the focus would be on diagnosis and prescriptions for a specific subsector, not generalizations across subsectors.

We will not attempt to apply Markham's approach here; that was not our objective in doing the subsector studies. We will draw some comparisons of the way these miniature economic systems work: their organization, coordination, and performance. Some common patterns and trends are apparent. And a few guarded conclusions are possible. We will leave it to others to examine the extent to which policy changes could improve the societal benefits resulting from specific subsectors.

Similarities and Differences in Subsector Organization and Coordination

Each subsector performs certain basic functions, including the acquisition or application of essential inputs (fertilizer, seed, land, labor, packaging supplies), commodity production and physical transformation, physical distribution, and establishing procedures for determining values and coordinating resource allocations. The last function is accomplished through a variety of exchange mechanisms along with information systems, government programs or actions, and, in some cases, industry self-regulation.

Although the basic functions performed are similar, the ways that they are accomplished vary widely across the subsectors studied. The unique characteristics of each commodity have a strong effect on the way the subsector is organized and the mechanisms used for coordination. Some subsectors, such as eggs and fresh potatoes, have relatively simple organizations; after production (and storage for potatoes), the commodities are graded, packed, and shipped to wholesalers and retailers. The coordinating task appears to be fairly easy within a market period (that period during which total supply is relatively fixed). Other subsectors, such as beef, that are complex in organization and in the nature of the coordination task pose a substantially greater challenge to synchronize the stages involved in transforming a calf into fed beef that ultimately reaches retail markets. Different mechanisms have evolved to deal with the coordination problems in various subsectors.

Temporal coordination—the process of trying to regulate the quantity supplied during different time periods so it is consistent with consumer preferences (and willingness to pay)—is *the* overriding coordination problem of agricultural subsectors. Because of the biological nature of agricultural production and the perishable nature of many commodities, temporal coordination in agricultural subsectors is fundamentally different and much more difficult than temporal coordination of the television, drug, or detergent subsectors. Temporal coordination within a market period, while not free of problems, is generally easier and has less effect on the welfare of participants than coordination across market periods. Where subsectors have volatile prices within a market period, producers may be able to realize the average price by selling at many different times. In a few commodities, participation plans accomplish this type of price averaging.

Coordination across years is particulary difficult in subsectors where supply and/or demand is unpredictable. The impact of weather is a major stochastic influence on the supplies of tart cherries and citrus and has some influence on nearly all the subsectors examined. Since the early 1970s, many U.S. agricultural commodities have been strongly influenced by world supply and demand forces and international trade. Of the subsectors reviewed here, that is particularly true for corn, wheat, and soybeans. Year-to-year variations in U.S. prices for these commodities have increased sharply since 1972–1973, reflecting shifts in international supply and/or demand from year to year (often because of weather conditions in other countries). Coordination of the U.S. subsectors proves difficult under these circumstances. Since the prices of corn and soybeans also have a major effect on the feed costs of livestock and poultry enterprises, the volatility of corn and soybean prices creates considerable uncertainty for livestock and poultry farmers.

International trade also has an important influence on the citrus subsector. In this case, imports of frozen concentrated orange juice are probably more important than exports of fresh fruit. As with grains and oilseeds, the strength of the U.S. dollar has had a strong influence on imports and exports. In the case of concentrated orange juice, imports tend to dampen the extent of price increases during short crop years.

Temporal coordination is also influenced by whether a commodity is a stock or flow commodity, by its storability, and by the length of the biological production period. The storage of raw or processed products to smooth out supplies across market periods, while technically feasible in several subsectors, involves substantial risk and tends to occur mainly in connection with government or industry-wide programs. The tart cherry marketing order and the Farmer Owned Reserve program for grains were developed as instruments to smooth out year-to-year variations in supply. Carry-over by the private sector from one year to the next occurs to some extent but is often unintentional (for example, potato freezers sometimes freeze more than they are able to sell at acceptable prices), ties up capital, and involves a substantial price risk. Without some type of risk-sharing arrangement, subsector participants have little incentive to carry inventory from one crop year to the next.

The coordinating mechanisms that have developed in the different subsectors are primarily concerned with coordination within a year—that is, of supply already produced or in the process of being produced. Most of these mechanisms were not designed to coordinate supply and demand across years.

In most of the subsectors studied, temporal coordination depends on the decisions of subsector participants. Decisions to increase or decrease future output are atomistically distributed; hundreds of farmers or contractors commit resources for future production based on current prices and expectations for future prices. In many cases, current price levels have a strong effect on the expectations for future prices. For example, in years when cherry prices are high, farmers plant more trees; when prices are disastrously low, trees are abandoned or destroyed. Perhaps farmers find it so difficult to predict future prices that they rely on current prices. Even in commodities where there are relatively few stochastic forces affecting supply and demand, such as eggs, price cycles continue to be a major problem.

Monthly prices of all commodities except tart cherries (data were not available) were analyzed for the 1961–1984 period. One-month, six-month, and twelve-month price variations were examined. The analysis allowed price variations to be partitioned into seasonal variations, trend-cyclical variations, and irregular or unpredictable variations. Regardless of the measure used, milk prices were consistently the least variable, and fresh potato prices were clearly the most variable. Twelve-month price variations for fresh potatoes averaged 37 percent compared to 6 percent for milk. Milk was the only commodity with average price variations below 12 percent. Before adjusting for seasonal or cyclical-trend patterns, year-to-year price variations were lowest (after milk) for fed cattle, broilers, and eggs, and highest (after potatoes) for hogs, wheat, and Florida oranges. After adjusting for seasonal and cyclical-trend patterns, fresh potatoes, Florida oranges, eggs, and soybeans had the largest variations in prices—whether compared across twelve-, six- or one-month intervals. Dairy, corn, beef, and wheat had the lowest irregular variations in prices. The commodities with the greatest price variability tend to be those in which prices are essentially market determined, whereas government programs had a major influence on dairy, corn, and wheat prices during the period examined. The magnitude of seasonal price variations declined for milk and eggs over this twenty-three-year period but remained roughly the same for the remaining commodities.

Long-run variations in price are extremely difficult to avoid in subsectors that are essentially market coordinated. Of the commodities studied, the only one that has avoided substantial price variations over time is dairy, where prices are administered through a combination of government price supports and milk marketing orders. Since 1980, this stability has come at a high cost, however, as government purchases of dairy products have mushroomed. During the 1960s, there were also relatively stable prices for corn and wheat due to price-support programs. Here, also, government-owned surpluses became a problem.

A variety of instruments and arrangements are used by the subsectors studied to shift or manage risk, to discover price, and to improve coordination. Several subsectors are strongly influenced by either government supply-management or price-support programs (dairy, corn, wheat) or by market orders that allow some type of industry-wide action to regulate supply, demand, or prices (dairy, fresh and processed citrus, and to a lesser extent tart cherries). Some of these are primarily aimed at orderly marketing within a market or production period (citrus). The recent government programs for corn and wheat have had more influence on farmer income protection than on supply or price control. The beef, pork, egg, broiler, soybean, and potato subsectors involve neither government programs nor marketing orders to a significant degree, although all are indirectly affected by government programs toward corn and wheat (either through feed costs or as substitute crops).

Collective action by farmers through their cooperatives can potentially reduce farmer risk and uncertainty, countervail market power, affect price discovery, and improve coordination. Cooperatives are most active in subsectors strongly affected by government programs or marketing orders. Cooperatives play a minor role in the beef, pork, egg, and broiler subsectors. Cooperative involvement is by far the strongest in dairy, where they bargain and/or assemble a major portion of U.S. milk production and are also involved in manufacturing and bottling milk. Although cooperatives handled over one-third of the grain and soybeans marketed in 1983, they are primarily involved at the early stages of these subsectors and have a relatively small presence in processing or international trade.

The heavy involvement of cooperatives in dairy is sometimes attributed to the vulnerability of dairy farmers in marketing a highly perishable product. However, the opportunities to manufacture cheese, butter, and nonfat dry milk—all of which can be stored—considerably enhance the ability of cooperatives to balance supply and demand and bargain over class I prices. Beef, pork, eggs, and broilers have few storage options. A classified pricing system, as in dairy, would not be feasible. Cooperative marketing activities (or marketing orders) to smooth out supply or to allocate the raw commodity to different end uses, which are possible in dairy, have limited potential in beef, pork, broilers, and eggs. Cooperatives could still bargain for their members over contract terms in broilers and eggs and could attempt to preserve farmer access in all these markets by integrating into the first handler or processing stages; however, this has not occurred to any great extent in these four subsectors.

Participation plans are used widely in citrus and tart cherries. Although there are a variety of arrangements, farmer returns are determined in most cases after the cooperative or corporate processor has sold the crop for a particular year. Processing and handling costs are deducted from receipts, and farmers receive the remainder. Under these arrangements, a transfer price is unnecessary at the time of harvest. Processors have little if any price risk. Growers shoulder all the price risk—benefiting on upswings and suffering when prices drop—but are assured of a market. A futures market contract exists for frozen concentrated orange juice but is used more for risk management than as a basis for price determination.

Production contracts and/or vertical integration are central features of the broiler, egg, and processed potato subsectors. Grower contracts are negotiated in advance of production, usually specify price or payment terms, and frequently involve some shifts in decision control. Production contracts in broilers and eggs usually involve some of the key inputs being provided by the integrator. Fewer production inputs are provided by potato processors. In all three cases, processors bear the risk of commodity price variations. Although contracts and vertical integration exist to some extent in the grain subsectors, most transactions are either spot or forward sale arrangements in which price is pegged to a futures market.

Futures contracts play a central role in pricing and risk management for corn, wheat, and soybeans. Beef, pork, orange concentrate, and fresh potato futures market contracts are available for risk management but are used little in price determination. Futures markets for eggs and broilers are no longer active.

Government programs, marketing orders, vertical integration, and production management contracts have minor roles in the beef, pork, and fresh potato subsectors. Open market prices and a variety of forward contracts are relied on to determine value and coordinate the various functions and stages.

Although many economists place a high priority on open markets in which buyer and seller negotiate price and the terms of transactions, one of the subsectors examined—eggs—has very few negotiated prices and has relied for years on fabricated prices. How can that be? Market clearing prices for eggs are estimated by Urner Barry, a private market report, based on the level of egg inventories. If inventories increase, egg prices are adjusted downward, and vice-versa. Since the vast majority of transactions in the subsector are tied to the Urner Barry price, the subsector operates with nearly 100 percent of the transactions formula priced. The high degree of egg price volatility suggests that this system of establishing prices leaves room for improvement. However, it has endured for many years and is apparently acceptable to egg producing and marketing firms.

Most of the subsectors have institutions and arrangements that are unique to those subsectors. To the extent that there are few impediments to the birth or death of these institutions and arrangements, economic forces largely determine whether they serve a useful function in the various subsectors. Indeed one of the conclusions from reading the case studies is that there are many ways of organizing and coordinating these economic systems, and all work well enough to survive.

Some Generalities

Although all subsectors are unique in many respects, there are also some common trends and characteristics that apply to most, if not all, the subsectors studied. These include:

Agricultural production has generally become more concentrated geographically.

Agricultural production has become more specialized and more concentrated in large farms.

The largest processing companies in most subsectors have increased their shares of the national market.

Agricultural marketing cooperatives have generally increased in importance both at the first handler and processing stages even though the number of cooperatives has declined.

There is generally a declining number of first handler buyers to compete for farm output; however, the geographic size of producer–first handler markets has also expanded. Thus, it is not clear whether commercial farmers have fewer alternative markets. Access of farmers to buyers is a problem for small producers in many commodities. It is also frequently a problem in fringe production areas.

The use of formula pricing and forward sale contracts has increased in most subsectors. The volume of open market trades with negotiated prices has declined, resulting in a thin price base in a growing number of subsectors. These trends indicate a shift toward exchange arrangements that have low transaction costs.

Production contracts with farmers in which price is negotiated prior to production commitments are relatively stable in usage. Since these increase the risk exposure of processors, there is a general reluctance of processors to enter into grower contracting unless necessary to meet their supply needs.

Production contracts are used only in commodities in which the production period is relatively short and where resources committed to production can change substantially from one production period to the next (examples are broilers, eggs, and processed potatoes).

Vertical integration has increased in the hog, citrus, egg, and tart cherry subsectors. In the last two, this has largely involved producers integrating forward into the first handling stage. There has generally been a decline in the importance of farms owned by agribusiness corporations.

Direct marketing has generally increased, resulting in a decline in the number of intermediaries.

Most subsectors have become operationally more efficient through genetic and cultural advances, greater mechanization, fewer middlemen, and improved vertical coordination.

Most subsectors have been reasonably responsive to changing consumer preferences by developing new products, improving packaging and convenience, modifying quality, or smoothing of supplies over time. The quality of products has improved in many subsectors.

Many of the subsectors have considered or implemented generic promotional programs in an effort to increase consumption and sales.

There is a need to improve grades and standards and market information in some subsectors to make them more consistent with commercial reality and to allow markets to reflect quality, form, and time preferences more accurately.

International markets have had a significant impact on most subsectors. This has generally increased the variability of commodity prices and the overall level of uncertainty. In some subsectors, imports have reduced the market power of U.S. processors.

Substantial price variations *within* a market period occur in many commodities. In some cases, this reflects seasonal shifts in supply or demand or temporary imbalances that most markets experience. In the case of crops such as potatoes, in which total supply for the year is largely known by fall harvest, substantial price variations within the year suggest the need for improved coordinating mechanisms. Improved information on supplies and demand may be called for. Futures contracts can also facilitate coordination within a market period.

Stability of prices and/or net returns over time remains a major problem for producers and/or first processors in most subsectors. In some cases, price variations at the farm level are exacerbated by relatively stable manufacturer and retail prices that only partially reflect shifts in commodity supply-demand conditions.

All of the subsectors continue to experience major problems of matching supply with demand at prices consistent with the opportunity cost of resources. Subsectors lack the mechanisms for subsector planning or balancing aggregate supply and demand. Government programs are frequently not designed to deal effectively with coordinating supply and demand across years. Contracts and marketing orders fail to organize supply at the national level. This basic long-run coordination problem results in substantial inefficiencies in the allocation of resources in agricultural subsectors.

Macroeconomic policies have a pervasive influence on all subsectors. Subsectors with a substantial exposure to international markets are particularly affected by macropolicies affecting the strength of the dollar and trade barriers. Macropolicies affecting interest rates have a substantial effect on farmers who are highly leveraged and on processors in those subsectors in which substantial product storage occurs.

Two major types of food manufacturing companies seem to be emerging. Large brand manufacturers that make heavy use of advertising are withdrawing from some commodity-oriented stages and subsectors and concentrating on merchandising functions such as new product development, advertising, and promotions. The second group of large firms are commodity oriented, tend to concentrate on supplying other manufacturers, private labels, and the food service market, and are diversifying across commodities. Whereas the first group emphasizes new products, branding, and promotions, the second emphasizes efficiency and risk management.

Concentration of sales has increased in the food wholesaling, food retailing, and foodservice industries. The balance of power between food manufacturers and food distributors has probably shifted some toward food distributors, although this varies considerably from product to product.

Concluding Comments

A number of problems are common to many of the subsectors and generally fall within one or more of the following areas: how best to establish the economic value of the product; how to transfer information throughout the subsector; how to reduce supply excesses and shortages across years and the resulting price variability; how to reduce price variability within a year; how to reduce the variability in the price of key inputs such as feed and credit; and how to deal with nodes of concentrated market power. Most of the subsectors have used a variety of exchange mechanisms or other institutions to address these problems, with varying degrees of success.

The case studies do not point to any one mechanism as the optimal way to address any of the problem areas. Formula pricing, for example, seems to reduce the complexity of pricing; however, formula pricing depends on a base price that accurately reflects market conditions. As formula pricing increases, it tends to undermine or make more fragile the base price on which it depends.

Definite trade-offs exist between the performance of subsectors largely coordinated by market prices versus those in which prices or supplies are significantly influenced by government programs or marketing orders. The former generally have markets that are allowed to clear; that is, price rises or falls until the available supply is sold. In these subsectors, supply and demand are kept in balance, but the level and variability of prices may be periodically unacceptable to farmers, middlemen, or consumers.

In subsectors in which prices or supplies are administered by a central authority (such as dairy, corn, and wheat), markets may or may not clear, depending on the program (price support versus supply restrictions) and the year. Price variability is generally reduced, but periodic surpluses often present problems. Government programs in dairy and grain have resulted in periodic high costs to taxpayers for either storing surpluses and/or for maintaining prices to farmers. Thus, the problems of balancing supply and demand are present in both types of subsectors, but the consequences are distributed differently.

Although production management or resource-providing contracts are not without problems, they do include several appealing characteristics. Producer returns are known before resources are committed to production. Price risks are transferred to processors, who can usually manage this risk exposure better than farmers; however, the terms of these contracts are not reported so that the quantities and prices are not public information. Contracts are also not standardized, making them difficult to compare. Producers often find themselves at a disadvantage in trying to negotiate contracts with the few processors in their area.

An alternative that retains most of the desirable features of production management contracts but eliminates most of their limitations is the forward deliverable contract market (FDCM). FDCMs have yet to be operationally tested. As conceived by Holder and Sporleder (1976), however, FDCMs would have many features of futures markets but would provide a market for contracts in which the product was always delivered. For commodities in which the FDCM became the dominant exchange mechanism, the more distant contracts could provide effective coordination of supply and demand at acceptable prices. There would likely be considerable resistance to FDCMs, as there has been to experimental electronic markets, but they hold sufficient promise to warrant additional investigation by producer and commodity organizations and the federal government.

Historically producers have borne most of the price and supply risk in the U.S. food system; however, food manufacturers and food distributors are generally in a better position than producers to influence and predict consumer demand and to manage periodic shortages or surpluses. From this standpoint, processor-grower contracts that shift some of the price and supply risk to processors should contribute to improved long-run coordination and a more equitable distribution of risk.

Marketing orders and agricultural cooperatives are means of reducing or redistributing producer risk. The degree of cooperative activity varies by subsector; however, cooperatives have gradually become more heavily involved in the processing and physical distribution of many commodities. Producers have also made greater use of generic promotional programs, usually in conjunction with marketing orders that also enable more orderly marketing. Although both cooperatives and marketing orders have been periodically criticized by nonfarm organizations, they are the primary vehicles farmers have available to deal collectively with problems of subsector instability.

The food distribution trade has a strong influence on the coordination and returns of many subsectors. Their merchandising decisions and their general lack of concern about individual commodities directly affect the long-run viability of some subsectors. Since food distributors have little vested interest in individual commodities, they generally leave management of demand and supply factors to other subsector participants. This observed behavior reinforces the importance of producers having the tools, expertise, commitment, and resources to continue to develop marketing options.

The subsector studies highlight the diverse nature of the U.S. food system. Each subsector is organized and coordinated in a somewhat different way. Yet all seem to work in a reasonably satisfactory manner. No one system stands out as clearly superior to others.

The subsector approach to research has proved of value in understanding the organization and coordination of different commodity systems, in diagnosing problems, and in identifying research opportunities. Generalities across subsectors are often hazardous, however. We have been unable to test hypothesized relationships of subsector organization, coordination, and performance. Although we know better how subsectors work, we have difficulty saying how well. Clearly much remains to challenge future researchers.

Part III
Food Manufacturing and Distribution

T he food manufacturing and distribution industries occupy powerful positions in the industrialized U.S. food system. A relatively small number of food manufacturers collect the domestic output of millions of farmers, process these commodities, and sell their products to hundreds of thousands of food distributors, which in turn supply millions of households.

The procurement requirements of food manufacturers have conditioned the geographic location, product specialization, financial structures, and ownership patterns of farming and first handlers of farm products. The selling strategies of food processors have also influenced warehouse and store designs, vertical integration by retailers, shelf allocation and pricing behavior, firm size, and other organizational characteristics of food distribution. The U.S. food and tobacco manufacturing industries utilize about 85 percent of the value of all domestically marketed farm products.

The vertical control exercised by food processors and manufacturers varies considerably by commodity. Backward integration by ownership or contractual arrangements by processors are greatest for broilers, turkeys, eggs, milk, hogs, and processed vegetables and fruits. These tend to be perishable commodities that maintain their identity throughout the marketing channels. In most cases there is relatively little value added to these commodities as they move from farm to consumers. Although manufacturer brands and advertising are used to some extent, in the main, food manufacturers have relatively little market power in selling these products to retailers and consumers.

The opposite is true for most commodities made from grains, oilseeds, sugar, cocoa, and coffee beans. These tend to be ingredient commodities that are frequently combined with other commodities to produce a significantly transformed consumer product. For example, flour, shortening, sugar, and salt are combined to produce Nabisco crackers, Keebler cookies, or Wonderbread. Wheat and sugar are combined to produce Sugar Frosted Flakes. Chocolate, sugar, nuts, and other ingredients are combined to produce Snickers candy

---

The coordinating authors for this part were Bruce Marion and John Connor.

bars. The identities of the original commodities are lost. For these commodities, food processor-manufacturers rarely use vertical ownership or contractual arrangements to gain control over farm production decisions. Most of these commodities are relatively unperishable and easily stored. Considerable value is added as they move from farmer to consumer. Brands and advertising provide manufacturers with considerable influence over retailers and consumers. Vertical control by manufacturers is primarily forward, not backward.

Thus, at this stage in the evolution of the food system, there is an illuminating, if overly simple, dichotomy of goods. The commodities where backward vertical control by food processors (by ownership or contractual integration) is most prevalent are those involving little processing and little market power at the manufacturing-processing stage. In contrast, market power by food manufacturers is most prevalent in the more highly processed products made from multiple ingredients, and it is wielded forward through the system.

Food wholesalers and retailers sell mainly processed foods, beverages, and tobacco products; however, about 10 percent of food store sales are unprocessed foods (mostly fresh produce and eggs). An additional 15 percent of sales come from nonfood grocery items (paper products, soaps, health and beauty aids, and others). Food wholesalers and retailers have the most influence over the vertical production and marketing systems for unbranded products (such as fresh meat and produce) and for private label (store brand) and generic products. These products account for 35 to 40 percent of grocery store sales. Manufacturer brands, where retailers and wholesalers exercise less backward vertical influence, represent the remaining 60 to 65 percent of grocery store sales.

During the post–World War II period, both food manufacturing and food distribution increased their share of the economic activity of the U.S. food system. As measured by value-added, their shares each increased by about 5 percent. However, only food distribution has increased in relative importance if employment is used as a criterion. In 1950, food wholesaling, retailing, and foodservice establishments accounted for about one out of every four persons employed in the U.S. food system. By 1980, this had increased to nearly two out of every three employed (figure III–1). The rapid increase in food consumed away from home has resulted in foodservice firms accounting for about one-third of food system employment. During 1950–1980, total food system employment increased only about 7 percent.

Since food retailing and foodservice firms provide the connection between the food system and consumers, they are in a critical position to transmit information and market signals in both directions. The rapid growth of electronic scanning and information processing technology may make retailer control over information even more important in the future. Food manufacturers are often the key transmitters of consumer-retail preferences to farmers and first handlers. In addition, food manufacturers frequently have the greatest influence over consumer preferences and buying behavior through ad-

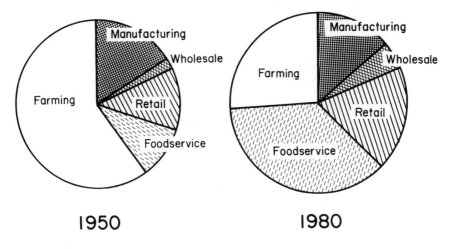

1950   1980

Source: Connor et al. 1985, pp. 22.

Figure III–1. Employment Trends in the U.S. Food System, 1950 and 1980

vertising, promotions, and new product development. Thus, in addition to the other functions they perform, food manufacturers and distributors have a vital influence on the information transmitted in the food system and hence on system coordination.

The analysis in both of these chapters relies primarily on the industrial organization paradigm. That model proposes a causal linkage flowing from basic supply and demand conditions to market structure to patterns of firm conduct to market performance. Both chapters include considerable descriptive material as well as analytical content. Finally, each chapter relies heavily on books that treat the subjects in much greater detail: chapter 4 on Connor et al. 1985 and chapter 5 on Marion et al. 1979.

4

The Organization and Performance of the Food Manufacturing Industries

T he food, beverage, and tobacco manufacturing industries occupy a central place in the U.S. food production and marketing system. In contrast to the rest of the system, the food manufacturing stage is dominated by large-scale, capital-intensive, highly diversified corporations that many believe may become the models for other stages of the food system. Although it is useful to view processing as part of a vertically articulated system, it is generally more instructive to analyze food manufacturing as a component of the manufacturing sector. In particular, the market structures of the food manufacturing industries are most comparable to other industries manufacturing consumer products. Differences in market structure, structural change, or competitive outcome between food and the rest of manufacturing are explained by the nearly unique dependence of food manufacturing on agricultural inputs and on certain special features of selling consumer nondurables, especially through grocery stores.

This chapter highlights three aspects of market organization of the food manufacturing industries. These features were chosen for emphasis because they are intimately related to the quality of economic performance of the food industries and because they sharply distinguish manufacturing from the rest of the food system. First, we analyze the levels of market concentration and the leading positions of large firms in the food industries; we show how these organizational characteristics are related to aggregate concentration. Second, advertising and other forms of sales promotion in the food system are examined; these are dominated by food manufacturers. Considerable evidence exists that product differentiation efforts by food manufacturers have important consequences for structural change and economic performance. Product differentiation is practically absent in agriculture, and enterprise differentiation is comparatively weak among food retailers. Third, product diversification by food manufacturers is examined; diversification has risen dramatically, as

The lead author for this chapter was John Connor; other authors were Richard Rogers, Bruce Marion, Willard Mueller, and Robert Wills.

has the participation in food manufacturing by companies whose principal businesses lie elsewhere. By contrast, food distributors have remained relatively specialized, and farming has become more specialized. A parallel rise has occurred in the number and width of geographic markets served by food manufacturers.

Considerable attention is devoted to quantitative studies of performance in the food industries. We are fortunate to be able to draw on a relatively large body of empirical studies of the relationship between market structure and profits, prices, productivity, and other dimensions of performance. These measures refer mainly to the horizontal (intraindustry or interfirm) dimensions of economic performance, although some vertical (subsystem) and noneconomic elements also are examined. The complex task of assessing overall performance of food manufacturing is addressed.

This chapter is patterned after the industrial organization paradigm (Scherer 1980). That model proposes a logical, causal linkage flowing from basic demand and supply conditions to market structure to patterns of industry conduct to performance outcomes. The chapter also proceeds from purely descriptive material to more analytic content; the later sections summarize research that measures the determinants of economic performance. Finally, the earlier sections of this chapter are primarily in the realm of positive economics, whereas the latter parts delve into the normative and prescriptive.

Basic Demand and Supply Conditions

This section provides descriptive information for the rest of the chapter, a prelude to the more compelling drama surrounding the denouement. Unless otherwise noted, we employ the industry definitions of food and tobacco manufacturing used by the Census Bureau in the late 1970s based on the Standard Industrial Classification (SIC) system.[1] We focus mainly on the 1947–1980 period; special census tabulations permit a more detailed analysis of the 1967–1977 period. Most data are keyed to census years.

Size and Linkages

Food and tobacco manufacturing ranked third in 1978 gross value-added among the nineteen major industry groups of manufacturing, after transportation equipment and nonelectrical machinery.[2] In 1958 food and tobacco ranked first, accounting for 14.2 percent of all value-added in manufacturing; this proportion fell to 10.8 percent in 1978 (Cremeans 1981). Total manufacturing value-added contributed about one-fourth of U.S. gross domestic product in both years. Value-added is considered the best measure of the relative size of industries, but based on shipments value (f.o.b. plant at manufacturers' prices), food remains the largest of the manufacturing groups. In 1982 shipments of food and tobacco manufacturing products totaled $297 billion, or 14 percent of all manufacturing.

Figure 4–1 places the contribution of food and tobacco manufacturing within the context of the U.S. food system. Using the somewhat narrow definition of the food production-marketing system underlying the figure, the 1982 food system accounted for about 8 percent of U.S. GNP. Food and tobacco processing generated $82 billion in value-added in 1982, which was 33 percent of the total value-added by the food system. In 1947, the $12 billion value-added by manufacturing was only 25 percent of the food system's total. From being far smaller than farming in 1947, the GNP contribution of food manufacturing had by 1982 easily surpassed that of agriculture.

A study of the world's food processing industries by the United Nation's Centre on Transnational Corporations (1982) concluded that among the market economies, the United States had by far the largest national industry. The United States accounted for 26.9 percent of food manufacturing output and 25.7 percent of value-added of all the market economies (evaluated at official or market rates of exchange).[3] U.S. food manufacturers' shipments were only slightly less than the ten EEC countries combined and were 80 percent of all shipments by the Western European countries.

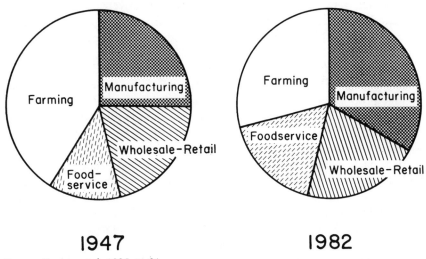

1947   1982

Source: Connor et al. 1985, p. 21.

Note: The food system as defined here excludes leather, textile, and clothing manufacturing; food transportation; manufactured inputs used by the above segments of the food system; and nonfood trade.

Figure 4–1. Contribution of the U.S. Food System to Gross National Product, 1947 and 1982

Major Marketing Channels

Shipments from food manufacturing plants pass through four distinct channels. Distinguishing among these channels is important because they conform to different demand segments for the same products. A few food products are sold through only one distribution channel; however, in most industries, firms (or divisions of firms) face multiple marketing channels and tend to specialize in sales through one channel. As a result, an industry often contains two or more submarkets or "strategic groups," each containing firms with distinct modes of conduct.

The sharpest distinction exists between processed *consumer* products and semiprocessed *producer* goods. The latter, intermediate foodstuffs, are virtually homogeneous commodities bought in large lots by well-informed purchasing agents working for manufacturers. Some food industries are mainly (flour and sugar) or exclusively (partly refined oils, leaf tobacco) producer goods industries. Approximately 26 percent of the value of shipments of food manufacturing establishments in 1977 were producer goods (Connor 1982a).

Finished consumer foods are sold by three main channels: foodservice, unbranded food store, and branded food store. Food and beverage products made for the foodservice channel have many of the characteristics of producer goods: they are purchased by well-informed buyers (foodservice wholesalers or chain retailers) and consumer brands are relatively unimportant (the main exceptions are carbonated and alcoholic drinks, candy, and tobacco products).[4] About 15 percent of processed foods were shipped to foodservice outlets in 1977.

It is the three-fifths of manufactured foods sold to food stores that is a primary focus of this chapter. Private label, generic, and unbranded food and beverage products accounted for 20 percent of the value of manufacturers' shipments in 1977. These products are made in the retailers' own plants or procured by food store buyers; consumers identify product quality with the food store operator. Finally, 39 percent of manufactured foods in 1977 were branded, packaged goods sold through food stores or the food departments of other retail outlets. Branded foods vary along a continuum from negligibly to highly differentiated. Branded food manufacturers use a variety of persuasive techniques, directed at both consumers and food store managers, to maintain brand distinctiveness. Consumers hold the manufacturers of branded foods primarily responsible for product quality.

Although some companies do both, manufacturers of branded foods tend to be larger than and different from manufacturers of distributors' brands. A model first suggested by Hoffman (1940) and elaborated by Handy and Padberg (1971) suggested that for most products, large manufacturers and large retailers avoid direct confrontation by each allowing the other to dominate different processed food marketing channels. Specifically, leading manufacturers follow a strategy of building consumer loyalty through media advertising and new product introductions. Leading grocery chains, on the other hand, build consumer patronage through extensive private label offerings of more standardized foods, obtained from either self-manufacture or smaller manufacturers. Smaller grocery retailers deal mainly with the major grocery manufacturers, according to Handy and Padberg. Their theory is less relevant today, however, because the growth of cooperative and voluntary wholesalers since the late 1940s permits most supermarket retailers to adopt effective private label programs. Moreover, major manufacturers use temporary price deals and other sales promotions in their relations with large as well as small grocery retail firms. Thus, the Handy-Padberg model is a somewhat oversimplified dichotomy, though it remains true that the modes of conduct for procurement of branded foods are quite different from that of private label items (Hamm 1981b).

Industry Growth and Demand Conditions

As late as the 1870s, the marketed value of unprocessed foods was greater than the value of manufactured foods and beverages. Today manufactures comprise over 90 percent of U.S. household purchases of foods and beverages. With the exception of a small amount of homemade (nonmarketed) preserved foods and imports, the U.S. food industries satisfy all U.S. demand for processed food and tobacco products.

Household food expenditures are a large but declining portion of disposable personal income (DPI). Personal consumption expenditures (PCE) for food, beverages, and tobacco reached $442 billion in 1982, of which 60 percent was for food to be consumed at home, 22 percent for food away from home, 11 percent for alcoholic beverages, and 6 percent for tobacco. When consumption expenditures are measured in constant dollars, the percentage distribution has remained about the same since the mid-1950s.

The PCE for food and tobacco declined steadily from 35 percent of DPI in 1949 to 21 percent in 1982. The decline occurred mainly because of reduced expenditures on food at-home, but the decline in the proportions spent on alcoholic beverages and tobacco was even steeper. Only away-from-home consumption has kept up with household incomes. In addition to PCE, foods and beverages away from home are purchased from funds provided by business and government or as part of other services (Prescott 1982).

Average annual real growth of production in the food manufacturing industries during 1947–1982 was 2.9 percent (compounded); this compares to 3.6 percent for all manufacturing and 3.3 percent for the entire economy (updated from Connor 1982b; Gordon 1980). Because of four recessions since 1969, the growth of the food industries has been about one-third greater than the rest of manufacturing since the mid-1960s. Food and tobacco manufacturing is relatively immune to annual shifts in demand, though there is a pronounced seasonality in demand for many foods and beverages.

Changes in inflation-adjusted PCE for food and tobacco products were slower during the post–World War II period than data on real production indexes indicate, partly because the latter include export and nonhousehold demand. During 1946–1982 U.S. household demand expressed in 1972 dollars rose from $102 billion to $198 billion, or 1.9 percent per year on average. Per capita real PCE increased by 0.5 percent per year; however, demand measured by the physical weight of food and nonalcoholic beverages consumed has shown no change; Americans have consumed about 1,500 pounds per capita annually since the earliest records began around 1900. The change in real per capita PCE is due to shifts in the composition of food purchases toward items that have higher real prices per pound. The changing demand mix is in turn explained by rising incomes, greater product variety, improved quality (for example, through more costly ingredients or greater convenience), sociodemographic changes, and changing national tastes.

The principal post–World War II demographic changes are well documented by Easterlin (1980). The 1945–1960 baby boom and subsequent bust introduced a strong age-profile cycle to the U.S. population. Families have become much smaller since 1960, divorce is more common, and the proportion of never-married, young adults living alone has risen six-fold. Longevity has increased the elderly population; the nonwhite population has more than increased proportionately; and the proportion of working women is up. Household real income nearly doubled over 1947–1977, and income distribution became slightly more equal (Blinder 1980). Relatively more male adults are shopping for and preparing foods at home.

These sociodemographic and income trends appear to be responsible for several postwar changes in the composition of demand for processed foods. There is less demand for infant food but a corresponding increase in geriatric formulations. Foods designed to be sold in groceries are increasingly convenient (kitchen-labor saving), compatible with even more sophisticated kitchen equipment, and packaged in smaller sizes. Processors have offered more preparations identified as natural, health, ethnic, low calorie, and, low fat. Consumption of regular bread, potatoes, variety meats, and other "inferior" foods has declined. Sales of frozen foods, sauces, dehydrated potatoes, pet foods, flour mixes, and many other convenience foods have expanded rapidly. Ingredients for baking and other traditional, labor-intensive home preparations have become less popular (Connor 1982a).

International Trade

International trade is a potential source of both increased demand and supply for the U.S. food industries. In some industries, both are simultaneously present, but most industries are predominantly import oriented or export oriented. Export sales may be regarded as an additional distinct marketing channel for some U.S. food and tobacco processors (Connor 1982a).

Despite their size internationally, the U.S. food manufacturing industries are relatively insulated from international trade. U.S. imports of processed foods and beverages in 1977 were $8.7 billion or 4.9 percent of domestic product shipments. This import ratio places food eighteenth among the twenty major manufacturing groups; only tobacco manufacturing and printing were lower. The import share for food manufactures has remained virtually constant since the 1960s, unlike much of manufacturing that has experienced increasing import penetration. About two-thirds of all U.S. food and agricultural imports are processed items (USDA 1984e).

Processed food exports were slightly less than imports: $7.8 billion in 1977, or 4.4 percent of domestic U.S. production. Exports of tobacco products added another $0.7 billion, or 8.2 percent of domestic product shipments. Thus, U.S. imports and exports of food and tobacco manufactures are nearly in balance. Food and tobacco products accounted for about 9.6 percent of all exports of U.S. manufactures, again ranking fifth among the nineteen industry groups. Since the late 1960s, food manufacturing has become more export prone, though the rate of increase has been less than the rest of manufacturing (Cremeans 1981). Slightly over one-third of all U.S. food and agricultural exports consist of manufactured products (USDA 1984e).

During the 1970s exports of U.S. processed foods and tobacco increased at a rate that was over 50 percent greater than the growth in total production (O'Brien et al. 1982); that is, export values grew at about 16 percent annually (compounded), compared to total value-of-shipments' growth of about 10 percent. Volume growth of exports averaged 4 to 6 percent per year. Yet because of a boom in world trade, the U.S. share of world trade in processed foods has fallen since the mid-1960s. This trend parallels the U.S. experience in world trade of all manufactures (Branson 1980), but it is in sharp contrast to U.S. export performance with respect to total agriculture-based products (foods, beverages, feeds, and fibers).[5] In processed foods and tobacco trade, the United States was a distant second in 1980 to the EEC, which originated 45 percent of the value of all such trade (17 percent if one excludes intra-EEC trade), up from 33 percent in 1970. The United States is failing to maintain its share of the most dynamic portion (41 percent) of agriculture-based trade: processed food and tobacco products.

Supply and Cost Conditions

The food and tobacco industries are important users of many U.S. resources: farm and fishery commodities, chemicals, packaging materials, labor, machinery, energy, advertising, and many other inputs. Compared with the rest of manufacturing, food processing is relatively materials, capital, and advertising intensive. A breakdown of various costs for selected food industries is shown in figure 4–2. Soybean oil processing, a producer good industry, has very high materials costs, low labor costs, and a low gross margin. Meat packing, bread, and cigarettes are low-, moderate-, and high-differentiation consumer food industries. Materials usage declines and margins increase with the degree of differentiation. Labor costs are high in the bread industry because of direct store delivery in that industry.

The principal materials used in food processing are agricultural or marine raw products. Connor (1980) estimated for 1975 that 68 percent of marketed U.S. farm output was purchased by the domestic food and tobacco manufacturing industries; in addition, nearly all of the 19 percent of farm sales exported in that year was processed by food and feed manufacturers abroad. Of

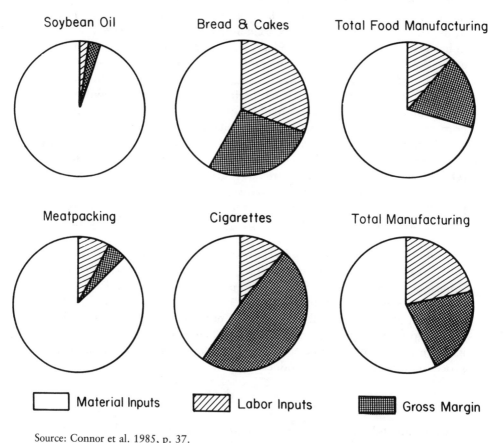

Source: Connor et al. 1985, p. 37.

Figure 4–2. Costs and Margins of Selected Manufacturing Industries, 1977

the remainder, about 8 percent of farm output is in the form of unprocessed foods (produce and eggs) and 5 percent in fibers other than tobacco. Dependence on farm raw materials leads to pronounced seasonal fluctuations in real output of some of the food industries. The seasonal adjustment factors developed by the Federal Reserve Board indicate a regular peaking (7 percent above the trend) of all food manufacturing in September and a trough (5 percent below the trend) in January. Seasonal fluctuations in the output of the beverage industries (peak in summer) and candy and liquor industries (peak before Christmas holidays) are largely demand induced.

Besides food ingredients, the other major material input is packaging. In 1980 the food and beverage manufacturing industries paid $34 billion for packaging and containers (Gallo and Connor 1981). This was 66 percent of the value of all such materials: 96 percent of all glass containers, 80 percent of textile bags, 71 percent of all metal cans, 62 percent of all paper packaging, and 46 percent of all other materials. For ten food manufacturing industries, the costs of packaging were found to outweigh manufacturers' costs of the food materials they contained.

Labor cost for food manufacturers accounted for 12 percent of shipments value. This was less than half the rate for all manufacturing. In 1972 the annual wages of food manufacturing production workers were about 5 percent below the all-manufacturing average; salaries of nonproduction workers were 17 percent lower. The phenomenon may be due to lower skill requirements, to the fact food processing plants tend to be located in rural areas, and to relatively weaker labor organizations.

Some food processing technologies require heavy use of heat or mechanical power; sugar refining, freezing, distilling, and brewing are outstanding examples. Energy costs represent only 2 percent of the costs of sales in the food industries, which is less than taxes or advertising. Yet by one estimate, the food and tobacco processing industries accounted for 40 percent of all the energy consumed by the commercial food production-distribution system (Federal Energy Administration 1974). The food system together with home preparation of foods utilized one-sixth of all U.S. energy output in 1974; this proportion rose substantially during the 1940–1970 period.

Expenditures for plants, equipment, office space, and other forms of capital are a relatively small portion of costs: about 3 percent. In 1977, about one-fifth of the new capital expenditures of food manufacturers was for plants, one-tenth for trucks, and the remaining 70 percent for other machinery and equipment. Because of extensive direct-to-store delivery systems, food manufacturers buy over one-fifth of the trucks purchased by all manufacturers. Food processing is more capital intensive than such heavy industries as machinery and transportation equipment. In fact, only four major industry groups are more capital intensive than food or tobacco manufacturing: paper, chemicals, petroleum, and primary metals.

Although many food industries experience significant seasonal fluctuations, aggregate domestic demand for established food products is very predictable from one year to the next. Partly as a result, capacity utilization is on average slightly higher and much steadier for food manufacturing than most other manufacturing industries.

The total costs of shipping agricultural food commodities and finished foods amounted to about $10 billion in 1977 (excluding intracity movements); shipping from food manufacturing plants cost about $8 billion, or 5 percent of the value of shipments. Processed foods were delivered an average distance of 300 miles from their points of manufacture in 1977; 80 percent (by value) were shipped less than 500 miles (Connor 1982b, appendix table 12). The average distance ranged from 1,469 miles for dried fruits and vegetables (most production is in California) to 7 miles for manufactured ice.

Product perishability, direct store delivery systems, territorial franchising, and high transportation costs imply the existence of local or regional markets for several food manufactures: cottage cheese, fluid milk products, ice cream, animal feeds, bread, ice, and soft drinks bottling. There are, for example, about 30 to 50 wholesale bread markets. These 7 are the only industries where 80 percent of the value of shipments was delivered within 200 miles of manufacturing points. The proportion of food manufacturing shipments in local markets exceeds that of the rest of manufacturing. Other food industries are essentially national in geographic scope: meat packing, most canned goods, dried and frozen fruits and vegetables, cigarettes, confectionery, and beverages (except beer and soft drinks). For national industries, closeness to sources of major materials plays a greater role in determining plant location than for the local market industries. Most food manufacturing industries fall in an intermediate category. There are, for example, three to five subnational markets for beer.

Market Structure

Market structure refers to the organizational characteristics of a market that largely determine where it falls in the competitive spectrum between monopoly and competition. The structure of a market is expected to influence the competitive *conduct* of sellers and buyers in the market, which in turn influences how well the market *performs*.

We examine three key structural characteristics: the number and size distribution of sellers and buyers, product differentiation, and conditions of entry. Research repeatedly has shown that these structural dimensions are crucial determinants of the market power in particular markets. We also examine, as a component of structure, the position occupied in particular markets by the large food manufacturing companies. Although this is often ignored in industrial organizational studies, large firms have characteristics that confer conduct options not attributable to the three structural characteristics.

Seller Market Concentration

Useful descriptions of market structure depend on sensible definitions of markets. Market definitions include both the geographic and product scope of the market. Markets vary in geographic scope from local (e.g., bread) to international (e.g., exported rice). The product scope of the market may include only a few or many products. Markets must be defined narrowly enough to exclude noncompeting products but not so narrowly as to omit truly competing products. Defining a market too broadly (or narrowly), either in its geographic size or its product scope, understates (overstates) the true level of market concentration. The Bureau of the Census (1977a) product classes, with some adjustments, are generally reasonable approximations of meaningful economic markets.

Company Numbers and Concentration Ratios. Several measures summarize the distribution of product sales among firms within a market. One measure, the number of firms selling the good, by itself tells little about competitive conditions unless the number becomes very small. Concentration ratios measure the importance of a few leading firms.

A large number of companies in a market may have a competitive influence even if concentration is high. Some of the small companies that operate on the fringe of the market have the potential to expand if market leaders restrict output and raise prices. In 1982 the number of companies in individual food industries varied greatly, ranging from 9 manufacturers of chewing gum to 1,863 wholesale bakers. The majority of food manufacturing firms are very small. Of the 17,000 companies that were primarily classified in food manufacturing in 1982, over half had fewer than ten employees and over 90 percent had fewer than one hundred employees.

Competitive conditions in a particular market are better measured by the four-firm concentration ratio (CR4) than by the number of companies. In 1977, nine of ninety-eight food and tobacco product classes had a CR4 over 80 percent (Connor et al. 1985). On the other hand, forty-one product classes had a CR4 below 40 percent. Concentration ratios for many of these product markets are understated, however. For example, the eight local-market product classes had average CR4s of about 25 percent. If corrections for the geographic size of markets were made, the concentration ratios of these product classes would average 50 percent to 70 percent.

Changing Seller Concentration. Average seller concentration in food and tobacco manufacturing has increased over time (table 4–1). By 1977, shipments

Table 4–1
Classification of National Food and Tobacco Product Classes by Bain's Concentration Types, 1958, 1967, and 1977
(percentage)

Bain's Concentration Type[a]	1958		1967		1977	
	Product Classes	*Value of Shipments*	*Product Classes*	*Value of Shipments*	*Product Classes*	*Value of Shipments*
I. Highly concentrated oligopolies	22.2	19.6	21.3	16.3	29.4	24.4
II. High-moderate concentrated oligopolies	20.4	14.2	25.0	21.6	25.2	26.1
III. Low-grade oligopolies	34.3	34.6	38.0	35.7	32.8	25.6
IV. Unconcentrated	23.1	31.6	15.7	26.4	12.6	23.9

Source: Bureau of the Census 1977c.

[a]Bain's (1968, pp. 124–133) concentration categories are as follows: Type I, CR8 ≥ 85 or CR4 ≥ 65; Type II, 70 ≤ CR8 < 85 or 50 ≤ CR4 < 65; Type III, 45 ≤ CR8 < 70 or 35 ≤ CR4 < 50; and Type IV, CR8 < 45 and CR4 < 35. In each year SIC 20999, other food preparations not elsewhere classified, was omitted.

from product classes in which the top four firms held less than 50 percent of shipments approximately equaled the shipments of product classes with CR4 ≥ 50 percent. Unconcentrated product classes probably have declined in the share of shipments since 1977 because of the dramatic restructuring of the beef packing industry, which accounted for 10.3 percent of 1977 processed food and tobacco shipments. New generation meat packers have sharply increased their share of the market, and many older companies have sold or closed plants. By early 1982, the two largest beef packers, IBP and Excel, were estimated to account for 35 percent of the beef slaughtered in the United States; the largest four firms slaughtered approximately 45 percent, which is about double the census CR4 in 1977 (Helmuth 1984). The rapid increases in concentration appear to have continued since 1982.

Average CR4 increased 4 percentage points (or about 9 percent) for eighty-five comparably defined food and tobacco product classes over the period 1958 to 1977 (figure 4–3). When the product classes are grouped into four advertising-to-sales categories, interesting differences become apparent. Product classes that used no media advertising actually decreased in concentration. As advertising intensity rose, the *increase* in CR4 became larger. The *level* of CR4 in each year also shows a positive relationship to advertising intensity. In 1977, the weighted CR4 for the high-advertising category was 70.2 percent, nearly twice the concentration level of the unadvertised or low-advertising-intensity group.

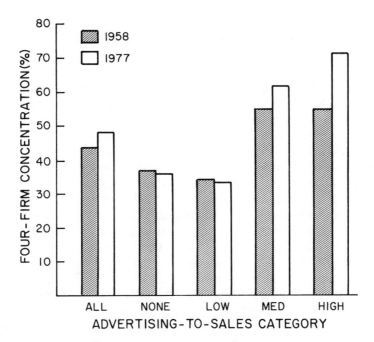

Source: Connor et al. 1985, p. 75.

Figure 4–3. Four-Firm Concentration Ratios by Advertising Intensity

Market Dominance. Economists have suggested that a 40 percent market share (in a relevant economic market) is sufficient to confer single-firm price leadership (Stigler 1968, p. 228; Scherer 1980). This can facilitate collusive price coordination by making explicit agreements unnecessary. Unfortunately, market shares of individual firms are rarely available to economic researchers.

The Nielsen early intelligence system (NEIS) report for 1980 provides one indication of market dominance. The NEIS product categories are frequently narrower than economic product markets; this may result in some overstatement of market shares. These data show that the leading brand held over 40 percent of category sales in 204 of the 378 NEIS product categories. In 39 product categories, private label brands as a group held over 40 percent of category sales. In the remaining 36 percent of product categories, neither a single brand nor private labels as a group held a dominant position (Connor et al. 1985, p. 77).

Product Differentiation

Product differentiation has an important influence on the conduct and performance of markets. The degree of product differentiation refers to the extent to which offerings of competing sellers are imperfect substitutes. When sub-stitutability is perfect, the products are undifferentiated, and no seller can charge a higher price.

Advertising is one of the major methods of differentiating food products. It is used as a proxy for product differentiation because the latter is difficult to measure directly. The advertising-to-sales ratio (ADS) is a widely used, if imperfect, proxy for advertising-created product differentiation.

The extent of product differentiation differs dramatically across products and brands. Brand names in themselves confer a degree of product differenti-ation. Generic products have little or no differentiation.

Physical differences are helpful but not necessary for product differentia-tion among brands. In many cases, product differentiation stems from images or other intangible differences. Although these illusory differences have many sources, most are created by firms' advertising efforts. Images are typically much harder to imitate or successfully counter than physically unique features.

Processed foods have several characteristics that encourage significant and often massive advertising expenditures (Greer 1980; Porter 1976b). They are generally packaged by the manufacturer under a brand name, bought fre-quently, sold with relatively low unit prices, and marketed predominantly through self-service retail outlets. These conditions help create an opportunity to develop consumer brand preferences through advertising.

Advertising Levels. In 1980, food and tobacco advertising expenditures ex-ceeded $8 billion according to data provided to the IRS. This was higher than any other broad manufacturing category and has been so since at least 1954. Chemicals and allied products, which includes such grocery items as house-hold cleaning products and health and beauty aids, was a distant second in advertising expenditures.

Mass media advertising is the main instrument for creating and main-taining food and tobacco product differentiation. In 1982, $4.5 billion was spent advertising food and tobacco products in six media reported by Leading National Advertisers (1983) (table 4–2). Television advertising dominated these six measured media expenditures with 70 percent of the expenditures. Magazines and newspaper supplements accounted for about 22 percent of the six-media advertising expenditures, outdoor advertisements accounted for nearly 7 percent, and network radio accounted for 1 percent.

The predominance of television is significant because television is widely held to be more effective than printed media in creating lasting impressions conducive to establishing and maintaining product differentiation (Porter 1976b). Moreover, the advantages large firms enjoy in advertising are greatest in television advertising (Levmore 1978; Rogers 1982).

Advertising by Industries. Advertising expenditures vary widely across food and tobacco industries. The heaviest advertising in 1977 was done by the

Table 4–2
Advertising Expenditures for Food and Tobacco Products by Media, 1972, 1977, and 1982

Year	U.S. Total	Television			Magazine	Newspaper Supplements	Network Radio	Outdoor
		Total	Network	Spot				
1972[a]	1,441	973	458	515	328	32	9	99
1977[a]	2,635	1,886	978	908	495	78	20	156
1982[a]	4,473	3,126	1,738	1,388	890	96	58	302
1972[b]	100	67.5	31.8	35.7	22.8	2.2	0.6	6.9
1977[b]	100	71.6	37.1	34.5	18.8	3.0	0.8	5.9
1982[b]	100	69.9	38.9	31.0	19.9	2.1	1.3	6.8

Source: Leading National Advertisers 1982, and earlier years.
[a]Millions of dollars.
[b]Percentages.

cigarette industry, with $338 million of media advertising. Six of the top ten food and tobacco advertising industries in 1977 also were among the ten heaviest advertisers in 1954 (Rogers and Mather 1983). Cigarette advertising was first in both years despite a prohibition on the use of television since 1971. Beer and breakfast cereals ranked two and three in 1977 and were also among the top ten in 1954. Distilled liquor was in the top ten in both years. Industries that moved into the top ten advertisers' list between 1954 and 1977 were pet food, soft drinks, candy, and chewing gum. Overall, the 1977 top ten advertisers might cause some anguish for those who believe that consumption of tobacco, alcohol, and sugar is related to health problems.

Many of the leading industries in dollars of advertising are also among the top industries in terms of advertising intensity (ADS); however, large industries like coffee and soft drinks had lower ADS rankings than their ranks based on absolute dollar expenditures, while some smaller industries, like wine and flavorings, rated higher in the ADS rankings.

Of the ninety-eight processed food and beverage product markets included in table B–8, twenty product markets had six-media ADS exceeding 3 percent. A nearly equal number (twenty-two) had ADS of zero. The product classes that are the most intense users of media advertising tend to be the most concentrated as well; examples are chewing gum, breakfast cereals, ready-to-mix desserts, and cigarettes. The most concentrated product class, canned baby food, is an exception, with an ADS of 1.4 percent, ranking thirty-eighth out of the ninety-eight products. Gerber has such a dominant position in baby foods (70 percent of sales according to Fierman 1984) that it can apparently maintain its market position and discourage entry with a relatively low level of advertising. As a rule high ADS occurs when the CR4 is either high or increasing and the market leaders have similar market shares.

Aggregate Concentration of Advertising Expenditures. Advertising expenditures are highly concentrated among a few large firms. In 1982, over 1,100 companies had measured media advertising for their food products, but 81.5 percent of the advertising originated from the fifty largest food advertisers (table 4–3). This was an increase of nearly 8 percentage points since 1967. The twelve largest food advertisers accounted for most of the increase as they increased their share from nearly 40 to 45 percent. Beyond the top fifty advertisers, the use of advertising falls off dramatically.

Concentration levels were even higher in network television advertising of food than for all six media combined (Rogers and Mather 1983). In 1982, twelve firms accounted for 59 percent of the network advertising of food. The top fifty food advertisers on network television held 95.5 percent, leaving no doubt that network television is dominated by the largest firms with nationally distributed brands. Spot television has lower concentration levels than network television because more firms with regional brands can afford to advertise on a spot basis. The top fifty food advertisers on spot television accounted for 75.2 percent of the total in 1982.

The top fifty advertisers have remained largely the same for a quarter-century, after allowing for mergers. Rogers and Mather (1983) compared the top fifty in 1954 and 1977. The most noticeable change was that the companies were less specialized in 1977. In 1954 the top fifty advertised in an average of 3.6 food industries, and by 1977 they advertised in 10.5 industries.

Total Selling Costs. Media advertising data present only a partial view of the sales promotion activities of food firms. First, some kinds of mass media advertising are not measured (such as ads in special interest, business, or trade publications) or cannot be classified. Second, much consumer-directed ("pull") advertising is not in the mass media. Gallo (1981) estimated that in 1979, such devices as premiums, package design, trading stamps, contests, sweepstakes, and free samples amounted to at least 65 percent of media ad-

Table 4–3
Concentration of Food Advertising Expenditures among the Fifty Largest Food Advertisers
(percentage)

	1967 Share	*1982 Share*
Four largest	20.97	21.05
Eight largest	30.94	34.38
Twelve largest	39.48	45.02
Twenty-five largest	57.73	65.04
Fifty largest	73.63	81.54

Source: Connor et al. 1985, p. 85.

vertising costs. Third, food manufacturers direct substantial selling efforts at food distributors in order to persuade them to stock their brands. Such "push promotions" as point-of-purchase displays for stores, direct field sales forces, trade deals, trade fairs and conventions, cooperative advertising, and liberal delivery and return practices, have been estimated at two to three times media advertising expenditures (Gallo 1981). Taken together, total U.S. food and beverage selling expenses (advertising and sales promotion) in 1980 amounted to at least $10 billion and possibly as high as $15 billion. In these totals, advertising in the six measured media represented 30 to 45 percent of selling expenses.

The FTC Line of Business Program provided data on both the media advertising and total selling expenses of nearly 500 large manufacturers (Connor et al. 1985). These data allocate enterprise sales and costs according to SIC industry definitions called lines of business (FTC 1979). For 1974–1976, the food manufacturing firms included in this program devoted 3.2 percent of their sales to media advertising, nearly three times the all-manufacturing average. Total selling expenses of food manufacturers averaged 13.0 percent of sales, about twice the all-manufacturing average.

Conditions of Entry

Barriers to entry refer to anything that provides established sellers in an industry an advantage over potential entrants. "Entry" in this context refers to "de novo" entry as opposed to entry by acquiring an established firm. The latter involves simply a change in ownership; no new capacity or additional competitors have been added to the industry.

If entry barriers are low, even firms in highly concentrated industries have little discretion to charge noncompetitive prices. Where both entry barriers and concentration are high, established firms may enjoy considerable discretion in their pricing and output decisions without attracting new entrants. There are five commonly recognized types of entry barriers.

1. *Absolute cost advantage* barriers exist if the unit costs of established firms are lower for all levels of output than the costs that can be achieved by a newcomer. Incumbents may have lower unit costs because of access to cheaper materials or purchased services, superior production technologies unavailable to entrants, or lower interest rates on borrowed capital.

2. *Scale* barriers exist if the minimum efficient scale (MES) of a plant or firm is large relative to industry size and suboptimal-sized firms are subject to significantly higher costs. When both of these characteristics are met, new entrants must enter at a size that adds significantly to total industry output. Unless total industry sales are expanding rapidly, sizable market shares will take time to acquire, and a new entrant will be at a cost disadvantage while it is building market share.

3. *Capital cost* barriers refer to the size of investment required for efficient entry. The absolute size of investment often determines the number of potential entrants. There are far fewer potential entrants when the initial investment required to operate an efficient plant is $1 billion than when it is $1 million. Unlike the first two barriers discussed, capital cost barriers disappear for those with a big enough bankroll.

4. *Product differentiation* barriers often involve substantial marketing costs for advertising and unique packaging. Incumbents with differentiated products may have advantages over new entrants because search costs and risk avoidance make consumers loyal to their old brands; the expenditures required to persuade consumers to try new brands or products are higher than the expenditures required to maintain brand loyalty; there are increasing returns to advertising and promotion activities over a wide range of expenditures; or the capital outlays for advertising and promotion campaigns are large and difficult to finance from debt capital (Comanor and Wilson 1974). Whereas the above barriers to entry arise from market structure, other barriers can be created by firm conduct.

5. *Strategic behavior* by incumbent firms can prevent or deter market entry by would-be sellers (Yip 1982). Steven Salop (1979, p. 335) defines strategic entry barriers as those "purposely erected to reduce the possibility of entry." The four structural barriers to entry he labels innocent because they are unintentionally erected as a side effect of profit-maximizing behavior.

Entry Barriers in Food Manufacturing. Barriers to entry are difficult to measure. We review here empirical evidence on the extent to which plant economies of scale, product differentiation, and firm economies of size create entry barriers in food and tobacco manufacturing.

Economies of scale refer to the relationship between the average unit cost of producing an item and the quantity produced. A minimum efficient scale (MES) plant is the smallest-sized plant at which minimum unit costs are achieved, where costs include both production and physical distribution activities.

Estimating a MES for an industry is a complicated and technical problem (see Scherer et al. 1975). The available evidence (National Commission on Food Marketing 1966b; Culbertson and Morrison 1983) suggests that plant economies are not substantial in food manufacturing and have increased relatively little over time. Although the MES estimates are not precise, they provide rough estimates. The average U.S. food manufacturing industry could accommodate roughly thirty-five to fifty efficient-sized plants. In approximately one-fifth of the industries, scale economies call for twenty or fewer efficient-sized plants nationally. Since a new MES plant would add a small amount to national industry output in most cases, the newcomer must take only a relatively small share from incumbents for products sold in national markets; for products sold in local or regional markets, the displacement effect of a new MES plant could be substantial.

Product differentiation is an important barrier to entry into the advertised brand segment of most food manufacturing industries. Product differentiation barriers derive in some cases from first-mover advantages, the fact that advertising effectiveness of new entrants is often less than the advertising effectiveness of incumbent firms (Folsom and Greer 1983).

There is also some evidence of increasing marginal returns to advertising up to a large size. The sales response per dollar of advertising for some products increases until advertising expenditures reach a large absolute amount. New entrants and smaller firms must devote a higher percentage of sales to advertising than do large firms to get the same effect. For example, Brown (1978) found that average costs of advertising fall sharply with sales and that returns to advertising capital increase with sales over a wide range, "implying that barriers to entry due to advertising do exist and are substantial" (p. 435). Although Brown's analysis dealt with the cigarette industry, his findings should apply to most highly advertised convenience consumer goods. Comanor and Wilson (1979, p. 470) in a review article concluded, "Taken together, these results suggest that economies of scale in advertising are generally present, which provides an important advantage to large advertisers. . . . These economies may be an important factor leading to the anti-competitive implications of heavy advertising expenditures."

In addition to increasing returns to advertising expenditures within a particular market, there is also evidence of economies resulting from large advertising expenditures for the firm as a whole. One advantage for large advertisers is their ability to buy advertising time and space cheaper than small advertisers. Until at least the mid-1960s, there were substantial volume discounts in television advertising (Blake and Blum 1965). The discriminatory discount structure of television advertising has been formally discontinued; however, Levmore (1978, pp. 28–29) found, "There is every reason to believe that although the fixed rates and discounts have been formally abandoned in favor of a system in which prices are established through case-by-case bargains, these current bargained-for rates contain in them these very discounts. In other words, the 'outdated' rate and discount system is an excellent predictor of the current rate system." Multiproduct firms receive additional discounts by buying blocks of advertising time for their various products. It is cheaper to buy one minute of network advertising time and advertise two products for thirty seconds each than to buy two thirty-second slots.

Large firms often purchase a mix of commercial television time that includes prime time, daytime, some excellent placement, and some nonpreferred time and then pay one price for the entire package. Such procedures make it difficult to uncover any price discrimination. One bit of evidence is that Columbia Pictures, after being acquired by Coca-Cola, found that the increased discounts available to it allowed it to obtain about 5 percent more network television time than with the same advertising budget prior to its acquisition (*Fortune*, December 26, 1983).

Unlike Levmore, Porter (1976a) concentrated on examining only the rate structure and not the bargained-for packages of advertising time. He found quantity discounts to be unclear for network television but present for spot television and for many magazines and newspapers. Moreover, he found great economies in using national as opposed to local television advertising, implying that a firm or a potential entrant will be at a cost disadvantage if it must use local advertising to compete with national advertising by national firms.

This last point is related to the quality of the advertising time purchased. Clearly not all advertising time is equally desirable. Prime time is exactly what the name implies, usually the evening hours when the greatest number of viewers are present. Much of the available prime time space, however, is limited to sale in package deals at prices that exclude most smaller companies. Scala (1973) noted that large advertisers appear to secure more favorable time slots than smaller advertisers. The time slot is critical for many products because certain programs are much more valuable than others. For example, if major sports events are foreclosed by major brewers, other brewers are disadvantaged even when they have access to other prime time programs at the same cost per minute. Network rules (found in other media as well) that prevent competing products from being advertised too close together exacerbate the difficulty in gaining access to such programs. Although these rules raise the private financial value of the advertisement, they limit the number of competing sellers that can advertise on a major program.

Large, diversified food advertisers also enjoy an advantage over small firms in being able to pool the risks from advertising several products. There is great variation in the success of advertising campaigns. Even if a firm spends the vast sums necessary to buy good advertising time and hire excellent artistic talent and other professional services, the campaign may fail. The specialized firm faces greater risk from failure than the multiproduct firm that can self-insure through multiple campaigns.

Financially, large firms are preferred clients by the larger advertising agencies. Advertising agencies avoid conflict of interests by not representing sellers of competing products. They may be reluctant to represent smaller firms since that may prevent them from taking on the more lucrative business of a larger competitor.

Relatively little is known about *multiplant or firm-level economies of size* in food manufacturing. Multiplant size advantages may result from operating a network of spatially decentralized and/or product-specialized plants. These economies—resulting from lower shipping costs, peak-load spreading, pooling of capacity reserves, product specialization, and optimal investment staging—often are significant. They are real or direct economies of size (lower production and distribution cost) that result in raised social welfare even if all the benefits go to producers and have no effect on consumer prices (Caves 1978). One study of the U.S. brewing and cigarette industries estimated that two to three plants were necessary to realize all direct advantages to size (Scherer et al. 1975, pp. 334–335).

In addition, there are advantages of size that may not result in real economies, though in many cases they may result in increased private financial returns. These result from increasing returns (both real and pecuniary) in nonproduction activities. Some of these are associated with the purchase of advertising services and other promotional activities. Advantages of size may also occur in materials procurement, backward or forward vertical integration, and financial capital acquisition. The returns from increasing size in these instances do not necessarily increase economic welfare.

Very little empirical research has been done on the minimum efficient firm size in any of the manufacturing industries; however, studies have been made of the brewing, cigarette, and ready-to-eat cereal industries. Allowing for both direct and derived advantages of size, Scherer (1980) concluded that one to two cigarette plants were needed for a firm to capture nearly all multiplant economies. Companies of this size would have held 6 to 12 percent of the 1967 cigarette market.

Scherer (1975) estimated that plant economies of scale in brewing were fully realized at about 4.5 million barrels of output, or 3 percent of U.S. total production in 1970. Because of the growth in beer sales during the 1970s, there was room for roughly 43 MES plants in 1982. If multiplant economies still required three to four plants as Scherer (1980, p. 336) estimated, then an efficient-sized firm in 1982 would have needed 6.9 to 9.2 percent of the beer market. Scherer did his analysis, however, when nearly all brewers were specialized (1970–1972). Shortly after, Miller—its advertising coffers brimming with tobacco profits from its parent Philip Morris—began to teach the brewing industry a lesson about the power of large-scale advertising and astute product positioning. The advantages of firm size in this case go beyond those considered by Scherer; they are closely tied to overall firm size and conglomerate cross-subsidization to finance massive advertising campaigns.

Multiplant economies in cereal manufacturing are apparently not great. Based on evidence for the 1960s and early 1970s, Scherer (1982) concluded that firms with efficient-sized plants (4 to 6 percent of market) suffer few disadvantages in relation to larger cereal companies.[6] While this may seem like a modest market share for a new entrant to achieve, in fact it represents an almost impossible task because of the high level of product proliferation in cereals. As brand crowding becomes great, it is increasingly difficult for a new brand to find a sizable niche in the market. In breakfast cereals, it would be unrealistic for an entrant with a new brand to expect to gain more than 1 percent of the market. Hence, a new entrant would be faced with successfully launching five or six new brands in a short time.

The beer, cigarette, and cereal industries probably have greater multiplant economies of size than the typical food manufacturing industry. The estimates indicate that in all three of these industries, multiplant economies of size are probably realized with 5 to 10 percent of the market, requiring at most a CR4 of 40 percent. However, these estimates are based only on industry-related economies. There are also private financial advantages of absolute firm size and conglomerate power that have not been measured.

Strategic behavior by incumbent firms with market power is often different when directed toward a prospective entrant than when aimed at established firms (Spence 1981; Salop 1979; Williamson 1977; and Yip 1982). Typically these strategies involve accepting short-term losses in expectation of larger long-term profits. The most straightforward strategic response is deep price cutting that sacrifices some of the short-run monopoly profits of the incumbents. If the potential entrants expect the lower-than-maximum prices to hold indefinitely, then entry may be prevented or, more likely, held to a manageable trickle (Gaskins 1971). Other strategies include building excess capacity, product proliferation, trade deals, and massive advertising. Each of these imposes added entry costs on the prospective entrant.

Such strategies are especially effective when engaged in by a multimarket or multiproduct firm. When such incumbents can discriminate in different geographic or product markets, they can sustain losses in one market with profits earned elsewhere. The incumbent may use such strategies to signal prospective entrants that they may expect a costly strategic response in any market occupied by the incumbent.

Conclusions Regarding Entry Barriers. Although entry barriers are difficult to study directly, the direct and indirect evidence available warrants some conclusions. Entry barriers into the manufacture of producer goods and undifferentiated consumer food products (unbranded and private label products) generally are low except for products with relatively small geographic markets. Entry barriers are much higher in the manufacture of branded food products sold through grocery stores. Product differentiation stemming from advertising and product proliferation is the major entry barrier in these industries; these are not contestable markets.[7] Plant economies of scale are generally modest in food manufacturing industries. Except in some local or regional market industries, plant economies of scale do not pose significant barriers to entry.

Indirect evidence confirms that entry barriers are substantial in some industries. The positive relationship between concentration and profits found in many empirical studies indicates that significant entry barriers exist. Furthermore, interviews with private label manufacturers indicate that there are substantial barriers to the mobility of private label manufacturers into the advertised brand business (Hamm 1980).

If there were no barriers to entry, firms in highly concentrated industries with high levels of advertising would be unable to charge prices exceeding costs and reap higher profits—the results presented later in this chapter. One can also observe the extent to which entry has occurred as indirect evidence of entry barriers. In those industries where high profits provide the greatest incentive for entry—highly concentrated products with high levels of advertising—new entrants into the branded product segment are few and far between (examples are: breakfast cereals, gelatin desserts, chewing gum, cigarettes, concentrated coffee, canned soup, beer, soft drinks, and baby food).

Concentration Change

Changes in concentration are especially revealing because they serve as a proxy for changes in other elements of structure. For example, if entry barriers increase, industry concentration will probably rise as well.

Rogers (1982, 1984b) constructed a model to explain concentration change in food and tobacco product classes between 1958 and 1977 and over intercensus subperiods. His model focused on the primary structural characteristics of these product classes that may promote concentration change but did not distinguish between concentration change caused by mergers (or divestitures) and by internal firm expansions (contractions). His results indicate that advertising-created and -maintained product differentiation is primarily responsible for structural change in the food manufacturing industries. Rogers found a consistent, significant positive relationship between major media advertising, especially television advertising, and concentration change. Product classes with high levels of television advertising experienced increased concentration even if they were initially highly concentrated.

The second major influence in Rogers's model was the level of initial concentration (ICR). If the product class did not use television or radio advertising, then predicted concentration change was negative except at very low initial concentration levels (see Connor et al. 1985, table 3–7). This concentration-decreasing pressure was offset by relatively low levels of television and radio advertising intensity (TVR), however. For example if initial CR4 was 80 and TVR was zero, the regression results predicted a drop in CR4 of 9.3 percentage points between 1958 and 1977; however, if the television-radio advertising-to-sales ratio was 2 percent, the model gives an increase in predicted concentration of nearly 1 percentage point. TVRs of 2 to 6 percent had the strongest effects on changes in concentration.

Other factors can work to erode concentration. Occasionally the ability of product differentiation to stimulate consumer loyalty wanes, for reasons that are not well understood. Examples in the food industries are canned milk, fluid milk, canned tuna, and family flour. In addition, when a market's sales growth outpaces the growth of the leading sellers, concentration will decline. Rogers (1982) has shown that this generally has not happened in food and tobacco industries. Those product classes with the largest increase in concentration also tended to have the most rapid growth rate.

In theory, high profits attract new firms into a market unless entry is impeded. Advertising-created and -maintained product differentiation has deterred entry in food product classes where entry would be most attractive. This evidence contradicts the argument made by some that advertising facilitates entry (Posner 1979). Although there is growing evidence that advertising may ease entry into some nonfood retail activities, there is no comparable evidence for manufacturing industries (Comanor and Wilson 1979). No study of concentration change in manufacturing industries has ever found a significant negative relationship between advertising and concentration change (Rogers 1982).

Advertising rivalry among marketing giants is common in differentiated products. At times an advertising war develops that is similar in some respects to a price war. Promotional rivalry compares well to a poker game where the bets continually increase until the smaller firms are forced to withdraw because the stakes have become too large. A familiar example of this is the periodic cola wars between the two dominant soft drink companies, Coca-Cola and PepsiCo. John Sculley, former president of PepsiCo was quoted in the *Wall Street Journal* (November 6, 1982, p. 1) as saying such struggles do not involve "some gladiatorial contest where one of us has to leave on a stretcher. We're both winning." Similarly, accelerating advertising expenditures in the beer industry in the late 1970s has led to increasing concentration of sales among the top two firms in the industry.

High labor costs (and fringe benefits) of incumbent firms have made entry easier in some industries, thereby leading to an erosion of concentration. High-wage-cost firms are particularly vulnerable to new entry if they produce an undifferentiated product. If brand loyalty exists for the leading firms, they may enjoy a price premium sufficient to cover higher labor costs. The most recent notable example of entry facilitated by entrants' cost advantages is the meat packing industry. In that industry, however, the deconcentrating effect of low-wage entrants appears to have run its course. The major entrants (IBP and Excel) are now the industry leaders and since the late 1970s have been contributing to increased concentration in beef slaughtering. Another potential deconcentrating force, the growth of imports, has been a minor factor in most food and tobacco manufacturing industries. There is no reason to expect a sharp increase in imports in most food industries.

The increase in the number of generic food and tobacco items in recent years could reduce the importance of advertising-created and -maintained product differentiation. If product differentiation were weakened, entry barriers would drop and with them seller concentration. But to date, generics appear to have had little influence on either product differentiation or seller concentration (Wills and Mentzer 1982). Generics and private label products have been least successful in highly advertised products with high levels of concentration, the products with the greatest competitive problems.

U.S. antitrust laws have had some success in preventing increased concentration by mergers among companies in the same market. They have been ineffective in deterring increased concentration from less direct sources, such as the intensive use of advertising, predation, and cross-subsidization. The antitrust laws have been ineffective in deconcentrating an industry once it has become highly concentrated.

In some important food and tobacco product classes, the forces contributing to greater market concentration more than offset the deconcentrating forces. There remain, however, many product classes with modest levels of seller concentration. Most of these have modest levels of advertising and low entry barriers. Thus, although we have focused particular attention on concentrated product classes with high advertising and barriers to entry, there remains a sizable portion of food manufacturing where market structures imply that competition is still alive and well.

Nature and Importance of Large Food Firms

Market concentration and other structural variables provide valuable insights into oligopoly or monopoly power. These structural variables fail to reveal the power of large corporations that are highly diversified, however. Some economists have argued that there is nothing unique in conglomerate power. It is not the absolute size of a corporation that confers power, these economists argue, but such basic structural characteristics as the nature of the markets in which it operates and its relative position in these markets (Adelman 1951, p. 243). But as Stocking (1955) emphasized, although many aspects of conglomerate power "can be fitted within traditional concepts," doing so "might tend to conceal rather than reveal their social and economic significance" (p. 358).

To gain added insight into the nature and significance of large food corporations, we note the share of food manufacturing done by the largest firms —that is, the level of aggregate concentration in food manufacturing. Then in order to comprehend better the unique economic power inherent in these firms, we examine the characteristics of the markets in which the largest firms operate and their positions in these markets.

Aggregate Concentration. Aggregate concentration measures the share of some large segment of the economy (such as all food manufacturing) controlled by the largest companies (such as the top 100 or 500). The measure is used here to quantify the changing importance of large corporations in the food manufacturing industries. It measures the top companies' share of the business across all markets combined rather than their share in individual markets.

Viewed solely in terms of firm numbers, food manufacturing appears to be highly decentralized. In 1982 preliminary census data show about 17,000 food manufacturing firms, down by well over half from 1947. Not only has there been a high mortality rate among small food manufacturers, but the share of food manufacturing assets held by the largest 100 companies has risen by over 60 percent since 1950 (Connor et al. 1985, table 3.8). A superior measure of aggregate domestic concentration in food manufacturing is the top companies' share of total domestic value-added by food manufacturers. Using value-added, the top 200 food manufacturers' (excluding alcoholic beverages) share rose from 49 percent in 1954 to 64 percent in 1977 (figure 4–4). During the period, the top 100 firms' share rose from 42 percent to 53 percent, or about one-fourth. The increases were centered mainly in the top 20 firms. By 1977, the top 20 firms towered above all others, holding a share about as great as the next 80 largest firms combined and considerably greater than the combined shares of the 101st to 500th largest food manufacturers (Connor et al. 1985, table 3.9). This trend probably has continued

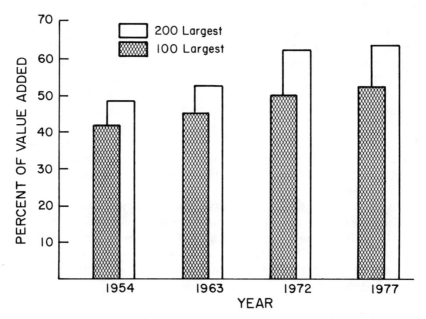

Source: Connor et al. 1985, p. 120.

Figure 4–4. Aggregate Concentration in Food Manufacturing

since 1977 because in recent years leading food and tobacco companies have been involved in several large mergers (ibid., figure 4–4), including the largest nonoil merger in history, Philip Morris' acquisition of General Foods (*Wall Street Journal*, September 30, 1985, p. 3). This created the largest U.S. consumer products company.

Despite the high levels of aggregate concentration, the centralization of control over decision making may be even greater than measures based solely on ownership. Caswell (1984) argues persuasively that the true level of aggregate concentration is higher because the largest food firms are linked to each other in a network of overlapping stockholdings, directors, financial ties, and other business contacts.

Characteristics of Markets in Which Large Firms Operate. Aggregate and market concentration in food manufacturing are related. The typical large food manufacturer is among the leaders in the markets where it operates, and it operates most extensively in large and highly concentrated markets and those in which product differentiation is most prevalent.

Leading Market Positions. In 1954 the top 100 food manufacturing companies occupied 63 percent of the top four positions in all census food product classes (excluding alcoholic beverages); by 1963 this had increased to 70 percent (National Commission on Food Marketing 1966b). More recent information from a special census tabulation shows that the top 100 have continued to hold the dominant positions in food manufacturing achieved in 1963. A leveling off of the portion of top positions held by the 100 largest companies occurred during 1963–1977 and may be explained by three factors. First, many of the product classes in which the top 100 did not hold leading positions are only marginally related to food manufacturing (such as ice manufacturing) or have small sales, and therefore may be of little interest to large companies. Second, attaining a third- or fourth-place position in a market may not be attractive if the top two positions are already occupied by other large firms with dominant shares, especially when this requires displacing another large conglomerate firm. Third, some product classes in which the top 100 companies held no leading positions are not meaningful economic markets. For example, the top 100 held no leading positions in SIC 20136, processed pork not made in meat packing plants, but held all four leading positions in SIC 20116, processed pork made in meat packing plants. These are both in the same economic market. Thus, the largest food manufacturers may now hold virtually all of the leading positions that are attractive for them.

The top 100 firms controlled the highest percentage of leading positions in the most concentrated product classes (figure 4–5). Holding leading positions in concentrated industries reflects greater market dominance than in

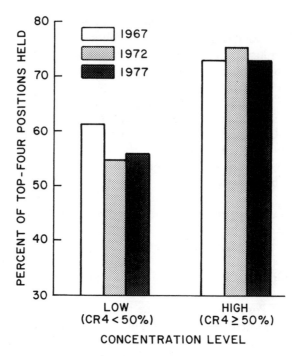

Source: Connor et al. 1985, p. 124.

Figure 4–5. Leading National Market Positions Held by the Top 100 Food and Tobacco Manufacturers

unconcentrated industries. Through their leading positions, the top 100 accounted for over 80 percent of the total shipments in markets with concentration ratios of at least 70 percent (Connor et al. 1985, p. 125).

Rogers and Schiferl (1984) found a significant positive relationship between the number of top four positions held by the 100 largest food companies and product class size (as measured by shipments). Nonetheless, the largest firms hold a large percentage of leading positions in smaller classes as well. For example, in 1977 the 100 largest firms held 48 percent of the leading positions in the smallest products. This reflects the pervasiveness of large food manufacturing companies.

The top 100 companies held a disproportionately high percentage of leading positions and shipments in highly differentiated products (figure 4–6). In 1977 the top 100 companies held 50 percent of the leading positions in undifferentiated product classes and 80 percent of such positions in the most differentiated product classes (Rogers and Schiferl 1984). Moreover, between 1967 and 1977, the percentage of leading positions held by the top 100 rose from 74 percent to 80 percent in the industries with the most product differentiation. In contrast, their relative positions declined in lower product differentiation classes.

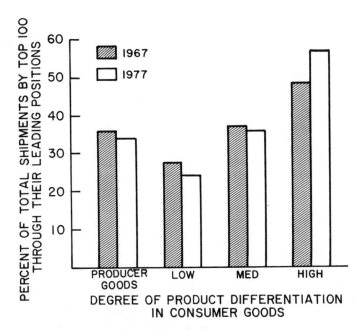

Source: Special Tabulation of 1977 Census of Manufacturers.

Figure 4–6. Percentage of Total Shipments by Top 100 through Their Leading Positions

Market Shares of the Largest Food Companies. Another way of looking at the potential market power of large firms is to examine their market shares in the products they sell. Table 4–4 shows various groupings of companies and the percentage of their sales that were made in products where they held those market shares. The largest companies held higher market shares than did smaller companies. In 1977, the 20 largest companies made 56 percent of their sales in markets where they had market shares of 20 percent or more. By comparison, the twenty-first to fiftieth largest firms made only 12 percent of their sales in such markets.

Between 1967 and 1977, the largest 20 companies increased the proportion of their business done in markets where they held large market shares, whereas smaller companies experienced the opposite trend. The proportion of total sales of the top 20 companies coming from product markets where they had market shares of 20 percent or more increased from 39 percent to 56 percent. In contrast, the next 480 companies as a group experienced a decline in their share of sales made in markets where they had shares of 20 percent or more.

Combined Effects of Market Characteristics. The overall conclusion is that the largest food and tobacco companies occupied most of the leading positions

Table 4–4

Share of Company Shipments in Various Market Share Categories, by Company Size Groups, 1967 and 1977

(percentage of group's shipments)

Company Size Group[a]	5 Percent or More		10 Percent or More		15 Percent or More		20 Percent or More		30 Percent or More	
	1967	1977	1967	1977	1967	1977	1967	1977	1967	1977
1– 20 largest	91	89	71	76	51	65	39	56	23	35
21– 50 largest	76	73	43	45	27	25	18	12	10	6
51–100 largest	63	65	32	41	21	16	13	8	6	4
101–200 largest	53	53	26	24	11	12	5	6	n.a.	0
201–500 largest	16	23	6	8	1	3	0	2	n.a.	1

Source: Connor et al. 1985, p. 128.

Note: Includes only products sold in national markets.

[a]Ranked by value-added in food and tobacco manufacturing.

n.a. = not available

in food and tobacco products and that their dominance was higher in those product classes that were more highly differentiated, more concentrated, and had larger sales. In a regression analysis explaining the percentage of a product class's shipments accounted for by the 100 largest food and tobacco companies, each of those characteristics of the markets was independently significant (Connor et al. 1985). For example, for an unconcentrated product class (CR4 = 20 percent) that does not advertise and has small shipments (VOS = $100 million), the regression results predict that the top 100 would control 19 percent of its shipments. For a concentrated product class (CR4 = 80 percent) with a high advertising-to-sales ratio (ADS = 10 percent) that had large shipments (VOS = $5,000 million), the equation predicts 100 percent control by the top 100 companies.

Between 1967 and 1977, the leading food and tobacco companies increased their share of shipments in those products with the highest concentration and advertising intensity. Overall, by 1977 there was very little opportunity for the largest firms to achieve additional leading market positions without displacing other large food firms. This was especially true in the most highly concentrated and differentiated products.

Today a mere 100 corporations control the greater part of all assets and value-added in food manufacturing. Their share has grown continuously and substantially over the past three decades. The economic power residing in these huge firms is reflected not only in their large financial resources but in their strong market positions. Thus there is a connecting link between the rising market concentration occurring in many individual product markets and the growing aggregate concentration in food manufacturing.

Diversification

Sales diversification is widespread today in the food manufacturing industries, particularly among large companies. While not unknown prior to World War II, manufacturing diversification accelerated greatly after 1945. The motives for and performance effects of diversification are not completely understood. The urge to diversify is often the result of corporate strategies to increase the rate or stability of growth or profits. When diversification occurs by means of mergers and acquisitions, the process is often controversial. Diversification among leading companies is one source of increasing aggregate concentration in food manufacturing. Moreover, sales diversification has probably contributed to reduced turnover among the largest industrial firms (Caves 1980). Whether this represents a case of economic hardening of the arteries or more efficiency in the allocation of capital resources is one of the most debated questions in industrial organization economics.

A firm diversifies its operations when it begins to sell in more than one market. Market boundaries are determined by the nature of the product and by geographic spread. *Product diversification* refers to the extent to which a firm sells a variety of goods or services in a single geographic area. Three types of product diversification may be conceptually distinguished: horizontal, vertical, and conglomerate. *Horizontal diversification* involves market extensions into industries that are similar in production technologies or marketing channels to the original or base industry of the firm. The movement of a Wisconsin butter manufacturer into Wisconsin cheese making constitutes horizontal diversification. In this chapter, special attention is devoted to horizontal diversification of food manufacturers into nonfood manufacturing industries whose products are sold largely through grocery stores. *Vertical diversification* by food manufacturers occurs through the ownership and control of successive stages of the food system—either sources of material inputs for manufacturing or distributors of finished food products. Vertical diversification as indicated by ownership is likely to exceed the extent of true vertical integration because some shipments from establishments that are vertically related to food processing may be sold outside the company. Ownership of product lines that are neither horizontally nor vertically related is called *conglomerate diversification*; butter and guns is an example.

The production of a food product in two or more spatially distinct markets is termed *geographic diversification*. Spatial separation of markets is determined by the interaction of demand and supply or by jurisdictional boundaries. Demand for most processed foods is remarkably uniform across the United States, though for some foods, distinct regional or ethnic differences exist. Supply conditions are likely to be a more important cause of geographic segmentation, particularly transportation costs of inputs or finished goods. State and national borders also may create geographically separate markets.

Measurement problems abound for all kinds of diversification. The usual approach is to classify firms according to their primary, principal, or historical base industry. These classifications are often mechanical or arbitrary, as is the division between the primary and secondary activities. In highly diversified firms, the primary industry may account for less than 10 percent of sales. Moreover, most data sets do not permit distinguishing among the major types of diversification.

Product Diversification

The earliest recorded instances of product diversification by U.S. food manufacturers occurred among the major meat packers between 1880 to 1920. By 1900 the five leading companies were producing in ten or more food industries and five or more other manufacturing industries that used meat packing by-products (soap, leather, and other products). In addition, the big meat packers were heavily vertically integrated into stockyards, railway cars, and wholesale and retail meat operations. During the late 1920s, two modern food conglomerates were formed by mergers: General Foods (now part of Philip Morris) and Standard Brands (now part of R.J. Reynolds). The arrays of leading brands of dry grocery products put together by those firms made it advantageous to set up their own direct field sales forces.

The best public data on levels of product diversification in food manufacturing are the enterprise statistics of the Bureau of the Census (1977a). All companies are assigned to one of 199 primary enterprise industry categories; firms primarily involved in food and tobacco manufacturing are placed in one of 15 categories encompassing from one to seven four-digit SIC industries. The primary industry of a firm is that enterprise industry that accounts for the largest share of company payroll. All other industries in which the firm is active are designated nonprimary or secondary industries. This classification procedure suggests an obvious measure of *outbound* diversification: the importance of nonprimary activity compared to total activity of the firm.

Some initial information concerning food and tobacco manufacturing diversification can be obtained with the use of several nonprimary employment or sales ratios. In 1977, 45 percent of food manufacturer employment was outside of the firms' principal enterprise industry (figure 4–7). This is higher than the average for all manufacturing firms, and food manufacturing as a group ranks eighth among the twenty manufacturing groups by this measure. Based on 1977 sales, outbound diversification for food and tobacco manufacturing is 59 percent, compared to 49 percent for all manufacturing, which places the food industries about sixth (Connor 1982b, p. 55).

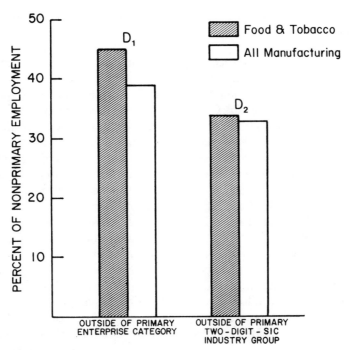

Source: Connor et al. 1985, p. 172.

Figure 4–7. Nonprimary Employment: Food and Tobacco Manufacturing versus All Manufacturing, 1977

Another measure is the share of total company employment outside the primary two-digit SIC group (in this case, food), a rough measure of vertical plus conglomerate diversification. Among food manufacturing firms, 34 percent of nonprimary employment is outside food manufacturing and 11 percent is in other food industries. Food is more diversified than the rest of manufacturing on average.

Target Industries of Food Manufacturers. More evidence concerning the direction of outbound diversification can be obtained from a recent study by MacDonald (1983, chap. 6). These data describe the distribution of sales of the 200 largest food and tobacco manufacturers in 1975. For 72 diversified firms with the food industries as their primary industry, approximately 44 percent of their nonfood manufacturing sales was in chemicals. Three other important directions of food manufacturer diversification stand out: vertical integration into containers (plastics, paper, can, and glass industries) and food machinery, and conglomerate diversification into other consumer products (apparel, furniture, and games). Very few firms diversified into heavy industrial goods. There were 53 food manufacturers with significant sales in wholesaling (mostly farm and food products) and retailing (grocery stores and eating places).

Most published data sources are inadequate to distinguish vertical from horizontal product diversification; however, there is one analysis of the extent of forward vertical integration based on a 1977 sample survey of manufacturers by the Census Bureau (Connor 1982a, table 5). Shipments to warehouses or sales branches from food manufacturing plants owned by the same company accounted for 14.7 percent of the total (as compared to 17 percent for all manufacturing). For five industries (breakfast cereals, flour and flour mixes, cookies and crackers, flavorings, and coffee) this ratio exceeded 40 percent. Forward integration into manufacturer-owned retail stores averaged only 4 percent. Finally, forward integration into other manufacturing also averaged only 4 percent of sales. Thus, vertical forward integration accounted for 23 percent of total shipments (including resales) from food manufacturing establishments (versus 32 percent for all manufacturing).

The discussion thus far has been limited to outbound diversification by firms primarily classified in food or tobacco manufacturing. It is also possible to gain insights into product diversification by analyzing *inbound* diversification: the extent of economic activity in the food industries controlled by firms classified primarily outside the industry. Connor and Mather (1978) identified 38 companies whose main business was outside food and tobacco manufacturing and yet whose total sales in those industries made them rank among the 200 largest of 1975. Of the 38, 18 were in other manufacturing industries (including 5 drug and 3 soap companies), 8 were wholesalers, 7 food retailers, and 5 others outside manufacturing. Enterprise statistics for 1977 show that on average, 31 percent of the sales of food and tobacco manufactures was by companies primarily classified outside the principal enterprise category. Of this total, 18 percent was by companies in other food and tobacco categories and 13 percent was by firms classified primarily outside food manufacturing (Connor 1980, 1982b). Inbound diversification has been directed mainly at the vegetable oil industries and some fast-growing consumer products industries (frozen foods, confectionery, and miscellaneous prepared foods).

Changes in Food Firms' Diversification. In 1950, most food manufacturer diversification was concentrated within food manufacturing. The vast bulk of food manufacturers' diversification into nonfood manufacturing consisted of vertical integration into packaging and machinery, by-product processing in leather and chemicals by meat packers, and some industrial chemicals operations. The nonmanufacturing activity of leading food processors consisted almost entirely of activities vertically related to food processing, such as agriculture, fishing, transportation, and food wholesaling and retailing. Since 1950 food manufacturers have diversified into a variety of conglomerate activities.

Vertical Diversification

This section and the two following report on the levels of domestic U.S. product diversification by the 500 largest food and tobacco manufacturers during 1967–1977. These data rely on a special tabulation of the Census of Manufactures sponsored by NC 117. Companies are chosen and ranked solely on the basis of their domestic value-added in food and tobacco manufacturing (SICs 20 and ⁻1). These data do not classify companies according to their principal enterprise category.

Diversification into Agriculture. However measured, the extent of diversification of food manufacturers into agricultural production, agricultural services, and commercial fishing is very slight. In 1977, all manufacturers had about 30,000 (full-time-equivalent) employees working on farms or ranches and an additional 5,600 in agricultural service establishments like soil and crop services, cotton ginning, and custom slaughtering. These employees represented only 0.16 percent of all employment of manufacturing companies and 2.7 percent of all hired farmworkers (Bureau of the Census 1977a; USDA 1984e). The 500 largest food firms in 1977 had 25,000 such employees on about 340 farms and ranches and 150 agricultural service establishments (plus about 1,000 fisheries workers).

The pattern of involvement in agriculture is interesting. Food firms among the 100 largest are more than twice as likely to participate in crop or animal raising as lower-ranking firms. The type of farms or ranches owned is not typical of agriculture in general. The farms owned by manufacturers are very large, averaging seventy employees in 1977. Manufacturers are relatively heavily involved in sugar, tobacco, grape, citrus, livestock feeding, and poultry operations. There was a substantial increase over the 1967–1977 period in the number and size of cattle, hog, and poultry operations; most of these farms and feedlots were owned by companies that also owned meat packing, meat processing, or poultry dressing plants. Food and tobacco manufacturers own about one-third of the true corporate farms (nonfamily corporations with ten or more stockholders), according to the 1978 Census of Agriculture, including about 80 percent of the corporate-owned poultry and egg farms. Thus, there are indications of a limited but growing amount of backward integration into agriculture through ownership; however, the available data do not permit inferences about integration achieved through long-term contracts or other binding relationships.

Backward Diversification into Manufacturing. Food and tobacco manufacturers own a wide variety of manufacturing plants that make inputs for food or tobacco manufacturing. Figure 4–8 shows that backward vertical manufacturing diversification by the 500 largest has hovered around 3 percent between 1967 and 1977, with the ratio falling slightly during the decade. In-

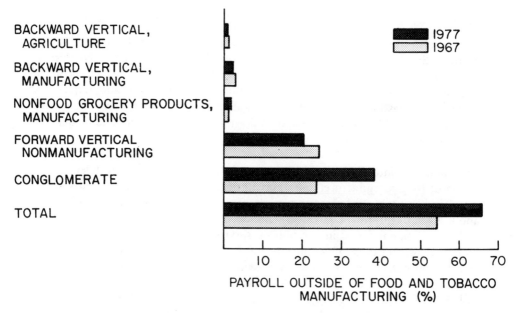

BACKWARD VERTICAL, AGRICULTURE

BACKWARD VERTICAL, MANUFACTURING

NONFOOD GROCERY PRODUCTS, MANUFACTURING

FORWARD VERTICAL NONMANUFACTURING

CONGLOMERATE

TOTAL

■ 1977
□ 1967

PAYROLL OUTSIDE OF FOOD AND TOBACCO MANUFACTURING (%)

Source: Connor et al. 1985, p. 179.

Figure 4–8. Diversification among the 500 Largest Food and Tobacco Manufacturers, 1967 and 1977.

dustries in which the 500 largest had actual shipments of $100 million or more in 1977 include paper bags, paperboard boxes, sanitary food containers, commercial lithographic printing, plastics resins, organic chemicals, plastic wrapping materials, glass jars, metal cans, and food machinery.

Forward Vertical Diversification. Forward vertical diversification was defined as transportation, wholesaling, or retailing industries specifically involved in handling food, beverage, and tobacco products. This category of product diversification accounted for one-fifth of the total 1977 payrolls of the 500 largest (figure 4–8).

About 1.5 percent of payroll goes to employees in trucking and water transportation; 76 of the 500 largest companies owned trucks and storage facilities in 1977. Another 5.5 percent of food manufacturers' activity involved grocery or farm product wholesaling, of which general-line grocery wholesaling is only one-twentieth. The most important form of diversification (15.2 percent of payroll) is directed toward food stores. About 80 percent of the food retailing payroll was attributable to 20 or so food retailing firms that qualify among the 500 largest manufacturers. Finally, eating places accounted for 2.2 percent of total company payroll, mostly national chains of fast food places (Connor 1980). Despite the increases in transportation, warehousing, and food service, between 1967 and 1977 the relative extent of forward vertical diversification for the leading food firms declined by about three percentage points.

Horizontal Diversification

The special census tabulation allowed us to examine product diversification into nonfood manufacturing industries that are dissimilar in terms of their production technologies but are similar in that a large proportion are marketed through grocery and other self-service stores. In 1977 such nonfood grocery products manufacturing accounted for 2.7 percent of the total payroll of the 500 largest food and tobacco manufacturers (figure 4–9). Though small, this ratio rose slightly in the decade after 1967.

Conglomerate Diversification

By the process of elimination, we are able to estimate the minimum extent of conglomerate diversification of the 500 largest food and tobacco processors (figure 4–9). Recall that conglomerate activity is measured by the proportion of company payrolls outside food and tobacco manufacturing, other grocery products manufacturing, and all industries potentially vertically related to food manufacturing. Recognizing that in 1977 about 15 percent of the 500 companies were primarily classified outside food and tobacco, these estimates are nonetheless reasonable indicators of conglomerate diversification of companies considered as food and tobacco manufacturers. Conglomerate activities rose from 24 percent of company payroll in 1967 to 39 percent in 1972, a period that included the peak of the conglomerate merger wave (Scherer 1980). Conglomerate diversification rose only insignificantly from 1972 to 1977, a period of relative merger quiescence (FTC 1981c). Even among the 100 largest firms, which are more specialized in food and tobacco manufacturing than the rest of the 500, over one-third of company payroll is in establishments carrying on unrelated activities.

Determinants of Product Diversification

MacDonald (1981) investigated the determinants of outbound product diversification of food manufacturers. Following Penrose's (1959) concept of expansion of a firm from its base or original primary industry, indexes of 1975 sales diversification based on four-digit SIC industry definitions were developed for 129 firms primarily engaged in food manufacturing. A regression analysis was performed to discover the major factors that influence product diversification.

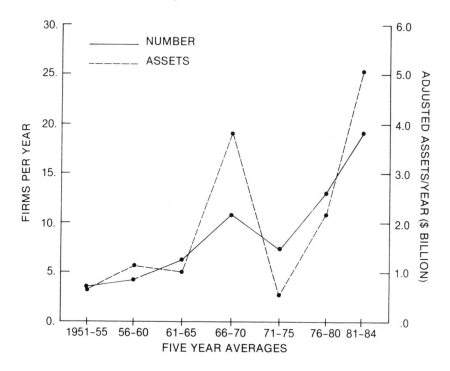

Source: Federal Trade Commission (1981c) and *Quarterly Financial Reports*. Data for 1980–1984 compiled from public records and therefore are understated relative to the earlier years.

[a]Assets were adjusted to reflect real and inflation-caused growth using the total average annual assets of food and tobacco companies in 1981–84 as a base. Thus, total assets of all companies acquired before 1981 were adjusted upward. For example, the actual value of assets acquired in 1951–55 were $342 million but were adjusted to $3,149 million, reflecting that total annual assets in 1951–55 were 10.86% as great as in 1981–84.

Figure 4–9. Large Food and Tobacco Manufacturing Companies Acquired, Numbers and Total Adjusted Assets, 1951–1984

The results provided strong support for several hypotheses concerning the incentives to diversify. The profitability and capital intensity of the firms' primary industries had a significant negative effect on product diversification, supporting the view that primary industry profits and scale requirements represent an opportunity cost of investment in secondary industries. On the other hand, profit risk (the coefficient of variation in price-cost margins during 1967–1975) and primary industry growth rates had no impact on diversification levels. Some economists hypothesize that primary industry risk would impel firms to diversify in order to smooth their profit records over time. Growth, if a proxy for expected profits, should have discouraged diversification. Because growth rates in food manufacturing are strongly affected by movements in raw materials prices, they are probably a poor proxy for expected profits.

Three other factors that capture some of the intangible assets of firms had strong positive influences on product diversification: R&D expenditures, advertising expenditures, and asset size. Following Chandler's (1982) reasoning, these variables were hypothesized to capture the technological capacity, marketing expertise, and efficiency or managerial experience of firms. The first two variables are also related to the extent of product differentiation in the industries in which the firms participate. Finally, some principal industries of firms were found to be associated with greater diversification; companies in the dairy, vegetable oil processing, and wet corn milling industries were significantly more diversified than those classified in other food manufacturing industries.

MacDonald's (1981) analysis focused primarily on firm-specific or primary-industry characteristics. A more complete analysis would include characteristics of target industries known to influence product diversification. Growth in the target industries encourages greater inbound diversification (Berry 1975; MacDonald 1983), whereas the height of entry barriers in target industries doubtless discourages it. Little is known about the special characteristics of diversification into industries vertically related to food manufacturing.

Role of Mergers

It is unlikely that the high levels of observed diversification in manufacturing would have been attained were it not so easy for corporations to buy, rather than build, assets and market position. Legal restrictions exist on horizontal mergers, particularly since 1950, and to a lesser extent on vertical and product extension mergers (Mueller 1978a). Partly as a result, of all the assets acquired, the proportion acquired through horizontal and vertical mergers fell from about 50 percent during 1948–1955 to only 21 percent during 1973–1977 (Caves 1980, p. 526). Contemporaneously, pure conglomerate mergers rose from 3 percent of large manufacturing and mining assets acquired to 49 percent of all such assets.

In manufacturing alone, about $125 billion of book assets were acquired during 1948–1979, of which 88 percent were large companies (assets of $10 million or more) (FTC 1981c). During that same period, over 200 large food or tobacco manufacturing firms were acquired, accounting for 11 percent of all the assets of large, acquired manufacturers. The number of acquisitions per year of large food firms rose throughout 1948–1970, dropped during the early 1970s, and reached a new higher peak in the late 1970s (figure 4–9). The adjusted dollar value of large food manufacturing companies acquired annually was $1.1 billion during 1956–1960 and reached $3.8 billion in 1966–1970.

After a brief hiatus in the early 1970s, asset values of acquired food companies rose again to new heights. During 1981–1984, an enormous $5.1 billion per year in food manufacturing assets were acquired. During that period many well-known companies—Oscar Mayer, Standard Brands, Jos. Schlitz Brewing, Heublein, Stokely-Van Camp, Carnation, Norton Simon, Esmark, and others—ceased to exist as independent entities. Relative to the total amount of assets potentially available to be acquired, on average about 0.8 percent of food manufacturer assets was actually acquired per year during 1948–1980; during 1981–1984 that proportion rose to 2.7 percent.

Food and tobacco processing companies have been active as acquirers of large companies as well as targets. During 1948–1984, food and tobacco firms bought at least 385 large manufacturers. Without mergers, the leading food manufacturers would have grown more slowly during the post–World War II period, leading to greater turnover and lower aggregate concentration. An analysis of the 1950–1975 merger record of the 100 largest food manufacturers in 1975 permitted the partitioning of asset growth into that part due to mergers by the companies and that part due to internal growth (Connor 1977). At least 40 percent of the 1975 total assets of the 100 largest could be attributed to merger-induced growth; this estimate is probably conservative in that not all mergers were publicly announced, no mergers before 1950 were examined, and the postmerger growth of acquired assets was assumed to be slower than premerger growth.

Geographic Diversification

Data on the spatial segmentation of domestic manufacturing markets are sparse. Proxies for geographic size of markets have been developed using unit transportation costs (Weiss 1972) or comparisons of plant locations with the distribution of population (Collins and Preston 1968). A correlated measure is the extent of multiplant ownership by leading firms in an industry. The operation of numerous plants per firm usually indicates fairly narrow geographic scope. Census data for 1977 show that the four leading sellers in each of the fifty-one food and tobacco manufacturing industries operated an average of 8.2 plants. The average numbers of plants per firm ranged from 48 in bread baking to 2.4 for cigarettes. Multiplant ownership is also high in the soft drink bottling industry because of the practice of exclusive territorial franchising in that industry.

Foreign direct investment (FDI) can be seen as the ultimate stage of national geographic expansion. FDI by U.S. firms abroad and FDI into the United States by foreign firms has been increasing rapidly since the early 1960s (Connor 1981a, 1981b). Over 20 percent of the assets of U.S. food manufacturers is deployed abroad (figure 4–10) and food manufacturing is the most internationalized of the stages of the food system. Food ranks about third in the accumulated amount of FDI among the twenty major manufacturing groups.

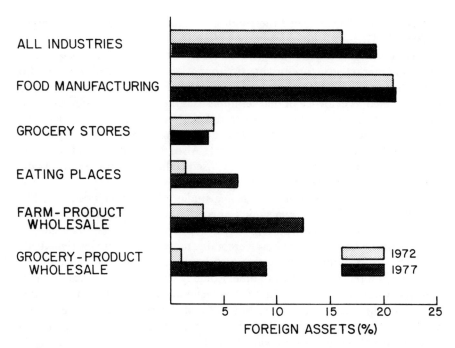

Figure 4–10. Foreign Assets as a Proportion of Total Book Assets of U.S. Companies, by Enterprise Industries, 1972 and 1977

Foreign-owned food affiliates tend to market highly differentiated products, like tea, cookies, chocolate, and alcoholic beverages. Counting both first-time investments and increases in ownership of existing investments, entry by foreign investors is predominantly by takeovers—90 percent of the 792 U.S. businesses in which foreign investment took place in 1979—with over four-fifths of the financing obtained in the United States by existing foreign affiliates. Direct investment by U.S. firms in the food manufacturing industries of other countries is about three times as large as FDI into the United States. The rate of increase in U.S. FDI (about 12 percent per year over 1966–1979) was greater than the increase in domestic investments by U.S. firms but less than the rate of increase of inward FDI.

Determinants of Foreign Direct Investment

The hypothesized explanations for the amounts, sources, and targets of FDI are essentially the same as for product diversification (Caves 1975). An additional wrinkle, however, is that international production may be influenced by the effects of different tax rules or other national policies and currency movements on profit maximization. Testing for the determinants of FDI is particularly challenging because firm-specific, industry-specific, home country, and host country factors must be incorporated.

Connor (1983) reviewed the empirical literature on the determinants of outbound FDI by manufacturers, including food manufacturers. All of the studies concur that R&D intensity, the extent of product differentiation efforts, and market structures giving rise to market power and elevated profits are all factors pushing U.S. investments abroad. These industry features may be interpreted as evidence of market imperfections or as market-level proxies for firm-specific assets easily transferred within the firm across national boundaries. Host countries with high per capita incomes or consumption expenditures were found to attract capital. Also, FDI into an industry was found to complement U.S. exports of those products, yet trade barriers did not impede the flow of FDI.

There are also a number of revealing studies of the other side of the FDI coin: the extent of foreign ownership or penetration in host country industries. Several analyses of inbound FDI in Canada support the idea that multinational manufacturing firms are adept at overcoming market-structure barriers to entry. There is also some evidence that high levels of concentration encourage a bunching of foreign investment in time. Roughly put, high concentration in the markets where multinationals are rivals facilitates the recognition of mutual dependence as revealed in herd instincts of global proportions. One empirical study of FDI specifically singled out food manufacturing firms, 120 large food processors with headquarters outside the United States (Connor 1981c). As with the studies already covered, FDI into the U.S. food industries was explained by the intensity of food advertising, firm sales diversification (worldwide), firm sales size, and home country weighted market share. All had positive effects.

Competitive Conduct

The structure of markets is an important determinant of the behavioral options open to companies. In competitive markets, firms have relatively few strategic options. Market forces are stern disciplinarians of the lax, slow-of-foot, or unlucky manager who fails to keep pace with cost-reducing possibilities. Firms in oligopolistic industries have many more strategic options available. They may have sufficient market power that, as Greer (1980) put it, "their owners and managers need not scratch and scrape for every penny of possible profit" (p. 226).

Market structure alone does not determine conduct. Government regulations and enforcement activities often define illegal and/or legal conduct (such as price fixing, product labeling, advertising claims) and provide varying types of penalties for nonconforming behavior. In addition, the motives and goals of owners and managers affect market conduct. Firms may seek to maximize short-run profits, sales, or growth, to maintain or increase market shares, to achieve a satisfactory level of profits and/or growth rate, or some variation of these goals. Even firms with the same objective may choose different paths to achieve their goals. Thus, market structure may be a poor predictor of specific types of conduct. It does, however, provide important clues concerning the likelihood that rivals behave independently and the discretion individual firms are likely to have in their competitive behavior.

In recent years, there has been a sharp increase in the attention given to strategic planning and behavior by businessmen, business school faculty, and industrial organization economists (Porter 1976b, 1985; Spence 1981; Buzzell, Gale, and Sultan 1975). The work of Porter, Spence, and others on strategic behavior is particularly helpful in understanding the various types of behavior that may be economically rational when placed in a long-run perspective and when uncertainties, imperfect information, market segments, and conglomerate power are recognized. Michael Spence (1981) contends that competition needs to be examined in an intertemporal setting. The evolution of an industry is frequently influenced not only by technology and economies of scale but also by strategic behavior that provides first mover advantages, erects entry barriers, or provides incumbents with significant advantages over a new entrant.

Michael Porter (1976b) developed the theory of *strategic groups* within industries. In the soft drink industry, for example, there may be a large number of strategic groups that differ because of customers serviced (foodservice versus retail stores), carbonated versus noncarbonated, advertised versus store brands, and type of containers. "Mobility theory" is concerned with the extent to which firms in different strategic groups can move into other strategic groups in the same basic industry. Porter (1981, p. 455) contends that all firms strive to drive other firms out of their strategic territory and to create sustainable mobility barriers. The intent to monopolize strategic groups is pervasive. Where there exist strategic groups (or submarkets) with high mobility barriers, *industry* structure may be misleading. As Porter states, "An industry need not be concentrated overall for a particular strategic group to have enormous market power" (1981, pp. 455–456).

Spence (1981) also points out that an incumbent firm can choose a variety of actions to strengthen its competitive advantages over a new entrant or fringe competitor. If it has a large market share, price reductions may be costly to the incumbent unless it can discriminate in different geographic market or product segments. It may choose instead to increase the costs of entry or to foreclose access to retail shelf space.

Strategic Groups in Food Manufacturing

Porter's (1976b) concept of strategic groups is useful in analyzing food manufacturing. There are at least four submarkets in some food manufacturing industries. These strategic groups correspond to the four major marketing channels identified earlier:

1. Producer goods markets: For many ingredient industries (such as flour, sugar, soybean milling, and wet corn milling), a major portion of industry output is sold to other manufacturers. Standardized quality, bulk shipping, an absence of brands, little advertising, and informed buyers generally result in considerable emphasis on efficiency and low prices in this submarket.

2. Foodservice market: This includes sales to commercial eating and drinking places, schools, hospitals, airlines, and other establishments that serve food away from home. This market has traditionally been highly fragmented and has been supplied by a fragmented wholesaling system. The nature of competitive behavior in this market depends on the product and the type of outlet (fast food restaurant versus white tablecloth restaurant versus hospital). However, except for products that consumers choose by brand, advertised brands are not important. Competitive prices, tightly specified quality, and reliable service are important in supplying large foodservice distributors or restaurant chains. Price is less important in serving smaller accounts, for which product quality, credit, and service may be the primary concerns.

3. Advertised brands sold through retail stores: The most important advertised brands are usually distributed nationally, and hence are called national brands. However, some regionally advertised and distributed brands hold important market positions in certain areas. Competitive conduct takes on many forms in this market. In general, key elements of success are consumer advertising, new product development, and the ability to obtain shelf space.

4. Private label, generic, and unbranded products sold through retail stores: Since these products are either unbranded (examples are fresh meat and generic grocery products) or carry the store or distributor's label, many manufacturers are potential suppliers. Consumer advertising and promotion are provided by retailers, not manufacturers, and generally emphasize price. Manufacturer success in this market depends on being efficient, price competitive, and reliable in quality and service. Production economies of scale are modest for most products. However, transportation economies and the large volume requirements of grocery chains and affiliated wholesalers place small manufacturers at a competitive disadvantage.

Pricing Behavior. Pricing in the four strategic groups varies considerably. Manufacturers of advertised brands generally develop price lists. These may be changed weekly or monthly where frequent variations in raw commodity prices have an important effect on the cost of the finished product, as with bacon, coffee, and sugar. List prices may remain unchanged for six months or more on other branded products. Manufacturers of national brands may have different list prices for the forty to fifty U.S. grocery marketing areas, depending on varying costs and competitive conditions.

Pricing of private label and unbranded products is subject to negotiations between buyers and sellers. Private label manufacturers often follow the price moves of leading brand manufacturers and try to maintain a certain price differential. Where there are several competing private label manufacturers (including in some cases the retailers themselves), these companies must also be responsive to the price of alternative suppliers. For products in which retailers have several potential suppliers of their private label, retail buyers sit in the driver's seat.

Pricing of unbranded products, such as fresh meat, and of semiprocessed products sold in producer goods markets are heavily influenced by agricultural commodity markets. For products such as soybean oil, sugar, beef, and pork bellies, there are active futures markets as well as cash markets. A variety of pricing and procurement arrangements is used in the sale of these products to other manufacturers, retailers, and foodservice customers. Some type of formula pricing procedure is frequently used. For example, most carcass beef is priced in relation to prices reported by the National Provisioner Yellow Sheet; long-term contracts for other products may specify prices tied to futures contract prices. Thus, the prices of these products generally reflect the prices in national commodity markets; individual manufacturers have little pricing discretion.

Because most of our research has dealt with the strategic groups supplying retail stores, we will concentrate in the following discussion on submarkets 3 and 4, which accounted for about 40 percent and 20 percent, respectively, of food manufacturing value of shipments in 1977.

Dual Branding. Manufacturers of advertised brands generally do not pack private labels or generics of the same products. This is particularly true if they market one of the leading brands. Thus, "dual branders" (firms that pack both advertised brands and private labels) are not the norm in most products; where they exist, they generally hold a weak position in the branded product market. While there are exceptions (the leading manufacturers of salt and teabags are reported also to manufacture private labels), they are relatively few.

Some companies are completely committed to branded products and refuse to manufacture any private label or generic products; Procter & Gamble (P&G) is one such company. P&G and a few other companies have responded to the growth of generics by offering lower-priced, less advertised products, such as Summit paper towels. Other companies, such as Heinz and

Ralston Purina, refuse to pack private labels on products where they have a leading brand (catsup and dry dog food, respectively) but do pack private labels of other products (canned soup by Heinz; ready-to-eat cereals and crackers by Purina).

The use of excess capacity is an important incentive for dual branding. For example, when Land O Lakes entered the margarine business, it manufactured private label margarine to employ plant capacity until the sales of Land O Lakes margarine expanded. The growth of generic coffee creamers resulted in 25 percent excess capacity for Borden, the manufacturer of the number two brand, Cremora (*Business Week*, March 23, 1981). Borden reluctantly entered the generic coffee creamer business, recognizing that it was contributing to the erosion of its brand's share. Brand manufacturers with relatively low market shares or that have lost market share are most likely to have excess capacity and hence are more interested in dual branding.

In a few cases, such as fluid milk, dual branding is the industry norm. In most industries, however, there is a strategic group of advertised brand manufacturers and a second strategic group of private label or generic manufacturers, with relatively few companies operating in both strategic groups.

Structure of Strategic Groups. Since firms compete most directly with other firms in their strategic group, it is important to examine the concentration of sales and mobility barriers of these groups. Advertised brand strategic groups are very highly concentrated (CR4 > 80 percent) for twenty-five of thirty-six products examined (Connor et al. 1985, p. 222).

Private label strategic groups are generally less concentrated and have considerably lower entry barriers than advertised brand strategic groups. Where private label products have a small share of the product market, however, a single firm may dominate the private label strategic group. Trade sources indicate this is true for several products, including canned soup, ready-to-eat cereals, cocoa beverage mixes, flavored gelatin desserts, and cake mixes. Where one firm dominates the private label strategic group, that firm may enjoy some pricing discretion. This is more likely if there are few potential entrants into the strategic group. Entry barriers into private label strategic groups are generally low except where the minimum efficient size plant is large relative to the size of the private label market.

Mobility barriers are generally low for established brand manufacturers to move into the private label business; however, incentives are often lacking. A Borden executive commented, "Making private label is a cancer. The better you do it the worse things get, because you erode your own brand's share" (*Business Week*, March 23, 1981, p. 76).

Market Penetration of Generics. In the late 1970s, several grocery chains began to carry plain label generic products. The idea for these products was not new; they had been distributed in Europe for several years. Their introduction in the United States coincided with increased retail price competition in certain areas and declining consumer real income. Generic products, box stores, and warehouse stores together created considerable price pressure on established brands and conventional retailers. Generics were manufactured mainly by the same companies manufacturing private label products. In some industries, such as processed fruits and vegetables, branded manufacturers were willing to pack generics in order to utilize lower-quality produce. But the introduction of generics was clearly the retailer's idea, not the manufacturer's.

Analysis of the 1980 market penetration of generics for a sample of processed food products indicates that generic market share was inversely related to the level of advertising and the market shares of the top four companies (Wills and Rosenbaum 1983). This parallels the findings concerning 1976 private label market shares (Parker and Connor 1979). Both advertising and market concentration are indicators of the barriers to entry for private label and generic products. The negative effect of advertising suggests that the consumer loyalty toward advertised brands in products such as breakfast cereals, beer, and cigarettes is sufficiently strong that it is difficult for generics to win much of the market, though the price savings are often substantial (typically 25 to 35 percent).

Manufacturer-Retailer Bargaining Behavior

The relationship between manufacturers and retailers on advertised brands is fundamentally different than in the case of private label products. In advertised brands, sellers bear the responsibility of product development, label design, quality control, developing consumer advertising, and helping retailers promote the product. Manufacturers try to persuade retailers to allocate sufficient shelf space in desired locations to the manufacturer's brands and to cooperate with periodic promotion, including in-store display, price reductions, and cooperative advertising. Retailers try to get manufacturers to give more trade deals that are of direct benefit to them. Retailers contend that large manufacturers can force distribution of a product by heavily advertising and promoting the product to consumers. This occurs most often when large branded manufacturers introduce new products or enter new geographic markets.

The private label manufacturer has little or no involvement in shelf allocation, advertising, or consumer promotions. These are the responsibility of the retailer. The primary concern of the manufacturer in this relationship is to meet the quality standards of the retailer (both parties are often involved in developing product specifications), fill orders as needed, and search for ways to reduce production or distribution costs. Because transportation costs are significant (about 5 percent of sales), manufacturers that have a product line broad enough to ship full truck or car loads to a retail chain have a significant cost advantage over firms that must ship partial loads. As a result, many private label companies have followed a strategy of product diversification.

Retailers have more influence over consumer responses to branded products and the competitive tactics of brand manufacturers than is often appreciated. Retailers determine whether a new product is made available to consumers and the merchandising support it receives. They determine whether two, three, or more brands of a product are carried, their shelf facings and location, and the extent to which they cooperate with manufacturer promotions.

The surest way for a manufacturer to gain favorable retailer treatment is to develop a leading brand through consumer advertising and promotions. Within a product category, the fastest-selling brand usually gets eye-level exposure on the retail shelf and is allocated more space (Hamm 1981b, p. 225). Favorable shelf placement boosts the sales of items whose purchase was unplanned or a last-minute decision. In addition, the higher the leading brand's market share, the more immune it becomes to retailer bargaining tactics. Retailers often are able to extract price and nonprice concessions from manufacturers with weak brands.

Retail pricing practices also can benefit leading brands. If a manufacturer succeeds in developing a leading brand that consumers use as an indicator of store prices, retailers may carry a lower margin on the brand; in some cases, price-sensitive items are regularly priced at or below cost to convey a low price store image to consumers. Thus, the manufacturer of a dominant brand may be in the enviable position of being able to charge a premium to retailers but having its brand sold for less to consumers (Wills 1985b; Albion 1983).

Brand manufacturers make extensive use of "trade deals" to promote their products. Trade deals usually involve lowering the product's list price for a specified time period to all competing retailers (a Robinson-Patman Act requirement) in a specific regional market in return for contractually specified merchandising actions by retailers. Manufacturers may require retailers to advertise the deal product, construct special displays, and/or drop the price on the product. In return, the retail (wholesale) buyer can buy at reduced prices for an extended time period. Often merchandising performance is accomplished in one or two weeks, while price reductions can be obtained for six to ten weeks. Precise numbers are not available, but industry sources estimate that deal allowances paid to grocery retail buyers ranged from $4 billion to $14 billion in 1981 (*Supermarket News*, November 15, 1982).

Transshipping Deal Merchandise

Manufacturers can establish different wholesale prices in different geographic markets. These differences are more pronounced when deals are offered in selected markets. If the net wholesale price differences in different areas are large relative to transport costs, arbitrage is profitable. Chains and wholesalers operating in multiple markets are capable of cross-hauling or transshipping deal merchandise between markets. More recently a new class of middlemen called "diverters" has arisen to provide similar opportunities to retail firms operating in single markets. Diverters buy deal merchandise from retailers in one market and divert that product to retailers in other markets. The potential profit is highest on those items with high value relative to transportation costs. If arbitrage is increased through transshipping and diverting, manufacturers will probably be forced toward uniform pricing in larger geographic areas.

Importance of Brand Market Share

A growing amount of evidence—some of it the result of research on strategic behavior—indicates a strong positive relationship between firm market share and profitability (Buzzell, Gale, and Sultan 1975; Imel and Helmberger 1971; Rogers 1978; FTC 1969b; Ravenscraft 1981). The evidence in food manufacturing indicates that high market share firms generally have higher prices (Wills 1983). To maintain or build market share, secondary brand manufacturers are usually forced to charge buyers no more, and often less, than the leading brand. Holding a leading market share also carries other benefits. It virtually ensures that retailers will carry the brand and give it preferred shelf space. In addition, advertising and promotion costs may be lower per dollar of sales without loss of market share.

As the importance of market share to firm profitability has become more apparent in recent years, there has been evidence of more firms withdrawing from markets in which they had low shares; such firms then concentrate their attention on products and markets in which they are either the leaders or have the potential to build market share. The growth of generic grocery products and the proliferation of sizes and flavors in branded products has expanded the demands for shelf space. The squeeze on retail shelf space has resulted in discontinuation of some weaker brands, thereby providing additional impetus for manufacturers to reconsider the future of their brands with low shares (*Business Week*, March 23, 1981).

Product Proliferation

Padberg and Westgren (1979) contend that product proliferation is one of the major modes of competitive conduct of leading food manufacturers. Not only does this dimension of conduct significantly affect economic performance, but it also may feed back on industry structure by increasing the market shares of leading firms or by elevating barriers to entry.

Underlying the concept of product proliferation is the notion that any product can be categorized according to several attributes or characteristics.

The various combinations of these attributes represent a product space, which may be empty or occupied at any time. For example, fat content is one attribute of fluid milk. In earlier decades, the product space for factory-skimmed milk was empty; now milk with four butter-fat levels is commonly available.

Theoretical analyses by Schmalensee (1978), Adams and Yellen (1976), and Koller (1979) suggest that new product development is a form of non-price business conduct related to the structure of the markets in which the firm operates. A firm that already holds a leading position in a market will find it advantageous to develop products to fill adjacent product spaces to 1) appeal to a new set of consumers, 2) leave fewer niches available for entering firms and therefore increase entry barriers, 3) eventually offer a full line of products using the same brand name and gain pecuniary economies of scale in advertising and promotion, and 4) increase the store shelf space devoted to the firm's products, resulting in less space for the products of new firms.

Couponing

Manufacturers use coupons to introduce new products, build brand loyalty, and ensure that price reductions are passed on to consumers. The number of cents-off coupons distributed by food manufacturers and retailers tripled from 30 billion in 1974 to 90 billion in 1980 (Gallo, Hamm, and Zellner 1982). To consumers who use them, coupons are analogous to a price reduction. However, since only about one out of twenty food coupons issued is redeemed, many consumers do not benefit from this form of price reduction. Coupons therefore discriminate among classes of consumers with different price sensitivities.

Coffee, breakfast cereals, prepared foods, flour, and flour mix products accounted for nearly two-thirds of the value of coupons redeemed. Coupons were used more heavily in product classes with high levels of advertising and high concentration of sales. However, unlike television advertising, which is almost solely the domain of large firms, couponing is an important promotional tool available to small manufacturers, particularly for new product introductions.

The average face value of coupons sampled by Gallo, Hamm, and Zellner (1982) was about 24 cents. The cost of producing, distributing, and handling coupons is high— estimated at 70 percent of the face value in 1978. Thus, the total cost to manufacturers for the average coupon redeemed was 41 cents: 24 cents to the consumer plus 17 cents for handling costs. With approximately 4.5 billion coupons redeemed in 1980, consumers received about $1.1 billion, and an additional $765 million was spent on the production, distribution, and handling of coupons.

Government-Sanctioned Conduct

While many businessmen voice their preference for less government regulation, this depends heavily on the perceived benefactor of the regulation. For example, the soft drink industry successfully sought national legislation to explicitly legalize exclusive territories in the bottling and distribution of soft drinks. The effect of this law is largely to eliminate intrabrand competition among bottlers. In a highly concentrated industry in which interbrand competition focuses largely on nonprice factors and a high level of interdependence exists, intrabrand competition could be an extremely important competitive force. Encouraged by the success of the soft drink industry, the beer industry is currently seeking national and state legislation that would permit exclusive territories for beer distributors.

Federal legislation also has an important effect on R&D efforts and product differentiation activities through the patent and trademark laws. Although Hoffman (1940) estimates that patents were important barriers to entry in a few instances in the early part of the century—the quick freezing process, for example—their role in restricting entry into food manufacturing today is thought to be minor. The perpetual rights extended to trademarks and trade names today have a much more important effect on industry conduct. Trademarks serve the socially useful functions of identifying the origin of foods and providing standards of quality. Trademarks and trade names also facilitate the development of market power when they become the sole or major source of quality assurance or the focus of images created by advertising (Greer 1980, p. 96). Proposals that have sought to retain the benefits while reducing the costs include limiting the length of exclusive trademark rights in a similar manner as the patent law. Greater use of government or industry grades and standards to provide consumers with more information about quality has also been proposed as a way of limiting the market power of brand names.

Conglomerate Behavior in Food Manufacturing

Practically all theoretical and empirical works in the field of industrial organization have examined business conduct and performance within particular industries or submarkets. Most attention has focused on the performance of oligopolistic markets. This is also true of most of the research results reported in this book. We turn our attention now to the competitive behaviors of multimarket conglomerate food manufacturers.

Conglomerate Theory. The preoccupation with oligopoly reflects developments in both economic theory and empirical research. Since the seminal works of Joan Robinson and Edward Chamberlin, theories of imperfect competition have been extended and refined. There is also much evidence that oligopoly, as opposed to monopoly or perfect competition, pervades most industrial sectors of the economy. An enormous empirical literature developed in this area because the theories of oligopoly presented many empirically stable hypotheses. Other sections of this chapter report the rather considerable empirical work of this type in the food manufacturing industries.

The theories of imperfect competition have been invaluable in exploring many dimensions of modern industrial organization. But because these theories examine conduct and performance within the context of particular industries, they cannot fully comprehend the many huge conglomerate corporations that operate across many different industries. The limits of these neoclassical theories in explaining the power of the modern conglomerate corporation have been lamented by Joan Robinson (1969), who contributed richly to these theories. Robinson believes that growing conglomeration has made her theories largely obsolete: "My old-fashioned comparison between monopoly and competition may still have some application to old-fashioned restrictive rings [cartels] but it cannot comprehend the great octopuses of modern industry" (ibid., p. ix). She further observed, "More and more, the great firms have a foot not only in many markets but in many industries, in several continents" (p. xi).

The organizational characteristics of conglomerates confer advantages that differ from the market power of the single-market monopolist or oligopolist that exploit their customers by raising prices considerably above costs. Although the conglomerate typically enjoys such market power in some markets, it also enjoys conduct options not open to the nonconglomerate. The conglomerate may use its power to engage in strategic behavior in one market to beget power in others. Corwin Edwards (1955) captured the essence of this dimension of the huge conglomerate:

> It can absorb losses that would consume the entire capital of a smaller rival.
> . . . Moment by moment the big company can outbid, outspend, or outlose
> the small one; and from a series of such momentary advantages it derives an
> advantage in attaining its large aggregate results. (pp. 334–335)

Earlier in this chapter we documented the extent to which the food manufacturing industries have skewed structures: relatively few huge conglomerate corporations and many smaller, usually specialized, companies. Not only do the largest firms overshadow in size their smaller competitors, but they also generally occupy the most concentrated industries and hold leading positions in these industries. Both of these characteristics (high market concentration and dominant market position) confer market power conducive to supracompetitive profits. Food conglomerates can use such profits to engage in competitive tactics not available to specialized firms. Most important, the conglomerate can engage in *cross-subsidization*: the practice of using profits earned in one market to subsidize competitive adventures in other markets. If sales in a subsidized market are small in comparison to the overall operations of the conglomerate, subsidization will have little impact on its overall profitability, while its more specialized rivals incur crippling losses.

Other competitive strategies of conglomerates include those of *reciprocal selling* and *conglomerate interdependence and forbearance* (Mueller 1982a). Reciprocal selling involves the business agreement, "I'll buy from you if you buy from me." Although all business may be inclined to favor suppliers that are also their customers, the multiproduct firm has more opportunities than the specialized firm to engage in the practice. As a result, conglomerate firms may engage in anticompetitive reciprocity.

Business reciprocity is symptomatic of a larger potential problem resulting from the communities of interest that develop among conglomerate corporations. Economic theory and industrial experience teach that when there are only a few sellers in a market, they tend to behave interdependently. The theory of oligopoly calls such conduct "oligopolist interdependence." Similarly when conglomerates meet as competitors in many markets, they may behave interdependently and may exercise competitive forbearance lest they trigger a retaliatory response in other markets where they meet. The result is that conglomerate firms tend to develop spheres of influence in which they are loath to act aggressively, especially against other conglomerates.

Empirical Evidence. The extent and uses of conglomerate power are not well understood. Indeed some economists argue that conglomerates have little unique market power and that they do not use what power they may have (Markham 1973). There is also a considerable body of empirical work that finds that firms achieving conglomeration through merger tend to be less efficient than the firms they acquire. In a comprehensive review of this literature, Dennis C. Mueller (1977, p. 339) concluded that conglomerate mergers occur for "corporate growth and other objectives not directly related to stockholder welfare and economic efficiency." These findings are not inconsistent with the conglomerate power hypothesis. All conglomeration is not motivated by a quest for market power, just as it is not always motivated by a quest for efficiency. Economic theory and industrial experience, however, teach that oligopolists or monopolists use their power irrespective of how the power was achieved. If conglomeration does confer market power on a firm, it may be expected that the firm will use such power.

Case studies were made of three large conglomerate enterprises in food manufacturing: Philip Morris–Miller Brewing Company, Procter & Gamble Company, and ITT–Continental Baking Company (Connor et al. 1985). These case studies were chosen because each involved one of the largest grocery product conglomerates, and public information was available that permitted examination of conglomerate-derived power. This is not to imply that all conglomerates use their power in these ways or that these companies use similar tactics in other industries in which they operate. Our purpose was to contribute to the literature of conglomerate power and behavior, particularly as it related to food manufacturing.

The case studies demonstrate that large grocery product conglomerates may use their economic power to restructure markets. Although generalizing from case studies is hazardous, each case revealed certain common characteristics worthy of emphasis.

1. Each involved a huge corporation ranking among the largest grocery product manufacturers. The smallest conglomerate (Philip Morris) had 1982 revenue exceeding $9 billion.

2. Each firm was highly diversified, operating across many product and geographic markets, including international ones.

3. Each conglomerate operated in some markets that were highly concentrated and in which the conglomerate held one of the leading positions.

4. Only a relatively small part of the conglomerate's business was committed to the product or geographic market selected for analysis. This meant that the conglomerate could pursue below-cost pricing or other strategies in these markets without threatening the profitability of its overall operations. This permitted pursuit of predatory conduct calling for forgoing profits in one period in anticipation of recouping lost profits after the market was restructured.

5. The industries involved were asymmetrically structured, with one or two large conglomerate corporations and a number of relatively small, specialized companies. In this environment, the specialized concerns were severely disadvantaged because their success depended entirely on their profitability in the markets involved.

6. In each of the cases there also existed another large corporation in the market. In two of the cases (Philip Morris–Miller and P&G), the largest incumbent firm countered the tactics that threatened its market position. The resulting confrontation between the industrial giants created an even more hostile environment for more specialized competitors.

Future Trends. These, then, are the organizational characteristics that confer conglomerate market power and permit strategic behavior not open to more specialized firms, even large ones. As more food industries become dominated by conglomerates, the surviving small companies often concentrate on serving narrower product or geographic market segments, thereby avoiding direct competition with their more powerful adversaries. Because many surviving small food companies operate in such market segments, statistics based on broad industry classifications tend to overstate the number of companies actually in competition with the conglomerate industry leaders.

The continuing trend toward greater conglomeration, fueled largely by mergers, raises the question of how well the food industries will perform in the future. Will conglomerate-based oligopolists compete more or less aggressively? The answer is not obvious. On the one hand, predatory pricing likely will become less commonplace, each conglomerate recognizing that its rivals are capable of a retaliatory response either in the target market or in some other market where the conglomerates meet. On the other hand, the aggrandizing instincts of conglomerates make increasing nonprice rivalry more likely. Evidence demonstrates that food conglomerates tend to prefer nonprice conduct made possible by advertising-created product differentiation. Not only will this tactic raise prices to consumers, but it may raise entry barriers as well.

Perhaps the most disquieting aspect of growing industrial conglomeration is that there are no forces impeding its expansion. Existing antitrust laws have been impotent before the swelling wave of merger-induced conglomeration that has pervaded the food industries during most of the period since World War II. Over two decades ago, in the early years of the conglomerate merger movement, Edwin G. Nourse (1963) observed the essentially irresistible trend toward increasing industrial conglomeration. As he saw it then:

> There is no demonstrable or discernible limit, national or international, at which such concentration of economic power, once fully underway, would automatically cease. It has insidious ability even to frustrate attempts of the Central Government to check or reverse its growth through legislative action. There are many political interests to overcome. [p. 255]

The experience of the past decades proves the wisdom of Nourse's pessimistic view. Several attempts have been made to slow the conglomerate trend through enforcing existing antitrust laws and through new legislation. For a brief period in the late 1960s and 1970s, it appeared that antitrust efforts might stem the conglomerate merger tide, but efforts were frustrated by the settlement of the ITT cases and by several hostile Supreme Court decisions (Mueller 1978a).

Performance

The concept of market performance has received a substantial amount of thoughtful attention by agricultural economists (Farris 1964; Sosnick 1958; Marion and Handy 1973; Brandow 1977; Shaffer 1979; Jesse 1978). These researchers have been particularly concerned about adapting general performance concepts for the specific conditions of the food system and developing operational criteria for assessing performance. There is a recognition that the overall level of performance is composed of several dimensions, some of which may be inconsistent with others. The dimensions of performance vary in their degree of measurability and in the implicit weighting given to each by society;[8] moreover, the weighting schemes also vary according to the training or viewpoint of the evaluator (Cox 1974).

Industrial organization theory traces the causes of performance outcomes to the structure of markets and the mode of industry conduct. The perfectly competitive market is a benchmark against which one can compare the structure and performance of naturally occurring markets. The perfectly competitive model is accepted by many economists because of its aesthetic appeal and analytical tractability. In its assumptions and derived equilibria, it comes reasonably close to widely accepted social and economic ideals. In practice, however, deviations from the competitive model must be accepted because of trade-offs that are found among performance dimensions and because actual markets almost always depart from the theoretical ideal. This gives rise to the looser standards of workable or effective competition (Sosnick 1958, 1968). As many as twenty specific performance criteria have been proposed to judge overall performance, though many of these might not apply to a particular industry.

In this section we summarize analyses of seven criteria of food industry performance.[9] Three elements of performance relate to static allocative efficiency: *profit, prices,* and *operational efficiency.* For full employment of all resources, it is socially desirable that profits be high enough to yield a risk-adjusted, normal, long-run return to venture capital and provide for sufficient future industry capacity. Yet profits should not be so high that they prevent the flow of equity capital to other industries with greater expected social rates of return. Similarly prices should be high enough to reward properly all factors of production but still reflect real relative costs across industries. Relatively high prices may be set in industries earning only normal profits if firms are technically inefficient or fail to minimize costs for other reasons. To examine the extent of technical or operational inefficiency, we present analyses of the relationship of market structure to *wage rates* and *labor productivity* in the food industries. Efficiency in the use of other inputs such as physical plant capacity or energy is not formally examined.

Many previous industry studies have been justly criticized for examining only static efficiency. In this section we present evidence on the *technological progressiveness* and *price stability* of the food industries, elements of performance that relate directly to the societal goals of growth and stability. Given the level of resources available and assuming some degree of technological opportunity, the more rapid the rate of technological change, the better. As Scherer (1980) has shown, even relatively high allocative losses can be rapidly overtaken by modest rates of productivity growth. Greater price stability (low inflation) is preferred for many social reasons and because it presumably lowers distortions in allocative efficiency over time that result from incorrectly anticipating levels of prices or outputs. Finally, we present some evidence on two previously unmeasured dimensions of performance: the influence of manufacturers on *consumption patterns and nutrition* and the *redistributive effects* of oligopoly in the food industries, criteria that primarily relate to societal values of consumer sovereignty, national health, and fairness.

Profit Performance

In long-run competitive equilibrium, economic profits are zero because price equals marginal cost. In the short run, transitory economic profits or losses may occur. In empirical applications, however, economists usually resort to proxies of economic profits derived from the financial reports of companies. Reported long-run profits are greater than economic profits because the former include returns to stockholders and managers for their invested capital and entrepreneurial risk taking.

Thus, accounting profits contain three returns: normal returns to equity capital, windfalls due to unanticipated changes in demand or supply conditions, and rents. Rents are supranormal returns and are of two kinds. *Pure rents* come from access to superior, more productive resources or from utilizing available resources more efficiently than rival firms. The remaining portion of profits is *monopoly rents*, both socially sanctioned (examples are patents or government regulation) and those arising from the exercise of market power. A traditional task of industrial organization studies has been to determine the rent portion of profits and the extent to which rents are due to market-structure sources. This task has been approached through empirical structure-performance studies. There are probably more published structure-profit studies for food manufacturing than for any other similarly narrow group of industries.

The profit rates of food manufacturers increased steadily over the period 1951–1980 (figure 4–11). Profit rates (after deducting taxes) in the late 1970s averaged twice their level in the early 1950s. Since 1970, the profits of food manufacturers have exceeded the rest of manufacturing in most years; in the twenty years before 1970 this had occurred only three times. The upward trend in nominal profit rates since 1970 has been slightly affected by inflationary conditions that abated during 1982. The important point is the rising profitability of food relative to the rest of manufacturing.

Relatively high profitability tends to be associated with large firm size (Connor 1980, p. 35) and with certain industries. The FTC's (1982a) line-of-

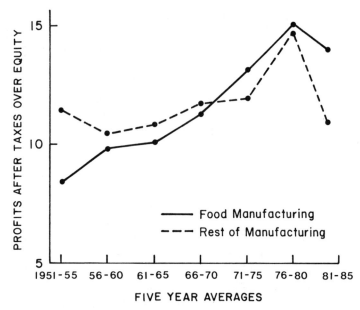

Source: Federal Trade Commission, *Quarterly Financial Reports*.

Notes: Data up through the fourth quarter of 1984. Five-year averages treat each year with equal weights.

Figure 4–11. Profitability of Food and Tobacco Manufacturing Compared to the Rest of Manufacturing, Five-Year Periods, 1951–1984

business data show that 1974–1976 operating income of major firms in food and tobacco lines of business averaged 15.5 percent of total assets. Food manufacturing profitability averaged 40 percent higher than the weighted average rate of return for all manufacturing. Unlike other profit series, these line-of-business data are especially appropriate because they match food manufacturing profits with food manufacturing operations only. A disadvantage is that these data are available for only three years, so some profit rates may be transitorily exaggerated; however, the ranking of most industries is in accord with what market structure would predict. Industries with high concentration, high product differentiation, and high barriers to entry generally display high profitability. Examples include canned specialties, breakfast cereals, pet foods, wet corn milling, and soft drink and other flavorings.

The data used for figure 4–11 also show that profit risk is lower for food and tobacco than for the rest of manufacturing. The average annual deviation from the linear time trend in nominal after-tax profits on equity over 1951–1981 was 0.70 percentage points for food and tobacco; it was 1.32 points for the average of the other eighteen industry groups in manufacturing.

Accounting Profits Studies. A large number of statistical studies have attempted to measure the extent and sources of the monopoly rents in reported profits or margins in food manufacturing. Using both aggregate industry and individual firm financial results, from one year or several years, and with data spanning the 1950–1975 quarter-century, the estimates are remarkably consistent. Monopoly profits or pure rents are inferred from the significant, positive associations between measured profits and several elements of market structure, notably concentration, advertising intensity, and barriers to entry. These estimates for food manufacturing are also compatible with scores of similar statistical profit-structure tests using other manufacturing data (see surveys by Weiss 1974, 1979).

1. One of the first empirical profit-market structure studies for food manufacturing appeared in a technical study by the National Commission on Food Marketing (1966b). By today's standards it was methodologically primitive, correlating net profits on equity (PE) of firms grouped by primary industry with CR4. It did have two good features, however; a large sample of firms (85) accounting for half the assets of all food companies and a CR4 weighted by company shipments in every product class in which it participated.

2. Kelly (FTC 1969b) subsequently used the same shipments data to develop weighted concentration, advertising, and growth variables. He regressed profits on assets (PA) as well as PE ratios against market structure data for 97 publicly owned firms from the universe of the 125 largest food manufacturers of 1950. To remove the effects of windfall profits, Kelly averaged profits over five years (1949–1953) and also included a variable for previous industry growth. The results indicated that three elements of market structure were significant positive determinants of profitability: CR4 (an upward-bending parabola), relative firm market share (cubic specification), and industry advertising intensity (ADS). In addition, firm sales diversification positively influenced profits, but asset size had no impact.

3. Imel and Helmberger (1971) estimated profit-structure relationships for 99 large companies primarily engaged in food and tobacco manufacturing. After-tax profits on sales were averaged over 1959–1967, but the authors did not have sufficient data on firm market shares to account for firm diversification across industries. They made three slight improvements in the Kelly study by including two more independent variables: testing for the sensitivity of industry definitions and applying an advanced generalized-least-squares procedure. Except for finding that company R&D intensity positively affected profits (replacing ADS in some models), their results were qualitatively the same as Kelly.

4. Rogers (1978) replicated the Kelly and Imel-Helmberger studies using a data set of 60 publicly owned food manufacturers. Average values of five different profit measures for 1964–1970 were used. Market structure variables were weighted by 1967 market share data derived from confidential

premerger notifications. Except for finding that firm size was negatively related to profits and some evidence that firm ADS positively interacts with industry ADS, the Rogers study essentially verifies the results of the previously published studies.

5. Ravenscraft's (1983) paper probably represents the finest methodological refinement in structure-profits studies to date. A new data source, the line-of-business reports to the FTC, permitted a more precise matching of the domestic performance of large firms to U.S. market structure characteristics than was previously possible in firm-level studies. Data on gross operating income-to-sales were available for over 3,000 business segments located in 257 manufacturing industries in 1975.[10] Profits were regressed on as many as 36 structural and control variables, and multiequation as well as single-equation models were examined. The major findings were the significant positive impacts of market share, MES, horizontal diversification, and vertical integration and negative impacts of import competition and supplier concentration. Thus, for all manufacturing, Ravenscraft concludes that the positive impact of CR4 in some previous studies may have been because CR4 was a proxy for large market shares of leading firms. However, in a further investigation of line-of-business profits *within* the 20 major industries, he finds evidence of collusion in six (the coefficients of both market shares *and* CR4 are significantly positive), of which food and tobacco manufacturing are two.

Price-Cost Margin Studies. Besides accounting profits, another approach to measuring economic profits is the establishment-based data on price-cost margins. Constructed from Census of Manufactures records, these margins are computed by deducting purchased materials and labor costs from shipments values. Thus, price-cost margins approximate pretax profit rates on sales but also include interest payments, executive compensation, and certain central office expenses, notably advertising expenses. The use of establishment price-cost margins to test the existence of market power overcomes two distinct estimation problems common in firm-based studies: correcting for firm diversification and precisely matching profits to the structural features of the markets in which they are made. When the difference between selling price and production costs is due to the exercise of market power, the price-cost margin approximates Lerner's index of monopoly; that is, the presence of monopoly pricing is inferred if the variation in price-cost margins across industries is explained by the variation in the structures of markets.

Price-cost margins for the 500 largest food and tobacco manufacturers of 1977 are shown in figure 4–12. These data suggest that firms with large enough shipments to rank among the top four producers in a market earn significantly higher profits than lower-ranking firms. Some of the differences may be due to the larger advertising expenditures or capital intensity of the top four firms. Because national market shares are less meaningful in the

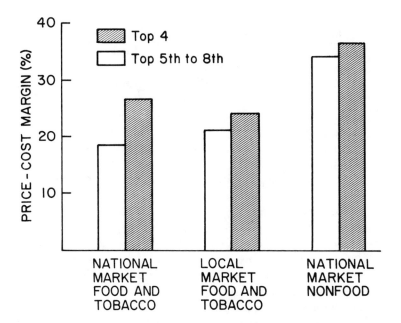

Source: Connor et al. 1985, p. 286.

Figure 4–12. Price-Cost Margins Earned by the 500 Largest Food and Tobacco Manufacturing Companies, by Rank in Industry, 1977

six local market food industries, their average margins do not vary as much by position rank.

There are five econometric studies of the relationship of price-cost margins to industry structure in the food processing industries.

1. Collins and Preston (1968) used 1958 census data on thirty-two food manufacturing industries. Controlling for capital intensity and geographic dispersion (a correction on CR4 for local markets), they found that CR4 and CR4² both had significant positive effects on industry margins. The fit for the food industries was the highest of all the two-digit SIC groups tried.

2. Parker and Connor (1979) repeated the Collins and Preston model with 1972 census data on forty-one industries; the results were qualitatively the same and the fit even closer (over 80 percent of the variance explained). They also improved the model by including ADS, which was significantly positive and caused the CR4² variable to become insignificant.

3. Pagoulatos and Sorenson (1979) introduced three sets of factors that were found to leave the influence of CR4 and ADS on margins unaltered: the price elasticity of demand (negative), the extent of international production by leading firms (positive), and the degree of U.S. tariff protection (positive).

4. Pagoulatos and Sorenson (1983) address the problem of potential endogeneity among margins, CR4, and ADS. Their three-stage, least-squares model applied to 1972 census data for forty-seven food and tobacco industries indicated the robustness of previous results based on single equations (the only difference was a negative sign on MES in their profit equation).

5. Rogers (1985) tested a similar model for 50 five-digit SIC product classes for the six census years during 1954–1977. In addition to reconfirming the industry models, an interesting finding was the rising statistical significance of CR4 over time and the corresponding falling significance of MES.

The various empirical studies of profit-structure relationships estimated for the food manufacturing industries show a remarkable consistency. Yet studies of profits alone have been justly criticized on a number of grounds (Phillips 1976; Demsetz 1974; Peltzman 1977). The principal objection is that high concentration may be associated with high profits either because of collusion-induced higher prices or because of lower average costs due to greater efficiency among leading firms. If the effect of concentration on costs outweighs the effect on prices, then high concentration could yield net social benefits. (That is, the gains to producers are greater than the losses of consumers.) On the other hand, if high concentration induces higher costs, then estimated profit-structure relationships understate net social losses due to market power. (In this case, both producers and consumers are worse off when concentration is high.) A related argument is that high market shares (and by extension, high concentration) are related to high profitability because of stochastic growth processes or luck among firms (Mancke 1974). These doubts about the existence of collusive conditions are partially refuted in the case of the food manufacturing industries by the surveyed studies using data from three different decades that included both market shares and concentration as explanatory variables (Kelly 1969; Rogers 1978; Ravenscraft 1981). In all three studies, both market shares (which should capture the greater efficiency or luck of leading firms) and industry concentration (a proxy for the potential to collude) have positive, significant effects on profits.

Price Performance

There is a relatively straightforward empirical approach to testing whether an industry's market structure actually is linked to measures of market power. "The predictions of oligopoly theory have to do with high prices, not high profits" (Weiss 1979, p. 1107). Estimates of the relationship of market structure to prices provide more direct tests of the exercise of market power by avoiding the possible influence of market structure on costs. Although the number of such tests is somewhat limited (Greer 1984, pp. 296–299), two price-structure studies of processed foods are available.

1. Parker and Connor (1978, 1979) used average U.S. relative national brand, private label retail price differences for 167 finely defined products. Weighted average price differences were developed for a sample of 45 census product classes. Average national private label prices were assumed to be proportional to costs of production (including a normal rate of return to manufacturers) because private label food manufacturers make homogeneous products in industry segments with insignificant barriers to entry. In addition, private label purchasing agents have the knowledge and incentives to search for lowest prices. Over 70 percent of the variation in retail price relatives was explained by manufacturing market structure and nonstructural factors included in their model. The portion of the price difference determined by values above certain critical levels of CR4 and ADS was attributed to manufacturers' market power (table 4–5).[11] The average price difference of the sample was 20 percent, about half of it (11.0 percent) estimated to be due to market power. The rest of the observed price difference was due to quality differences, higher ingredient or packaging costs of national brand manufactures, retailer margins, and other nonstructural factors. A similar model was estimated using U.K. food prices by Nickell and Metcalf (1978), with results comparable to Parker and Connor.

2. Wills (1985) examined price differences among 1,687 brands of 145 processed food product categories. His results indicate that retail prices are relatively high for brands of higher-rated quality, with larger market shares, and with higher measured media advertising expenditures, especially electronic media. He concluded that the impact of advertising exceeds the impact of quality on relative prices. In short, advertising of packaged foods is more persuasive than informative—an expensive guide to quality and a faulty guide to value. Omission of a variable representing product quality is likely to bias advertising coefficients in price-performance equations upward by less than 5 percent. Wills extended and confirmed these findings using wholesale-level prices of 76 categories of branded foods.

These two studies indicate that *prices* of processed foods are higher in markets with high concentration and product differentiation. Therefore the influence of market power on prices explains at least in part the market structure-profit relationships in the food industries.

Consumer Overcharges

The predicted excess price differences shown in table 4–5 were used by Parker and Connor to derive an estimate of the extent to which consumers overpay for national brands due to the exercise of market power. The wholesale price elevations (above prices predicted with a workably competitive market structure) can be multiplied by estimates of the shipments value of domestically

Table 4–5
Predicted Manufacturers' Brand Price Elevation Due to Market Power in the U.S. Consumer Food Manufacturing Product Classes, 1975
(percentage)

Groups of Product Classes[a]	National-Brand Price Enhancement Above Competitive Levels[b]
Meatpacking	0.2–0.3
Meat processing	1.0–1.3
Poultry and egg products	2.7–3.3
Other dairy products	8.7–10.7
Canned fruits and vegetables	4.6–5.5
Other canned and dried foods	8.5–11.3
Frozen foods	8.2–9.5
Four mixes	20.5–24.1
Breakfast cereals	23.9–30.4
Pet foods	19.5–21.8
Other grain mill products	13.4–15.4
Crackers and cookies	16.2–19.3
Sugar	6.7–10.4
Candy and chewing gum	11.8–13.7
Oils and margarine	17.9–20.6
Beer	16.3–18.9
Wine and brandy	10.6–13.8
Other alcoholic beverages	15.3–19.2
Soft drinks and flavorings	24.4–29.3
Coffee	17.5–21.7
Other processed foods	8.1–10.0
Tobacco products	21.8–22.3
Total food and tobacco	11.7–13.5

Source: Connor et al. 1985, p. 291.

[a]Fluid milk and bread industries omitted.

[b]Expressed as a percent of shipments value of domestic consumer products only (excludes export and producer-goods sales). These percentages were calculated using three critical levels for the three market structure factors. Based on previous research on the critical concentration level, CR4 = 40 percent was chosen as the workable-competition level; then critical levels for advertising intensity and geographic dispersion were derived. All other independent variables were held at their means. The ranges indicated are the minimum and maximum estimates from four models; they lie within confidence bands of unknown width.

produced national brands to arrive at a consumer overcharge for each industry. For 1975, Parker and Connor estimated that overcharges for all food manufactures totaled $10 billion to $15 billion per year. In addition, the higher prices cause a reduction in output that results in a deadweight social loss; based on reasonable demand elasticities, the deadweight loss to consumers amounted to $500 million per year.

Unlike the deadweight loss, the overcharge is an income transfer from one set of participants in the food system (households considered as consumers) to other sets of participants. Further analysis of the Parker-Connor results led to the conclusion that the income redistribution from consumers of food went in roughly equal amounts to three sets of beneficiaries: (1) owners of firms with market power in the form of monopoly profits (less than one-half of which were in turn paid to the government as income taxes), (2) recipients' excess advertising and promotion expenditures, and (3) individuals receiving factor payments accruing from "X-inefficiency" due to inadequate cost controls, excess production capacity, unjustified managerial perquisites, excessive wage settlements, and other unknown sources. The existence of X-inefficiency is inferred from the fact that estimates of price elevations are greater than previously predicted monopoly profit margins.

Income Redistribution

Economists have traditionally focused on the net social losses due to monopoly; however, estimates of income transfers due to oligopoly in food manufacturing are at least twenty times the deadweight welfare loss to society. Recent estimates of the distributive incidence of price changes by McElroy, Siegfried, and Sweeny (1982) permit the calculation of the direct and indirect income distribution effects of consumer overcharges due to market power in the food manufacturing industries.

The key finding is that eliminating monopoly overcharges would be *progressive*; that is, the increase in incomes resulting from the discontinuance of the exercise of monopoly power is proportionately greater for lower-income households. For example, the removal of monopoly pricing in the canned and cured meat industry would effectively raise the 1981 income of the poorest (fifth percentile) by 0.28 percent, whereas for the richest households (ninety-fifth percentile) income would increase only 0.15 percent. For all food, beverage, and tobacco manufactures, returning consumer overcharges to consumers with $10,000 incomes would raise their incomes by 1.09 percent; for relatively wealthy households with $60,000 income, the analogous increase is only 0.73 percent. However, in absolute dollar terms, households with $10,000 in income would have gained only $109 in 1981 income due to the elimination of market power of all food and tobacco manufacturers; by contrast, households with $60,000 gross income would have gained about $413 per year.

These data demonstrate the regressive income redistribution that occurs annually due to monopoly power in the food industries. In some industries the impact is virtually neutral with respect to income class, but in none are the price increases progressive. In a country committed to the ideal of greater income equality (as symbolized by a progressive income tax), such findings provide an additional rationale for public interventions that reduce market power.

Wage Rates, Productivity, and Industry Structure

It is often argued that firms in oligopolistic industries pay higher wage rates than those in more competitive markets. Firms in oligopolistic industries are better able to pay higher wages and grant higher wage increases, especially if they can largely pass on these higher costs to consumers. In addition, concentrated industries are more likely to be the targets of unionization campaigns than are unconcentrated ones.

Market structure-wage relationships affect several performance dimensions. First, the estimated allocative inefficiency implied by empirical results from numerous structure-profits studies may understate the actual inefficiency induced by oligopolistic structure; allocative inefficiencies also result from unnecessarily high wages and salaries. Second, higher wage rates in highly concentrated industries may distort firms' input mix decisions. If labor unions are in stronger bargaining positions than sellers of other inputs, the amount of labor employed (compared to other inputs) will be lower than it would be under competition. Third, the higher wage costs may be indicative of operational slack or technical (X-) inefficiency because oligopolistic firms may be under less pressure to minimize costs than are competitive firms. Finally, because unit labor costs are, in general, such an important component in unit variable costs, wage changes that exceed productivity changes affect prices and macroeconomic stability, especially the rate of inflation. Interindustry ratchet effects (see Kahn 1975) can add to the importance of initial wage changes. One such effect embedded in many collective bargaining agreements in the food system is the cost-of-living adjustment (COLA) provision.

Empirical Studies of Wages and Productivity. The empirical approaches taken to evaluate the wage-market structure relationship are varied, including both time-series and cross-sectional studies and including both intra-industry and interindustry analyses.[12] Most of the wage-rate studies have found a positive relationship between wage rates and concentration. The estimated relationship weakens but still remains significant when other industrial, as well as labor-market, characteristics are included in the models and when a simultaneous-equations model is employed. Much less attention in the literature has been focused on an interindustry comparison of wage-rate and productivity *changes*.[13]

Two studies examined wage rates and labor productivity in different food-related industries. McEowen (1982) examined 397 collective bargaining agreements that covered 1.6 million food industry employees in 1981. Using a relatively simple regression model, he found a significant positive association between industry concentration and wage rates, with or without fringe benefits. Higher rates of increase in compensation were also associated with more concentrated industries. Wage increases also were higher for unionized workers covered by a COLA provision than for those who were not.

McEowen's analysis of collective bargaining agreements indicated numerous provisions that reduce labor productivity or increase labor costs. Wage rates were higher in contracts with work restrictions and limitations than in contracts where such restrictions were absent. McEowen found that seniority is given precedence over productivity and job preservation over new technology; short-run considerations prevail over long-run considerations. He concluded that a longer-run perspective by both union and management might lead to agreements that give more consideration to the trade-offs among wage rates, work restrictions, worker productivity, and employment. At present, unions and employees fully face these trade-offs only in the extreme case of plant closings.

Factors Affecting Wages and/or Productivity. Whereas McEowen relied on a case analysis of collective bargaining agreements, Kelton (1983) used more aggregated data from the Census of Manufactures for 1958 to 1977. The cross-sectional analysis was based on a sample of fifty-nine product classes in food and tobacco manufacturing that did not undergo serious definitional changes. Her regression results are summarized in table 4–6. We will comment here only on the influence of CR4, change in concentration, and the level of unionization.

As with most previous studies, Kelton found that hourly wages were significantly higher in concentrated product classes. Wage rates also increased faster over time in concentrated product classes. Since labor productivity tended to increase more slowly (though not significantly) in concentrated product classes, it is not surprising that unit labor costs increased more rapidly in more concentrated product classes.

Change in CR4 over time was significant in only one of the four models; it was positively related to the change in average wage rate across census periods. The unionization variable was positively related to the change in average hourly earnings and negatively related to the change in labor productivity.

Of the four dependent variables Kelton examined, the analysis of change in unit labor cost is perhaps the most instructive. Unit labor cost is simply the production worker wage bill divided by the units of output produced. It is affected by both average hourly earnings and labor productivity. If hourly wages and productivity increase at the same rate, unit labor costs remain constant. For the fifty-nine product classes Kelton studied, unit labor cost dropped slightly from 1958 to 1963 but increased at an increasing rate after 1963. For the entire 1958–1977 period, unit labor cost increased 82 percent.

The evidence presented on average hourly earnings supports the allocative and technical inefficiency hypotheses discussed at the beginning of this sec-

Table 4–6
Regression Results Explaining Hourly Earnings and Productivity in Fifty-nine Food and Tobacco Product Classes, 1958–1977
(direction of effect)

Independent Variables	Dependent variables			
	Average Hourly Earnings[e]	*Percentage Change in Average Hourly Earnings*	*Percentage Change in Unit Labor Productivity*	*Percentage Change in Unit Labor Cost*
1. Four-firm concentration in product class	(+)[a]	(+)[c]	(−)	(+)[b]
2. Change in concentration over time		(+)[a]	(+)	(+)
3. Percentage of large establishments in product classes	(+)[a]	(+)[b]	(−)	(+)
4. Percentage of production workers in South	(−)[a]	(+)[b]	(+)	(−)
5. Median years of education	(±)	(−)	(+)	(−)
6. Percentage male	(+)[a]	(+)		(+)[c]
7. Percentage white	(+)[d]	(+)[a]		(+)
8. Percentage union coverage	(+)	(+)[c]	(−)[c]	(+)
9. Percentage change in quantity of output			(+)[a]	(−)[b]
10. Percentage change in labor productivity		(+)		
R^2	.68	.46	.19	.29

Source: Kelton 1983.

Notes: Data for variables 3, 4, and 6 were available only at four-digit level; data for variables 5, 7, and 8 were available only at three-digit level. The values for the four-digit industries or three-digit industry groups were assigned to all product classes that fell within these broader classifications.

   Empty cells represent omitted variable.

[a]Significant at .01 level.

[b]Significant at .05 level.

[c]Significant at .10 level.

[d]Significant in two out of five years.

[e]Average hourly earnings were expressed in natural logarithms.

tion. Average hourly earnings are significantly higher in concentrated product classes, even controlling for other variables that are expected to affect hourly earnings. The analysis also supports the macroeconomic stability hypothesis. The most concentrated product classes and product classes that have increased most in concentration have generally experienced higher wage rate *increases* without offsetting gains in productivity. As a result, these product classes experienced significantly higher increases in unit labor cost from 1958 to 1977 than less concentrated product classes, thereby contributing to inflationary forces.

Technological Performance

In recent years, the food manufacturing industries have experienced about the same increases in labor productivity as have other manufacturing industries, averaging 2 to 3 percent annually. In 22 percent of the food manufacturing industries, however, labor productivity increased by more than 5 percent per year, whereas only 9 percent of nonfood manufacturing industries experienced such increases. Labor productivity change has been much higher in manufacturing than in other stages of the food marketing system. Based on the evidence reported above, only a small proportion of the change in labor productivity is explained by industry concentration or labor market conditions in the food industries.

The productivity performance record of the food industries may surprise many because the food companies spend very little on research and development (R&D). In 1975, food and kindred product industries were tied with textile and apparel for the smallest R&D expenditures as a percentage of sales. Here we shall summarize briefly research that has examined this paradox of low R&D expenditures and relatively high productivity growth, as well as various factors that influence the extent and origins of R&D inputs and outputs (Mueller, Culbertson, and Peckham 1982).

Regression analysis of the relationship between the competitive structure of industry and R&D inputs and outputs found that industry structure does indeed make a difference. The findings *do not* support hypotheses that substantial market power and larger firm size best promote R&D effort. Rather, in food manufacturing, increasing returns to firm scale in R&D occur until a firm has assets of about $125 million (in 1970 dollars) and thereafter returns to scale decrease. Almost 200 food manufacturers were larger than this technologically optimal size. Also R&D inputs and outputs increase until CR4 reaches 50 to 60 percent and then declines. These findings reject the notion that huge firm size and near-monopoly industry structures best promote technical progress.

An analysis of the sources of patents in six food manufacturing industries found that most (90 percent) did not originate with U.S. food manufacturing firms. An example illustrates the point. Many of the important patents that contributed to the evolution of high-fructose corn syrup came from laboratories of the Japanese government and from U.S. and foreign firms outside the wet-corn-milling industries.

Examination of the sources of innovations identified as making significant contributions to the efficiency of food manufacturing yielded the same general results as the study of patents. A study of 265 award-winning innovations found that only a very small share (13 percent) of the innovations were made by food processors and food ingredient manufacturers. The largest share (55 percent) originated with firms that manufactured food machinery, provided plant maintenance, sanitation, and designs, and developed instrumentation and control systems. Paper and packaging companies (6 percent), chemical firms (4 percent), and miscellaneous corporations and government laboratories (21 percent) accounted for the remainder. Smaller firms made a very large percentage of the innovations studied: 44 percent were by companies with annual sales under $10 million and 63 percent by companies with sales under $100 million in 1975 (Mueller, Culbertson, and Peckham 1982, p. 69). This is a surprising finding since the 100 largest food manufacturers of 1975, each with sales exceeding $100 million, controlled about 70 percent of all food manufacturing assets.

In sum, most inventions and innovations affecting efficiency originate outside the food manufacturing industries. This explains the paradox of the extremely low R&D efforts in food manufacturing and the relatively high technological growth it experienced as measured by increasing labor productivity. For example, the beer industry, which has enjoyed one of the greatest increases in productivity of all manufacturing industries in recent years, ranked among the very lowest supporters of R&D. The reason for its productivity increases is to be found in the technological contributions of parties outside the industry. Only 7 percent of relevant beer patents originated within U.S. beer companies.

The sources of inventive and innovative activity were found to be diverse. Firms of all sizes within and outside the food manufacturing industries, foreign firms, individual inventors, independent research laboratories, and government-sponsored research laboratories have made meritorious inventions. Smaller enterprises have been especially productive in this regard. Many such enterprises were subsequently acquired by larger firms.

These findings support a public policy that promotes multiple sources of research effort: diversity as opposed to centralization of research and innovative effort. The findings also suggest that when there are significant relationships between industrial structure and technological performance, as have been found here and in other cross-sectional industry studies, these findings must be placed in a broader context that includes the sources of all inventions and innovations affecting an industry. In many food processing industries, alternative industrial structures (either more or less concentrated) would have an insignificant impact on total inventive effort influencing technical efficiency. Public policy decisions concerning the need for industrial restructuring should be based on concerns other than technological progressiveness—concerns such as the impact of market power on income distribution or allocative efficiency.

Administered Pricing

The theory of administered pricing has evolved since Gardner Means's first study in 1935. Postwar emphasis has focused on explaining administered or seller-push inflation. It has been argued that firms in oligopolistically structured markets both intensify the severity of recessions by reducing output and employment rather than price during these periods (the business-cycle hypothesis) and contribute to cost-push or seller inflation because oligopolistic firms have more pricing discretion than perfect competitors.

A general statement of the business cycle hypothesis is that administered prices exhibit different behavior during the various phases of the business cycle from prices in the market or auction sector of the economy. Means (1935) noted that many prices that were administered did not fall significantly during the Great Depression years in response to the decrease in national demand; in contrast, producers in the market sector had no choice but to reduce prices. Numerous empirical studies have tested the business cycle hypothesis, but there is no empirical consensus.

On the other hand, the seller-push inflation hypothesis suggests that administered prices rise more over the long term than competitive or market-determined prices and hence contribute more to inflation. The basic argument in this case has two parts. First, prices in oligopolistic markets tend to rise more slowly than prices in competitive markets during periods of general inflation. When general inflationary pressures abate, firms in oligopolistic markets then engage in catch-up pricing. Moreover, as prices and profits of oligopolistic firms climb, generous wage concessions are granted. Second, as prices and wages in oligopolistic markets rise, labor agreements in competitive industries are also affected, as are the costs of inputs purchased from oligopolistic industries. Thus, interindustry interdependence results in a ratchet effect spreading throughout the economy, following the price catch-up behavior of oligopolistic firms.

A basic empirical question from seller-push inflation theory is whether products produced in the more concentrated industries have shown greater price increases than those produced in more competitive industries. The conclusion from numerous empirical studies is that the hypothesis is time dependent.

To test the seller-push inflation hypothesis, Kelton (1982) used data from fifty-nine food and tobacco manufacturing product classes that experienced no serious definitional changes over the years 1958–1977. Implicit prices were computed for each product class for each census year, 1958 through 1977. (An implicit price is the product class value of shipments divided by quantity shipped.) The average price increase for all fifty-nine product classes rose consistently from − 1.0 percent for 1958 through 1963 to 66.2 percent for 1972 through 1977. For the entire time period, average food and tobacco implicit prices rose 107 percent.

Kelton (1982) examined the factors affecting percentage price change using regression analysis. The percentage change in unit variable cost had a strong positive influence on 1958–1977 price change. This variable measured the change in materials and production worker wage bill per unit of output. Since agricultural commodities are a major input to many food manufacturing industries and vary considerably in price over time, a strong relationship was expected. The materials cost component of this variable was eleven times the labor cost component for the product classes examined. The *level* of concentration (CR4) exerted a negative but insignificant effect on price changes in food and tobacco manufacturing, a result that does not support the seller-push inflation hypothesis. However, *change* in concentration had a positive and significant effect on price change. Firms in markets that were increasing in concentration tended to have higher price increases than firms in markets that experienced stable or declining concentration.

One of the important findings was the positive, significant effect of *advertising intensity* on price change. When advertising intensity was measured using two separate variables, electronic media and print media, only electronic media intensity had a significantly positive effect on long-term price change. The barriers to entry created by advertising in some food manufacturing industries apparently allowed producers in those industries to increase prices more rapidly.

Change in advertising intensity had a significant negative effect on price change. This finding may reflect successful advertising campaigns in which food sales and prices rise faster than advertising expenditures, resulting in a decline in advertising per dollar of sales.

These empirical results provide no direct support for the traditional seller-push inflation hypothesis, at least in food and tobacco industries. Higher price rises were not observed for the most concentrated food and tobacco product classes. The analysis does indicate, however, that market structure has a strong influence on price changes. Product classes that experienced sharp increases in concentration also had higher price rises. It may be that industries that were already oligopolistic were charging prices that resulted in joint profit maximization or that deterred entry and hence had less incentive or flexibility to increase prices sharply. Moreover, an important link has been shown empirically between advertising intensity (especially electronic media advertising) and price changes. Products that were heavily advertised enjoyed the greatest price increases between 1958 and 1977. These results indicate that policies that slow or reverse the trend toward increased concentration or that encourage lower levels of advertising may also help control the rate of price increases, at least in food and tobacco manufacturing.

Food Advertising, Consumption Patterns, and Nutrition

Concerns about nutrition in the United States are numerous and growing, stemming in part from the realization that several leading causes of death are related either to excessive food consumption or to the types of foods consumed. Obviously many factors determine food choices and consumption. Individual taste preferences, economic variables such as income and price, life-style characteristics such as the decline in size of households and the number of meals eaten at home, and nutritional knowledge probably all have some effect on consumption patterns. There also is growing evidence, however, that television advertising and programming have a definite effect on viewer attitudes, values, and behavior. If advertising has the capacity to influence patterns of food and beverage consumption, then it also has the potential to influence health and nutrition—for good or ill.

Advertising varies considerably by product and type of industry (Comanor and Wilson 1979). Advertising by retailers tends to have a high informational content and has been found to be pro-competitive, at least in some situations (Benham 1972; Bond et al. 1980). Advertising by manufacturers tends to have lower informational content (Costa 1983). Consumer durable goods generally receive less advertising by manufacturers than consumer nondurable goods (Albion and Farris 1981, p. 131). Because durable goods require larger outlays by consumers, on average, there tends to be greater buyer search and involvement in the decision process.

Porter (1976b) suggested a dichotomy between "convenience" and "non-convenience" consumer goods. Because of the fundamental differences in purchasing procedures, Porter contends that (1) advertising is a more powerful determinant of sales and profits in the convenience goods sector and (2) advertising messages that influence buyer behavior in convenience goods industries are less likely to be based on objectively measurable product attributes.

Porter's conclusions have particular relevance to food products and are consistent with evidence presented earlier in this chapter on the disproportionate share of total advertising accounted for by food and tobacco manufacturers and the effects of advertising on profits, prices, and market concentration. Television advertising appears to have a particularly strong influence on consumer food purchasing behavior. Television is the dominant medium for advertising food and tobacco products, accounting for $2 out of every $3 spent on media advertising by food manufacturers (Rogers and

Mather 1983). For these reasons, the following discussion will focus on television advertising.

Krugman (1965) observed that the recall of television commercials was similar to the recall of nonsensical or unimportant messages. He noted that the common element in receiving nonsensical or unimportant messages is a lack of involvement. Thus, he hypothesized that the impact of television advertising is due to the low involvement of viewers, who become passive recipients of information. This lack of resistance and perceptual defenses explains the effectiveness of advertising in low-involvement situations.

Because of low viewer involvement, frequent repetition of television ads is necessary to maintain consumer awareness, positive attitudes, and brand loyalty. Analyzing the effects of repetition of a given stimulus, Zajonc (1968, p. 1) concluded, "Mere repeated exposure of the individual to a stimulus is a sufficient condition for the enhancement of his attitude toward it."

Television advertising of consumer goods contains little factual information (Resnick and Stern 1977). Rather, through the use of implied claims and endorsers, television advertisements associate commercial products with the fulfillment of basic human needs such as love, acceptance, and happiness. Through sociopsychological implied claims, advertising attempts to transform products into objects that satisfy deep human needs. This type of advertisement does not result in a conscious decision to buy the product; rather, an unconscious shift in viewer attitude occurs that becomes evident only when the consumer faces a purchasing decision.

Food Advertising and Obesity. Obesity is one of the most widespread health problems in the United States. Costa's (1983) survey of the major obesity theories and empirical evidence indicates that overeating is the foremost cause of obesity. Two major theories may explain overeating behavior. Bruch (1973), a psychiatric expert on obesity, proposed incorrect learning experiences as the cause of overeating. Bruch contends that the most important type of incorrect learning experience today stems from the lack of parental limits to the self-indulgent eating behavior of children. In contrast, Schachter (1971) has developed considerable evidence to support his theory that overeating is triggered by external food-related stimuli such as the smell, sight, and taste of food.

Television advertising and programming can affect the learning experiences of children and can also provide external food-related stimuli. Children spend an average of 3.75 hours per day watching television and are tempted to eat irrespective of their hunger sensations. Moreover, foods that are heavily advertised appeal fundamentally to pleasure instincts and in most cases are not high in nutrition. Dussere (1977, p. 77) concluded from her research, "The more television viewing children did, the more likely they were to eat heavily-sugared cereals, the more often they ate between meals, the more total snack foods they ate, the more they ate candy and chips, and the more often they ate empty-calorie foods."

Empirical Analyses. The relationship between advertising and food consumption was examined by Costa in two ways. The first was a time-series analysis for 1953–1979 in which caloric intake per capita per year was regressed on an index of food prices, per capita income, total food advertising, total advertising except for food, population age distribution, and time trend. All variables were statistically significant. Both total food advertising and total nonfood advertising had a significant positive relationship with caloric intake per capita.

Although the aim of advertising is primarily to influence consumers to buy a particular brand, the cumulative effects of advertising for all brands within a product class may increase the total demand for that product class relative to other food classes with less advertising. Costa's second analysis examined the impact of advertising on the composition of the American diet using consumption data from the USDA nationwide food consumption surveys conducted in 1965 and 1977. Both change in advertising and the advertising-to-sales ratio had a significant positive relationship to change in quantity consumed (for parallel results, see Gallo and Connor 1982). Together they explained about one-third of the variance in consumption changes. Research on the effects of generic advertising is consistent with these findings. Generic advertising is used not to promote particular brands but to expand the total sales of a product. At least for dairy and citrus products, generic advertising has been found to be effective in expanding total sales (Morrison 1984).

These statistical results do not establish causality; they do indicate that a relationship exists between food advertising and both the total caloric intake and the composition of the American diet. Some may argue that advertising increases are the *result* of increased sales (and consumption) of a product or that advertising expenditures are concentrated on growing product categories. While this may be true in some cases, there is also considerable evidence that advertising also *affects* behavior, including food consumption.

The available evidence supports the proposition that advertising exacerbates the problem of obesity in the United States. The other nutritional consequences of advertising are less clear. However, if the consumption patterns of Americans are significantly influenced by television advertising, then concerns about the long-run nature of that influence are appropriate. It seems unlikely that the nutritional and health consequences will be neutral.

Product Proliferation

One aspect of the product performance of an industry is the variety of products available in a market. More variety is generally preferred to less, but at some point the rate of new product introductions and the resulting stock of highly substitutable items may become excessive. A.C. Nielsen (1982) data indicate that new item introductions through grocery stores dropped from 6,700 in 1975 to 4,750 in 1978 and then steadily increased to 6,100 in 1981. Between 1975 and 1981, 68 percent of the new items were classified by Nielsen as "item proliferation of established brands."

The performance consequences of product proliferation are particularly difficult to evaluate. Critics of product proliferation make five basic charges (summarized by Connor 1980):

1. Product proliferation is deceptive because most new products are mere imitations or minor variants of existing products and are often marketed by the same large companies.

2. Proliferation contributes to inflation because new products often have higher price-quality ratios than existing substitutes.

3. Proliferation results in waste from self-cancelling advertising and operating plants at suboptimal production levels.

4. Proliferation creates consumer confusion and undermines rational decision making by making trial purchases and personal evaluation costly.

5. Product proliferation creates or exacerbates competitive problems by strengthening product differentiation and raising entry barriers for more specialized potential entrants.

Product proliferation is embraced by others who argue that it broadens consumer choice and allows consumers to match their preferences more precisely with market offerings.

Welfare analyses of optimal product diversity lead to no clear-cut judgment of the net effects of proliferation. Schmalensee (1978) also argues that there are not necessarily too many products for a given market, though proliferation deters entry that could lead to lower prices. The greatest concern about proliferation should be in the product categories with very high levels of concentration. The main hope of increasing competition in these categories is from new entrants; however, extensive proliferation by incumbent firms may leave no profitable market niches for a new firm to occupy. Antitrust enforcement should be sensitive to the fact that a product proliferation strategy may be one of a mix of strategies by which entrenched firms reinforce barriers to entry.

Multidimensional Assessment of Performance

In this chapter, we analyzed seven dimensions of performance in the U.S. food and tobacco manufacturing industries. What have we learned about the performance of these industries?

Perhaps the major theme that permeates these analyses is that market structure has a strong effect on nearly all of the performance dimensions examined. Market concentration, market share, change in concentration, and media advertising affect one or more aspects of performance. The effects vary. Some performance dimensions are influenced by certain structural measures, while other aspects of performance are affected by different elements of market structure. But the overall conclusions are compelling and difficult to refute: market structure has a significant influence on the multidimensional performance of the food and tobacco manufacturing industries.

Table 4–7 provides a general summary of the market structure-performance relationships found in the various empirical studies reviewed in this chapter. Of those dimensions that have been studied, only productivity change and R&D activity seem to be influenced little by market structure. Given the evidence that technological opportunities vary considerably across different food manufacturing industries and that most important technological changes in food manufacturing are developed by other industries, these results are not surprising.

Because a central conclusion of this chapter is the pervasive influence of market structure on performance, we have classified seventy-five food manufacturing product classes by three important structural measures: four-firm concentration (CR4), change in CR4 (Δ CR4), and media advertising-to-sales ratio (ADS) (table 4–8). Change in concentration is divided into three categories. Product classes where concentration increased or decreased by 5 percentage points or more from 1967 to 1977 were placed in the increasing or decreasing categories. The remaining product classes were considered relatively stable. Product classes were placed in one of three product differentiation categories based on the simple average of their ADS in 1967, 1972, and 1977. CR4s for 1977 were used to divide the product classes into five categories.

Out of seventy-five product classes, eight are classified as shared monopolies. At the opposite extreme, fourteen product classes are unconcentrated. Hardly surprising given the evidence presented in this chapter, the more concentrated product classes also tend to have high levels of advertising and stable or increasing levels of concentration. Low-grade oligopolies and unconcentrated product classes generally do little advertising; moreover, they more frequently have declining concentration ratios than product classes in the top three categories. There is no evidence of a natural erosion of concentration in the top two categories (shared monopolies and highly concentrated oligopolies). Indeed, of the nineteen product classes in these two categories, nine increased in concentration (> 5 percent) from 1967 to 1977. Ten of the nineteen product classes had high levels of advertising, including five in which advertising exceeded 6 percent of sales.

How are we to interpret table 4–8? Are the eight product classes shown as shared monopolies acting like monopolists? We cannot answer that ques-

Table 4–7

Summary of Structure-Performance Relationships Found in Empirical Studies of Food Manufacturing

Performance Measure	Industries					
	CR4	CR4^2	ΔCR4	ADS	ΔADS	Firm Size
Accounting profits	pos	—	—	pos	—	—
Price-cost margins	pos	—	—	pos	—	—
National brand/private label price difference	pos	neg	—	pos	—	—
Brand prices						
Wage levels	pos	—	—	—	—	pos
Δ in wages	pos	—	pos	—	—	pos
Δ in productivity	n.s.	—	n.s.	—	—	n.s.
Δ in unit labor cost	pos	—	n.s.	—	—	n.s.
R&D expenditure/firm						
R&D employment/firm						
Patents registered per firm						
Rate of price increases	n.s.	—	pos	pos	neg	—
Change in consumption	—	—	—	pos	pos	—
Product proliferation	pos	—	—	pos	—	—

Note: pos = significant positive relationship in most or all studies over the relevant range.
  neg = significant negative relationship in most or all studies over the relevant range.
  n.s. = not significant in most or all studies over the relevant range.
  — = not included in models.
[a]Effect is positive until CR^4 reaches 50–60 percent; thereafter effect declines.
[b]Effect is positive until ADS reaches 7 percent, thereafter it declines.
Source: Connor et al. 1985, p. 322–323.

tion based on this table alone. The various structure-performance studies reviewed deal with average relationships across many products. They tell a great deal about probabilities but may do a poor job of predicting the performance of individual product classes.

We caution readers that some product classes closely approximate a relevant geographic and product market, and others do not. This can affect the level of structural variables and may lead to errors in classification. For example, "mayonnaise and salad dressings" (SIC 20354), includes mayonnaise, spoonable salad dressing (such as Miracle Whip), and pourable salad dressings. Pourable salad dressings do not compete directly with the other two. If this product class were split into "spoonable salad dressings and mayonnaise" and "pourable salad dressings," both would have higher concentration than with the present census definitions.

Our earlier discussion of strategic groups indicated that often segments or submarkets within an industry behave very differently from the industry in total. For example, the private label submarket of many product classes is relatively competitive. Although the margarine product class is a moderately

				Firms				
Industry		Industry		Firm or Brand		Market	Firm	Firm
CR4	CR4²	ADS	ADS²	ADS	$Ad.	Share	Size	Size²
pos	—	pos	—	n.s.	—	pos	n.s.[e]	—
—	—	—	—	pos	pos	pos	—	—
pos[a]	neg[a]	pos[b]	neg[b]	—	—	n.s.[d]	pos	neg[c]
pos[a]	neg[a]	n.s.	n.s.	—	—	n.s.[d]	pos	neg[c]
pos[a]	neg[a]	pos[b]	neg[b]	—	—	n.s.[d]	pos	neg[c]

[c]Effect is positive until firm reaches asset size of about $125 million (1970) dollars; thereafter effect declines.

[d]Not significant because the relationship is linear. Hence, a monopolistic industry would have the same total R&D as a competitively structured industry.

[e]Some negative.

[f]Industry structure variables generally represent weighted averages of industries in which firm participates.

concentrated oligopoly with high levels of advertising and increasing concentration, approximately 23 percent of margarine sales through grocery stores are accounted for by store brands or private labels. This segment of the product class appears to be effectively competitive.

As these caveats suggest, we are well aware of the limitations of the classifications shown in table 4–8. We believe, however, that the table is a useful general portrayal of the competitive characteristics of seventy-five food manufacturing product classes. Although there are several product classes that, because of their market structure, are probably performing subcompetitively, there are also a large number of product classes with structural characteristics that encourage competitive or near-competitive performance.

Major Conclusions and Issues

A relatively small number of manufacturing firms are in many respects the prime movers of the U.S. food system. The discretionary power of manufac-

Table 4-8
Classification of Seventy-five National Market Food and Tobacco Product Classes by Three Market Structure Characteristics

Concentration Class	Change in[a] CR4	Degree of Product Differentiation[b]		
		Low	Medium	High
Shared monopolies (CR4 ≥ 80)	↑		Canned baby foods	Chewing gum (11.9) Cigarettes (6.6)
	↑		Bottled and canned soft drinks[c]	Breakfast cereals (11.6) Desserts, ready-to-mix (6.4) Concentrated coffee Canned soup
	→			
Highly concentrated oligopolies (65 ≤ CR4 < 80)	↑		Chewing and smoking tobacco Canned milk products	Dried soup mixed (6.5) Dried beverage mixes
	↑	Refined sugar Tobacco stemmed and dry	Cocoa and cocoa mixes[d] Crackers and pretzels	Tea
	→			
Moderately concentrated oligopolies (50 ≤ CR4 < 65)	↑	Malt Chocolate coatings	Chips (potato, corn, and so forth)	Dog and cat food (6.5) Margarine Mayonnaise and salad dressings
	↑	Wet-corn milling Corn mill products Lamb and mutton	Frozen pies and baked goods Catsup and tomato sauces Other frozen specialties Roasted coffee Cookies Canned dry beans	Bottled liquors (9.7) Cigars Sweetening syrups/molasses
	→	Processed cheese Soybean oil mill products		
Low-grade oligopolies (35 ≤ CR4 < 50)	↑	Pickles Turkeys	Confectionary products Jams and jellies Frozen fruits and juices	

	Canned meats	Milled rice	Wines and brandy
	Canned vegetables	Frozen dinners and ethnic foods	Meat sauces
	Canned fruits	Canned and cured seafood	
	Wheat mill product except flour	Dry milk products	
	Wheat flour		
	Sugar cane products (unrefined)		
	Pork, fresh and frozen		
	Cottonseed oil mill products		
↓		Shortening and cooking oil	Flour mixes/refrigerated dough
↑	Young chickens and hens[e]		
	Ice cream mix		
↑	Canned fruit juices	Frozen vegetables	Macaroni and noodles
	Sausages		
	Processed pork except sausage		
	Beef, fresh		
	Concentrated milk, bulk		
Unconcentrated (CR4 < 35)	Natural cheese		
↓	Butter		
	Liquid and dried eggs		
	Veal		
	Vegetable oil mill products, NEC		

Source: Connor et al. 1985, p. 324–325.

Note: To simplify this table, product classes with value of shipments below $250 million, all animal feed product classes, and all local market product classes were excluded. A few product classes with the most serious definitional problems (such as dehydrated fruits and vegetables) were also excluded, although some in table 4–8 are still too broadly or narrowly defined. All product classes included operate in regional or national markets.

[a] Product classes that increased or decreased five percentage points or more from 1967 to 1977 are placed in increasing (↑) or decreasing (↓) categories.

[b] The simple average of the product class advertising-to-sales (ADS) ratios for 1967, 1972, and 1977 were used, where ADS < 1% = low differentiation; ADS ≥ 1% < 3% = medium differentiation; ADS ≥ 3% = high differentiation. Within each concentration-product differentiation cell, product classes are listed in descending order of ADS. ADS over 6 percent are shown in parenthesis.

[c] Because bottled and canned soft drinks are distributed in local markets, the CR4 for SIC 20873 (flavoring syrups for use by soft drink bottlers) was used. Media advertising by syrup manufacturers and bottlers was divided by value of shipments in SIC 20860 (bottled and canned soft drinks) to determine the advertising-to-sales ratio. Because of the exclusion territories for soft drink bottlers, we believe both the syrup manufacturing product class and soft drink bottling markets have the characteristics of shared monopolies.

[d] Represents a combination of product classes 20668 and 20998.

[e] Represents a combination of product classes 20161 and 20162 to allow comparisons with earlier census years.

turers in relation to farmers is most evident in commodity-type product markets, but it extends to more extensively processed consumer goods. Most of the items consumers recognize as edibles first take form in manufacturer's hands. Within certain boundaries prescribed by custom, processors are predominantly responsible for the physical design of foods. In addition, food manufacturers influence consumers' concepts of what constitute appropriate end uses and create or exploit deeply rooted emotive associations of foods. Extensive processing of increasingly numerous and unfamiliar food materials creates the impression among household consumers that foods originate from factories rather than farms. For a broad line of highly prepared foods especially, the close substitutability of one variety for another may give manufacturers considerable leverage over farmers and their bargaining associations. If Michigan cherries are expensive, the frozen pie manufacturer may make do with Georgia peaches. Retailers often must accommodate themselves to the merchandising thrusts of manufacturers of branded consumer foods.

The focus of this chapter is the competitive performance of the U.S. food manufacturing industries. The structure-conduct-performance paradigm was used as an analytical framework. Our major conclusion is that roughly 60 to 70 percent of the output of the food manufacturing industries is sold in markets that are workably competitive. The remaining 30 to 40 percent of output is produced in industries in which competitive forces are hobbled by the exercise of market power. Shortfalls in performance can be traced largely to the market structures of those industries: sales concentration, market shares, change in concentration, and advertising. Generally, food industries with relatively few producers selling differentiated consumer products through grocery stores are the ones most likely to display some market power, operational inefficiencies, or other deviations from desirable economic or social performance.

There are manifold reasons for this dichotomy in performance outcomes. On some points we are fairly confident about causal linkages; however, a number of issues need to be resolved by further study and open debate. In this final section, we focus on six recurring themes of the chapter—topics that are mixtures of relatively certain knowledge and questions awaiting resolution through future research.

Product Differentiation and Performance

Advertising wears the sole triple crown of the industrial-organization paradigm. As a surrogate for the degree of product differentiation, it is an element of market structure; as one of several nonprice business options open to firms, it is a mode of conduct; and as a major component of selling costs, it is a dimension of performance. In empirical tests, advertising expenditures were found to play a crucial and powerful role in the food manufacturing industries.

Advertising influences the conduct and strategies of firms in the food industries. Advertising was found to be a significant determinant of food product proliferation, sales diversification, and the degree of foreign direct investment. Advertising expenditures are calculated to be far more concentrated among the leading fifty or one hundred food manufacturers than are sales or value-added. Similarly the largest food firms hold proportionately more leading positions in industries or product classes characterized by the most intense advertising. Measured-media advertising expenditures are known to be positively correlated with some other forms of selling effort, such as couponing and are very likely complementary with other selling efforts as well (point-of-purchase displays, cooperative retailer advertising, free samples, deals, and so on).

Advertising has a pervasive influence on the performance of the food manufacturing industries. Along with sales concentration, advertising at the firm or industry level is the most consistent direct determinant of supranormal profits and prices (table 4–7). Excess advertising used to defend a monopoly position is considered a socially wasteful resource expenditure; it was estimated to be about one-third of the consumer loss due to market power. Some of the most highly advertised products (including cigarettes and soft drinks) are those associated with the greatest regressiveness in income redistribution. In most of the postwar period, advertising intensity was positively associated with administered price inflation. Finally, food advertising appears to contribute to obesity and other national nutritional problems. In short, except for the possibility that advertising-prone firms may be more technologically progressive, the performance impacts of advertising are not sanguine. This summary judgment applies with double force to advertising by the electronic mass media, presumably because television and radio lend themselves to conveying emotive, image-filled appeals.

Advertising has feedback effects on market structure. Because advertising itself enjoys technological economies of scale and pecuniary advantages of size, as well as threshold effects, it raises barriers to entry. Because of its effects on brand sales and consumer loyalty, advertising can be used to restructure markets; in particular, advertising was found to increase significantly levels of sales concentration in the food industries during the 1954–1977 period. This in turn may be one of the causes of the secular rise in the profit rates of food manufacturers. Advertising, particularly on television, also may undermine the assumptions of consumer sovereignty and in the long run alter the responsiveness of demand to price or income changes.

But what is the essential nature of advertising? Why is it used in some industries but not others? How does it work? And what can public policymakers do about it? These are some of the unresolved issues facing economists, behavioral scientists, and advertising practitioners. Measurement of advertising expenditures, trends, and intensities has reached new heights in food-system research (Connor and Ward 1983). But no social scientist has as yet been entirely successful in separating the "informative" from the "persuasive" content of messages.

Economists have spent little effort in establishing whether advertising intensity is a defensible proxy for the average degree of product differentiation in a market. The use of advertising expenditures in empirical applications is partly a matter of pragmatic acquiescence: the results are robust and the alternatives few. However, the differentiability of products may be in part an inherent quality, arising from the physical characteristics or culturally determined functions of the product. If so, advertising or selling effort is as much symptom as cause, and operationally the two roles are difficult to distinguish.

This brings us to another conundrum, the determinants of advertising. Although some work has been done on this question by business school researchers, little satisfactory work is available by economists working in the industrial organization framework. To some extent advertising may be jointly determined by profitability or price changes, but little is known about its roots in the basic conditions facing markets. For example, advertising intensity is probably affected by product durability (storability or frequency of purchase in the case of foods), type of packaging, health risks, type of store, delivery arrangements, perceived convenience services, and so forth.

Perhaps the hardest question of all is the policy treatment of advertising. Because it is a two-edged sword—both potentially barrier raising and barrier busting, improving informed choice as well as spreading obfuscation—policy choices are very difficult. Outright bans, upper limits, and countervailing information are among the proposals. Many suggestions are at variance with the constitutional protections extended to commercial free speech. At least for the present, the once-popular consumer protection approach is in abeyance, if not actual retreat.

Information and Rationality

One of the implications of our research is that there is a lack of adequate or reliable information for rational decision making by consumers, especially in channels dominated by branded, packaged foods and beverages. The discretionary, price-setting behavior of retailers and manufacturers makes prices unreliable guides to what is rare and costly to produce. We find that, contrary to Phillip Nelson's (1974) predictions, advertising is an uncertain and at times perverse index of quality-price relationships. Retailers have more information than consumers but except for their private label programs have little incentive to use it fully to benefit customers.

Human beings are creatures of habit. Their purchasing behaviors are conditioned both by subconscious feeling or emotional make-up and by the rational calculus of utility maximization. Indeed given substantial search costs relative to contemplated expenditures, some repetitiveness and unwillingness to change from satisfactory products may be entirely rational behavior. Because grocery products are sold in small units through self-service outlets and are purchased frequently, they are especially susceptible to highly repetitive buying patterns reinforced by image advertising. Early entrants (pioneering brands) into a product class can set the quality norms (taste, color, packaging, and formulation) to which following brands must attain. It may be cost-effective for risk-averse consumers who find their needs satisfied by early or leading brands to avoid experimenting with or gathering data on follower brands. In other words, for many food products consumers *learn to like what they buy* initially rather than *learn to buy what they like* after systematic sampling and comparison of alternative brands. Moreover, product proliferation exacerbates the costs of gathering information on numerous market alternatives. Under some conditions, it is a profitable long-run strategy for firms to make exaggerated claims about product quality or to let a brand's objective quality slip, given some degree of consumer lethargy or myopia.

The nature of consumer loyalty has not yet been fully explored by economists or behavioral scientists. Such research is pregnant with implications for firm strategies and industrial performance and can shed light on proposals to improve preference articulation through objective or scientific information programs.

Entry Conditions

Rigorous thinking about the conditions of entry and exit took a quantum leap with Bain's 1956 book. Beginning in the late 1970s, reconsiderations or perhaps refinements of Bain's concept appeared. The view of advertising as a barrier to entry was challenged. The idea of strategic investment in excess capacity was suggested as a superior alternative to limit pricing. The importance of strategic groups of firms within industries was proposed as a source of mobility barriers. The emphasis on entry barriers was accompanied by greater attention to exit conditions, a key feature of recent work on *contestable markets*. Most of these newer models remain untested, and the difficulty of measuring barriers and gross entry rates may frustrate research for some years.

This chapter devoted considerable attention to the roles of market shares and concentration. Under conditions of costless and instantaneous entry and exit, the height and stability of concentration or shares is of little policy relevance. For those devotees of the revisionist view of industrial organization, our emphasis on these structural features may seem a trifle old-fashioned; however, the evidence from the food manufacturing industries persuades us to adhere to them. The demonstrated stability of leading firm market shares and persistently high levels of concentration in the food manufacturing industries seem inconsistent with "ultra-free entry and exit." In our judgment, most food manufacturing industries are not characterized by costless and instantaneous entry and exit. We agree with Shepherd (1984) that the theory of contestable markets appears to have limited relevance. In addition to our personal knowledge of these industries, the studies that have found prices to be positively related to market shares and advertising indicate that entry barriers exist. We have included some preliminary findings of efforts to test Porter's (1976b, 1979, 1985) theory of strategic groups and mobility barriers. We believe this theoretical framework holds considerable promise for better understanding the food manufacturing industries and would encourage efforts to test Porter's concepts.

Diversification and Conglomeration

This chapter is in the form of an industry case study. Yet the data base consists of fifty or more distinct food and tobacco manufacturing industries. This level of analysis, while unusual in an industrial organization study, is dictated in part by the feverish (some would say vigorous) diversification trends of food firms in the post–World War II period. Sales diversification was partly the result of merger activity. Conglomeration is an extreme, possibly terminal, case of diversification.

Diversification is interesting as a topic, and it is essential to come to grips with the phenomenon in order to analyze performance at the firm level. But its principal fascination lies with the potential for restructuring markets. A key theme of this chapter is the impact on nonprice behavior, predatory tactics, and industry concentration that the presence of conglomerates can have and is having in the food industries. Our conclusions on conglomerate restructuring are based on a limited number of especially well-documented episodes. More systematic approaches are likely to lead to more generalized inferences.

Regulation Assessment

Numerous public policies impinge on the competitiveness of markets. Consumer protection measures have probably reduced the incidence of fraudulent and misleading advertising claims, and a few steps have been taken to ensure affirmative disclosure of factual information to facilitate value comparisons. Regulations governing the use of food grades, food standards of identity, and labeling have the potential for expanding usable information for consumers; each has had some effect on reducing the scope of product differentiation in the food system. Several government agencies collect and publish information on market structure and financial performance. Many others have been discontinued since 1980. These data are valuable to researchers and also can provide signals to potential entrants about the expected profitability of a particular line of business. In principle, the value of such information can be estimated; by comparing these benefits with known costs, the social returns to public investments in information can be calculated. Such exercises are rare, but where they have been performed, the benefit-cost ratios are quite large (see Oster 1981 for one good example).

Other laws and regulations affect the conditions of entry. For a few foods, imports widen the area of competition and provide needed price discipline. The increasing openness of the U.S. economy is cited as a principal reason for increasing U.S. competitiveness in the post–World War II era (Shepherd 1982). The Reagan and Carter administrations have largely resisted the protectionist appeals of domestic food processors' lobbying groups, but the pressures to erect import barriers appear to be growing. The special subsidies and tax treatment of small businesses and cooperatives are another set of policies that maintain company numbers or encourage entry. But these regulations must be set against others that favor large or incumbent firms. The effects of trademarks and exclusive territorial franchising in raising entry barriers have already been mentioned. Many tax and accounting rules encourage large firm size, product diversification, certain types of mergers, and increased income from foreign invstments. This chapter was able to assess competitive impact only on the basis of deductive reasoning or studies applied to other sectors.

We were able to devote more attention to assessing the federal antitrust laws. These laws are well analyzed for the food system in part IV of this book. They are the main bulwark against the monopolistic restructuring of markets, but they are ill equipped to ameliorate the effects of entrenched market power and conglomerate behavior.

Deconcentrating or Countervailing Forces

Lest we end on an unfashionable note of pessimism, it is appropriate to identify several forces or trends with potentially procompetitive effects.

Countervailing market power exists to some extent in the food system. The foodservice industry provides distant competition for such highly convenient grocery products as frozen pizza. The growth of diverters may help to blunt the promotional effects of deal merchandise offered by the major manufacturers. Food retailers have a great deal of discretion over new product acceptance and placement. Perhaps more important for competition are the private label and generic programs of retailers, which support a large number of small and medium-size processors. Manufacturers' advertised brands compete in varying degrees with store brands, but in those product categories where private labels are available, they provide at least a modicum of price discipline. For example, store brands of sugar, flour, and salt are very likely seen as nearly perfect substitutes for branded equivalents, whereas store brands of frozen waffles and soft drinks offer relatively distant or weak competition for the major brands. In most product classes, the share of unbranded or store labels has been nearly constant for years, and in some product lines, such as poultry and bottled water, branding is taking on new significance. The generic movement that began around 1977 appears stalled eight years later. The organized consumer movement, on the other hand, after a period of retreat in the early 1980s, appears to have matured and stabilized. For example, the quality testing activities of the Consumers' Union continues to be a widely used information source for consumers.

Technological change is an important deconcentrating force in some industries. In the long run, it can create new industries, restructure existing industries, and redefine the boundaries of existing product markets. To the extent that an oligopolistic consensus encourages passive or lethargic responses to technological opportunities, the sale of new products or processes by firms outside the oligopoly core is a welcomed destabilizing force. Unfortunately, except for the wet corn milling and frozen foods industries, there have been few instances of dramatic industrial redefinition among the food industries since 1945. Also, the leading food manufacturers are often quick to take advantage of the successes of small, dynamic firms in burgeoning industries by acquiring them. Finally, the restructuring of markets does not always imply deconcentration. This is attested by the recent (and still ongoing) conversion of the beef packing industry from traditional carcass to boxed beef methods. Similarly, the restructuring of the brewing industry has propelled it from a moderately concentrated to a highly concentrated industry in a mere decade.

Technological change can occur on the buying side of a market as well. Computerized information systems within retail stores, especially when combined with household computing capacity, hold promise for more routine, lower-cost, and more rational consumer buying decisions in the future. Consumers may be able to program their buying decisions by setting up certain nutritional, price, and quantity criteria in advance of purchase. If household computers could interact with food item data banks, the shopping process could be further routinized. Such fanciful systems of food purchasing could use cost-minimizing programs that would reduce the extent of impulse buying and the effects of product proliferation. Although there may be merchandising considerations that will cause less than full disclosure, similar systems can be feasibly operated presently by food retailers as a service to shoppers; retailers' own private labels will often look like the best value with instore price comparison systems.

Another relevant area of technological change is kitchen technology. The rapid growth of the frozen foods industry would not have been possible had not households acquired freezers. The modern household food processor is a form of backward vertical integration. The countertop pasta machine may replace some of the output of pasta factories just as the household refrigerator-freezer replaced the iceman. The advent of modular kitchen equipment that combines heating, cooling, and mechanical devices in coordinated units will likely make increasingly sophisticated, flexible, and convenient household food processing equipment possible. Much of this equipment will be adapted from the foolproof, automated machinery being developed for use by unskilled laborers in the foodservice industry. The importance for food industries competition is the return to basics that such changes imply. The kitchen of the future may use generic bags and bottles of commodity-type products that can be purchased infrequently in large units: wheat berries, potatoes, coffee beans, frozen meats, liquid sweeteners, starches, and bland oils. Such units could be programmed with favorite recipes and maintain records of calories, sodium units, or other nutrients consumed. A return to cooking from scratch using one's own miniature food processing unit is one way to avoid the unpalatable effects associated with consuming highly differentiated foods.

Notes

1. The food, beverage, and tobacco manufacturing industries span SICs 20 and 21, two of the twenty major industry groups of the manufacturing sector. In the 1977 version, food manufacturing contained 47 four-digit SIC industries and tobacco manufacturing 4 industries; these 51 industries were further broken down into 176 five-digit SIC product classes, of which 154 were well defined. All manufacturing has 452 industries and about 1,500 product classes. For values of shipments using constant industry definitions for selected census years 1849–1982, see appendix table 3 of Connor (1982b, pp. 97–113). More detail on sources of data is given in Connor et al. 1985.

2. There are twenty two-digit SIC major industry groups. Separating tobacco manufacturing from food would place it nineteenth among the twenty, and food would rank fourth. Tobacco is usually considered along with food in this chapter because the major tobacco firms are also leading food firms and because tobacco products share many of the same marketing characteristics as processed food products.

3. Using official rates of exchange, the Soviet Union's food and beverage industries are calculated to be 7 percent larger than that of the United States. If market rates of exchange existed, the Soviet Union's industry could doubtless be smaller. The U.N. data exclude the output of the centrally planned economies of Asia; assuming a population of 1 billion and a level of development equal to India's, output would be $17 billion, raising the global total to $712 billion.

4. Foodservice items are generally packaged in large units, but some condiments are packaged in individual serving sizes. Brands are used in this channel by manufacturers, but they are often not the same as foodstore brands. Delivery conditions promised by foodservice wholesalers are probably more important than quality images created by trademarking.

5. Branson (1980) estimates that in 1950 the United States produced 60 percent of world output of manufactures, 40 percent in 1963, and 35 percent in 1979. The U.S.-

originated share of world exports of manufactures also fell from 29 percent in 1953, to 17 percent in 1963, and to 13 percent in 1976. West Germany's share surpassed the United States' around 1970.

6. Recent changes in cereal manufacturing technology have substantially altered the MES of cereal plants. Using an extrusion process, one private label manufacturer estimated a plant with approximately 10 million pounds in annual output could be cost competitive (roughly 0.5 percent of 1977 industry shipments). This may have a significant effect on the entry of private label manufacturers. It appears, however, that brand manufacturers may still need 4 to 6 percent of the market to realize marketing economies of size.

7. This theory is similar to the theory of perfect competition in at least two respects: perfectly contestable markets produce equilibrium results that are essentially the same as perfect competition, and both models rest on extreme assumptions and may have limited relevance to the real world.

In perfectly contestable markets, entry is absolutely free (in Stigler's sense; entrants suffer no disadvantage in relation to incumbents). Exit is absolutely costless. Firms can leave the market and recoup any costs incurred in the entry process. Finally, potential entrants can evaluate the profitability of entry from incumbent firms' preentry prices; that is, the lag in incumbent price adjustment is sufficient to allow entry, profit reaping, and exit.

The crucial feature of perfectly contestable markets is their vulnerability to hit-and-run entry. A potential entrant can exploit even temporary profit opportunities by quickly entering, collecting profits by charging slightly lower prices than the incumbents, and exiting before incumbent firms can lower prices. To prevent hit-and-run entry, incumbents must produce efficiently and earn zero economic profits.

The relevance of this theory appears to be severely limited. There are very few markets that even approach the assumptions of perfect contestability. In addition, preliminary analysis indicates that when some of the assumptions of perfect contestability are relaxed slightly, the results can differ dramatically from those obtained under perfect contestability (Schwartz and Reynolds 1982).

In our judgment, the theory of contestable markets has little relevance to the food manufacturing industries. Hit-and-run entry is clearly out of the question for branded grocery products. The only situations where hit-and-run entry makes any sense in food manufacturing is in the supply of producer goods, private labels, or unbranded products. In these cases, companies with compatible equipment already in place (such as a company making cocoa beverage mix) could conceivably use that equipment to hit and run another industry (perhaps soft drink mixes). However, the markets for private label, unbranded products, and producer goods tend to be relatively competitive already. In addition, most manufacturers and retailers recognize that a sound business is not built on "one-night stands." Hamm (1981) found that private label buyers had a strong preference for private label manufacturers that provided consistent quality and reliable performance over time. Finally, few incumbent firms will stand by and let a new entrant take their business without a fight. All in all, contestable market theory offers no additional tools to understand the competitive characteristics of the food manufacturing industries.

8. Economic performance norms ultimately derive from broad societal values. U.S. political ideals are descended mainly from the Jeffersonian view of democracy as

pluralistic, agrarian, liberal, and dispersed in its decision making. Widely accepted American personal values include security, privacy, equality of opportunity, wide consumer choice, and a belief in pragmatic solutions to conflicting aims. These societal principles have been translated into more specific economic goals: economic efficiency, rapid growth of income and consumption, relative stability of prices, low unemployment, and greater equality through income taxation and transfers. Noneconomic goals are enshrined in social programs, criminal codes, public monuments, and elsewhere.

Operational measures of allocative efficiency are based on applied welfare theory (Just, Hueth, and Schmitz 1982). This aspect of performance is improved if there is an increase in consumers' or producers' welfare due to a change in prices, output, product quality, or other market outcomes. Performance related to income distribution or noneconomic goals can be inferred from the value judgments implicit in the outcome of political processes.

9. These seven dimensions are more complete than is typical of most other industry case studies, yet they are neither a comprehensive set nor a random selection of performance elements. The seven were selected mainly because they are quantifiable and available for all the industries. They present reasonably tractable analytical problems, arguably within the domain of industrial economics. Omitted valid performance elements include: local community welfare (such as the net effects of corporate philanthropy and the distance or anonymity of corporate control), the exercise of political power derived from market power, employee satisfaction in large firms or establishments, conservation of natural resources, and ethical standards of buyers and sellers. For surveys of research on these dimensions of performance, see Siegfried (1980).

10. Operating income is net profits plus income taxes plus interest payments. In 1975 there were 376 lines of business averaged for the food and tobacco industries (Connor 1982b, p. 73).

11. Identification of the critical value for an industry or sector is a much debated topic among industrial organization economists. It appears to be an empirical question rather than one that can be settled by theoretical arguments. Some estimates for manufacturing have ranged as high as 50 to 55 percent, and some analyses have found the relationship between concentration and performance to be continuous (Geithman, Marvel, and Weiss 1981). The critical concentration level for a particular industry may depend on mode of conduct. It also depends on the degree of buyer concentration.

12. The single equation wage-rate model has come to have the general form:

$$w = (fS, I, L)$$

where w is the individual or average industrial wage rate or average hourly earnings; S is a vector of structural variables, such as market sales concentration; I is a vector of additional industrial variables, including such factors as the proportion of large establishments in the industry and the percentage of workers covered by collective bargaining agreements; and L is a vector of employee characteristics related usually to education or skill. As examples of such studies, see Bailey and Schwenk (1971), Dalton and Ford (1977, 1978), Haworth and Reuther (1978), Masters (1969), Pugel (1980), and Weiss (1966).

13. The models that have been estimated tend to be variations of the following prototype:

$$\Delta w = f(S, \Delta S, I, \Delta I, L, \Delta L)$$

where Δ refers to change, measured either in absolute or percentage terms, and all other variables are defined as in note 12. A wage change model emphasizes the performance implications for macroeconomical stability or inflation. See Allen (1968), Garbarino (1950]), Greer (1975), Hamermesh (1972), and Schwenk (1980) for wage change models; also see Allen (1969), Greer and Rhoades (1976), and Gisser (1982) for cross-sectional productivity-change studies.

5
The Organization and Performance of Food Distribution Industries

T he food distribution industries encompass firms in food wholesaling, food retailing, and away-from-home foodservice. In addition to providing the linkage between the earlier stages of the food system (food production, assembly, and manufacturing) and consumers, food distribution companies play an important role in interpreting and influencing consumer preferences and in influencing the organization and competitive behavior of food production and manufacturing. As consolidation in these industries has occurred, the influence of large wholesalers, retailers, and foodservice firms within the food system has also increased.

The organization of channels of distribution can have an important influence on oligopolistic coordination in food manufacturing industries. Scherer (1971) contends that the greater the diversity in the distribution channel (such as, discount stores competing with full-service stores and mail order firms; branded products competing with private labels and generics), the greater the likelihood of price cutting by oligopolistic manufacturers. Clair Wilcox (1950) recognized the impact of distributors on manufacturer behavior in his quip, "The formula for competition is simple: add one part of Sears Roebuck to twenty parts of oligopoly."

Thus, the organization and behavior of the food distribution industries are important to understand, both to determine how well the distribution function is being performed and to assess the impact of these industries on the rest of the food system.

This chapter first examines the organization, trends, and competitive characteristics of the food retailing industry, followed by an examination of food wholesaling and then the foodservice industry. Because of its importance and the larger amount of research and data available on retailing, the chapter devotes more space to this industry than to food wholesaling or foodservice.

The lead author for this chapter was Bruce Marion; other authors were Russell Parker and Charles Handy.

Food Retailing Industry: Historical Perspective

Two major innovations have dominated the evolution of food retailing during this century: the development and growth of food chains and supermarkets. From its first store in 1859, A&P—the first major food retailing chain—grew to 200 stores by 1900; rapid growth resulted in 16,000 stores by 1930 and over $1 billion in annual sales (Hampe and Wittenberg 1964). Other chain organizations developed during the late nineteenth century and numbered 21 by 1900. By 1928, there were 315 chains (defined until 1948 as four or more stores operated by the same company); their share of grocery store sales rose from 8 percent in 1900 to 32 percent in 1929.

The rapid growth of food chains during this period stemmed in part from a hospitable environment. Food wholesaling and retailing were made up of many small, specialized firms with high costs. Several chains integrated into wholesaling; because of efficiencies and buying power, they were able to reduce subtantially the cost of products delivered to their stores. Many chains eliminated credit and delivery and reflected these cost savings in lower retail prices. Thus, during this formative period, lower prices were the primary source of food chain growth, although chain stores also tended to have greater selection and higher-quality products.

The rapid growth of food chains was temporarily interrupted during the 1930s by the second major innovation, the development of the supermarket. The supermarket combined cash and carry, self-service, and a broad selection of products with a strong emphasis on low prices and high turnover. The greater prevalence of automobiles and refrigerators plus the hard times of the 1930s were conducive to this low-price, one-stop shopping approach. Supermarkets grew rapidly from 1 in 1930 to 3,066 in 1937, 6,175 in 1940, and 14,217 in 1950 (Hampe and Wittenberg 1964). During this period, supermarkets were defined by Super Market Institute and trade publications as "a departmentalized retail food store consisting of four departments—self-service groceries, meats, produce and dairy products—with any number of other departments, doing a minimum annual volume of $250,000" (Ibid., p. 328). Supermarkets (using this definition) had captured 24 percent of grocery store sales by 1940 and 40 percent by 1950.

Supermarkets were initially developed by independent businessmen. Food chains, however, found that their stores, with average sales of $60,000 per year and gross margins of 20 percent, were no match for supermarkets that averaged nearly ten times the volume at gross margins of about 12 percent. Several food chains began replacing conventional stores with supermarkets in the late 1930s. A&P dropped from 16,000 stores in 1930 to 9,000 in 1939 to fewer than 5,000 stores by 1949; company sales declined modestly during the 1930s but nearly tripled during the 1940s. The Kroger Co. cut its store numbers by more than half during this twenty-year period (Hampe and Wittenberg 1964).

The supermarket share of grocery store sales increased most rapidly during the 1940s and 1950s. Since 1960, the share held by supermarkets has continued to increase but at a more gradual pace. Figure 5–1 shows the share of grocery store numbers and sales by supermarkets with the same real sales per store in 1954, 1963, 1972 and 1982. (Current dollar sales for the four years were $703,400 or more, $762,900 or more, $1 million or more, and $2,355,900 or more respectively.) In 1963, supermarkets accounted for 9 percent of all grocery stores but did 60 percent of all grocery store sales. By 1982, this had increased to 14 percent of store numbers and 74 percent of grocery store sales.[1]

The growth of food chains, which reached a plateau during the 1930s, picked up steam in the 1940s, especially after World War II. In 1948, chains with eleven or more stores accounted for 34 percent of total grocery store sales; by 1982, their aggregate market share had increased to 62 percent, an increase of nearly 1 percent per year (table 5–1). Chains have normally enjoyed a larger share of supermarket sales than of all grocery store sales. For example, in 1972 grocery chains accounted for about three-fourths of all supermarket sales, whereas they held 57 percent of grocery store sales (Grinnell, Parker, and Rens 1979).

Independents (operators with fewer than eleven stores) dropped from two-thirds of all grocery store sales in 1948 to 38 percent in 1982. The sharpest decline in national market share has occurred among single store operators; whereas they did 59 percent of grocery store sales in 1948, by 1982 they did 26 percent (figure 5–2). The growth in market share of chains and decline in share of independents is in part due to the shift of some independents into the chain category. The number of firms classified as chains (eleven or more stores) increased from 299 in 1967 to 468 in 1982.

The increasing share of grocery store sales captured by supermarkets and food chains occurred during a time when grocery stores were gaining a larger and larger part of all food store sales. Whereas specialty stores, such as bakeries, meat and produce markets, did approximately 30 percent of all food store sales in 1930, they declined to 11 percent in 1958 and 6 percent in 1982 (table 5–1). The growth in quality-conscious consumers has sparked a recent renaissance in specialty stores in many communities, which may increase the market share of these stores.

Independents reacted to the rapid growth of food chains between 1910 and 1930 by affiliating with voluntary and cooperative chains, which were organized during this period. Red and White, IGA, and Clover Farm were founded during the 1920s. Several cooperative buying organizations existed earlier. Voluntary and cooperative buying organizations have continued to grow as a means of offsetting the advantages of chain organizations. While independent food retailers have steadily lost market share since the late 1940s, this has been particularly true of unaffiliated independents whose share of grocery store sales dropped from 30 percent in 1948 to 7 percent in 1972 (*Progressive Grocer* 1973). Later data are not available.

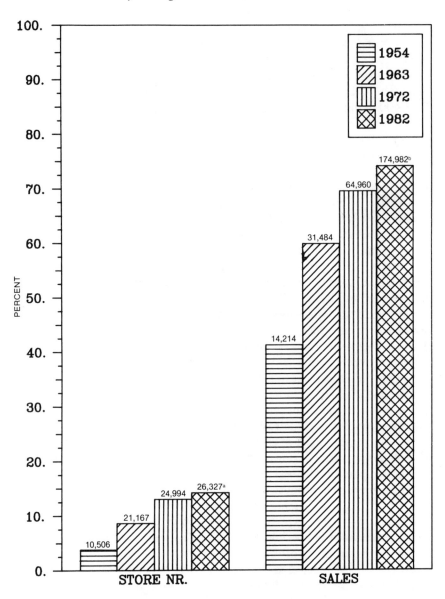

Source: Table B–1.

[a]Figures at top of bars are total number of supermarkets in United States.

[b]Figures at top of sales bars are total sales done by supermarkets, in millions.

Figure 5–1. Supermarkets as a Percentage of Grocery Store Numbers and Sales

Table 5–1
Number and Sales of Food Stores, Selected Years

	Number of Food Stores						
	1954	1958	1963	1967	1972	1977	1982
Total retail food stores	384,616	353,072	319,433	294,243	267,352	252,853	262,901
Grocery and combination stores	279,440 (73%)	259,796 (74%)	244,838 (77%)	218,130 (74%)	194,346 (73%)	179,042 (71%)	184,363 (70%)
Independent	262,535 (94%)	242,173 (93%)	223,549 (91%)	191,833 (88%)	160,782 (83%)	142,424 (80%)	144,603 (78%)
Chain (11 or more stores)	16,905 (6%)	17,623 (7%)	21,289 (9%)	26,297 (12%)	33,564 (17%)	36,411 (20%)	39,760 (22%)
Specialty	105,176 (27%)	93,276 (26%)	74,595 (23%)	76,114 (26%)	73,006 (27%)	73,811 (29%)	78,538 (30%)

	Sales of Food Stores (millions of dollars)						
	1954	1958	1963	1967	1972	1977	1982
Total retail food stores	39,762	49,022	57,079	70,251	98,605	158,444	246,782
Grocery and combination stores	34,421 (87%)	43,696 (89%)	52,566 (92%)	65,074 (93%)	91,574 (93%)	148,116 (93%)	230,824 (94%)
Independent	20,868 (61%)	24,483 (56%)	27,845 (53%)	31,638 (49%)	39,376 (43%)	59,246 (40%)	88,867 (38%)
Chain (11 or more stores)	13,553 (39%)	19,213 (44%)	24,721 (47%)	33,436 (51%)	52,198 (57%)	88,870 (60%)	141,957 (62%)
Specialty	5,341 (13%)	5,326 (11%)	4,513 (8%)	5,178 (7%)	7,031 (7%)	10,328 (7%)	15,958 (6%)

Source: Bureau of Census, Census of Business 1954, 1958, 1963, 1967; Census of Retail Trade 1972, 1977, 1982.

Shifts in Competitive Emphasis

The initial growth of supermarkets was due largely to their low price appeal. During the 1950s, many supermarkets began to emphasize such nonprice factors as larger stores, more services, trading stamps, and other promotions. Increasing gross margins during the 1950s and early 1960s reflected this shift (figure 5–3). Starting in the mid-1960s, supermarket percentage gross margins remained relatively steady for ten to fifteen years. From the late 1970s to the mid-1980s, however, gross margins moved sharply higher.

The retail gross margin represents the cost to society of the retailing function and is influenced by many factors: the cost of labor and other inputs, the adoption of new technology, the services provided by retailers, and the effectiveness

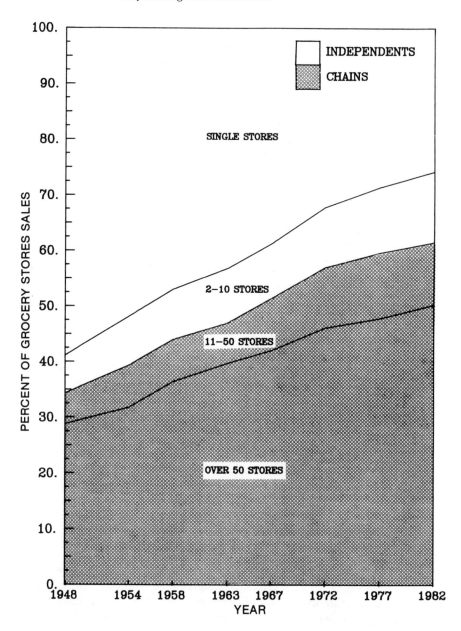

Source: Table B–2.

Figure 5–2. Distribution of Grocery Store Sales by Size of Firm, 1948–1982

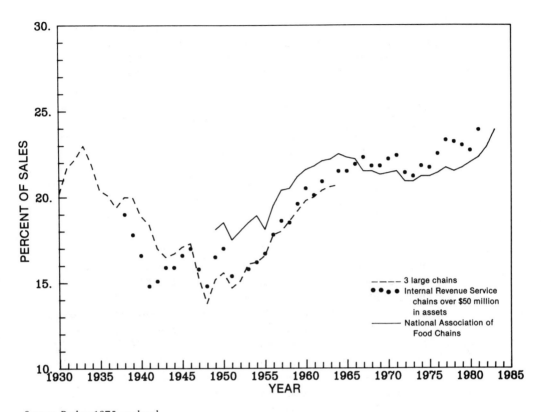

Source: Parker 1975, updated.

Figure 5–3. Trend in Food Chain Gross Margins as Percentage of Sales

of competition. The largest single expense item, store labor, has risen rather steadily from 10.4 percent in the mid-1960s to 13.1 percent in 1983–1984 (Cornell University 1984). This has been partially offset by a decline in other expenses. Net earnings before taxes for grocery chains have exhibited no clear trend from 1965–1966 to 1983–1984. During this period net earnings ranged from 0.8 to 2.4 percent of sales, with the low point occurring between 1972–1973 and 1977–1978.

Although discounting and no-frills retailing continued as competitive strategies for some retailers after the mid-1950s, in the main the competitive focus was on larger and fancier stores, greater breadth and variety of products, and increased services. The number of items handled by supermarkets grew from about 1,000 in 1930 to 3,750 in 1950 to 6,800 in 1963 to 11,000 in 1984 (*Progressive Grocer* 1985).[2] Whereas the early supermarkets were about 10,000 square feet in size, new supermarkets in 1983 were 38,000 square feet (Food Marketing Institute 1984).

As supermarkets grew in size, they became less desirable for fill-in shopping trips by consumers. A modern version of the Mom & Pop store emerged in the late 1950s: the convenience store. Estimated at 4,100 in 1963, the number of convenience stores increased roughly tenfold by 1982. Estimates of the share of grocery store sales held by convenience stores in 1982 range from 6 percent (*Progressive Grocer* 1983) to 15 percent (National Association of Convenience Stores 1983). Convenience store chains seldom operate supermarkets, and vice-versa. The largest convenience store chain (Southland Corp.) operated nearly 7,000 stores in the United States in 1982, more than the next seven convenience chains combined, and accounted for nearly one-fifth of all convenience store sales (Southland Corp. Annual Report 1982).

Supermarket Formats

The 1960s and 1970s witnessed considerable effort to differentiate stores by size, product assortment, and product-service-price combinations. Supermarkets—the general term used to refer to multidepartmental grocery stores of a certain annual sales volume—took on several different forms.

The differences among conventional supermarkets, superstores, combination stores and warehouse stores—the four predominant formats for supermarkets—are difficult to define precisely. *Progressive Grocer* (1982) defined a superstore as a supermarket with more than 30,000 square feet of space, annual volume of $8 million or more, and offering an expanded selection of nonfoods plus specialty departments. If such a store has more than 40 percent of the selling area devoted to nonfood, it is called a combination store.

A warehouse store is a low-amenity supermarket carrying more than 1,500 items. Dry groceries are emphasized. Customer services are severely curtailed. Gross margins are often one-third to one-half less than conventional supermarkets because of no frills and nonunion labor.

As firms seek to differentiate their stores, there is constant experimentation and blending of the various store formats. One of the newest and fastest growing formats is the hybrid or super warehouse store, essentially a combination of the superstore and the warehouse store.

The operating characteristics of four supermarket formats are summarized in table 5–2. Although superstores and super warehouse stores are the most rapidly growing formats, conventional supermarkets still accounted for 59 percent of supermarket sales in 1984 (*Progressive Grocery* 1985). Super stores held 25 percent of supermarket sales.

Warehouse and super warehouse store numbers mushroomed from 350 in 1978 to about 2,700 in 1984; they were estimated to hold about 10 percent of U.S. grocery store sales by 1984 (*Progressive Grocer* 1985). Of the 2,700 stores, 70 were estimated to be super warehouse stores and the remainder

Table 5–2
Median 1983 Operating Data, by Store Format

Average	*Conventional*	*Superstores*	*Combination*	*Warehouse*
Weekly sales	100,000	186,200	291,230	202,330
Weekly sales/checkout	19,200	26,850	27,400	23,100
Sale/customer transaction	14.02	18.61	17.40	22.15
Sales/labor hour	88.20	91.00	87.00	130.80
Weekly sales/sq. ft. of selling area	7.15	6.15	6.85	8.00
Total size/sq. ft.	17,235	30,200	45,875	28,700
Retail price/item[a]	1.27	1.25	1.55	1.18
Number of items carried	12,500	18,000	25,000	9,000
(Number of stores reporting)	(4,422)	(1,381)	(746)	(217)

Source: Food Marketing Institute 1984.

[a]Differences in average retail price per item are largely due to the mix of products sold and should not be interpreted as indicators of the price levels in different store types.

regular warehouse stores. Regular warehouse stores have low investments (one-tenth to one-fourth that of conventional supermarkets), little if any advertising, and low payroll expense (about one-half of conventional supermarkets) because of nonunion labor, reduced services, and the use of productivity-increasing practices, such as stocking by case or pallet, eliminating price marking, and scanning. As a result, the operating expenses per dollar of sales of warehouse stores are substantially lower than conventional supermarkets. In addition, warehouse stores make very heavy use of manufacturer deals to reduce their cost of goods sold. The combination of lower operating costs and heavy use of deals allows warehouse stores to offer savings to consumers of 5 to 20 percent on market baskets of food (*Chain Store Age Supermarkets* October 1980; Handy and Stafford 1980).

Conventional supermarket chains sometimes employ *zone pricing* (charging lower prices in selected stores) in an attempt to block the market penetration of warehouse stores. For example, in a study of the Atlanta market, Allvine found that Kroger prices were 10 percent lower in stores located near warehouse stores than in other Kroger stores in the market (*Chain Store Age Supermarkets* March 1982). In Chicago, the three major chains instituted lower price zones in their supermarkets located near warehouse stores (*Competitive Edge* 1982). Handy and Stafford (1980) found that some of the established chains in Washington, D.C., used zone pricing to combat the entry of limited assortment stores. Despite zone pricing, warehouse stores have generally been successful in their market entry efforts. They appear to have many opportunities for future growth. Although they account for about half of all grocery store sales in cities such as Milwaukee and Minneapolis, they have a small presence in most metropolitan areas.

The national growth of generic products has benefited greatly from competitive pressures posed by warehouse and limited assortment stores. Although generics had been successfully used by Loblaw Ltd. in Canada and by Carrefour in France, Jewel was the first U.S. chain to stock this economy version of many products as a competitive response to Aldi's box stores. By 1981, two-thirds of the largest 100 chains stocked generics; however, the sales of generic products appear to have reached a plateau at about 3 percent of sales of the products tracked by SAMI (1983). In companies that have carried generics since at least 1979, SAMI found generic share dropped about 17 percent from 1982 to 1983. Thus these products appear to be losing their sales momentum.

Grocery Retailing Markets

Nature of Relevant Markets in Food Retailing

In order to understand competition in food retailing, one must first define the relevant geographic and product markets. There is widespread agreement that food retailers sell in geographic markets that are inherently local. Consumers do not travel from one region to another, or even one city to another, to shop for groceries. Surveys show that most supermarket customers travel less than 2 miles although super warehouse stores draw customers from much larger areas. In metropolitan areas, this means that customer trading areas are small relative to the overall size of the market.

Although individual stores draw customers from small areas, the trading areas of individual supermarkets overlap with those of competing supermarkets, creating a degree of competitive interrelationship throughout a metropolitan area. Competition on a metropolitan-area basis is also fostered by the advertising medium used by supermarkets—newspapers and, to a growing extent, television. Newspaper advertising is the primary instrument of rivalry among supermarket firms in metropolitan areas. The circulation areas of the principal metropolitan papers are often coextensive with Standard Metropolitan Statistical Areas (SMSAs) defined by the federal government. Court testimony and the trade literature indicate the strategic plans of grocery chains are typically formulated on an SMSA basis and in some cases by smaller trading areas within SMSAs. The federal courts and the FTC have accepted SMSAs as relevant geographic markets for grocery retailing (FTC 1979, 1983).[3]

Defining relevant product markets is more difficult. Here, Michael Porter's (1976b, 1979) theory of strategic groups and mobility barriers provides a useful framework. Porter's basic notion is relatively simple. In any industry, there is a continuum of firms with different strategies regarding products, prices, and services. Some may appeal to customers desiring low prices; others may appeal to customers seeking high quality or services. In addition, firms are often clustered in groups along the continuum of strategies; hence the term *strategic groups*. Firms compete most directly with other firms in their strategic group and less directly with firms in other strategic groups. Strategic groups that are sufficiently distant from one another are only indirect competitors; for antitrust purposes, they are in separate product markets.

The concept of strategic groups is useful in understanding the competitive characteristics of food retailing. For example, nine retail store formats are classified by price and service levels and by breadth of product assortment in figure 5–4. While stores might be classified by other attributes, these three are probably the most important in trying to visualize the "space" between different store formats. In general, low-priced stores have low service and vice-versa, but this is not always the case. Included in service is the pleasantness of the shopping environment, as well as customer services, such as carry-out, check cashing, and special departments.

Each store format can be viewed as a strategic group. For each to survive in a market, there must be a segment of customers who prefer that cluster of products, services, and prices. Box stores, for example, have met with limited success in most markets and may not survive as a strategic group.

All of these strategic groups compete to some degree with each other if they are located in the same geographic market. Consumers can buy ground coffee at a conventional supermarket, a warehouse store, a convenience store, or a specialized coffee-tea shop. But does that mean all strategic groups are in the same product market for economic analysis or for antitrust purposes?

Estimates of the cross-elasticity of demand between different store types would provide an indication of the extent to which consumers perceive these stores as close substitutes. Unfortunately such estimates are not available. The Justice Department has proposed an approach that is conceptually similar in its 1984 merger guidelines: "The Department will include in the product market a group of products such that a hypothetical firm that was the only present and future seller of those products ('monopolist') could profitably impose a 'small but significant and nontransitory' increase in price" (U.S. Department of Justice 1984, p. 2).

In the case of food retailing, the "product" is the product-service-price bundle provided by various retail stores. Thus, the question becomes whether consumers perceive the bundles of various types of stores as close substitutes. For consumers, are convenience stores or meat markets close substitutes for supermarkets? Are warehouse stores close substitutes for superstores? Are fast food outlets close substitutes for convenience stores or supermarkets?

Although such judgments are subjective, we believe stores primarily selling food for consumption at home are in a distinct product market from stores

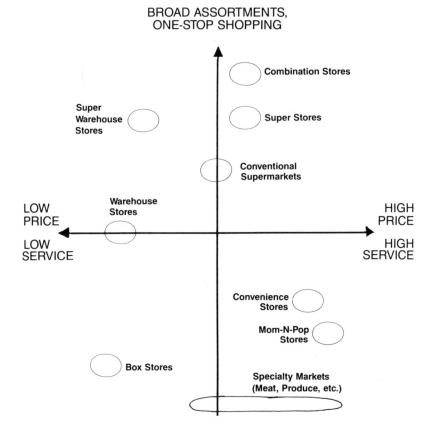

**BROAD ASSORTMENTS,
ONE-STOP SHOPPING**

Combination Stores

Super Warehouse Stores

Super Stores

Conventional Supermarkets

Warehouse Stores

LOW PRICE

HIGH PRICE

LOW SERVICE

HIGH SERVICE

Convenience Stores

Mom-N-Pop Stores

Box Stores

Specialty Markets (Meat, Produce, etc.)

**LIMITED ASSORTMENT,
FILL-IN AND SPECIALTY SHOPPING**

Figure 5–4. Retail Food Store Formats

that primarily sell food for consumption away from home. In addition, within stores that sell food for consumption at home, we believe there are at least two product markets: 1) stores that provide the breadth of assortment and price levels to compete for the major shopping trips of consumers and 2) stores that primarily compete for fill-in and supplemental shopping trips. In the first category are those store formats on or above the horizontal line in figure 5–4: conventional supermarkets, super stores, combination stores, warehouse stores, and super warehouse stores. All would be classified by the trade under the general umbrella of "supermarkets". In the second category are convenience stores, specialty markets, and Mom and Pop grocery stores.

Not all agree that supermarkets and convenience stores are in separate product markets. This was a critical issue in the FTC–Grand Union case, which challenged Grand Union's acquisition of Colonial Stores—a geographic market extension merger between two of the top twenty grocery chains in the U.S. The Administrative Law Judge (ALJ) concluded that supermarkets are a relevant product market, that entry into this product market in many SMSAs is difficult and that Grand Union's acquisition of Colonial Stores was anticompetitive and in violation of the antitrust laws. Regarding the relevant product market, the ALJ (FTC 1981b) concluded:

> The record in this case is replete with evidence that supermarkets, by and large, compete with other supermarkets. [p. 204]

> Convenience stores are not generally price-checked by supermarket firm operators. They carry little, if any, produce and meat, and indeed, average only 500–3000 items. Supermarkets stock from 8–12,000 items. Convenience stores generally have only one employee per shift and they average sales of from $1–3 per customer, as compared to the $11–15 average sale for supermarkets. Convenience stores are generally not considered in supermarket expansions and store location studies. Basically, the only competition they offer to supermarkets is in terms of hours of operation. [p. 204]

> Grand Union's and Colonial's supermarkets averaged over $3 million dollars in annual sales per store, while convenience stores averaged from $140 thousand to $325 thousand per store. [p. 201]

The Federal Trade Commission, on appeal, concluded that *all grocery stores* in an SMSA are the more appropriate product market definition, found several instances of entry by various types of grocery stores, and concluded that entry was easy and that the merger was not a violation of the law (FTC 1983). Had the commission been able to apply accurately the approach suggested by the Justice Department, we believe they would have agreed with the Administrative Law Judge on the relevant product market.

Using the Justice Department procedures, one would need to answer the following hypothetical question: If one firm was the only present (and potential) operator of various types of supermarkets (conventional, superstores, warehouse stores, and so forth) in Madison, Wisconsin, or Washington, D.C., could that firm profitably increase its price? For example, could that firm raise prices by 2 or 3 percent and increase profits? Or would customers transfer enough patronage to convenience stores, small grocery stores, and specialty markets that the supermarket firm's profits would decline? Assuming supermarket gross margins of 20 percent of sales, a 2 percent price increase would represent a 10 percent increase in gross margins. Since there would be no apparent change in costs, sales would have to decline by roughly

10 percent for no change to occur in profits. Given the much higher gross margin of convenience stores and the one-stop shopping appeal of supermarkets, it is doubtful that the supermarket chain in this example would lose enough sales to make the price increase unprofitable.

The correct definition of relevant product markets and submarkets is obviously critical in antitrust cases. It is also critical in attempting to study structure-performance relations. For example, entry into the convenience store submarket is much easier than into the supermarket submarket. Compared to supermarkets, desirable convenience store sites are more numerous, initial investment is much less, advertising is relatively unimportant, and zone pricing by incumbent retailers to deter entry is highly unlikely. In short, entry conditions into the convenience store submarket are not an accurate indicator of entry conditions into the supermarket submarket, and vice-versa.

Local Market Concentration

Data on the percentage of SMSA sales accounted for by the top four and eight firms (concentration ratios) are available for the census years 1954 through 1977. For 1972 and 1977 only, data are available on the percentage of supermarket sales accounted for by the largest four and eight supermarket firms in each SMSA and on both grocery store and supermarket Herfindahl indexes. In earlier years, only concentration ratios for grocery store sales are provided by the Bureau of the Census.[4]

Concentration figures for supermarket firms correspond reasonably well to one of the two product markets identified earlier: those stores that compete for the major shopping trips of consumers. A large number of empirical studies in a wide variety of industries have found that seller concentration is positively related to seller prices and profits (Weiss 1974; Marion 1984). Therefore the level and trends of concentration are important to understand. The effects of concentration on competitive behavior may vary considerably in the short run and particularly when a new store format is being introduced. For example, the entry of warehouse stores into some relatively concentrated markets may result in lower market prices than would be expected given the level of concentration. This is generally a temporary phenomenon, however. Over the long term, concentration is expected to be an important indicator of the effectiveness of competition in different metropolitan areas.

On average, local market concentration in grocery retailing increased between each of the six census years from 1954 to 1977. Moreover, the rate of increase has accelerated since 1967. The market share held by the largest four grocery firms (CR4) in each of 173 SMSAs that could be compared from 1958 to 1977 rose persistently from an average of 48.7 in 1958 to 56.4 in 1977 (table 5–3).[5] In the 1958–1963 and 1963–1967 periods, the increase was relatively small, about 1 percentage point. For 1967–1972, average CR4

Table 5–3
Average Four-Firm Concentration for 173 SMSAs Classified by 1958 Four-Firm Concentration Level, 1958–1977

SMSA Population and Level of Four-Firm Concentration Level in 1958	Number of SMSAs	Four-Firm Concentration					Average 1977 Market Sales (thousand dollars)[a]
		1958	1963	1967	1972	1977	
SMSAs over 500,000[b]							
CR4 less than 40	11	34.10	36.31	39.60	43.61	48.64	1,416,351
40.0–49.9	24	46.16	46.64	45.17	49.28	52.53	931,670
50.0–59.9	11	54.16	53.80	51.74	49.35	54.63	1,274,795
60.0 and over	8	63.75	61.38	60.98	62.40	66.43	1,069,074
Total and average	54	47.94	48.18	47.71	50.08	54.22	1,120,653
SMSAs under 500,000[b]							
CR4 less than 40	22	35.51	38.35	42.61	46.19	49.75	180,594
40.0–49.9	47	46.00	46.77	48.95	50.43	55.72	159,648
50.0–59.9	32	54.50	54.69	53.60	54.73	58.74	162,512
60.0 and over	19	63.32	63.34	63.07	65.44	67.72	167,899
Total and average	119	49.11	49.99	51.28	53.20	57.34	165,608
Average all SMSAs		48.74	49.42	50.17	52.23	56.37	463,715

Source: Bureau of Census. Special tabulations of Census of Retail Trade, various years.
[a]Grocery store sales for establishments with payroll.
[b]Population in 1970.

rose 2 percentage points; for 1972–1977 the average increased 4 percentage points. This upward trend in concentration was evident in all of the studied SMSAs, regardless of population size; SMSAs with 1970 population less than 500,000, however, experienced a higher rate of increase.

Concentration increased most in SMSAs with relatively low initial concentration (CR4 in 1958 less than 40). Average CR4 in these SMSAs went from 35.0 in 1958 to 49.4 in 1977, an increase of almost 41 percent. SMSAs with initial concentration greater than 50 experienced smaller increases or even a slight decline in CR4 during the 1958 to 1972 time span; however, these SMSAs also experienced a jump in average CR4 between 1972 and 1977.

The shift toward higher levels of local market concentration is further illustrated by the changes in the percentage distribution of SMSAs classified by four-firm concentration (figure 5–5). For an identical sample of 173 SMSAs, the proportion of markets with CR4 below 50 declined from 59.2 percent in 1958 to 32.8 percent in 1977. Half of this decline occurred between 1972 and 1977. The proportion of highly concentrated markets (CR4 ≥ 60) expanded from 15.5 percent in 1958 to 42.0 percent in 1977. This increase was most dramatic for 1972 to 1977. The proportion of very highly concentrated markets (CR4 ≥ 70) rose from 0.6 percent in 1958 to 4.6 percent in 1972 to 14.4 percent in 1977.

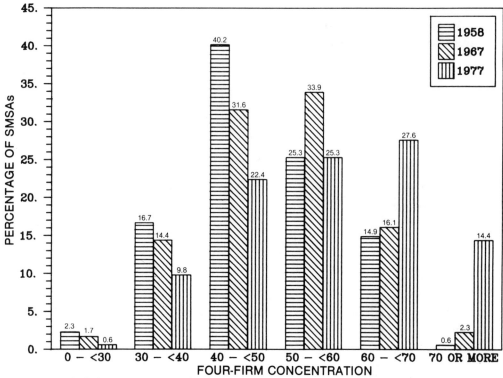

Source: Special tabulations of Census of Retail Trade, various years.

Figure 5–5. Distribution of 173 SMSAs by Level of Concentration of Grocery Store Sales

Another measure of market concentration is the Herfindahl-Hirschman Index (HHI). Well over half of the SMSAs examined had estimated HHI values in 1977 above the threshold level defined in the Department of Justice merger guidelines (HHI = 1,000); about a fourth had values greater than the highly concentrated dividing line defined in the guidelines (HHI = 1,800). This is especially significant since the new guidelines represent a relaxation of merger policy.

The trend toward increasing average four-firm concentration in SMSAs has been accompanied by a slowing of the growth of the combined shares of the fifth to eighth and ninth to twentieth firms in SMSAs. In the 1950s through the late 1960s, eight- and twenty-firm concentration increased faster than four-firm concentration. Since 1972, however, market share increases have been limited mainly to the four largest firms in each SMSA.

Supermarket Concentration. Although concentration of *grocery store* sales in SMSAs has often been used as an indicator of competitive conditions because of the availability of these figures, concentration of SMSA *supermarket* sales is preferable as a measure of the competitive environment of supermarkets. Supermarket concentration figures for SMSAs were developed by census for 1972 and 1977 (supermarkets were defined as grocery stores with sales of $1 million or more in 1972 and $1.5 million or more in 1977). For 240 SMSAs that were comparable in the two years, average four-firm supermarket concentration (SCR4) increased from 69.6 to 70.9, whereas average four-firm grocery store concentration (CR4) increased from 52.6 to 56.1 (table 5–4). SMSAs were classified into six categories according to their CR4 in 1972. Grocery store concentration increased in all classes from 1972 to 1977; supermarket concentration increased except in the two most concentrated classes.

When SMSAs were classified by supermarket concentration (SCR4) in 1972, 57 of the 240 SMSAs examined had SCR4 levels of 80 or above. Average SCR4 in these markets dropped from 87.8 to 85.4. Thus, some erosion of supermarket concentration occurred in those markets with extremely high levels of concentration in 1972. However, for all classes in which SCR4 was less than 80 in 1972, average SMSA supermarket concentration increased.

A decline in SCR4 from 1972 to 1977 was most likely in markets in which supermarket sales in 1972 accounted for less than 65 percent of all grocery store sales. In these SMSAs, total supermarket sales grew faster than the sales of the largest four supermarket companies on average (table 5–5). In SMSAs in which supermarket sales accounted for a higher proportion of grocery store sales, the two measures of concentration tended to change in similar ways.[6]

Table 5–4
Comparison of Four-Firm Grocery Store and Supermarket Concentration Figures, 240 SMSAs, 1972 and 1977

Grocery Store Concentration in 1972 (CR4)	Number of SMSAs	Grocery Store Concentration		Supermarket Concentration	
		Mean CR4 in 1972	Mean CR4 in 1977	Mean SCR4 in 1972	Mean SCR4 in 1977
< 30	5	27.86	32.20	38.40	41.42
30 < 40	17	35.07	40.02	48.65	51.51
40 < 50	81	44.90	49.71	61.84	64.87
50 < 60	77	54.69	58.05	72.12	73.30
60 < 70	45	64.72	66.02	83.44	82.52
≥ 70	15	74.93	76.89	90.40	88.49
Total	240	52.58	56.09	69.55	70.93

Source: Bureau of Census, Special tabulations of Census of Retail Trade, 1972 and 1977.

Table 5–5

Change in Supermarket and Grocery Store Concentration in SMSAs by the Percentage of Grocery Store Sales Accounted for by Supermarkets

Percentage of Grocery Store Sales Held by Supermarkets	Number of SMSAs	Average Change in SCR4, 1972–1977	Average Change in CR4, 1972–1977
Less than 65	43	−1.9	+3.5
65 < 75	77	+2.3	+4.5
75 < 85	101	+1.8	+2.8
≥ 85	19	+3.0	+3.5
Total	240	+1.4	+3.5

Source: Bureau of Census, special tabulations of Census of Retail Trade, 1972, 1977.

Entry Conditions

The ease with which a new firm may enter an industry is another indicator of the nature of competition in the industry. Scherer (1971, p. 10) comments on the importance of barriers to entry: "Entry barriers are the *sine qua non* of monopoly and oligopoly, for . . . sellers have little or no enduring power over price when entry barriers are nonexistent."

Entry is defined as a new firm coming into a market and operating new capacity. It therefore excludes entry by acquisition. This definition is consistent with Bain's (1968) usage of the term (p. 252), as well as the meaning of entry in antitrust cases (Utah Pie Co. 1967). In applying this concept to food retailing, several grey areas exist. Established firms in a market periodically spin off older stores, replacing them in some cases with newer and larger stores. Independent operators frequently acquire or take over the leases of spun-off chain stores and operate them as independent supermarkets. In the main, we would not classify this as entry even if the independent operator is new to the market since existing capacity is simply changing hands. In some instances, this is part of an upgrading process for independent operators in which they give up small stores and move into stores previously operated by chains.

A second grey area is the purchase by an outside firm of one or more stores in the market—accounting for a small share of the market—where those stores are the base for substantial future expansion of capacity by the outside company. In the vocabulary of antitrust, these are toehold acquisitions. Since these are similar to de novo entry in adding capacity to the market, we would include these as entry. Thus, in reality, there are a variety of ways for a new firm to develop a presence in a new market; some are clearly entry, some are not, and still others require a judgment call. In the following discussion of barriers to entry, the focus will be on de novo entry of stores that compete for the major shopping trips of consumers.

Barriers to Entry in Grocery Retailing. The height of entry barriers is measured in terms of the cost or selling price advantages that established firms have relative to the least disadvantaged outside firms. The least disadvantaged potential entrants to metropolitan-area grocery markets are usually supermarket chains that operate a warehouse within about 200 miles and are a "competitive factor" in a nearby city.

Barriers to entry need to be considered at both the trading-area and metropolitan-area levels. The entry of a new firm usually occurs one store and one trading area at a time. Independent operators may be satisfied to enter and operate one or two stores in certain trading areas. Their entry will affect competition in those areas but will affect competition market-wide only in small cities (and in medium-sized cities in the case of super warehouse stores). When a grocery chain enters a metropolitan area, however, it is usually interested in gradually penetrating all or most of the market. If it is successful in entering and building market share, it influences competition first in the trading areas directly affected by its stores; at some point as it expands, its competitive influence is sufficient to affect competition at the market level. In the jargon of the trade, it has become a competitive factor in the market.

Barriers to entry vary for the various strategic groups (or store formats) shown in figure 5–4. The ease of de novo entry into a strategic group is likely to depend on the extent to which incumbent firms in that group have fully exploited the market potential. Older strategic groups, such as conventional supermarkets, have probably gained about as much of the market as they can in most SMSAs. There may be few easily gained sales for a new conventional supermarket.

By contrast, the warehouse and super warehouse store strategic groups are far short of their market potential in many SMSAs. Based on their success to date, a sizable segment of consumers prefers these store formats. If successful in entering, warehouse stores will attract this segment of consumers. At some point, these strategic groups will also achieve their market potential, and at this point new entry will be more difficult.

Significant new strategic groups emerge only rarely in food retailing. When they do, as in the case of warehouse and super warehouse stores, de novo entry into that strategic group may be easier than it is into older strategic groups. Where the new strategic group poses a substantial threat to other strategic groups, entry-deterring action can be expected, especially when the new strategic group is expected to introduce nontrivial price competition.

A new entrant that is able to define a poorly served geographic area or market segment and enters to fill that niche may face modest entry barriers, particularly if the niche is a small part of the market (for example, filling the demand for ethnic or gourmet foods). Although small market niches offer opportunities for independents, supermarket chains generally aim at the major segments of a market. The entry barriers confronting these chains are often substantial. George Yip (1982, p. 27) comments, "Frequent entry of minor competitors does not indicate low barriers for firms wishing to become major competitors. There is also the public policy implication that easy entry into an industry's fringe may have little effect on the forces of competition in the core of the industry."

Conventional supermarkets, superstores, and combination stores accounted for about 90 percent of supermarket sales in 1984 and clearly still are the core of the industry (*Progressive Grocer* 1985). Barriers to de novo entry by these stores stem from (1) store economies of scale; (2) multistore economies, some of which are related to market shares in individual markets (such as advertising costs), while others are related to firm size nationally or in a region (such as self-manufacture of private label products); (3) capital costs and risk; (4) the difficulty of obtaining desirable store sites; and (5) strategic behavior by incumbent chains such as zone pricing and geographic preemption. Because warehouse-type stores represent a new strategic group with a different mix of strategies (for example, little if any media advertising), they are less affected by some of these barriers at the present time. The discussion that follows focuses primary attention on the barriers faced by nonwarehouse-type stores.

Store Economies of Scale. Because of the sharp increase in the number of items carried and consumer preference for store features such as service delicatessens and wide aisles, the minimum desired size of supermarkets has steadily increased. Larger stores require large capital expenditures and substantial sales to break even.

Supermarkets averaged $6.6 million in annual sales in 1984 (*Progressive Grocer* 1985). A city of 25,000 people could support four supermarkets of this size; a small SMSA of 50,000 people could support about eight. Thus, in small cities and SMSAs, a new entrant faces the challenge of taking substantial sales from existing firms (a "displacement" effect). In general, the larger the displacement effect of a new entrant, the stronger the resistance from incumbent firms. Because the average cost curve of supermarkets is sharply downward sloping at low volumes, new entrants are usually at a substantial cost disadvantage unless they are able to achieve the desired store volume. For the new entrant, sales volume is the key to survival.

Research on store-level cost functions indicates that capacity utilization is the most important determinant of short-run operating costs (National Commission on Food Marketing 1966a; Marion et al. 1979a, p. 135; Mallen and Haberman 1975). Operating costs per dollar of sales exhibit a curvilinear relationship to sales per square foot, dropping sharply at first and gradually leveling off as sales per square foot increase. The effect of absolute store size on operating costs is unclear, with the NCFM finding a significant relationship in the early 1960s (as store size increased from 4,000 to 16,000 square feet, operating expenses per dollar of sales declined 1.4 percentage points) and Marion et al. finding no statistical relationship a decade later.

This is not to say that store size has no influence on store costs, however. A larger number of cost-reducing technologies are economically feasible in large stores. In addition, store size (in square feet) affects the ability of different types of stores to attract customers, which determines capacity utilization, which affects operating costs. The size of store required varies by store format and the competitive appeal. For example, "bare-bones" warehouse stores carry a moderate number of items, have restricted perishable departments, and can effectively implement their low price–low amenity strategy in stores that are 10,000 to 20,000 square feet in size. Superstores and combination stores carry a large number of items (including many nonfood items), feature extensive departmentalization, and emphasize spacious stores and a pleasant shopping environment. To carry out this strategy, stores exceeding 30,000 square feet are generally required. Super warehouse stores, such as Cub and Edwards, are often even larger (40,000 to 80,000 square feet). When these stores enter a market, the displacement effect is many times that of a conventional supermarket entrant. Whereas the latter may take $6 million per year in sales from incumbent firms, some super warehouse stores do $25 million to $50 million in sales per year.

The displacement effect of a new warehouse store in a relatively small SMSA is documented in *Shoppin' Bag* v. *Dillon* case (U.S. District Court for Colorado, No. 81-Z-1548, 1979). In March 1979, Shoppin' Bag opened a warehouse store in Pueblo, Colorado (Mueller 1984a). The first warehouse store in Pueblo, it had little difficulty attracting sales with its substantially lower prices. With annual sales of approximately $30 million, King Soopers was the market leader in the Pueblo SMSA with a 30 percent market share. Safeway was second with 27 percent of the market. Assuming no price response by incumbent firms, King Soopers estimated the Shoppin' Bag store would take 14 percent of its sales, 11 percent of Safeway's sales, and 26 percent of Albertson's sales. Although King Soopers' losses were less than predicted during its first nine weeks after the Shoppin' Bag store opened, King Soopers lowered prices on thousands of grocery items to meet or beat Shoppin' Bag prices. Shoppin' Bag sales dropped by about one-half, resulting in substantial losses. It was on the verge of closing the store when an FTC investigation led King Soopers to raise its prices. Because warehouse stores are a new format, they have successfully entered many SMSAs in spite of their substantial displacement effect.

Multistore Economies: Market Share Related. Multistore economies derived from vertical integration into warehousing and self-manufacture will be discussed later under economies of firm size. Here we focus on market-level multistore economies.

Industry witnesses in the Grand Union case testified that multiple store entry was necessary for a supermarket chain that intended to become a competitive factor in an SMSA. The size of the SMSA is positively related to the number of stores necessary for effective entry. William Stewart, a former president of Colonial Stores and former vice-president of Grand Union, estimated the number of stores necessary for de novo entry into each of the thirteen SMSAs involved in the Grand Union case. "His estimate of the number of conventional supermarkets necessary for profitable entry ranged from a low of two in Fayetteville, North Carolina, to a high of twelve in Atlanta, Georgia" (Federal Trade Commission 1981a, p. 37). Bert Thomas, president of Winn-Dixie Stores, also provided estimates; the number of stores he considered necessary for successful de novo entry was generally one-half to three-fourths those of Stewart.

Multistore economies accrue from the costs and effects of advertising in medium and large SMSAs. In addition, the reactions of incumbents, such as zone pricing, are better borne by companies entering with multiple stores. A new entrant that provides a combination of products, prices, and services that fill an unmet need in the market may have little difficulty attracting customers from established stores. Within established strategic groups, however, advertising is usually a major vehicle to attract the sales necessary for an entrant to operate its stores at low unit costs. Area-wide newspaper advertising (or television) is very expensive, particularly in large metropolitan areas. New entrants can expect to spend as much as 5 percent of sales on advertising during their initial years in such markets, placing them at a substantial cost disadvantage relative to established firms, which are more likely to spend about 1 percent of sales on advertising. New entrants must rapidly increase store numbers and total sales if they are to eliminate this cost disadvantage.

This situation is similar to what Willig (1979) has called an "economy of scope" entry barrier. The established firm can expand by building additional stores, one by one, as demand expands and market niches are discovered. In contrast, a new entrant must enter the market at minimum efficient scale, which in large cities may require building simultaneously ten or more stores. The entrant then faces a displacement problem not faced by the established firm.

In addition, the leading firms in a market can more fully take advantage of advertising allowances offered by manufacturers than fringe firms or new entrants. This accentuates the advertising cost disadvantage faced by entering firms. Alternative advertising media, such as handbills and direct mail, can be used but have less consumer impact per dollar of cost.

The advertising costs and difficulty of quickly building a sufficient sales base over which to spread these costs can be a major reason why regional chains will not attempt to enter a large SMSA. This was the main reason given by the general manager of Ingles Markets for not attempting to enter Atlanta (FTC 1981a, p. 40). Grand Union executives indicated that advertising per dollar of sales in their expansion areas (Baltimore and west coast of Florida) was two and a half times that in areas where Grand Union was established (Ibid., p. 41).

Capital Costs and Risk. In order to open a new 25,000 to 30,000 square foot supermarket in 1980, between $500,000 and $1 million was required to equip and stock the store (FTC 1981b, p. 216). In addition, supermarket firms must obligate themselves for leases on new stores; this liability is approximately $3.0 million to $3.5 million per store. Thus, roughly $4 million per new store is at risk.

Drawing on the estimates of industry members in the Grand Union case, approximately nine conventional supermarkets are necessary for effective de novo entry into the Atlanta SMSA core; nine times $4 million is $36 million at risk. This does not include advertising and promotional expenditures incurred during entry. Fewer super warehouse stores would be required for effective entry, but the investment cost per store is much higher than for conventional supermarkets.

The magnitude of capital costs and investment risk is generally a direct function of the SMSA size. Whereas Atlanta may require an at-risk commitment of roughly $36 million, Fayetteville or Gainesville may require only $4 million to $8 million for effective entry.

Store Sites. A major element in attracting sales to a store is a good location. Store sites for supermarkets are mostly made available through developers. The best sites are usually in or adjacent to shopping centers where customer traffic is concentrated. It is a typical practice for developers to sign a supermarket tenant before they attempt to recruit other tenants and often before obtaining financing. The supermarket may be used as a selling point. The leading chain in the market is the most proven traffic builder in that area. New entrants are often uncertain traffic builders and represent substantial risk. If a new entrant fails, leaving its site in the shopping center closed for a time, the entire shopping center will be hurt. Because of this risk, a new entrant able to get a site in a shopping center is likely to pay higher rental costs than the leading chains in the market. Where the new entrant has something unique to offer that has been highly successful in other markets, the above may not be true (for example, a warehouse store in a market without any).

Strategic Behavior by Established Chains to Forestall Entry. Raising entry barriers by engaging in entry-forestalling practices differs in an important respect from the barriers listed above. Whereas the latter entry barriers are unintentionally erected as a side effect of innocent profit maximization, "strategic entry barriers" are purposely erected to reduce the possibility of entry (Salop

1979). Established firms lose sales and profits if a new firm enters the market and becomes established. The seriousness of the perceived threat will largely determine how established firms respond. If the new entrant fills a relatively small niche in the market and is not perceived as a major threat to conventional supermarkets, the response may be relatively mild. But if established firms perceive the new entrant as a strong threat to their sales, they may attempt to forestall its successful entry or cause it to incur large costs, thereby impeding subsequent expansion. A new entrant is particularly vulnerable to an aggressive competitive response during its entry phase because its stores are on the sharply declining section of their average cost curves. If the established firms can successfully limit an entrant's sales growth in the initial phase, they can impose heavy losses on the entrant.

The costs and benefits to the established firms of undertaking aggressive action are generally related to its market position and the extent to which the entrant is expected to affect its sales. The following example, based on the regression results of the Marion et al. (1979a) study, illustrates the profit incentives for established firms to block a new entrant from becoming established.[7] In the example the entrant is assumed to achieve a moderate 8 percent market share in a market in which the top four firms have an initial 70 percent combined share. It is assumed that the market share lost to a new entrant is proportional to the market share of established firms. The size of market assumed for the example is $1 billion of annual grocery store sales, which is about the size of Memphis now or Washington, D.C., in the early 1970s.

Market Share of Established Chain		Firm's Profit Rate			Annual Profit Reduction Due
Before Entry	*After Entry*	*Before Entry*	*After Entry*	*Change*	*to Entry*
10%	9.2%	1.45%	1.39%	−0.06%	$ 171,200
30	27.6	2.94	2.76	−0.18	1,202,400

Under these assumptions, a firm with a 10 percent initial share stands to lose $171,200 in profits per year if the new entrant gains an 8 percent market share. A firm with an initial share of 30 percent would suffer profit reductions seven times as great. Although this illustration is based on market share-profit relationships during 1970–1974 and therefore may be somewhat dated, it indicates the strong incentive that an established firm has to block or retard the entry of a new firm. The stakes are particularly high for the market leader.

Two kinds of entry-forestalling practices deserve comment. One is zone pricing, increased advertising, and other tactical responses immediately prior to or after a new entrant opens its stores. The second is to create excess capacity and prevent access to preferred new sites by building stores ahead of sales. The latter is a general preemptive strategy aimed at all new entrants.

The former takes place only when a new entrant has one or more sites and has taken definite action to enter the market.

The action taken by incumbents depends on the strategic group of which the entrant is expected to be a part. In some cases, incumbents may decide store remodelings are a better response than reducing prices. However, increased advertising and promotions and reduced prices are frequent tactics used to counter a new entrant. This is particularly likely in SMSAs with one or more dominant chains. These chains have a strong incentive to deter entry and can employ zone pricing in stores near the new entrant to force the new entrant to carry low prices and sustain large losses while it tries to attract sales.[8] Multistore entry by large chains is less likely to be subjected to zone pricing by incumbents because the new entrants have the financial resources to withstand such actions; in addition, incumbents would have to drop prices more broadly in the market and possibly trigger a price war. Occasionally, deep and prolonged price cutting may result from entry, particularly when an established dominant firm responds strategically. Bill Saporito (1983) describes Kroger's entry into the San Antonio market:

> Like a thunderstorm off the Gulf of Mexico, it rolled in with 14 stores and a warehouse in two years. It was betting an estimated $100 million that it could take a big bite of the market. . . . Lo and behold, H.E. Butt Grocery Co. the then and present market leader, knew how to play defense Kroger-style. . . . [It] matched Kroger new store for new store, price for price, precipitating a price war the like of which the city had never seen. Two smaller chains went to the bottom. (p. 80)

Four years later Kroger held only 11 percent of this market compared to H.E. Butt's market share of 26 percent (Metro Market Studies 1984).

Entry-forestalling tactics of this type raise the cost of entry, sometimes prevent successful entry, and can also serve an important strategic role in signaling other potential entrants that the incumbent firm will extract a heavy toll from new entrants. Thus, zone pricing, massive advertising campaigns, and other aggressive responses to new entrants may be aimed not only at the entrant in question but also as a warning to future potential entrants (Spence 1981).

The competitive response of established firms may constitute predation, the practice of forgoing profits in the short run in order to restructure markets in expectation of greater profits in the long run. Public policies concerning predation are discussed in part IV.

Another tactic to forestall entry in the supermarket industry is geographic preemption, or building stores ahead of sales. Since the growing parts of metropolitan areas are most susceptible to entry, it may be profitable in the long run for a leading firm to build stores in prime locations in anticipation of future population growth. Although substantial losses may be incurred for a year or so, this practice makes new entry more difficult and enables a leading firm to protect its market position.

Large chains can overcome entry barriers more easily than small. For example, "Grand Union management, in outlining a Florida West Coast Development Program for 1976–1980, anticipated operating their eighteen stores on the West Coast of Florida at a substantial loss for at least five years" (FTC 1981b, p. 216). Large chains can cross-subsidize from other markets and have greater total resources on which to rely during an entry attempt.

Because de novo entry can be slow, costly, and uncertain, entry by acquisition is often preferred by chains when antitrust laws and enforcement permit. "The surest route around other San Antonios led to the acquisition of Dillon, the 11th largest U.S. chain, which has a lock on established markets, much like Kroger's own. At some $600 million in Kroger stock, Dillion was the priciest supermarket acquisition in history. But Everingham figures it was a bargain. To crack Denver from scratch, as it did in San Antonio, Kroger would have had to lay out $500 million, facing price wars and no guarantee of market share" (Saporito 1983, p. 80).

Entry barriers are clearly higher in large SMSAs. All else the same, entry barriers are also higher in SMSAs in which a high percentage of grocery store sales are held by supermarkets indicating that there is little unmet demand for supermarkets; supermarket sales are highly concentrated; there is one or more dominant supermarket chains in the market; there are several multimarket regional or national chains that can subsidize strategic behavior in particular markets; and there is little or no growth in SMSA grocery store sales.

Entry is facilitated where the new entrant has a significant competitive advantage over incumbent firms. This is true for the first warehouse stores to enter a market. In some cases, new entrants have significantly lower labor costs than incumbent firms, which helps the entrants overcome entry barriers. The labor cost advantages of some relatively young firms have resulted in numerous efforts by older chains to negotiate labor concessions.

Structure-Performance Relationships in Local Markets

The conduct and performance of food retailers in consumer markets involve many factors. Annual surveys by Burgoyne, Inc., indicate that consumers consider several factors in selecting a store to patronize. Grocery prices, the quality of meats and produce, store location, the selection of merchandise available, and store cleanliness and attractiveness are usually cited as important considerations in selecting a store. From the standpoint of the consumer, retailer performance is clearly multidimensional. Surveys of consumers also indicate that, on average, they are relatively satisfied with the retail food stores available to them.

From a public policy standpoint, however, there are other conduct and performance factors of interest. Is the retailing function performed efficiently with no unnecessary cost to consumers? Is the industry progressive in adopting new processes or products? Are prices in line with costs so that only normal profits are realized? Is competition effective and fair? Are consumers offered sufficient alternatives? Are consumers adequately informed to make intelligent choices among food stores?

In this section, we cannot examine all the factors of importance. Data are simply not available on many factors. We will concentrate on those aspects of retail competitive behavior of particular concern to public policy and on which there are available data.

Food Retailing Prices and Profits. Retail food prices and profits vary considerably from one metropolitan area to another. Within a metropolitan area, different retailers also charge different prices and realize different levels of profits. Several studies have examined the factors related to food retailing prices and/or profits in metropolitan areas. The results have varied, in part because of methodological differences and in part because of differences in data. To clarify this issue, a brief digression on data and methodology is necessary.

Food is retailed through many types of stores, each providing a certain bundle of goods and services. Store gross margins and prices vary with the mix of goods and services offered. Whereas a traditional supermarket may have a gross margin of about 20 percent, a warehouse store may have a gross margin of 12 percent, and a convenience store may have a gross margin of 28 percent.

In analyzing the prices of food retailers, a researcher must decide whether to compare the technical efficiency and costs of different store types, determine the effects of the competitive environment on the pricing behavior of certain store types, or both. Comparing the prices of convenience stores in one market with the prices of supermarkets in another market may reveal little about the competitive environments of the two markets or the technical efficiency of the two types of stores.

Problems also can exist in the products priced and the weights used. National brands are generally priced higher than store brands of the same product. A market basket that is not held constant across stores and markets with respect to the national brand and store brand content may frustrate efforts to isolate the effect of the competitive environment.

For these reasons, the most straightforward price comparisons are between stores of the same type (such as conventional supermarkets) for the same brands and types of products. Because the stores of individual grocery chains tend to be similar in different markets, comparing the prices in one chain's stores across metropolitan markets is the simplest method to determine the effects of market structure on prices. With this type of analysis, many of the factors that can influence prices are held constant.

Only two studies of retail food prices have used this research design. The first and most extensive was done for the Joint Economic Committee (JEC) of the U.S. Congress. Done in part as a response to widespread concerns about rising food prices in the early 1970s, the "JEC study" has been widely distributed and critiqued (U.S. Congress 1977a, and 1977b; Marion et al. 1979a, 1979b; the report has also been the subject of extensive testimony in several antitrust cases). A second study used similar methodology to analyze the market structure-price relationship in rural Vermont grocery markets.

Results of JEC Price and Profit Analysis. For the JEC price analysis, the weighted average cost to consumers was calculated for a grocery basket of ninety-four comparable grocery products for three chains in thirty-six SMSAs. Multiple regression analysis indicated that a chain's "relative firm market share" (the chain's market share divided by the sum of the market shares of the top four firms) and the CR4 were positively and significantly related to a chain's grocery price level. The results indicate that if a firm has a strong position in a market relative to its major competitors, it has greater discretion to raise prices. Although a dominant firm might achieve some efficiencies from a large market share, the results indicate these are not reflected in lower prices to consumers. Indeed chains charged higher prices in markets where they had large market shares.

Four-firm concentration (CR4) was also positively and significantly related to grocery prices across SMSAs. CR4 is expected to measure the degree of competitive interdependence. When a few firms have most of the sales in a market, they recognize their mutuality of interest. Thus, there is a tendency for either explicit collusion or a live-and-let-live environment (tacit collusion) to develop in markets with high levels of concentration. This expectation was supported by the positive relationship found between grocery prices and CR4 in the JEC study.

Other factors also affected price levels in different markets. Grocery prices were negatively related to the rate of growth of SMSAs. Supermarket chains may charge lower prices to forestall entry or to build market share in rapidly growing markets. The amount of market rivalry (measured by changes in the market shares of the leading firms) was also found to have a significant negative effect on prices. At any time, several SMSAs in the United States may be experiencing moderate or severe price wars with temporarily depressed prices.

The profit analysis in the JEC study related the profit-to-sales ratio before taxes to the structure of markets and several control variables. SMSA profit data from six supermarket chains were examined across forty-nine metropolitan areas (there were seventy-one observations since several SMSAs had more than one of the six chains). Division profit data were provided by twelve chains (ninety-six divisions in total). The models used for the SMSA and division profit analyses were similar.

In the profit analysis, relative firm market share (RFMS) and CR4 were also found to be positively and significantly related to chain profits, in both the SMSA and division analyses. In both analyses, the profit-CR4 relationship was strongest when CR4 was expressed in curvilinear form; that is, profits rose rapidly as concentration increased at low and moderate levels of concentration and tended to level off at high levels of concentration. The predicted price and profit levels for different combinations of relative firm market share and CR4, based on the JEC regression analyses, are shown in table 5–6.

The profit analysis also indicated that firms entering an SMSA de novo experience lower profits in the years immediately following entry. Profits were higher in rapidly growing markets, perhaps because higher store utilization results in lower costs in these markets. The caliber of chain management, as measured by firm growth, was also found to be positively related to firm profits.

Results of the Vermont Price Analysis. During 1981 a court challenge to the Vermont blue law provided an opportunity to replicate the JEC study's market structure-price analysis. The Vermont market basket of price-checked items contained the ninety-four grocery products analyzed in the JEC study, plus frozen foods, dairy products, and health and beauty aids. Prices were aggregated to produce a weighted price index value for each firm in each local market. (See Cotterill 1984 for a full description of the study.)

Table 5–6
Estimated Index of Grocery Prices and Pretax Profit-Sales Ratios Associated with Various Levels of Market Concentration and Relative Firm Market Share

	CR4							
	40		50		60		70	
Relative Firm Market Share (RFMS)	Index of Grocery Prices[a]	Profits as Percentage of Sales[b]	Index of Grocery Prices	Profits as Percentage of Sales	Index of Grocery Prices	Profits as Percentage of Sales	Index of Grocery Prices	Profits as Percentage of Sales
10	100.0	.36	101.0	.96	103.0	1.18	105.4	1.23
25	100.7	1.14	101.7	1.74	103.7	1.96	106.1	2.01
40	102.2	1.92	103.2	2.52	105.2	2.74	107.6	2.79
55	103.2	2.70	104.2	3.30	106.2	3.52	108.6	3.57

Source: Marion et al. 1979a, p. 131.

[a]The estimated grocery basket cost for each combination of RFMS and CR4 was calculated using equation 1h, table 4–3, in Marion et al. and holding other independent variables at their respective means. The index was constructed by setting the grocery basket computed for RFMS = 10, CR4 = 40 equal to 100.0.

[b]Profits as a percentage of sales were estimated for each combination of RFMS and CR4 using equation 1d, table 3.7, in Marion et al.; all other variables except API were introduced at their means; the binary variable API was introduced with a value of 1. Equation 1d was developed using the average division profit levels for 1970, 1971, and 1974. The grocery price models were based on 1974 prices.

The Vermont study differed from the JEC study in that it focused on cities and towns too small to be classified as SMSAs. Burlington is the only SMSA among the eighteen local food retailing markets identified in the state. The product market, as in the more advanced models of the JEC study, was defined as supermarket sales.

The food retailing business in small cities and towns in Vermont (and elsewhere) is significantly more concentrated than in metropolitan areas. In three instances local markets were served by only one supermarket, with the closest competitor being as much as twenty-five miles away. The market share of the leading firm averaged 51.8 percent; the Herfindahl index averaged 4,270 in the eighteen markets. Supermarket CR4 in the eighteen markets averaged 96.1 percent in 1980. By comparison, supermarket CR4 in SMSA markets nationwide averaged 70.9 percent in 1977.

The price level indexes for thirty-five firm-market observations were regressed on several explanatory variables. Several measures of market structure were used: the Herfindahl index, one- through four-firm concentration, and relative firm market share (the firm's market share as a percentage of the measure of concentration used; for example, CR3, CR4). Nearly all measures were positively and significantly related to price levels. In markets as small as those in Vermont, the market share of the leading firm appears to be a better determinant of individual firm pricing behavior than CR2, CR3, or CR4; however, the Herfindahl index was the best structural predictor of price levels.

Prices were also found to be significantly higher (about 2 percent higher) in independent than in chain supermarkets, holding all else constant. Growth was negatively related to price levels as in the JEC report but was not significant. Per capita income, included in an attempt to isolate demand influences, was not statistically significant. The same was true for a distance-from-the-warehouse variable. Wholesale-retail transportation costs appeared to have little impact on retail prices in different markets.

The data also allowed for an indirect measure of store operating costs and merchandising strategies. Sales per square foot, a measure of capacity utilization, was positively and significantly related to the price level. Although retail operating expenses have been found to decline as sales per square foot go up (National Commission on Food Marketing 1966a, pp. 139–152; Marion et al. 1979a, pp. 135–137), high sales per square foot may reflect the lack of alternative stores for consumers or a strong preference for a particular store. The last two factors would allow retailers to charge higher prices even though their costs may be lower than less-utilized stores. Store size, measured by square feet of selling space, was significantly related to price level when store size was introduced quadratically. Small stores had high prices, supermarkets in the 14,000 to 18,000 square foot range tended to have lowest prices, and still larger stores had higher prices. The store size-price relationship may reflect a combination of long-run average cost levels and merchandising strategies.

The Vermont results are similar to the JEC study conclusions. Rural and small city markets may face even more serious competitive problems in food retailing than metropolitan markets. Although nonmetropolitan markets account for only about one-fourth of the nation's food sales, they can be a rich profit lode for supermarket companies. For example, the Grand Union Company, which had 39 percent of Vermont's supermarket business in 1980, enjoyed a pretax profit-sales ratio of 5.9 percent on its Vermont operations. While only 3 percent of Grand Union's 1980 sales were in Vermont, 15 percent of its pretax profits came from Vermont.

Other Structure-Price Studies. Although the results of the JEC and Vermont studies are consistent with the vast majority of industrial organization research, these studies have been challenged by industry spokespersons and a small percentage of the thirty or more academicians who have reviewed the JEC study. It is appropriate to consider whether other studies of food retailing have found similar results.

Lamm (1981, 1982) examined a very different data set, the Bureau of Labor Statistics's (BLS) market basket price for food consumed at home. Using a pooled cross-sectional time-series analysis, Lamm found a positive and significant relationship between market concentration and food prices across eighteen SMSAs during 1974 to 1977. BLS data collection and analysis procedures would be expected to yield prices that are biased toward a negative relationship to supermarket concentration (Geithman and Marion 1978). For this reason, Lamm's findings are somewhat surprising. In one analysis (1981), Lamm found BLS prices were positively related to the union wage rate of journeymen clerks in various SMSAs. In a subsequent analysis (1982), he used the percentage of grocery store employees in an SMSA who were unionized instead of union wage rate and found a positive and significant relationship to BLS prices. Although in most respects Lamm's data set was inferior to that employed in the JEC study, we would expect this to bias his results toward zero. His results are consistent with the findings of the JEC and Vermont studies concerning the impact of market concentration on retail prices.

In another study using BLS data, Hall, Schmitz, and Cothern (1979) employed a simple three-variable model to examine retail price-cost margins for beef in nineteen SMSAs over the seven-year period 1967–1973. Retail market concentration and wage rates were both positively and significantly related to retail beef margins. Holding all other things constant, a 10 percent increase in CR4 was found to cause a 4 percent increase in beef price-cost margins, more than double the effect on grocery prices found in the JEC study. Although this study has important limitations in the data set and econometric model employed, the results are consistent with the JEC and Vermont studies concerning the influence of market concentration on prices.

Two earlier studies found results in possible conflict with the above studies. Mori and Gorman (1966) examined the prices of a 151-item market basket in 1965 in twenty-two relatively small and highly concentrated cities. Using a simple two-variable model, they found a positive but insignificant relationship between four-firm concentration and prices. Had a more appropriate econometric model been used, the concentration-price relationship might have been significant.

The National Commission on Food Marketing (1966a) examined the 1963 gross margins of the individual stores of eight chains across several SMSAs. Stepwise multiple regression analysis indicated a chain's SMSA market share had a significant positive relationship to individual store gross margins for two of the eight chains, while CR4 was never significant in any of the models. Although a large data set was available for this analysis, there are serious questions about the methodology employed (Cotterill 1977, pp. 31–38; Helmberger, Campbell and Dobson 1981, p. 531). When store results were averaged by market, there was a significant positive correlation between chain market share and both gross margin and net profits.

The Gorman-Mori and NCFM studies are critiqued in greater detail elsewhere (U.S. Congress 1977b, pp. 94–96). While careful researchers will want to examine these two studies, the bulk of the evidence indicates that market concentration and a retailer's position in the market have a strong influence over that firm's prices and profits.

Approximately twenty studies have examined concentration-price relationships for product-services such as gasoline retailing, auto loans, commercial loans, life insurance, drug retailing, and securities. Greer (1984, p. 296) concludes from these various studies, "Prices and concentration *are* positively related."

Influence of Information on Retailer and Consumer Behavior. There is a growing interest in the role and adequacy of market information. The 1980 Economic Report of the President (p. 127) said, "Increasing the information consumers can draw upon sometimes complements more traditional structural remedies as a means of fostering competition in the market."

In selecting a food store at which to shop, consumers are expected to have inadequate information for several reasons. Food retailers stock several thousand items, frequently change prices due to weekly specials, and vary in their emphasis on prices, product quality, and store services. Because of this complex purchase environment, buyer search is discouraged.

Several studies have examined the effects of increasing consumer information on food prices. Although the results have varied some in different cities, the studies have consistently shown procompetitive effects from publicly provided comparative price information that provides consumers with a better basis for selecting food stores.

A study of the Ottawa, Canada, metropolitan market produced the most dramatic results (Devine and Marion 1979). Price information on a market basket of sixty-five food products in twenty-six Ottawa supermarkets was published weekly in the daily newspaper for a five-week period. Average prices in the market dropped sharply, and the dispersion of prices across stores declined during the information period. The estimated and perceived benefits to consumers far exceeded the cost of the program.

Because comparative price information was provided to consumers for only five weeks, one of the questions unanswered by this study was the long-run consequences. Would comparative price information provided over a longer period continue to have procompetitive effects, or given the concentrated nature of food retailing in many metropolitan areas, would it lead to tacit or explicit price collusion?

A follow-up Canadian study sought to answer this question by publishing comparative price information weekly in two cities (Regina and Saskatoon) for five consecutive months while also monitoring prices in six control markets (Devine 1978). In Regina, similar though less dramatic results occurred as in Ottawa. The dispersion of prices narrowed and average prices declined more rapidly than in Calgary, the paired control market.

In Saskatoon, a highly concentrated market in which the leading chain held over 50 percent of the market and the top four firms had over 95 percent, a different scenario emerged. Prior to the comparative price information program, prices in Saskatoon stores were tightly grouped (2 to 3 percent spread). The information program had no significant effect on the dispersion of prices in Saskatoon. Although average prices in Saskatoon declined more rapidly than in the paired control market (Winnipeg) during most of the information period, this was reversed during the last six weeks of the program.

In part as a follow-up to the Canadian studies, Purdue researchers examined the effects of comparative price information in four U.S. cities in 1979–1980 (Uhl, Boynton, and Blake 1981). Price information was published in the local newspapers for periods ranging from six to twelve weeks. Prices were also monitored in four control cities. The study found, first, that the comparative price reports reduced food price levels in the test cities, relative to price levels in the control markets, during the period that prices were published. The percentage decline for the 100-item market basket ranged from 0.8 percent in Des Moines to 5.2 percent in Springfield, Missouri. Second, the competitive effects of the food price reports were neither triggered nor reinforced by changes in consumer behavior in the test cities. The publicity effect of the price reports apparently caused retailers to change prices in anticipation of consumer reaction.

The market perfecting effects of the Purdue study were generally consistent with the Canadian studies; however, consumer response was quite different. In Ottawa, consumers made significant shifts in stores as a result of the information program. Why consumers in the Purdue study did not respond to the price information by shifting stores is not clear.

One comparative price reporting program in the United States has been in operation since 1971. The Indiana Public Interest Research Group has published monthly the prices for Bloomington, Indiana, grocery stores in the University of Indiana newspaper. Although Bloomington is more concentrated than several other Indiana markets, surveys during 1979 and 1980 consistently found prices in Bloomington to be lower than in Indianapolis, Lafayette, and four surrounding towns (Loescher 1983). Retail chains reportedly used their lowest price zone in Bloomington because of the information program.

These studies provide evidence that in most markets, the dispersion of prices across stores is greater than justified by differences in the product-service offers of those stores and that credible comparative price information for consumers will reduce price dispersion and average retail prices in a metropolitan area. Put another way, these findings support the hypothesis that consumers have insufficient information to vote accurately their preferences for food stores in the marketplace. Increased information generally leads to more efficient allocation of resources.

Technological Progressiveness and Labor Productivity. One basis for judging the efficiency of an industry is the sources and adoption rates of cost-saving technology. Overall the food retailing industry has been relatively slow to adopt potential cost saving innovations. The amount of research and development funding supplied by the industry for technological improvements is very low when compared to other sectors. Such innovations as are introduced—a recent major one has been scanning cash registers—typically originate from equipment suppliers rather than from the industry itself. Leading-edge management systems such as the highly touted ScanLab are far below the technical possibilities offered by microprocessing and scanning systems. Ricker (1981, p. 99) summarizes the situation as follows: "The net result is inattention to wasteful practices in distribution, processing and retailing." Overall the dynamic efficiency of food retailing must be described as modest.

BLS data indicate that labor productivity in both food stores and eating and drinking places generally declined during the 1970s and early 1980s (figure 5–6). Hours worked in food retailing rose 20.7 percent from 1970 to 1980, while output increased only 6.5 percent. At least in part, this reflects the trend during the 1970s for supermarkets to be open on Sundays and to add service-oriented operations such as in-store bakeries and delicatessens.

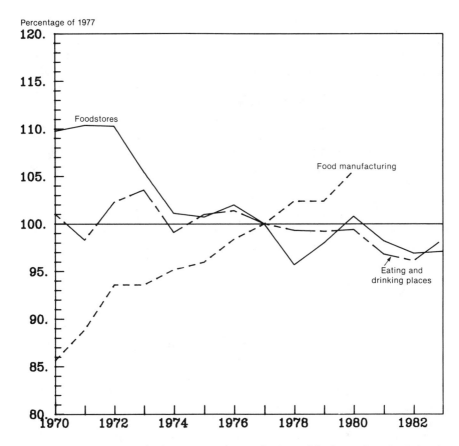

Source: U.S. Department of Labor, 1985. Labor productivity of food manufacturing industries were estimated by USDA using BLS data.

Figure 5–6. Food Industry Labor Productivity Trends

Warehouse stores, with much lower labor requirements, may counter this downward trend in labor productivity if their share of U.S. grocery store sales continues to increase. More rapid adoption of new technology and a stronger orientation of the industry toward ways of cutting costs is most likely if strong price competition exists. Warehouse stores are important because of the efficiencies they trigger in other retailers, as well as the option they provide to consumers.

Labor unions and retail employees are currently under considerable pressure in several markets to make wage or fringe benefit concessions. In part, this reflects the present or anticipated competitive pressure from warehouse stores that pay lower wages. In part, it may also be a sign of the times; employee concessions have been obtained in many industries. In some cases, companies have been absolved from union contracts by changes in owner-ship; substantial reductions in wages have followed.

In many cases, labor contracts place older firms or firms that are declin-ing in market share at a significant disadvantage in relation to young growing companies. For example, seniority clauses in many contracts allow senior employees from a closed store to "bump" employees at other stores in a chain's division. If a chain is in trouble and closes its poorest stores, its oldest and highest paid employees end up at its remaining stores. As a result, labor con-tracts can hasten the demise of firms that are in trouble. New labor agree-ments such as A&P's Super Fresh program overcome this problem and pro-vide for profit sharing with employees.

Reductions in employee compensations by grocery chains may reduce one of the important advantages traditionally enjoyed by independent re-tailers. *Progressive Grocer* (1985) reported that in 1984, independent super-markets were far less unionized and paid wages roughly 20 percent lower than chains.

Causes of Structural Change

Given the evidence that market structure (seller concentration and entry bar-riers) has a significant effect on market performance in grocery retailing, an obvious question is what factors determine the structure of markets. Why are some metropolitan areas highly concentrated, while others are unconcen-trated? How are SMSAs changing in concentration and entry barriers? Is there evidence of a natural erosion of highly concentrated markets? What role do mergers play?

Because entry barriers are impossible to measure directly, the change in entry conditions cannot be examined empirically in the same way as change in seller concentration. Measures of SMSA seller concentration are provided by the Bureau of Census for the census years 1954 to 1977 and make possible studies of the factors affecting retail concentration.

Two econometric studies have examined the change in SMSA grocery store concentration. Cotterill and Mueller (1980) studied the change in CR4 in eighty-six SMSAs over the period 1967–1975. Parker (1985) attempted to improve on the earlier analysis by Cotterill and Mueller (C-M). In addition to a larger sample of SMSAs and a longer time period, Parker divided market extension mergers into two types, toehold and leading firm, depending on whether the acquired firm ranked among the top four in an SMSA. De novo entry and market extension mergers by the 100 largest chains were examined by Parker, whereas C-M focused on entry and mergers by the largest twenty-two chains. Because Parker's study is more recent and more comprehensive, we will concentrate on summarizing his findings, making note where ap-propriate of important differences from the C-M study.

Parker employed multiple regression analysis to measure the net influence on change in SMSA grocery store concentration of market characteristics such as market size, market growth and the initial level of concentration, and the effects of conduct factors such as mergers and entry.

Equations were fitted for each of five intervals between regular census years: 1954–1958, 1958–1963, 1963–1967, 1967–1972, and 1972–1977. A progression of equations was fitted because the whole period spans major changes in grocery retailing such as the ending of the "supermarket revolution," the development of shopping centers, and important demographic shifts that likely affected the way the explanatory variables related to concentration change. The division of the long period into shorter intervals was also necessary since several variables, such as those relating to mergers, were available for only the final ten years of the twenty-three-year span. Herfindahl-Hirschman concentration indexes, to which federal antitrust policy is currently tied, were available only for the final five years.

A basic model relating SMSA size, growth, level of initial concentration, and SMSA definition change was fitted to all five periods and to data for all SMSAs. SMSA population size was found to be negatively related to concentration change.[9] A negative relationship was expected. The increasing size of new supermarkets during the 1954–1977 period limited the feasible number of supermarket companies in small SMSAs, provided an upward pressure on concentration, and made entry more difficult.

A negative relationship was found between SMSA growth and concentration change. This is consistent with the standard industrial organization hypothesis that rapid growth creates favorable conditions for entry of new firms and expansion of small, established firms. Growth became more significant over time as opportunities for displacing traditional small stores disappeared and as increasing scale economies made entry more difficult. The slowdown in SMSA growth rates after 1967 may explain part of the sharp increase in average SMSA concentration from 1972 to 1977.

The level of initial concentration was negatively related to concentration change. Metropolitan areas with low levels of concentration tended to increase substantially in concentration, whereas SMSAs with very high levels of concentration had a tendency to decline slightly in CR4.

A final variable in the basic model was the percentage change in the size of an SMSA due to a change in the official SMSA definition. This variable had a strong negative relationship to change in concentration. In census periods with a large number of definition changes, such as the 1967–1972 period, the increase in average concentration was significantly lower than if there had been fewer changes.

To this basic model, Parker added variables measuring merger activity and entry during the final two periods. Data for the merger variables, available for 118 larger SMSAs, came from mandatory FTC premerger notification reports and from trade publications. A variable for horizontal mergers measured the percentage point increase in CR4 (using the combined pre-merger shares) resulting from a merger. Only horizontal mergers that increased CR4 were considered. As in the C-M study, horizontal mergers were positively and significantly related to change in four-firm concentration. For the 1967–1977 period, the coefficient on this variable was .95, indicating little erosion in the combined market shares.

There was a difference, however, in the mergers consummated in the first half of the decade and the second. In the first five years, the horizontal merger variable coefficient was statistically insignificant, and its value indicated that a third of the immediate increase in concentration was eroded within the five years. Furthermore, there was continued erosion of the combined shares in the following five years. The mergers consummated in the second half were in sharp contrast. The regression coefficient was statistically significant and at 1.5 indicated a 50 percent increase over the combined market shares. The difference between the mergers of the two halves of the decade suggests that screening of mergers by the antitrust agencies may have changed after 1972 to permit economically stronger firms to combine.

Substituting Herfindahl-Hirschman index (HHI) values for concentration ratios as the dependent variable for the 1972–1977 period did not greatly affect the statistical fit of the explanatory variables. For each 1 percent the combined shares of merged firms initially increased CR4, the HHI levels by the end of the period had gone up 58 points.[10]

In addition to horizontal mergers, C-M examined the effects of conglomerate mergers (market extension mergers by the largest twenty-two chains plus acquisitions of food retailers by large nonfood corporations), whereas Parker distinguished between leading firm and toehold market extension mergers by the largest one hundred grocery chains and ignored pure conglomerate mergers. In Parker's analysis, if the firm acquired was one of the top four firms in an SMSA, the merger was a leading firm merger; firms acquired that ranked below the top four were regarded as toehold acquisitions.

C-M found a significant positive effect on concentration of conglomerate mergers. Parker found that leading firm acquisitions in the 1967–1977 period, on average, led to a statistically significant 5 percentage point increase in CR4; however, he found toehold acquisitions by the top one hundred chains during 1967–1977 tended to erode CR4 by about 3 percentage points in concentrated markets (CR4 over 50 in 1967). Toehold acquisitions in unconcentrated markets (CR4 less than 50) during this ten-year period had no significant effect on CR4.[11]

The effects of de novo entry in the two studies differed but may be largely due to the samples involved. The C-M data set had fifty-three instances of entry into thirty-eight relatively unconcentrated SMSAs (average CR4 = 43). De novo entry had a significant positive effect on CR4. However, the C-M results shed little light on the effects of de novo entry into concentrated SMSAs or de novo entry by chains smaller than the largest twenty-two. Parker found that de novo entry by the top one hundred chains into concentrated SMSAs (CR4 > 50) had a significant negative effect on CR4 (a decline of 3 percentage points during 1967–1977, on average). De novo entry into unconcentrated markets (CR4 < 50) had no significant effect on CR4 in Parker's models.

The effects of de novo entry into unconcentrated markets are of less concern from an antitrust standpoint than de novo entry into concentrated markets. Since C-M provided evidence primarily on the former, Parker's results on the latter are of particular value.

Both C-M and Parker found the number of large national chains (top twenty, roughly) in an SMSA to have a significant positive effect on change in concentration. It was hypothesized that very large multimarket chains have conglomerate power not possessed by smaller companies. Their greater resources make them better able to rebuff entry, to outspend and outlast smaller rivals, and to pursue costly share-enhancing strategies not available to smaller retailers.

Both studies also found A&P's market share in 1967 to be negatively related to change in concentration during the periods studied. A&P was included as a variable because of its extraordinary decline during 1967–1977, resulting in its complete withdrawal from many SMSAs. A&P was also unlike other national chains in that it had tended to concentrate on developed areas of cities following World War II while other chains directed their growth to the suburbs. As a consequence, its stores were much smaller than those operated by other chains when it began to lose market share rapidly in the 1960s.

The results of these studies concerning the effects of various types of mergers may understate the effects of present-day mergers. During the period examined by both C-M and Parker, the FTC had an industry-specific merger policy directed toward the grocery retailing industry. Thus, the mergers in both data sets were screened by the federal antitrust agencies for their concentration-increasing potential. Had the data set been of mergers not subject to an antitrust screening, the regression results could have been quite different.

National Size Distribution of Firms and Firm-Scale Economies

Competition among food retailers as sellers occurs in local markets; however, the national size distribution of firms may influence competition among retailers as buyers and the overall economic power of companies. National concentration is affected by merger activity as well as the advantages and disadvantages of large firm size. In this section we will examine the level and trend of national concentration in grocery retailing, several indicators of firm economies of size, and the role of mergers in shaping the size distribution of U.S. food retailing companies.

Trends in National Concentration

The share of U.S. grocery store sales held by the largest twenty food chains increased from 27 percent in 1948 to 34 percent in 1958. From 1958 to 1982, this market share increased very little, in part because of a precipitous decline in A&P's national market share from 11.1 to 1.7 percent. When A&P is excluded, the remaining nineteen of the top twenty increased their national market share by 50 percent during this twenty-five-year period (table 5–7). All U.S. grocery chains did about 62 percent of 1982 grocery store sales. Thus, the largest twenty chains did over half of chain store sales.

Table 5–7
Share of U.S. Grocery Store Sales Held by the Twenty Largest Grocery Chains, Census Years 1948–1981
(percentage)

Firm Size	1948	1954	1958	1963	1967	1972	1977	1982
Four largest	20.1	20.9	21.7	20.0	19.0	17.5	17.4	17.8
Fifth to Eighth largest	3.6	4.5	5.8	6.6	6.7	6.9	7.0	7.3
Eight largest	23.7	25.4	27.5	26.6	25.7	24.4	24.4	25.1
Ninth to twentieth largest	3.2	4.5	6.6	7.4	8.7	10.4	10.1	10.4
Twenty largest	26.9	29.9	34.1	34.0	34.4	34.8	34.5	35.6
A&P	10.7	11.3	11.1	9.4	8.3	6.6	4.2	1.7
Twenty largest excluding A&P	16.2	18.7	23.0	24.6	26.1	28.2	30.3	34.3

Source: Data for 1948 through 1963 prepared by the FTC for the National Commission on Food Marketing and published in Organization and Competition in Food Retailing, Technical Study No. 7, June 1966. Data for 1967 are tabulated from a 1969 FTC special survey of food chains. Data for 1972 and 1977 are based on U.S. Bureau of the Census, Census of Retail Trade, Subject Series, *Establishment and Firm Size* (1972, 1977), tables 2c, 6. Data for 1982 are based on *Food Institute Report*, May 6, 1984, p. 3; *1982 Census of Retail Trade* RC82-I-8(P), U.S. Department of Commerce, Bureau of the Census, May 1984; and the Southland Corporation 1982 Annual Report.

Notes: The census 1982 preliminary report provides grocery sales only for establishments with payroll. These figures were adjusted upward based on the ratio of total sales to payroll sales for the 1977 census. The total estimated grocery sales for 1982 is $231,646,700. The Southland Corporation's sales were included in the top eight and top twenty grocery chain sales. These sales included gas sales. If gas sales were excluded CR8 = 25.0 percent and CR20 = 35.1 percent.

Economies of Firm Size

When retail chains reach a certain size, they vertically integrate into wholesaling by developing their own warehouse, store delivery fleet, and procurement system. Food Marketing Institute (1982, p. 58) data reveal that $200 million to $300 million in 1981 retail sales (roughly forty to sixty stores) were required to justify owning a warehouse. Smaller companies obtained the majority of their supplies from general line grocery wholesalers. In 1982, 138 retail chains operated 50 or more grocery stores (Bureau of Census 1982c). Most of these companies probably had their own warehouses.

The National Commission on Food Marketing (1966a) estimated the minimum efficient volume for a warehouse in the mid-1960s was $75 million to $100 million. This is equivalent to $200 million to $270 million in 1981 dollars, a volume consistent with the Food Marketing Institute data. The advantages from operating one's own warehouse appear to have declined in recent years, however. Interviews with industry personnel and the trade literature indicate that more medium to large grocery chains have turned to general line grocery wholesalers to supply at least some of their stores in recent years.

The National Commission on Food Marketing also estimated that economies of firm size exist up to about $500 million in annual sales. The commission stated, "Economies accruing from combining several warehouses in a single firm arise primarily from manufacturing operations, the procurement of private label merchandise, and field buying of perishables" (1966a, p. 140). Five hundred million dollars in sales in the mid-1960s is equivalent to about $1.5 billion in 1984 sales, a level of sales achieved by about sixteen grocery chains.

Data on food manufacturing by grocery chains indicate two clusters of chains that are actively involved. The top eight chains in 1977 supplied about 10 percent of their store needs from their own manufacturing plants. The ninth through fortieth largest chains supplied about 5 percent of their store volume from their own plants. Smaller chains appear to have little involvement in manufacturing. These data suggest that some firm economies in food manufacturing may be present at higher volumes than estimated by the National Commission; for example, the largest eight chains in 1977 each had sales of $2.4 billion or more.

The size required for a sound private label program has probably dropped over the last fifteen to twenty years. Private label programs offered by firms such as Topco and Shurfine have eliminated many of the advantages of very large chains. Private label manufacturers have also become larger, more sophisticated, and better able to provide assistance to small and medium-sized chains in running a private label program. Thus, we expect that economies of firm size due to private label programs (in real terms) have declined since the NCFM report, although we have no way of estimating a sales level at which available economies are realized.

Based on these data, the largest forty chains probably enjoy some economies from self-manufacturing, while the largest hundred or so chains may also benefit from having their own warehouses; however, these advantages have probably declined over time. An additional advantage of large firm size is the ability to cross-subsidize operations from one market to another. Cross-subsidization can be used defensively or offensively. In either case, a large chain that is profitable in some of its markets can use those profits to finance entry into new markets, to restructure markets through zone pricing or heavy promotions, or to endure in unprofitable markets until firms with fewer resources withdraw from the market.

Characteristics of Retail Procurement Markets

The relevant geographic market within which manufacturer-retailer (wholesaler) transactions take place varies by product from relatively local markets to national markets. As transportation has improved and barriers to the flow of products have been reduced or eliminated, the size of the relevant geographic markets has increased. Fluid milk and bread were at one time supplied by manufacturers within each metropolitan market. To an increasing extent, this is no longer true. Milk in consumer packages may now travel 300 miles or more to supply retail customers.

Concentration figures are seldom available for either the buying or selling side of manufacturer-retailer markets that are local or regional in nature. While national concentration is generally increasing in both food manufacturing industries and food retailing, the geographic broadening of some local markets may mean that buyer or seller concentration in those markets has not increased. The concentration trends depend on the extent to which the national market structure is reproduced in local and regional markets.

Advertised Brand Procurement. With an advertised brand, the manufacturer is responsible for most aspects of the production and marketing of a product (including product specification, quality control, label design, and advertising). However, a product's success still depends on retailers' stocking it, giving it favorable shelf location, and cooperating with the manufacturer's price adjustments and promotions.

In recent years, the use of deals by manufacturers has increased greatly as a method of promoting advertised brands. Every week, buyers may have 200 to 400 manufacturer deals from which to choose. Because deal prices can be substantially lower than regular list prices, retailers operating warehouse stores rely heavily on deals to maintain low prices. As one deal expires, these stores change to another brand on deal. The competitive pressure of warehouse-type stores has probably forced full-service retailers to pass on deal savings to consumers to a greater extent than would be true without these competitors.

Private and Generic Label Brands. Procurement of private label (retailer) brands and generic or no name brands is similar. For both, the retailer buying organization provides most of the marketing support. Whereas the merchandising of advertised brands is basically the responsibility of the manufacturer, with retailer brands and generics, this responsibility resides with the retailer or wholesaler. Retailers and wholesalers establish product specifications, design labels, provide advertising, and set retail pricing strategies (Hamm 1981b). Because of these differences, distributor private label procurement departments are often separate from their brand procurement systems. Private label procurement is heavily price oriented, though other considerations such as quality consistency, supplier reliability, and personalities also influence the manufacturers selected.

For many years, large private label buyers have had a strategic bargaining advantage over the manufacturers of undifferentiated private label products. The lowest-cost processors have generally gotten the business. The trend is toward fewer, larger, and more diversified private label suppliers. Some national brand manufacturers also pack private labels of products in which they do not have one of the top brands. It appears that retailer buyers will be dealing in the future with a smaller number of relatively large private label suppliers.

Vertical Integration

Vertical integration refers to the linking together within a single firm the activities of two or more successive stages of production or distribution. One motive for vertical integration is to reduce costs. In the early development of grocery chains, this was an important motive for retailers integrating into warehousing. High market transaction costs were replaced by internal transfers. Currently most supermarket chains with sufficient sales within a radius of 200 miles to support a warehouse are vertically integrated into that activity. Two hundred miles is the practical distance that can usually be served by a truck in a single day.

Data on food manufacturing by food chains indicate a decline from 1954 to 1967 in the percentage of food sales of the forty largest chains supplied by their own manufacturing plants (figure 5–7). A modest increase occurred from 1967 to 1977. The ninth through fortieth largest chains are approximately half as active in food manufacturing as the top eight chains, supplying about 5 percent of their store volume from their own plants (table 5–8). Manufacturing by chains smaller than the top forty is relatively unimportant.

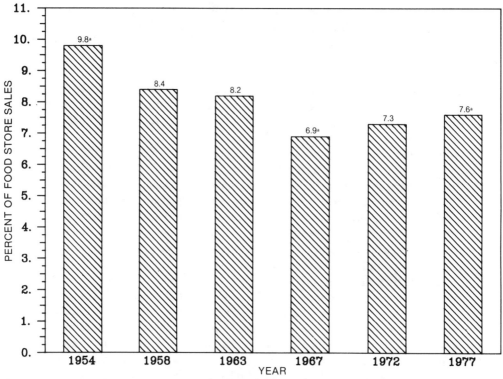

Source: FTC, 1954–1967; U.S. Bureau of the Census special tabulation, 1972, 1977.

[a]About 0.6 percentage point of the decline between 1954 and 1967 was due to increasing retail gross margins. Another 0.3 percentage point was due to increasing nonfood sales of food stores. These two influences have had negligible effects since 1967. In combination they may have reduced the 1977 ratio by 0.1 percentage point. That is, the 1977 ratio if adjusted to be comparable to 1967 could be 7.7.

Figure 5–7. Food Products Manufactured by Largest Forty Food Chains as a Percentage of Their Food Store Sales, 1954–1977

Fluid milk, fresh and processed meats, and bread products accounted for two-thirds of the value of food manufactured by the largest fifty chains in 1977 (table B–3). All three are high-volume categories in which retailer brands have a large share of category sales. The average number of SIC 20 product classes in which the largest chains were involved in manufacturing declined slightly from 1972 to 1977 (table 5–9). The ninth through fortieth largest chains were involved in many fewer food manufacturing product classes than the top eight chains. The largest chains may have sufficient total retail volume to justify their integrating into some of the smaller-volume product classes.

Vertical integration into food manufacturing is primarily the domain of the largest eight grocery chains. The relative importance of food manufacturing by the top forty chains may have stabilized in recent years after declining for many years.

Table 5–8
Value of Shipments of Food Products Manufactured by Fifty Largest Food Chains, 1972 and 1977

Rank	Value of Shipments		Percentage of Firms' Food Store Sales	
	1972	*1977*	*1972*	*1977*
4 largest	1,535	2,615	9.4	10.1
5–8 largest	511	892	7.9	10.4
9–20 largest	490	785	4.9	5.2
21–40 largest	324	497	5.0	4.8
41–50 largest	NA	45	NA	1.4
50 largest	NA	4,933	NA	7.57

Source: U.S. Bureau of the Census, special tabulation 1972, 1977.
[a]Millions of dollars.

Mergers Involving Food Retailing Firms

Mergers have played an important role in the national structure of the food retailing industry. Figure 5–8 indicates the pattern of merger activity since 1949. Acquired sales are converted to 1967 dollars. The thirty-five-year period can be broken into four distinct subperiods: the period prior to 1955, 1955–1964, 1965–1974, and 1975–1984. Prior to 1955, merger activity was slight as retail firms grew primarily by internal expansion. By the mid-1950s, there were fewer opportunities for growth by building new supermarkets. Mergers became a more common method of growth from 1955 on; mergers between 1955 and 1964 significantly increased the national market shares held by the largest twenty chains (National Commission on Food Marketing 1966a).

In 1959, the FTC initiated the first of a series of actions to challenge mergers by large food chains when it challenged twenty-six acquisitions by National Tea. This was followed by complaints challenging acquisitions by Kroger (1959), Vons (Justice, 1960), Grand Union (1962), Winn Dixie (1966), Consolidated Foods (1968), Bohack (1968), and Grand Union

Table 5–9
Average Number of Food Products Manufactured by Forty Largest Chains, 1930–1977

Rank	Average Number of Product Classes Integrated During:					
	1930	*1940*	*1950*	*1963*	*1972*	*1977*
4 largest	18.3	22.3	29.3	33.5	44.0	39.2
5–8 largest	6.7	9.7	15.8	22.8	19.2	20.0
9–20 largest	1.9	1.9	3.6	9.7	10.4	8.2
21–40 largest	.9	1.9	3.3	6.3	6.4	5.6

Source: FTC 1930–1963; U.S. Bureau of the Census, special tabulation 1972, 1977.

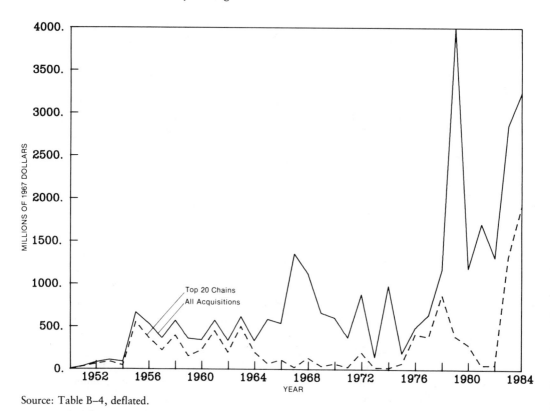

Source: Table B–4, deflated.

Figure 5–8. Acquisitions of Food Retailers in Constant Dollars, 1950–1984

(1968). The FTC issued its opinion in National Tea in 1966, which prohibited the company from making further acquisitions of food retailers for ten years without prior approval of the commission. Consent agreements were subsequently reached with six other chains, most of which imposed a similar restriction on future mergers (Mueller 1978a).

The actions of the FTC and Department of Justice toward mergers by large food chains during this period changed the pattern, if not the tempo, of total mergers in food retailing. Between 1965 and 1974 merger activity by the top twenty chains was sharply lower than during the prior decade (figure 5–8).

The 1965–1967 FTC actions toward mergers by large grocery chains occurred on the eve of the great merger movement that swept U.S. industry between 1967 and 1971. Total merger activity in food retailing, as measured by acquired sales, peaked during the first two years of this period (1967 and 1968), dropped to a level similar to 1955–1956 during the next three years, and then peaked again in 1972 and 1974. Until 1975, the effect of the FTC enforcement policies was to channel this accelerated merger activity away from the top twenty chains but not to stop it.

By the mid-1970s, the FTC was at a public policy crossroads. As the commission's consent orders with leading chains began expiring, the industry waited for signals indicating the direction of future commission merger policy. The FTC had ample opportunity to act during 1975 and 1976 when five substantial mergers occurred:

1. In 1975 Lucky Stores acquired Arden-Mayfair's grocery stores located in Seattle and Tacoma. This was a horizontal merger.
2. In 1976 Winn Dixie, the leading food retailer in the South, acquired Kimbell Stores, Inc., the largest market extension acquisition in food retailing up to that time.
3. In 1976 Allied Supermarkets acquired Great Scott Supermarkets, a substantial horizontal merger in Detroit.
4. In 1976 A&P acquired sixty-two stores of National Tea in Chicago, another substantial horizontal merger.
5. In 1976 Food Town announced its intention to acquire Lowe's Food Stores. This would have been a horizontal and market extension merger between two modest-size food chains in North Carolina.

Of these, the only merger challenged was the last. The FTC obtained a temporary restraining order from the Fourth Circuit Court of Appeals, after which Food Town abandoned the merger.

The failure of the FTC to challenge these mergers, especially the horizontal merger between Lucky and Mayfair and the market extension merger between Winn Dixie and Kimbell, evidently led some large chains to infer that the FTC had abandoned the policy adopted in the 1960s. As *Supermarket News* (1977) put it, the "FTC looked the other way when Winn-Dixie swallowed Kimbell, Inc."

The post-1975 pace of mergers by large chains hit an all-time high in 1978 when the top twenty chains made nine acquisitions that totaled nearly $2 billion in retail sales. The sharp decline in 1981 and 1982 may have stemmed in part from the 1978 challenge by the FTC of Grand Union's acquisition of Colonial Stores and the decision by the administrative law judge in October 1981 declaring the merger illegal. That decision was reversed by the commission in 1983, an action greeted with speculation that it "will certainly spark some firms to look into areas which might have been passed over because of possible FTC intervention" (*Supermarket News*, August 1, 1983, p. 31). Two recent mergers dwarf any previous acquisitions among U.S. supermarket chains. In 1983, Kroger, the second largest food retailer, acquired Dillon Co., which had sales of $2.8 billion in 1982. In 1984, American Stores became the nation's third largest food retailer by acquiring the Jewel Co., which had sales of $5.7 billion in 1983. Acquisitions by the top twenty chains during 1983 and 1984 far exceeded those of any previous year even when converted to 1967 dollars (figure 5–8).

Retrenchments and Divestitures. Prior to the 1970s, supermarket chains in the United States generally followed a strategy of expanding into more metropolitan areas. In the last decade, however, several chains, including some with serious financial problems, have undergone significant retrenchment. A&P withdrew from a large number of markets; Food Fair and National Tea pulled out of several markets. Even some of the more successful chains, such as Kroger, withdrew from some metropolitan areas during the 1970s. The better stores of exiting chains were usually sold to other firms already operating in that market or converted to other types of retail outlets.

The importance and characteristics of divestitures were examined for the five years, 1978–1982. Stores sold as a result of the complete withdrawal of a chain from a market were the primary cases included in the analysis. Divestitures accounted for 18 percent of all acquisitions of food retailers during the five-year period examined. The largest twenty chains made 95 percent of the divestitures during this period and acquired 10 percent of all divested sales.

The sales of stores divested by the top twenty chains totaled $3.88 billion during 1978–1982. Acquisitions by these chains totaled $4.01 billion for the same period, including the $402 million of divested sales acquired. Thus, during this period, the effect on national concentration of acquisitions by the largest twenty chains was almost completely offset by divestitures by these chains. During 1983 and 1984, acquisitions by the top twenty chains far surpassed divestitures.

Foreign Investment in U.S. Food Retailing

A unique aspect of the recent merger activity in grocery retailing has been the purchase of several U.S. food chains by foreign companies. As of March 1982, nineteen foreign companies held 10 percent or more of the stock of U.S. food retailing affiliates. Most of the parent companies were large and were either primarily food retailing companies or had investments in food retailing prior to their investments in the United States. In total, foreign-owned food retailers held 10 percent of all SMSA grocery store sales in 1980 (Marion and Nash 1983). With the exception of the Canadian firm George Weston, foreign direct investment in U.S. food retailing did not occur until the 1970s. A substantial weakening of the U.S. dollar in the late 1970s together with a depressed stock market created an ideal buying environment for European companies. The variation in the value of European currencies against the dollar appears to correspond to both the time pattern of investments in U.S. food retailing and to the prominent role of certain countries in this investment (Marion and Nash 1983).

While foreign investment in U.S. food retailing mushroomed during the 1970s, U.S. food retailing companies have been content to be homebodies for the most part. By 1980, inward foreign investments were nearly four times as large as outward foreign investments in food retailing. Of the major U.S. grocery chains, only Safeway, A&P, Jewel, and Southland had investments in foreign food retailing operations in 1981.

Most of the foreign investments in U.S. food retailing have been by acquisitions by foreign food retailing companies; to some extent they are analogous to geographic market extension mergers by U.S. food retailing companies. As the U.S. dollar has strengthened in the 1980s, foreign investments in U.S. food retailing have dropped sharply, both in dollar sales acquired and as a percentage of food retailing sales acquired. For example, during the three-year period 1978–1980, food retailers acquired by foreign companies accounted for about half of the sales of U.S. food retailing companies acquired. In 1982, the proportion acquired by foreign companies dropped to 9.4 percent.

Looking Ahead

The food retailing industry is in the midst of the most significant transformation in twenty or more years. Although warehouse stores account for only about 10 percent of supermarket sales, they have brought renewed price competition to several metropolitan areas and have stimulated efforts by conventional supermarkets to increase efficiency and reduce operating costs. On the fringe of many markets, "upscale" specialty stores (bakeries, produce markets, cheese and meat shops, and so forth) are enjoying a surge in popularity. The food retailing market has become more segmented.

Super stores and super warehouse stores are the most rapidly growing store formats. A common feature of both is their very large volume. Over time, as these two store types increase in numbers, the concentration of sales and entry barriers are likely to increase in many small and medium-sized SMSAs because they can support only so many very large stores.

Although, on balance, medium-sized chains are probably the most effective-sized competitors, these chains will continue to be acquired by large chains and thereby eliminated as future sources of competition if present antitrust enforcement policy continues. Large chains, although often less aggressive and slower to act than smaller chains, have financial, procurement, and multimarket advantages that cannot be matched by smaller firms. While large chains are rarely innovators in developing new store formats, they have the capital to acquire innovative firms or to develop stores with the new format rapidly. Thus, the enormous resources of the large chains will allow most of them to survive even though they periodically encounter hard times. Independent store operators will probably have the greatest difficulty surviving; neighborhood-type markets may be their best prospect for the future.

The rapid change in information technology will have a substantial effect on food wholesaling and retailing. As a growing proportion of retail stores have electronic scanning tied to computers, reordering and inventory control from the retail store through to manufacturers will be controlled electronically to an increasing extent. The capacity to develop extensive information about consumer behavior and the many factors affecting product movements is rapidly increasing. This will vastly improve understanding of consumer demand and the ability of retailers to meet the preferences of shoppers. It will also provide more opportunities for food manufacturers and retailers to manipulate consumer demand through advertising and merchandising activities. The access rights to this great pool of information are likely to become an important future public policy issue. Will private industry have sole access to this information? Or will universities, governments, and public interest organizations share in the access to and the power of this new information?

Future information systems could be developed to benefit shoppers who have home computers. For example, store computers could accumulate purchase information for each family, which would be accessed by home computers. Computers could also be used to facilitate prepurchase search. The direction that information systems take will depend on the property rights to information, the technology to develop, transmit, and analyze information, and the value that consumers, manufacturers, and others place on such information.

Most consumers and most visitors from other countries would probably give the U.S. food retailing industry high overall grades for its performance. In general, we agree, but there are also present and potential problems in this industry. Competition in a growing number of metropolitan areas and small cities is not as effective as it would be if the leading retailers were less dominant. Entry barriers in some markets are high and are likely to increase in the future. And the recent wave of acquisitions by leading grocery chains has eliminated several viable competitors while yielding few if any benefits to the public. Public-sector actions and decisions on matters such as mergers, predatory behavior, and the property rights to information are likely to affect significantly the future organization and performance of this industry.

Organization of Food Wholesaling

The food wholesaling function consists of the procurement, warehousing, and physical distribution of food products. It is carried out by wholesaling companies, although some food manufacturers and food retailers also perform the function. Most large and many medium-sized retail grocery chains operate their own warehouses and purchase directly from manufacturers. These vertically integrated wholesaling operations, however, are not part of the food wholesaling industry discussed here. Food wholesalers referred to here operate establishments that supply other firms.[12]

Types of Wholesalers

Food wholesalers differ greatly in the services provided, the products handled, and the buyers served. In 1982, approximately 38,500 food wholesaling establishments serviced three-quarters of a million retail food stores and food service operations. Wholesalers are classified by type of operation and kind of business. Types of operation include merchants, brokers, and manufacturers' sales branches and offices. A merchant wholesaler takes title to products and usually has warehouse facilities. A broker sells on the account of others for a commission and normally does not take title or handle products. Manufacturers' sales branches and offices are the field sales forces of manufacturers. A sales branch has storage facilities, whereas a sales office does not. Almost 80 percent of food wholesaling establishments are classified as merchants. The remaining establishments are about equally divided between brokers and manufacturers' sales branches and offices (table 5–10). This chapter will focus primarily on merchant wholesalers.

Wholesalers are also classified by kind of business as either general line or specialty products. General line wholesalers handle a broad line of food and related products and include voluntary and cooperative affiliated wholesalers and unaffiliated wholesalers. Specialty food wholesalers are classified by the products handled (table B–5). Food wholesalers also may specialize by catering to a particular type of customer, such as convenience stores, supermarkets, restaurants, or institutions.

Characteristics

Although 90 percent of all merchant establishments are classified as specialty wholesalers, general line wholesaling establishments are typically much larger (table 5–10).[13] General line merchant wholesalers derive most of their sales (86 percent in 1977) from food retailers, particularly small chain supermarkets and independent stores (figure 5–9). These wholesalers also sometimes supply the supermarkets of large chains that are too distant from the chain's own distribution centers. In 1984, approximately one out of every four chain stores was supplied by affiliated general line wholesalers (*Progressive Grocer* 1985).

Table 5–10

Sales, Establishments, and Employment of Grocery Wholesalers, 1963–1982

Sales, Establishments, Employees, and Type of Wholesaler	*1963*	*1967*	*1972*
Sales (in billions of dollars)			
Specialty merchants	23.0	27.9	42.4
General line merchants	11.7	15.5	21.6
Manufacturers' sales offices	12.4	15.1	21.7
Agents and brokers	13.8	15.9	20.6
Total	60.9	74.4	106.4
Establishments (in thousands)			
Specialty merchants	31.3	28.8	27.1
General line merchants	2.5	2.5	2.8
Manufacturers' sales offices	4.2	4.3	4.0
Agents and brokers	4.5	4.4	4.6
Total	42.5	40.0	38.5
Employees (in thousands)			
Specialty merchants	295.6	305.3	335.9
General line merchants	83.4	92.7	101.3
Manufacturers' sales offices	93.3	97.8	102.0
Agents and brokers	36.5	39.0	40.3
Total	508.8	534.8	579.5

Sources: U.S. Bureau of the Census, *U.S. Census of Business, 1958, Wholesale Trade, United States Summary*, BC58-WA1, U.S. Govt. Print. Off., 1961; U.S. Bureau of the Census, *Census of Business, 1963, Wholesale Trade: United States Summary*, BC63-WA1, U.S. Govt. Print. Off., 1965; U.S. Bureau of the Census, *Census of Business, 1967, Vol. III, Wholesale*

By contrast, 30 percent to 50 percent of the sales of specialty merchant wholesalers, brokers, and manufacturer sales offices were to other wholesalers and 10 to 20 percent to foodservice firms in 1977 (figure 5–9). Sales to food retailers accounted for one-third to one-half of the sales of these wholesalers—roughly one-half the proportion for general line merchant wholesalers.

While over 90 percent of all wholesalers are single establishment firms, multiestablishment firms dominate general line merchant wholesaling. Sysco Corp., the leading general line wholesaler supplying foodservice outlets, operates about sixty distribution centers. The next five largest foodservice wholesalers each operate over twenty distribution centers. Among those general line merchant wholesalers that primarily serve food stores, Super Valu, Fleming, and Wetterau—the top three with roughly one-fifth of this $71 billion submarket in 1984—operated nearly seventy distribution centers between them (*Progressive Grocer* 1985; telephone interviews with company executives). There is widespread agreement that census figures significantly understate the sales of general line merchant wholesalers and overstate specialty merchant sales.

		Percentage				
1977	1982	1963	1967	1972	1977	1982
75.7	113.3	37.7%	37.5%	40.0%	41.4%	39.3%
35.9	59.7	19.2	20.8	20.3	19.6	20.7
41.6	69.3	20.4	20.3	20.3	22.8	24.0
29.7	46.2	22.7	21.4	19.4	16.2	16.0
182.9	288.5	100.0	100.0	100.0	100.0	100.0
26.5	25.8	73.5	72.0	70.4	69.9	67.0
2.7	3.3	5.9	6.2	7.3	7.1	8.6
4.2	4.6	10.0	10.8	10.4	11.1	11.9
4.5	4.8	10.6	11.0	11.9	11.9	12.5
37.9	38.5	100.0	100.0	100.0	100.0	100.0
341.9	373.9	58.1	57.1	57.9	56.8	56.0
110.2	124.4	16.4	17.3	17.5	18.3	18.6
106.8	121.4	18.3	18.3	17.6	17.8	18.2
43.0	48.3	7.2	7.3	7.0	7.1	7.2
601.9	668.0	100.0	100.0	100.0	100.0	100.0

Trade—Subject Reports, U.S. Govt. Print. Off., 1971; U.S. Bureau of the Census, Census of Wholesale Trade, 1972, Area Series, United States, WC72-A-52, U.S. Govt. Print. Off., 1975; and U.S. Bureau of the Census, 1977 Census of Wholesale Trade, Geographic Area Series, United States, WC77-A-52, U.S. Govt. Print. Off., 1980.

Of the two submarkets of general line merchant wholesaling, foodservice and food retailing, the latter is far larger in total sales. "Affiliated" wholesalers, which serve voluntary or cooperative groups of retail stores (examples are IGA, Foodland, and Super Valu), account for most of the sales by general line merchant wholesalers to food retailers. To be competitive with chain supermarkets, independents depend on the numerous services provided by large affiliated wholesalers, (among them site selection, store engineering and layout, financing, accounting, computer support, merchandising, advertising, recommended prices, employee training, and trouble shooting. Some wholesalers buy supermarkets formerly operated by chains and refinance them to independent owner-operators. According to Forbes, Super Valu has almost $100 million loaned to its customers for operating needs (Forbes 1983, p. 203). The larger wholesalers help retailers select scanning equipment and software, provide host computer support at the warehouse level, and provide analysis of item movement data from stores with scanning equipment. Such analysis can improve buying, merchandising, and labor scheduling. Large wholesalers offer their retail customers extensive private label and generic products and consolidated perishable procurement programs that

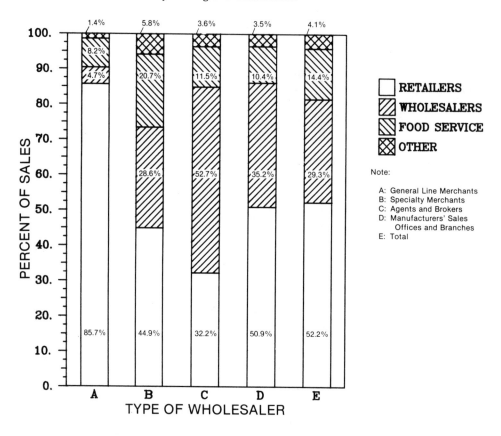

Source: U.S. Bureau of the Census, Census of Wholesale Trade, Subject Series (1977-WC77-S3).

Figure 5–9. Percentage of Sales to Different Customers by Type of Food Wholesaler, 1977

rival similar programs run by the integrated chains. Organizations such as IGA, Shurfine, Red & White, and Foodland provide product specifications, package design, and quality control for private label and generic products and contract with manufacturers to supply these products.

Whereas large, general line merchant wholesalers have been an important factor in supplying independent food stores for many years, a more recent development has been large wholesalers that provide foodservice companies with a complete line of products. Sysco/Sayles, Inc., by far the largest foodservice wholesaler with estimated 1984 sales of $2.5 billion, supplies 90,000 customer outlets from over sixty warehouse locations. Over 80 percent of Sysco's sales are to foodservice firms. Martin-Brower Co. ranked second, with estimated 1984 sales of $1.8 billion. Martin-Brower is a major supplier of McDonald Corp. and other limited-menu chains and has grown very rapidly. CFS Continental, acquired by A.E. Staley in 1984, had estimated sales of $1.4 billion in 1984. PYA/Monarch ranked fourth (1.3 billion), followed by Rykoff-Sexton ($850 million) and Kraft ($826 million) (*Food Institute Report*, February 9, 1985). Except for Consolidated Foods (PYA/Monarch) and Kraft, Inc., few large food manufacturing firms have diversified into general line food wholesaling. Beatrice Foods sold its John Sexton Co. subsidiary to S.E. Rykoff and Co. in 1984.

Trends in Firm Size and Industry Concentration

Between 1963 and 1982, the number of food wholesaling establishments declined by 9 percent while sales increased 374 percent (67 percent after adjusting for inflation). Real sales rose by 87 percent for general line wholesalers and by 70 percent for specialty wholesalers. Because of the decline in establishments operated by specialty merchants, average real sales per establishment increased 75 percent compared to a 36 percent increase in average establishment sales for general line merchants. Real sales per employee increased more for specialty wholesalers (35 percent) than for general line wholesalers (20 percent) during this twenty-year period.

The nation's twenty largest general line wholesale firms accounted for 33 percent of all general line wholesale sales, while the fifty largest firms accounted for 51 percent in 1977 (table B–6). These figures disregard the submarkets served by general line merchant wholesalers. Within the subset of wholesalers that primarily supply food stores, the national concentration of sales is much higher. The leading four companies accounted for about 22 percent of this submarket in 1984 (*Progressive Grocer* 1985 and industry estimates). Similarly, concentration is much higher among general line wholesalers serving the foodservice submarket. The national share held by the fifty largest specialized wholesalers ranged from 22.1 for fresh fruit to 46.8 for dairy wholesalers. National concentration consistently increased from 1972 to 1977 for all types of wholesalers.

Wholesale establishments regularly service retail clients within a 200 mile radius and sometimes service clients as far away as 300 to 400 miles. A 1982 trade study showed that the average distance between general line wholesaler warehouses and stores served was 113 miles; the most distant stores served averaged 271 miles from the warehouse (Food Marketing Institute 1982, p. 4). Since wholesalers operate in relatively local markets, national concentration ratios provide no indication of market power or dominance in relevant economic markets but do indicate the size of the largest wholesalers.

Concentration in local geographic areas gives a better indication of potential market power and the alternatives available to retailers in selecting wholesale suppliers. In an effort better to approximate geographic markets faced by wholesalers, USDA researchers defined fourteen grocery marketing areas (GMAs) for the special tabulation of the 1972 census of wholesale trade. GMAs included at least two and as many as nine SMSAs. For example, the Boston GMA was a combination of four SMSAs: Boston, Lawrence-Haverhill, Lowell, and Brockton.

CR4 for general line food wholesalers across the fourteen GMAs averaged 73 percent in 1972, ranging from a low of 58 percent in the San Francisco GMA to a high of 89 percent in Cleveland and Seattle GMAs. Among the specialty wholesalers, meat, other grocery, and fresh produce wholesalers were least concentrated, with CR4s ranging from 32 to 35 percent. Combined market shares of the four leading confectionery firms were highest, averaging 63 percent across the fourteen GMAs.

It is not clear how one should interpret these relatively high concentration ratios. Since wholesaler growth is heavily dependent on the growth of their retail clients, competition between independent retailers and integrated chains provides indirect constraints on the ability of large wholesalers to charge higher prices, even in areas where they may enjoy some market power. A wholesaler that raises prices to supermarket customers to the extent that they are unable to compete with chains will gradually lose its customer base. In this regard, it is important to distinguish between general line wholesalers that primarily serve independent supermarkets and small chains and the general line wholesalers primarily serving convenience stores, other small grocery stores, and foodservice outlets. The former may be constrained in their pricing to a greater extent than the latter.

In addition, large general line wholesalers supply substantially more services than their smaller counterparts. These support services are becoming more expensive and sophisticated. Economies of size in providing a full range of support services have contributed to the growing number of acquisitions of general line wholesalers. It has also led to formation of a few groups of noncompeting wholesalers that work together to develop common computer systems and certain other services. The provision of electronic services and financial assistance to retail customers is cited by industry representatives as the two major factors requiring larger firm size. One wholesale executive estimated that affiliated wholesalers serving supermarket accounts need to have annual sales of at least $1 billion in order to provide these services. The benefits of economies of size and increased services in general line wholesaling *may* be sufficient to outweigh the losses in competitive rivalry as wholesalers become larger and fewer. At this point, the data needed to assess this trade-off are not available.

Mergers and Acquisitions

Mergers have substantially increased the size of several large general line wholesalers. According to the Food Institute (1985), food wholesaling firms initiated 335 acquisitions between 1973 and 1984. These data do not include instances where wholesalers were acquired by nonwholesalers. Of the total acquisitions, 60 percent involved food wholesalers acquiring all or part of other wholesalers; 27 percent were acquisitions of groups of retail food stores; and 13 percent were acquisitions of other firms, such as trucking companies, food manufacturers, and nonfood retailers.

Food wholesalers averaged twenty-two acquisitions each year during the 1970s (figure 5–10). The merger pace then quickened to thirty-six mergers per year between 1980 and 1984. There has been a sharp increase in mergers between large wholesalers since 1980.

Super Valu (ranked first) acquired Western Grocery in 1982, West Coast Grocery Co. in 1985, and four chain distribution centers. Fleming, the second largest wholesaler, acquired McLain Grocery Co. in 1981, Waples Platter Co. in 1982, American-Strevell in 1983, Giant Wholesale in 1983, and United Grocers in 1984. Wetterau, ranked third in 1984, acquired Milliken-Tomlinson Co. in 1980, Fox Grocery in 1981, and Creasey Co. in 1985.

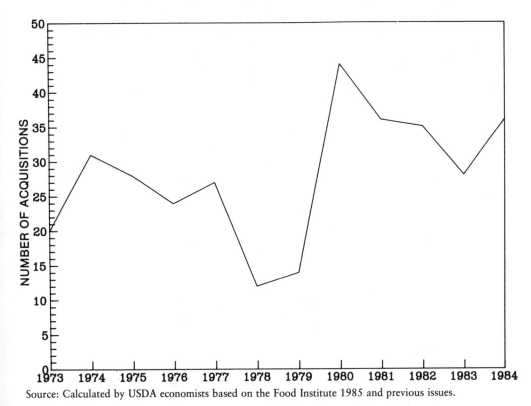

Source: Calculated by USDA economists based on the Food Institute 1985 and previous issues.

Figure 5–10. Total Number of Acquisitions by U.S. Food Wholesalers, 1973–1984

Farm House Foods, Scrivner, and Roundy's are other wholesalers that significantly increased their sales through acquisitions in the 1980s. Most mergers have been among voluntary wholesalers, but several cooperative wholesalers have also merged. Clearly grocery wholesaling has not been immune from merger mania.

According to *Progressive Grocer*'s 1982 *Marketing Guidebook*, most major local wholesale markets are served by three to six large affiliated general line wholesalers. Horizontal mergers among large wholesalers with warehouses serving the same local market would reduce the number of alternative suppliers available to retailers in that market area. To the extent that the larger affiliated wholesalers already realize the available economies of size, horizontal mergers between these firms probably are not in the public interest. To date, most mergers have been geographic market extensions of the acquiring firms. Where the acquired wholesaler is considerable distance from the area served by the acquiring wholesaler, the acquisition may provide the latter with a foothold in a new region from which it will expand internally. Each acquisition must be examined case by case to determine the likely competitive consequences. Market extension mergers contribute to the increase in national concentration among general line wholesalers, which may increase their power as buyers.

Entry barriers are high for affiliated general line wholesalers; in fact, de novo entry for these firms has been almost nonexistent in recent years. It is extremely difficult for a wholesaler entering a market to attract retail customers away from their current general line wholesaler in large enough numbers and quickly enough to make de novo entry feasible. Retailers become tied to a particular wholesaler's private label products, store name (such as IGA), computer support services, and merchandising programs. Switching to a new primary supplier may disrupt store operations and might require store customers to become familiar with a new store name and different private label brands. Barriers to entry for specialty wholesalers, however, are relatively low. Size of operations is much smaller, and firms typically offer few, if any, customer support services.

Integration and Diversification

Most firms engaged in food wholesaling have not diversified into other lines of business, nor have they generally integrated forward into retailing or backward into manufacturing. A few large affiliated wholesalers do own numerous retail stores.

In 1977, of the 513,766 employees of food wholesaling firms, 70 percent were employed by companies engaged only in food wholesaling. The remaining 30 percent were employed by food wholesalers that had integrated or diversified into other industries. In contrast, in 1963 only 13 percent of employees of all food wholesaling firms were employed by food wholesalers with operations in other industries. The share of food wholesaler employment located in other industries increased from 3 percent in 1963 to 10 percent in 1977. Thus, although the overall level of diversification is relatively low, diversification among food wholesalers is growing quite rapidly. Most of the employment outside wholesaling has occurred in retail trade and food manufacturing.

Operating Expenses

Operating expenses in 1977 (the latest data available) averaged 7.3 percent of sales for general line merchants, 11.6 percent for specialty merchants, 3.8 percent for brokers, and 7.9 percent for manufacturers' sales branches and offices (table B–7). Differences reflect functions performed; those with higher operating expenses generally provide more product handling, storage, refrigeration, and transportation services. Large operations in general have substantially lower operating expense ratios than comparable but smaller wholesalers. Some small establishments serve a particular need (such as small orders, special services, or frequent deliveries) for which customers are willing to pay a premium.

Brokers neither own nor handle the products they sell, so they have the lowest operating expenses. Specialty merchant wholesalers store, transport, and take title to the products they sell, and many deliver small quantities to scattered customers. General line merchants primarily sell to retail food stores and foodservice customers. Voluntary and cooperative general line wholesalers, which sell mainly to supermarkets, enjoy scale economies and low operating expenses (6.0 percent of sales). The remaining general line wholesalers, which sell to other food stores, restaurants, and institutions, generally are smaller, fill smaller orders, and have higher operating expenses (9.9 percent of sales in 1977). Manufacturers' sales branches often operate much like specialty merchant wholesalers, while manufactuers' sales officers operate more like brokers. As a result, average operating expenses of manufacturers' sales branches and offices fall between those of specialty merchants and brokers, averaging 7.9 percent in 1977.

Operating expenses as a percentage of sales were about the same in 1972 and 1977 for general line merchant wholesalers. Operating expenses as a percentage of sales decreased for manufacturers' sales branches and increased slightly for agents and brokers.

In addition to firm economies of size, there are also significant economies of scale in general line grocery warehousing. A USDA study found that per unit operating expenses in dry grocery warehouses declined as weekly volume increased from 100,000 cases to 500,000 cases (about $475 million per year in 1984 dollars) (Crawford and Grinnell 1976). A Cornell study reported that per unit costs continued to decline for warehouses handling over 900,000 cases per week (Roller and Lesser 1983).

Labor productivity in dry grocery warehouses (tons handled per hour of direct labor) increased only 5 to 10 percent during the 1970s according to the National American Wholesale Grocers' Association. Since real hourly earnings rose more than 15 percent, real labor costs per unit of output probably increased 5 to 10 percent.

A recent USDA study found a sizable gap between actual and potential labor productivity for a cross-section of nine dry grocery warehouses (Grinnell and Friedman 1982). By achieving a more balanced warehouse workload, improving work methods and assignments, adopting new equipment, and encouraging unitized shipments from suppliers, it was estimated that the sample warehouses could reduce their labor requirements by nearly 50 percent. Roller and Lesser (1983) estimated potential per unit cost savings ranging from 5 to over 50 percent for a sample of thirty-nine grocery warehouses. Both studies conclude that there are significant technical and managerial inefficiencies in the food wholesaling industry. Competitive pressures from other wholesalers and integrated chains apparently have not been strong enough to result in prompt adoption of available technology.

Profit Margins

In 1976, gross margins for all voluntary and cooperative general line merchant wholesalers averaged 7.6 percent of sales (table 5–11). Gross margins declined slightly for firms in the $50 million to $99.9 million sales class and then increased somewhat for firms with sales of $100 million or more. The higher gross margin for the largest sales class may, in part, reflect the greater array of support services typically provided by the larger wholesalers. Net profits before taxes averaged 1.7 percent for voluntary wholesalers and increased as the size of firm increased. Unfortunately, even the largest sales

Table 5–11
Gross Margins and Profits of Grocery Wholesalers as a Percentage of Sales, 1976

Type of Merchant and Sales	Gross Margin	Profits
Voluntary and cooperative	7.6	1.7
$50 million sales or less	7.5	0.5
$50–99.9 million sales	6.6	0.8
$100 million sales or more	7.8	2.2
All specialty merchants	14.4	2.9
$10 million sales or less	17.7	3.4
$10–24.9 million sales	11.7	2.3
$25 million or more	8.4	2.1

Source: Special survey. U.S. Bureau of the Census, 1976.

class used by census for the 1976 survey was much too small to provide useful information on the larger firms in grocery wholesaling.

Specialty merchant wholesalers' gross margins averaged 14 percent, while net profit margins averaged 2.9 percent of sales. Both gross margins and profits as a percentage of sales declined as the size of firm increased.

Food wholesaling is essentially a pass-through industry; most wholesalers do little manufacturing or retailing, and a firm's success is strongly linked to its efficiency in meeting customers' particular product and service needs. Profit margins as a percentage of equity for many large wholesalers are among the highest in the food distribution system. For example, the five-year (1978–1982) average return on equity for eleven leading general line wholesalers ranged from 28.0 percent to 9.0 percent, with a median value of 15.5 percent (table 5–12). In spite of the attractive profits, there has been virtually no entry by nonwholesaling companies.

Outlook

Voluntary and cooperative wholesalers will continue to grow larger due to the size required to provide the services demanded by retail customers. The electronic revolution that is affecting all industries will require substantial technical involvement and support by wholesalers. Analysis of retail scanning data, computer warehouse management systems, and the uniform communication system (UCS), which will facilitate computer-to-computer ordering and billing, are examples of the increasing role of computers and electronic communication. This will result in a more tightly coordinated distribution system and allow lower inventory levels to be maintained at both wholesale and retail.

Table 5–12
Profits as a Percentage of Equity for Leading General Line Wholesalers

Company	Return on Equity, Five-Year-Average
Super Valu Stores	28.0%
Fleming	18.0
Malone & Hyde	17.5
Wetterau	12.5
SYSCO	19.2
S.M. Flickinger	15.5
Super Food Services	12.1
Scot Lad Foods	9.0
Pacific Gamble Robinson	10.3
Nash Finch	14.9
Farm House Foods	19.8

Source: *Forbes*, "Wholesalers" in 35th Annual Report on American Industry, January 3, 1983, p. 203.

Many larger general line wholesalers are picking up additional chain accounts as the latter focus financial resources on expanding and upgrading retail operations. As large wholesalers expand their retailer support services, they will increasingly seek to influence and even direct trends in retailing rather than just react to their customers' needs. Wholesalers are now developing and refining new store formats, operating these stores in test markets, and then seeking independent retailers to purchase the stores and expand to new locations.

As affiliated general line wholesalers increase in size, there is likely to be a trade-off between operational efficiency and allocative efficiency. Most relevant geographic markets will support only a small number (say, one to four) of general line wholesalers of the size necessary to achieve economies of scale. To a considerable extent, effective competition in food wholesaling depends on effective competition in retail markets. If retail competition is soft, wholesalers are likely to receive less pressure from their customers to trim costs, keep prices low, and so forth. Similarly, if all the major retailers in a metropolitan area are supplied by two or three wholesalers, there may be less pressure on wholesalers than if one or more of the leading retail firms is an integrated chain supplied by an efficient warehouse. Thus, the effectiveness of competition among affiliated wholesalers may well depend on the characteristics of the retail market areas in which their customers operate.

Foodservice Industry

The foodservice industry can be loosely defined as those firms that dispense prepared meals and/or snacks for on-premise or immediate consumption. The industry can be divided into the commercial and noncommercial segments (table 5–13). The commercial segment is comprised of foodservice operations that are readily accessible to the public at large; examples are fast food operations, restaurants, and cafeterias. With the exception of the foodservice operations of hotels, recreational facilities, and some retail stores, commercial foodservice operations are not run as subsidiary or complementary operations to other business activity.

The noncommercial segment of the industry includes foodservice operations that are run primarily as subsidiary or complementary operations to other business or service activities, such as schools and universities, hospitals, airlines, and in-plant feeding. Access to these foodservice facilities is largely confined to persons who either work in or are users of the primary service or business activity.

Van Dress (1984) has estimated the meal and snack sales of establishments in the commercial and noncommercial segments for 1977 through 1984. His estimates indicate 73 percent of these sales were done by commercial foodservice firms in 1984 and 27 percent by noncommercial (table 5–13).

Table 5–13
Estimated Meal and Snack Sales of Various Segments of Food-Service Industry, 1977–1984
(millions of dollars)

Segments of the Food-Service Industry	Estimated Meals and Snacks Sales		
	1984	1980	1977
Commercial feeding			
Separate eating places[a]	99,582	67,557	47,426
Restaurants, lunchrooms	(48,419)	(35,615)	(24,720)
Fast food outlets[b]	(47,319)	(28,706)	(20,334)
Cafeterias	(3,022)	(2,426)	(1,813)
Lodging places	7,264	5,235	3,613
Retail hosts[c]	4,779	3,535	2,691
Recreation, entertainment[d]	3,394	2,362	1,915
Separate drinking places	1,076	1,100	979
Total commercial feeding	116,095	79,812	56,624
Noncommercial feeding			
Schools and universities	12,239	10,833	8,242
Plants, office buildings	6,793	5,145	3,576
Hospitals and care facilities	11,098	8,521	6,099
Vending	3,553	3,094	2,508
Military services	2,366	1,934	1,595
Transportation	1,922	1,563	1,079
Other	4,418	2,975	2,052
Total noncommercial feeding	42,389	34,065	25,151
Total	158,484	113,877	81,775

Source: Van Dress 1984.

[a]Sales for separate eating places exceed the sum of sales for the three segments listed because the sales of social caterers are included in the total but not in any of the three segments. The sales of contract feeders are excluded from the sales of separate eating places and are included with the segment in which they operate.

[b]Includes the sales of ice cream stands.

[c]Foodservice operations within retail establishments such as department stores, variety stores, drugstores, retail bakeries, delicatessens, and gasoline stations.

[d]Foodservice operations in sporting and recreation camps, commercial sports establishments, bowling alleys, golf courses, athletic clubs, amusement parks, theaters, and similar places.

Within the commercial segment, separate eating places accounted for 86 percent of sales (or 63 percent of commercial and noncommercial sales).[14]

During the past twenty years, significant shifts have occurred in the sales accounted for by various types of commercial foodservice operations. Limited menu operations (fast food firms) have increased sharply in relative importance. Census data indicate limited menu operations accounted for 19 percent of commercial feeding sales in 1967 and 36 percent in 1977. Their market share increased to 39 percent in 1982, indicating a tapering off of growth rates; however, the sales growth of limited menu establishments was still somewhat faster than full menu establishments between 1977 and 1982.

Establishment Size

The average annual sales (in 1972 dollars) of eating place establishments increased from $106,490 in 1967 to $149,982 in 1982, a 41 percent increase. Although full menu establishments had larger average sales, limited menu establishments (fast food establishments) grew much faster in average size during this fifteen-year period. In 1967 the average sales of limited menu places was 60 percent of the sales of restaurants and lunchrooms; by 1982, this had increased to 86 percent.

Multiunit Operations

In 1967, multiunit operations accounted for 24 percent of sales and 10 percent of eating place establishments. By 1982, these shares had increased to 48 percent and 27 percent, respectively (table 5–14). Over 85 percent of the increase in multiunit sales was attributable to the expansion of fast food operations.

Table 5–14
Single and Multiunit Restaurant Sales by Type of Establishment, Census Years 1967, 1972, and 1982, Current Dollars

Classification	Sales (millions of dollars)			Percentage Sales		
	1967	1972	1982	1967	1972	1982
Eating places	17,955.5	28,208.9	90,671.3	100.0	100.0	100.0
Fast food places[a]	3,417.6	8.208.9	34,803.1	19.0	29.1	38.4
Single units	2,603.0	4,825.0	14,240.3	14.5	17.1	15.7
Multiunits	814.6	3,383.9	20,562.7	4.5	12.0	22.7
2–5 units	363.8	1,059.3	5,014.1	2.0	3.8	5.5
6–10 units	74.6	265.0	2,005.5	0.4	0.9	2.2
11 or more units	376.2	2,059.7	13,069.3	2.1	7.3	14.4
Other eating places[b]	14,537.9	20,000.0	55,868.2	81.0	70.9	61.6
Single units	11,087.1	14,475.3	33,021,4	61.7	51.3	36.4
Multiunits	3,450.7	5,524.7	22,846.9	19.2	19.6	25.2
2–5 units	981.1	1,567.2	4,706.9	5.5	5.6	5.2
6–10 units	282.9	477.7	1,168.7	1.6	1.7	1.3
11 or more units	2,186.7	3,479.9	15,953.9	12.2	12.3	17.6

Source: Bureau of the Census, 1982 Census of Retail Trade (and previous years).

Note: Includes only those establishments with payroll that were operating at the end of the year. The 1967 data do not exclude sales for establishments closed during the year.

[a]Fast food places correspond to the census classification "Refreshment Places."

[b]Includes cafeterias, catering places, and restaurants/lunchrooms.

Foodservice chains (eleven or more units) accounted for 32.0 percent of all eating places sales in 1982, up from 14.3 percent in 1967. During this fifteen-year period, the share of full menu eating place sales captured by chains increased from 15 percent to 29 percent. The share of fast food sales accounted for by chains rose from 11 percent to 38 percent during this period.

Firm Size

The dramatic changes in the commercial foodservice business have rapidly eroded the position of small firms. In 1982, 144,000 firms with annual sales of less than $500,000 accounted for nearly two-thirds of eating place establishments but only 26 percent of eating place sales, down from 41 percent of sales in 1977 (Bureau of the Census 1982c). In 1982, forty-nine foodservice firms with sales of $100 million or more accounted for 21 percent of eating place sales and only 10.3 percent of total establishments. Although this market share is still relatively low, large firms are making rapid inroads.

Fast food firms accounted for nearly 42 percent of the sales by all commercial foodservice firms with sales of $100 million or more in 1982 (Bureau of the Census 1982c). This percentage would have been much higher if the sales of all franchisees had been included with those of franchisors in the calculations.

Advertising by foodservice firms is much more concentrated than sales. Twenty-five foodservice chains did 87 percent of all media advertising by foodservice firms in 1982 (Leading National Advertisers 1983). McDonalds alone accounted for 28 percent of foodservice media advertising (table 5–15). Twelve of the twenty-five largest advertising chains are owned by large food manufacturing companies.

Franchising

Franchising is an important activity for many foodservice firms. Franchise restaurant operations had aggregate sales of $44.1 billion in 1984 (table 5–16), accounting for approximately 39 percent of eating place sales. This represented a 16 percent increase over their share in 1972. The largest franchise systems—those with more than 500 establishments—accounted for about 72 percent of franchise sales in 1982, up from 62 percent a decade earlier. Franchisor-owned operations (top half of table 5–16) were responsible for 34.8 percent of franchise system sales and 30.8 percent of all franchise establishments in 1984.

Concentration of Sales in Foodservice

Census data indicate that commercial foodservice sales are highly fragmented at the national level. In 1977, the four largest firms accounted for 4.5 percent of all eating place sales (up from 3.6 percent in 1972); the largest twenty firms held

Table 5–15
Six-Media Advertising Expenditures by Twenty-five Foodservice Chains with Largest Advertising in 1982
(thousands of dollars)

Parent Company and Food Service Chain	Chain Advertising Rank	6-Media Total	Spot TV	Network TV	Other
McDonalds	1	161,067.8	94,156.0	59,875.9	7,035.9
Pillsbury					
Burger King	2	65,062.7	82,758.7	35,400.4	903.5
Steak & Ale	16	5,659.6	2,824.0	2,798.7	36.9
R.J. Reynolds					
KFC	3	42,630.8	14,845.5	27,184.3	601.1
Pepsico					
Pizza Hut	4	35,736.3	22,402.8	13,282.5	51.0
Taco Bell	10	11,508.0	11,473.8		34.2
Wendy's	5	32,289.8	17,790.2	13,817.3	682.3
General Mills					
Red Lobster	6	25,958.7	25,866.4		92.3
York Steak	22	2,583.3	2,560.6		22.7
Jerrico					
Long John Silver's	7	20,187.0	20,159.0		28.0
Dennys	8	17,132.3	4,470.5	12,426.5	235.3
Royal Crown					
Arby's	9	12,434.1	7,398.4	4,801.9	233.8
Imasco					
Hardee's	11	11,190.9	10,794.5		396.3
Burger Chef	18	5,042.8	4,968.6		74.2
Dairy Queen	12	9,071.7	8,744.1		327.6
Ralston Purina					
Jack-in-the-Box	13	8,8178.8	8,795.7		22.1
Collins Foods					
Sizzler Steak Houses	14	8,670.0	8,644.8		25.2
Godfather's Pizza	15	5,904.5	5,855.4		49.1
Marriott					
Big Boy	17	5,228.5	5,223.8		4.7
Roy Rogers	21	3,193.0	3,172.9		20.1
Brock Hotel Co.					
Show Biz Pizza	19	4,084.1	4,021.2		62.9
Carl Karcher					
Carl's Jr.	20	3,412.4	3,246.9		165.5
Hershey					
Friendly Ice Cream	23	2,533.3	2.056.9	476.4	
Holiday Inns					
Perkins	24	2,410.0	2,324.3		85.7
Pizza Inn	25	2,202.9	2,188.9		14.0
Top 25 chains total		504,012.3	322,744.0	170,063.9	11,204.4
Top 4 chains		304,497.6	160,163.0	135,743.1	8,591.5
Top chain		161,067.8	94,156.0	59,875.9	7,035.9
Leading National Advertisers total		578,085.8	386,462.0	170,104.1	21,519.7

Source: Leading National Advertisers 1983.

a combined market share of 12.4 percent. Even within more narrowly defined market segments, national concentration levels tend to be low. For example, the four largest fast food firms accounted for 9.1 percent of U.S. fast food sales in 1977; the twenty largest accounted for 19.3 percent of sales (Schmelzer 1981).

Although these figures are of some value, they provide no indication of the level of concentration in relevant economic markets. Competition among foodservice firms as sellers occurs primarily at the local level—that is, in towns, cities, and metropolitan areas. In selecting an eating place, consumers in Chicago rarely consider traveling to New York or Philadelphia; rather, they choose from the eating places in the Chicago metropolitan area, and often from establishments in their part of Chicago. As with most other types of retailing, concentration figures for local markets and submarkets are needed.

Defining relevant product markets also poses problems. Are hamburger fast food outlets, pizza parlors, and full menu restaurants direct competitors? In the minds of consumers, are they close substitutes? Alternatively, do pizza outlets primarily compete with other pizza establishments, hamburger fast food outlets with other hamburger fast food outlets, and so on? Or do food-service firms compete primarily on price and service levels—that is, low-priced fast service firms compete in one submarket while high-priced full service firms compete in a separate submarket? Although we each might have a judgment on this from our own experience no empirical data are available to help cluster those eating places that are close substitutes for consumers and therefore direct competitors.

Further compounding the problem of developing useful concentration figures is the extensive use of franchising. Census calculates concentration figures on the basis of ownership. Thus, in a franchise system, only the sales of outlets owned by the franchisor are added together. To the extent that the franchisor largely controls the operations and buying-selling behavior of franchisees, this results in an understatement of concentration. If franchisees have considerable independence in their buying and selling behavior, the census procedure may be appropriate.

Excluding franchisee sales probably results in a significant understatement of the actual level of national buyer concentration in the foodservice business. Many franchisors secure favorable purchasing arrangements with their suppliers on the basis of their total system-wide product usage. While franchisors are largely prohibited from forcing their franchisees to participate in such arrangements, the lower prices resulting from these arrangements are often an inducement for franchisee participation.

Based on system-wide sales data, the four largest fast food firms accounted for an estimated 41 percent of all fast food sales in 1977. This combined share was about 6 percent larger than the share the four largest firms held in 1972 and about twice as large as their share in 1964. The combined sales of the twenty largest fast food firms represented 71 percent of fast food sales in 1977, up from 42 percent in 1964 (Schmelzer 1981). Clearly national

Table 5–16
Franchisor and Franchisee Restaurant Numbers and Sales Classified by Major Menu Offering, Selected Years

Classification	Units		
	1972	*1977*	*1984*
Franchisor owned	6,319	14,527	23,087
Chicken	816	1,729	3,197
Hamburger/roast beef	2,399	4,293	6,952
Pizza	781	2,756	4,464
Mexican	270	1,300	1,611
Seafood	183	878	1,602
Pancakes, waffles	134	273	508
Steak/full menu	1,724	3,136	4,294
Sandwich and other	12	162	459
Franchisee owned	26,219	37,445	51,755
Chicken	3,745	4,708	6,292
Hamburger/roast beef	16,925	20,529	23,706
Pizza	1,604	4,003	9,033
Mexican	636	847	2,072
Seafood	304	1,469	1,764
Pancakes, waffles	601	1,080	1,190
Steak/full menu	2,169	4,117	5,633
Sandwich and other	235	692	2,065
Total	32,538	51,972	74,842

Source: *Franchising in the Economy*, selected years.
[a]In current dollars. Column entries may not add to totals due to rounding error.

concentration among fast food firms has increased rapidly. Although these concentration figures do not accurately measure the level of buyer concentration (other foodservice firms are also buyers, and some buying takes place in regional rather than national markets), they do suggest that large fast food firms have become a more powerful influence in the food system. Companies like McDonalds have had a significant influence on the vertical production and processing system that supplies them with french fried potatoes, ground beef, and other products.

Vertical Integration in Commercial Foodservice

Vertical integration by ownership is not prevalent throughout the commercial foodservice sector, and there is no clearly identifiable trend toward either vertical integration or disintegration by foodservice firms. Some firms have vertically integrated backward into the foodservice wholesaler-distributor stage and/or operate commissary facilities. These firms tend to be the largest

Sales[a] (millions of dollars)			Sales/Unit (thousands of dollars, 1972)[b]		
1972	1977	1984	1972	1977	1984
1,753.3	5,653.2	15,360.8	277.464	254.705	261.628
194.1	569.2	1,652.6	237.868	215.460	203.265
711.9	2,242.2	5,635.0	296.749	341.850	318.729
90.5	556.1	1,916.8	115.877	132.056	168.846
40.7	238.3	906.4	150.741	119.953	221.239
25.2	224.8	1,098.0	137.705	167.562	269.511
30.1	103.5	294.2		248.214	227.728
656.6	1,703.5	3,761.8	380.858	355.531	344.485
4.3	15.7	96.1		63.512	82.329
5,044.1	12,527.2	28.786.8	192.383	218.969	218.715
819.6	1,519.7	2,757.6	218.852	211.272	172.337
3,055.6	6,858.6	15,680.4	180.538	218.671	260.097
209.0	860.2	3,248.5	130.299	140.649	141.413
72.6	256.8	828.0	114.151	198.436	157.137
35.3	354.3	866.3	116.118	157.856	193.111
144.6	448.6	635.1		271.857	209.861
686.6	2,119.2	4.311.2	316.551	336.905	300.951
20.7	109.9	459.5		103.919	87.499
6,797.4	18,180.4	44,167.6	208.907	228.958	231.952

[b]The food-away-from-home component of the CPI was converted to a 1972 base and used to deflate sales.

firms that operate coffee shops, family restaurants, and foodservice management operations. Firms that operate fast food facilities and dinner house or theme restaurants are less likely to be vertically integrated. Even the largest firms with these types of foodservice operations are not vertically integrated. For example, only six of the eighteen largest fast food firms in 1979 operated distribution and/or commissary facilities. This is in sharp contrast to grocery retailing, where nearly all of the top one hundred chains are vertically integrated at least through the wholesale distribution stage.

There are a number of reasons for this pattern of integration. Large firms that operate coffee shops and family restaurants tend to rely less on franchising as a vehicle for expansion than do large fast food firms. Thus, a single management team directly controls the restaurant operations and ordering procedures of all of their outlets. This provides a captive market that often can be served efficiently by integrated wholesale facilities operated by the parent organization. In a franchise system, by contrast, the individual franchisees maintain considerable autonomy with respect to purchasing decisions.

Franchisors cannot be certain that their franchisees would buy from franchisor-owned distribution facilities if they were available.

The emergence of multimarket foodservice distributors that specialize in the service of fast food restaurants is another reason why large fast food firms have not integrated backward. The development of these distributors, which began in the late 1960s, has simplified the interfirm coordination process. Instead of dealing with different, nonspecialized distributors in each local or regional market area, large fast food firms can now develop distribution agreements with fewer but more specialized foodservice wholesalers. This enables fast food operators to concentrate their purchasing among fewer firms and may allow them to negotiate lower margins on purchased items than would be possible if they dealt with individual distributors in each market area.

General Procurement Practices

Among limited menu firms, it is common practice to negotiate fixed price contracts directly with food and paper processors and then enter into separate distribution agreements with distributors. The distributors perform the general wholesaling function for the foodservice firm and coordinate retail level deliveries with store managers. Distributors order products from designated food and paper processors as specified by the retailer. Cost-plus distribution arrangements are common in these relationships. Franchisors often use this type of distribution arrangement and generally make it available to their franchisees on a voluntary basis.

Although such arrangements are voluntary on the franchisee's part, franchisors usually maintain some control by limiting the available sources of supply, typically accomplished through the use of supplier or distributor approval programs run by franchisors. These programs serve a dual purpose for franchisors: they assist in maintaining quality standards throughout the franchise system and permit the franchisor to concentrate purchases among fewer processors and thereby increase franchisor buying power. These programs are important to franchisors, as evidenced by the fact that each of the twenty largest franchisors imposed such restrictions on their franchisees in 1979 (Schmelzer 1981).

Conditions of Entry

At the individual store level, entry barriers into the foodservice business appear to be modest. In any metropolitan area, there is almost continual entry and exit of various types of eating places. Entry conditions vary considerably by market segment and the extent to which consumer preferences are being satisfied. The first Mexican or French restaurant in an area may find entry relatively easy, whereas later entry may be difficult.

Entry by an independent eating establishment is quite different from entry by a franchised outlet. The latter can frequently rely on the expertise and support of the franchisor for site selection, store layout and equipment, advertising and promotions, menu, sources of supply, and other services. However, franchise systems vary greatly in their appeal to consumers. Thus, becoming a franchisee is not always the easier method of entry.

Franchisee start-up costs are relatively modest. According to a Department of Commerce study, median start-up cash for franchisee operations in 1980 was $60,000. Total investments for such operations ranged from $40,000 to $2 million, with a median investment of $175,000.

As fast food firms have rapidly increased their share of eating place sales, good sites have become an important barrier to entry and expansion. Established foodservice firms such as Hardee's and Marriott Corporation have recently purchased or merged with other foodservice operators (Burger Chef and Gino's) for the express purpose of gaining access to the attractive real estate holdings of the acquired firms. If future expansion opportunities are conditional on the acquisition of existing store locations, entry by small or medium-sized operations may be curtailed.

Entry by a new foodservice chain or the development of a new foodservice system is more difficult than entry at the individual outlet level. The established market position of firms such as McDonalds, Wendys, or Kentucky Fried Chicken may constitute sizable barriers for new hamburger or chicken chain entrants into a metropolitan area. Most foodservice chains will enter a new metropolitan market only if they feel they can successfully develop a number of outlets in the market. This often means directly challenging encumbent foodservice firms, which may yield market share grudgingly.

Mergers in Foodservice

Mergers and acquisitions involving large foodservice firms have been commonplace since the mid-1960s. The growth opportunities within the industry and the accompanying demand for capital to sustain individual firm growth have been important factors influencing merger activity.

Between 1976 and 1980, thirty-two of the one hundred largest commercial foodservice firms of 1979 were involved in at least one merger or acquisition. This included nine of the ten largest firms and twenty-four of the fifty largest firms. Vertical and conglomerate mergers resulted in the acquisition of over 6,100 establishments with total sales in excess of $2.75 billion. Market extension-type mergers (between firms in different segments of foodservice industry) resulted in the acquisition of an additional 1,750 establishments with sales of over $820 million. If the establishments and sales of franchisee-operated businesses are included with those of acquired franchisors, about 12,000 establishments with sales in excess of $4.7 billion were affected by vertical, conglomerate, and market extension mergers during this five-year period (Schmelzer 1981).

Mergers and acquisitions have been the primary vehicles used by food and tobacco processors to enter the foodservice industry. Between 1965 and 1980, thirty-eight of the two hundred largest food and tobacco processors of 1975 made seventy vertical acquisitions of foodservice firms. Slightly over $3 billion in sales and nearly 10,000 establishments were acquired. Although foodservice firms operating in all segments of the industry were acquired, approximately one-third of acquired sales and about 45 percent of acquired establishments were in the limited menu segment (Schmelzer 1981).

The significance of mergers as an entry vehicle can be more fully appreciated by noting that the foodservice holdings of thirty-six of the forty-six large processors with such operations in 1979 were directly attributable to mergers. This included all of the twenty-three franchise systems sponsored by processors. In recent years, some food processors have sold their foodservice operations, while other processors have expanded their holdings.

All segments of the foodservice business, from wholesale distribution to eating places and institutional feeding, appear to have important changes still facing them in the future.

Notes

1. There is no official definition of a supermarket. *Progressive Grocer* used $500,000 in sales or more in 1972, $1 million or more in 1977, and $2 million or more in annual sales in 1982. Some industry associations used $1 million as the minimum sales in 1972 and $1.5 million in 1977. A special census tabulation for 1977 used $1.5 million as the cut-off, and found that 73 percent of grocery store sales were done by supermarkets. The figures used in figure 5–1 were estimated by Alden Manchester of the Economic Research Service, USDA, using census data.

2. The term *item* refers to the smallest breakdown of products in a store. Differences in size, brand, flavor, or type of package result in different items; for example, 1 liter and 2 liter bottles of Seven-up are two items. *Stock keeping unit* (SKU) is synonymous with *item*.

3. Although SMSAs are generally reasonable approximations of relevant geographic markets, this is not always the case. The evidence presented in the FTC–Grand Union case indicated that the Raleigh-Durham and Greenville-Spartanburg SMSAs should be divided into two relevant markets.

4. The difference between supermarket sales concentration ratios and all grocery store sales concentration ratios is principally the values of their denominators. The denominators of the grocery store sales concentration ratios are larger by the sales of small stores, which in 1977 averaged 25 percent of total grocery store sales in the average SMSA. The values of the numerators differ little because in almost every SMSA the four largest firms are supermarket companies whose operations are highly specialized to supermarkets. The largest convenience store chain in an SMSA often ranks among the fifth through eighth in grocery store sales but rarely ranks in the top four.

5. These are SMSAs for which CR4 data are available for each census year between 1958 and 1977 and whose geographic redefinition (if any) during that time period resulted in less than a 20 percent addition to food store sales. Definitions changed for 80 of the 173 chosen SMSAs. Markets with no definition change experienced a slightly higher increase in concentration (48.69 to 57.18) than did SMSAs that were redefined (48.80 to 55.42).

6. During the 1972–1977 period, supermarket concentration increased only 40 percent as fast as grocery store concentration. If this was true during earlier periods, there may have been little, if any, increase in SMSA supermarket concentration from 1958 to 1972, a period when grocery store concentration increased by 3.5 percentage points. The steady increase in grocery store CR4 since 1958 may partially reflect the shift in sales from small stores to supermarkets.

7. These figures were calculated by inserting the assumed market share and concentration figures into the SMSA profit regression model of Marion, et al. (1979a, p. 82), holding all other variables constant.

8. For a description of the tactics used by Safeway and Giant to deter the entry of Shop Rite into Washington, D.C., see FTC Staff Report (1969a). Allvine examined zone pricing in Atlanta and Nashville (*Supermarket News* 1984). The use of separate price zones by Kroger and Colonial for their stores located near warehouse stores received testimony in the Grand Union trial. The below-invoice-cost selling of Safeway in two Texas divisions in 1954–1955 is documented in chapter 3 of FTC Staff Report (1966).

9. In the later periods the best-fitting form for SMSA size was one that declined sharply over the range of population sizes up to about 150,000 and then became quite flat. Above 1 million, the slope turned slightly upward, making the overall relationship somewhat U shaped. The tendency for concentration to increase faster in large SMSAs may have been due to the high absolute cost of SMSA-wide advertising, which requires firms to face the disadvantages of entering with large numbers of stores in order to achieve quickly advertising scale economies.

10. The increase was greater when the regression equation was run separately for SMSAs with HHI levels greater than 1,000. This is the level the Department of Justice Merger Guidelines specify as sufficiently concentrated that mergers that increase the HHI by as little as 100 points are likely to be challenged.

11. Interestingly, the effects of toehold entry during 1967–1972 on concentration change in the 1972–1977 period were positive and statistically significant. This suggests that within five years after being acquired, the average toehold had increased in share sufficiently to rank among the top four and that its subsequent growth caused concentration to go up rather than down. De novo entry did not experience this change and continued to cause concentration to decline even after five years.

12. The activities of food wholesalers are reported under SIC code 514, Wholesale Trade, Groceries and Related Products. Excluded from this SIC group are Farm-Product Raw Materials Wholesalers (SIC 515) and Beer, Wine, and Distilled Alcoholic Beverages Wholesalers (SIC 518).

13. Bureau of Census officials indicate that general line wholesale figures may be slightly understated since some general line establishments were misclassified as specialty grocery due to incomplete reporting of product lines on census forms.

14. Van Dress's definition of separate eating places is essentially the same as the Bureau of Census's Eating Places (SIC 5812), except that Van Dress excludes contract

feeding, which represented about 6 percent of census's total in 1977. Eating Places are divided by census into six subcategories: restaurants and lunchrooms, social caterers, cafeterias, refreshment places, contract feeding, and ice cream and frozen custard stands. Industry analysts often partition foodservice industry data according to full menu, limited menu, and other services offerings. The census categories of restaurants, lunchrooms, and cafeterias are generally identified in the full menu (full service) group, refreshment places are equated with limited menu (fast food) establishments, and contract feeding, caterers, and ice cream establishments fall into variously defined other categories.

Part IV
The Legal Environment of the U.S. Food System

Many parties have a stake in the organization and performance of the U.S. food system, especially consumers, farmers, and the numerous food processors and distributors who transform raw agricultural products into consumable goods. Although many parties have an interest in these matters, often their interests conflict. Such conflicts are ultimately resolved within a legal framework that represents the public policy constraints placed on the system in a democratic society.

Public policies reflect the citizen's inherent interest in the performance of the U.S. economic system. A venerable tenet of a democratic society is that the legitimacy of particular economic actions derives from the public's perception that such actions serve its interest. While this is well recognized and acknowledged in the public behavior of private individuals, it applies equally to the large private enterprises that play increasingly important roles in the food system. This principle of publicly derived legitimacy of corporate behavior has long been recognized though sometimes overlooked. It was proclaimed forcefully eight decades ago by President Theodore Roosevelt at his first inaugural: "Great corporations exist only because they are created and safeguarded by our institutions; and it is therefore one's right and duty to see that they work in harmony with these institutions."

Food system participants work in harmony with the public interest when their practices are consistent with socially derived choices. A society's economic choices reflect the political and economic preferences of the society. In the United States, economic choices are made largely in the context of a capitalistic economy operating within a system of democratic institutions that establish rules governing private enterprise.

Desirable economic performance may be represented by the maximization of public or consumer welfare as measured by such criteria as the public may designate, such as efficient manufacturing and distribution processes, rapid technological progress, diversity and nutritional quality of product

---

This part was coordinated by Dale Dahl and Willard F. Mueller.

offerings, equity in the distribution of the fruits of economic progress, free choice by consumers, and fair competition among market participants.

To govern private enterprise so as to achieve desired performance, systems of rules have historically been used. Among these are a system of laissez-faire in which government has virtually no control over business behavior; a system of private enterprise regulated by antitrust laws designed to achieve or maintain effectively competitive market structures and conduct; a system of private enterprise with direct regulation of certain aspects of conduct and performance; and public ownership of key industrial sectors, particularly natural monopolies.

Americans have experimented with each of these approaches in the food system and elsewhere. Farm leaders were in the forefront of efforts to regulate the railroads through the establishment of the Interstate Commerce Commission in 1887 and to promote competition in other areas with passage of the Sherman Antitrust Act in 1890. The Clayton Act of 1914 and the Capper-Volstead Act of 1922 gave agricultural cooperatives a limited exemption from the antitrust laws. The land grant college system and the Tennessee Valley Authority are examples of publicly owned and operated institutions. The Pure Food and Drug Act of 1906 represented an early policy involving direct regulation of business behavior. These and many other actions are reflections of what public policymakers viewed as the public interest as it affected the food system.

Several members of NC 117 have conducted legal-economic research examining the effects of existing policies and exploring the needs for alternative policies. It is beyond the scope of this summary to discuss the law pertaining to the food system. Rather, this introduction briefly highlights several of the major legal-economic studies conducted by members of NC 117 and introduces readers to the main legal-economic research of the regional research group: antitrust policy economics.

In the earlier stages of the project, some effort was devoted to a categorization and biographical survey of legal studies dealing with the U.S. food system (Dahl 1975, 1979; Grant and Dahl 1978). Subsequent research focused on four areas: farm business organization, farm labor policy, economics of regulation, and antitrust policy and enforcement.

The first major NC 117 monograph dealt with a study of the use of the limited partnership as a financing and tax shelter device in U.S. agriculture (Matthews and Rhodes 1975). At the time of the study, public offerings of limited partnership investment interests had been made in cattle feeding and breeding, citrus, vineyards, nuts, and eggs. The study reviewed the limited farm partnership in terms of federal tax policy, concluding that unless tax incentives were altered, large investments could be expected with accounting losses, rather than profit, as a major economic goal.

A subsequent study of limited farm partnerships in upper Midwest agriculture revealed the existence of increasing numbers of farms using this business organization tool (Dahl and Burke 1979). The principal reason for limited partnerships was not as a financing or sheltering device but to resolve difficult farm estate planning problems.

A 1976 monograph analyzed public policy toward mergers in the dairy processing industry. It reviewed past enforcement efforts, evaluated their effects on industry structure, and proposed alternative policy initiatives (Mueller, Hamm, and Cook 1976).

A more comprehensive analysis of public policy toward mergers was published in 1978 (Mueller 1978a). The study was undertaken at the request of the House Subcommittee on Monopolies and Commercial Law, Committee of the Judiciary. The resulting monograph analyzed the nature, scope, and effectiveness of the first twenty-seven years of enforcement of the Celler-Kefauver Act of 1950. The monograph examined merger enforcement in five food industries, as well as other manufacturing industries.

The economics of regulation as a potential research focus in agricultural economics was explored in a conference cosponsored by NC 117 in 1979. The proceedings were published as part 2 of the November 1979 issue of the *American Journal of Agricultural Economics*. Public awareness of the cost and complexity of a growing body of federal and state regulations became a political issue in the 1970s. Professional recognition of this trend also raised questions concerning the benefits, costs, complexity, and outcomes of much regulation (Shaffer 1979).

A comprehensive review was made of agriculture employment law and policy in a historical and comparative context (Pederson and Dahl 1981). Hired farmworkers had been systematically excluded from many areas of legal protection developed for nonfarm labor in the United States. Much of this exemption was rationalized by the low income position of farmer-employers. Starting in the 1960s, many aspects of labor regulations were extended to include hired farm labor: minimum wage, social security, unemployment compensation, housing conditions, and worker safety. These laws still are not available to most farm labor.

Several legal-economic studies involved the Capper-Volstead Act of 1922, which gave limited antitrust exemption to agricultural cooperatives (Jesse et al. 1982; Jesse 1983; Paterson and Mueller 1984b). These studies examined the purpose, scope, and consequence of the act and made recommendations concerning future enforcement and possible amendment.

The greater part of the legal-economic studies published by NC 117 dealt with antitrust law and its related economic questions. For that reason, chapter 6 focuses on antitrust policies and enforcement. Antitrust law, more than any other, conditions competitive behavior in the food system and elsewhere in the U.S. capitalistic economy. In addition to summarizing previous legal-economic research, chapter 6 presents previously unpublished statistical materials on the patterns of antitrust enforcement actions in the food industries, an evaluation of the effectiveness of these actions, and several alternative policies designed to improve the effectiveness of competition policy.

6
Policies to Promote Competition

The U.S. antitrust laws are the center of public policy designed to promote fair and effective competition in the marketplace. These laws reflect a historic U.S. concern with excessive economic power, both private and public. Although Jefferson and Jackson articulated a philosophy of egalitarianism, the philosophy of laissez-faire dominated economic and political thinking about business affairs during the nineteenth century. But as technological and other forces dramatically restructured the economic order after the Civil War, many Americans feared developments they did not understand and over which they had little control. The giant corporations and trusts of the day had amassed economic power dwarfing that of farmers, most merchants, and individual laborers.

Agrarian interests in the West and South were particularly vociferous in their criticism of the changing industrial structure. As Hans Thorelli (1955, p. 55) put it, "To the farmer it appeared as if all non-agricultural elements of the economy had suddenly entered a conspiracy against him, and his legitimate interests." Many farmers showed their discontent in the Granger movement, which sought reform through state legislation. By 1880, at least fourteen states, predominantly in the West, had adopted constitutional or statutory prohibitions against monopoly. Because state efforts proved largely ineffective, reformers were therefore forced to look to their federal government for legislation.

Antimonopoly sentiment reached a fever pitch in 1890 when, among other happenings, a Senate select committee report exposed the manipulations of the "big four" meat packers (Thorelli 1955, pp. 159–160). This was the environment that gave birth to the Sherman Act of 1890.

After over nine decades, the Sherman Act remains an essential part of U.S. public policy aimed at controlling the possession and use of economic power. The underlying premise of the Sherman Act and subsequent antitrust

---

This chapter was written by Willard F. Mueller and Thomas W. Paterson.

laws remains the same: effective business performance requires the prohibition of certain business practices and, if necessary, the alteration of industrial structure.

Nature of Various Antitrust Laws

Sherman Act of 1980

The Sherman Act does not mention competition, yet its primary concern is the protection of the competitive process. Section 1 of the act prohibits "every contract, combination in the form of a trust or otherwise, or conspiracy in restraint of trade." The Supreme Court has defined the congressional purpose of section 1 as treating

> as illegal all contracts or acts which [are] unreasonably restrictive of competitive conditions, whether from the nature or the character of the act or where the surrounding circumstances [are] such as to justify the conclusion that they [have] not been entered into or performed with the legitimate purpose of reasonably forwarding personal interest and developing trade.[1]

This language declares that only unreasonable restraints are illegal. In subsequent decisions the Supreme Court concluded that certain restraints are always unreasonable and hence should always be considered illegal as they "lack any redeeming virtue."

Among the conclusively presumed, or per se, unlawful restraints of trade are fixing prices, allocating territories among competitors, and tying the purchase of one product to the purchase of another. Restraints not included in the per se category are judged doctrinally by the rule of reason, whereby each restraint is examined within its industrial context to determine whether the restraint on trade is more restrictive than necessary to achieve a legitimate business objective.

Section 2 of the Sherman Act provides that "every person who shall monopolize, or attempt to monopolize, or combine or conspire . . . to monopolize any part of trade . . . shall be guilty of a felony." There are different legal standards for "monopolization" and an "attempt to monopolize."

Clayton Act of 1914

The Clayton Act proscribes specific trade practices thought to injure competition even though they fall short of attempts to monopolize, as defined by the courts. The act seeks to reach—in their incipiency—acts or practices that might eventually lead to adverse economic effects. The types of conduct covered by the act are: price discrimination in section 2; exclusive dealing and

tying contracts in section 3; mergers in section 7; and interlocking director-
ates in section 8.

The two most significant parts of the act are sections 2 and 7. The Robinson-Patman Act of 1936 amended section 2 of the Clayton Act. The current
version of section 2 prohibits discrimination in price "between different pur-
chasers of commodities of like grade and quality . . . where the effect of such
discrimination may be substantially to lessen competition or tend to create a
monopoly in any line of commerce, or to injure, destroy, or prevent competition with any person who either grants or knowingly receives the benefit
of such discrimination, or with customers of either of them."

The Celler-Kefauver Act of 1950 amended section 7 of the Clayton Act.
The current section 7 provides that no person who is engaged in commerce or
in activities affecting commerce may directly or indirectly acquire the stock or
share capital or the assets of another who is also engaged in commerce when
the effect of the acquisition "may be substantially to lessen competition, or to
tend to create a monopoly."

The objective underlying amended section 7 is to prevent merger-induced
structural changes falling far short of actual monopoly. The law was designed
to forestall anticompetitive mergers in their incipiency, before adverse effects
were experienced. In a sense, amended section 7 is to the nation's industrial
market structure what preventive medicine is to the nation's health.

Many authorities believe that section 7 of the Clayton Act has been the
most important antitrust statute in the period since 1950, as measured in
terms of litigation and impact on industrial structure.

Federal Trade Commission Act of 1914

The FTC Act overlaps and extends the Sherman Act concerns with restraints
of trade and monopolization of trade. Also passed in 1914, the FTC Act gives
federal sanction to the common law principle that businesspersons must not
only compete but must compete within certain bounds of conduct.

Section 5 of the FTC Act prohibits "unfair methods of competition." The
Congress intended that the FTC, as a body of experts, give substance to the
meaning of this language. As the conference report on the act states, unfair
competition can best be prevented

> through the action of an administrative body of practical men . . . who will
> be able to apply the rule enacted by Congress to particular business situa-
> tions, so as to eradicate evils with the least risk of interfering with legitimate
> business operations. . . . In thus divining that there is no limit to business in-
> genuity and legal gymnastics the Congress displayed much foresight.[2]

Accepting this congressional mandate, the Supreme Court has held that
the FTC has great discretion in finding which business practices are unfair.

Today the FTC Act is generally recognized as encompassing practices that are presumably covered by other antitrust statutes, as well as some that are not covered.

With the extension of the FTC Act by the Wheeler-Lea Act of 1938, the FTC has authority to protect consumers as well as competitors. The amended FTC Act attempts to ensure that the consumer's decision to elect between alternative suppliers will be based on the value to the consumer of the goods and services, not on unacceptable influence created by advertising or other means.

Packers and Stockyards Act

The Packers and Stockyards Act of 1921 gave the Department of Agriculture general supervisory authority over the meat packing industry. In addition to various public utility regulatory responsibilities, the act includes provisions modeled after the Robinson-Patman Act. The enforcement of these provisions has involved relatively few antitrust actions and is not discussed below.[3]

Enforcement of the Antitrust Laws

Two federal government agencies have primary responsibilities for enforcing the antitrust laws: the Antitrust Division of the Department of Justice (established in 1903) and the FTC (established in 1915).

The FTC has responsibility for enforcing the FTC Act and, concurrently with the Antitrust Division, the Clayton Act. The Antitrust Division enforces the Sherman and Clayton acts. Interagency clearance procedures have been developed to determine which agency initiates a particular action.

Various types of remedy may be achieved by parties bringing antitrust cases. The Sherman Act is both a criminal and a civil act. The criminal provisions penalize illegal conduct through fines and imprisonment, though these remedies are sought only in cases involving clear-cut violations (such per se violations as conspiracies to fix prices). In civil cases the government may ask the courts for divestiture (most common in merger cases) or other actions that provide adequate relief.

A private party injured by the violation of the Sherman or Clayton acts also may enforce these acts and may receive treble the amount of monetary injury sustained. The policy underlying the provision for treble damage awards to private parties is to create an incentive for private parties to aid in enforcing these laws (acting as private attorneys general) and a deterrent to would-be violators. In recent years private parties have initiated many more antitrust cases than the two federal agencies combined.

Exceptions to the Antitrust Laws:
Agricultural Cooperatives

An agricultural marketing cooperative is an association of agriculturally related business firms that performs some function in the marketing process. Such an association of independent business firms engaged in cooperative marketing is a combination that can arguably restrain trade or tend to monopoly. The potential for conflict between the Sherman Act and the cooperative form of business organization prompted the passage of section 6 of the Clayton Act of 1914, the Capper-Volstead Act of 1922, the Cooperative Marketing Act of 1926, and the Agricultural Fair Practices Act of 1967. Each of these statutes provides certain exemptions to the antitrust laws. Here we shall be concerned primarily with the Capper-Volstead Act.

The Capper-Volstead Act consists of two sections. Section 1 explicitly grants producers the right jointly to market their agricultural commodities through cooperatives. Without this provision, virtually all agricultural marketing cooperatives would be in jeopardy of violating section 1 of the Sherman Act (Mueller 1979). The section also permits cooperatives to use marketing agencies in common and to make "the necessary contracts and agreements to effect such purposes." To qualify for these rights (that is, to be recognized as a Capper-Volstead cooperative), an association must operate for the mutual benefit of members, practice "one member-one vote" or pay no more than 8 percent interest on stock or membership capital, and limit nonmember business to less than 50 percent of total volume.

Whereas section 1 gives cooperatives a degree of exemption from the antitrust laws, section 2 of the act was designed to place limits on a cooperative's ability to enhance prices. If the secretary finds, after a hearing, that a marketing cooperative has unduly enhanced price by monopolization or restraint of trade, the secretary shall issue an order directing the cooperative to cease and desist from such monopolization or restraint of trade. The legal interpretation of these provisions is discussed below.

Agricultural Marketing Agreement Act

The Agricultural Marketing Agreement Act of 1937 (AMAA) is the enabling legislation for federal marketing orders and agreements. Unlike Capper-Volstead, the AMAA has been frequently amended, mainly to add eligible commodities and permit new provisions. Different provisions apply to milk and other eligible products (primarily fresh fruits and vegetables and tree nuts). Milk orders allow producers to impose classified pricing for milk according to end use. Orders for other commodities allow a variety of quality and quantity controls but do not permit direct price setting.

Relative to the antitrust exemption granted cooperatives under Capper-Volstead, the AMAA antitrust exemption is unequivocal:

> The making of such agreement shall not be held to be in violation of any of the antitrust laws of the United States, and any such agreement shall be deemed lawful: Provided, that no such agreement shall remain in force after the termination of this Act. [7 U.S.C. 608b]

However, as noted by the FTC (1975), the legitimization of activities does not necessarily legitimize anticompetitive practices within these activities. For example, dairy cooperatives are permitted under the AMAA to pool receipts in markets in which they operate and pay all producers an associated blend price. But when reblending is done for the purpose of harming competition (pool loading), it is subject to prosecution (Masson, Masson, and Harris 1978, pp. 202–204).

The AMAA grants the secretary of agriculture oversight responsibility for marketing orders, including the authority to terminate or suspend an order or provision that "does not tend to effectuate the declared policy of this title" (7 U.S.C. 608c (16)(A)). Since declared policy is phrased in such terms as "the interest of consumers and producers," "orderly marketing," and "unreasonable fluctuations in supply and price," the secretary has broad discretion in deciding whether to allow certain practices under orders. In reality, this authority has been exercised sparingly; oversight is largely delegated to the Dairy and Fruit and Vegetable Divisions of USDA's Agricultural Marketing Service, whose personnel are the source of counsel concerning public interest implications of regulatory recommendations.

Enforcement Experience of Various Antitrust Provisions in Food Industries

Federal Antitrust Enforcement in the Food System, 1950–1984

Tables 6–1, 6–2, and 6–3 provide one measure of the extent of federal antitrust enforcement in the food system. The tables summarize Department of Justice (DOJ) and FTC cases in the food system from 1950 through 1984. Table 6–1 gives the number of DOJ complaints, informations, and indictments, as well as the number of FTC complaints and consent orders by statutory provision for six periods from 1950 through 1984. Table 6–2 shows the major industries in the food system where these antitrust cases were instituted, also for six periods from 1950 through 1984. Table 6–3 combines the statutory provisions in table 6–1 and the major industries in table 6–2 to reveal the distribution of cases by statute and industry for 1950 through 1984. The three tables therefore distinguish statutory enforcement over time (table 6–1), the industries in which these cases have focused over time (table 6–2), and statutory enforcement by industry for the entire period (table 6–3).

Several qualifications are necessary for interpretation of the tables. The summary statistics simply count cases that have directly affected the competitive environment of the food system as measured at the farm level and forward through manufacturing and distribution industries. It would be misleading, however, to consider all cases as having the same impact on competition in the food system. A monopolization challenge is qualitatively much more significant than an isolated price discrimination case.

A total of 901 cases are represented in the tables. One case may allege more than one statutory violation; however, each statutory provision alleged in a complaint has been treated separately in tables 6–1 and 6–3. Hence, table 6–1 shows that the 901 cases charged 961 violations of the various statutory provisions. And, as noted in the tables, some of the 901 cases represent the same or similar situations because the DOJ may institute both criminal and civil charges on the same facts. Finally, it should be noted that tables 6–2 and 6–3 do not include food system cases which do not fit within the major industries listed.

The tables do not indicate why the DOJ or FTC brought a specific action. Past antitrust enforcement can be evaluated, however, in terms of the structure and conduct dimensions of the industrial organization paradigm. Market structure involves buyer and seller concentration, barriers to entry, product differentiation, the size of sunk costs, and the growth rate of market demand. Market conduct includes a firm's policies toward price setting, product quality, and competitors. Certain market structures facilitate certain conduct; certain conduct in turn may change market structure (for example, predatory conduct may increase concentration or raise entry barriers). An analysis of antitrust enforcement in the food system therefore breaks down conveniently into a consideration of alleged structural or conduct violations. A *structural violation* refers to a case involving attempted or actual changes in market structure. This is used to include a charge of monopoly or attempted monopolization under section 2 of the Sherman Act or section 5 of the FTC Act or a merger challenged under section 7 of the Clayton Act. A *conduct allegation* is used here to include charges of price fixing or other restraints of trade under section 1 of the Sherman Act or section 5 of the FTC Act, unfair trade practices (other than monopolization cases) under section 5, and price or promotion discrimination or unlawful brokerage payments under section 2 of the Clayton Act (referred to hereafter as R-P for the Robinson-Patman Act). What is termed a structure-related case will involve conduct, and conduct-related cases are expected to reflect market structure.

Table 6–1
FTC and Department of Justice Antitrust Cases in the Food System,
by Statute, 1950–1984

| | Clayton Act | | | | FTC Act |
	§2	§3	§7	§8	§5
1950–1955	48	1	3	2	51
1956–1960	210	1	18	0	38
1961–1965	47	0	11	0	39
1966–1970	15	0	14	0	24
1971–1975	7	1	16	2	72
1976–1980	1	1	18	0	19
1981–1984	0	0	7	0	11
Total	328	4	87	4	254

Source: Compiled from Commerce Clearing House *Trade Regulation Reporter* and *Blue Book*.
[a]This column, a horizontal sum of the columns to its left, gives the total number of times all statutory provisions shown have been alleged for the indicated time period. This column is to be contrasted with the column giving the total number of actual cases. The differences between the two columns stem from cases alleging more than one statutory violation.

The great bulk of all complaints involved conduct-related cases. Fully 328 (34.1 percent) challenges involved section 2 of the Clayton Act, and 249 (25.9 percent) challenges involved section 1 of the Sherman Act. Moreover, practically all of the 254 (26.4 percent) challenges under section 5 of the FTC Act also involved conduct cases. Although fewer in numbers, the structure-related cases under Clayton Act section 7 and Sherman Act section 2 represented a sizable enforcement effort, whether measured by resource commitment or probable affects on market structure.

The most notable aspect of the enforcement pattern portrayed by table 6–1 is the decline in recent years in the number of complaints. Although the number of attorneys employed by the DOJ and the FTC rose between the early 1950s and the late 1970s, just over one-third as many complaints were issued in 1976–1980 as in 1950–1955. The number of cases brought during 1981–1984 declined sharply, especially those brought by the FTC. During 1983 and 1984; the FTC brought only thirteen antitrust cases in food, a historic low; it brought no price discrimination, resale price maintenance, monopolization, or attempt to monopolize cases.

While the greatest decline occurred in R-P section 2 cases (from forty-eight in 1950–1955 to none in 1981–1984), the number of Sherman Act section 2 challenges also declined sharply (from nineteen to zero). The most consistent area of enforcement involved challenges of mergers under section 7 of the Clayton Act, although activity in this area also was down sharply since 1980 despite a great increase in merger activity.

Sherman Act					
§1		§2			*Actual*
Civil	*Criminal*	*Civil*	*Criminal*	*Total*[a]	*Cases*[b]
19	32	10	9	175	158
11	19	2	0	299	290
14	21	5	5	142	130
10	11	1	0	75	70
33	26	3	0	160	152
15	17	0	0	71	64
12[c]	9	0	0	39	37
114	135	21	14	961	901

[b]This column shows the total number of complaints, consent orders, and indictments. The totals given for the Clayton Act derive from Department of Justice cases and FTC complaints and consent orders. The Department of Justice often institutes both civil and criminal actions in the same facts. Hence two complaints may correspond to what is really one set of facts, particularly for Sherman Act section 1 cases.

[c]The Department of Justice issued four price-fixing complaints in 1984 involving Waldbaum, Inc. This was counted as one complaint.

Private Antitrust Actions

The preceding summary of enforcement activity covered only actions brought by the two federal antitrust agencies. While these actions represent the major continuing public commitment to the enforcement of these laws, numerous private antitrust actions are initiated each year. For example, whereas during the 1970s the two antitrust agencies brought an average of 75 cases per year, private parties brought an average of 1,400 cases per year. No systematic information has been developed of the overall patterns of private enforcement.[4] It would be a mistake, however, to infer that private cases are not significant or involve only small plaintiffs. Many cases in the food industries, as elsewhere, involve large food corporations. For example, large food retailers and food manufacturers were the major recipients of millions of dollars in damages awards paid when private corporations challenged an alleged price-fixing conspiracy among sugar manufacturers.[5] Similarly, large food manufacturers received most of the damages paid by paper companies that allegedly had fixed prices on paper cartons.[6] More recently, leading meat packers brought suit against Eli Lilly and other companies for allegedly fixing prices in the purchase of pancreas glands used in the manufacture of insulin.[7]

We now discuss in more detail the nature of the enforcment effort as reflected in leading government and private antitrust cases, the apparent

Table 6–2
FTC and Department of Justice Cases in the Food System, by Leading Industry, 1950–1984

	Bakery Products	Beer and Liquor	Milk and Dairy Products	Fish and Seafood	Fruits and Vegetables	Tobacco and Tobacco Products	Total
1950–1955	4	15	28	12	21	13	93
1956–1960	20	9	29	39	77	17	191
1961–1965	10	13	18	0	31	8	80
1966–1970	8	5	7	0	4	5	29
1971–1975	28	13	10	1	2	9	63
1976–1980	5	8	11	1	2	6	33
1981–1984	4	4	1	4	8	1	22
Total	79	67	104	57	145	59	511

Source: Compiled from Commerce Clearing House *Trade Regulation Reporter* and *Blue Book*.
Note: The totals given are from Department of Justice cases and from FTC complaints and consent orders.

competitive significance of various kinds of enforcement effort, and the current legal status of the various antitrust provisions.

Price-Fixing Agreements

Price-fixing agreements among competitors are per se illegal under section 1 of the Sherman Act. Since 1950 many price-fixing cases have been brought in various food industries, especially in baking, fluid milk, and beer and liquor. Cases in these three industry groups involved price fixing in local or regional markets consisting of relatively few sellers, a condition conducive to price fixing.[8]

The *Bakers of Washington* conspiracy illustrates how antitrust enforcement may result in significant price reductions in a conspiracy-prone industry.[9] This case involved a tightly knit, long-lived conspiracy of the leading wholesale bakers in the state of Washington.[10] Only one member of the group, the dominant grocery chain, Safeway, was allowed to deviate from the prices set by the association of bakers. The record of the case showed that "while all the other bakers, wholesale and retail, were pressured to retail their bread for the same price that Continental (the largest wholesale baker in Seattle) got for its 'Wonder' bread Safeway was permitted to sell for 1¢ less."[11] Strict discipline was maintained. When necessary, threats of "drastic price retaliation to anyone who would not keep their prices in line" were used. It was further found that the conspirators were almost completely successful in bringing price cutters in line and that each time the price leader raised the price, it stuck. Other bakers followed quickly.

The conspirators successfully raised prices over the period 1955–1964. Prior to 1954, Seattle bread prices very nearly equaled national average bread

Table 6-3
FTC and Department of Justice Cases in the Food System, by Leading Industry and Statute, 1950-1984

	Bakery Products	Beer and Liquor	Milk and Dairy Products	Fish and Seafood	Fruits and Vegetables	Tobacco and Tobacco Products	Total[b]
Clayton Act							
Section 2	3	4	18	32	111	10	178
Section 3	1	0	3	0	0	0	4
Section 7	8	16	11	1	3	3	42
Section 8	1	0	0	0	0	0	1
FTC Act							
Section 5	19	5	35	10	14	28	111
Sherman Act							
Section 1	42	42	43	15	18	17	177
Section 2	2	0	9	3	7	2	23
Total[a]	76 (79)	67 (67)	119 (104)	61 (57)	153 (145)	60 (59)	536 (511)

Source: Compiled from Commerce Clearing House *Trade Regulation Reporter* and *Blue Book*.

[a]If a complaint or indictment challenged a firm on several statutory provisions, each provision has been entered separately. For this reason, a vertical summation of the cases for an industry may exceed the total number of cases in the industry; the actual number of cases in an industry is given in parentheses.

[b]Because other products are also involved, this column does not equal totals given in table 6-1.

prices. But commencing in mid-1954, Seattle bread prices rose sharply and over the next decade averaged between 15 and 20 percent above the national average. Shortly after the FTC's decision in December 1964, Seattle bread prices began to tumble, continuing to fall until they were below the national average.

Significantly, although the price conspiracy increased bread prices by over 15 percentage points, there was not a corresponding increase in the profits of wholesale bakers because their costs, especially selling costs, rose more rapidly than those of bakers in other parts of the country. This is an example of the kind of X-inefficiency that Leibenstein has predicted will occur when competition is suppressed.

During the period of the conspiracy, consumers in the state of Washington paid about $35 million more for bread than if prices had remained at the national average. Had bakers nationally succeeded in raising prices by this amount over the period of the conspiracy, U.S. consumers would have paid over $2 billion more for bread than they actually did.

This example illustrates that successful enforcement of the law prohibiting price fixing can save consumers enormous amounts. It is impossible, of course, to determine how many potential conspiracies are deterred by this prohibition. But experience in nations that do not prohibit price fixing indicates that such behavior becomes commonplace if it is not prohibited.

Price Discrimination

Section 2 of the Clayton Act as amended by the R-P Act prohibits various kinds of discrimination and its inducement by large buyers. Here we shall consider only price discrimination: the practice of selling at different prices to different buyers.

There are two broad categories of price discrimination cases. *Primary line* cases involve injury to parties competing with the seller practicing discrimination. *Secondary line* cases involve injury to competitors of the buyers that receive a discriminatory price.

Many of the precedent-setting R-P cases involved food companies. The Supreme Court's *Morton Salt* decision in 1948 provides a key precedent in secondary line cases.[12] It established a virtual per se rule for such cases by shifting the burden of proof to the alleged discriminator. Morton Salt Company had used a discriminatory price discount schedule that gave maximum discounts to only the five largest food chains. Even other chains buying in carload lots paid 11 percent more than did the five largest. Some economists have argued that the discriminatory prices given by Morton Salt were not anticompetitive because salt represents an insignificant part of a retailer's total sales. But such reasoning overlooks the fact that only a few grocery products represent as much as 5 percent of total sales. So should the law permit discriminatory pricing in such cases, large buyers would receive a large cumulative advantage, a point emphasized by the Supreme Court: "Since a grocery store consists of many comparatively small articles, there is no possible way effectively to protect the grocer from discriminatory prices except by applying the prohibitions of the Act to each individual item in the store."

Utah Pie Company v. *Continental Baking Company* is an important precedent in primary line cases.[13] After a jury trial, the defendants were found guilty of violating the R-P Act and were directed to pay treble damages. When a court of appeals reversed the jury's decision, the Supreme Court heard the case, finding for Utah Pie.

Briefly, the facts are these. Utah Pie entered the frozen pie business in 1957. At the time, three large multimarket companies dominated the Salt Lake City market, serving it from plants in California. Utah Pie was an immediate success, capturing 66.5 percent of the market. The established companies responded by deep price cuts that were below their costs. Utah Pie was viewed by the largest established firm, Pet, as an "unfavorable factor," one that "dug holes in our operations" and posed a constant "check" on pricing. Pet went so far as to send an industrial spy to seek information to discredit Utah Pie with its largest customer. But despite these acts, Utah Pie retained a 45 percent market share and earned modest profits in 1961, the last year in the record. The supreme Court asserted these facts were sufficient to establish a violation of the R-P Act: "We believe that the Act [reaches] price discrimination that *erodes* competition as much as it does price discrimination that is intended to *have immediate destructive impact.*"

This case illustrates why the R-P Act is the most controversial antitrust statute. Its critics disagree with the Supreme Court, arguing that the events in Salt Lake City were manifestations of the kind of "hard competition" essential to the competitive process. Supporters of the decision emphasize that the statute is devised to prevent discrimination that *may* substantially lessen competition, what framers of the Clayton Act called "catching the [monopoly] weed in the seed." The policy debate will continue as to whether proper R-P rules can be framed that protect the competitive process without preventing desirable price competition.

Whereas *Utah Pie* and other Supreme Court primary line cases required only a substantial probability that competition was injured by price discrimination, recent cases appear to have raised the level of injury to that approaching the standards for predation or an "attempt to monopolize" under section 2 of the Sherman Act. Indeed, in its most recent R-P Act decision, *ITT Continental Baking Co,* (1984), the FTC applied stricter standards for a finding of predation under the R-P Act than some courts have used to identify predation under section 2 of the Sherman Act.[14]

The R-P Act has received less and less attention by the antitrust agencies, resulting in a persistent decline in the number of cases brought under section 2 of the Clayton Act. This reflects a growing sentiment in the antitrust agencies and among some economists that price discrimination does not represent a serious threat to competition. Another reason is that in the 1930s and for a time after, there was great disparity in buying power among food retailers because of the asymmetrical size distribution of food retailers. Since then the number of large food chains has risen, and practically all independent retailers have become affiliated with large wholesalers that can match the buying power of even the largest chains. These structural changes together with the strict legal standards developed for secondary line injury have eliminated practically all of the gross sorts of price discrimination that existed prior to the enactment of the R-P Act in 1936. Thus, the battle against secondary line injury in food retailing, the main concern of the proponents of the R-P Act, has largely been won: strict legal rules prohibiting discriminatory conduct in secondary line cases have been abetted by structural changes that reduced business incentives to discriminate.

But the battle against primary line price discrimination is less certain. Despite the antitrust agencies' disinclination to pursue such cases, the large number of private cases suggests that a problem remains, at least as measured by violation of existing legal rules. In recent years the number of private R-P actions was much greater than the number brought by the antitrust agencies.[15]

Merger Enforcement

The first mergers challenged by the FTC and DOJ following the 1950 Celler-Kefauver Amendment to section 7 of the Clayton Act involved food companies. The FTC's first case challenged Pillsbury Mills, Inc.'s acquisition in 1952 of Ballard & Ballard Co. and the Duff's Baking Mix Division of American Home Products. The DOJ's first case involved Schenley Industries, Inc.'s acquisition in 1955 of Park & Tillford Distillers. Both cases involved horizontal mergers, the acquisition of direct competitors. Neither action resulted in divestiture. The Pillsbury case, initially pursued aggressively, ultimately became part of a marathon legal battle extending over fifteen years. In 1966 the FTC dismissed the case for lack of public interest, recognizing that divestiture of the long-scrambled assets was impractical.[16] The Schenley case was settled with a consent agreement in 1955 providing that Schenley not make any further liquor acquisitions for ten years without prior approval of the DOJ.

During the first five years following enactment of the Celler-Kefauver Act, only three food manufacturing mergers were challenged. This reflects in large part the fact that very few large mergers (assets over $10 million) occurred during the early 1950s (table 6–4). When merger activity accelerated in the mid-1950s, nearly 50 percent (measured by acquired assets) of all large food manufacturing companies acquired were challenged by the antitrust agencies, and a sizable proportion of large mergers in food retailing were challenged during the period. In subsequent years a declining percentage of acquired assets was challenged, except during 1971–1975 when merger activity measured in adjusted assets fell to levels near that of 1951–1955. Despite a record volume of food manufacturing acquisitions during 1981–1984, the agencies challenged only five of the acquisitions. These challenged acquisitions represented only 6.9 percent of all recorded food manufacturing mergers involving acquired companies with assets of $10 million or more, an all-time low since 1950 (table 6–4).

Changes over time in the nature of the mergers occurring were primarily responsible for the decline in the share of mergers challenged. Whereas during the 1950s most large acquisitions involved horizontal, vertical, or geographic market extension mergers, these kinds of mergers declined in relative importance after 1960 because of the strict legal rules established toward them in the late 1950s and early 1960s.[17] Although horizontal mergers declined in relative importance, since 1973 practically all of the antitrust agencies' efforts have continued to be directed at such mergers in the food industries (table 6–5), as well as in other industries (Mueller 1978a).

During the 1960s the Supreme Court ruled several conglomerate-type mergers illegal, and in 1969 the head of the antitrust division, Richard McLaren, launched a vigorous assault against conglomerate mergers as he

Table 6–4
Total Food Manufacturing Companies Acquired and Total Food Manufacturing Acquisitions Challenged by the Antitrust Agencies, 1951–1955 to 1981–1984
(millions of dollars)

Period	Total Mergers[a]		Total Mergers Challenged		Challenged Mergers as Percentage of Total Mergers	
	Number	Assets[c]	Number	Assets[c]	Number	Assets[c]
1951–1955	17	$ 3,149	3	$ 497	17.6%	15.8%
1956–1960	21	5,613	15	2,659	71.4	47.4
1961–1965	31	4,968	9	1,292	29.0	26.0
1966–1970	54	19,147	11	833	20.4	4.4
1971–1975	36	2,989	15	1,332	41.7	44.6
1976–1980	65[b]	10,875[b]	9	703	13.8	6.5
1981–1984	76[b]	20,296[b]	5	1,098	6.6	5.4
Total	300	67,037	67	8,414	22.3	12.6

Source: FTC 1981c (and previous years) and secondary sources.

[a]Includes acquired companies with assets of $10 million or more.

[b]Mergers for these years are understated relative to earlier years. For 1950–1979 the FTC published merger data for manufacturing acquisitions of $10 million or more. Because that source is no longer available, the mergers reported for 1979–1984 include primarily those reported in *Fortune* magazine, *Moody's Industrial Manual, Mergers and Acquisitions,* and the *Food Institute Report.* The latter sources probably reported a high percentage of the acquired assets of companies with assets exceeding $10 million but understated by a significant percentage the number of acquired companies of this size.

[c]Assets were adjusted to reflect real and inflation-caused growth using the total average annual assets of food and tobacco companies in 1981–1984 as a base. Thus, total assets of all companies acquired before 1981 were adjusted upward. For example, the actual value of assets acquired in 1951–1955 was $342 million but was adjusted to $3,149 million, reflecting that total annual assets in 1951–1955 were 10.86 percent as great as in 1981–1984.

sought to determine the reach of the law in this area.[18] McLaren's effort was aborted in 1971 when he was persuaded to settle, rather than appeal to the Supreme Court, the three conglomerate cases he had initiated against International Telephone and Telegraph (Mueller, 1973). The most important result of the ITT settlement was to deprive the Warren Court of an opportunity to rule on broad-based conglomerate theories. The emergence of the Burger Court's "new antitrust majority," with its allegedly anti-antitrust bias, virtually closed the door in 1973–1974 on the use of existing law to challenge conglomerate acquisitions.[19]

Nearly half of the food industry merger complaints challenged acquisitions in three industries: food retailing, dairy processing, and beer (table 6–6). Several others involved conglomerate mergers by grocery products manufacturers. Here we review briefly the enforcement effort in these three industries and the apparent effect of this effort on the structure of these industries, as well as enforcement efforts toward conglomerate-type mergers in grocery manufacturing.

Table 6–5
Total Merger Complaints by Type of Merger in Food and Grocery Products Manufacturing, 1951–1984
(millions of dollars)

Type of Merger	1951–1960		1961–1970	
	Number	Assets[a]	Number	Assets[a]
Horizontal	12	$1,031	13	$1,105
Vertical	1	133	1	43
Conglomerate				
Market extension	4	2,195	2	170
Product extension	1	8	4	718
Other (pure)	0	0	0	0
Total	18	$3,367	20	$2,036

Source: FTC 1981c (and previous years); and secondary sources.
[a]Assets for 1951–1980 were adjusted to reflect inflation and real growth in total assets over the period, as explained in table 6–4, note c.

Food Retailing. Both antitrust agencies challenged mergers in food retailing: the DOJ issued three merger complaints and the FTC fifteen complaints.[20] The DOJ's challenge in 1959 of the Von's–Shopping Bag merger in Los Angeles set an important precedent for horizontal mergers in all fields. In this 1966 decision, the Supreme Court made it manifestly clear that even mergers involving small, combined market shares were prohibited by section 7 when they involved leading sellers in a market experiencing a trend toward concentration.[21] This and subsequent actions by the two agencies thereafter stopped virtually all significant horizontal mergers among food retailers.

In 1959 the FTC initiated the first of a series of actions designed to halt a merger movement in the food retailing industry involving mainly geographic market extension mergers. These mergers tend to concentrate the industry nationally and eliminate potential competition among retailers in geographically adjacent markets. In that year, the FTC challenged mergers by the National Tea Company and the Kroger Company. These actions were followed by complaints during the 1960s challenging acquisitions of other large chains.

In 1966 the FTC issued its opinion in *National Tea*, holding that National Tea's acquisitions were unlawful. The commission prohibited National Tea from making further acquisitions without commission approval for a period of ten years. Similar consent orders were entered with several other chains. In 1967 the commission issued merger guidelines and required merger notification by leading food chains. The goals of efficiency and competition could best be pursued, in the commission's view, if large chains did not make additional acquisitions. It therefore concluded, "Mergers and acquisitions by retail food

1971–1980		1981–1984		1951–1984	
Number	Assets[a]	Number	Assets[a]	Number	Assets[a]
20	$1,217	5	$1,098	50	$4,451
1	491	0	0	3	667
0	0	0	0	6	2,635
3	188	0	0	8	914
0	0	0	0	0	0
24	$1,896	5	$1,098	67	$8,397[b]

[b]This total differs slightly from the total in table 6–4, column 4, because an adjustment index based on ten-year averages was used in this table, whereas a five-year average was used in table 6–4.

chains which result in combined annual food store sales in excess of $500 million annually raise sufficient questions regarding their legal status to warrant attention and consideration by the commission under the statutes administered by it" (FTC 1967, p. 4).

The effects of these various policies were virtually to stop all but very small mergers by the leading ten food chains, despite a rise in the overall level

Table 6–6
Merger Complaints Challenging Acquisitions in Food Manufacturing, Grocery Manufacturing, and Food Retailing, 1951–1984
(millions of dollars)

Industry Group	Number of Complaints	Sales of Acquired Companies	Assets of Acquired Companies[d]
Food manufacturing			
Dairy processing	9	$1,641	$ 564
Beer	14	1,572[b]	963[b]
Other	44	2,964[b]	1,371[a]
Food retailing	19	1,256[d]	438[c]
Total	86	$7,433	$3,336

Source: FTC 1981c (and previous years) and secondary sources.
[a]Information available for thirteen of fourteen acquisitions.
[b]Information available for thirty-one of forty-three acquisitions.
[c]Information available for twelve of eighteen acquisitions.
[d]These assets have not been adjusted, as was done in tables 6–4 and 6–5.

of merger activity in the industry. Merger activity by large chains did intensify for a time in the mid-1970s when the FTC appeared to have changed its policy. Then in 1979 the FTC reasserted its concern with market extension mergers by challenging Grand Union's acquisition of Colonial Stores, a large potential competitor in the Southeast.

Today policy toward mergers in food retailing is at a historic crossroads. In 1981 an FTC administrative law judge found illegal the merger between Grand Union and Colonial Stores because it eliminated substantial potential competition.[22] The new commission, which to date has challenged only horizontal mergers, did not rule on the *Grand Union* decision until July 1983. In early 1983 the Kroger Company acquired Dillon Company, which had 1982 sales exceeding $1 billion, making this the largest merger in the history of the food retailing industry; the merger also gave Kroger greater sales within the United States than any other food chain.

The commission did not challenge the Kroger-Dillon merger, though it appeared to pose the same danger for eliminating potential competition as did the Grand Union–Colonial merger. This inaction presaged the commission's decision on July 18, 1983, dismissing the administrative law judge's opinion. The commission concluded that the relevant markets involved all grocery stores, not just supermarkets. When so viewed, the commission concluded that *actual* competition within the markets involved in the merger was sufficiently intense that there existed no substantial danger that the merger would eliminate *potential* competition. The *Grand Union* decision and the failure to challenge the Kroger-Dillon and the American Stores–Jewel mergers could well trigger a new wave of mergers in food retailing (see chapter 5).

Beer Industry. Since 1958 about 100 breweries have been acquired by other brewers. The early pattern of this merger activity was shaped significantly by the DOJ's challenge between 1958 and 1964 of acquisitions by the nation's three largest brewers of that period: Anheuser-Busch, Schlitz, and Pabst. These actions stopped further acquisitions by these brewers until 1982. The bulk of merger activity involved a dozen or so regional brewers. Although the DOJ challenged several mergers by regional brewers, it generally took a tolerant attitude toward such mergers. Economists evaluating mergers by brewers other than the top three generally agree that such mergers were either procompetitive or had no significant adverse competitive effects (Weiss 1965).

The only large conglomerate acquisition in the industry, the 1969–1970 acquisition of Miller Brewing Company by Philip Morris, was not even investigated by the antitrust agencies (see chapter 5). However, this merger drastically upset the balance of power in the industry, triggering a massive industry restructuring. Until Philp Morris–Miller began expanding rapidly in the early 1970s, it appeared that merger policy and the basic economics of the industry would permit the emergence of a fairly large number of viable brewers. But the Philip Morris–Miller expansion upset the emerging structure, causing even large brewers to merge for survival. In 1982 alone, Stroh acquired Schlitz and Pabst acquired Olympia; subsequently, Heileman acquired three of Pabst's breweries and the remaining Pabst properties were acquired by the Kalmanovitz brewing interests.

As leading brewers recently sought to merge with one another, the DOJ appeared to be following a policy designed to create sufficient balance among the survivors so that there would exist four viable national companies in addition to the big two, Anheuser-Busch and Philip Morris–Miller. While prohibiting Heileman's (the fifth largest brewer in 1981) proposed 1981 acquisition of Schlitz (the third largest brewer), which would have given the combined company the largest market position in the large midwestern market, Justice did permit Stroh (the seventh largest brewer nationally) to acquire Schlitz in 1982 on the condition that Stroh divest one of the Schlitz's plants in the South. And, in 1982 the DOJ did permit Pabst (the sixth largest brewer nationally) to acquire Olympia Brewing (the eighth largest brewer). It subsequently permitted Heileman to acquire three brewing plants from Pabst-Olympia.[23]

It is still too early to determine the effects of the DOJ's recent efforts to channel merger activity to achieve a preferred market structure. However, the central role that the Philip Morris–Miller merger played in restructuring the beer industry illustrates how the best-intentioned and -executed policies toward horizontal mergers may be frustrated by conglomerate mergers that cannot be challenged under existing law, at least as currently interpreted.

Fluid Milk Processing. In the dairy processing industry, the FTC's issuance of four complaints in 1956 slowed the extent of merger activity by large dairy processors, which had made over 400 mergers during 1950–1956 and about 2,000 acquisitions in the preceding decades (Mueller, Hamm, and Cook 1976). After the FTC issued its initial decision in these cases in 1962, the eight largest dairy companies virtually stopped acquiring other fluid milk processors. The effect of the policy was not to stop all mergers but to channel them away from the top eight dairy processors to regional and smaller companies. Thus, whereas the overall rate of merger activity in the industry was not changed, merger activity by regional and local dairy companies rose.

Without the policy the large dairy processors probably would have continued to increase their share of national sales; instead their share has gradually eroded over the past two decades. Because of the increasing size of fluid milk markets and the importance of large food retailers in fluid milk manufacturing and distribution, the balance of power has shifted from large dairy processors to large food distributors (Parker 1977). These changes warrant a relaxation of the strict rules that had their origins in the industrial structure of the 1950s and early 1960s.

Conglomerate Grocery Manufacturing Mergers. Most acquisitions of grocery manufacturers involve product-extension-type conglomerate mergers. Yet enforcement efforts toward such mergers have had only a minimal effect (Mueller 1978a, pp. 50–63). Many substantial mergers have gone unchallenged, and at least one has been challenged without resulting in adequate relief. This is true despite a number of landmark court decisions during the 1960s regarding mergers in the industry, especially *Procter & Gamble*[24] and *General Foods*,[25] and the issuance in 1968 of an FTC merger enforcement policy statement with respect to conglomerate-type mergers among grocery product companies (FTC 1968). The commission's unexplained withdrawal in December 1976 of its grocery products merger guidelines was interpreted by the industry as a lack of conviction by the FTC that these mergers can or should be challenged under section 7. As in food retailing, an apparent relaxation in the FTC's enforcement policy was followed by an acceleration in mergers, so that thereafter large grocery product market extension mergers reached record levels.

Merger Guidelines. In addition to the merger guidelines issued by the FTC in specific food industries, grocery retailing (1967), grocery products manufacturing (1969) and dairy processing (1973), the DOJ in 1968 issued merger guidelines to be applied generally. In 1982 the antitrust agencies issued new merger guidelines that were subsequently revised in 1984.

The new DOJ and FTC merger guidelines are considerably more permissive toward horizontal mergers than were earlier guidelines. In effect, the Justice guidelines promise that the DOJ will never challenge mergers in a market with a four-firm market share of about 40 to 45 percent, but it is very likely to challenge mergers that raise concentration significantly in industries with CR4 of about 70 percent.[26] These standards are substantially less restrictive than the earlier DOJ merger guidelines, as well as the rules enunciated in several Supreme Court merger decisions. Moreover, the new merger guidelines give a green light to virtually all vertical and conglomerate-type mergers.

Summary of Merger Enforcement. Experience with merger enforcement indicates that usually the most important impact of such enforcement policy is deterrence. For example, in the first twelve months following the 1964 initial decision that dismissed the *National Tea* case, the ten largest food chains made market-extension acquisitions of firms with total sales of over $500 million. This was greater than all such acquisitions challenged to that date by the commission. However, leading chains virtually stopped making acquisitions following the reversal in 1966 of the initial *National Tea* decision and the other enforcement initiatives pursued in the industry. Without these actions, the largest chains almost certainly would have continued to be leading acquirers during the massive economy-wide merger movement in the late 1960s. Similarly, were it not for the FTC's enforcement policy toward mergers in the dairy industry, the eight largest dairies may well have acquired hundreds of dairies since 1960. Instead merger activity has been channeled to smaller firms.

Experience with merger enforcement policy in several areas demonstrates that merger activity in a particular industry may respond directly and quickly to an antitrust agency's announcement of its enforcement intentions toward mergers in that industry. The success of such policy statements, however, requires that the agency give credibility to the announced policy by vigorous enforcement. This was illustrated dramatically in food retailing. When during 1975–1976 the FTC left unchallenged a number of substantial mergers falling within its guidelines, large food chains renewed their merger activity. Although the FTC had not publicly rescinded the enforcement policy initiated in the 1960s, businesspeople inferred from the commission's inaction that it had changed its policy toward market extension mergers in food retailing.

Finally, the 1982 merger guidelines of the FTC and DOJ, as revised in 1984, are more permissive of horizontal mergers and would permit virtually all nonhorizontal mergers. They remove any doubts business may have had regarding the agencies' views on the legality of conglomerate mergers by food manufacturers and food retailers. Conglomerate mergers, which reached record highs after 1980 (table 6–4), will likely remain high unless there is a change in enforcement policy or in the law.

Attempt to Monopolize

Section 2 of the Sherman Act prohibits attempts to monopolize. There are three elements in a charge of an attempt to monopolize: (1) specific intent, (2) predatory or anticompetitive conduct, and (3) dangerous probability of success. Some courts view the key element in this triad as predatory conduct since the other two elements may be inferred from it.

Courts have relied on various kinds of evidence from which to infer whether a particular kind of conduct is predatory. In recent years several economic and legal scholars have attempted to develop objective criteria that can be used to identify the existence of specific intent of predation. One of the first and more comprehensive efforts to develop such rules was that of Phillip Areeda and Donald F. Turner (1975). Areeda and Turner argue that predatory intent may be inferred only when firms sell below their marginal costs:

> The monopolist is not only incurring private losses but wastes social resources when marginal costs exceed the value of what is produced. And pricing below marginal costs greatly increases the probability that rivalry will be extinguished for reasons unrelated to efficiency of the monopolist. Accord-

ingly, a monopolist pricing below marginal cost should be presumed to have engaged in predatory or exclusionary pricing. [p. 712]

This standard has been adopted by a number of courts.

Many legal and economic scholars reject the Areeda-Turner marginal cost rules as being too narrow. These critics would accept the marginal cost rule as a *sufficient* but not a *necessary* condition of predation. They believe predation may occur when firms sell above average variable costs but below average total costs and, in some circumstances, even when selling above average total costs. However, the economists and lawyers who reason that predation may occur when firms sell above marginal costs believe such pricing should be considered predatory only when accompanied by additional evidence of intent to monopolize.[27] Economic analysis has come to play an important role in antitrust decisions involving predatory conduct (Dirlam 1981).

Although the government has brought relatively few attempt-to-monopolize cases involving food companies, there have been a number of private actions. Two of the most important recent attempt cases, one brought by a private party and the other by the FTC, involved the same company, International Telephone and Telegraph Co.-Continental Baking (ITT-Continental).[28] Here we shall discuss briefly both the private and the FTC cases.

The private action was brought in 1971 when Inglis, a local baker, charged ITT-Continental with predatory pricing in northern California. After a jury trial, ITT Continental was found guilty. The case was then heard on appeal by the Court of Appeals for the Ninth Circuit. Because the Supreme Court refused to hear the case on appeal, the Ninth Circuit opinion provides an important precedent.

The Ninth Circuit's opinion repudiated "rigid adherence to a particular cost-based rule," rejecting the Areeda-Turner marginal cost standard as necessary to a finding of predatory intent:

> A plaintiff must prove that the anticipated benefits of defendant's price depended on its tendency to discipline or eliminate competition and thereby enhance the firm's long-term ability to reap the benefits of monopoly power. If the defendant's prices were below average total cost but above average variable cost, the plaintiff bears the burden of showing defendant's pricing was predatory. If, however, the plaintiff proves that the defendant's prices were below average variable cost, the plaintiff has established a prima facie case of predatory pricing and the burden shifts to the defendant to prove that the prices were justified without regard to any anticipated destructive effect they might have on competition.[29]

This decision essentially accepts the reasoning of those economists who would treat the Areeda-Turner marginal cost rule as a special case, concluding that predation may occur at prices between marginal cost and average total cost when there also exists evidence demonstrating an intent to monopolize.

On October 30, 1981, an FTC administrative law judge found ITT-Continental guilty of an attempt to monopolize. This decision was reversed by a majority of FTC commissioners July 25, 1984.[30] In addition to making sales below average variable costs presumptively illegal, the FTC majority also stated, "Sales at prices that equal or exceed average variable cost should be strongly, often conclusively, presumed to be legal."[31] This is a more difficult standard for identifying predation than that applied by the *Inglis* court.

This and other aspects of the majority's opinion caused dissenting commissioner Patricia P. Bailey to conclude that the FTC majority had sent a signal to the business community that "anything goes." Bailey added, "It would be simpler, and surely a great saving of everybody's time if the Commission today had simply announced that it does not believe predatory pricing exists."[32]

Thus, the law on attempt to monopolize remains unsettled because the various appellate courts (Dirlam 1981) and the FTC have applied a variety of rules. Until the Supreme Court agrees to hear a predation case, the law will remain at odds in the various lower courts.

Monopolization

There are two elements to a finding of monopolization: "(1) the possession of monopoly power in the relevant market and (2) the willful acquisition or maintenance of that market power as distinguished from growth or development as a consequence of a superior product, business acumen, or historic accident."[33] Thus the mere possession of monopoly power is not per se unlawful. The monopolist runs afoul of the law when it engages in certain deliberateness of purpose to maintain its monopoly position. The practices engaged in need not themselves be independently unlawful; rather they must be undertaken with the general intent to maintain monopoly power.

Two recent antitrust cases dealt with the possession and use of monopoly power by food manufacturers. The first case challenged single firm monopoly, and the second challenged so-called "shared monopoly." Not surprisingly, both cases involved industries where product differentiation had been successful in achieving and maintaining market power. This is significant because the main source of market power in food manufacturing is advertising-created product differentiation.

The ReaLemon Case. In 1976 an administrative law judge (ALJ) of the FTC found the Borden Company, a large multiproduct corporation, guilty of monopolizing the processed lemon juice industry. The case was brought under section 5 of the FTC Act, but the standards of section 2 of the Sherman Act were used in determining legality. The FTC upheld this decision in 1978 but modified the judge's order on relief. In 1982 the Sixth Circuit affirmed the FTC's decision and order.[34]

Evidence of the strength of Borden's ReaLemon brand is that it held up to 90 percent of the market and generally commanded a 40 to 50 percent price premium over brands of products of equal quality. This is probably one of the greatest price premiums ever enjoyed by a dominant brand in the U.S. food industry. Borden's own documents speak eloquently as to the strength and source of the brand. A Borden marketing plan said that ReaLemon is "one of the greatest brand names in the history of the supermarket." It had, as Borden put it, "an almost imaginary *image* superiority," despite the fact that "from a technical standpoint, ReaLemon has no apparent advantage over the juice of any of its competitors. Processed lemon juice is processed lemon juice." (FTC 1976, fact 83).

The FTC had little difficulty concluding that Borden enjoyed monopoly power; it met the legal test of having power over product price and had the power to exclude competitors. This decision was based on Borden's large market share and high degree of product differentiation. It further found that Borden willfully maintained its monopoly position through predatory geographic price and promotional discrimination to destroy competitors. The commission did not find that Borden sold at prices below its costs but rather an "intent to hold on to its monopoly share of the market by sacrificing somewhat higher prices over the short run to assure continued monopoly returns over the long haul."[35]

While the commission found that the ReaLemon brand gave Borden market power, its decision focused particularly on Borden's predatory practices. This difference in emphasis proved important when it came to remedy. The ALJ remedy called for compulsory licensing of the ReaLemon brand and placing some restraints on anticompetitive price and promotional conduct. The commission, with only its chairman dissenting, abandoned the ALJ's compulsory licensing as being unnecessarily severe; it believed a prohibition against predatory pricing and promotion would be sufficient to prevent Borden's use of monopoly power.

In affirming the commission's decision, the Sixth Circuit concluded that Borden had monopoly power because it held a "dominant" market share, had a highly differentiated product, and had a "substantial resource advantage over its competitors."[36] It further found that "when a monopolist, through brand identification or otherwise, can and does manipulate price in such a way as to exclude equally efficient competitors by requiring them to sell below their average variable costs, such price manipulation is an unreasonable use of power to maintain the monopolist's market position."

Following the FTC's victory in the Sixth Circuit, Borden appealed to the Supreme Court. In May 1983, the FTC took the unprecedented action of asking the Supreme Court not to review the case because the commission had entered into a settlement with Borden.[37] One of the most important features of the settlement was the commission's adoption of a below-variable-cost pricing rule. Although the commission said it was not "deciding that the standard imposed by this order is necessarily the appropriate standard in all instances," its action is generally viewed as indicating that the current commission majority intends to apply the Areeda-Turner marginal cost rule for identifying predation.[38] In his dissenting opinion, Commissioner Michael Pertschuk asserted that the commission majority "is trying to point predation law in a different direction—toward a solely cost-based standard that will be infrequently violated in real life and even less frequently proved. While it may appeal to some as embodying the height of economic rationality, as a practical matter, the standard in this order would take the commission out of the business of policing predation."[39]

Shared Monopoly. Section 2 of the Sherman Act is aimed at monopoly: a single firm possesses power independently of other firms in the market. Narrowly defined, this generally immunizes from attack tightly knit oligopolies, the most common manifestation of monopoly power in the food industries. Although very few food firms achieve the sort of dominant position held by Borden in ReaLemon processed lemon juice, there are a number of highly concentrated, tightly knit oligopolistic food industries, and this number promises to increase. Because firms in such industries may through joint conduct behave very similarly to a single dominant firm, the antitrust laws appear to provide no safeguards against the most serious monopoly problem found in the food industry.

To close this gap in the antimonopoly law, legal-economic scholars developed the concept of shared monopoly. This concept asserts that tightly knit oligopolists in industries with high entry barriers have the same ability to monopolize a market as does a single dominant firm (Scala 1973). This innovative theory was first applied in the *Kellogg* case, in which the FTC in 1972 charged the three largest ready-to-eat (RTE) cereal manufacturers with holding a shared monopoly.[40]

The FTC staff attempted to show that the RTE cereal industry was highly concentrated (four-firm market share of 91) and had high entry barriers. In the staff's view the three leading cereal companies had engaged in tacit collusion and had cooperated to maintain and exercise monopoly power. The staff then attempted to demonstrate that the defendants had attained and maintained their monopoly through a variety of explicit monopoly practices, including massive advertising (12 percent of sales), brand proliferation, and allocation of shelf space. As a result of their monopolization, the defendants allegedly enjoyed enormous monopoly profits, "overcharging" consumers $1,037,980,000 during the years 1957–1972.

The defendants argued in response that the heavy advertising and product proliferation were manifestations of keen competition and that there was no evidence of tacit or overt collusion. Thus, the RTE sellers asserted that they neither possessed the requisite monopoly power nor manifested a general intent to maintain their power.

After a prolonged trial, in which prominent economists testified on both sides, the FTC administrative law judge dismissed the case, concluding that complaint counsel had failed to demonstrate monopolization. In essence, the judge concluded that the defendants had acted like independently behaving rational oligopolists, which is not sufficient to constitute monopolization. In early 1982 the commission refused to hear the case on appeal, thereby sustaining dismissal of the case.

Thus ended the first and, to date, last shared monopoly case. The disposition of this case reflects the reluctance of the FTC or the courts to use the antitrust laws to deal with product-differentiation-created market power held by more than a single dominant firm. Indeed it is questionable whether the antitrust laws, even under the best of circumstances, provide an effective means for dealing with this problem, which is the most common source of market power in the food industries. This raises the question of whether new initiatives are required to deal with the problem of product differentiation-created market power.

Antitrust Treatment of Agricultural Cooperatives

The Capper-Volstead Act grants agricultural cooperatives a partial exemption from the antitrust laws. Section 1 of the act permits "farmers, planters, ranchers, dairymen, nut and fruit growers" to act together in marketing such products. This language has raised two basic issues. First, who are persons engaged in agricultural production? Second, what can these persons do?

Persons engaged in agricultural production include partnerships and corporations, as well as natural persons organized as sole proprietorships. Given this disregard for a producer's organizational form, eligibility for section 1 treatment largely depends on who is an agricultural producer. The Supreme Court addressed this issue in *National Broiler Marketing Association* v. *United States* (1978).[41] In that case, the government charged the National Broiler Marketing Association (NBMA) with horizontal price fixing and with restricting production to increase prices. NBMA members were vertically integrated companies generally owning and operating processing facilities, feed mills, hatcheries, and breeding flocks for the production of broiler eggs. The actual responsibility for raising chicks to maturity was contracted out to growers, with the integrated companies usually retaining ownership of the chicks. The Supreme Court rejected NBMA's claim to Capper-Volstead protection. The Court held that an agricultural producer is someone who is directly involved in animal husbandry and who assumes the risks of production and market fluctuations. Capper-Volstead does not protect all those who bear costs and risks of a fluctuating market, only those directly involved in production of livestock and, presumably, crops. Left unanswered in the case law is whether Capper-Volstead extends to all persons directly involved in production agriculture or strictly to those whose only effective response to market forces is through a cooperative.

Section 1 of Capper-Volstead gives agricultural producers the option to join together for the purposes of, among other things, cooperative processing, preparing for market, handling, and marketing of production. Cooperative associations may have marketing agencies in common, and the cooperatives and their members may make the necessary contracts and agreements to accomplish its purpose.

The cases indicate that there is a wide range of activity that a cooperative can pursue under section 1 with protection from antitrust charges concerning those activities. While price fixing is a per se violation of section 1 of the Sherman Act, the Supreme Court held in *Maryland and Virginia Milk Producers Association* v. *United States* (1960) that a cooperative can fix the price at which it will sell members' produce.[42] The Second Circuit has extended this holding to allow an association of cooperatives to fix price, even if that is the association's primary function.[43] Reasoning that marketing comprehends price fixing, the Ninth Circuit had earlier held that a cooperative can bargain to establish the price at which members will sell, even though the cooperative performs no other function.[44]

But the exemption provided by section 1 is not absolute. Although a cooperative can enter into a price-fixing agreement with another cooperative,[45] similar agreements with noncooperatives are unlawful.[46] Lower courts have further held that a cooperative may not lawfully engage in boycotting, predatory refusals to deal, blacklisting, unfair pricing policies, picketing, and acts of violence.[47] Several cases have treated the application of Sherman section 2 to cooperative monopoly. In *Maryland and Virginia Milk Producers Assn.,* the Supreme Court held that an allegation that a cooperative has used its legitimately acquired monopoly power in a variety of specified ways to drive out competitors is sufficient to state a section 2 cause of action.[48] Recently the Second Circuit held that Capper-Volstead allows for cooperative monopolies, but a cooperative cannot acquire or exercise monopoly power in a predatory fashion such as through picketing and harassment, coerced membership, and discriminatory pricing.[49]

A general policy is apparent in the case law treating what a cooperative can or cannot do under the Capper-Volstead Act. Farmers acting through cooperatives should have the same legal-organizational advantages and liabilities as the firms to which they sell their production or with which they compete. Indeed the courts recognize that "farmers' legitimate desires for unity of effort" necessarily involve "a concept of corporate aggrandizement."[50] Also, intracooperative activity is largely immune from antitrust scrutiny. As with noncooperative intracorporate activity, intracooperative activity will generally be viewed as deriving from an entity, not from separate members. The court decisions indicate that just as a noncooperative corporate entity can bargain for or fix the price at which it will sell, so can a cooperative entity. Corresponding to this, cooperatives are generally subject to the application of the antitrust laws for extracooperative activity involving anticompetitive conduct and structure.

Section 2 of Capper-Volstead was enacted to prevent the abuse of market power by cooperatives as a result of practices permitted by section 1. Specifically the secretary of agriculture is authorized to prohibit cooperatives from monopolizing or restraining trade to such an extent that they "unduly enhance" prices.

To date, enforcement has involved periodic analyses of third-party complaints by USDA task forces. In 1979 Secretary Bob Bergland proposed the establishment of a USDA cooperative monitoring unit, which would receive and evaluate third-party complaints and initiate investigations based on ongoing monitoring of cooperative behavior. Implementation of the plan proceeded only to the publication of agency rules concerning cease-and-desist proceedings.[51]

Since no complaints have been issued under the act, there are no court interpretations of the concept of undue price enhancement. Most legal analyses generally point to the lack of section 2 enforcement, often providing explanations for this.[52] Most also contend that the law ought to be enforced more aggressively, making suggestions for change. The 1979 Report of the National Commission for Review of the Antitrust Laws and Procedures to the President and the Attorney General addressed these issues.[53] The commission urged that section 2 be amended to clarify the meaning of undue price enhancement and that the secretary of agriculture be either relieved from enforcement responsibility for section 2 or this responsibility be divorced from promotion responsibility within the USDA. Some critics advocate that the DOJ or the FTC should assume an exclusive or an expanded role with respect to the antitrust treatment of cooperatives.

Economic analyses of section 2 have focused both on the theoretical conditions required for a cooperative to enhance price and on what is an unduly enhanced price (Jesse et al. 1982; Mueller 1979). The various definitions of undue price enhancement that have been proposed in recent years require a reference price for evaluating what is undue price enhancement. Most definitions recognize that undue price enhancement requires more than that a price be above a perfectly competitive price. It has also been suggested that the concept of undue price enhancement should be viewed within a broader industrial concept that considers the price-cost levels that exist elsewhere in the economy (Mueller 1979). Wills (1985a) has applied this concept and found that in food manufacturing industries, cooperatives generally have lower prices than proprietary concerns operating in similarly structured industries.

This suggests that undue price enhancement is not a significant problem in these industries, although it might occur in isolated instances.

Some economists urge that an unduly enhanced price is a price corresponding to the exercise of substantial market power. But they would not, for the purpose of section 2, include in this high prices that result from "superior products, brand loyalty, innovative management, or better services," provided that once attained, such prices are not maintained with anticompetitive tactics. Their reference point, discussed in terms of the price that would prevail in a workably competitive market, is the price expected under similar market conditions but absent the cooperative's influence.

Summary of Antitrust Enforcement

Antitrust enforcement in the food industries has been quite active over the past three decades, serving as the focus of several precedent-setting antitrust cases. As in other industries, the most important enforcement area involved mergers, though there also were important price-fixing, price discrimination, and monopoly cases. In recent decades a substantial percentage of the antitrust agencies' resources were devoted to antitrust actions in the food industries. Although many business people are critical of the antitrust laws, support remains strong among consumer groups, organized labor, small business, and some large businesses.

What is the significance of this effort? To what extent did it alter market structure and business conduct? Is there a need to strengthen these laws? Should they be supplemented by or replaced with other forms of social control of business? Or should the laws be repealed or substantially curtailed, relying instead on a laissez-faire policy that assumes natural competitive forces are sufficiently powerful to discipline effectively the attainment and the use of private economic power?

Answering most of these questions requires an excursion in normative economics, reflecting the values of those proposing change. Here we only attempt to summarize the state of the various antitrust laws and their apparent effects. We then set forth several policy alternatives that might make these laws more effective in promoting competition in the food industries.

Price-fixing and related restraints among competitors remain per se unlawful. These prohibitions appear to have been enforced quite effectively in the most conspiracy-prone food industries. Although one never knows how many conspiracies go undetected, the law is certainly effective in preventing the kinds of elaborate schemes required in cartels, as well as many less formal enduring price-fixing arrangements. Some economists would limit the antitrust laws essentially to prohibiting price fixing.[54] Dewey (1979) has even suggested that this most basic restriction be relaxed; this clearly extreme view has been strongly rebutted by others. Extensive relaxation of existing laws seems unrealistic because it would permit, indeed encourage, the emergence of monopolies through merger and predation that could set excessive prices with impunity.

The agencies and the courts have taken a dim view of horizontal mergers, though less so in recent years. This strict policy doubtless has challenged or otherwise prevented some mergers that did not injure competition and, perhaps, even some that were procompetitive. But historical experience makes a strong case for erring on the side of a too strict merger policy rather than a too lenient one. Whereas firms blocked or discouraged from merging always still have the alternative of growing by internal expansion, once a merger occurs, it may bring about irreversible structural change, perhaps triggering other mergers whose cumulative effect drastically and unnecessarily increases concentration and decreases competition.

Available evidence indicates that the tough horizontal merger policy has, on balance, prevented many industries from becoming more concentrated. Given the insatiable appetite for growing by mergers, including conglomerate mergers that make little or no economic sense, the absence of strict legal constraints would certainly have resulted in many more anticompetitive horizontal and market extension mergers. Examination of the effects of merger enforcement in several food industries indicates that it had quite dramatic and salutary effects. Though not stopping all mergers or even materially slowing overall merger activity, it has sharply channeled this activity away from the industry leaders, resulting in more decentralized market structures without any obvious impairment of efficiency; indeed, the policy doubtless helped many smaller firms to achieve more efficient size.

In sum, horizontal merger policy seemingly has contributed to more competitive market structures, particularly in producer goods industries; significantly, market concentration has not risen in these industries in the decades following World War II (Mueller and Rogers 1980). But the policy has been less effective in preventing rising concentration in consumer goods industries where advertising-created product differentiation is instrumental in raising concentration (ibid.). Although conglomerate mergers also have played a role in concentrating these industries, merger policy has become increasingly permissive in this area.

We have not attempted to quantify the effectiveness of the R-P Act. In our judgment, however, prohibitions against secondary line price discrimination have been largely effective in eliminating most of the anticompetitive price discrimination arising because of the superior market power of large retail buyers, the main objective of the framers of the R-P Act. The act has been less effective in addressing primary line discrimination, conduct that falls short of the predatory behavior prohibited by section 2 of the Sherman Act. This is partly due to the antitrust agencies' reluctance to enforce the act in recent years because of their lack of sympathy for the act, a view shared by many economists.

In recent years there have been several attempt-to-monopolize and monopolization cases brought under section 2 of the Sherman Act and section 5 of the FTC Act. Defendants have almost invariably prevailed in these cases.

The law with respect to attempt to monopolize is currently unclear, with several appellate courts applying different standards. If the Areeda-Turner marginal cost rule accepted by several appellate courts when identifying predatory conduct is endorsed by the Supreme Court, it will be extremely difficult for plaintiffs to prevail in such cases. The present law in this area is, at best, effective in preventing only the most egregious types of predatory conduct destructive of competition.

The present reach of the law of monopolization appears to encompass only situations of single firm dominance. Since relatively few food industries have such structures, the law does not have much application here. Moreover, the FTC's decision to settle the *ReaLemon* case indicates that the current commission is disinclined to challenge practices that could be challenged under existing law.

The greatest gap in existing antitrust law is the inability to deal with the possession and use of market power by oligopolists. Although innovative approaches have been proposed that would treat tightly knit oligopolies as shared monopolies, this approach has been rejected to date. This immunizes those oligopolistic industries that can exercise monopoly power without explicit agreement and can maintain their power without illegal acts. This presents the greatest anomaly in the U.S. antitrust laws: loosely knit oligopolies that must conspire to achieve market power are proscribed by per se standards of section 1 of the Sherman Act, but tightly knit oligopolies that can reach a monopoly result without conspiring are immune from antitrust prosecution under section 2 of the act.

Recommendations Regarding Public Policy

Advertising and Concentration

The main industries experiencing increasing concentration in food manufacturing are those that lend themselves to extensive advertising, especially television advertising. Existing antitrust laws have had minimal effect on the advertising-related increases in concentration. Because the increases can occur without resort to acquiring competitors, the harsh antitrust strictures toward mergers have little application. When a food conglomerate acquires a company that is a leader in the industry, the acquisition may be vulnerable to antitrust challenge; indeed, several such mergers have been successfully challenged. But when a conglomerate acquires a company that is not a market leader, the merger is generally thought to be beyond the reach of the merger law even when there is evidence that the power has been used to restructure the acquired company's industry. Thus it appears that the growing market concentration in industries with heavy advertising is essentially beyond the reach of existing antitrust laws. Nor have antitrust scholars come forth with many recommendations for reform.

One way in which antitrust could be made more effective would be to develop stricter standards for predatory advertising. Food conglomerates may engage in costly subsidized advertising when launching new products or expanding their market shares over existing products. This practice is viewed as promotional advertising and is virtually untouchable under existing interpretations of the law dealing with attempts to monopolize. As Areeda and Turner (1978, p. 336) observe when speaking of predatory pricing, "The basic thrust of the classic rule is the presumption that attempt [to monopolize] does not occur in the absence of a rather significant market share." These authors would make the standard even higher for alleged predatory advertising than for predatory pricing. Such a view may counsel for amending existing law toward predatory pricing and advertising conduct.

Other policies not involving the antitrust laws may significantly improve performance in industries where advertising-created market power exists. These policies are aimed primarily at improving consumer information. These initiatives include (1) *affirmative disclosure* of product characteristics and limitations, (2) *corrective advertising* to eliminate misinformation conveyed by past advertising claims, (3) *substantiation* of the truthfulness of advertising claims, and (4) *counteradvertising*. In the 1960s and 1970s the FTC initiated programs involving all but the last of the above approaches. In recent years the special interests affected displayed increasing resistance to these efforts. The current FTC chairman, James Miller III, has been quite unsympathetic to these approaches. Recently he proposed weakening the FTC's existing program requiring advertisers to be prepared to substantiate their advertising claims.[55]

The fourth approach, counteradvertising, has considerable potential, as demonstrated by the brief period when the Federal Communications Commission required, under the fairness doctrine, television stations to provide free time to public groups to counter cigarette advertising. Based in part on this experience, the FTC suggested to the FCC that media licenses might make available regular prime time for counter-advertisements directed at broad general issues raised by advertising involving certain products "as a way of fulfilling this aspect of their public service responsibilities." The current FCC has shown no interest in this approach.

In sum, the antitrust laws have a limited role in dealing with advertising-created market power. Strengthening these laws may help in dealing with predatory advertising. However, an eclectic approach wherein antitrust is supplemented by policies that increase consumer information may be the most promising way of dealing with the problem. Because of the important role of advertising in modern capitalistic economies, continuing efforts must be made to develop alternative policies in this area that do not impair other performance dimensions of the food system.

Merger Policy

Merger enforcement in the food manufacturing and food retailing industries, while not effective in preventing all anticompetitive increases in concentration, generally has had a salutary effect on industry structure and performance. The legal rules established by the Supreme Court in the 1960s prevented many horizontal mergers that otherwise would have unnecessarily increased market concentration in food manufacturing and food retailing. Similarly, in both food retailing and food manufacturing, the merger law prevented many product- and geographic market-extension mergers that might have eliminated potential competition. Commencing in the mid-1970s and especially in the early 1980s, the antitrust agencies enforced less aggressively the legal precedents of the 1960s. In 1982 the FTC and the DOJ issued new merger guidelines that greatly enlarged the area of permissible horizontal mergers and virtually gave a green light to all nonhorizontal mergers. The guidelines, which permit many of the mergers declared illegal by the Supreme Court in the 1960s, represent explicit decisions by the antitrust enforcement agencies not to enforce the existing antitrust laws.

Our analysis of the application of the merger law to the food industries indicates that this diminution of enforcement is not justified by empirical evidence. Prior enforcement policies had been successful in promoting competition and did not do so at the expense of economic efficiency.

Thus the congressional oversight committees should carefully scrutinize present antitrust enforcement policy to determine whether the antitrust agencies are properly fulfilling their respective mandates to enforce the laws enacted by the Congress and subsequently interpreted by the Supreme Court.

Predatory Conduct and Attempts to Monopolize

There is empirical evidence that predatory conduct, the practice of employing price or other strategies to destroy, weaken, or discipline competitors, has been used in both grocery manufacturing and grocery retailing. A public policy problem exists because the antitrust agencies have not been diligent in enforcing the laws designed to prevent anticompetitive predatory conduct, and there exists considerable disagreement among the various appellate courts as to the appropriate standards proscribing predatory conduct under existing laws.

Predatory conduct can be challenged under either section 2 of the Sherman Act or under the R-P Act, which prohibits anticompetitive price discrimination under certain circumstances. The current FTC administrators, which have primary responsibility for enforcing the R-P Act, have not challenged a single instance of discriminatory conduct under the act, either in food or any other industry. Although the act has not always proved effective in dealing with anticompetitive price discrimination, the enforcement record of the current FTC reflects its chairman's basic antipathy toward the act. The failure to carry out the FTC's enforcement mandate warrants careful oversight hearings by the Congress to determine whether the Congress agrees with the FTC's current enforcement policy. If the Congress does agree with FTC policy, the R-P Act should be repealed or amended; if the Congress disagrees with current FTC policy, the Congress should take appropriate action to ensure effective enforcement of the act.

Section 2 of the Sherman Act prohibits attempts to monopolize if three conditions are met: (1) evidence of a specific intent to monopolize, (2) conduct undertaken to achieve this purpose, and (3) evidence showing a dangerous probability of success. Various courts have established rules that make it very difficult to prevent conduct that many economists (and lawyers) view as clearly anticompetitive.

First, there has been widespread acceptance by the courts of the Areeda-Turner rule that intent should be inferred from pricing conduct and that an attempt to monopolize can only be presumed to have occurred if an alleged predator sells below its marginal costs (Areeda and Turner 1975). Economic authorities generally agree that the Areeda-Turner rule represents only one special case of predation. These authorities argue that predation may also occur at prices between marginal costs and average total costs and, in exceptional cases, at prices above average total costs.[56]

Second, many courts have equated the dangerous probability standard with actual monopolization. Such a standard permits "plainly predatory or vicious anticompetitive conduct [to go] unchecked under the antitrust laws."[57]

If the attempt to monopolize standards were applied to the *ITT-Continental* case discussed in chapter 4, no attempt to monopolize could have occurred unless ITT-Continental's prices were below its marginal cost. Moreover, "a dangerous probability of success" would not have existed because even if ITT-Continental destroyed all its rivals except Campbell-Taggert, the largest seller in the market, ITT-Continental would not have achieved a monopoly.

Because of the narrow approach some courts have taken on these issues, the President's National Commission to Review the Antitrust Laws and Procedures recommended in 1979 that section 2 of the Sherman Act be amended. This proposal would require that in determining intent, "the fact that prices were not below either average variable costs or marginal costs should not be controlling but is a factor which may properly be considered in assessing the defendant's intent and the competitive effects of particular conduct" (National Commission for Review of Antitrust Laws and Procedures 1979, p. 151). The commission also proposed that in determining whether "a dangerous risk of monopoly exists" the courts weigh the following factors: "(1) the defendant's intent; (2) the defendant's present or probable market power; and (3) the anticompetitive potential of the conduct involved." Taken together "these factors are intended to measure and predict the likely effects such conduct would have on competition" (ibid., p. 151). The recommendations of the National Commission deserve careful consideration.

Shared Monopoly

Earlier chapters indicated that a growing number of markets in grocery retailing and food manufacturing are highly concentrated and that such markets result in substantial monopoly overcharges to consumers. Existing antitrust case law is virtually silent on the monopoly power that results from such highly concentrated industries with substantial entry barriers. Section 2 of the Sherman Act contemplates a single firm with monopoly power, not the shared monopoly power that exists when several firms together possess a predominant share of the market. Thus, there is a gap between the reality of monopoly power and the law designed to deal with it.

This gap lends credence to the criticism that these laws and their enforcement are little more than a charade played out to legitimize market power. Galbraith (1967, p. 187) speaks for many critics when he asserts, "We discriminate against those who, as a result of their numbers and weakness, must use crude or overt methods to control their markets and in favor of those who, because of achieved size and power, are under no such compulsion." He further observes (p. 185) that whereas monopoly is illegal, "oligopoly, which is agreed to have the same consequences but with diminished force, is not."

Because the market power of shared monopolists is conferred by the market structures in which they operate, competition can only be helped by industrial restructuring. Various initiatives have been pursued to restructure concentrated industries. One approach has been to apply, without success, the existing law. The recent attempt to challenge the shared market power held by the leading cereal companies failed. Nor is it likely that existing law will be used effectively in the future.

Legal authorities generally agree that, given the state of the case law, new legislation is required if shared monopoly is a serious public policy concern. The most recent efforts to obtain new legislation originated in the recommendations made in the 1968 *Report of the White House Task Force on Antitrust Policy,* which proposed enacting a concentrated industries act.[58] The proposed act applied only where four or fewer firms accounted for 70 percent or more of industry sales in important industries. A specialized panel of judges would have been established to hear proceedings under the act.

In 1971, the proposed Concentrated Industries Act (S.2614) was introduced, but no hearings were held on the proposal. In 1972, Senator Philip A. Hart introduced a similar bill, the Industrial Reorganization Act (S.3832). Extensive hearings were held on the bill over several years, but it never was voted out of the Senate Antitrust Subcommittee.

Although no progress has been made in dealing with shared monopoly, not only does the problem remain, but it is growing in several food industries. Those concerned with the competitive performance of the economy will continue to search for public policy solutions that will reduce (or control) the market power of shared monopolists in the food industries and elsewhere in the economy.

Conglomerate Corporations

The huge food conglomerates possess market power not fully contemplated by the antitrust laws. The power of these enterprises cannot be captured by simple economic models and defies careful empirical examination. What we have learned about them, however, shows they often enjoy power not vulnerable to challenge under existing law. Today the antimerger laws deal almost exclusively with horizontal combinations, and section 2 of the Sherman Act deals only with the use or enhancement of horizontal market dominance.

The typical food conglomerate corporation derives its power from huge size and multiproduct and multimarket operations, often extending over many nations. Its power is augmented by horizontal market dominance in some markets, though not necessarily in those in which it exercises its power. These organizational characteristics enable the conglomerate to engage in strategies not always open to specialized firms, even powerful ones.

The dimensions of conglomerate power require new public policy initiatives. The available evidence suggests that most mergers among huge conglomerates are not motivated by economic efficiency, nor is this their effect. Various proposals have been made that would closely monitor and limit conglomerate mergers. One such approach was a bill (S.600) introduced in 1979 by Senator Edward Kennedy and others. It would have prohibited mergers among large corporations and acquisitions of firms holding large market shares. Briefly the bill would have prohibited mergers among companies where each had sales of $350 million or more in a significant market. The bill provided the following affirmative defenses: (1) the merger "will have the preponderant effect of substantially enhancing competition; (2) the merger will result in substantial economies; and (3) within one year before the merger the parties shall have divested one or more viable businesses with revenues at least equal to the revenues of the smaller merger partner." Hearings were held on this bill, but no action was taken. In 1983 Congressman Peter Rodino introduced a similar bill.

Another approach to conglomerate power would require federal chartering (as opposed to state chartering) of huge conglomerates, placing publicly appointed directors on their boards, and requiring greater public disclosure of their operation. This approach derives from recognition that large corporations are not purely private enterprises but quasi-public institutions affecting the lives of millions of people. Such corporations become imbued with a public interest and are legitimized only if they serve the public's goals. Determining whether such corporations are operating in the public interest requires greater knowledge of their operations than is now available. Indeed, each time one corporation is absorbed by another, our knowledge of corporate affairs is diminished. The need for greater disclosure was recognized by Theodore Roosevelt at his first inaugural. Speaking of what he viewed as the corporate giants of his day, he said, "The first requisite is knowledge, full and complete; knowledge which may be made public to the world."

Not surprisingly, corporate officials are virtually unanimous in opposing publicly appointed directors. Robert Townsend, former chairman of Avis, Inc., and one-time official of ITT, is an exception. In his view, "If implemented properly, a public director could be a vehicle to make a real dent into corporate unaccountability," adding, "it is very hard to build a good case *against* public directors for these corporate giants" (Townsend 1973, p. 257).

Agricultural Cooperatives

The secretary of agriculture has never formally challenged under section 2 of the Capper-Volstead Act the practices of any cooperative. Some critics have argued that this fact alone is sufficient to demonstrate that the secretary should not be entrusted to enforce the act. Others have reasoned that the secretary's inaction is consistent with evidence showing that cooperatives, acting alone, generally do not possess an essential element of substantial market power, control of supply.

Some economists have demonstrated that some cooperatives possess, in the short run at least, sufficient power to raise prices above perfectly competitive levels; it is highly questionable, however, that the resulting price enhancement is "undue" when viewed within the broader context of pricing behavior commonplace elsewhere in the economy, including food manufacturing.

Public policymakers should view skeptically any broad generalizations charging inadequate enforcement by the secretary of agriculture. It seems desirable, however, for the secretary to divorce enforcement responsibility for section 2 from persons having responsibility for promoting cooperatives within the USDA, as recommended by the President's National Antitrust Commission.

Given the likelihood of infrequent violations of section 2, it does not seem necessary to establish a special monitoring unit in the USDA along the lines contemplated in 1979. Creating such a new bureaucratic organization within USDA would necessarily consume significant resources, both within the department and for cooperatives submitting compliance reports. Rather, adequate enforcement could be achieved if the department examines complaints of alleged undue price enhancement; such complaints could originate from customers or competitors of cooperatives, consumer groups, the antitrust agencies, and congressional committees. This would result in at least as much surveillance as there exists in the enforcement of the antitrust laws. The department possesses sufficient legal and economic resources to investigate such ad hoc complaints and, when warranted, to enforce the provisions of section 2.

Treble Damage Actions by Farmers

The Supreme Court's decision in *Illinois Brick Co.* v. *Illinois,* 431 U.S. 720(1977), prevents indirect victims of antitrust violations to sue for treble damages. This has prevented farmers and consumers from maintaining actions against indirect buyers or suppliers of their commodities. The structure of the food industries, as well as the hundreds of antitrust cases brought in these industries since 1950, indicates that they are prone to collusive behavior. Although various objectives have been raised to overruling *Illinois Brick,* these are not of overriding significance given alternative ways of satisfying these concerns in the food industries (Mueller 1984b). We therefore favor an amendment to the antitrust laws that would reverse the *Illinois Brick* decision, at least as it applies to the food industries.[59]

Statistical Reporting Programs

A market-directed economy is premised on informed responses of business and investors to profit opportunities. Moreover, a market economy relies on the self-correcting mechanism of the marketplace to promote competition. When firms hold strong market positions that confer high profits, this attracts entry. And firms with high costs and low profits may attract entry of more efficient firms. These signals cannot be received by potential entrants when the financial statements of large conglomerate enterprises mask both profits and losses of various lines of business.

The extent of information loss resulting from the increasing conglomeration of U.S. industry was documented by a 1972 FTC study (FTC 1972b, pp. 87–126). Subsequently the FTC initiated an annual Line of Business (LB) program, which developed detailed financial data by significant product categories. While information for individual companies was not disclosed, many independent researchers were able to use the data in analyzing various aspects of the organization and performance of manufacturing industries (FTC 1982a, pp. 349–403).

In 1982, the FTC announced the suspension of data collection for its LB program in order to give its staff "sufficient time and resources to conduct an extensive analysis of the benefits and costs of the LB program" (Miller 1982, p. 9). To date, the suspension has continued despite considerable analysis by the FTC's staff; businesses affected by the program have submitted extensive reports in opposition to the LB program.

It would be unfortunate if the LB program were to be suspended permanently. The sorts of information it developed are essential to a meaningful analysis of many dimensions of industrial performance and are unavailable from any other source.

Review of Antitrust Policy

The maintenance of effective competition is essential to the proper functioning of a market-directed economy. Not only does competition policy have a direct bearing on the goals of rapid economic growth, efficient allocation of resources, and the distribution of those resources, but it reflects important social values, particularly those associated with a system of decentralized economic and political power.

Antitrust policy, as embodied in the Sherman, Clayton, and Federal Trade Commission acts, remains the primary policy aimed at maintaining a competitive economy. During most of the period since 1950, there has been vigorous enforcement of these laws as they applied to horizontal mergers in the foods manufacturing and other industries. This effort demonstrates that the antitrust laws can play a central role in preserving and enhancing competition. Other areas of antitrust have also been successful to varying degrees. Since 1981, however, there has been a virtual suspension of federal antitrust enforcement in areas outside price fixing and horizontal mergers involving large market shares in already highly concentrated industries. The change in enforcement policy has resulted from the decisions of the FTC and DOJ to interpret the antitrust laws contrary to how the Supreme Court has interpreted their legislative intent. This represents a historic departure from past antitrust enforcement. Because of its great significance for competition policy, there should be a comprehensive debate, under the aegis of the appropriate congressional oversight committees, as to whether the direction of antitrust policy should be changed; if so, the antitrust laws should be modified accordingly. Based on our survey of the application of these laws to the food manufacturing and related industries, these laws should not be repealed but strengthened.

Notes

1. Standard Oil Co. v. United States, 221 U.S. 1, 58 (1911).

2. FTC v. Cement Institute, 333 U.S. 683, 693 (1948).

3. For a discussion of the enforcement of the Packers and Stockyards Act *see* Walter J. Arbruster, Dennis Henderson, & Ronald Knutson (eds.), *The Federal Marketing Programs in Agricultural: Issues and Options* 239–268 (1983).

4. The only study of the patterns of private actions covers cases brought in the Southern District of New York. *See infra* note 15.

5. Sugar Antitrust Litigation, 73 F.R.D. 322 (E.D. Pa. 1976).

6. Folding Cartons Antitrust Litigation, 88 F.R.D. (N.D. Ill. 1980).

7. Wilson Foods Corporation v. Eli Lilly and Company, No. 81C1812 (N.D. Ill. 1982).

8. Before fluid milk markets became larger, this industry also was conducive to price fixing.

9. Bakers of Washington, Inc., 64 F.T.C. 1079, 1109 (1964), *aff'd sub nom,* Bakers of Washington v. Federal Trade Commission, 306 F.2d 795 (9th Cir. 1966).

10. This discussion is from Willard F. Mueller, "Effects of Antitrust Enforcement in the Food Industry: Price Fixing and Merger Policy," 2 *Antitrust L. & Econ. Rev.* 83 (Winter 1968–1969).

11. Bakers of Washington, Inc., 64 F.T.C. at 1126. Typically chain label bread sells at prices 10 percent to 15 percent below the brands of wholesale bakers.

12. Federal Trade Commission v. Morton Salt, 334 U.S. 337 (1948).

13. Utah Pie Company v. Continental Baking Co., 386 U.S. 685 (1967). Earlier precedent-setting primary line cases were also in food. *See, e.g.,* Moore v. Mead's Fine Bread, 348 U.S. 115 (1954); Anheuser-Busch, Inc. v. Federal Trade Commission, 359 F.2d 487 (8th Cir. 1966).

14. ITT Continental Baking Co., supra note 30. The FTC ruled that sales at prices equal to or exceeding average variable costs "cannot ordinarily satisfy the predation element of primary line injury to competition." *Ibid.* p. 292.

15. Data are not available of the number of private R-P cases. A study that examined 299 private cases brought in the Southern District of New York in 1973–1978 found that 12.2 percent of allegations involved R-P cases. If this percentage is applied to all private actions filed during 1973–1978, private parties brought about 884 Clayton section 2 and R-P cases during this period. NERA, *A Statistical Analysis of Private Antitrust Litigation: Final Report,* prepared for the American Bar Association, Section of Antitrust Law by National Economic Research Associates, Inc., New York, Oct. 1979, at 1, 27. In contrast, during 1971–1980 the two antitrust agencies brought only eight cases alleging violations of the R-P Act.

16. 69 F.T.C. 482 (1966).

17. *See esp.* Brown Shoe Co. v. United States, 370 U.S. 294 (1962); United States v. Bethlehem Steel Corp., 168 F. Supp. 576 (S.D.N.Y. 1958).

18. *See esp.* Federal Trade Commission v. Procter & Gamble Co., 386 U.S. 568 (1967); Federal Trade Commission v. Consolidated Foods Corp., 380 U.S. 594 (1965); United States v. Penn-Olin Chemical Co., 378 U.S. 158 (1964).

19. Justice White's dissenting opinion in United States v. Marine Bancorporation, Inc., 418 U.S. 602, 642 (1974), characterizes the majority as constituting a "new antitrust majority."

20. This summary of mergers in food retailing draws heavily from W.F. Mueller (1978a, pp. 38–50).

21. United States v. Von's Grocery Co., 384 U.S. 270 (1966).

22. Grand Union, F.T.C. Docket No. 9121 (Initial Decision, October 30, 1981).

23. United States v. G. Heileman Brewing Co., U.S. Dept. of Just. Docket No. 3027 (Nov. 22, 1982).

24. FTC v. Procter & Gamble Co., 386 U.S. 568 (1967).

25. FTC v. Consolidated Foods Corp., 380 U.S. 592 (1965).

26. The actual numerical standards are not expressed in CR4s but as Herfindahl indexes, which measure the sum of the squares of individual firm market share in a relevant market. *Justice Department Merger Guidelines and FTC's Policy Statement on Horizontal Mergers,* Special Supplement, *Antitrust & Trade Regulation Report,* Bureau of National Affairs, June 17, 1982, pp. S-6, S-7.

27. Sullivan (1977, p. 113) believes the hallmark of predatory conduct is that "the predator is acting in a way which will not maximize present or foreseeable future profits unless it drives or keeps others out or forces them to tread softly."

28. William Inglis & Sons Baking Co., Inc. v. ITT-Continental Baking Co., Inc., 668 F.2d 1014 (9th Cir. 1981); ITT Continental Baking Co., F.T.C. Docket No. 9000 (Initial Decision May 1, 1981).

29. Inglis, 668 F.2d at 1035–1036.

30. ITT Continental Baking Co., F.T.C. Docket No. 9000, 7/25/1984. Citations to decision reported in BNA *Antitrust & Trade Reg. Rep.* vol. 47, No. 1177, August 9, 1984, pp. 283–313.

31. Ibid., p. 286.

32. Ibid., p. 311.

33. United States v. Grinnell Corp., 384 U.S. 563, 570–571 (1966).

34. Borden, Inc. v. Federal Trade Commission, 674 F.2d 498 (6th Cir. 1982).

35. Borden, Inc., 92 F.T.C. 778 (1978).

36. 674 F.2d at 515–516.

37. "FTC Asks Supreme Court Not to Review Borden," 44 *Antitrust & Trade Rep.,* May 5, 1983, p. 922.

38. "FTC's Proposed Settlement of Borden Case," 44 *Antitrust & Trade Reg. Rep.,* March 3, 1983, p. 525.

39. Ibid., p. 528.

40. Kellogg Co., F.T.C. Docket No. 8883 (Initial Decision, Sept. 10, 1981). Quaker Oats Co. was named in the initial complaint but was subsequently dismissed.

41. 436 U.S. 816 (1978).

42. 362 U.S. 458, 466 (1960).

43. Fairdale Farms, Inc. v. Yankee Milk, Inc., 635 F.2d 1037, 1040 (1980).

44. Treasure Valley Potato Bargaining Association v. Ore-Ida Foods, Inc., 497 F.2d 203, *cert. denied,* 419 U.S. 999 (1974). *See also* Northern California Supermarkets, Inc. v. Central California Lettuce Producers Cooperative, 413 F. Supp. 984 (N.D. Cal. 1976), *aff'd,* 580 F2d 369 (9th Cir. 1978) (per curiam), *cert. denied,* 439 U.S. 1090 (1979).

45. Fairdale Farms, Inc., 635 F.2d at 1039-1040. In Sunkist Growers, Inc. v. Winckler & Smith Citrus Products Co., 370 U.S. 19, 29 (1962), the Supreme Court held that de minimis organizational distinctions among cooperatives should be disregarded. There the Court upheld an agreement among three cooperatives to process and market members' citrus products.

46. United States v. Borden, 308 U.S. 108, 205 (1939).

47. Treasure Valley, 497 F.2d at 216–217 n.11.

48. 362 U.S. at 854.

49. Fairdale Farms, 635 F.2d at 1043–1044.

50. *Id.* at 1043.

51. "Rules of Practices Governing Cease and Desist Proceedings under Sec. 2 of the Capper-Volstead Act," 44 Fed Reg. 39,409 (1979) codified at 7 C.F.R. 2.27(a)(13)(1985).

52. *See, e.g.,* Note, "Trust Busting Down on the Farm: Narrowing the Scope of Antitrust Exemptions for Agricultural Cooperatives," 61 *Va. L. Rev.* 341 (1975); Folsom, "Antitrust Enforcement under the Secretaries of Agriculture and Commerce," 80 *Colum. L. Rev.* 1634 (1980).

53. Reproduced at [Jan.-June] *Antitrust & Trade Reg. Rep.* (BNA) No. 897, Spec. Supp. (January 18, 1979).

54. Lester Thurow (1980, p. 150) would rely mainly on prohibitions against price fixing by banning "explicit or implicit cartels that share either markets or profits. Firms can grow by driving competitors out of business or by absorbing them, but they cannot agree to not compete with each other." For a critique on Thurow's views, see Willard F. Mueller (1981, pp. 27–38).

55. "FTC Chairman Wants to Weaken Its Rule Requiring Proof of Truth of Ad Claims," *Wall Street Journal,* November 10, 1982, at 10.

56. For a review of much of this literature *see* Joskow and Klevorick (1979).

57. Donald I. Baker quoted in National Commission for the Review of Antitrust Laws and Procedures, p. 145.

58. A copy of this report appears in the *Antitrust L. & Econ. Rev.* 11–12 (Winter 1968–1969).

59. One such proposal is currently being reviewed by the Senate Judiciary Committee, S.2835, "A Bill to Amend the Clayton Act to Allow Certain Sellers of Agricultural Products to Bring Antitrust Actions" (Mueller 1984b).

Part V
Conclusions

As this book goes to press, several issues in the food system have high visibility. Clearly the crisis in farming is one. Not since the Great Depression have so many farms been poised on the brink of financial disaster. An associated issue is the decline in the ability of the United States to compete in world markets. In agricultural commodities, this appears to be largely attributable to the increasing prevalence of protectionist policies and the international strength of the U.S. dollar. From 1979 to 1984, the value of the dollar increased about 50 percent relative to the currencies of those countries buying U.S. agricultural products. However, there is also a growing fear that U.S. companies in many industries are no longer the most progressive and most efficient. What do the Japanese have that we do not have? The massive number and size of mergers and take-overs is a third issue. Although previous merger waves have affected the food system, none involved as many mergers on the scale of Nestles-Carnation; Beatrice-Esmark; American Stores-Jewel; Kroger-Dillon; Reynolds-Nabisco Brands; or Phillip Morris-General Foods. A fourth and related issue is the strong push by the Reagan administration toward deregulation, laissez-faire economics, and "market" solutions. We are in a period of free enterprise permissiveness in which great confidence is placed in the rationality of business and the workings of the market. The turmoil in labor markets is a fifth issue. Since 1980, there has been persistent high unemployment, with a 7 percent rate now considered low, whereas only a decade ago, such a rate was considered unacceptable. In addition, wage concessions or give-backs have been negotiated in several U.S. industries. Since World War II, blue-collar workers have been able to look forward to increasing wages and a rising standard of living. This may no longer be true for many. And it seems unlikely that white-collar employees will remain immune from the downward pressures on remuneration. Sixth, the huge and growing national debt is a pervasive issue affecting all parts of the U.S. economy.

The coordinating author for this part was Bruce Marion, who wrote the introduction.

This list of high-visibility issues is in sharp contrast to the list that might have been developed only ten years ago: sharply increasing oil prices and widespread inflation, international food shortages and high world grain prices, the need for U.S. farmers and the marketing system to gear up to serve international markets and to "feed the world," sharply higher U.S. food prices, and concerns about the lack of competition in food marketing industries.

The striking change in high visibility issues over ten years creates a certain sense of humility as we try to identify some of the important policy implications of our research. The focus of our research has not been insensitive to the shifting priorities of various national issues; however, our overriding objectives have remained much the same: to develop a better understanding of how the food system is organized, how it is changing, the factors affecting its performance, and the effects of present and alternative public policies. The organization and performance of the food system is not currently a hot topic; however, we believe it is a fundamental issue that calls for basic and applied long-term research. Sooner or later, it will once again move to the front burner on the policy agenda.

The research in this book contributes more than an analysis of the U.S. food system. We believe it also contributes to our knowledge of how markets work and provides evidence that is consistent with certain industrial organization theories and inconsistent with some alternative theories.

Chapter 7 is organized to correspond to the first three parts in the book. Because the policy implications of the three parts differ greatly, we briefly summarize some of the key findings and present the policy implications of each part: first for agricultural production, then for pricing, coordination, and the organization of agricultural subsectors, and finally for the food manufacturing and distribution industries. The discussion of competition policies for the food manufacturing and food distribution industries builds on the analysis of antitrust policies in part IV.

7
Summary and Policy Implications

Agricultural Production

Farming, composed mainly of owner-operated units that are price takers, is unique. Crop farmers' assets are mainly land; the value of land depends largely on rather insubstantial expectations about future farm incomes. The farm business is largely internally refinanced each generation by new entrants coming usually from sons and daughters of the owners.

Most crop farms, as measured by acres and/or value of sales, have become steadily larger since the 1940s. Many kinds of livestock (except cow-calf) and poultry operations have had even more rapid increases in average size as measured by value of sales in the same period. Increasingly farms have specialized in either crops or livestock and in fewer species of them.

Farm assets appreciated more rapidly than the GNP implicit deflator during the 1960s and 1970s. Aggregate assets in nominal terms tripled from 1970 to 1980. Their value as a potential source of capital gains influenced potential investors and lenders and caused farmers to be willing to accept fairly low current cash incomes and cash rates of return on present value. Farm asset values have been falling, quite sharply in many areas, since 1981 because of the higher real interest rates, the fall in farm prices and incomes, and changed inflationary expectations. While farmers typically have a low ratio of debts to assets, the average ratio has risen in the 1980s. In 1985, as many as 143,000 farms (6.6 percent of all farms) had debt-asset ratios above 70 percent; a high proportion of them were in financial jeopardy. Another 243,000 farms with debt-asset ratios above 40 percent had serious cash-flow problems.

U.S. crop agriculture has become heavily dependent on the vagaries of world demand. Shocks from shifts in demand for U.S. crops are readily transmitted through the market mechanisms to most other subsectors. The coefficient of variation for annual cash receipts during 1972–1983 for crops was

---

The first two sections of this chapter were written by V. James Rhodes; the last section was written by Bruce Marion.

27.4 percent and 25.5 percent for livestock. Both rates were much higher than those of preceding periods. Net farm income has become highly unstable. Producers have essentially the same set of government price supports and marketing orders (to help absorb these shocks) that were developed in the 1930s. The degree of protection varies greatly for different commodities.

Different subsectors of agriculture have relied to varying degrees on government programs to stabilize and/or raise their incomes. Producers of grains, tobacco, cotton, and, to a lesser extent, soybeans have generally had price supports. The dairy farmers have utilized import controls and marketing orders, as well as price supports. Several other subsectors have utilized import controls, including sugar, wool, beef, and pork (pending in 1985). Producers of numerous fruits, vegetables, and specialty crops have utilized marketing orders to supplement the vertical coordination provided by market prices. Because of the resource substitutions possible within agriculture, some of the benefits of any commodity program eventually spread to other groups. On the other hand, governmentally instigated increases in feed grain prices hurt the animal subsectors in the short term.

While there may be ready agreement on a dozen or more factors that influence structural changes in farm production, there is less consensus concerning their relative importance. Certainly technology ranks high. The four-wheel-drive tractor increased optimal crop acreage; better disease control and the automated chicken house led to egg factories. Federal programs that reduce downside price risk and indemnify against crop disasters may have increased the rate of growth of larger farms due to more highly leveraged financing. Yet the opposite hypothesis has also been voiced: instability of incomes increases the rate of consolidation of farms into large units because of large tax-savings-inspired investments in favorable years. Certain income tax provisions such as cash accounting and investment credits have encouraged the plowing back of earnings into depreciable assets so that the big get bigger. The capital barriers to entry of new owner-operators have been increased by income and estate tax policies that turn farm assets into attractive tax shelters.

The mix of agricultural inputs in the past half-century has changed greatly while becoming more productive. Total output increased 150 percent in the past half-century while total inputs rose only 7 percent. Labor use declined rapidly, land use remained stable, and capital use rose. Improved genetics of plants and animals and increased use of fertilizer, mechanization, pesticides, and irrigation were among the main sources of increased productivity.

Technical economies of scale encourage large farm size but do not require it from a societal point of view; that is, most economies of size seem to taper off at the medium-size farm. The operator of a large farm can obtain greater total profits although not necessarily lower per unit costs. Two caveats apply. First, economies of size probably extend to large size for a few commodities. Second, purely pecuniary economies from quantity discounts on input purchases probably increase profits for many large-size operations. Larger units may also obtain some pecuniary gains from more astute timing of sale of their output.

Sole proprietorships are still the dominant type of organization, although sales of corporate farms (mainly family controlled) rose to a 24 percent share in 1982 from an 18 percent share eight years before.

Considerable interest was displayed in the 1960s and 1970s in the structure of agriculture and the welfare implications of the rapid changes underway. Correcting the size distribution for changes in inflation, and changes in the labor input required as the technology changes, shows a significant change in the distributions of farm numbers and proportion of production. The percentage of total output from "small family farms" fell from 22 percent in 1960 to 9 percent in 1982 as the percentage from "larger-than-single-family farms" rose from 33 percent to 49 percent. The share of total sales by the largest 5 percent of farms rose from 41.5 percent in 1960 to 50.1 percent in 1982. The commodities with their production most highly concentrated in larger units are eggs, fed cattle, fruits, and vegetables. The least-concentrated enterprises are cash grain and dairy.

Agribusiness control of agricultural production by ownership vertical integration or production contracts increased only slightly from 1960 to 1980. This type of control is confined mainly to vegetables for processing, sugarcane, citrus, and poultry. Some additional production contracting in commodities such as hogs developed in 1984–1985 in response to the farm financial crisis.

Major Policy Issue 1: The Goals of the Farm Program of the 1980s

Farmers are operating in an increasingly uncertain environment. Many in 1985 were struggling to survive financially. Government policies to dampen inflation were a very important cause of farmers' difficulties in the early 1980s. How much shall government help farmers in financial crisis? How shall the huge financial losses associated with falling values of farm assets be distributed among farmers, lenders, agribusinesses, and taxpayers? How much effort simply to stabilize the farming sector is justified?

There are no easy answers. Some farmers deepest in debt are land speculators, but others are beginning farmers who bought land at its peak price. Failure to provide any bail-out may engulf many agricultural lenders, including the farmer-owned Farm Credit System, and thus spread the problem to a widening circle of farmers and agribusinesses. Any program to improve the incomes of family farmers seems inevitably to help disproportionately the larger-than-single-family farmers. Thus, programs to help the family farms may simply diminish their future role as the larger farms continue to increase their share of agricultural output. Considering the massive instability in agriculture, the current financial crisis, and the considerable contributions of governmental fiscal and monetary policies to both, there is some justification for trying to reduce the instability in U.S. agriculture. Such programs as the Farmer-Owned Reserve for grains, crop insurance, and price supports at near-world-price levels can provide some stability without excessive costs to taxpayers. On the other hand there are strong pressures to allow Darwinian survival to develop a set of farmers that are presumed to be able to compete effectively in world markets. The decisions will be heavily influenced by non-farmers because farmer influence is divided and waning.

Pricing, Coordination, and the Organization of Agricultural Subsectors

Vertical coordination as a process includes activities internal to vertically integrated firms and the market transactions among firms at different market stages. Our interest in vertically integrated activities has pertained less to how they are governed and implemented within the organization structure of the firm and has pertained more to why they are not market transactions. Unified control of production and marketing by vertical integration or production contracts has been confined mainly to a few commodities.

A market transaction involves a buyer and a seller. The transaction generally involves the participation of alternative, potential buyers and sellers. A transaction occurs within a context of regulations, customs, and industry practices that makes routine the setting of many of the terms of trade. A market transaction has four important elements:

1. Making the deal (specification of terms of performance by each participant).
2. Transfer of ownership.
3. Establishing a price.
4. Physical delivery to the buyer.

All four elements may be completed simultaneously, or they may be fulfilled in varying places at varying times. In the terminal markets for livestock and produce, the seller often ships to the buyer's doorstep before any deal is made. Then in the livestock terminal, price is established as the deal is made, the ownership is transferred, and physical delivery is completed by the drive to the scales. Contrast a contractual deal to sell hogs in 90 days at a fixed price. The deal has been made, and price has been established. A few of the rights of ownership are transferred immediately, but the seller retains possession of the hogs (and the physical risks of disease and disaster) until they are delivered and the transaction is finally completed. In citrus the transfer of ownership and delivery takes place months after the deal is made and months before the final price is determined by settling the participation pool.

A traditional market transaction involved face-to-face dealing of a buyer and seller in the presence of the commodity and the immediate completion of all four elements of the transaction. In the twentieth century, many variations have developed: buyer and seller may deal over the telephone; the commodity is described rather than displayed and so is not necessarily in the presence of either the buyer or seller; or one or more of the elements of the transaction occurs at a different time or place than other elements. This new flexibility usually results in a reduction in market transaction costs. It also allows for various allocations of risk.

Market transaction costs are all those costs associated with the various elements of a transaction, including an appraisal of alternative deals, the communication and transportation costs directly associated with making the deal, transferring ownership, setting price, and delivery, plus those occasional negotiational costs when one or both parties complain about some aspect of the transaction. Transaction costs are increased by uncertainties that complicate the appraisal of alternatives: questions of prevailing prices, actual quality of the commodity, likely cost of delivery, and reliability of the potential buyer or seller.

An important theoretical insight is that, other things equal, activities equivalent to market transactions occur within firms or within markets (between firms) depending on where the transaction costs are less (Coase 1937). Thus retail food chains found that they should obtain warehouses and do much of their wholesaling. Independent wholesalers countered by developing special affiliations with independent retailers that reduced their market transaction costs and allowed them to compete with the vertically integrated chains.

A parallel observation is that a transaction method that has lower costs will prevail eventually in the marketplace over its more costly alternatives, other things equal. Thus direct marketing of eggs has replaced the more cumbersome market system prevailing through World War II. Direct marketing of livestock has eroded the market shares of terminal markets over the past sixty years. Formula pricing of carcass beef became popular in the past quarter-century, replacing a system that negotiated price at the time of the deal. Much earlier when packers were powerful and retailers were not, beef carcass prices were listed by the packers. The negotiated price system that replaced it may have been no less costly, but it was more acceptable to the chain retailers. Thus, other things (than cost) are not always equal. Milk producers developed bargaining cooperatives and voted for marketing orders to secure such objectives as continuous market access and fair prices rather than to lower transaction costs; however, the entire transaction process has been routinized in milk so that costs are low.

With production contracts and most marketing contracts, the deal is usually made some weeks or months prior to delivery of the commodity. Contracting sellers seek assurance of market access for highly perishable commodities. Sellers may also contract because of pressure from lenders, to secure technical knowledge and equipment, or to establish a price before undertaking production. Contracting buyers usually have specific product needs—so many tons of a specific quality of green beans each day during the canning season. The costs explicitly associated with such a contracting system may appear large; however, these contract transactions may implement vertical coordination better than that available with any other transaction alternative so that system costs are less. Contracts may also relate to the power balance among competing buyers and between the contracting parties; the stronger party is usually the writer of the contract.

Most market participants gather considerable market news in the process of market negotiations. Additional market news is usually gathered by a specialized agency and distributed to market participants. Market participants usually can reduce their transaction costs by utilizing this additional market information rather than by extended search. Because of the public good nature of market news, it is usually argued theoretically that market news should be handled by a publicly supported agency that will provide more information than market participants are willing to buy. In fact, in the livestock and meat industry, the larger participants are willing to buy a great deal of market news (the Yellow and Pink Sheets) beyond the news provided publicly by the USDA. The egg industry places heavy reliance on market news purchased from a private agency. The reasons for this apparent conflict of theory and fact are not clear.

Numerous equity issues have long arisen in market transactions. The seller may be wrongfully deprived of all or part of the market value of his or her property by means employed by the buyer: physical force, a rubber check, misinformation about the market value of the commodity, or monopsony power. Or a buyer might be coerced by physical threats, defrauded by watering the milk, or exploited by monopoly power. Laws and regulations have evolved over the centuries to curb the recognized inequities. However, some smaller enterprises still seem to receive a less than equitable treatment.

The increasing fragmentation of the transaction's four elements has given rise to new possiblities of inequity. Contractual transactions with several months intervening between the deal and its completion provide ample time for one or both sides to regret the deal. The rising prices associated with a drought-shortened crop motivate a seller to break an earlier agreement to deliver at a fixed price. The failure to deliver, however, may leave the buyer in an exposed position. Another example is that the bankruptcy of an elevator may occur after a farmer's grain is delivered but before payment is received. In a third example, erratic fluctuations of base prices may cause sellers and/or buyers to be shocked by the actual formula price set for their earlier deal. If there are associated suspicions that the base prices may have been manipulated to a seller's or buyer's advantage, feelings of inequity are heightened. As a final example, a green bean producer may claim inequity when he or she is not allowed to deliver beans from part of his or her contracted acreage because the processor is facing excess supplies.

The developments in the flexibility of the market transaction as to place, timing, and so on have numerous positive aspects. These developments encourage the expectation of technically efficient markets. The flexibility of transactions and the futures markets available in many commodities encourage competition by allowing many participants to bid for the particular terms that they find attractive. Degree of market risk can be enlarged or diminished, within bounds, according to one's preferences. A participant with little confidence in pricing skills can likely find a transaction providing a formula price. The presumption is that a mix of transaction mechanisms is appropriate in the food system. Whether any existing mix is optimal in a subsector is an open question.

While each subsector has significant unique features, those subsectors studied by NC 117 have several commonalities. Generally the number of firms at all stages is declining. The number of farm producers is still large enough to provide an atomistic structure on the selling side even in local markets. Agricultural production is becoming more commodity specialized and more capital intensive. There is usually some market power among the agribusiness firms, especially in first-handler buying in local markets. Producers have tried cooperatives with varying degrees of success. Growth of direct marketing has led to a decline in the importance of intermediaries.

A subsector is a set of enterprises from farm to retail linked together by various ownership and contractual ties, markets, rules, and transaction arrangements involved in producing and marketing a commodity. In most subsectors, there has been a trend away from open, anonymous trading to more selective, personal coordination. Generally market participants before the retail stage do not deal with strangers. The expected repetition of transactions among the same market participants (farmer and canner, meat packers and retail chains, food processor and fast food chain) is evidence that transactions are generally part of a continuing relationship. Certain institutions have developed that facilitate ongoing relationships rather than isolated transactions. Such relationships and institutions usually have low transaction costs. In other words, they are technically quite efficient; however, they may not be as favorable to open market price discovery, full market-wide competition, and optimal allocative efficiency.

Coordinating arrangements of a continuing nature between buyer and seller reduce uncertainties of market supplies or outlets. When there is a big disparity in the size and number of buyers and sellers, as is typical when farmers are sellers, the market power balance favors the side of the fewer and larger. Producers often address their problem of market weakness by cooperative integration into first handling and even processing. The divergent successes of cooperatives in such subsectors as dairy and hogs suggest that cooperatives can achieve more where close farmer-handler coordination is essential than where the traditional open market functions well.

Farmers produce commodities; consumers mostly buy products. Some commodities such as eggs move through the subsector relatively unchanged. There are many challenges in linking consumer product markets to farmer commodity markets. In summarizing some of those challenges in terms of problem and policy areas, it should be emphasized that the accomplishments are large indeed.

Suppose the entire marketing system of a particular subsector were wiped out? Would we expect it to be replaced with all the same institutions and the same structure of firms at each level and coordinated vertically as before? Probably not. Yet most of us would be cautious in pressing forward possible improvements. In learning more about how market institutions work in the various subsectors, we have had to recognize an important diversity. It is no longer so tempting for a commodity specialist to assume that an institution that works well in one subsector will work equally well in others.

We choose to highlight certain broad problem areas that relate to two or more of the subsectors studied. These problem areas may also be seen as major policy issues.

Major Policy Issue 2: Achieving an Accurate Redefinition
and Vertical Coordination of Commodity Quality

It is often erroneously assumed that a commodity (in contrast to a manufactured product) is a gift of nature with unchangeable characteristics. In fact, a commodity can usually be redesigned considerably through changes in breeding and production practices. Some commodity changes can occur as an unintended by-product of changes in breeding and/or production to increase productive efficiency. The changes of present interest are those made deliberately in a commodity in the interests of maintaining or increasing demand.

The difficulties stem first from the fact that producers must be persuaded to undertake some fundamental changes in breeding and/or production techniques and, second, that there may be conflicting messages as to the desirability of redesign.

It is useful to contrast the experiences in the dairy, hog, and beef subsectors. Shortly after World War II when the market for farm-separated cream disappeared, the high-butterfat-producing breeds largely disappeared from dairy herds. The message was clear, and dairy farmers reacted promptly.

More recently, concerns have developed about better payment for nonfat solids in milk. This message has not been as clear, and little has happened. In hogs, low lard prices signaled a demand for leaner hogs; however, the message was not clear. Most of the gain in meatiness required genetic changes, and it was not immediately clear what was being given up in desirable production capabilities. In a quarter of a century, however, remarkable changes in lean pork have been achieved. The message in beef has been even less clear. Consumers say they want lean, nonwasty beef. More meatiness would also reduce production costs, but what would it do to palatability? The industry has slowly and cautiously moved leaner. Today's Choice grade that is the target for most fed beef production is roughly equivalent to the Good grade of pre–World War II that was then regarded as inferior and too lean. Some of the opposition to further leanness of beef stems from genuine fears about reducing demand through hurting palatability, and some stems from vested interests including fancy restaurants, feedlots, and breeders.

It would appear rather obvious that a buyer would pay more for a more valuable (to him or her) unit of a commodity than a less valuable unit. If the buyer fails to do so, he or she risks losing the more valuable units to a competing buyer. To facilitate this process, new carcass yield grades were developed for both beef cattle and for hogs. But providing increased clarity about quality requires extra transaction costs. Most cattle and hogs are priced per pound of live weight rather than carcass weight. Typically an average price for the pen or the truckload is settled rather than an inconvenient and separate price for each animal or each grade group. While average prices between two producers may vary accurately with the differences in average qualities (grades), the difference is usually small. The average market price does not drive home to the farmer the price that he or she could have received if all of the animals had been as good as the top quartile. In fact, the pricing mechanism does not necessarily indicate anything to the producer as to which animals are superior. Hence agricultural economists and other educators have often supported a pricing system that attaches values to individual animals, both for the value demonstration effect and because it is then easy for all to see that price incentives actually exist. Pricing on a carcass basis is usually the most expedient way to manage pricing of individual animals. Carcass pricing has been supported by educators but has been implemented slowly. Governments in some other advanced countries have often taken stronger actions than has the USDA.

The debate about quality pricing techniques continues. Some economists allege market failure with average lot pricing even if the mean price accurately reflects the mean quality. Other economists argue that such mean pricing does recognize quality and that slow progress has been more the fault of conflicting messages (as in beef) than of the pricing system.

The policy mechanisms for achieving commodity redesign at the producer level include changes in commodity descriptions, such as federal grades, education of market participants, and price incentives. The three are complementary. The education provided by private and public sources through numerous industry channels provides the specific details of what, how, and why. Price differentials in favor of the new, improved commodity provide the essential profit incentives.

Sometimes federal grades are used by market participants to describe and communicate quality variations. Debates have focused on grade characteristics for several of the commodities studied. It appears to be increasingly difficult politically to obtain consensus of producers, agribusiness, and consumers on grade redefinitions. Perhaps industry standards with their greater flexibility will replace grades.

Present grain grades need revision to describe better the quality factors of importance to traders. These grading inadequacies are one of the reasons that contractual and vertical integration has been developed by those processors with very specific quality requirements.

Major Policy Issue 3: The Temporal Coordination
of Quantities Produced and Marketed

In the U.S. food system, commodity prices ration available supplies so that there are few queues when supplies are short and minimal spoilage when supplies are long. Thus market pricing seems to perform its market clearing tasks quite well. When one studies the large price variations that occur, however, and the confusing ways in which a price change passes the length of a subsector, one must ask whether improvements are possible. The large price variations essential to market clearing are confusing to production planning. While producers may seldom naively extrapolate current prices to expected prices, the optimism of high current prices or the pessimism of low current prices is difficult to avoid.

Agricultural production is less amenable than industrial production to quick corrections. Agricultural production is typically a batch process with long biological lags before completion. The obvious examples are crops in which a fall harvest follows planting decisions in early spring. Even the apparently continuous flow of pork arises from a succession of batch decisions associated with ten month lags.

The process of vertical coordination of agricultural commodities is affected by: (1) the biological lags between production decisions and actual output; (2) the economics that generally motivates a producer to complete a batch production process once begun regardless of large, unexpected drops in price; (3) the fact that production decisions are made with incomplete knowledge of the aggregate impact of the simultaneous decisions of other producers; (4) the unpredictable and largely uncontrollable impacts of weather, disease, and other variables on domestic and world output; (5) the relative perishability or storability of the commodity and any derived products; and (6) the relative elasticities of demand and supply for the commodity.

The long biological lags in getting a cherry or citrus orchard into production contrasts with the shorter lags of producing more eggs or more hogs. Generally the longer the biological lag, the longer the actual output may deviate from the output desired by producers and by consumers. Beef has a special problem because of its high ratio of breeding stock to output and the fact that heifers may go to slaughter or to the breeding herd. Hence an industry attempt to reduce output leads to slaughter of more heifers and greater output for two or three years; the same perverse supply response applies to an attempt to increase output.

Price fluctuations would generally be least if both supply and demand were highly elastic. In that case, an unplanned large output can be readily absorbed in an elastic market. Also an output shortfall is handled without much change in price. Of course, there may be effects on the costs and profits of other firms in the subsector when there is a shift in the amounts to be handled, processed, and merchandised.

Price cycling is reduced to the extent that supply is less elastic than demand, a circumstance that seems likely for a slow response crop such as citrus. Large variations in both output and prices are disruptive of efficient operation of all market participants.

Many producers realize prices far different than they expected when making earlier production decisions. Some of the disappointments are individual failures to interpret correctly the available outlook data. More of the disappointments result from unforeseen shifts in demand (especially foreign demand for grains) or in output because of good or bad weather or some other factor. But beyond all those is the fundamental problem in a competitive industry with batch production lags that there is no institution by which producers can assess the aggregate decisions being made by others and then modify their decisions through a series of iterations that would have a high probability of making realized prices equal to anticipated ones. Economists have solved this equilibrium problem theoretically with a mythical auctioneer who took bids and rebids until all buyers and sellers had arrived at a mutually acceptable price and total output. In agriculture, there is no auctioneer, no rebidding process, and no certainty as to future wants or outputs. The problem manifests itself in different forms in the various subsectors depending on the biology of the production process, the lags involved, and so forth. Producers of a few commodities are able to transfer much of the problem to processors by means of preproduction contracts with firm prices. A transferred problem is still a problem. Moving independent production decisions up through the subsector is no solution for society as long as the ignorance of others' decisions remains; witness the continued cycles in a broiler industry populated by vertically integrated processors.

Generally shifts in the volume of an agricultural commodity moving into consumption require an opposite shift in retail price. A rather quick adjustment at retail is particularly important to producers of the perishables, such as fresh meats, eggs, and poultry. A continuing problem has been the slow response of retail prices. Farm prices are thereby made to fluctuate more severely as they balance changing supplies and demands. The process works as follows. An increase in farm volume of a perishable seems to go unnoticed by retailers. Processor inventories build, and farm and wholesale prices fall; the retail margin widens. Weeks later, retail prices finally adjust, and the retail margin returns to normal. The process is similar when farm volume falls, although the lag by retailers may be shorter.

The management of excess supplies is a frequent problem handled quite differently among the subsectors. Storage of commodities such as grains, processed fruits and vegetables, and orange juice concentrate is profitable to the individual enterprise when excess supplies are not chronic. In beef, pork, broilers, potatoes, and eggs, the basic disposal mechanism is a price falling low enough to clear the current market. A few subsectors such as beef, broilers, and citrus have faced the favorable circumstances of chronically falling costs or rising demand.

Unfortunately excess supplies may become chronic in some subsectors because specialized resources are relatively immobile once committed. The industrialization of hog production is presumably reducing the downward flexibility of the supply response. Poultry and dairy production have a similar degree of industrialization. Dairy producers in the 1980s have an overproduction problem stemming from several years of too high price supports. Tree fruits represent a long-term commitment. Excess facilities in associated agribusinesses are also fairly common. On the one hand, overcapacity represents resource misallocation; on the other, it may lead to more aggressive competition in purchasing farm commodities.

Clearly prices alone perform only part of the vertical coordination needed in food subsectors. Prices do determine rewards to market participants. Thus the setting of prices raises equity issues. Marketing orders, government price supports, contracts, and vertical integration often supplement market pricing. They may affect vertical coordination as much as do prices. More institutions need to be invented as subsectors evolve toward less dependence on prices as a vertical coordination device.

Marketing orders have been of some stabilizing value in a number of commodities. Marketing orders allow some extra supplies of commodities such as milk and some fruits to be diverted into a secondary market with a fairly elastic demand. A marketing order for tart cherries permits interseasonal storage aimed at reducing interseasonal price variation; however, a few marketing orders have been criticized for propping up prices from year to year and leading to chronic overproduction. In any case, marketing orders are not adapted to the pricing problems of the major commodities such as grains and oilseeds.

Cooperative bargaining, ordinarily in conjunction with a marketing order, is another institution for supplementing price as a choice for vertical coordination. Although the effects of cooperative bargaining are usually relatively modest, they sometimes include a moderation of price fluctuations and uncertainty. Bargaining cooperatives facilitate coordination by gathering and disseminating information on supplies, demand, and price and by working out various marketing problems as they arise. If marketing orders and/or governmental price supports were eliminated, producers of several commodities would likely try to rely more on cooperative bargaining.

Governmental programs involving price guarantees and supply management can aid in stabilizing agricultural prices and outputs. In the 1950s and 1960s, government-supported corn prices seldom deviated much from $1 a bushel. The considerable economic problems of this approach are complicated immeasurably by the political issues as to levels of price supports, storage stocks, and government payments. This approach is so widely used in Europe that "marketing" is basically the study of government price guarantees and supply management. While the political environment of the early 1980s was strongly against this approach, its long use around the world as well as in the United States suggests that it will continue to be considered as an option. At this point, we simply remind that government programs could be used to facilitate production planning and market clearing without being used to make sizable income transfers from consumers to producers.

Another option for improving vertical coordination is forward contracting by producers. Some experts have hopes for the usefulness of a forward deliverable contract market (FDCM) in some commodities, but the FDCM is as yet untested. Proponents of the FDCM would have producers, prior to initiation of production, make firm price, marketing-type contracts with processors or retailers, who should know most about prospective demand. Those contracts could then, if desired, be resold through the season—changing who delivers to whom. Retailers as contract recipients would have far greater incentives to adjust prices and merchandising quickly to the inventories available, thus eliminating troublesome lags. It is not clear, however, that processors or retailers have sufficient incentives for taking the risks posed in such contracts. Nor is it clear that the process would solve adequately the crucial set of bids and rebids essential to producers determining how much to produce in that brief, final period before resources are put into production, unless regulations required all producers to forward contract or otherwise register and fulfill their production plans. This mandatory feature would likely greatly hinder initial acceptance, although it is hardly as restrictive as the marketing quotas that some producers have accepted in certain price support programs.

*Major Policy Issue 4: Transaction Mechanisms
and Thin Markets*

Price posting, decentralized individual negotiation (private treaty), marketing
and production contracts, administrative decisions within vertically integrated
firms, collective bargaining, pooling, public auctions, offer and acceptance,
formula pricing, and electronic trading are the principal transaction mechanisms found in the U.S. food system. Attention in recent years has focused on
the last two: formula pricing and electronic trading. The first is much practiced, while the second is used more as a theoretical concept.

The frequent use of formula pricing at the processor–retailer pricing
interface and occasional use at the producer–first handler interface is due to
several advantages. Search costs are reduced for buyers and sellers. Delivery
follows the rest of the transaction in many types of wholesaling. Formula
pricing allows a price to be set at or near delivery that is the going market
price being paid (and received) by one's competitors. Formula pricing fits
especially well those account-supplier relationships in which seller S regularly
sells to buyer B. Such continuing relations develop because uncertainties and
transaction costs are reduced. B may like to rely on S because he provides
quick, reliable service; he consistently provides the particular commodity
specifications desired at the times promised. S may like to sell to B because
she has been found to be a reliable purchaser, who buys regularly, does not
reject shipments on trumped-up excuses, and pays promptly. Formula pricing
provides a neutral, noncontroversial, easy, and cheap way for S and B to set a
series of prices that reflect the market around them.

Why isn't formula pricing used universally given its impressive advantages? We may not know the complete answer to that question, but the pricing and subsector research have given some clues. One technical answer
might be that some other form of pricing must coexist in order to form the
price base for formula pricing. That answer is not necessarily true, as will be
explained.

More generally there are situations in which other transaction mechanisms are apparently more acceptable to market participants. Price posting is
common when the numbers of buyers and sellers are vastly unequal, as is true
at the retail-consumer interface and frequently at the farmer–first handler interface. Price posting is operationally efficient; it sometimes reflects some
degree of market power held by the price posters. Resistance by farmers to
price posting and/or other exercise of market power by buyers has sometimes
led to collective bargaining, cooperative marketing, pooling, or development
of other transaction mechanisms such as auctions and electronic trading, and
to a marketing order-cooperative-price-support framework for milk pricing.
Very large producers of flow commodities such as hogs and eggs may sell
regularly enough to develop a continuing relationship that includes formula

pricing, but smaller producers typically do not. Custom feeding in large feed-lots with its many separate owners of cattle discourages development of a continuing relationship of producer and packer. In wholesale situations such as grains where transactions vary greatly in regularity and volume, price posting or the individual negotiation of price (with reference to the related futures prices determined by double auction) is more acceptable to participants than formula pricing.

Considerable attention of both market participants and economists has focused on the thin markets that sometimes arise with extensive formula pricing. As those firms negotiating and reporting prices become fewer, confidence in the resulting base price can erode. One early hypothesis was that formula pricing would tend to self-destruct when everyone in a market tried to formula price. An alternative hypothesis was that some traders would quickly revert to negotiations whenever they distrusted the base, so that formula pricing could be self-perpetuating. A third alternative is that a base price can be provided either with no negotiated prices or by a specially contrived negotiation.

The price series reported in eggs is based largely on the size of producer inventories rather than on the prices in the tiny number of negotiated transactions that usually are regarded as nonrepresentative trades. A price reporting agency, or a committee of experts, can apparently perceive inventory changes and adjust a fabricated price base accurately enough to achieve market clearing for eggs, and likely for some other commodities. In these cases all of the transactions can be formula priced. There have been many participant complaints about egg pricing, suggesting that the pricing mechanism is not optimal, but it has persisted for years. The wholesale trading in cheese proceeds quietly, with more than 99 percent priced by formula. The weekly base price is set by an instructive technique. At a public cheese exchange, participants meet once weekly and make at least one transaction. The publicly negotiated price becomes the base for formula pricing for the following week. The general acceptance of this base price may be because the forces of supply and demand are publicly registered in the cheese exchange plus the fact that any other pair of participants could challenge the negotiated price by immediately negotiating a different one at the weekly base-setting session.

There is a high proportion of formula pricing of beef carcasses and fresh pork cuts at the wholesale level and also many participant complaints. While negotiated transactions are much more numerous in beef and pork than in cheese or eggs, the negotiations are in private, and their reporting tends to be selective and infrequent. Consequently the formula base prices arising from reported negotiated prices may sometimes appear unrealistic to market participants.

Suggested policy options in wholesale beef have varied from banning formula pricing to making mandatory a certain percentage of negotiated and reported prices, to encouraging or requiring electronic trading. Formula pricing is so technically efficient in many situations that banning is strictly a last resort. The term *mandatory* arouses subsector opposition. A mandatory percentage of negotiated prices could probably be made to work in some situations, although there might be strong incentives for some participants to try to manipulate the base prices.

Electronic trading appears to combine the operational efficiencies of direct trading with the competition-enhancing mechanism of the auction. Search costs are reduced; more distant traders can participate. Concerns about price manipulation and pricing inaccuracies are reduced. Allocative efficiency is increased further by electronic trading, which facilitates the use of detailed descriptions of the commodities traded. Theoretical interests have been sharpened by recent USDA-financed trials in marketing several farm commodities, as well as wholesale meat. Electronic trading can help farmers deal with the problems of market access and buyer market power. Electronic trading at the wholesale level could eliminate the thin market problem while conceivably having transaction costs nearly as low as formula pricing.

It is unlikely, however, that electronic trading will rapidly and extensively replace other transaction mechanisms. Start-up costs are high, with a large cooperative or the government the most likely sponsor. An important policy question is to what extent government shall encourage electronic trading and in what interfaces of what subsectors it shall do so. Contrary to some first thoughts, electronic trading may not fit well where formula pricing seems to fit best. Electronic trading is anonymous and transaction focused. It works best when the buyer and seller focus entirely on that transaction and its price, disregarding the identity of the other party. For example, it works well in cotton where the buyer can acquire specific qualities without knowledge of the seller's identity. Farmer sales of livestock where there is a regular, large aggregate volume but individual sales are infrequent and irregular fits electronic trading. Electronic trading will not fit well where supplier-account relationships are important unless it is used in a minority of transactions to establish the base price.

Much the same supply and demand forces are at work regardless of the transaction mechanism. Large differences in long-term average prices by transaction mechanism are hardly to be expected. Savings in transaction costs may be shared by buyers and sellers. Short-term differences by transaction mechanism in the level and flexibility of prices and other terms of trade are more likely. More important may be ways in which the best-adapted transaction mechanism meets market needs of participants at low transaction costs and thus facilitates market exchange rather than vertical integration. The movement toward vertical integration has frequently been a quest for greater technical efficiency. Unfortunately, it has been at the cost of some inflexibility in the allocation of resources. This research suggests that there may be innovative ways to achieve greater technical efficiency without sacrificing allocative efficiency.

Major Policy Issue 5: Agribusiness Market Power

How to deal with agribusiness market power is a problem for those without it and for society. Much of the market power in the commodity part of the food system is not concentrated enough that society is likely to do much about it. Nevertheless, farmers facing that power have incentives to neutralize or match it.

Farmers throughout U.S. history have complained about a lack of active competition among local buyers of their commodities. The improved highway network in the past half-century has reduced but not eliminated some of those local oligopsony problems. Producers in major production areas face the least problems. Fringe-area producers (a sunflower producer in Missouri, a hog producer in Texas, or a cattle feedlot in Montana) frequently have problems obtaining competitive bids on their output. Producers of milk, a highly perishable item, have traditionally felt that they must have help in dealing with the one outlet on which they depend. Consequently dairy producers have long relied on bargaining cooperatives and marketing orders to provide them with countervailing power. There have been power problems also with eggs; they have been largely eliminated by the growth of large producers that are frequently integrated into egg packing.

Producers faced with agribusiness power have two basic policy options: try to develop more competition by antitrust and/or the development of more price-competitive institutions such as electronic trading or try to develop countervailing power through cooperatives, marketing orders, and government price supports. Much more reliance has been placed on the second group of options by both the subsectors studied here and also most of agriculture. Because fewness of competitors is economically justified in many first handler markets, the competition furnished by a farmer cooperative is frequently beneficial. Of course, devices such as cooperatives and price supports offer farmers additional benefits besides countervailing power.

Another problem is very different; it is the disequilibrating force of a sizable wage differential in an industry associated with uneven bargaining power of labor unions. When labor costs are major in an industry, those firms with much lower labor costs may obtain a dominant position over higher-wage firms. The result is a massive restructuring of the industry as high-cost firms exit or reorganize or find ways of escaping their high-wage contracts. The beef industry has been going through a major reorganization of this type since about 1970 and the pork industry since about 1980. There have been social and human costs associated with long strikes, closings or sales of plants and/or firms, and bankruptcies. One of the low-wage firms has obtained a large market share in several regional procurement areas. One policy option would be an incomes policy that allows government to affect directly prices and incomes in concentrated industries. Although our research has been far ranging, it does not encompass an analysis of the pros and cons of such an option.

Organization and Performance of Food Manufacturing and Distribution Industries

Food manufacturing and distribution industries are the primary orchestrators of the food system. Not only do these industries perform essential tasks themselves, but they also have significant influences over the rest of the food system: backward on agricultural production and forward on consumers.

Although many firms are involved in food and tobacco manufacturing and distribution, a relatively small number account for most of the business. The largest fifty food and tobacco manufacturers accounted for 43 percent of the value-added in food manufacturing in 1977. In food wholesaling, the largest fifty general line merchant wholesalers accounted for 57 percent of that industry's sales. The largest fifty corporate chains accounted for 44 percent of all grocery store sales in 1977.

In 1977, 26 percent of food manufacturer value of shipments were producer goods. These intermediate foodstuffs are essentially homogeneous commodities that are sold to other manufacturers for further processing. An additional 35 percent of food manufacturer shipments were either sold to foodservice outlets or were unbranded products (such as fresh meat) or generic or private label products sold to food stores. Thus, approximately 60 percent of the value of shipments by food manufacturers were from commodity-type products—that is, products with little or no product differentiation. We make this point at the outset since these products tend to be produced in competitive industries in which price competition is emphasized. The most serious competitive problems occur in the 40 percent of food manufacturer sales that are from advertised brands of products.

Although the output of a few food manufacturing industries is entirely producer goods (examples are animal feed and wet corn milling) or branded products (such as canned baby foods and chewing gum), most produce a combination of outputs: producer goods, unbranded or private label consumer products, and branded consumer products.

Industries that primarily produce branded products tend to be highly concentrated, spend a high percentage of sales on advertising, have relatively high entry barriers, and enjoy relatively high profit rates. These are the industries into which large food manufacturers have tended to diversify as they have reduced their involvement in commodity-type industries and sought opportunities for growth, profits, and greater control over markets.

Advertising plays a major role in food and tobacco manufacturing. Of eighty-five food manufacturing product classes that could be compared over time, a sharp dichotomy occurred between the thirty-five classes in which advertising exceeded 1 percent of sales and the remaining fifty classes with little or no advertising. In the latter fifty classes, the top four sellers made on average only 42 percent of sales, and concentration remained about constant between 1958 and 1977. In the other thirty-five classes the top four sellers controlled on average about 62 percent of sales by 1977, a significant increase over 1958 (Connor et al. 1985, p. 160).

As these figures suggest, high levels of concentration in food manufacturing are closely tied to the importance of advertised brands and the level of advertising. There is little evidence that economies of size in food manufacturing at the plant, multiplant, and firm level are responsible for this high concentration found in many industries.

This book examines the influence of industry organization on several aspects of performance in food manufacturing. The analysis of profit, price, and technological progressiveness is consistent with many other studies in industrial organization. Profits, regardless of the measure used, tend to be higher in highly concentrated industries and in industries with high levels of advertising. When individual firms are the unit of analysis, firm profits are also positively related to firm market share.

Analysis of prices reveals that the higher profits realized by firms with high market shares and high advertising are at least in part the result of higher prices. Demsetz (1974) has argued that the positive relationship found in many studies between profits and seller concentration and/or firm market share is the result of firm efficiency, not higher prices. This argument receives no support from the research reported here. Rather, the results indicate that tacit or explicit collusion and/or leading firm price leadership in industries with high entry barriers results in supracompetitive profits *and* prices in some food manufacturing industries.

Analysis of other performance dimensions reveals few redeeming benefits from concentrated food manufacturing industries. Technological progressiveness depends primarily on research and development activities of companies supplying food manufacturers, such as food machinery firms. Roughly 90 percent of the patents and award-winning innovations having a significant effect on the efficiency of food manufacturing came from outside these industries. R&D investments by food manufacturing companies are relatively low. Within food manufacturing, medium-sized firms and moderate levels of concentration appear to provide the best environment for R&D activity.

Monopoly rents from concentrated food manufacturing industries are shared to some extent with their workers. The level of wages and the rate of change of wages were found to be higher in more concentrated industries and in industries with high union representation; however, these industries did not have higher rates of labor productivity increases. The net result is that more concentrated food manufacturing industries experienced higher increases in labor costs per unit of output than less concentrated industries.

Industry structure was also found to have a significant influence on the rate of price increases in food manufacturing. Industries with high levels of advertising and those that had *increased* most in seller concentration tended to have higher rates of price increases during 1958–1977. This suggests that policies that affect industry structure will also influence macroeconomic stability. The level of concentration had no significant effect on price increases. It may be that industries that are already oligopolistic are charging prices that deter entry or result in joint profit maximization and hence have less incentive or flexibility to raise prices sharply.

One of the fundamental questions about food advertising that has received little attention is the extent to which it influences consumer preferences, consumption habits, and nutrition. Galbraith (1967) has contended that large companies in the United States attempt to manage consumer demand for their products through advertising. In Galbraith's scenario, the notion of consumer sovereignty has little relevance in his "planned" part of the economy.

Changes in the consumption of various food products from 1965 to 1977 were found to be positively related to the level of advertising and the change in television and radio advertising. The results do not prove causality; however, there are stronger theoretical reasons to expect that advertising affects consumption than vice-versa. Since there is no reason to expect that highly advertised products are more wholesome or nutritious than unadvertised products (nutritionists tend to argue the opposite), the long-run impact of advertising on consumption patterns must be a point of concern.

The effects of industry structure on various measures of performance indicate there are few detectable benefits to society from food manufacturing industries that are highly concentrated and/or that have high levels of advertising. The lack of competition in some food manufacturing industries results in substantial overcharges to consumers. These overcharges fall relatively more on low-income families and are akin to a regressive consumption tax.

Large companies increasingly dominate the food manufacturing industries. In 1977, the largest one hundred food manufacturing companies produced 53 percent of the value-added in food manufacturing and held 66 percent of all product class leading positions (top four positions). These companies held an even higher proportion of the leading positions in product classes that were highly differentiated or highly concentrated. In 1982, nearly 91 percent of the measured media advertising expenditures of manufactured food products were made by the one hundred largest food advertisers. Because of their strong positions in highly differentiated and highly concentrated product classes, large companies are the primary beneficiaries of supracompetitive profits in food manufacturing.

The largest food manufacturers are highly diversified on average, operating not only in several food manufacturing industries but in many industries outside food manufacturing. These companies thus have the ability to cross-subsidize from one market or industry to another and have greater opportunities for reciprocity and mutual forbearance. These are conduct options unavailable to smaller, specialized firms.

There are, however, important areas of food and tobacco manufacturing where there is effective competition. Approximately 50 percent of the value of shipments in 1977 were from unconcentrated or moderately concentrated product classes. About 60 percent of the value of shipments were producer goods or relatively undifferentiated consumer goods. For many products, private label and generic products provide an important low-price alternative for consumers and an opportunity for survival for many small and medium-sized companies.

Because entry barriers and economies of scale are usually low for private label manufacturing, price competition is generally keen. The numerous small and medium-sized companies in food manufacturing largely concentrate on producer goods, private label and generic consumer goods, and products for the foodservice market. Although some large manufacturers of advertised brands also produce some private label goods, small and medium-sized manufacturers are seldom able to compete in the branded product business. The entry barriers into the advertised brand segment of the market are too high for most of these companies to overcome. Mobility within food manufacturing is therefore not symmetrical.

Although competitive problems in food manufacturing are largely associated with advertised brands, we would be remiss if we did not acknowledge the positive contribution of advertised brand manufacturers. Many product innovations are developed and/or commercially implemented by large branded manufacturers. The variety of products and packaging available to consumers would be substantially less but for the efforts of these companies. Thus, there is a role for branded, private label and unbranded products in the food system.

Food Distribution

Approximately 75 percent of the shipments of food manufacturers in 1977 went to foodservice firms, food retailers, or the wholesalers that supply foodservice or food retailing companies. (The remaining 25 percent of shipments were producer goods sold to other manufacturers.) The 60 percent sold (eventually) through retail food stores accounted for 75 percent of retail sales. Retail food stores sell many products that are either unprocessed foods and hence are not supplied by firms classified as food manufacturers (such as fresh fruits and vegetables) or that are supplied by nonfood manufacturing establishments (such as soap and paper products, health and beauty aids, and various household products). These two groups of products make up about one-fourth of supermarket sales (nonfoods account for about 15 percent).

At the typical supermarket, unbranded (for example, fresh meat), generic, and private label (store brand) products, which tend to be relatively undifferentiated commodity-type products, represent 35 to 40 percent of store sales. The remaining 60 to 65 percent of sales come from manufacturer brands of food and nonfood products, most of which are advertised to some extent.

Although unbranded, generic, and private label products tend to be *produced* in competitive industries, they are not necessarily sold to consumers in competitive retail markets. By the same token, branded products that may be produced in noncompetitive industries may be sold to consumers in competitive retail markets. The point may be obvious; it is important to understand competition at both the manufacturing and distribution levels. Grocery retailers that enjoy market power in particular markets may increase the prices for private label and unbranded products, as well as prices for manufacturer brands.

The competitive behavior of food distributors has often stimulated increased competition by food manufacturers. Food chains and grocery wholesalers were responsible for the development and growth of private label and generic products. These products have provided a low-price alternative to consumers and reduced the pricing discretion of national brand manufacturers. Recently transshipments by retailers and "diverters" have frustrated manufacturer efforts to employ geographic discrimination on prices or deals. In their procurement activities, large food distributors have often provided a procompetitive force in the food system.

Supermarkets are the dominant factor in food distribution. In 1977, these stores did about three-fourths of all grocery store sales. The organization of food retailing changed rather slowly from the late 1950s to the late 1970s. Corporate chains (firms with eleven or more stores) steadily increased their share of all grocery store sales to 60 percent in 1977; their share rose to 62 percent by 1982. The share held by the largest twenty chains was relatively stable from 1958 to 1982 at about 35 percent of grocery store sales.

Although supermarkets gradually became larger and fancier from the mid-1950s to the mid-1970s, there was no dramatic change in the type of store. In the late 1970s and 1980s, limited assortment and warehouse stores were introduced in several markets. Their success triggered widespread experimentation with store types and cost-cutting methods. Warehouse stores, with approximately two-thirds the gross margins of conventional supermarkets, have introduced aggressive price competition in several markets. Some so-called hybrid or super warehouse stores have been extremely successful, realizing sales of $25 million to $50 million per store. Warehouse and super warehouse stores held about 10 percent of U.S. grocery store sales by 1984.

Concentration of food retailing sales in local metropolitan markets increased at an increasing rate between 1967 and 1977. In 1977 the four leading firms, on average, did 56 percent of grocery store sales in 173 SMSAs examined. Over 40 percent of these SMSAs had CR4s over 60 percent. The proportion of SMSAs with very high levels of concentration more than doubled from 1972 to 1977. Concentration of supermarket sales was significantly higher, with the top four firms accounting for 71 percent of SMSA supermarket sales in 1977, on average. Entry barriers into many SMSAs are substantial.

As in food manufacturing, research has demonstrated that concentrated retail markets tend to have higher prices and yield higher profits than unconcentrated markets. This has been found to be true for both small cities and towns and for major SMSAs. A firm's market share has also been found to be positively related to the prices it charges and profits it realizes. Thus, the trend toward more concentrated retail markets is bad news for consumers. The good news for consumers in some markets has been the introduction of warehouse stores, which may ameliorate to some degree the effects of high concentration, at least temporarily.

Because of their substantially lower prices, warehouse stores threaten the sales, profits, and oligopolistic interdependence of conventional supermarkets. Warehouse stores have grown rapidly in fragmented markets and in markets where the market leaders have not engaged in entry-deterring strategies. In some instances, however, the market leaders have employed zone pricing and other competitive tactics to deter the entry and growth of warehouse stores. To date, these tactics have not been successfully challenged as predatory. Although established firms may be able to slow the growth of warehouse stores, the success of these stores suggests that, in time, they will be an important competitive factor in most markets. While warehouse stores were initially developed primarily by independents and small chains, several leading grocery chains are now developing them.

Advertising in food retailing plays an important but somewhat different role than in food manufacturing. Economies of scale of advertising are an important barrier to entry in both food retailing and food manufacturing. Advertising in food retailing emphasizes information, whereas advertising in food manufacturing emphasizes image creation. Product differentiation in food manufacturing is heavily dependent on advertising. Enterprise differentiation in food retailing depends more on the nature of the product-service-location-price combination being offered than on advertising. Still, advertising in food retailing does contribute to enterprise differentiation. Newspaper and television advertising by grocery retailers generally provides price information for only a small percentage of items sold. As a result, the use of massive advertising by the leaders in a market may convey misimpressions of aggressive price competition.

The progressiveness of food retailers and wholesalers in adopting cost-reducing techniques is not impressive. These industries are generally more strongly oriented toward factors that affect sales than factors affecting costs. This explains in part the slowness of these industries to adopt cost-reducing technology. Labor productivity in food stores and eating and drinking establishments declined during the 1970s.

The potential of the electronic information revolution is just beginning to be tapped by food distribution companies. Retail scanning tied to central computers holds great potential for synchronizing the flow of products from food manufacturer to consumers and for providing far more accurate and timely information than previously existed. Retailers, as the generators of this information, will be in a stronger bargaining position with manufacturers. Scanning data are being used in collaborative research between food manufacturers and retailers to examine the impact of alternative advertising and promotion programs by manufacturers. Although such research holds potential to improve the understanding of consumer demand, it also carries the potential danger that it may allow greater manipulation of consumers. Scanning and centralized computers could potentially provide much greater information to consumers on their food purchasing choices and the nutrient characteristics of their purchases, but little work is being done in this area at the present time. Food manufacturers and retailers may have few incentives to initiate these types of information programs.

Data limitations preclude a comprehensive analysis of the structural trends and competitive conditions in food wholesaling and foodservice industries. Food wholesalers that primarily supply supermarket accounts have experienced considerable consolidation in recent years. In many areas, independent and small chain retailers have few wholesalers from which to choose. Given substantial economies of scale and very high barriers to de novo entry, this submarket of food wholesaling seems to be moving toward duopolies or monopolies in some markets. The structure of markets needed for technical efficiency appears to be in sharp conflict with the structure needed for effective competition.

A growing number of large general line wholesalers concentrate on supplying foodservice accounts. The structure in this submarket of wholesaling is much more fragmented than the submarket supplying supermarkets. Large foodservice distributors have probably increased operational efficiency at both the wholesale and foodservice outlet levels. There are substantial opportunities for further rationalization of the wholesale supply system for the foodservice segment.

The foodservice industry itself has undergone dramatic changes. Away-from-home food expenditures increased twice as fast as food-at-home expenditures between 1954 and 1984. This rapid growth attracted a wide variety of eating establishments, ranging from hamburger or chicken fast food outlets, to seafood, pizza, or steak restaurants, to Mexican or French restaurants, to pancake or baked potato restaurants. Many of these have been developed as either restaurant chains or franchised systems. Multiunit firms, franchise firms, and fast food firms now dominate the foodservice industry. By 1984, fast food firms accounted for 48 percent of the sales of separate eating places and 41 percent of the sales of commercial feeding establishments. Together, multiunit firms and franchised systems, including fast food firms, held about 60 percent of eating place sales in 1982.

Relative to food retailing, the foodservice industry is still quite fragmented nationally. Data at the local market level are not available. Entry barriers are low for individual units although substantial for new franchise systems. Because low barriers allow a fairly steady flow of firms into and out of the commercial foodservice market, instances of market power are likely quite limited.

Mergers have played an important role in the food manufacturing, food wholesaling, food retailing, and foodservice industries and have increased in importance in recent years. Mergers in food wholesaling and foodservice have essentially been ignored by the antitrust agencies. The actions of the FTC in the mid-1960s in challenging several mergers by large grocery chains and issuing merger guidelines for food retailing firms largely stopped acquisitions by the top twenty chains for approximately a decade. Although the FTC also issued merger guidelines for grocery product manufacturing companies, these did not have the same dampening effect as in food retailing. In the mid-1970s, the FTC adopted a more lenient enforcement policy toward large mergers in food manufacturing and distribution and rescinded in December 1976 its grocery product merger guidelines. As a result, the number of large acquisitions by leading grocery manufacturers and distributors has increased substantially. Although the ultimate effects of these mergers are still not clear, there is little evidence that mergers involving large food manufacturers or retailers are in the public interest. Mergers involving the largest food wholesaling firms may also be of questionable public benefit, whereas mergers by medium-sized wholesalers may be necessary to realize economies of scale.

Policy Options

The research reported in this book indicates that important portions of food manufacturing and distribution are exposed to the currents of effective competition. There are also important segments where market power is sufficient to stifle competitive forces. In the latter cases, performance is suboptimal for nearly every dimension examined. Scholarly assessments of the consequences of market power reveal few benefits. What, then, are the options for the social control of the U.S. economic system?

Different countries have chosen different instruments to control their economies and to deal with problems of economic power. Among predominantly market economies, antitrust laws are an important means by which governments attempt to harmonize the profit-seeking behavior of private enterprise with the public interest. Compared to U.S. antitrust laws, Corwin Edwards (1967) found that the antitrust laws of other countries tend to be more permissive in the treatment of horizontal agreements and combinations, such as price fixing and mergers, as long as prices and performance are considered "fair"; similar in the treatment of collective activity designed to coerce independents, exclude enterprises from markets, or impose discriminatory disadvantages on them; and more restrictive in treating refusals to sell, vertical price fixing, and prices charged by powerful firms.

In several countries, government has the power to intervene in a firm's pricing behavior if previous prices or price increases are judged unreasonable. For example, the EEC treaty prohibits "any improper exploiting . . . of a dominant position" affecting Common Market trade. In a 1975 decision, the European Commission fined the United Brands Company $1.2 million and ordered it to reduce banana prices 15 percent in West Germany and 30 percent in Belgium, the Netherlands, and Luxembourg (Greer 1980, p. 220). Although part of this order was later overturned, it demonstrates the differences in policies pursued by the United States and European nations.

In addition to antitrust policy, countries may also rely on a mix of other policies as part of an overall competition policy. These include taxation and tariff policies, information programs, public regulation, public ownership of industry, moral suasion, and preferential treatment and subsidies for small business or certain industries. Government programs and policies in a large number of areas affect the organization and performance of the economy.

Although numerous scholars and government commissions have recommended modifications in the policies toward competition in the United States (Neal Report 1968–1969; Stigler Report 1969; Hoffman 1980; Mueller 1983), the relatively minor changes that have been made have had little effect on the major competitive problems in the food system. There are many ways of fine-tuning the present system; however, something more comprehensive may be required, particularly for industries with entrenched monopoly power that is largely derived from advertising and/or conglomerate power.

Major Policy Option 6: Advertising in Food Manufacturing

Past research on a large number of industries has found that advertising has a strong positive relationship to profits of manufacturers of consumer nondurable experience goods like soap, beer, and most foods (Porter 1974; Nelson 1975); has either a negative or insignificant relationship to profits of manufacturers of durable experience and search goods like autos, furniture, and clothing (Porter 1974; Nelson 1975); and has a weak negative relationship to profits in the retail and service trades (Boyer 1974).

Experience goods, especially nondurables, in which quality may be judged only by consumption, lend themselves to exhortative advertising, which increases brand loyalty and reduces consumer price elasticity. Advertising by retail and service trades tends to be more informative concerning prices, availability, and location. The beneficial effects of advertising in drug and eyeglass retailing have been documented (Greer 1980, p. 392). These findings suggest that approaches to deal with the competitive problems associated with advertising should be tailored to the type of industry.

Existing policies in the United States that affect product differentiation are of three general types (Greer 1980, p. 396):

1. Forced disclosure of information, such as contents and grade labeling.
2. Prohibitions against unfair or deceptive sales promotion.
3. Direct regulation of product features affecting safety, quality, and efficacy.

We shall not attempt to evaluate these policies as they affect the food system. The first and second types of policies have most often been proposed as ways of dealing with advertising-created product differentiation. To the extent that these policies have been used, they have affected product differentiation of grocery products. Their application has been relatively uneven, however, particularly prohibitions against unfair and deceptive sales promotion.

Trademarks are fundamental to the process of product differentiation. They are also essential for consumer information and product accountability. A comparison of television sets by Consumer Reports would be of little value if there were no brands. Trademarks also tell to whom to turn if a product we purchase is unsatisfactory. Consumers also find trademarks useful to identify product quality. Greer (1980) contends that if quality identifications could be made independent of trademarks, the market power generated by trademarks would weaken and in some instances even die.

Government grades for food have served to some extent as an indicator of quality in lieu of brands. This is particularly true for beef, eggs, and fluid milk. Without government grades, stronger manufacturer brands probably would have developed. Consumers make little use of the grades approved for some products, however. In addition, grades are difficult to develop or of questionable value to consumers for products such as ready-to-eat cereals, soft drinks, and cigarettes—products for which brand names are very important. It is questionable whether government standards of quality for these products would erode the market power of such trademarks as Wheaties, Coca Cola, and Marlboro.

There may be some products, however, where government grades would diminish the market power of existing trademarks. ReaLemon is a case in point. Borden, the producer of ReaLemon acknowledged in internal documents, "From a technical standpoint, ReaLemon has no apparent advantage over the juice of any of its competitors. Processed lemon juice is processed lemon juice" (FTC 1976, fact 83).

Quality grades developed for consumers might facilitate comparisons of dominant brands such as ReaLemon, Minute Maid frozen orange juice, Miracle Whip salad dressing, and Sun Maid raisins with other brands, including private labels. To the extent that dominant brands are of superior quality, government grades might have little effect on their market shares or prices. Where no significant quality difference exists among brands (such as in household bleach), grades might help consumers discover this. The more highly processed and fabricated the product, however, the less likely that meaningful grades can be developed.

Two other categories of products warrant comment regarding trademarks: private label products and products such as beer and detergent on which consumers have difficulty distinguishing quality differences even after use. Private label or retailer brand products are an important potential means of keeping in check the price premiums charged by leading advertised brands, and, even where having failed this, they do provide some consumers with an alternative. In many product categories, they have accomplished one or both. These products, however, tend to have the smallest penetration and are discounted the most in products with high seller concentration and advertising: the products where sellers enjoy the greatest market power. For most products, major private label distributors such as Topco and Surefine and the leading chains such as Safeway and Kroger seek to match or exceed the quality of the leading brand in their first-line private label. Consumers are generally unaware of this, however. Nor do they know that some of the leading branded manufacturers may also produce much of the private label in some products. For example, Purina is the major producer of private label breakfast cereals. H.J. Heinz is the major producer of private label soup. Falstaff is the major producer of private label and generic beer. Food distributors have done little to inform their customers of these facts. Food editors and others involved in consumer education have also tended to maintain a low profile on distributor brands. Perhaps one problem is the variation in private label quality from one distributor to another. For example, whereas Topco maintains high and consistent quality in its private labels, some other firms do not. Standards of quality, where they can meaningfully be developed, would provide consumers with useful information in comparing the quality of private labels and national brands and the quality of private labels sold by different distributors.

The final group of products that deserve comment are those in which consumers cannot judge quality differences even after consumption. At least in part because of advertising, consumers may have strong psychological attachments to particular brands, even when objective tests demonstrate they cannot detect quality differences. Blind taste tests of brands of beer and cigarettes indicate consumers cannot tell the difference among major brands, yet many consumers have strong brand loyalty. Heavy-duty laundry detergents are very similar, but consumers have definite brand loyalty and pay sizable premiums for some of the leading brands.

One can attribute this behavior to uninformed consumers. If they knew there were no detectable differences, they would choose the low-priced brands. A West German study casts doubt on this simple explanation, however. Scherhorn and Wieken (1972) examined the buying behavior of consumers before and after authoritative information was distributed to them indicating that most laundry detergents are alike and should be purchased on the basis of price. Although one-third of the consumers were convinced, two-thirds remained ready to pay a premium for their preferred brand.

Consumers may be reluctant to accept the judgment of others on what product is best for them to buy. Buying decisions are personal and individual in nature and to some extent may be sheltered from objective comparisons. Thus, even if a beer taste test was conducted by Consumer Reports between halves of the next Super Bowl to convince beer drinkers that unadvertised brands are as good as advertised brands, a substantial proportion might still cling to the brand with which they identify psychologically. Increased information may help but is not likely to eliminate the influence of advertising.

Trademark Licensing. Trademarks have perpetual legal life. A policy alternative is to grant a limited period, say twenty years, when a company has exclusive rights to a trademark. Thereafter exclusivity would depend on whether the trademark was being used in the public interest. In cases like ReaLemon where extremely high price premiums were received that were not justified by quality differences, licensing might be required. This would be a major change in property rights and would pose major administrative difficulties. However, it might be applied in extreme cases where a seller, having achieved a virtual monopoly in a product, charges prices far above costs. This approach was accepted by an FTC administrative law judge in the case involving Borden's ReaLemon processed lemon juice brand. The Federal Trade Commission subsequently reversed the decision.

In cases where the trademark truly has become the generic name for the product, anyone can use the name freely. There is the legal question, however, of when a trademark becomes generic. For example, aspirin and shredded wheat are one-time trademarks that have been declared generic. Should trademarks like Jello and Ritz Crackers be considered generic? The FTC can bring cases to establish that a trademark has become a generic term. More aggressive action by the FTC on this issue is needed.

Unfair and Deceptive Advertising. Section 5 of the FTC Act states that "unfair methods of competition in commerce, and unfair or deceptive acts or practices in commerce, are declared unlawful." Unfair, deceptive, or false advertising is explicitly prohibited in later sections of the act.

Although no proof of actual harm to consumers is required, the government bears the burden of proving that a sales claim possesses the *capacity or tendency to deceive*. Recent Supreme Court decisions applying the constitutional protection of free speech to advertising may limit the scope of government regulation (Wills 1983). Timothy Muris, the current director of the FTC's Bureau of Consumer Protection, and FTC chairman James Miller recommended that the FTC drop its requirement that companies be able to substantiate advertising claims. Muris recommended challenging inaccurate claims only if they are *likely to injure* consumers.

These proposed and actual changes in applicability and enforcement of restrictions on unfair advertising would result in a substantial dilution of the government's role in policing advertising. The advertising industry has opposed the changes proposed by Muris and Miller as not being in the best interest of the public or of industry. Howard H. Bell, president of the American Advertising Federation, stated:

> I don't subscribe to the view that a lie is okay if nobody is hurt. . . . We feel very strongly that there be prior substantiation of claims. It has had a salutary effect on protecting the marketplace—consumers as well as advertisers—making sure that competitors don't make false claims to unfairly gain a share of the market. [Mayer 1982, p. A29.]

Although it is not clear what changes will be made in the ad substantiation program, the present majority of the FTC has a strong predisposition to assume that information provided by unregulated markets is accurate and sufficient. Chairman Miller, in statements supporting changes in the FTC Act, has indicated that the presumption of accurate market information is especially strong in markets for cheap, frequently purchased, and easily evaluated products. If this orientation is reflected in enforcement priorities, relatively little attention will be focused on unfair and deceptive advertising of grocery products under the current leadership of the FTC.

In addition to advertising substantiation, the FTC has previously used a number of policy approaches to improve consumer information about products. Affirmative disclosure led to health warnings on cigarette packages and posting the octane level of gasoline. Corrective advertising was used to offset prior misinformation in advertisements, such as with Profile bread. Counteradvertising was used briefly to allow public groups to counter cigarette television advertising. These approaches require more direct involvement of the FTC in the competitive conduct of businesses, a role inconsistent with the present leadership at the commission. Although these approaches may receive little use in the current FTC they remain instruments that can be used in the future to deal with deceptive or unfair advertising.

Direct Intervention to Reduce Advertising or Prices. Although several European countries have the power to order companies to reduce prices or advertising if they are judged unfair, U.S. regulatory agencies do not have this power. Given the difficulty under current laws of dealing with monopoly power that is largely due to product differentiation, new policy approaches may be needed.

Attempts to regulate directly conduct or performance are more cumbersome and less efficient than less interventionist approaches; however, direct intervention could be useful in policing extreme cases. Where there are clear instances of firms exploiting their monopoly positions, there may be greater public support for government action to reduce the exploitation than to correct the underlying structural problem.

Such a regulation might be similar to section 2 of the Capper-Volstead Act, which empowers the secretary of agriculture to intervene if an agricultural cooperative monopolizes or restrains trade to such an extent that prices are *unduly enhanced*. Although the court interpretation of this wording has never been tested, it is no more vague or imprecise than the language of other statutes that courts have learned to interpret, such as establishing fair rates for public utilities. Regulatory agencies might also be empowered to challenge excessive selling costs, as well as unduly enhanced price.

*Major Policy Issue 7: Concentrated Markets and
Industries with High Entry Barriers*

For the most part, existing antitrust laws are effective in addressing competitive problems in food manufacturing industries whose output is producer goods or undifferentiated consumer goods. These industries tend to be lower in concentration and entry barriers and to make little use of advertising. In these industries, horizontal conspiracies are more of a temptation, particularly in local markets, since they cannot resort to advertising to gain more discretion over pricing. Laws challenging horizontal conspiracies continue to receive widespread support.

Monopoly power that results from highly concentrated industries with substantial entry barriers is beyond the reach of existing antitrust law as long as the firms avoid illegal behavior. Sales in food retailing are highly concentrated in a rapidly increasing proportion of metropolitan areas. Large SMSAs, in particular, have high entry barriers. In food manufacturing, highly concentrated industries also tend to have high levels of advertising. Nearly half of the value-added in food manufacturing comes from industries with significant structural problems. In food manufacturing, analysis reveals a tendency for highly concentrated industries to decline in concentration if advertising and mergers are not used by leading companies to maintain their market shares. Rogers (1984a) found that product classes with a CR4 of 70 tended to decline in concentration from 1967 to 1977 if the advertising-sales ratio was 3 percent or below. Thus, policies to reduce the level or influence of advertising may be beneficial in reducing market concentration in food manufacturing.

Industrial restructuring may be the only policy alternative to restore competitive structures in some markets. This would require new legislation; however, there has been little evidence that the United States is willing to take such drastic action. Short of action to restructure noncompetitive industries, the best that can be done is to try to discourage further concentration using existing laws, reduce the level of entry barriers through tax or trade policies, and/or consider direct intervention to regulate blatantly noncompetitive behavior. Calling for more vigorous enforcement of the antitrust laws may be futile at the present time; however, more vigorous enforcement is one option that has had important payoffs in the past.

Recent court interpretations and antitrust enforcement policies have reduced the reach of existing antitrust laws. Since the mid-1970s, market extension and product extension mergers have become progressively more difficult to challenge successfully. The legal requirements to challenge predatory conduct and attempts to monopolize are in a state of flux. Exclusive territorial arrangements for soft drink bottlers and distributors have been given explicit immunity from the antitrust laws. The beer industry is currently seeking similar special treatment. For differentiated products sold by highly concentrated industries, exclusive territorial arrangements are particularly questionable since they eliminate potential intrabrand competition at the wholesale level (as among Coca Cola bottlers) and reduce interbrand competition.

The Illinois Brick decision has also restricted the reach of the antitrust laws since it prevents indirect victims of antitrust violations from suing for damages. This has particular significance for farmers, who are now unable to leap over food processors to seek damages from food retailers. Since intermediate firms may be able to pass on higher prices (or other injuries) to their customers, they may have no incentive to take legal action against the antitrust violator. Thus, congressional action that would overturn Illinois Brick would be helpful to farmers and others who are now unable to seek restitution for injuries resulting from antitrust violations.

Other options, if competitive structures cannot be restored, include various types of direct public control over prices, wages, and advertising. Finally, if no other options are chosen, various degrees of state ownership of production or marketing facilities could be considered. Although most Americans will find neither of the last two options to their liking, it is important to recognize that these alternatives have had their greatest appeal when citizens have lost confidence in other means of social control. Thus, those who would abandon or greatly weaken the antitrust laws may be unwittingly increasing the attractiveness of more direct government intervention to attain desired performance.

Major Policy Issue 8: Conglomerates
in the Food System

The theoretical and legal grounds for controlling the growth and impact of conglomerates (large multimarket firms) are weak. Although empirical evidence demonstrates the power of conglomerates to restructure markets, subsidize massive advertising campaigns, and engage in reciprocity, the economics profession has done little to develop or test theories of conglomerate conduct and performance.

Large conglomerate enterprises are most often created by acquisitions. Conglomerate acquisitions are facilitated by tax and accounting rules. In his criticism of "paper entrepreneurialism" in the United States, of which conglomerates are a manifestation, Robert Reich (1983) contends:

> Conglomerate enterprises rarely, if ever, bring any relevant managerial, technical, or marketing skills to the new enterprises they acquire. Their competence lies in law and finance. . . . Dextrous tax and accounting manipulation can extract paper profit from economically senseless acquisitions [p. 52].

A growing number of businessmen and journalists have become critical of the merger mania sweeping across U.S. industry. In a recent cover story on the subject, *Business Week* observed that a remarkable number of mergers—between a half and two-thirds—never pan out. One out of three mergers is later undone (*Business Week*, June 3, 1985).

Although some economists have contended that conglomerates provide superior management, synergism, and more efficient allocation of capital, little evidence supports these contentions. Indeed large diversified organizations appear to be less efficient in the operation of businesses acquired than prior owners. Conglomerate firms do possess important conduct options not available to specialized companies. Reciprocity and cross-subsidization are particularly questionable when viewed from the standpoint of what is fair, what is beneficial to competition, or what is good for society. However, these practices are difficult to challenge under existing laws unless they are deemed predatory.

Policies to control the growth of conglomerates must deal with the central role of mergers. Few conglomerate mergers violate section 7 of the Clayton Act, as currently interpreted. Indeed, despite the sharp increase in very large conglomerate mergers since 1980, none has been challenged. New legislation will be required if these acquisitions are to be controlled effectively. The incentives to make such acquisitions could also be reduced by changes in tax and/or accounting rules. For example, tax codes make interest payments on loans for any purpose tax deductible. Companies would be encouraged to grow by internal investments if tax laws were changed to allow interest deductions only for the purchase of new assets or modernization of old ones. In a similar way, tax laws concerning loss carry-forwards, depreciation, and depletion allowances of acquired companies could be changed to eliminate these as incentives to make acquisitions.

The growth of conglomerates seriously erodes the amount of public information available on various industries. The FTC's Line of Business program was developed in large part to meet this informational need. This program has enjoyed widespread support among economists and policymakers. The primary opponents of the program have been the large companies required to submit data under the program. The current FTC has suspended this program and shows no inclination to reinstate. This action is difficult to justify unless one believes that public policies are best formulated in an information vacuum. Action by Congress may be necessary if this program is to be saved.

Finally, the reach of section 2 of the Sherman Act could be broadened, commensurate with the recommendations of the National Commission to Review the Antitrust Laws and Procedures in 1979. The suggested changes would make predatory conduct and attempts to monopolize more vulnerable to challenge. This would reduce the ability of conglomerates to use cross-subsidization to restructure markets and eliminate competition.

Major Policy Issue 9: Information

The electronic information revolution is just beginning. The effects on the competitive organization and performance of markets are still far from clear. Much will depend on who has access to the massive amount of information generated and how it is used.

Electronic scanning information from supermarkets provides considerable opportunities to increase consumer information. Assuming that in time most consumers will have computers that can access a wide variety of data banks, consumers could theoretically identify a list of products to be purchased and receive information on the cost of buying them at various stores. Past research on the provision of comparative price information to consumers has found that price competition has been helped.

As another example, consumers could obtain information on individual products using such a system. Visualize a search procedure to select a heavy-duty detergent with certain measurable characteristics. The information system could identify the brands that have those characteristics, where they can be purchased, and the best buy. This type of use would require more rating of products on important characteristics.

These systems could also be used to provide nutritional and budgetary information for families. The nutritional characteristics and costs of all foods could be accumulated at a central data bank. The nutritional content of purchases over certain periods could be compared to the estimated nutritional needs of the family. Expenditures for various categories of foods could be analyzed to determine potential savings from buying other brands or products or shopping at other stores.

At this point, these are largely "pie in the sky" possibilities. One of the critical issues is who should hold the property rights to various types of information. Do consumers have the right to know? If the potential for improved consumer information is realized, consumers will be able more intelligently to police the performance of food manufacturers and distributors, rewarding some and penalizing others through their purchases. Advertising would be expected to lose some of its noninformational, persuasive influence. Entry barriers for new firms would be reduced. The marketplace would become a more open arena in which government officials and the public would gain access to much information now available only to the companies involved.

A related information issue is the extent to which proprietary information on the effects of advertising should be available to public agencies conducting investigations of advertising. The effects of advertising on children, smoking, and alcoholic beverage consumption are highly controversial yet of enormous significance for the public welfare. Investigations into such issues by regulatory agencies often are affected by the sharp disparity in the information available. Those defending advertising—whether the advertising industry or the users of advertising—have access to a growing amount of information on the effects of advertising. This evidence is generally not fully available to public agencies.

At present, for example, there are several proposals to restrict or ban the advertising of alcoholic beverages because of the alleged contribution to alcohol abuse and drunk driving. Rhetoric flows from both sides. But those who are in the best position to have evidence on the subject—the advertising or alcoholic beverage industries—are not required to provide this evidence to investigating agencies or to cooperate on research that attempts to develop scientific documentation. On complex and controversial issues, asymmetries in the access to information are particularly damaging to efforts to serve the public interest.

One alternative policy approach that may be particularly appropriate to the advertising of alcoholic beverages and tobacco products is to establish an advertising evaluation fund that would be financed by a mandatory check-off from industry. For example, companies might be required to contribute 1 percent of their advertising expenditures on alcoholic beverages. The evaluation fund would be used to finance research on the impacts of advertising.

There may be other ways of overcoming the problems of trying to develop sound public policy when the relevant information base is very inadequate. Actions to provide policymakers with more research on the effects of advertising should be supported by industry if they too want policies based on scientific evidence.

*Major Policy Issue 10: Impediments to
System-Wide Efficiencies*

Some of the major improvements in the efficiency of the food marketing system depend on system-wide adoption or cooperation. The universal produce code (UPC) and scanning at the supermarket checkout illustrate the interdependence of manufacturers and distributors in implementing certain types of technological change. The standardization of package, case, and pallet size has long been identified as another important potential source of increased efficiency. However, gains in efficiency depend on the vast majority of companies adopting uniform sizes. Individual companies have little incentive to adopt such changes even though there is universal agreement that the changes, if made by most companies, would improve the food system and benefit society.

It is difficult to define policy alternatives that would encourage system-wide cooperation in making these types of changes. To the extent that companies are deterred by fears of antitrust allegations, the law should be clarified or modified.

The appropriate public policy may vary with the types of system-wide change. In some cases, such as standardized containerization, a combination of legislative mandate and investment tax credit might be the appropriate policy action. In other cases, a different mix of policies might be called for. Care should be exercised to avoid policies that unnecessarily place smaller companies at a competitive disadvantage.

One way of dealing with this issue would be to establish an office in the executive branch to facilitate system-wide changes. The Office of Technological Assessment (OTA) could be used to analyze proposed system-wide changes and recommend appropriate policy actions. The new office would be an action agency that would work closely with industry groups and various government agencies to implement OTA recommendations.

Public versus Private Interests in the Policy Arena

This discussion has ignored the policymaking and enforcement process. It is important to recognize that this process is heavily influenced by the various interest groups affected. Large companies, industry trade associations, farm organizations, organized labor, consumer organizations, public interest groups, and the public at large may all have some influence over the development or implementation of public policies. Consumer and public interest organizations generally have relatively few resources and are most effective on selected policy issues about which their constituents feel strongly. They are ill equipped to represent the interests of the public on many policies that are of vital interest to certain industries or labor groups.

Although government regulation of industry is often viewed as primarily for the protection and benefit of the public at large, Stigler (1971) has argued that industries and professions seek the use of public resources and powers to increase profits through direct subsidies, control over the entry of new rivals, reducing the threat of substitutes, and price fixing. The "supply" of such regulations is controlled by political parties and office holders. Since there are normally conflicting interests involved in most regulation, the question becomes whose interests will be served. Stigler (1971, p. 12) comments: "The political system is calculated to implement all strongly felt preferences of majorities and many strongly felt preferences of minorities but to disregard the lesser preferences of majorities and minorities."

There is widespread evidence of the influence of industry, farm, and labor groups on market rules and regulations. Price-support levels, import quotas, the regulation of pesticides, the regulation of certain types of advertising, antitrust enforcement, food health and safety regulations, programs requiring certain types of information from companies, and efforts to gain exemptions from the antitrust laws are but a few examples within the food system that quickly come to mind. The strong and persistent opposition of large corporations resulted in the shelving of the Line of Business program by the FTC. Following a lobbying effort by a coalition of food firms, the broadcasting industry, and advertising agencies that reputedly cost between $15 million and $30 million, the Congress in 1981 directed the FTC to cease work on a rule for children's ads. The soft drink industry was successful in gaining special legislative exemption from the antitrust laws so as to allow exclusive territories for soft drink bottlers and distributors. The beer industry is currently seeking a similar exemption and is also opposing efforts to regulate the advertising of alcoholic beverages. Large dairy cooperatives were in part responsible for an increase in the price-support level for manufactured dairy products in the 1977 farm bill, which led to serious surplus problems in the 1980s.

A less direct influence of vested interests occurs in the financial support provided for research at universities and federal research agencies. This influence may be registered both by encouraging certain allocations of public monies and by private grants to conduct research on selected topics. The health-related consequences of certain chemicals (such as pesticides and PCB), food additives (such as cyclamate and artificial colorants), and certain products (such as sugared cereals, animal fats, tobacco, and alcoholic beverages) are but a few examples where strong vested interests have sought to influence the amount and agenda of public research.

The investment policies of federal and state governments in the infrastructure of the food system can also affect the organization and performance of the system. Roads, canals, port facilities, public markets, public elevators and warehouses, credit programs, and public information programs are some examples. These seldom have a neutral effect on the industries affected. They may reduce entry barriers and enhance competition, or they may have the opposite effect. Food system participants can be expected to try to influence these policies so that they serve their interests.

Thus, although we have identified some policy issues on which we believe changes could lead to improved food system performance, we recognize the hazards of policymaking and enforcement. Nearly all of the changes we have suggested will be opposed by strong vested interests. Most will require strong public support in order to overcome the opposition of private interests.

The major policy issues discussed in this book reflect our perspective of the public action needed to deal with the most important problems in the U.S. food system. By intent, they have focused on areas where substantial improvements can be made. We have not discussed policy alternatives that would help maintain good performance where there are few problems.

In many respects, the U.S. food production and marketing system has performed well. Abundant supplies of a wide variety of relatively safe food products are offered to consumers at reasonable prices. When compared to the food systems in other countries, the performance of the U.S. system would be ranked very high by most observers. But economic systems improve not by resting on their laurels but by building on strengths and eliminating weaknesses. The U.S. food system, while admirable in a comparative sense, also has some deficiencies that threaten its long-run ability to serve well the public interest.

Both the strengths and weaknesses of the system stem from its capitalistic nature. The most important safeguards in such a system are informed consumers, competitive behavior among existing firms, and the ability of new firms to seize untapped opportunities. The trends toward increased concentration of economic power in the food system endanger these safeguards. The American public and its elected representatives must decide whether to initiate policy changes aimed at reversing these trends.

Appendix A
Conceptual and Institutional
Evolution of NC 117

T he formation of NC 117 as an institutional entity in 1973 was preceded by a series of developments with roots extending several decades into the past. Economic changes in agriculture and the general economy in the 1930s and 1940s focused increasing attention on marketing. Rising awareness of marketing problems helped bring about passage of the Research and Marketing Act of 1946, which provided stimulus and support for greatly expanded programs of research and education in marketing over the following several years.

Antecedents from the 1950s

Early post–World War II work in marketing was centered primarily on problems of efficiency. A great deal of this work was concerned with marketing at the firm level, although some related to marketing systems, primarily raw product assembly. Within the marketing channel, attention was given principally to marketing and processing activities not far removed from the farm gate. A few studies of wholesale distribution, storage, transportation, and retailing were undertaken.

By the late 1950s, the substantial increase in marketing work was being sharply criticized. Criticisms were of three major types. First, the numerous studies of marketing were quite fragmented. They dealt with a variety of problems but were not integrated to provide better understanding of marketing systems as wholes. Second, the work in marketing was not dealing effectively with organizational changes in production and marketing systems. Integration in the poultry industry was proceeding rapidly, but marketing economists had little to say in response to questions about integration. Third, marketing research was not guided by theoretical frameworks that seemed adequate or relevant.

The concerns about the state of marketing work led to the following recommendation by the heads of departments of agricultural economics in the north central states (Regional Administrative Committee NCA-12) in January 1958: "That an NCR Committee be created on Economics and Management in Marketing. . . . It is the intent that such a committee would give major attention to methodology and program in areas not necessarily bounded by commodity lines."

NCR and Marketing Issues in the 1960s

The North Central Agricultural Experiment Station directors responded positively to this recommendation by establishing Regional Research Study Committee NCR-20, Economics and Management in Marketing. In January 1959, NCA-12 suggested that NCR-20 schedule its first meeting to make possible a joint session with NCR-4, an ongoing regional research study committee that dealt with farm management and production economics. It was believed that the two groups might find mutual interest in discussing the integration of production and marketing systems.

The Farm Foundation was highly supportive of the formation of NCR-20. It provided funds to help the committee get started, and it contributed limited continuing support for several years afterward.

The first meeting of NCR-20 was held in March 1959. Those attending were the managing director of the Farm Foundation and faculty members in the north central states and the USDA who had interests in problems of marketing. This initial meeting was characterized by discussion of a wide range of topics, research methods, committee purposes, and committee organization. Experiences of NCR-4 helped NCR-20 conclude that it might best contribute by becoming an idea-generating, problem-identifying, and methods-improving group to guide research in agricultural marketing. The committee would attempt to accomplish its objective by organizing and conducting seminars, workshops, and symposia.

At this meeting, five NCR-20 subcommittees were established as follows: pricing systems; integration; consumer behavior; risk, uncertainty and management problems; and market organization and economic adjustment. At the next meeting of NCR-20 in November 1959, the subcommittee areas evolved further into four subcommittees that replaced the previous five: demand and consumer analysis; market structure; management; and long-range planning.

The market structure subcommittee became the most active group, and was the most direct antecedent of NC 117. The first visible product of the market structure subcommittee was "A Report on Market Structure Research in Agricultural Economics," by Robert L. Clodius and Willard F. Mueller, published in the August 1961 *Journal of Farm Economics* (43:513–553). That report, relying heavily on the recently published book by Joe S. Bain, *Industrial Organization* (New York: John Wiley, 1959), provided illustrations of empirical work and suggestions for applying industrial organization ideas in research.

Publication of the report was followed by a workshop on market structure research at Purdue University in June 1962. The purpose of the workshop was to build on current market structure ideas and to suggest useful research applications. Participants comprised mainly some one hundred agricultural marketing research workers in the North Central region and the USDA. Proceedings of the workshop were published as a book, *Market Structure Research,* ed. Paul L. Farris (Ames: Iowa State University Press, 1964).

Activities of NCR-20 during the 1960s proceeded essentially along two lines. One was the continuation of workshops and seminars oriented toward perceived high-priority problems in several areas of industrial organization and performance of the agricultural economy. The other was the development of specific research project proposals. The seminar activity produced additional proceedings publications:

Research in Management and Operating Problems in Agricultural Marketing Firms, Vernon L. Sorenson, ed., Agricultural Economics Mimeo. 939 (Ann Arbor: Department of Agricultural Economics, Michigan State University, 1963).

Research on Coordination of Production and Marketing in Agriculture, Paul L. Farris, ed., NCR-20-64 (West Lafayette, In.: Department of Agricultural Economics, Purdue University, 1964).

Federal, State and Local Laws and Regulations Affecting Marketing, David C. Nelson, ed., Regional Research Bulletin 168, published as Bulletin 455 (Fargo: North Dakota Agricultural Experiment Station, North Dakota State University, 1965).

Proceedings of Market Structure Workshop, W.S. Farris, ed., North Central Regional Extension Marketing Committee (W. Lafayette, In.: Purdue University, 1966) (in coordination with NCR-20).

Implications of Changes (Structural and Market) on Farm Management and Marketing Research, A. Gordon Ball, chairman of Conference Planning and Program Committee, CAED Report 29 (Ames: Iowa State University, 1967) (in coordination with NCR-4, Farm Management).

Agricultural Organization in the Modern Industrial Economy, Paul L. Farris, ed., NCR-20-68 (Columbus, Ohio: Department of Agricultural Economics and Rural Sociology, Ohio State University, 1968 (in coordination with NCR-56, Agricultural Policy).

Economics of Conglomerate Growth, Leon Garoyan, ed., (Corvallis: Agricultural Research Foundation, Oregon State University, 1969).

Economics of Consumer Protection, Loys L. Mather, ed., (Danville, Ill.: Interstate Printers and Publishers, 1971).

The seminars appeared to have an influence on research orientation in agricultural marketing through activities of workshop participants and through the availability of the written proceedings.

National Commission on Food Marketing

A related development also contributed in significant ways to the eventual formation of NC 117. The developing economic forces in the 1950s and early 1960s, which led to the creation of NCR-20 and the subsequent activities of that group, had an important influence on legislation that in 1964 established the National Commission on Food Marketing (Public Law 88-354, 89th Congress). Also contributing to formation of the commission were demands by farmers and other groups for answers to questions that were of such scope and urgency that the information was not being provided by academicians and other members of the professional research establishment. Duties of the commission were to study and appraise the marketing structure of the food industry. Objectives included determining changes in policies to achieve a desired distribution of power as well as desired levels of efficiency.

The National Commission on Food Marketing was a significant milestone in the history of agricultural marketing research. The commission took advantage of its unique opportunity to mobilize agencies of the federal government in helping to assemble information about the food sector and to counsel with numerous individuals in analyzing and interpreting the findings. New data and insights were obtained by the commission and its staff through special surveys and hearings. The technical reports of the commission provided basic information about market structures, behavior patterns, and performance characteristics in important agricultural industries, and they added a great deal to the understanding of organization and competition in food marketing. Several conclusions of the commission influenced public policy, especially in the areas of competition and consumer protection.

The commission's one and one-half years of operation was too short a period to analyze in depth many of the broad and complex problem areas. The benchmark studies showed a need for continuing research, and they provided clearer perspectives about the importance of particular kinds of future work. The approach of the commission also served to emphasize the value of research organization on a scale large enough to deal effectively with some types of marketing problems.

USDA Initiatives and Project Conceptualization

Following the conclusion of the commission's work and publication of its reports, the USDA contributed significantly to the marketing research dialogue and to conceptualizations about research organization. One step was to arrange with James D. Shaffer, Michigan State University, to allocate some of his time to develop ideas about marketing research. The result was "A Working Paper Concerning Publicly Supported Economic Research in Agricultural Marketing" (Economic Research Service, USDA, March 1968). Another step, which built on Shaffer's work along with that of the National Commission on Food Marketing and previous activities of NCR-20, was the organization of "A Seminar toward Better Economic Research on the U.S. Food and Fiber Industry" in May 1968. The seminar was attended by some fifty researchers and research administrators from throughout the United States. It emphasized both problem conceptualization to deal with industrial organization questions and research organization alternatives that might be considered in addressing such questions.

The extensive professional concerns about industrial organization questions in the agricultural economy and how the questions might be answered through research led to initiatives within NCR-20 in the late 1960s to develop a large-scale research proposal. Several discussions followed, involving primarily James D. Shaffer, Michigan State University; Marshall R. Godwin, Texas A&M University; Paul L. Farris, Purdue University; William T. Manley, USDA; R. James Hildreth, Farm Foundation; and Elmer R. Kiehl, dean of agriculture, University of Missouri, who was serving as administrative adviser to NCR-20. A group comprised of Shaffer, Godwin, and Farris prepared a large-scale project proposal that incorporated the salient features being discussed that were believed to be necessary for the success of such a venture. The project proposal, dated May 8, 1970, was entitled "Organization and Control of the U.S. Food Production and Distribution System." The proposed duration of the project was five years, from July 1, 1971, to June 30, 1976.

Major changes were proposed in the organization and funding of this project from patterns traditionally found in regional projects. It was recognized that the research contemplated would likely be sensitive, difficult, and complex. Professionals of varying backgrounds and experience would be required. Further, the scale of the project was such that no single state agricultural experiment station could undertake a project of this magnitude and complexity, and participation by appropriate federal agencies would be highly desirable. Initially a consortium of five or more state agricultural experiment stations in the North Central Region was suggested. The project would be financed and administered through the Association of North Central Directors. Ongoing operations of the project would be managed by an executive director. The research program would be carried out through an organizational arrangement involving a core group of professional staff researchers who would work closely with the executive director; state contributing projects related to the overall research objectives; and an advisory group. The executive director would have considerable administrative latitude to negotiate for needed professional talent and to organize, initiate, coordinate, and monitor work under the project.

Although the project would be formed as a North Central Regional Research Project, invitations to participate would also be extended to state agricultural experiment stations outside the region and to interested federal government agencies. This recognized the fact that the project was directed at many questions that were interregional and national in scope. Initially funding was proposed to come from two sources: special grant funds from CSRS, USDA, in the amount of $150,000, and off-the-top allocation of $150,000 of regional research funds by the North Central Agricultural Experiment Station directors. The $300,000 budget was considered the minimum amount necessary to launch the venture.

Project Approval and Activation

The project proposal then began a long and torturous course on its way toward eventual activation as a regional research project in July 1973. An early delay resulted from a reorganization of North Central regional research committees.

The reorganization came about through the work of a task force established in 1969 by the North Central Agricultural Experiment Station directors to examine marketing aspects of the regional research program. The task force had the function of "reviewing the present agricultural marketing research program in the North Central Region, to consider emerging needs for marketing research in agriculture, and to recommend appropriate organizational devices for carrying out future research work in agricultural marketing in the North Central Region." One recommendation of the task force was that procedures be established for financing and conducting large-scale, complex projects that would likely best be handled outside the traditional regional research framework. Another recommendation, which would facilitate implementation of the large-scale concept, was that existing NCR committees be dissolved and three new ones established in commercial agriculture, natural resource development, and community and human resource development. The North Central Agricultural Experiment Station directors approved the recommendation, naming the three new committees, respectively, NCRS-1, NCRS-2, and NCRS-3. Plans for implementing the new structure were formulated in 1970, and a joint meeting of the three new committees was held in February 1971.

As NCR-20 was phased out in 1970, in line with the new regional organization pattern, one of the suggestions that NCR-20 made to NCRS-1, the committee on commercial agriculture, was that procedures for implementing the large-scale project idea be continued. A task force on organization and control of agriculture was established under NCRS-1, with Willard F. Mueller, University of Wisconsin, as chairman. That task force recommended the development of a broad research proposal dealing with various issues in the organization and control of agriculture, as proposed by NCR-20 to NCRS-1. In 1971, the task force reworked the large-scale research proposal of May 8, 1970, and submitted it to the North Central Agricultural Experiment Station directors in early 1972, recommending that the project be approved and commence in 1972–1973.

In March 1972, the directors approved formation of NCT-105, "Organization and Control of U.S. Food Production and Distribution System," for one year beginning July 1982. This procedure was in keeping with the established administrative practice in the North Central region of forming temporary committees to develop formal regional research project proposals before approving them as projects under which the actual research would be conducted. Willard F. Mueller served as chairman of NCT-105. During late 1972 the project proposal was reworked again, put in final form, and submitted to the North Central Agricultural Experiment Station directors.

In April 1973, the directors approved the proposal for five years, beginning July 1, 1973. The proposal then became Regional Research Project NC 117. The directors also approved "without prejudice" the unique organizational feature of the project: a full-time executive director plus a core research staff group located at one state agricultural experiment station. But the directors did not approve off-the-top regional research funding. They suggested that funding be sought from other sources.

Funding from several potential sources was explored but without success. Initial financial support for the core group was eventually obtained in 1974 through the efforts of Kenneth R. Farrell, deputy administrator of the Economic Research Service, USDA. A combined pledge of $30,000 per year for a three-year period was made by the Economic Research Service, the Farmer Cooperative Service, and the Cooperative State Research Service, USDA, provided that the sum would be matched with $30,000 off-the-top funding by the North Central directors. The directors agreed to this funding arrangement, and a major hurdle to launching the project was overcome. After the project was underway, a special request was made to the U.S. Congress for support under PL89-106. The U.S. Congress designated $150,000 of PL89-106 funds, through CSRS, USDA, to be available beginning in the spring of 1976 for support of the research. As time passed, other agencies of the U.S. government, including the Agricultural Marketing Service and the FTC, contributed funds and/or personnel to the venture. The largest single source of funds continued to be congressional support through PL89-106.

The project was organized similar to the concept that had been outlined in the first proposal prepared three years earlier and under active discussion for some years prior to that. Important features were creation of a core group and an executive director to provide continuity and coordination among collaborating institutions, and adoption of a renewable three-year project horizon for planning and budgetary purpose with evaluation, respecification of project priorities, and recommitment of financial and collaborative project support at the end of each three-year cycle.

Bruce W. Marion, Ohio State University, was hired as executive director of NC 117 in September 1974. He and the core staff of personnel from the Economic Research Service and University of Wisconsin were located at the University of Wisconsin-Madison. An executive committee was established, with Willard F. Mueller as chairman. Researchers at individual state agricultural experiment stations, both within and outside the North Central states, developed contributing projects and participated in various ways in the research of the project. Thus the project was launched on what was to become a unique large-scale organizational experiment in regional research and a productive research venture in dealing with important problems of the agricultural economy.

Conceptual Development in Marketing Research

The fifteen-year span from the initiation of NCR-20 in 1958 to the activation of NC 117 in 1973 was a highly significant and intellectually stimulating period in agricultural marketing research. It was a time when conceptual frameworks were broadened and elaborated, problems of industry organization and competition were identified, and issues involving policy for the agricultural economy were seen to encompass marketing, distribution, and exchange, as well as production.

The rapid organizational changes that occurred in several industries during this period served as continuing reminders to marketing researchers of the relevance of their work. Numerous requests for knowledge and guidance intensified the efforts of researchers to respond effectively to the developing needs. There was a substantial change in the kinds of research topics undertaken during the period. Increasingly, professional activity was oriented toward industrial organization issues. Thus when NC 117 began, participants had the benefit of having been through a great deal of professional discussion and conceptualization. The problem areas were real, and there was enthusiasm for trying a new research program in solving perceived important problems of the agricultural economy.

Appendix B
Supporting Tables

Table B–1
Distribution of Grocery Stores and Grocery Store Sales by Store Size, Selected Years

Store Size in Annual Sales (thousands of dollars)	1954	1958	1963	1967	1972	1977	1982
			Percentage of Sales				
5,000+			2.1	4.9	13.5	37.1	56.9
2,000–4,999	33.0	45.6	21.7	29.0	38.9	35.3 ⎱	25.3
1,000–1,999			29.0	27.4	19.9	9.3 ⎰	
500–999	16.1	15.7	16.1	13.7	18.7	5.7	6.4
100–499	28.9	23.5	20.0	16.9	15.3	11.1	10.7
50–99	11.7	7.8	6.3	5.1	2.5	1.2	0.5
Less than 50	10.8	7.5	4.9	3.1	1.4	0.5	0.2
			Percentage of Establishments				
5,000+			0.1	.2	1.0	4.4	8.1
2,000–4,999	2.3	4.3	1.8	3.1	6.4	9.6 ⎱	13.6
1,000–1,999			4.6	5.8	6.7	5.7 ⎰	
500–999	2.8	3.7	5.0	5.7	5.9	7.3	11.8
100–499	18.0	19.7	21.6	24.4	35.9	41.5 ⎫	
50–99	20.7	18.8	20.2	22.4	16.7	14.8 ⎬	66.5
Less than 50	56.2	53.6	46.7	38.5	27.4	16.6 ⎭	

Source: Census of Retail Trade, 1982, 1977, 1972; Census of Business, 1967, 1963 and 1958 and estimates by authors for 1982.

Table B-2
Distribution of U.S. Grocery Store Sales by Size of Firm, 1948–1977

Size of Operation	1948 Sales ($)	1948 Sales (%)	1954 Sales ($)	1954 Sales (%)	1958 Sales ($)	1958 Sales (%)	1963 Sales ($)	1963 Sales (%)
Independent								
Single units	14,552	58.8	17,838	51.8	20,556	47.0	22,677	43.1
2–3 units	899	3.6	1,664	4.8	2,084	4.8	2,630	5.0
4–10 units	787	3.2	1,365	4.0	1,842	4.2	3,538	4.8
Total	16,238	65.6	20,867	60.6	24,482	56.0	27,845	53.0
Chain								
11–25 units	805	3.3	1,232	3.6	1,454	3.3	2,191	4.2
26–50 units	567	2.3	1,365	4.0	1,903	4.3	1,659	3.1
51–100 units	372	1.5	818	2.4	1,750	4.0	2,752	5.2
100 + units	6,788	27.4	10,137	29.4	14,105	32.3	18,118	34.5
Total	8,532	34.4	13,552	39.4	19,212	44.0	24,720	47.0
Grand total	24,770	100.0	34,421	100.0	43,696	100.0	52,566	100.0

Source: Bureau of the Census, *Census of Retail Trade*, various years.
Note: Sales are in millions of dollars.

1967		1972		1977		1982	
Sales ($)	Sales (%)	Sales ($)	Sales (%)	Sales ($)	Sales (%)	Sales ($)	Sales (%)
25,301	38.9	29,483	32.2	41,752	28.6	58,838	25.8
3,243	5.0	4,681	5.1	7,482	5.1	12,880	5.6
3,094	4.8	5,211	5.7	9,611	6.6	16,250	7.1
31,638	48.6	39,375	43.0	58,845	40.3	87,968	38.5
3,383	5.2	4,416	4.8	8,332	5.7	13,590	5.9
2,653	4.1	5,565	6.1	8,926	6.1	12,177	5.3
3,901	6.0	5,923	6.5	10,403	7.1	18,976	8.3
23,499	36.1	36,293	39.6	59,320	40.7	95,940	42.0
33,436	51.4	52,197	57.0	86,981	59.6	140,683	61.5
65,074	100.0	91,574	100.0	145,828	100.0	228,651	100.0

Table B–3
Vertical Integration into Food Manufacturing Industries by the Largest Food Chains, by Industry, 1958–1977

Product Area	Number of Integrated Chains among Forty Largest					Fifty Largest, 1977	
	1959	1963	1967	1972	1977	Number Integrated	Value of Shipments
Food manufacturing	n.a.	n.a.	n.a.	31	31	34	$4,933,437
Meat packing	4	4	5	7	4	4	484,699
Prepared meats	7	9	10	8	6	6	322,675
Poultry dressing	5	3	2	3	1	1	14,564
Butter	7	5	4	3	1	1	
Cheese	5	8	5	5	3	4	77,769
Concentrated milk	7	9	5	9	5	6	40,854
Ice cream	10	7	16	15	12	13	169,421
Fluid milk	8	13	13	16	16	17	1,820,025
Canned specialties	4	3	4	4	3	3	38,259
Canned fruit and vegetables	12	10	10	11	14	14	77,040
Dehydrated fruit and vegetables	2	2	1	2	1	1	n.r.
Pickles, sauces, salad dressing	10	10	11	10	8	9	28,538
Frozen fruit and vegetables	6	10	12	2	2	2	7,552
Frozen baked goods	n.a.	n.a.	n.a.	10	10	10	n.r.
Flour milling	0	3	1	1	1	1	n.r.
Wet corn milling	0	1	2	1	2	2	n.r.
Pet food	n.a.	n.a.	1	3	2	2	n.r.
Bread products	22	30	28	27	28	28	730,530
Cookies and crackers	12	16	20	18	12	12	n.r.
Confectionery products	7	9	11	7	3	4	n.r.
Chocolate products	1	1	1	1	1	1	n.r.
Soybean oil	1	1	0	1	2	2	n.r.
Vegetable oil	1	1	0	0	1	1	n.r.
Animal oil	n.a.	n.a.	n.a.	4	4	4	n.r.
Shortening and cooking oil	2	2	1	2	2	2	n.r.
Bottled and canned soft drinks	4	6	7	14	15	16	n.r.
Flavoring	6	6	7	4	6	6	n.r.
Canned seafood	2	2	1	1	1	1	n.r.
Packaged fish	2	2	2	1	2	2	n.r.
Coffee	21	21	19	9	9	9	n.r.
Manufactured ice	n.a.	n.a.	n.a.	2	2	2	n.r.
Macaroni and spaghetti	1	1	1	2	2	2	452,339
Miscellaneous total	13	13	20	18	15	17	150,986
Ready-mix desserts	n.a.	n.a.	n.a.	3	4	4	n.r.
Potato and corn chips	n.a.	n.a.	n.a.	7	4	4	n.r.
Syrups and sweetenings	n.a.	n.a.	n.a.	6	6	6	n.r.
Tea	n.a.	n.a.	n.a.	6	8	8	n.r.
Vinegar and cider	n.a.	n.a.	n.a.	3	4	4	n.r.
Other	n.a.	n.a.	n.a.	14	10	11	n.r.
Other common grocery store products[a]							
Cigarettes						1	n.r.
Apparel						1	n.r.
Soap and detergent						4	n.r.
Polishes and sanitation goods						2	n.r.
Miscellaneous plastic products						3	n.r.
Footwear						1	n.r.

Table B–3 continued

Product Area	Number of Integrated Chains among Forty Largest					Fifty Largest, 1977	
	1959	1963	1967	1972	1977	Number Integrated	Value of Shipments
Products needed to operate stores[a]							
Wood partitions and fixtures						2	n.r.
Metal partitions and fixtures						3	n.r.
Paper bags						1	n.r.
Paper boxes						4	n.r.
Printing labels, wrappers, advertising, etc.							n.r.
Refrigeration and heating equipment						2	n.r.

Source: FTC, special surveys 1959, 1965, 1969; special tabulation of U.S. Bureau of Census, 1972, 1977.

Notes: n.a. = data for category not tabulated.

  n.r. = Bureau of the Census did not release data because of the possibility they would disclose information about individual companies.

[a]These items were not surveyed by the FTC.

Table B-4
Acquisitions of Food Retailers, 1949–1984

Year	By All Acquirers: Sales of Acquired	By Twenty Leading Food Chains[a]: Sales of Acquired	By Twenty Leading Food Chains[a]: Percentage of Total Acquired Sales	By Ten Leading Food Chains[a]: Sales of Acquired	By Ten Leading Food Chains[a]: Percentage of Total Acquired Sales
1949	$66	$47	71%	$47	71%
1950	4	3	75	1	25
1951	28	25	89	19	68
1952	71	55	77	53	75
1953	88	77	88	61	69
1954	76	37	49	31	41
1955	559	465	83	267	48
1956	450	310	69	141	31
1957	319	194	61	170	53
1958	517	361	70	261	50
1959	319	136	43	24	8
1960	307	201	65	36	12
1961	518	407	79	292	56
1962	306	179	58	157	51
1963	568	463	82	416	73
1964	312	188	60	153	49
1965	558	61	11	35	6
1966	539	110	20	73	14
1967	1,350	21	2	0	0
1968	1,155	139	12	24	2
1969	715	41	6	13	2
1970	688	74	11	22	3
1971	435	28	6	28	6
1972	1,069	242	23	3	1
1973	206	29	14	11	5
1974	1,591	30	2	14	1
1975	337	127	38	84	25
1976	882	742	84	738	84

1977	1,218	728	60	350	29
1978	2,456	1,835[b]	75	1,067	43
1979	9,315[d]	911	10	680[c]	7
1980	2,975	730	25	696	23
1981	4,599	142	3	142	3
1982	3,667	156	4	124	3
1983	8,067	3,737	46	3,737	46
1984	9,475	5,593	59	4,843	51

Source: Nominal sales data for 1949–1977 from Mueller 1978a, p. 44. Nominal sales data for 1978–1984 from various secondary sources.

Note: Dollar amounts in millions.

[a]For 1949–1966, data are for largest chains of 1963. For 1967–1981, data are for the largest chains of 1975. Subsequent data are for the largest chains of 1982.

[b]Pick N Pay–First National merger is included here; acquired sales of $424.12 million are those of Pick N Pay.

[c]Skaggs–American merger is included here; acquired sales of $300 million are those of Skaggs.

[d]Includes acquisition of A&P by Tengelman. Acquired sales were $5,558 million.

Table B–5
Number of Establishments and Sales of Food Wholesalers by Kind of Business and Type of Operation, 1977

	Merchants			
	Establishments		Sales	
Kind of Business	(no.)	(%)	(millions of dollars)	(%)
General line	2,744	9.4	35,896	32.2
Voluntaries	459	1.6	12,528	11.2
Cooperatives	214	.7	11,347	10.2
Unaffiliated	2,071	7.1	12,021	10.8
Specialty				
Frozen foods	2,032	6.9	7,559	6.8
Dairy products	2,842	9.7	7,964	7.1
Poultry products	1,746	6.0	5,522	4.9
Confectionery	2,027	6.9	2,249	2.0
Seafood products	1,735	5.9	3,374	3.0
Meat products	4,443	15.2	17,487	15.7
Fresh fruits and vegetables	5,033	17.2	11,812	10.6
Coffee, tea, and spices	601	2.1	5,673	5.1
Bread and baked goods	1,043	3.6	958	.9
Canned goods	932	3.2	4,459	4.0
Food and beverage basic material	273	.9	822	.7
Other grocery specialties	3,816	13.0	7,791	7.0
Total	29,267	100.0	111,567	100.0

Source: U.S. Bureau of the Census, *1977 Census of Wholesale Trade, Geographic Area Series, United States,* WC77-A-52, U.S. Department of Commerce, June 1980.

Note: Empty cells indicate not applicable.

Brokers				Manufacturers' Sales Branches and Offices			
Establishments		Sales		Establishments		Sales	
(no.)	(%)	(millions of dollars)	(%)	(no.)	(%)	(millions of dollars)	(%)
434	9.6	5,143	17.3				
434	9.6	5,143	17.3				
572	12.6	3,803	12.8	105	2.5	1,526	3.7
237	5.2	933	3.2	845	20.3	6,130	14.7
78	1.7	330	1.1	75	1.8	762	1.8
389	8.6	1,249	4.2	204	4.9	2,624	6.3
127	2.8	427	1.4	13	.3	46	.1
247	5.4	1,681	5.7	435	10.5	5,843	14.1
743	16.4	2,942	9.9				
75	1.7	784	2.6	203	4.9	4,745	11.4
119	2.6	251	.8	1,122	27.0	3,257	7.8
495	10.9	4,183	14.1	201	4.8	4,901	11.8
96	2.1	549	1.9	28	.7	96	.2
924	20.4	7,434	25.0	929	22.3	11,699	28.1
4,536	100.0	29,709	100.0	4,157	100.0	41,630	100.0

Table B–6
Concentration of Largest Wholesale Firms by Type of Operation and Kind of Business, 1972–1977
(percentage of category sales accounted for by largest firms)

Type of Operation and Kind of Business	1972				1977			
	Four Largest	Eight Largest	Twenty Largest	Fifty Largest	Four Largest	Eight Largest	Twenty Largest	Fifty Largest
General line groceries	9.9	16.2	29.8	47.5	13.1	19.6	32.7	50.6
Merchants					15.0	22.4	36.8	56.6
Manufacturers' sales branches								
Agents and brokers					20.4	27.9	41.5	60.2
Specialty merchants								
Frozen foods	9.8	15.0	25.7	41.0	11.3	17.5	28.7	43.3
Dairy	11.0	15.9	25.9	38.6	14.0	21.6	34.2	46.8
Poultry	6.2	9.5	15.9	27.7	8.6	13.9	21.0	34.2
Confectionery	6.8	11.2	18.4	29.8	11.9	17.3	25.5	37.1
Fish	4.8	8.3	15.8	28.5	15.5	20.4	28.9	39.6
Meat	5.2	8.0	13.7	22.9	6.8	10.8	17.9	29.1
Fresh fruit	6.6	8.6	12.2	17.9	7.0	10.4	15.0	22.1
Groceries	10.4	21.7	30.7	42.3	13.3	19.4	31.4	46.6

Sources: Bureau of the Census, *Census of Wholesale Trade*, Subject Series (1972-WC72-S1; 1977-WC77-S1).
Note: Empty cells indicate no data available.

Table B–7
Operating Expenses of Grocery Wholesalers by Type of Wholesalers and Kind of Business, 1972 and 1977

| Kind of Business and Year | Operating Expenses as a Percentage of Sales | | | |
	All Establishments	Merchants	Manufacturers' Sales Branches	Agents and Brokers
1977				
All grocery wholesalers	8.3	9.7	7.9	3.8
General line	6.8	7.3		3.4
Voluntary	6.2	6.2		
Cooperative	5.8	5.8		
Unaffiliated	8.0	9.9		3.4
Specialty				
Frozen foods	8.8	11.8	7.1	3.5
Dairy	8.6	8.8	9.2	3.5
Poultry	8.3	9.0	6.0	2.6
Confectionery	10.1	15.2	8.2	4.9
Fish	9.8	10.5	11.4	4.1
Meat	9.0	10.0	7.7	2.7
Fresh fruit	12.6	14.1		6.6
Other groceries	7.5	9.9	7.7	3.4
1972				
All grocery wholesalers	8.6	10.0	9.6	3.3
General line	7.1	7.1		
Voluntary	6.3	6.3		
Cooperative	5.4	5.4		
Unaffiliated	9.2	9.2		
Specialty				
Frozen foods	7.8	11.8	5.9	3.1
Dairy	11.1	11.9	12.9	2.4
Poultry	10.3	10.9	8.6	4.0
Confectionery	9.2	15.3	9.1	2.4
Fish	11.7	13.1	5.8	4.4
Meat	8.3	9.1	8.2	1.8
Fresh fruit	13.4	16.9		4.7
Other groceries	7.6	10.5	9.3	3.3

Source: U.S. Bureau of the Census, *Census of Wholesale Trade* 1972, (WC72 A52), *Census of Wholesale Trade* (WCyy A52).

Note: Empty cells: not applicable or data not available.

Table B–8
Market Structure Data for Food and Tobacco Product Classes, Sorted by SIC

SIC	SIC Description	Code	NL	CR4 1954	CR4 1958
20111	Beef	0	0	36	31
20112	Veal	0	0	49	41
20113	Lamb and Mutton	0	0	61	60
20114	Pork	0	0	42	39
20115	Lard	0	0	45	41
20116	Pork, processed or cured	9	0	40	30
20117	Sausage and similar products	9	0	24	22
20118	Canned meats	9	0	46	42
20119	Hides, skins, and pelts	0	0	43	33
20151	Broilers	27	0	18	12
20163	Turkeys	51	0	22	23
20172	Liquid, dried, and frozen eggs	52	0	34	30
20210	Creamery butter	60	0		
20221	Natural cheese, except cottage	0	0		
20222	Process cheese and related products	0	0		
20231	Dry milk products	0	0		22
20232	Canned milk products	0	0	79	78
20233	Concentrated milk, bulk shipped	0	0	45	38
20234	Ice cream mix and ice milk mix	0	0	24	23
20240	Ice cream and ices	0	1	33	35
20261	Bulk fluid milk and cream	0	1	18	16
20262	Packaged fluid milk	0	1		26
20263	Cottage cheese	0	1		32
20264	Buttermilk, chocolate drink, etc.	0	1		30
20321	Canned baby foods	53	0	95	94
20322	Canned soups	38	0	89	90
20323	Canned dry beans	3	0		46
20331	Canned fruits	3	0		
20332	Canned vegetables	3	0		
20333	Canned hominy and mushrooms	3	0		37
20334	Canned fruit juices, nectars	3	0		
20335	Canned vegetable juices	3	0	58	58
20336	Catsup and other tomato sauces	3	0		55
20338	Jams, jellies, and preserves	3	0	26	28
20341	Dried fruits and vegetables	0	0		
20342	Soup mixes, dried	0	0		
20352	Pickes and other pickled products	3	0	18	20
20353	Meat sauces (not tomato)	3	0		35
20354	Mayonnaise and salad dressings	3	0		
20371	Frozen fruits, juices, and ades	7	0	40	34
20372	Frozen vegetables	3	0	52	45
20381	Frozen pies	0	0		
20382	Frozen dinners	0	0		
20383	Other frozen specialties	0	0		
20411	Wheat flour (not flour mixes)	0	0		
20412	Wheat mill products (not flour)	0	0	42	40
20413	Corn mill products	0	0		
20415	Flour mixes and refrigerator doughs	9	0		
20430	Cereal breakfast foods	0	0	78	80
20440	Milled rice and byproducts	0	0	40	44
20460	Wet corn milling	0	0		68

CR4 1963	CR4 1967	CR4 1972	CR4 1977	CR8 1977	CR20 1977	ADS	VOS 1977
26	26	30	25	36	53	.00	14096
36	37	27	32	56	85	.00	319
54	57	55	58	82	97	.00	330
36	33	37	37	55	78	.00	5648
33	33	37	39	59	83	.01	214
25	22	22	18	30		.24	3779
20	19	17	22	31		.62	4680
39	34	41	36	51		.99	1256
33	32	30	23	35	53	.00	808
14	17	18	23	35		.06	4191
23	28	40	42	59		.54	927
33	43	36	30	49	85	.03	313
		37	30	42	64	.12	1110
34	38	36	32	41	56	.68	2727
67	72	60	59	76	88	.45	2519
22	35	45	38	52	69	1.71	1735
66	62	69	72	91	100	1.80	672
41	31	29	33	50	80	.00	264
17	15	16	22	36	60	.00	293
34	32	27	27	36	53	.57	2229
15	17	23	25	38	57	.00	2124
25	25	19	18	30	46	.09	7346
32	36	27	25	38	62	.62	546
31	31	29	32	44	60	1.06	852
95	93	95	98	100	100	1.40	401
92	93	95	95	99	100	3.66	762
44	49	50	51	68	90	1.20	557
37	34	35	37	51	78	.64	1298
34	38	35	38	49	70	.70	1651
34	39	39	53	73	96	.77	150
31	31	29	34	47	69	.71	1223
55	62	62	67	81	95	1.47	252
49	55	56	52	71	88	2.85	1350
31	35	40	49	63	84	1.23	397
39	32	32	39	56	82	1.15	899
84	73	75	78	88	98	6.54	225
23	29	38	40	53	78	.58	553
45	47	50	49	65	85	4.30	262
56	55	52	60	67	79	3.66	1292
28	30	41	36	50	75	1.06	1154
39	34	35	34	56	79	1.02	1798
		51	52	72	88	2.96	770
		58	45	58	80	2.21	1298
		35	58	72	88	2.21	718
40	37	37	38	66	88	.21	2209
38	35	37	39	64	88	.26	455
	62	60	62	85	96	.25	413
60	59	61	48	64		3.35	1492
82	82	84	81	95	99	11.57	1833
46	45	42	47	72	94	1.12	1242
65	64	63	61	86	99	.34	1946

Table B–8 continued

SIC	SIC Description	Code	NL	CR4 1954	CR4 1958
20471	Dog and cat food	29	0	32	38
20472	Other pet and specialty feed	0	0		
20480	Prepared feeds, N.E.C.	0	1		
20510	Bread, cake, and related products	0	1	19	21
20521	Crackers and pretzels	0	0		77
20522	Cookies and ice cream cones	0	0		
20610	Sugar cane mill products	0	0		
20620	Refined cane sugar	30	0		67
20650	Confectionery products	0	0	18	17
20661	Chocolate coatings	0	0		46
20662	Choc. and chocolate-type confectionary	0	0		88
20668	Other chocolate and cocoa products	9	0		62
20670	Chewing gum	55	0	84	83
20740	Cottonseed oil mill products	0	0	44	44
20750	Soybean oil mill products	0	0	37	37
20760	Vegetable oil mill products	0	0		61
20770	Animal and marine fats and oil	0	0		19
20791	Shortening and cooking oils	0	0	55	50
20792	Margarine	0	0	39	46
20820	Beer	19	0	27	29
20830	Malt and malt byproducts	0	0	47	50
20840	Wines, brandy, and brandy spirits	28	0	38	35
20851	Distilled liquors (not brandy)	3	0		55
20853	Bottled liquors (not brandy)	3	0	67	61
20860	Bottled and canned soft drinks	31	0	89	89
20871	Flavoring extracts and emulsions	0	0	35	28
20872	Liquid beverage bases	0	0	83	63
20874	Other flavoring agents	21	0	38	44
20910	Canned and cured seafood	3	0		
20922	Fresh packaged fish	0	0		
20923	Frozen packaged fish (not shell)	0	0		
20924	Frozen packaged shellfish and seafood	0	0		
20951	Roasted coffee, whole or ground	0	0		
20952	Concentrated coffee	32	0		
20970	Manufactured ice	0	1	26	32
20980	Macaroni, spaghetti and noodles	0	0	25	25
20991	Desserts (ready-to-mix)	33	0	80	81
20992	Chips (potato, corn, etc.)	0	0		35
20993	Sweetening syrups and molasses	21	0	65	64
20994	Baking power and yeast	0	0		78
20995	Tea in consumer packages	0	0		
20996	Vinegar and cider	0	0	46	41
21110	Cigarettes	34	0	82	80
21210	Cigars	3	0	45	54
21310	Chewing and smoking tobacco	3	0	56	53
21411	Tobacco, redried	3	0	82	72
21412	Tobacco, stemed	3	0	89	86

Notes: NL: national market, 0; local market, 1. ADS: average advertising-to-sales ratio for the years 1967, 1972, and 1977. In 1972 and 1977 six-media (network and spot television, magazines, newspaper supplements, outdoor, and network radio) were used, in 1967 newspapers and spot radio were included with the other six-media. VOS: value of shipments in 1977, in millions of dollars.

CR4 1963	CR4 1967	CR4 1972	CR4 1977	CR8 1977	CR20 1977	ADS	VOS 1977
42	46	54	58	76	87	6.55	2717
		26	34	47	70	.00	268
		22	21	30	44	.00	8350
22	25	27	32	40	53	.85	7966
71	71	68	70	80	92	1.60	1169
52	51	55	55	66	82	1.25	1578
47	42	43	42	61	86	.00	708
64	63	62	65	93	100	.17	3328
15	24	32	36	46	63	2.03	4170
45	56	54	62	90	99	.00	341
82	82	82	82	98	100	1.45	565
60	70	69	69	81		1.77	888
86	81	84	93	97	100	11.89	649
40	44	42	42	59	81	.00	763
48	55	52	50	71	93	.00	6117
54	46	45	33	53	84	.00	401
18	18	17	19	29	46	.00	2102
51	53	50	47	63	87	1.05	3166
50	47	54	60	84	99	5.15	1070
34	40	52	65	83	98	3.41	6613
37	42	49	60	81	98	.00	489
44	48	53	49	62	84	4.99	1363
51	50	49	54	81	99	.00	206
58	53	51	54	72	94	9.66	1703
89	89	89	86	91	96	2.83	8504
27	18	23	21	38	67	.02	226
73	74	65	78	91	99	1.53	213
51	59	68	76	81	88	3.57	1063
33	34	38	37	53	71	1.53	1026
			10	16	29	.00	461
			36	52	76	.27	744
			27	42	65	.01	888
51	56	60	57	71	90	1.66	3675
81	85	88	88	98	99	5.37	1388
32	32	29	22	36	47	.00	141
28	31	34	32	51	76	4.22	752
86	81	80	81	87	97	7.16	413
41	41	49	52	61	76	2.52	1797
63	54	53	52	69	86	3.45	297
86	81	89	78	89	99	.72	170
		79	79	88	97	3.83	617
49	53	48	54	71	88	.40	123
80	80	84	88	100	100	6.63	6098
59	58	55	54	75	94	4.02	256
53	50	60	65	91	99	2.08	401
77	65	60	67	92	100	.00	171
82	76	72	72	90	99	.00	1532

Code explanations are as follows:

0   No problems with the data. Census data are as found in table 9 of the *1977 Concentration Ratios in Manufacturing (Census, 1977b)*, (hereafter the concentration book).

Table B-8 continued

3   The census substitutes value of production for value of shipments.

7   Code 3 applies and a 1972 census revision caused a loss of comparability between the 1972 data and earlier years, but the loss was estimated by the census to be less than 3 percent; hence the observation was included in the sample.

9   Census data were taken from table 10 of the 1977 concentration book. This change was made because the census recognized that a substantial portion of the product classes' value of shipments was primary to more than one industry. For example, table 7 combines SIC 20116, Processed Pork Made in Meatpacking Plants, and SIC 20136, Processed Pork Not Made in Meatpacking Plants. The relevant economic market is processed pork; whether it was manufactured in a meatpacking plant is irrelevant.

19   Since five-digit product class data are too disaggregated, the four-digit industry data are used. For example, canned beer and bottled beer are nearly perfect substitutes for each other and should not be viewed as separate economic markets.

21   1958 concentration ratios are not available and were estimated by Rogers (1982).

27   Concentration ratios for 1977 are weighted averages of two new 1977 SIC product classes, 20171 and 20172. Concentration ratios for 1972 are weighted averages of 20161 and 20162.

28   Concentration ratios and VOS are from table 5 of 1972 concentration book and table 8 of 1977 concentration book.

29   1977 and 1972 concentration and VOS data are for SIC 20471; previous years used SIC 20423.

30   Since refined sugar made from sugar cane or sugar beets is indistinguishable to the consumer, SICs 20620 and 20630 were combined to form one observation. Value of shipments data were summed and concentration ratios for the two SICs were averaged.

31   The soft drinks industry has a two-tier market structure (Katz 1978), with the syrup manufacturers classified in SIC 20873, Flavoring Syrups for Use by Soft Drink Bottlers, and the soft drink bottlers classified in SIC 20860, Bottled and Canned Soft Drinks. Both SIC 20860 and SIC 20873 were combined to form one meaningful observation. Concentration data were taken from SIC 20873, and value-of-shipments data were taken from SIC 20860 (shipments from SIC 20873 are inputs to SIC 20860). SIC 20873 was then omitted from the study. See chapter 4 and Scherer (1980, pp. 63–64) for more information concerning census data for the soft drinks industry.

32   CR4 in 1972 was estimated by Parker and Connor; CR4 in 1977 is from *Advertising Age*, April 13, 1981, p. 74.

33   CR4s in 1972 and 1967 were estimated by Rogers (1982).

34   1963 and 1967 CR4s were estimated by Rogers (1982). Code 3 also applies. 1977 CR8 estimated to be 100.

38   CRs estimated by Rogers (1982).

51   1977 CRs and VOS are for SIC 20173 in table 10 of the 1977 concentration book.

52   1977 SIC is 20179.

53   CR8 in 1977 estimated to be 100. Code 7 applies also.

55   CR20 in 1977 estimated to be 100.

60   CRs prior to 1972 are unreliable due to census handling of dairy cooperatives.

Appendix C
Lists of NC 117 Publications and Participants

Monograph Series

1. Matthews, S.F., and V.J. Rhodes, *The Use of Public Limited Partnership Financing in Agriculture for Income Tax Shelter*, July 1975.
2. Marion, B.W., ed., *Coordination and Exchange in Agricultural Subsectors*, January 1976.
3. Mueller, W.F., L.B. Hamm, and H.L. Cook, *Public Policy toward Mergers in the Dairy Processing Industry*, December 1976.
4. Marion, B.W., ed., *Agricultural Cooperatives and the Public Interest*, September 1978.
5. Cook, H.L., L. Blakley, R. Jacobson, R. Knutson, R. Milligan, and R. Strain, *The Dairy Subsector of American Agriculture: Organization and Vertical Coordination*, November 1978.
6. Schrader, L.F., H. Larzalere, G.B. Rogers, and O.D. Forker, *The Egg Subsector of U.S. Agriculture*, June 1978.
7. Hayenga, M.L., ed., *Pricing Problems in the Food Industry (with Emphasis on Thin Markets)*, February 1979.
8. Ward, R.W., and R.L. Kilmer, *The United States Citrus Subsector: Organization, Behavior and Performance*, December 1980.
9. Hayenga, M.L., A.C. Johnson, Jr., and B.W. Marion, eds., *Market Information and Price Reporting in the Food and Agricultural Sector*, August 1980.
10. Pederson, D., and D. Dahl, *Agricultural Employment Law and Policy*, August 1981.
11. Mueller, W.F., J. Culbertson, and B. Peckham, *Market Structure and Technological Performance in the Food Manufacturing Industries*, February 1982.
12. Ricks, D., L. Hamm, and W.C. Chase-Lansdale, *The Tart Cherry Subsector of U.S. Agriculture: A Review of Organization and Performance*, July 1982.
13. Dahl, D.C., W. Grant, and L. Geyer, *Federal Antitrust Policy and the U.S. Food System*, August 1983.
14. Connor, J.M., and R.W. Ward, eds., *Advertising and the Food System*, September 1983.
15. Jesse, E.V., ed., *Antitrust Treatment of Agricultural Marketing Cooperatives*, September 1983.

Special Reports

1. Grant, W.W., and D.C. Dahl, *Bibliography of Agriculture and Food Law, 1960–1978,* August 1978.
2. Connor, J.M., and L.L. Mather, *Directory of the 200 Largest Food and Tobacco Processing Firms, 1975,* July 1978.

Working Paper Series

1. Campbell, G.R., and T.S. Clevenger, "An Institutional Approach to Vertical Coordination in Agriculture," August 1975.
2. Henderson, D.R., "Toward a Theory of Vertical Market Behavior," October 1975.
3. Sporleder, T.L., "Algorithms for Vertical Integration Indices," October 1975.
4. Clevenger, T.S., and G.R. Campbell, "Vertical Market Organization and the Structure-Profits Relationship," December 1975.
5. Schmelzer, J.R., G.R. Campbell, and A. Yuen, "Production and Consumption Trends in the U.S. Fruit and Vegetable Subsectors," June 1976.
6. Parker, R.C., "The Status of Competition in the Food Manufacturing and Food Retailing Industries," August 1976.
7. Marion, Bruce W., "Application of the Structure-Conduct-Performance Paradigm to Subsector Analysis," November 1976.
8. Raikes, Ronald, and Lynn Dippold, "Design and Evaluation of a Simultaneous Auction for Slaughter Cattle," December 1976.
9. Schmelzer, J.R., and D.R. Henderson, "An Analysis of the Impact of Collective Bargaining on Grower Prices and Integrative Efficiency—A Case Study of the Ohio Concord Grape Industry," December 1976.
10. Marion, B.W., and W.F. Mueller, "The Structure and Performance of Food Retailing," Testimony for Joint Economic Commission, March 1977.
11. Mueller, W.F., "The Social Control of Economic Power," June 1977.
12. Lang, Mahlon G., "Vertical Coordination and Vertical Coordination Mechanisms: Analysis and Case Studies," September 1977.
13. Henderson, D.R., and R.B. Schwart, Jr., "Vertical Coordination between Cow/Calf Enterprises and Feedlots in the United States," November 1977.
14. Ward, C.E., "Vertical Coordination in Cattle Feeding and Slaughtering in the Cattle and Beef Subsector System," December 1977.
15. Jesse, Edward V., "Measuring Market Performance: Quantifying the Non-Quantifiable," March 1978.
16. Miller, Katherine S., and Ronald Raikes, "A Risk-Processing Analysis of Cattle Procurement by Beef Packers," May 1978.
17. Mueller, W.F., and R.T. Rogers, "The Role of Advertising in Changing Market Concentration," May 1978.
18. Mueller, W.F., "The Need for Vigorous Antitrust Enforcement," May 1978.
19. Parker, R.C., and J.M. Connor, "Estimates of Consumer Loss Due to Monopoly in U.S. Food Manufacturing Industries," September 1978.

20. Campbell, G.R., and M.L. Hayenga, "Vertical Organization and Coordination in Selected Commodity Subsectors," August 1978.

21. Marion, B.W., "Government Regulation of Competition in the Food Industry," September 1978.

22. Hayenga, M.L., "Vertical Coordination in the Beef Industry: Packer, Retailer and HRI Linkages," October 1978.

23. Hayenga, M.L., "Risk Management in Imperfect Markets: Commodity Procurement Strategy in the Food Manufacturing Sector," October 1978.

24. Connor, J.M., and W.F. Mueller, "Market Structure and Performance of U.S. Multinationals in Brazil and Mexico," November 1978.

25. Devine, G.D., and B.W. Marion, "The Influence of Consumer Price Information on the Structure, Conduct and Performance of Food Retailing," December 1978.

26. Dahl, D.C., "Recent Developments in Agricultural Law," February 1979.

27. Mueller, W.F., "The Capper-Volstead Exemption," February 1979.

28. Mueller, W.F., "Federal Milk Marketing Orders," February 1979.

29. Connor, J.M., "Competition and the Role of the Largest Firms in the U.S. Food and Tobacco Industries," February 1979.

30. Parker, R.C., and J.M. Connor, "Conglomeration and Consumer Loss in the Food Manufacturing Industries," April 1979.

31. Mueller, W.F., "Conglomerate Mergers in the Food Industry," April 1979.

32. Hayenga, M.L., "Formula Pricing and Price Reporting Problems in the Markets for Beef and Pork," May 1979.

33. Cotterill, R.W., and W.F. Mueller, "The Impact of Firm Conglomeration on Market Structure: Evidence for the U.S. Food Retailing Industry," May 1979.

34. Ward, C.E., "Meat Marketing and Pricing—An Evaluation of Current and Proposed Systems," June 1979.

35. Henderson, D.R., "Some Considerations in the Application of Electronic Marketing to Meat," June 1979.

36. Mather, L.L., "Advertising and Mergers in the Food Manufacturing Industries," July 1979.

37. Hayenga, M.L., "Pork Pricing Systems: The Importance and Economic Impact of Formula Pricing," August 1979.

38. Hayenga, M.L., "Cheese Pricing Systems," August 1979.

39. Hayenga, M.L., ed., "Commodity Pricing Systems: Issues and Alternatives," August 1979.

40. Shaffer, J.D., "Food System Organization and Performance: Toward a Conceptual Framework," December 1979.

41. Connor, J.M., "Food Product Proliferation: A Market Structure Analysis," March 1980.

42. Cotterill, R., "Group Purchasing, An Analysis of Performance and Economies of Size in Preorder Food Cooperatives," June 1980.

43. Kelton, C.M.L., "The Administered-Price Thesis: Literature Review and Methodological Discussion," June 1980.

44. Mueller, W.F., "The Social Control of Private Economic Power," June 1980.

45. Lesser, W., "Vertical Exchange Relationships and Performance in the Great Lakes Yellow Perch Industry," July 1980.

46. Jesse, E.V., and A.C. Johnson, "Marketing Cooperatives and Undue Price Enhancement: A Theoretical Perspective," October 1980.
47. Culbertson, J.D., and W.F. Mueller, "The Influence of Market Structure on Technological Performance in the Food Manufacturing Industries," October 1980.
48. Schrader, L.F., and D.R. Henderson, "Auction Pricing: Options and Implications," November 1980.
49. Marion, B.W., "Future Organization of U.S. Food System: Implications for Agriculture," November 1980.
50. Kilmer, R.L., and R.W. Ward, "Exchange Performance Contrasted between Coordinated and Spot Markets," November 1980.
51. Jesse, E.V., A.C. Johnson, and B.W. Marion, "Interpreting and Enforcing Section 2 of the Capper-Volstead Act," February 1981.
52. Mueller, W.F., "Conglomerates: A 'Nonindustry,'" March 1981.
53. Mueller, W.F., "The Anti-Antitrust Movement," June 1981.
54. Cook, H.L., and M.L. Hayenga, "Environmental and Structural Characteristics of the Dairy Subsector," July 1981.
55. Hayenga, M.L., D.L. Boyd, and L.L. Christian, "The Changing Economic Structure and Behavior of the Swine Breeding Stock Market," August 1981.
56. Schmelzer, J.R., "The Commercial Foodservice Sector: Trends in Growth and Market Structure," September 1981.
57. Culbertson, J.D., "The Policy Interpretation of Econometric Tests of the Schumpeterian Hypothesis," October 1981.
58. Hamm, Larry, G., "The Impact of Food Distributor Procurement Practices on Food System Structure and Coordination," October 1981.
59. Carl, C.K., and R.L. Kilmer, "Analyzing the Prices from a Vertical Exchange Mechanism: An Implicit Price Approach," November 1981.
60. Kelton, Christina M.L., "The Effect of Market Structure on Price Change for Food Manufacturing Product Classes," February 1982.
61. Mueller, Willard F., "Public Policy and Economic Power: The American Antitrust Laws and Some International Comparisons," February 1982.
62. Henderson, Dennis, "Electronic Markets for Agricultural Commodities: Potentials and Pitfalls," March 1982.
63. Mueller, Willard F., "Food Conglomerates," March 1982.
64. Hamm, Larry G., "Retailer-Manufacturer Relationships in the Food Sector—Some Observations from the U.S.A.," April 1982.
65. Mueller, W.F., and D.F. Greer, "The Effect of Market Share Distribution in Industry Performance—Reexamined," May 1982.
66. Holder, Dave, Tom Sporleder, and Allen Paul, "Ownership of Electronic Commodity Exchanges," November 1982.
67. Marion, B.W., and H.J. Nash, "Foreign Investment in U.S. Food Retailing Industry," December 1982.
68. Isaksen, Geir P., "Political Support for Farmer Cooperatives," March 1983.
69. Mueller, W.F., and R.T. Rogers, "Changes in Market Concentration of Manufacturing Industries, 1947–1977," March 1983.
70. Connor, John M. "Determinants of Foreign Direct Investment by Food and Tobacco Manufacturers," March 1983.

71. Roberts, Tanya, "Benefit Analysis of Selected Slaughterhouse Meat Inspection Practices," August 1983.
72. Kelton, Christina M.L., "Operational Efficiency in Food and Tobacco Manufacturing," September 1983.
73. Combs, Robert P., and Bruce W. Marion, "Food Manufacturing Activities of 100 Large Agricultural Marketing Cooperatives," April 1984.
74. Rogers, Richard T., "Concentration Change in Food and Tobacco Product Classes, 1958–1977," September 1985.
75. Rogers, Richard T., "A Structure-Price-Cost Margin Model Estimated Over Time for Food and Tobacco Product Classes, 1954–1977," June 1985.
76. Wills, Robert L., "A Comparison of Price Enhancement Practices of Cooperative and Proprietary Brands," June 1984.
77. Wills, Robert L., "Advertising and Quality as Sources of Price Heterogeneity among Brands of Food Products," September 1984.
78. Mueller, W.F., "Alleged Predatory Conduct in Food Retailing," September 1984.
79. Paterson, Thomas W., and Willard F. Mueller, "State Sales-Below-Cost Laws: An Econometric Analysis of Effectiveness," September 1984.
80. Paterson, Thomas W., and Willard F. Mueller, "State Sales-Below-Cost Laws: A Legal-Economic Analysis of Effectiveness," September 1984.
81. Marion, Bruce W., "Strategic Groups, Entry Barriers and Competitive Behavior in Grocery Retailing," September 1984.
82. Mueller, Willard F., "Clarifying the Rights of Farmers to Seek Damages in Antitrust Actions," October 1984.
83. Cotterill, Ron, "Modern Markets and Market Power: Evidence from the Vermont Retail Food Industry," November 1984.
84. Paterson, Thomas W., and W.F. Mueller, "Agricultural Marketing Cooperatives and Section 1 of the Capper-Volstead Act: Conditioning (Limited) Antitrust Immunity on Capper-Volstead Policy," December 1984.
85. Paterson, Thomas W., and W.F. Mueller, "Sherman Section 2 Monopolization for Agricultural Marketing Cooperatives," December 1984.
86. Rosenbaum, David I., "Predatory Pricing and the Reconstituted Lemon Juice Industry," March 1985.

Reprint Series

1. Mueller, W.F., and L. Hamm, "Trends in Industrial Market Concentration, 1947 to 1970, *Rev. of Econ. and Stat.,* November 1974.
2. Meisner, J.C., and V.J. Rhodes, "The Changing Structure of U.S. Cattle Feeding," *Spec. Rep. 167,* U. of Missouri, November 1974.
3. Dahl, Dale C., "Public Policy Changes Needed to Cope with Changing Structure," *AJAE,* May 1985.
4. Padberg, D.I., "Emerging Effectiveness of Competition and the Need for Consumer Protection," *AJAE,* May 1975.
5. Mueller, W.F., "Antitrust in a Planned Economy: An Anachronism or an Essential Complement," *J. of Econ. Issues,* June 1975.

6. Marion, B.W., and T.L. Sporleder, "An Evaluation of the Economic Basis for Antitrust Policy in the Food Industry," *AJAE*, December 1976.

7. Parker, Russell C., "Antitrust Issues in the Food Industries," *AJAE*, December 1976.

8. Clevenger, T.C., and G.R. Campbell, "Vertical Organization: A Neglected Element in Market Structure-Profit Models," *Ind. Org. Rev.*, February 1977.

9. Kilmer, R.L., and D.E. Hahn, "Effects of Market-Share and Antimerger Policies on the Fluid Milk-Producing Industries," *AJAE*, August 1978.

10. Geithman, F.E., and B.W. Marion, "A Critique of the Use of BLS Data for Market Structure-Price Analysis," *AJAE*, November 1978.

11. Mueller, Willard F., "The Control of Agricultural Processing and Distribution," *AJAE*, December 1978.

12. Marion, Bruce W., "Government Regulation of Competition in the Food Industry," *AJAE*, February 1979.

13. Hayenga, M.L., "Risk Management in Imperfect Markets: Commodity Procurement Strategy in the Food Manufacturing Sector," *AJAE*, May 1979.

14. Devine, D.G., and B.W. Marion, "The Influence of Consumer Price Information on Retail Pricing and Consumer Behavior," *AJAE*, May 1979.

15. Padberg, D.I., "Non-Use Benefits of Mandatory Consumer Information Programs," *J. of Consumer Policy*, January 1977.

16. Marion, B.W., W. Mueller, R. Cotterill, F. Geithman, and J. Schmelzer, "The Price and Profit Performance of Leading Food Chains," *AJAE*, August 1979.

17. Leuthold, R.M., and P.A. Hartmann, "A Semi-Strong Form Evaluation of the Efficiency of the Hog Futures Market," *AJAE*, August 1979.

18. Padberg, D.I., and R.E. Westgren, "Product Competition and Consumer Behavior in the Food Industries," *AJAE*, November 1979.

19. Parker, R.C., and J.M. Connor, "Estimates of Consumer Loss Due to Monopoly in the U.S. Food Manufacturing Industries," *AJAE*, November 1979.

20. Mueller, W.F., and R.T. Rogers, "The Role of Advertising in Changing Concentration of Manufacturing Industries," *Rev. of Econ. and Stats*, February 1980.

21. Dahl, D.C., and T.J. Burke, "The Use of Limited Partnership in Upper Midwest Agriculture," *Agric. Law J.*, Fall 1979.

22. Hayenga, M.J., and L.F. Schrader, "Formula Pricing in Five Commodity Marketing Systems," *AJAE*, November 1980.

23. Cotterill, R.W., and W.F. Mueller, "The Impact of Firm Conglomeration on Market Structure: Evidence for the U.S. Food Retailing Industry," *Antitrust Bulletin*, Fall 1980.

24. Connor, J.M., "Advertising, Promotion and Competition: A Survey with Special Reference to Food," *Agric. Econ. Research*, January 1981.

25. Lang, M.G., "Marketing Alternatives and Resource Allocation: Case Studies of Collective Bargaining," *AJAE*, November 1980.

26. Lang, M.B., "Economic Efficiency and Policy Comparisons," *AJAE*, November 1980.

27. Hoffman, A.C., "The Rise of Economic Power: Some Consequences and Policy Implications," *AJAE*, December 1980.

28. Geithman, F.E., H.P. Marvel, and L.W. Weiss, "Concentration, Price and Critical Concentration Ratios," *Rev. of Econ. and Stat.*, August 1981.

29. Connor, J.M., "Food Product Proliferation: A Market Structure Analysis," *AJAE*, November 1981.
30. Jesse, E.V., A.C. Johnson, Jr., B.W. Marion, and A.C. Manchester, "Interpreting and Enforcing Section 2 of the Capper-Volstead Act," *AJAE*, August 1982.
31. Jesse, E.V., A.C. Johnson, Jr., and A.B. Paul, "User Fees, Deregulation and Marketing Efficiency," *AJAE*, December 1982.
32. Connor, John M., and W.F. Mueller, "Market Structure and Performance of U.S. Multinationals in Brazil and Mexico," *J. of Developmental Studies*, April 1982.
33. Connor, J.M., "Determinants of Foreign Direct Investment by Food and Tobacco Manufacturers"; Pagoulatos, Emilio, "Foreign Direct Investment in U.S. Food and Tobacco Manufacturing and Domestic Economic Performance"; Marion, Bruce W., and Howard J. Nash, "Foreign Investment in U.S. Food-Retailing Industries" (series of three articles), *AJEA*, May 1983.
34. Mueller, W.F., "Market Power and Its Control on the Food System," *AJAE*, December 1983.
35. Mueller, W.F., and D.F. Greer, "The Effect of Market Share Distribution on Industry Performance Reexamined," *Rev. of Econ. and Stat.*, May 1984.
36. Mueller, W.F., and R.T. Rogers, "Changes in Market Concentration of Manufacturing Industries, 1947–1977," *Rev. of Ind. Organization*, Spring 1984.
37. Parker, R.C., and J.M. Connor, "Estimates of Consumer Loss Due to Monopoly in the U.S. Food Manufacturing Industries: Second Reply," *AJAE*, November 1984.
38. Schrader, Lee F., "Implications of Electronic Trading for Agricultural Prices," *AJAE*, December 1984.

Books, Congressional Committee Prints, and Miscellaneous Publications

Dahl, D.C., and W.W. Grant, ed., "Antitrust and Agriculture," *Misc. Rept. 137*, Minnesota Agr. Sta., 1975.

Marion, B.W., W.F. Mueller, R.C. Cotterill, F.E. Geithman, and J.R. Schmelzer, *The Profits and Price Performance of Leading Food Chains, 1970–74*, Joint Economic Committee, April 1977.

Hearings before the Joint Economic Committee, U.S. Congress, "Prices and Profits of Leading Retail Food Chains, 1970–74," Government Printing Office, 1977.

Mueller, W.F., *The Cellar-Kefauver Act: The First 27 Years*, House Judiciary Committee, U.S. Congress, December 1978.

Marion, B.W., W.F. Mueller, R.W. Cotterill, F.E. Geithman, and J.R. Schmelzer, *The Food Retailing Industry: Market Structure, Profits and Prices*, Praeger 1979.

Lang, M.G., "Collective Bargaining in Agricultural Product Markets: Findings of a Survey," *Station Bull. 241*, Purdue University, September 1979.

"Proceedings, Economic Research Conference on U.S. Food System Regulation," *AJAE* 61:4, Part 2, November 1979.

Leuthold, R., and P. Dixon, ed., *Livestock Futures Research Symposium,* Chicago Mercantile Exchange, 1980.

Sporleder, T., ed., *Proceedings, National Symposium on Electronic Marketing of Agricultural Commodities,* Texas A&M University, March 1980.

Connor, J.M., R.T., Rogers, B.W. Marion, and W.F. Mueller, *The Food Manufacturing Industries: Structure, Strategies, Performance and Policies,* Lexington Books, 1985.

Hayenga, Marvin, V. James Rhodes, Jon A. Brandt, and Ronald E. Deiter, *The U.S. Pork Sector: Changing Structure and Organization,* Iowa State University Press, 1985.

NC 117 Participants

Senior Adviser	A.C. (Oscar) Hoffman*
California	Leon Garoyan
Connecticut	Ronald W. Cotterill* (and Wisconsin, Michigan)
Cornell	Olan D. Forker William Lesser*
Florida	Richard L. Kilmer* Ronald W. Ward*
Illinois	Raymond M. Leuthold* Daniel I. Padberg (and Cornell)
Iowa	Ronald Raikes Marvin Hayenga* (and Wisconsin)
Kansas	Milton Manuel Mark Newman Orlen Grunewald*
Kentucky	Loys Mather* Jerry Skees
Massachusetts	Julie Caswell* (and Wisconsin) Richard Rogers* (and Wisconsin)
Michigan	James D. Shaffer* Donald Ricks Larry Hamm (and ERS) Harold Riley*
Minnesota	Dale C. Dahl* Winston Grant

---

*Indicates current member.

Missouri	V. James Rhodes*
	Stephen Matthews
Nebraska	Lynn Lutgen
	Emilio Pagoulatos*
New Mexico	Thomas Clevenger
North Dakota	Donald Scott
Ohio	Dennis Henderson*
Purdue	John Connor* (and ERS, Wisconsin)
	Paul L. Farris*
	Mahlon G. Lang
	Lee C. Schrader*
South Dakota	Robert Olson
	John Hanson
Texas	Thomas L. Sporleder*
	Ronald D. Knutsen
Wisconsin	L.J. Butler*
	Gerald Campbell
	Hugh L. Cook
	Frederick Geithman*
	A.C. Johnson
	Christina Kelton
	Willard F. Mueller*
	Robert L. Wills* (and ERS)

U.S. Department of Agriculture

Agricultural Cooperative Service	Jack Armstrong
	Randall Torgerson*
	Marshall Godwin
	James Haskell*
Agricultural Marketing Service	Richard Heifner (ERS)
	William Manley
	James Pearson
	Harold S. Ricker*
Economic Research Service	Clark Burbee
	John Culbertson
	Kenneth Farrell
	Robert Frye
	Charles Handy*

David Harrington*
George Irwin
Edward Jesse (Wisconsin)
John Lee*
Lester Myers*
James Zellner

Cooperative State
Research Service

Lloyd C. Halvorson
Ken McIntosh
Eldon Weeks*

U.S. House of Rep-
resentatives, Com-
mittee on Small
Business

John Helmuth

Federal Trade
Commission

Russell C. Parker* (and Wisconsin)

Farm Foundation

Neill Schaller
Walter Armbruster*

Administrative
adviser

Elmer R. Kiehl (Missouri)
Walter L. Fishel (Ohio)
Kenneth Schneeberger (Missouri)*

Executive director

Bruce Marion (ERS/Wisconsin)*

References

Adams, W. James, and Yellen, Janet L. 1976. "Commodity Bundling and the Burden of Monopoly." *Quart. J. Econ*. 90:475–498.

Adelman, Morris. 1951. "The Measurement of Industrial Concentration." *Rev. Econ. & Stat.* 33:285–290.

Albion, Mark S. 1983. *Advertising's Hidden Effects: Manufacturers' Advertising and Retail Pricing*. Boston: Auburn House.

Albion, M., and Farris, P. 1981. *The Advertising Controversy: Evidence on the Economic Effects of Advertising*. Boston: Auburn House.

Allen, Bruce T. 1968. "Market Concentration and Wage Increases: U.S. Manufacturing, 1947–1964." *Industrial and Labor Relations Review* 21:353–366.

———. 1969. "Concentration and Economic Progress: Note." *Amer. Econ. Rev.* 59:600–604.

Areeda, Philip, and Turner, Donald. 1975. "Predatory Pricing and Related Practices Under Section 2 of the Sherman Act." *Harvard L. Rev.* 88:697–733.

———. 1978. *Antitrust Law*. Boston: Little, Brown.

Armbruster, W., and Jesse, E.V. 1983. "Fruit and Vegetable Marketing Orders," in W. Armbruster, D. Henderson and R. Knutson (eds.), *Federal Marketing Programs in Agriculture*. Danville: The Interstate Printers and Publishers, pp. 121–158.

Babb, E.M., and Bohall, Robert. 1979. "Marketing Orders and Farm Structure," in *Structure Issues of American Agriculture*. AER438. Washington, D.C.: USDA, Economics, Statistics and Cooperative Services.

Bailey, William R., and Schwenk, Albert E. 1971. "Wage Differences among Manufacturing Establishments." *Monthly Labor Review* 94:16–19.

Bain, Joe S. 1956. *Barriers to New Competition*. Cambridge: Harvard University Press.

———. 1968. *Industrial Organization*. 2d ed. New York: Wiley.

———. 1972. *Essays on Price Theory and Industrial Organization*. Boston: Little, Brown.

Baligh, Helmy, and Richartz, Leon. 1969. *Vertical Market Structures*. Boston: Allyn and Bacon.

Beales, H.; Craswell, R.; and Salop, S.C. 1981. "The Efficient Regulation of Consumer Information." *J. of Law and Econ.* 24:491–539.

Benham, Lee. 1972. "The Effect of Advertising on Price of Eyeglasses." *J. of Law and Economics* (October):337–352.

Berry, Charles H. 1975. *Corporate Growth and Diversification*. Princeton: Princeton University Press.

Blake, Harlan, and Blum, Jack. 1965. "Network Television Rate Practices: A Case Study in the Failure of Social Control of Price Discrimination." *Yale Law Journal* 74:1339–1401.

Blinder, Alan S. 1980. "The Level of Distribution of Economic Well-Being." In Martin Feldstein (ed.), *The American Economy in Transition*. Chicago: University of Chicago Press.

Blobaum, Roger. 1980. "Maximizing Rural Values through Dispersed Agriculture." In *Increasing Understanding of Public Problems and Policies—1980*. Chicago: Farm Foundation.

Boeckenhoff, E.; Janssen, H.; and Plate, R. 1976. "Wie steht es mit der Preisbildung auf den Agrarmaerkten." *Agrawirtschaft* 25(5):125–129.

Boehlje, Michael D., and Krause, Kenneth R. 1981. "Economic and Federal Tax Factors Affecting the Choice of a Legal Farm Business Organization." AER468. Washington, D.C.: USDA, Economics and Statistics Services.

Bond, Ronald S., et al. 1980. *Staff Report on Effects of Restrictions on Advertising and Commercial Practice in the Professions: The Case of Optometry*. Washington, D.C.: FTC, Bureau of Economics.

Boxley, Robert F., and Walker, Larry. 1979. "Impact of Rising Land Values on Agricultural Structure." In *Structure Issues of American Agriculture*. AER438. Washington, D.C.: USDA, Economics, Statistics, and Cooperative Services.

Boyer, Kenneth D. 1974. "Informative and Goodwill Advertising." *Rev. Econ. & Stat.* 56:541–548.

Brandow, George E. 1977. "Appraising the Economic Performance of the Food Industry." In Clark Edwards (ed.), *Lectures in Agricultural Economics*. Washington, D.C.: USDA, Economic Research Service.

Branson, William H. 1980. "Trends in United States International Trade and Investment Since World War II." In Martin Feldstein (ed.), *The American Economy in Transition*. Chicago: University of Chicago Press.

Breimyer, H.F. 1976. *Economics of the Product Markets of Agriculture*. Ames: Iowa State University Press.

Brewster, David. 1979. "The Family Farm: A Changing Concept." In *Structure Issues of American Agriculture*. AER438. Washington, D.C.: USDA, Economics, Statistics, and Cooperative Services.

———. 1979. "Historical Notes on Agricultural Structure." In *Structure Issues of American Agriculture*. AER438. Washington, D.C.: USDA, Economics, Statistics, and Cooperative Services.

Broiler Industry. 1982. "Nation's Top Broiler Firms." Mt. Morris, Ill.: Watt Publishing Co., December.

———. 1984. "Nation's Top Broiler Firms." Mt. Morris, Ill.: Watt Publishing Co., December.

Brown, Randall S. 1978. "Estimating Advantages to Large-Scale Advertising." *Rev. Econ. & Stat.* 60:428–437.

Bruch, Hilde. 1973. *Eating Disorders.* New York: Basic Books.

Bureau of the Census. 1977a. *1977 Census of Manufactures: General Summary.* MC77-SR-1 and previous editions. Washington, D.C.: U.S. Department of Commerce (issued April 1981).

——. 1977b. *1977 Census of Retail Trade* (and previous years). Washington, D.C.: U.S. Department of Commerce.

——. 1977c. *General Report on Industrial Organization.* ES77-1. Washington, D.C.: U.S. Department of Commerce.

——. 1977d. *1977 Census of Manufactures: Concentration Ratios in Manufacturing.* MC77-SR-9. Washington, D.C.: U.S. Department of Commerce (and previous years).

——. 1977e. *1977 Census of Manufactures: Industry Report Series.* Washington, D.C.: U.S. Department of Commerce (and previous years).

——. 1977f. *1977 Census of Manufactures.* Vol. II, Industry Statistics. Washington, D.C.: U.S. Department of Commerce.

——. 1982a. *1982 Census of Agriculture.* Washington, D.C.: U.S. Department of Commerce (and previous issues).

——. 1982b. *Money Income and Poverty Status of Families and Persons in the United States: 1982.* Series P-60, No. 140, July.

——. 1982c. *1982 Census of Retail Trade.* Washington, D.C.: U.S. Department of Commerce.

Bureau of Labor Statistics. 1977. *Productivity Indexes for Selected Industries.* 1976 ed. Washington, D.C.: Department of Labor.

Business Week. 1981. "No-Frills Food: New Power for the Supermarkets." March 23, p. 72.

——. 1985. "Do Mergers Really Work? Not Very Often—Which Raises Questions about Merger Mania." June 3, pp. 88–100.

Buzzell, Robert; Gale, B.T.; and Sultan, R. 1975. "Market Share—A Key to Profitability." *Harvard Business Review* 53:97–106.

Campbell, G.R. 1981. "Experimental Contract Reporting." In *Agricultural Bargaining Process-Problems-Potentials.* ACS Service Rep. 6. Washington, D.C.: USDA, Agricultural Cooperative Service.

Carlin, Thomas A., and Ghelfi, Linda M. 1979. "Off-Farm Employment and the Farm Sector." In *Structure Issues of American Agriculture.* AER438. Washington, D.C.: USDA, Economics, Statistics, and Cooperative Services.

Caswell, Julie, A. 1984. "Direct and Network Control of Firms in the Agribusiness Sector." Ph.D. dissertation, University of Wisconsin.

Caves, Richard E. 1975. *Diversification, Foreign Investment and Scale in North American Manufacturing Industries.* Ottawa: Economic Council of Canada.

——. 1978. Review of *Economics of Multi-Plant Operation. J. Econ. Lit.* 16: 627–628.

——. 1980. "The Structure of Industry." In Martin Feldstein (ed.), *The American Economy in Transition.* Chicago: University of Chicago Press.

Centre on Transnational Corporations. 1982. *Transnational Corporations in Food and Beverage Processing.* New York: United Nations.

Chain Store Age Supermarkets. 1980. "Barebones Formats Abound." October, pp. 29–31.

Chain Store Age Supermarkets. 1982. "Zone Pricing Prompts 'Predator' Charge." March, pp. 16–21.

——. 1983. "1983 Supermarket Sales Manual." July.

Chamberlin, Edward H. 1962. *The Theory of Monopolistic Competition.* 8th ed. Cambridge, Mass.: Harvard University Press.

Chandler, Alfred D. 1982. "The M-Form: Industrial Groups, American Style." *European Economic Review* 19:3–24.

Chavas, Jean-Paul. 1983. "Structural Change in the Demand for Meat." *Amer. J. Agric. Econ.* 65:148–153.

Clark, F.E., and Weld, L.D.H. 1932. *Marketing Agricultural Products in the United States.* New York: Macmillan.

Coase, R.L. 1937. "The Nature of the Firm." *Economica* 4:386–405.

Cochrane, Willard W. 1979. *The Development of American Agriculture: A Historical Analysis.* St. Paul: University of Minnesota Press.

Coffman, George W. 1979. "Entry and Exit: Barriers and Incentives." In *Structure Issues of American Agriculture.* AER438. Washington, D.C.: USDA, Economics, Statistics, and Cooperative Services.

Collins, Norman, and Preston, Lee. 1966. "Concentration and Price-Cost Margins in Food Manufacturing Industries." *J. Ind. Econ.* 14:226–242.

——. 1968. *Concentration and Price-Cost Margins in Manufacturing Industries.* Berkeley: University of California Press.

Comanor, William S., and Smiley, R.H. 1980. "Monopoly and the Distribution of Wealth: Revisited." *Quart. J. Econ.* 94:185–198.

Comanor, William S., and Wilson, Thomas A. 1974. *Advertising and Market Power.* Cambridge, Mass.: Harvard University Press.

——. 1979. "The Effect of Advertising on Competition: A Survey." *J. Econ. Lit.* 17:453–476.

Combs, Robert P., and Marion, Bruce W. 1984. "Food Manufacturing Activities of 100 Large Agricultural Marketing Cooperatives." Working Paper 73. Madison, Wis.: NC117.

Competitive Edge. 1982. Vol. III, No. 4, December. Barrington, Ill.: Willard Bishop Consulting Economists Ltd.

Connor, John M. 1977. "Mobility among the Largest Food Processing Firms, 1950–75." Paper presented at the annual meeting of the American Agricultural Economics Association, San Diego.

——. 1980. "The U.S. Food and Tobacco Industries: Market Structure, Structural Change, and Economic Performance." AER451. Washington, D.C.: USDA, Economics, Statistics, and Cooperative Services.

——. 1981a. "Foreign Direct Investment—An Overview." *National Food Review* 15 (Summer):7–9.

——. 1981b. "Foreign Direct Investment in U.S. Food Manufacturing: How Much, by Whom, and Why." *National Food Review* 16(Fall):20–26.

——. 1981c. "Foreign Food Firms: Their Participation in and Competitive Impact on the U.S. Food and Tobacco Manufacturing Sector." In Glenn Johnson and Allen Maunder (eds.), *Rural Change: The Challenge for Agricultural Economists.* Farnborough, England: Gower.

———. 1982a. "Estimates of Manufacturers' Food and Beverage Shipments Among Major Marketing Channels, 1977." Staff Report AGES820416. Washington, D.C.: USDA, Economic Research Service.

———. 1982b. "Structural Adjustment of the Food Industries of the United States." ERS Staff Report AGES820723. Washington, D.C.: USDA, Economic Research Service.

———. 1983. "Determinants of Foreign Direct Investment by Food and Tobacco Manufacturers." *Ar.. J. Agric. Econ.* 65:395–404.

Connor, John M., and Mather, Loys L. 1978. *Directory of the 200 Largest U.S. Food and Tobacco Processing Firms.* Special Report 2. Madison, Wis.: USDA, Economics, Statistics, and Cooperative Services and NC 117.

Connor, John M.; Rogers, Richard T.; Marion, Bruce W.; and Mueller, Willard F. 1985. *The Food Manufacturing Industries: Structure, Strategies, Performance, and Policies.* Lexington, Mass.: Lexington Books.

Connor, John M., and Ward, Ronald W. (eds.). 1983. *Advertising and the Food System.* NC 117 Monograph 14. Madison, Wis.: NC 117.

Cook, H.L.; Blakley, L.; Jacobson, R.; Knutson, R.; Milligan, R.; and Strain, R. 1978. *The Dairy Subsector of American Agriculture: Organization and Vertical Coordination.* NC 117 Monograph 5. Madison, Wis.: NC 117.

Cook, H.L., and Marion, B.W. 1981. "The Impact of Price Stability on Farm Structure." *Economic Issues,* no. 53. Madison, Wis.: Dept. of Agricultural Economics, University of Wisconsin-Madison.

Coppinger, V.; Smith, V.L.; and Titus, J. 1980. "Incentives and Behavior in English, Dutch and Sealed Bid Auctions." *Economic Inquiry* 18(1):1–22.

Cornell University. 1984. "Operating Results of Food Chains, 1983–84" (and previous years). Ithaca, N.Y.: Department of Agricultural Economics.

Costa, Jose. 1983. "Advertising, Food Consumption, and Obesity." Ph.D. dissertation, University of Wisconsin.

Cothern, James H.; Peard, R. Mark; and Weeks, John L. 1978. "Economies of Scale in Beef Processing and Portion Control Operations: Northern California-1976." Leaflet 21027. Division of Agriculture Sciences, University of California.

Cotterill, Ronald. 1977. "Market Structure, Performance and Market Restructuring." Ph.D. dissertation, University of Wisconsin.

———. 1985. "Modern Markets and Market Power: Evidence from the Vermont Retail Food Industry." Working Paper 83. Madison, Wis.: NC 117.

Cotterill, Ronald, and Mueller, W.F. 1980. "The Impact of Firm Conglomeration on Market Structure: Evidence for the U.S. Food Retailing Industry." *Antitrust Bulletin* (Fall):557–582.

Cox, C.C. 1976. "Futures Trading and Market Information." *J. Political Econ.* 84: 1215–1237.

Cox, Steven R. 1974. "An Industrial Performance Evaluation Experiment." *J. Industrial Econ.* 22:199–214.

Cox, Thomas L. 1984. "An Analysis of Price Effects in Cross-Section Data." Ph.D. dissertation, Texas A&M University.

Crawford, Terry L., and Grinnell, Gerald E. 1976. "Performance Comparisons of Conventional, Batch-Pick-to-Conveyor, and Vending Types of Dry Grocery

Warehouses." Presented at National Association of Wholesale Grocers of America (NAWGA) Productivity Conference, Minneapolis, Minnesota, October 24–27.

Cremeans, John E. 1981. "Economic Perspective—Trends in the United States Economy: 1968–1978." *1981 U.S. Industrial Outlook.* Washington, D.C.: U.S. Department of Commerce.

Culbertson, John D., and Morrison, Rosanna Mentzer. 1983. "Economies of Scale Data for the Food Manufacturing Industries." Unpublished manuscript. Washington, D.C.

Dahl, Dale C. 1975. "Public Policy Changes Needed to Cope with Changing Structure." *Amer. J. Agric. Econ.* 57(2):206–213.

———. 1979. "Recent Developments in Agricultural Law." Working Paper 26. Madison, Wis.: NC117.

Dahl, D.C., and Burke, T.J. 1979. "The Use of Limited Partnership in Upper Midwest Agriculture." *Amer. Law Journal* (Fall):345–367.

Dalton, James A., and Ford, E.J., Jr. 1977. "Concentration and Professional Earnings in Manufacturing and Utilities." *Industrial and Labor Relations Review* 31:45–60.

———. 1978. "Concentration and Professional Earnings in Manufacturing." *Industrial and Labor Relations Review* 31:379–394.

Davenport, Charles; Boehlje, Michael D.; and Martin, David B.H. 1982. *The Effects of Tax Policy on American Agriculture.* AER480. Washington, D.C.: USDA, Economic Research Service.

DeBraal, J. Peter, and Majchrowica, T. Alexander. 1983. *Foreign Ownership of U.S. Agricultural Land Through December 31, 1982.* Staff Report AGE830310. Washington, D.C.: USDA, Economic Research Service.

Demsetz, Harold. 1974. "Two Systems of Belief about Monopoly." In Harvey L. Goldschmid et al. (eds.), *Industrial Concentration: The New Learning.* Boston: Little, Brown.

Devine, D. Grant. 1978. "A Review of the Experimental Effects of Increased Price Information on the Performance of Canadian Retail Food Stores in the 1970s." *Can J. Agr. Econ.* 26:24–30.

Devine, D. Grant, and Marion, Bruce W. 1979. "The Influence of Consumer Price Information on Retail Pricing and Consumer Behavior." *Amer. J. Agr. Econ.* 61:228–237.

Dewey, Donald. 1979. "Information, Entry and Welfare: The Case for Collusion." *Amer. Econ. Rev.* 69:587–594.

Dirlam, Joel B. 1981. "Marginal Cost Pricing Test for Predation: Naive Welfare Economics and Public Policy." *Antitrust Bull.* 26(Winter):769.

Dobson, William, and Buxton, Boyd. 1977. "Analysis of the Effects of Federal Milk Orders on the Economic Performance of U.S. Milk Markets." Research Bulletin R2897. Madison, Wis.: University of Wisconsin.

Dorner, Peter. 1980. "Agriculture within the U.S. Economy: Integration and Interdependence." In *Farm Structure: A Historical Perspective on Changes in the Number and Size of Farms.* Washington, D.C.: Committee on Agriculture, Nutrition, and Forestry, U.S. Senate, April.

Dussere, Sally. 1977. "Edible TV: Your Child and Food Commercials." In Hearings by U.S. Senate Select Committee on Nutrition and Human Needs. Washington, D.C.: U.S. GPO.

Easterlin, Richard A. 1980. "American Population Since 1940." In Martin Feldstein (ed.), *The American Economy in Transition*. Chicago: University of Chicago Press.

Edwards, Corwin. 1955. "Conglomerate Bigness as a Source of Power." In G. Stigler (ed.), *Business Concentration and Price Policy*. Princeton: Princeton University Press.

———. 1967. *Control of Cartels and Monopolies: An International Comparison*. Dobbs Ferry, N.Y.: Oceana Publications.

Elzinga, Kenneth G., and Hogarty, Thomas F. 1973. "The Problem of Geographic Market Delineation in Antimerger Suits." *Antitrust Bull.* 18:45–81.

Ericksen, Milton H.; Clayton, Kenneth C.; Johnson, James; and Collins, Keith J. 1981. "Commodity Programs and Policies," *Agricultural-Food Policy Review: Perspectives for the 1980's*. AFPR4. Washington, D.C.: USDA, Economics and Statistics Service.

Ewart, N.W. 1972. "The Impact of Information on Commodities Pricing—A Simulation Study." Ph.D. dissertation, Purdue University.

Faminow, M.D., and Sarhan, M.E. 1983. "Economic Analysis of the Location of Fed Cattle Slaughtering and Processing in the United States." AERR189. Urbana: University of Illinois.

Farris, Paul L. (ed.). 1964. *Market Structure Research: Theory and Practice in Agricultural Economics*. Ames, Iowa: Iowa State University Press.

Federal Energy Administration. 1974. *The U.S. Food and Fiber Sector: Energy Use and Outlook*. Washington, D.C.: U.S. GPO.

Federal Trade Commission. 1966. *Food Retailing: Market Structure and Competitive Behavior*. Washington, D.C.: U.S. GPO.

———. 1967. *Enforcement Policy with Respect to Mergers in Food Distribution*. Washington, D.C.: U.S. GPO.

———. 1968. *Enforcement Policy with Respect to Product Extension Mergers in Grocery Products Manufacturing*. Washington, D.C.: U.S. GPO.

———. 1969a. *Economic Report on Food Chain Selling Practices in the District of Columbia and San Francisco*. Washington, D.C.: U.S. GPO.

———. 1969b. *Economic Report on the Influence of Market Structure on the Profit Performance of Food Manufacturing Companies*. Washington, D.C.: U.S. GPO.

———. 1972a. *Statistical Report: Value of Shipments Data by Product Class for the 1,000 Largest Manufacturing Firms of 1950*. Washington, D.C.: U.S. GPO.

———. 1972b. *Conglomerate Merger Performance*. Staff Report. Washington, D.C.: U.S. GPO.

———. 1975. "A Report on Agricultural Cooperatives." Mimeographed. Washington, D.C.: Bureau of Competition, September.

———. 1976. *In the Matter of Borden, Inc.* FTC Docket 8978, Initial Decision, Washington, D.C.: FTC.

———. 1977. *Statistical Report on Mergers and Acquisitions, 1977*. Washington, D.C.: Bureau of Economics.

———. 1979. *In the Matter of National Tea Co.* 603 F.2d (8th Cir.).

———. 1981a. *In the Matter of the Grand Union Co.* FTC Docket 9121, Proposed Findings of Fact, Conclusions of Law, and Order. Atlanta, Ga.: FTC Regional Office.

Federal Trade Commission. 1981b. *In the Matter of the Grand Union Co.* FTC Docket 9121, Initial Decision, Washington, D.C.

———. 1981c. *Statistical Report on Mergers and Acquisitions, 1979.* Washington, D.C.: FTC, July.

———. 1982a. *Annual Line of Business Report, 1976* (and previous years). Statistical Report of the Bureau of Economics to the Federal Trade Commission. Washington, D.C.: U.S. GPO.

———. 1982b. *Benefits and Costs of the Federal Trade Commission's Line of Business Program.* Vol. 1. Washington, D.C.: FTC, September.

———. 1983. *In the Matter of The Grand Union Co.* FTC Docket 9121. Final Order. Washington, D.C.

Fierman, Jaclyn. 1984. "Beech-nut Bounces Up in the Baby Market." *Fortune*, December 24, p. 56.

Florida Citrus Mutual. 1985. "Annual Statistical Report: 1983–84 Season." Lakeland: Florida Citrus Mutual.

Florida Crop and Livestock Reporting Service. 1985. "Florida Agricultural Statistics: Citrus Summary, 1984" (and previous years). Orlando: Florida Crop and Livestock Rept. Service, January.

Folsom, Roger N., and Greer, Douglas F. 1983. "Advertising and Brand Loyalty as Barriers to Entry." In J. Connor and R. Ward (eds.), *Advertising and the Food System*. NC 117 Monograph 14. Madison, Wis.: NC 117.

Food Institute. 1985. *Food Business Mergers and Acquisitions, 1984* (and previous years). Fairlawn, N.J.: American Institute of Food Distribution.

Forbes, Jan. 3, 1983. "Wholesalers" in 35th Annual Report on American Industry, p. 203.

Food Marketing Institute. 1982. "The Food Marketing Industry Speaks, 1982." Detailed Tabulations. Washington, D.C.: Food Marketing Institute.

———. 1984. "Statement of Food Marketing Institute before the Bureau of Competition, Federal Trade Commission." Milwaukee, Wis., September 11.

Fortune. 1983. "Coke Tries Selling Movies Like Soda Pop." December 26, pp. 119–126.

Gabriel, Steve. 1982. "The Degree of Financial Leverage in the Farm Sector: A Measure of Financial Stability." ERS Staff Report AGES821015. Washington, D.C.: USDA.

Galbraith, John K. 1967. *The New Industrial State.* Boston: Houghton Mifflin.

Gallo, Anthony. 1981. "Food Advertising." *Nat. Food Review* 13 (Winter).

Gallo, Anthony, and Connor, John M. 1982. "Advertising and American Food Consumption Patterns." *National Food Review* 20 (Fall):10–12.

Gallo, Anthony; Hamm, Larry G.; and Zellner, James. 1982. *Couponing's Growth in Food Marketing.* AER486. Washington, D.C.: USDA, Economic Research Service.

Garbarino, Joseph W. 1950. "A Theory of Interindustry Wage Structure Variation." *Quart. J. Econ.* 64:282–305.

Garoyan, L., and Thor, E. 1978. "Observations on the Impact of Agricultural Bargaining Cooperatives." In B.W. Marion (ed.), *Agricultural Cooperatives and the Public Interest.* NC 117 Monograph 4. Madison, Wis.: NC 117.

Gaskins, Darius W. 1971. "Dynamic Limit Pricing: Optimal Pricing under Threat of Entry." *J. Econ. Theory* 10:306–322.

Geithman, F., and Marion, B.W. 1978. "A Critique of the Use of BLS Data for Market Structure-Price Analysis." *Am. J. Agri. Econ.* 60:701–705.

Geithman, Fredrick; Marvel, Howard; and Weiss, Leonard. 1981. "Concentration, Price, and Critical Concentration Ratios." *Rev. Econ. & Stat.* 63:346–353.

Gisser, Micha. 1982. "Welfare Implications of Oligopoly in U.S. Food Manufacturing." *Am. J. Agri. Econ.* 64 (November):616–624.

Goldberg, R.A. 1968. *Agribusiness Coordination: A Systems Approach to the Wheat, Soybean and Florida Orange Economies.* Boston: Graduate School of Business Administration, Harvard University.

Gordon, Robert J. 1980. "Postwar Macroeconomics: The Evolution of Events and Ideas." In Martin Feldstein (ed.), *The American Economy in Transition.* Chicago: University of Chicago Press.

Grant, W.W., and Dahl, D.C. 1978. *Bibliography of Agriculture and Food Law, 1960–78.* NC 117 Special Report 1. Madison, Wis.: NC 117.

Gray, R.W. 1963. "Onions Revisited." *J. of Farm Econ.* 45(2):273–276.

Greer, Douglas F. 1975. "Market Power and Wage Inflation: A Further Analysis." *Southern Economic Journal* 41:466–479.

———. 1980. *Industrial Organization and Public Policy.* New York: Macmillan.

———. 1984. *Industrial Organization and Public Policy.* 2d ed. New York: Macmillan.

Greer, Douglas F., and Rhoads, Stephen. 1976. "Concentration and Productivity Changes in the Long and Short Run." *Southern Econ. J.* 43:1031–1044.

Grinnell, G., and Friedman, L. 1982. "Productivity Potential in Dry Grocery Centers." AER484. Washington, D.C.: USDA, Economic Research Service.

Grinnell, G.; Parker, R.; and Rens, L. 1979. *Grocery Retailing Concentration in Metropolitan Areas, Economic Census Years 1954–72.* Washington, D.C.: FTC and USDA.

Guither, H.D. 1980. *The Food Lobbyist.* Lexington, Mass.: Lexington Books.

Haidacher, Richard C. et al. 1982. *Consumer Demand for Red Meats, Poultry, and Fish.* ERS Report AGES820818. Washington, D.C.: USDA, Economic Research Service.

Hall, Lana; Schmitz, Andrew; and Cothern, James. 1979. "Beef Wholesale-Retail Marketing Margins and Concentration." *Economica* 46:295–300.

Halloran, John M. 1983. "An Economic Evaluation of Computerized Markets in Future Delivery Contracts as a Coordination Mechanism for the U.S. Potato Subsector." Ph.D. dissertation, Michigan State University.

Hamermesh, Daniel S. 1972. "Market Power and Wage Inflation." *Southern Econ. J.* 39:204–212.

Hamm, Larry, G. 1980. "Food Distributor Procurement Practices: Some Implications for Food Price Policy." Presented at the American Agricultural Economics Association meetings, University of Illinois, July.

———. 1981a. "Food Distributor Procurement Practices: Their Implications for Food System Structure and Coordination." Ph.D. dissertation, Michigan State University.

Hamm, Larry, G. 1981b. "The Impact of Food Distributor Procurement Practices on Food System Structure and Coordination." NC 117 Working Paper 58. Madison, Wis.: NC 117.

———. 1982. "Retailer-Manufacturer Relationships in the Food Sector—Some Observations from the U.S.A." Working Paper 64. Madison, Wis.: NC 117.

Hampe, Edward C. Jr., and Wittenberg, Merle. 1964. *The Lifeline of America: Development of the Food Industry.* New York: McGraw-Hill.

Handy, Charles R., and Padberg, Daniel I. 1971. "A Model of Competitive Behavior in Food Industries." *Amer. J. Agr. Econ.* 53:182–190.

Handy, Charles, and Stafford, Tom. 1980. "Supermarket Reaction to New Competition." Paper presented at Food Distribution Research Society Annual Meeting, Lexington, Ky., October 12–15.

Harrington, David H. 1983. "Cost and Returns: Economic and Accounting Concepts." *Agricultural Economics Research*, 35(4):1–8.

Harrington, David H.; Reimund, Donn A.; Baum, Kenneth H.; and Peterson, R. Neal. 1983. *U.S. Farming in the Early Eighties. Production and Financial Structure.* AER504. Washington, D.C.: USDA, Economic Research Service.

Harrington, David H., and Schertz, Lyle P. 1981. "Inflation and Agriculture," *Agricultural-Food Policy Review: Perspectives for the 1980's.* AFPR4. Washington, D.C.: USDA, Economics and Statistics Service.

Harris, Harold M., Jr.; Jesse, Edward V.; Torgerson, Randall E.; Shaffer, James D.; and Garoyan, Leon. 1983. "Cooperatives and Bargaining in Federal Marketing Programs in Agriculture: Issues and Options." In W.F. Armbruster, D.R. Henderson, and R.D. Knutson (eds.), *Federal Marketing Programs in Agriculture.* Danville, Ill.: Interstate Printers and Publishers.

Haworth, Charles, and Reuther, Carol Jean. 1978. "Industrial Concentration and Interindustry Wage Determination." *Rev. Econ. & Stat.* 60:85–95.

Hayenga, M.L. (ed.), 1979a. *Pricing Problems in the Food Industry.* Monograph 7, North Central Regional Publication 261. Madison, Wis.: NC 117.

———. 1979b. "Cheese Pricing Systems." Working Paper 38. Madison, Wis.: NC 117.

Hayenga, Marvin; Rhodes, V. James; Brandt, Jon A.; and Deiter, Ronald E. 1985. *The U.S. Pork Sector: Changing Structure and Organization.* Ames, Iowa: Iowa State University Press.

Hayenga, Marvin, and Schrader, L.F. 1980. "Formula Pricing in Five Commodity Marketing Systems." *Amer. J. Agric. Econ.* 62(4):753–759.

Heller, Walter. 1981. "Economy Store Census." *Progressive Grocer* (May):89–91.

Helmberger, P.; Campbell, G.; and Dobson, W. 1981. "Organization and Performance of Agricultural Markets." In L.R. Martin (ed.), *A Survey of Agricultural Economics Literature.* Minneapolis: University of Minnesota Press.

Helmberger, P.G., and Hoos, S. 1965. *Cooperative Bargaining in Agriculture.* Berkeley: University of California, Division of Agricultural Sciences.

Helmuth, J.W. 1977. "Grain Pricing." Washington, D.C.: Commodity Futures Trading Commission.

———. 1984. "Update on Cattle and Hog Slaughter Data." Memorandum to Congressman Neal Smith, U.S. House of Representatives, June 12.

Henderson, D.R. 1975. "Toward a Theory of Vertical Market Behavior." Working Paper 2. Madison, Wis.: NC 117.

—— . 1982. "Electronic Markets for Agricultural Commodities: Potentials and Pitfalls." Working Paper 62. Madison, Wis.: NC 117.

Henderson, D.R.; Schrader, L.F.; and Rhodes, V.J. 1983. "Public Price Reporting." In W.J. Armbruster, D.R. Henderson, and R.D. Knutson (eds.), *Federal Marketing Programs in Agriculture: Issues and Options*. Danville: Interstate.

Henderson, D.R., and Schwart, R.B., Jr. 1977. "Vertical Coordination between Cow/Calf Enterprises and Feedlots in the United States." Working Paper 13. Madison, Wis.: NC 117.

Hill, Lowell D., and Leath, Mack N. 1985. *A Subsector Study of the U.S. Grain Industry*. Champaign-Urbana: University of Illinois (forthcoming).

Hoffman, A.C. 1940. *Large-Scale Organization in the Food Industries*. Monograph 35. Washington, D.C.: U.S. Temporary National Economic Committee.

—— . 1980. "The Rise of Economic Power: Some Consequences and Policy Implications." *Am. J. Agric. Econ.* 61:866–872.

Hoffman, George, et al. 1981. "Estimating Costs of Production: Some Problems and Issues." Paper presented at the Cost of Production Seminar, Washington, D.C., June 2.

Hofkin, M.G. 1976. *A Perspective Piece of the Major Brewers*. Milwaukee: Robert W. Baird & Co., March.

Holder, D.A., and Sporleder, T.A. 1976. "Forward Deliverable Contract Markets." Leaflet No. 7-4, Marketing Alternatives for Agriculture. Ithaca, N.Y.: Cooperative Extension, New York State College of Agriculture and Life Sciences, Cornell University.

Holt, James S. 1979. "Farm Labor and the Structure of Agriculture." In *Structure Issues of American Agriculture*. AER438. Washington, D.C.: USDA, Economics, Statistics, and Cooperative Service.

Hoos, Sidney. 1970. "Economic Possibilities and Limitations of Cooperative Bargaining Associations." In *Cooperative Bargaining*, Service Report 113. Washington, D.C.: USDA, Farmer Cooperative Service.

Hottel, Bruce, and Harrington, David H. 1979. "Tenure and Equity Influences on the Incomes of Farmers." In *Structure Issues of American Agriculture*. AER438. Washington, D.C.: USDA, Economics, Statistics, and Cooperative Services.

Houg, J.T., and Plott, C.R. 1982. "Rate Fixing Policies for Inland Water Transportation: An Experimental Approach." *Bell J. of Econ.* 13(11):1–19.

Houthakker, H.S. 1967. *Economic Policy for the Farm Sector*. Washington, D.C.: American Institute for Public Policy Research.

Hulse, F.E. 1976. "Joint Ventures Involving Cooperatives in Food Marketing." In B.W. Marion (ed.), *Coordination and Exchange in Agricultural Subsectors*. Monograph 2. Madison, Wis.: NC 117.

Imel, Blake, and Helmberger, Peter. 1971. "Estimation of Structure-Profit Relationships with Application to the Food Processing Sector." *Amer. Econ. Rev.* 61: 614–627.

Institute for Research on Poverty. 1981. "Poverty in the United States: Where Do We Stand?" *Focus* (2) (Winter).

Jensen, Harold R.; Hatch, Thomas C.; and Harrington, David H. 1981. *Economic Well-Being of Farms*. AER469. Washington, D.C.: USDA, Economics and Statistics Service.

Jeremias, Ronald A., and Durst, Ron L. 1984. *The Effects of Social Security Taxes on Farm Operations and Investments.* Unpublished Paper. USDA, Economic Research Service. February.

Jeremias, Ronald A.; Hrubovcak, James M.; and Durst, Ron L. 1983. *Effective Income Tax Rates for Farm Capital, 1950–1984.* Staff Report AGES830621. Washington, D.C.: USDA, Economic Research Service.

Jesse, Edward V. 1978. "Measuring Market Performance: Quantifying the Non-Quantifiable." Working Paper 15. Madison, Wis.: NC 117.

———. 1980. *Thin Markets for Agriculture Products: Causes, Effects and Public Policy Options.* National Economics Division Staff Report. Washington, D.C.: USDA, Economics, Statistics, and Cooperative Service.

———. 1983. *Antitrust Treatment of Agricultural Marketing Cooperatives.* Monograph 15. Madison, Wis.: NC 117.

Jesse, Edward V., and Johnson, Aaron C., Jr. 1981. *Effectiveness of Federal Marketing Orders for Fruits and Vegetables.* AER471. Washington, D.C.: USDA, Economics and Statistics Service.

Jesse, Edward V.; Johnson, Aaron C., Jr.; Marion, Bruce W.; and Manchester, Alden C. 1982. "Interpreting and Enforcing Section 2 of the Capper-Volstead Act." *Amer. J. Agr. Econ.* 64(3):431–443.

Johnson, A.C. 1973. *Effects of Futures Trading on Price Performance in the Cash Onion Market, 1930–68.* ERS Technical Bulletin 1470. Washington, D.C.: USDA.

Johnson, James D.; Ericksen, Milton H.; Sharples, Jerry A.; and Harrington, David H. 1979. "Price and Income Policies and the Structure of Agriculture." In *Structure Issues of American Agriculture.* AER438. Washington, D.C.: USDA, Economics, Statistics, and Cooperative Service.

Johnson, James D., and Short, Sara D. 1983. "Commodity Programs: Who Has Received the Benefits?" *Amer. J. Agri. Econ.* 65:912–921.

Johnson, R.K., and Schrader, L.F. 1981. *An Analysis of Prices Paid and Received by Farmers in Indiana, Illinois and Iowa.* Station Bulletin 357. West Lafayette, Ind.: Department of Agricultural Economics, Agriculture Experiment Station, Purdue University.

Jones, Eugene. 1984. "An Econometric Model of Structural Changes in the U.S. Potato Industry." Ph.D. dissertation, University of Florida.

Jones, Eugene, and Zepp, G. 1985. "Changes in the U.S. Potato Industry." *Vegetable Outlook and Situation Report.* Washington, D.C.: USDA, Economic Research Service, February.

Joskow, Paul L., and Klevorick, Alvin K. 1979. "A Framework of Analyzing Predatory Pricing Policy." *Yale L. Rev.* 89:213.

Judge, Edward and Sons. 1983. *The Almanac of the Canning, Freezing, Preserving Industries.* Westminster, Md.: Edward Judge and Sons.

Just, R.E., and Rausser, G.C. 1981. "Commodity Price Forecasting with Large Scale Econometric Models and the Futures Market." *Amer. J. Agric. Econ.* 63:197–208.

Just, Richard E.; Hueth, Darrell L.; and Schmitz, Andrew. 1982. *Applied Welfare Economics and Public Policy.* Englewood Cliffs, N.J.: Prentice-Hall.

Kahn, Alfred. 1975. "Market Power Inflation: A Conceptual Overview." In Gardiner Means, et al. (eds.), *The Roots of Inflation.* New York: Burt Franklin.

Kauffman, D.E. 1983. *A Pork Contract Market: An Investigation into Attitudes about and Possibilities of Such a Market for Slaughter Hogs.* East Lansing, Mich.: Department of Agricultural Economics, Michigan State University.

Kautz, J.H. 1978 "Why Bargaining Associations are Important to Processing Cooperatives." In *New Dimensions of Cooperative Bargaining.* ESCS Report 31. Washington, D.C.: USDA.

Kelton, Christina, M.L. 1982. "The Effect of Market Structure on Price Change for Food Manufacturing Product Classes." Working Paper 60. Madison, Wis.: NC 117.

———. 1983. "Operational Efficiency in Food and Tobacco Manufacturing." Working Paper 72. Madison, Wisc.: NC 117.

Koller, Roland H. 1979. "Predatory Pricing: The Tip of the Iceberg." Paper presented to the American Economics Association annual meeting, Atlanta, Ga., December.

Krause, Kenneth R. 1982. *Indirect Farm Labor and Management Costs.* AER469. Washington, D.C.: USDA, Economic Research Service, December.

Krause, Kenneth R., and Burbee, Clark R. 1982. *Federal Tax Policies of Special Importance to Agriculture.* ERS Staff Report AGES811204. Washington, D.C.: USDA, Economic Research Service, January.

Krause, Kenneth, and Kyle, Leonard R. 1970. "Economic Factors Underlying the Incidence of Large Farming Units: The Current Situation and Probable Trends." *Amer. J. Agri. Econ.* 52(5):748–761.

———. 1971. *Midwestern Farms: Economic Status and the Potential for Large and Family Size Units.* AER216. Washington, D.C.: USDA, Economic Research Service, November.

Krugman, H. 1965. "The Impact of Television Advertising: Learning without Involvement." *Public Opinion Quart.* 29:349–356.

Kwoka, John E. 1975. "Pricing Under Federal Milk Market Regulation: Theory, Objectives and Impact." Unpublished manuscript. Chapel Hill, N.C.: University of North Carolina.

———. 1979. "The Effects of Market Share Distribution on Industry Performance." *Rev. Econ. & Stat.* 61:101–109.

Lamm, McFall. 1981. "Prices and Concentration in the Food Retailing Industry," *J. Ind. Econ.* 30:67–78.

———. 1982. "Unionism and Prices in the Food Retailing Industry." *J. Labor Research* 3 (Winter):69–79.

Lang, M.G. 1978. "Structure, Conduct, and Performance in Agricultural Product Markets Characterized by Collective Bargaining." In B.W. Marion (ed.), *Agricultural Cooperatives and the Public Interest.* NC 117 Monograph 4. Madison, Wis.: NC 117.

Lasley, Floyd. 1983. "The U.S. Poultry Industry: Changing Economics and Structure." AER502. Washington, D.C.: USDA, Economic Research Service, July.

Leading National Advertisers, Inc. 1983. *Company/Brand$* (1983 and previous years). New York: Leading National Advertisers.

Lee, John E. 1981. "Food and Agricultural Policy: A Suggested Approach." *Agricultural-Food Policy Review: Perspectives for the 1980's,* AFPR4. Washington, D.C.: USDA, Economic and Statistics Service, April.

Leibenstein, Harvey. 1966. "Allocative Efficiency vs. 'X-Efficiency,' " *Amer. Econ. Rev.* 56:392.

Leuthold, R.M. 1973. *Futures Market Contracts as Vertical Coordination Instruments: A Status Report.* AE4334. Urbana: University of Illinois, Department of Agricultural Economics.

———. 1976. "Relationships between Futures Contracts and Alternative Contractual Arrangements in Agriculture." In B.W. Marion (ed.), *Coordination and Exchange in Agricultural Subsectors.* NC 117 Monograph 2. Madison, Wis.: NC 117.

Leuthold, R.M., and Hartmann, P.A. 1979. "A Semi-Strong Form Evaluation of the Efficiency of the Hog Futures Market." *Amer. J. Agric. Econ.* 61:482–489.

———. 1981. "An Evaluation of the Forward-Pricing Efficiency of Livestock Futures Markets." *North Central J. of Agric. Econ.* 3:71–80.

Leuthold, R.M., and Tomek, W.G. 1982. "Developments in the Livestock Futures Literature." In R.M. Leuthold and P. Dixon (eds.), *Livestock Futures Research Symposium.* Chicago: Chicago Mercantile Exchange.

Levmore, Saul. 1978. "Small Firm Disadvantages in Television Advertising." Ph.D. dissertation, Yale University.

Lin, William; Johnson, James; and Calvin, Linda. 1981. *Farm Commodity Programs: Who Participates and Who Benefits?* AER474. Washington, D.C.: USDA, Economic Research Service, September.

Lins, David A. 1979. "Credit Availability Effects on the Structure of Farming." In *Structure Issues of American Agriculture.* AER438. Washington, D.C.: USDA, Economics, Statistics, and Cooperative Service, November.

Lins, David A., and Barry, Peter. 1980. "Availability of Financial Capital as a Factor of Structural Change in the U.S. Farm Production Sector." In *Farm Structure: A Historical Perspective on Changes in the Number and Size of Farms.* Committee on Agriculture, Nutrition, and Forestry, U.S. Senate, April.

Loescher, Samuel M. 1983. "The Effects of Disseminating Comparative Grocery Chain Prices by the Indiana Public Interest Research Group: A Case Study." In J. Connor and R. Ward (eds.), *Advertising and the Food System.* Monograph 14. Madison, Wis.: NC 117.

Lu, Yao-Chi. 1979. "Technological Change and Structure." In *Structure Issues of American Agriculture.* AER438. Washington, D.C.: USDA, Economics, Statistics, and Cooperative Service, November.

Lurie, H.R. 1978. "Mergers under the Burger Court: An Anti-Antitrust Bias and Its Implications." *Vill. L. Rev.* 23:213.

MacDonald, James M. 1981. *Determinants of Diversification in Food Manufacturing.* ESS Staff Report (AGESS810714). Washington, D.C.: USDA, Economics and Statistics Service.

———1983. "Product Diversification in U.S. Manufacturing." Ph.D. dissertation, State University of New York at Buffalo.

McElroy, K.M.; Siegfried, J.J.; and Sweeny, G.H. 1982. "The Incidence of Price Changes in the U.S. Economy." *Rev. Econ. & Stat.* 64:191–203.

McEowen, Jack L. 1982. "Compensation Differentials, Restrictive Labor Practices, and Food Industries Structure." Ph.D. dissertation, Michigan State University.

Mackie, Arthur B. 1983. *The U.S. Farmer and World Market Development.* AGES830810. Washington, D.C.: USDA, Economic Research Service.

Mallen, Bruce, and Haberman, M. 1975. "Economies of Scale: A Determinant of 'Overstoring and Superstoring'?" In Canadian Association of Administrative Sciences Conference Proceedings, Edmonton, Alta.

Manchester, Alden. 1974. "Market Structure, Institutions, and Performance in the Fluid Milk Industry." AER248. Washington, D.C.: USA, Economic Research Service.

———. 1982. *The Status of Marketing Cooperatives Under Antitrust Law*. ERS673. Washington, D.C.: USDA, Economic Research Service.

———. 1983. *The Public Role in the Dairy Economy. Why and How Governments Intervene in the Milk Business*. Boulder, Colo.: Westview Press.

Mancke, Richard B. 1974. "Cause of Interfirm Profitability Differences: A New Interpretation of the Evidence." *Quart. J. Econ.* 88:181–193.

Mann, Jitendar S. 1977. "Techniques to Measure Social Benefits and Costs in Agriculture: A Survey." *Agric. Econ. Res.* 29:115–126.

Marion, B.W. 1976. "Application of the Structure, Conduct, Performance Paradigm to Subsector Analysis." Working Paper 7. Madison, Wis.: NC 117.

———. 1984. "Strategic Groups, Entry Barriers and Competitive Behavior in Grocery Retailing." Working Paper 81. Madison, Wis.: NC 117.

Marion, B.W., and Handy, Charles R. 1973. *Market Performance: Concepts and Measures*. AER244. Washington, D.C.: USDA, Economic Research Service.

Marion, B.W.; Mueller, W.F.; Cotterill, R.W.; Geithman, F.E.; and Schmelzer, J.R. 1979a. *The Food Retailing Industry: Market Structure, Profits and Prices*. New York: Praeger.

Marion, B.; Mueller, W.F.; Cotterill, R.W.; Geithman, F.E.; and Schmelzer, J.R. 1979b. "The Price and Profit Performance of Leading Food Chains." *Amer. J. Agr. Econ.* 61 (August):420–433.

Marion, B.W., and Nash, H.J. 1983. "Foreign Investments in U.S. Food Retailing Industry." *Amer. J. Agr. Econ.* 65:413–420.

Markham, Jesse W. 1950. "An Alternative Approach to the Concept of Workable Competition." *Amer. Econ. Rev.* 40:349–361.

———. 1973. *Conglomerate Enterprise and Public Policy*. Boston: Division of Research, Graduate School of Business Administration, Harvard University.

Martin, L., and Garcia, P. 1981. "The Price-Forecasting Performance of Futures Markets for Live Cattle and Hogs: A Disaggregated Analysis." *Amer. J. Agric. Econ.* 63:209–215.

Masson, A.; Masson, R.T.; and Harris, B.C. 1978. "Cooperatives and Marketing Orders." In B. Marion (ed.), *Agricultural Cooperatives and the Public Interest*. Monograph 4. Madison, Wis.: NC 117.

Masters, Stanley H. 1969. "An Interindustry Analysis of Wages and Plant Size." *Rev. Econ. & Stat.* 51:341–345.

Matthews, S.F., and Rhodes, V.J. 1975. *The Use of Public Limited Partnership Financing in Agriculture for Income Tax Shelter*. Monograph 1. Madison, Wis.: NC 117.

Mayer, Carolyn R. 1982. "Admen Back Deregulation, Up to a Point." *Washington Post*, November 12, p. A29.

Means, Gardiner C. 1935. *Industrial Prices and Their Relative Inflexibility*. Senate Document 13. Washington, D.C.: U.S. GPO.

Melichar, Emanuel. 1979. "Capital Gains versus Current Income in the Farming Sector." *Amer. J. Agric. Econ.* 61(5):1085–1092.

Metro Market Studies. 1984. *1984 Grocery Distribution Analysis and Guide.* Weston, Mass.: Metro Market Studies.

Mighell, R.L., and Jones, L.A. 1963. *Vertical Coordination in Agriculture.* AER19. Washington, D.C.: USDA, Economic Research Service.

Miller, James C. III. 1982. Prepared testimony before the Subcommittee on Monopolies and Commercial Law, Committee on the Judiciary, U.S. House of Representatives, June 3.

Miller, S.E., and Kenyon, D.E. 1980. "Empirical Analysis of Live-Hog Futures Price Use by Producers and Packers." In R.M. Leuthold and P. Dixon (eds.), *Livestock Futures Research Symposium.* Chicago: Chicago Mercantile Exchange.

Miller, Stephen, and Harris, Harold. 1982. "Monopsony Power in Commodity Procurement: The Case of Slaughter Hogs." Working Paper 012281. Clemson, S.C.: Department of Agricultural Economics, Clemson University.

Miller, Thomas A. 1979. "Economies of Size and Other Growth Incentives." In *Structure Issues of American Agriculture.* AER438. Washington, D.C.: USDA, Economics, Statistics, and Cooperative Service, November.

Miller, Thomas A.; Rodewald, Gordon E.; and McElroy, Robert G. 1981. *Economies of Size in U.S. Field Crop Farming.* AER472. Washington, D.C.: USDA, Economics and Statistics Service, July.

Miller, Thomas A., and Sharples, Jerry A. 1979. "Issues Concerning the Level of Price and Income Supports." In *Structure Issues of American Agriculture.* AER438. Washington, D.C.: USDA, Economics, Statistics, and Cooperative Service, November.

Milling and Baking News. 1982. "Milling Directory/Buyer's Guide." Kansas City: Sosland Publ. Co., December 1982 (and previous issues).

Monfort of Colorado v. Cargill, Inc. and Excel Corp. U.S. District Court (Colorado). 1983. Civil Action 83-F-1818, Opinion and Order.

Mori, Hiroshi, and Gorman, William. 1966. "An Empirical Investigation into the Relationship Measured by Prices." *J. of Farm Econ.* 48:1496–1502.

Morrison, Rosanna Mentzer. 1984. *Generic Advertising of Farm Products.* Agricultural Information Bulletin 481. Washington, D.C.: USDA, Economic Research Service.

Mueller, Dennis C. 1977. "The Effects of Conglomerate Mergers: A Survey of the Empirical Evidence." *J. Banking & Finance* 1:315–347.

Mueller, Willard F. 1973. "The ITT Settlement: A Deal with Justice?" *Indus. Org. Rev.* 1:67.

——1978a. *The Cellar-Kefauver Act: The First 27 Years.* A study prepared for for the Subcommittee on Monopolies and Commercial Law of the Committee on the Judiciary, House of Representatives. Washington, D.C.: U.S. GPO.

———. 1978b. "The Control of Agricultural Processing and Distribution." *Am. J. Agric. Econ.* 60:848–855.

———. 1978c. Prepared statement on Hearings on Conglomerate Mergers. U.S. Senate. Judiciary Committee. May 12.

———. 1979. "The Capper-Volstead Exemption." Report to the President and the Attorney General of the National Commission for the Review of Antitrust Laws and Procedures, Vol. II, January 22.

——. 1981. "The Anti-Antitrust Movement." In John V. Craven (ed.), *Industrial Organization, Antitrust and Public Policy*. Boston: Kuwer-Nijhoff Publishing Co.

——. 1982a. "Conglomerates: A Non-Industry." In W. Adams (ed.), *The Structure of American Industry*. New York: Macmillan.

——. 1982b. "Public Policy and Economic Power: The American Antitrust Laws and Some International Comparisons." Working Paper 61. Madison, Wis.: NC 117.

——. 1983. "Market Power and Its Control in the Food Industry." *Am. J. Agric. Econ.* 65:855–863.

——. 1984a. "Alleged Predatory Conduct in Food Retailing." Working Paper 78. Madison, Wis.: NC 117.

——. 1984b. "Clarifying The Rights of Farmers to Seek Damages in Antitrust Action." Working Paper 82. Madison, Wis.: NC 117.

Mueller, Willard F.; Culbertson, John; and Peckham, Brian. 1982. *Market Structure and Technological Performance in the Food Manufacturing Industry*. Monograph 11. Madison, Wis.: NC 117.

Mueller, Willard F.; Hamm, Larry; and Cook, Hugh. 1976. *Public Policy Toward Mergers in the Dairy Processing Industry*. Studies in the Organization and Control of the U.S. Food System. Monograph 3. Madison, Wis.: NC 117.

Mueller, Willard F., and Rogers, Richard. 1980. "The Role of Advertising in Changing Concentration of Manufacturing Industries." *Rev. Econ. & Stat.* 62:89–96.

National Association of Convenience Stores. 1983. "1983 State of the Convenience Store Industry." Falls Church, Va.: NACS.

National Commission on Food Marketing. 1966a. *Organization and Competition in Food Retailing*. Technical Study 7. Washington, D.C.: U.S. GPO.

——. 1966b. *The Structure of Food Manufacturing*. Technical Study 8. Washington, D.C.: U.S. GPO.

National Commission for the Review of Antitrust Laws and Procedures. 1979. *Report to the President and the Attorney General*. Washington, D.C.: U.S. GPO.

Neal Report. 1968–1969. "Report of the White House Task Force on Antitrust Policies." *Antitrust Law and Economic Review* 2(2) (Winter):11–70.

Nelson, K.E. 1980. "Market Information and Pricing Mechanisms in Livestock and Meat Industry: Issues and Alternatives." In *Market Information and Price Reporting in the Food and Agricultural Sector*. Monograph 9. Madison, Wis.: NC 117.

Nelson, Phillip. 1974. "Advertising as Information." *J. Polit. Econ.* 82:729–754.

——. 1975. "The Economic Consequences of Advertising." *J. of Business* (April): 237.

Newman, Mark D., and Riley, Harold M. 1982. *Coordinating Exports by Farmer Cooperatives*. ACS Research Report 15. Washington, D.C.: USDA.

Nichols, J.P.; Hill, L.D.; and Nelson, K.E. 1983. "Food and Agricultural Commodity Grading." In W.J. Armbruster, D.R. Henderson, and R.D. Knutson (eds.), *Federal Marketing Programs in Agriculture: Issues and Options*. Danville, Ill.: Interstate.

Nickell, Stephen, and Metcalf, David. 1978. "Monopolistic Industries and Monopoly Profits or, Are Kellogg's Cornflakes Overpriced?" *Econ. J.* 88:254–268.

Nielsen, A.C. Co. 1980. *Nielsen Early Intelligence System (NEIS): April/May 1979 and 1980*. Northbrook, Ill.: A.C. Nielsen Co.

Nielsen, A.C. Co. 1982. "New Item Introductions—NEIS Alert." Northbrook, Ill.: A.C. Nielsen.

Nourse, Edwin G. 1963. "Government Discipline of Private Economic Power." In Subcommittee on Antitrust and Monopoly, Committee on the Judiciary, U.S. Senate, *Administered Prices: A Compendium on Public Policy*. Washington, D.C.: U.S. GPO.

O'Brien, Patrick, et al. 1982. *World Trade in High Value Agricultural Products: U.S. Export Opportunities in the 1980s*. Draft Staff Report. Washington, D.C.: USDA, Economics and Statistics Service.

Oellermann, C.M. 1985. "Futures and Cash Price Relationships for Beef Cattle." Ph.D. dissertation, Purdue University.

Oster, Sharon. 1981. "Product Regulations: A Measure of the Benefits." *J. Indus. Econ.* 29:395–411.

Padberg, Daniel, and Westgren, Randall. 1979. "Product Competition and Consumer Behavior in the Food Industries." *Amer. J. Agric. Econ.* 61:620–625.

Pagoulatos, Emilio, and Sorenson, Robert. 1979. "Foreign Trade, Protection, and Multinational Activity in U.S. Food Processing Industries." *So. J. Agric. Econ.* 11:119–125.

——— . 1981. "A Simultaneous Equation Analysis of Advertising, Concentration, and Profitability." *So. Econ. J.* 47:728–741.

——— . 1983. "The Competitive Impact of Advertising in the U.S. Food Industries: A Simultaneous Equation Approach." In John M. Connor and Ronald L. Ward (eds.), *Advertising and the Food System*. Monograph 14. Madison, Wis.: NC 117.

Parker, Russell C. 1975. "Staff Economic Report on Food Chain Profits." Washington, D.C.: FTC, Bureau of Economics.

——— . 1977. "Federal Trade Commission Merger Policy with Respect to the Dairy Industry." Midwest Milk Marketing Conference, Louisville, Kentucky, March 22.

——— . 1985. *Concentration, Integration and Diversification in the U.S. Grocery Retailing Industry*. Washington, D.C.: FTC, Bureau of Economics, Forthcoming.

Parker, Russell, and Connor, John M. 1978. "Estimates of Consumer Loss Due to Monopoly in the U.S. Food Manufacturing Industries." Working Paper 19. Madison, Wis.: NC 117.

——— . 1979. "Estimates of Consumer Loss Due to Monopoly in the U.S. Food Manufacturing Industries." *Am. J. Agric. Econ.* 61:6628–6639.

Pasour, E.C., Jr.; and Bullock, J.B. 1975. "Implications of Uncertainty for the Measurement of Efficiency." *Amer. J. Agric. Econ.* 57(2):335–339.

Paterson, Thomas W., and Mueller, Willard F. 1984a. "State Sales-Below-Cost Laws: A Legal-Economic Analysis of Effectiveness." Working Paper 80. Madison, Wis.: NC 117.

——— . 1984b. "Agricultural Marketing Cooperatives and Section 1 of the Capper-Volstead Act." Working Paper 84. Madison, Wis.: NC 117.

Pederson, D., and Dahl, D. 1981. *Agricultural Employment Law and Policy*. Monograph 10. St. Paul, Minn.: Minnesota Agricultural Experiment Station, University of Minnesota.

Peltzman, Sam. 1977. "The Gains and Losses from Industrial Concentration." *J. Law & Econ.* 20:229–264.

Rogers, Richard, and Schiferl, E. 1984. "Control of Leading Market Positions in Food Manufacturing by the 100 Largest Food Companies." Paper presented at American Agricultural Economics Assn. meeting, Ithaca, N.Y., August.

Roller, V., and Lesser, W. 1983. "Evaluating Warehouse Efficiency Using Residual Analysis." *J. of Food Distrib. Res. Soc.* 44:83–88.

Salop, Steven C. 1979. "Strategic Entry Deterrence." *American Economic Review* 69:335–338.

Salop, Thomas R. 1979. "Concentration Ratios and the Degree of Monopoly." *International Econ. Rev.* 11:139–146.

SAMI. 1983. *Generic and Private Labels.* New York: Selling Areas-Marketing, September.

Saporito, Bill. 1983. "Kroger, The New King of Supermarketing." *Fortune*, February 21, pp. 74–80.

Scala, James R. 1973. "Advertising and Shared Monopoly in Consumer Goods Industries." *Colum. J.L. & Soc. Probs.* 9:241–278.

Schacter, S. 1971. *Emotion, Obesity and Crime.* New York: Academic Press.

Scherer, F.M. 1971. *Industrial Market Structure and Economic Performance.* Chicago: Rand McNally.

———. 1980. *Industrial Market Structure and Economic Performance.* 2d ed. Chicago: Rand McNally.

———. 1982. "The Breakfast Cereal Industry." In Walter Adams (ed.), *The Structure of American Industry.* 5th ed. New York: Macmillan.

Scherer, F.M., et al. 1975. *The Economics of Multi-Plant Operation.* Harvard Economic Studies, Vol. 145. Cambridge, Mass.: Harvard University Press.

Scherhorn, G., and Wieken, K. 1972. "On the Effect of Counter-Information on Consumers." In B. Strumpel, J. Morgan, and E. Zahn (eds.), *Human Behavior in Economic Analysis.* San Francisco: Jossey-Bass.

Schertz, Lyle P., and others. 1979. *Another Revolution in U.S. Farming?* AER441. Washington, D.C.: USDA, Economics and Statistics Service.

Schmalensee, Richard. 1978. "Entry Deterrence in the Ready-to-Eat Breakfast Cereal Industry." *Bell. J. Econ.* 9:305–327.

Schmelzer, John. 1981. "The Commercial Foodservice Sector: Trends in Growth and Market Structure." Working Paper 56. Madison, Wis.: NC 117.

Schrader, L.F.; Heifner, R.G.; and Larzelere, H.E. 1968. "The Electronic Egg Exchange: An Alternative System for Trading Shell Eggs." Agriculture Economics Report 119. E. Lansing: Michigan State University.

Schrader, L.F., and Henderson, D.R. 1980. "Auction Pricing: Options and Implications." Working Paper 48. Madison, Wis.: NC 117.

Schrader, L.F., and Lang, M.G. 1980. "The Potential Effects of Proposed Commodity Grade Specification Changes: BCFM in Corn and FM in Soybeans." *N.C. J. of Agric. Econ.* 2(1):31–40.

Schrader, L.F.; Larzalere, H.; Rogers, G.B.; and Forker, O. 1978. *The Egg Subsector of U.S. Agriculture.* NC 117 Monograph 6. W. Lafayette: Purdue University Agricultural Experiment Station.

Schwartz, Marius, and Reynolds, Robert. 1982. "Contestible Markets: An Uprising in the Theory of Industrial Structure: Comment," Economic Policy Office Discussion Paper EPD82-1. Washington, D.C.: U.S. Department of Justice, June 17.

Schwenk, Albert E. 1980. "Profit Rates and Negotiated Wage Changes." *Quart. Rev. Econ. & Bus.* 20:63–75.

Shaffer, James D. 1979. "Observations on the Political Economics of Regulations." *Am J. Agric. Econ.* 61:721–31.

Shepherd, William G. 1982. "Causes of Increased Competition in the U.S. Economy, 1939–1980." *Rev. Econ. & Stat.* 64(4):613–626.

———. 1984. " 'Contestability' vs. Competition." *Amer. Econ. Rev.* 74(4):572–587.

Siegfried, John J. (ed.). 1980. *The Economics of Firm Size, Market Structure, and Social Performance*. Washington, D.C.: FTC, Bureau of Economics.

Simunek, Richard W., and Poirier, Lise. 1983. "Comparing IRS Farm Data Trends with USDA Measures of Farm Income." *Economic Indicators of the Farm Sector. Farm Sector Review 1982*. ECOFS 2-1. Washington, D.C.: USDA, Economics Research Service.

Skinner, R.A. 1981. "Economic Implications of the Michigan Bargaining Law." In *Agricultural Bargaining Process-Problems-Potentials*. ACS Service Report 6. Washington, D.C.: USDA, Agricultural Cooperative Service.

Smith, V.L. 1976. "Bidding and Auctioning Institutions: Experimental Results." In Yakov Amihud (ed.), *Bidding and Auctioning for Procurement and Allocation*. New York: New York University Press.

———. 1981. "An Empirical Study of Decentralized Institutions of Monopoly Restraint." In G. Horwich and J. Quirk (eds.), *Essays in Contemporary Fields of Economics*. West Lafayette, Ind.: Purdue University Press.

———. 1982. "Microeconomic Systems as an Experimental Science." *Amer. Econ. Rev.* 72(5):923–955.

Sosnick, Stephen. 1958. "A Critique of Concepts of Workable Competition." *Quart. J. Econ.* 72:380–423.

———. 1968. "Toward a Concrete Concept of Effective Competition." *Am. J. Agric. Econ.* 50:827–853.

Southland Corporation. 1983. 1982 Annual Report. Dallas, Tex.: Southland Corp.

Spence, Michael. 1981. "Competition, Entry and Antitrust Policy." In Steven Salop (ed.), *Strategy, Predation and Antitrust Analysis*. Washington, D.C.: FTC.

Stigler, George J. 1966. "The Effects of the Antitrust Laws." *J. of Law and Econ.* 9:225.

———. 1968. *The Organization of Industry*. Homewood, Ill.: Richard D. Irwin.

———. 1969. "Report of the Stigler Committee on Productivity and Competition." *Antitrust Law and Economic Review* 2(3)(Spring):1–52.

———. 1971. "The Theory of Economic Regulation." *Bell J. Econ. and Management Science* 2:3–21.

———. 1982. "The Economists and The Problem of Monopoly." *Amer. Econ. Rev. Proc.* 72:1–11.

Stocking, George W. 1955. "Comment on Conglomerate Bigness." In George Stigler (ed.), *Business Concentration and Price Policy*. Princeton, N.J.: Princeton University Press.

Sullivan, Lawrence. 1977. *Antitrust*. St. Paul: West Publishing Company.

Supermarket News. 1977. "Premerger Notifying Rules in Effect Today." February 28, p. 12.

———. 1982a. "Market Profiles '82." September 13, sec. II.

———. 1982b. "Deals Eroding Consumer Trust, Twin Country Executive." November 15, p. 4.

———— . 1983. "FTC Seen Flexible on Future Mergers." August 1, p. 31.

———— . 1984. "Kroger, Safeway Labeled Wreckers of Competition." October 8, p. 1.

Swanson, Earl R., and Sonka, Steven T. 1980. "Technology and the Structure of U.S. Agriculture." in *Farm Structure: A Historical Perspective on Changes in the Number and Size of Farms*. Committee on Agriculture, Nutrition, and Forestry, U.S. Senate, April.

Talburt, W.F., and Smith, O. 1975. *Potato Processing* Westport, Conn.: AVI Publishing Co.

Taylor, G.S., and Leuthold, R.M. 1974. "The Influence of Futures Trading on Cash Cattle Price Variations." *Food Research Institute Studies* 3:29–35.

Thor, Peter K., and Jesse, Edward V. 1981. *Economic Effects of Terminating Federal Marketing Orders for California-Arizona Oranges*. TB1664. Washington, D.C.: USDA, Economics Research Services, November.

Thorelli, Hans B. 1955. *The Federal Antitrust Policy: Origination of an American Tradition*. Baltimore: Johns Hopkins Press.

Thurow, Lester. 1980. *The Zero-Sum Society*. New York: Basic Books.

Tomek, W.G. 1971. "A Note on Historical Wheat Prices and Futures Trading," *Food Research Institute Studies* 10:109–113.

———— . 1980. "Price Behavior on a Declining Terminal Market." *Amer. J. of Agric. Econ.* 62(3):434–444.

Tomek, W.G., and Gray, R.W. 1970. "Temporal Relationships Among Prices on Commodity Futures Markets: Their Allocative and Stabilizing Roles." *Amer. J. Agric. Econ.* 52:372–380.

Townsend, Robert. 1973. "A Modest Proposal: The Public Director." in R. Nader and M.J. Green (eds.), *Corporate America*. New York: Grossman Publishers.

Tweeten, Luther. 1983. "The Economics of Small Farms," *Science*, 219-1037-41, March 4.

Uhl, J.M.; Boynton, R.D.; and Blake, B.F. 1981. *Effects of Comparative Foodstore Price Information on Price Structures and Consumer Behavior in Local Food Markets*. West Lafayette, Ind.: Department of Agricultural Economics, Purdue University.

U.S. Congress. 1977a. "The Profit and Price Performance of Leading Food Chains, 1970–74." Washington, D.C.: Joint Economic Committee, U.S. GPO.

———— . 1977b. Joint Economic Committee Hearings, March 30 and April 5. *Prices and Profits of Leading Retail Food Chains, 1970–74*. Washington, D.C.: U.S. GPO.

U.S. Department of Agriculture. 1979a. *Report of the Secretary's Meat Pricing Task Force*. Washington, D.C.: USDA.

———— . 1979b. "U.S. Tax Policy and Agricultural Structure." In *Structure Issues of American Agriculture*. AER438. Washington, D.C.: USDA, Economics, Statistics, and Cooperative Service.

———— . 1981a. *A Time to Choose: Summary Report on the Structure of Agriculture*. Washington, D.C.: USDA, January.

———— . 1981b. *A Review of Federal Marketing Orders for Fruits, Vegetables and Specialty Crops: Economic Efficiency and Welfare Implications*. AER477. Washington, D.C.: USDA, Agricultural Marketing Service.

———— . 1983a. "Cattle on Feed." Washington, D.C.: Crop Reporting Board, Statistical Reporting Service, January (and previous issues).

————. 1983b. "Dairy Products Annual Summary, 1982." Washington, D.C.: Crop Reporting Board, Statistical Reporting Service.

————. 1983c. "Livestock and Meat Statistics: Supplement for 1982." Washington, D.C.: USDA.

————. 1983d. "Milk: Production, Disposition, Income: 1980–82." Washington, D.C.: Crop Reporting Board, Statistical Reporting Service.

————. 1984a. "Dairy Outlook and Situation Report." Washington, D.C.: USDA, December (and previous issues).

————. 1984b. "Milk Production, Disposition, and Income: 1983 Summary Milk Production Series." Washington, D.C.: USDA.

————. 1984c. *Packers and Stockyards' Statistical Resume*, P&SA Statistical Report Nr. 84-1. Washington, D.C.: Packers and Stockyards Administration, September.

————. 1984d. "Potatoes and Sweet Potatoes: Production, Disposition, Value, Stocks and Utilization," Statistical Bulletins #291 (1961), #409 (1967), #490 (1972), #583 (1977), #645 (1980), #709 (1984). Washington, D.C.: Crop Reporting Board.

————. 1984e. *Agricultural Statistics, 1984* (and previous editions). Washington, D.C.: USDA.

————. 1984f. *Economic Indicators of the Farm Sector: Income and Balance Sheet Statistics, 1983,* EC/FS 3. Washington, D.C.: Economic Research Service.

————. 1984g. "Agricultural Finance Outlook." Nr. AF025. Washington, D.C.: Economic Research Service, December.

————. 1985a. "Livestock and Poultry Outlook and Situation Report." Washington, D.C.: USDA, March (and previous editions).

————. 1985b. "Crop Production, 1984 Summary." Washington, D.C.: Crop Reporting Board, Statistical Reporting Service (and previous editions).

————. 1985c. "Feed Outlook and Situation Report." Washington, D.C.: Economic Research Service (and previous issues).

————. 1985d. "Oil Crops Outlook and Situation Report." Washington, D.C.: Economic Research Service (and previous issues).

————. 1985e. "Wheat Outlook and Situation Yearbook." Washington, D.C.: Economic Research Service (and previous issues).

————. 1985f. "Foreign Agriculture Circular; Grains." Washington, D.C.: Foreign Agriculture Service (and previous issues).

————. 1985g. "Foreign Agriculture Circular, Oilseed and Products." Washington D.C.: Foreign Agriculture Service (and previous issues).

————. 1985h. *Financial Characteristics of U.S. Farms.* AIB495. Washington, D.C.: Economic Research Service, July.

————. 1985i. "Noncitrus Fruits and Nuts: 1984 Summary" (and previous years). Washington, D.C.: Statistical Reporting Service.

U.S. Department of Commerce. 1983. *Franchising in the Economy.* Washington, D.C.: U.S. GPO (and previous years).

U.S. Department of Justice. 1968. *Merger Guidelines.* Washington, D.C.

————. 1984. *Merger Guidelines.* Washington, D.C., June 14.

U.S. Department of Labor. 1985. "Productivity Measures for Selected Industries, 1954–1983." Bulletin 2224. Washington, D.C.: Bureau of Labor Statistics.

U.S. House of Representatives. 1978. *Small Business Problems in the Marketing of Meat and Other Commodities* (Part I-Meat Pricing), Report of the Subcommittee on SBA and SBIC Authority and General Small Business Problems, No. 95-1787.

U.S. Office of Management and Budget. 1984. *Budget of the United States Government, FY1985,* February.

Utah Pie Co. v. Continental Baking Co. 1967. 386 U.S. 685.

Van Dress, Michael. 1984. "Definition of the Foodservice Industry and Methodology for Estimating Selected Statistics." Washington, D.C.: USDA, Economic Research Service.

Wall Street Journal. 1982. November 6.

——. 1984. September 15, p. 3.

Ward, Ronald W. 1982. "Asymmetry in Retail, Wholesale, and Shipping Point Pricing for Fresh Vegetables." *Amer. J. Agric. Econ.* 64:205–212.

Ward, R.W., and Kilmer, R.L. 1980. *The United States Citrus Subsector: Organization, Behavior and Performance.* Monograph 8. Madison, Wis.: NC 177.

Weiss, Leonard W. 1965. "An Evaluation of Mergers in Six Industries." *Rev Econ. & Stat.* 47:172–181.

——. 1966. "Concentration and Labor Earnings." *Am. Econ. Rev.* 56:96–117.

——. 1972. "The Geographic Size of Markets in Manufacturing." *Rev. Econ. & Stat.* 54:245–252.

——. 1974. "The Concentration-Profits Relationship and Antitrust." In Harvey J. Goldschmid (ed.). *Industrial Concentration: The New Learning.* Boston: Little, Brown.

——. 1979. "The Structure-Conduct-Performance Paradigm and Antitrust." *Univ. of Pennsylvania Law Review* 127:1104–1140.

Wilcox, Clair. 1950. "On the Alleged Ubiquity of Oligopoly." *Amer. Econ. Rev.* 40: 71.

Williamson, Jeffrey G. 1977. " 'Strategic' Wage Goods, Prices and Inequality." *Amer. Econ. Rev.* 67:29–41.

Williamson, O.E. 1975. *Markets and Hierarchies: Analysis and Antitrust Implications.* New York: Free Press.

Willig, Robert. 1979. "Multiproduct Technology and Market Structure." *Amer. Econ. Review* 69:346–351.

Wills, Robert L. 1982. "Determinants of Price Differences Among Brands of Food Products." Paper presented at the annual meeting of the American Agricultural Economics Association, Logan, Utah.

——. 1983. "Economic Regulation v. First Amendment Protection of Commercial Speech." Paper presented at the Law and Society Association Meeting, Denver, Colo., June 3.

——. 1985a. "Evaluating Price Enhancement by Processing Cooperatives." *Amer. J. Agric. Econ.* 67:183–192.

——. 1985b. *Brand Pricing in Processed Foods.* USDA Technical Bulletin. Washington, D.C.: USDA, Economic Research Service, forthcoming.

Wills, Robert L., and Mentzer, Rosanna L. 1982. "The Effect of Generics on Food Market Structure." *Nat. Food Rev.* 18 (Spring):7–10.

Wills, Robert L., and Rosenbaum, David I. 1983. "Measures of Barriers to Entry into Food Processing Industries." Presented to Eastern Economics Association Meeting, Boston, March.

Wissman, Roger. 1985. "Coop Share of Marketing, Purchasing Stabilizes After Period of Growth." In *Farmer Cooperative*. Washington, D.C.: USDA, Agricultural Cooperative Service.

Working, H. 1953. "Hedging Reconsidered." In *Selected Writings of Holbrook Working*. Chicago: Chicago Board of Trade.

———. 1960. "Price Effects of Futures Trading." *Food Research Institute Studies* 1:3–31.

Yip, George. 1982. *Barriers to Entry*. Lexington, Mass.: Lexington Books.

Zajonc, R. 1968. "Attitudinal Differences of Mere Exposure." *J. of Personality & Social Psych. (Monograph Supplement)* 9(2,Pt.2):1–27.

Name Index

Subject Index

About the Author

Bruce W. Marion is an agricultural economist with the Economic Research Service of the U.S. Department of Agriculture and professor of agricultural economics at the University of Wisconsin-Madison. He was a member of the Ohio State University faculty from 1963 to 1974. Since 1974 he has been executive director of NC 117, the multiuniversity research effort responsible for this book. He is coauthor of *The Food Retailing Industry: Market Structure, Profits and Prices* (Praeger, 1979) and *The Food Manufacturing Industries: Structure, Strategies, Performance, and Policies* (Lexington Books, 1985). He has written numerous articles and monographs on the organization and performance of the food marketing system and has received awards for outstanding research from the American Agricultural Economics Association and the American Council on Consumer Interests. As executive director of the NC 117 project, he received the American Agricultural Economics Association award in 1980 for distinguished policy contribution.